Derek A. Sanders
State University of New York at Buffalo

AURAL REHABILITATION

A Management Model

SECOND EDITION

PRENTICE-HALL, INC., Englewood Cliffs, New Jersey 07632

Library of Congress Cataloging in Publication Data

SANDERS, DEREK A.
Aural rehabilitation.

Bibliography
Includes index.
1. Deaf—Rehabilitation. 2. Audiology. I. Title.
RF297.S35 1982 362.4'283 81-13915
ISBN 0-13-053215-0 AACR2

To my wife, Cynthia,

and my daughters,

Jennifer and Hilary

PRINTED IN THE UNITED STATES OF AMERICA

10 9 8 7 6 5 4 3 2 1

ISBN 0-13-053215-0

PRENTICE-HALL INTERNATIONAL, INC., *London*
PRENTICE-HALL OF AUSTRALIA PTY. LIMITED, *Sydney*
PRENTICE-HALL OF CANADA, LTD., *Toronto*
PRENTICE-HALL OF INDIA PRIVATE LIMITED, *New Delhi*
PRENTICE-HALL OF JAPAN, INC., *Tokyo*
PRENTICE-HALL OF SOUTHEAST ASIA PTE. LTD., *Singapore*
WHITEHALL BOOKS LIMITED, WELLINGTON, *New Zealand*

Contents

The Human Communication System

Physical Aspects of The Speech Signal

A Model for the Management of Problems Resulting From Hearing Impairment

Assessment and Management of The Hearing-Impaired Adult

Preface

In writing this book I have tried to achieve several goals. My primary purpose has been to develop a model of professional service that will be effective in helping hearing-impaired children and adults to function as close to their ideal as possible. The model I propose is based upon my belief that the major resource in the task of reducing a handicap is the individual who experiences it.

The role of the professional is that of a facilitator. While our knowledge and experience constitute expertise, they do not make us experts. Each individual faces problems and situations unique to himself or herself, problems that will not respond to generalized rehabilitation procedures. Thus I have offered a model of management of resources based upon a specific problem-solving approach, the most important factor of which is relevance. To achieve relevance we must understand people's needs in terms of the demands made upon them in their own particular environment. A reduction of difficulties will occur only if individuals effect a relevant change in their perception of the problem and identify new ways of meeting demands and satisfying needs.

For the young child, parents and professionals must create conditions that stimulate the development of effective behaviors. Even then, the goal is to encourage self-reliance. The task requires cooperation among those who contribute to the management program; most important, it places the ultimate responsibility for decision making in the hands of the client, or the parents of the young child.

A second goal I hope I have achieved was to show the enormous potential we have for positively influencing the quality of life for the hearing-impaired person. When we each make the client the center of our concern, setting aside personal prejudices about professional roles or rigid commitment to particular methods, we constitute a powerful resource. I have attempted to describe the contribution we each can make and the ways in which it might be achieved. My overriding concern at all times has been to demonstrate that the maintenance of the integrity of the client should be central to our management program. Through the enhancement of the client's sense of self-confidence and independence, we justify our role as a true helper.

No author who works with people can claim full credit for the originality of his or her ideas. The concepts presented here derive from many people. The only experts on the effects of hearing impairment are those who experience it and their families, who see their loved ones handicapped by it. These people have helped me to acquire a sensitivity to the breadth of problems created by a hearing deficit. To them I also owe my awareness of the great potential individuals have for surmounting their difficulties. To my many students over the years and to colleagues in aural rehabilitation, I owe the refinement of my ideas, which resulted from the questions they asked and the stimulation they provided.

In the actual production of the book I received much help from graduate student assistants who were responsible for many of the most tedious tasks of manuscript preparation. I wish to express my thanks also to my copy editor, Louisa B. Hellegers, and to my production manager, Serena Hoffman, who both contributed so much to the style and attractiveness of the book.

I am grateful for the useful criticism provided by the following reviewers, who saw portions of the rough manuscript: Daniel Ling, McGill University; Paul W. Dodge, Temple University; and Linda L. Smith, Michigan State University.

Finally, I am indebted to the schools and agencies that allowed me to take photographs, to the parents who authorized their use, and to the skill of James A. Ulrich, photographer. For much of the artwork, I owe thanks to Donald E. Watkins.

DEREK A. SANDERS

Introduction

1

Understanding Hearing Impairment

The task of meeting the needs of hearing-impaired children and adults is a complex one, for an impairment of hearing affects all aspects of an individual's life. It also affects the hearing-impaired person's family, creating a need for support and guidance for those close to the handicapped person. The very complexity of the problem makes approaches to its resolution complicated and demanding. Yet the satisfactions of solving the problems effectively will more than reward the effort.

For a child, a hearing impairment makes it difficult to develop naturally without help. For an adult, it creates problems in maintaining an established life style, in retaining a job, and in preserving satisfying personal and social relationships, both within and outside the family. A program of habilitative or rehabilitative management seeks to minimize such effects. Your concern as an audiologist, hearing therapist, special teacher, or counselor is to improve the quality of life of the hearing-impaired person. In order to achieve this goal, you will need a broad perspective on the difficulties created by hearing impairment.

The root of the problem lies in the impact of the hearing deficiency on the communication process. This is itself a complex topic upon which much of our discussion will center. However, it is not reasonable to isolate a single component, even of the communication process, and to concentrate remedial efforts on that aspect alone. We cannot assume, for example, that our role is to concentrate only on providing intensive auditory and visual training for the client, leaving to other professionals the task of improving learning ability, developing linguistic skills, teaching speech articulation, or facilitating better attitudinal adjustment.

When you work with a hearing-impaired child, you are confronted with someone who needs help in growing and learning in a society in which normal hearing is taken for granted. It is a society which, for the most part, neither understands the special developmental and learning problems created by hearing impairment, nor knows how to accommodate them. When a hearing-impaired adult seeks your help, that person needs to understand to what extent he or she must live differently as a result of the hearing impairment, to learn what adjustments he or she must make, and to realize how to make them. These are people who, without help, will experience difficulty and frustration beyond that experienced by their normal-hearing counterparts. They are people with practical problems of everyday living, problems that need direct intervention procedures.

The effectiveness of those procedures can be judged only in terms of the extent to which they effect a noticeable change in the client's ability to meet the demands of daily living. This may result either from an improvement in the ability to process auditory and visual speech information, or from learning new strategies for influencing the communication situation, or it may be a factor of changes in attitude and personal adjustment. Whatever the specific source of the improvement, it is likely to occur only if we know the nature of the individual child's and adult's needs. These needs must be defined and understood within the larger framework of the client's social contacts. We must know what is expected of the client at home, at school, at work, at play, and in social situations. It is upon this knowledge of personal needs that intervention procedures must be based. Understanding the problem, therefore, becomes your first task.

Unlike the diagnostic component of audiology, the rehabilitative management of the client's problem cannot be readily reduced to a set of quantifiable test results which together permit diagnosis. When performing a clinical diagnostic assessment, audiologists focus their attention on the integrity of the client's auditory system. They seek to obtain objective measure of this system; then they compare the data with the norms for each test to determine the extent of the deviance. The more objective the test procedures, the greater will be the validity of the results. Involvement of the client in the test is unavoidable in many procedures, but it is undesirable because the subject's judgments represent independent variables that must be controlled for in evaluating responses. Audiologists involved in the clinical diagnostic stage are only incidentally concerned with the client's perceptions and function.

In the habilitative/rehabilitative stage, by contrast, the focus of attention *is* the client, his or her perceptions and behavior. The process is far less controlled, far less scientific than in clinical diagnosis. The procedures we use are often of necessity pragmatic, concerned with practical results rather than with measured performance on standardized tests. For example, it may be possible to train individuals to improve their scores on a speech-reading test without in any way influencing their actual communicative proficiency.

Rehabilitation management involves the effective coordination of available resources in order to effect a broad-based change in a person's adaptive behavior. However, before these resources can be effectively marshaled, the problem must be understood both in general and specific terms. Therefore the first seven chapters of the text are devoted to the essential information you must have if you are to meet the needs of hearing-impaired children and adults successfully. I reject the idea that we "train" audiologists, speech and language therapists, or teachers to work with persons with impaired hearing. Our concern must be to educate, not train. Techniques, methods, and skills are of secondary value. What is important is that, as an educator, you develop a keen curiosity about the task, that you gain the information necessary to think logically, systematically, and creatively about it, and that you are able to approach the task with a problem-solving attitude. Above all, you must respect your role. To achieve this level of security, you must be knowledgeable, but open-minded; structured, yet flexible.

THE HUMAN COMMUNICATION SYSTEM

It is not possible to engage in problem solving without an understanding of the nature of the problem and a rationale for the procedures to use to resolve the problem. Your role in habilitative/rehabilitative management of hearing-impaired persons involves finding ways to reduce the negative impact that the hearing deficit has on communication. Management necessitates a rationale. That rationale must be based upon a model of your understanding of the normal communication process and the ways in which hearing impairment disrupts its function. Our first need, therefore, is to understand what is involved in normal human communication. To do this we will examine a model.

A communication model consists of a schematic representation of the stages and functions that a particular theory suggests are involved in human communication. The model is theoretical because we have virtually no concrete evidence of what actually occurs within the communicating individual. The theory can be developed only by carefully comparing observed changes in behavior associated with a specific stimulus presented to the listener. A model generally results from a consolidation of experimental and empirical data supported by philosophical reasoning. Although a model may prove to be an imperfect representation of what actually happens, it provides a valuable basis for understanding how a hearing deficit disrupts the normal process of communication. It also helps us to understand how information encoded into different physical forms—for example, light waves, sound waves, pressure waves—can interact to increase comprehension. This knowledge will have important implications for the later discussion of the role of vision and audition in communication training of the hearing-impaired person.

Physical Aspects of the Speech Signal

The one segment of the human-communication model that we can study objectively and that we do know a great deal about is the physical signal by which speech is transmitted from speaker to listener. This acoustic signal is distorted by a hearing impairment. In order to understand the effects of this distortion, you need to know how the signal is produced and how information about linguistic values is encoded into it.

Neither ideas nor language can be transferred physically between persons. Comprehension is dependent, therefore, upon the ability of the listener to receive information that permits him or her to reconstruct *equivalents* of the language patterns which *represent* those ideas. The information transmitted and received is encoded into the physical signal which travels between the speaker and listener. Hearing impairment distorts the signal received. This distortion limits the ability of the listener to reconstruct an equivalent of the message which the speaker wishes to convey. If the hearing-impaired person's hearing deficit is so severe as to prevent adequate monitoring of his or her own speech production, then the production and transmission of correct speech sound patterns will also be affected. This will compound the interpersonal communication problem. Studying those aspects of the acoustic speech signal which are relevant to a basic understanding of how two people talk with each other will help you to understand the extent to which amplification can and cannot compensate for the deficit in acoustic information. Such knowledge is also necessary for you to realize why hearing impairment does not distort all sounds equally, and will help you to consider how to approach the teaching of speech to hearing-impaired children.

Even with amplification, many hearing-impaired persons are still unable to derive enough information from the acoustic signal to comprehend a given message. Because information about the thought or idea is also encoded by the speaker into the visual channel, vision has the potential of serving a valuable role in the reception of additional information. The production of speech sounds involves the use of the speech articulators whose movements are visible to varying degrees. Visible articulatory patterns, therefore, constitute a potential source of valuable information about the speech code. The common auditory-visual link of speech articulation frequently provides enough information from both sensory channels to reconstruct a spoken message not recoverable through acoustic information alone. Behavioral cues to meaning are also often transmitted simultaneously with the spoken message. This additional source of visual information, together with cues which may be generated by such situational constraints as dress, tools, equipment, environment, helps the hearing-impaired person to make use of all available cues to meaning. Your understanding of the nature of the visual stimulus in communication and the extent to which it can contribute to the comprehension of spoken language should directly affect the way you design communication-training strategies.

Perception and the Effects of Hearing Impairment

Information processing, if successful, leads to perception. When information processing proves inadequate, comprehension does not occur. The creative act of perception is, therefore, of prime importance. How does a hearing impairment interfere with this process? In order to understand how this occurs, we must examine some perceptual processes fundamental to communication. We will begin a very basic consideration of the role of the senses in human beings. Too often we treat hearing impairment only within the narrow confines of its effect on speech comprehension. We tend to neglect the profound effect it can have upon a person's contact with the world. A hearing impairment alters the perception of reality, depriving a person of a full complement of information about his or her relationship to the environment. The psychological and social ramifications of such an alteration can be profound. Once again we will use a theory and a model to examine the process of perception. This model will be helpful in understanding the types of problems a hearing-impaired person encounters when trying to follow a conversation about an unfamiliar topic, learning new information in school, paying attention in class, remembering what was said a few sentences ago.

We have already suggested that the ability to integrate auditory and visual cues to speech will significantly enhance the hearing-impaired person's understanding of the message. This topic is so important that a separate chapter has been devoted to it so that you can become familiar with the research on how vision contributes to speech recognition and the factors that affect this ability in hearing-impaired persons. This topic has direct relevance to how we train or retrain hearing-impaired persons to understand spoken language. Controversy exists about how young hearing-impaired children should be taught. Some specialists advocate a predominately auditory approach to teaching, whereas others advocate an auditory-visual approach that encourages speech reading as well as listening. As a professional you will often encounter such unresolved issues. You will also learn that others have polarized these issues so that supporters are divided into camps, rapidly losing their objectivity in undertaking or evaluating research on the topic. In time, you should be able to reach your own independent conclusions concerning the criteria you will use in selecting a particular approach to working with preschool children. Our goal in considering perception is a better understanding of some of the effects that hearing impairment has on both perception and language.

AMPLIFICATION FOR THE HEARING-IMPAIRED PERSON

The most important tool to help the hearing-impaired person surmount the handicap is a hearing aid or educational amplification unit. No system of amplification can restore hearing, but it can make useful residual hearing, which could not otherwise be reached. Using amplification, your clients or pupils will be able to achieve goals unattainable without it. Three chapters are devoted to this invaluable aid to management in order to provide the key concepts essential to understanding what the manufacturer of a particular amplication system tells you about the instrument and its use. The practical application of this information ensures that your client will obtain maximum benefit from amplification. We will also consider some of the questions a client is likely to raise about his or her aid, or questions parents may ask about their child's hearing aid. We do not expect you to become expert in either hearing aids or educational amplification systems. The purpose is to make you feel reasonably secure in counseling clients concerning amplification and in making best use of it in your management of a habilitation or rehabilitation program. In this section, we will also examine the uses of amplification in the educational setting. Increasingly, teachers and therapists are working in settings that provide some form of group or individual amplification systems for use with children. We will consider the types of equipment you may encounter and discuss the advantages and disadvantages of each type.

A MODEL FOR THE MANAGEMENT OF PROBLEMS RESULTING FROM HEARING IMPAIRMENT

In the first part of the book our concern will be to acquire an understanding of the nature of the task that confronts us. In the second part of the book we will consider how to apply that insight to the organization and implementation of a plan of management designed to meet the needs of individual children and adults with impaired hearing. Our first consideration will be to understand what is meant by management and the rationale that supports it. We will discuss the philosophy of management before we examine the procedures it involves.

At each stage of our discussion of procedures, you must critically evaluate what is being suggested. In the light of previously acquired information, you must decide whether the procedures suggested are logical and supportable. You will also have to decide whether you consider the suggestions to be practical. Above all, you must decide for yourself how to help the people who seek your counsel. This text is intended to be a guide for you, not a blueprint for all situations.

The goal of a management program is to facilitate maximal adjustment of the handicapped person to his or her immediate environment. In most cases the hearing disability will remain constant. The resulting handicap, however, will vary constantly. A handicap represents the discrepancy between what a situation demands and a person's ability to meet those demands. As the complexity of a situation increases, as a person seeks higher levels of function, the handicap will increase, unless specific ways are devised to reduce the person-environment impedance. No communication-skills training program alone can be expected to achieve this. The effective management of all resources offers the only route to success.

The major resource lies within the individual. It consists of a person's potential for changing the perception of a problem and for developing targeted problem-solving strategies. Valuable resources also exist within the individual's family, at school, and to some extent in the working environment. Educational and even social environments may be modified by creative use of technical resources. For example, I am involved in a research project aimed at providing access to the arts for the hearing-impaired person. We are achieving this through the use of radio-frequency amplification in concert halls, theaters, and museums. In a management role, you too are a resource. Your creativity in the marshaling and effective utilization of resources will greatly influence the child's or adult's success in adaptation.

The Preschool Child

Although each hearing-impaired child and adult requires an individualized plan of management, a general outline for meeting the needs of particular age groups can be developed. It is appropriate to consider preschool children as a group and to discuss their common needs. The preschool years can be divided further into infancy (birth to 3 years) and nursery-school years (3 to 6 years), the upper limits of which include kindergarten. This division hinges on the observation that from birth to 3 years, the focus of need is on the parents, whereas for the later preschool years, focus shifts to the child. During the first three years of life, the infant's dependency on the parents is high. The most effective intervention techniques, therefore, are those that affect the parents' understanding of the child's learning needs and that increase their ability to create a rich cognitive and linguistic learning environment for their child. Three-year-old children not only benefit from a stimulating home environment, but they also are capable of responding to a more intense, structured learning experience. The emphasis thus shifts from a parent-centered management model to a child-centered model with continued parent involvement.

We will examine these two management models both in terms of how to assess the needs of the parents and their child, and how to structure a program specifically designed to address these needs. We will consider both the information and personal adjustment needs of the family and the audiologic, communicative, and behavioral needs of the child. We will continue to address these needs in our discussion of the older preschool child. We will concentrate, however, on meeting cognitive and linguistic needs in a more structured approach than we will adopt through parent training. We will be particularly concerned with the integration of individualized speech and language stimulation with the broader, ongoing stimulation occurring within the classroom.

Once the child approaches school age, important decisions must be made concerning what will be the most appropriate educational placement. A procedure by which this decision must be reached has now been laid down by law. We will review the process as it involves the parents and you, and we will consider the types of educational opportunities currently available to hearing-impaired children in many communities.

The Primary School Child

Entrance to primary school creates a whole new set of demands for every child. The early grades are structured to facilitate the adaptation process. Most normal children are able to make the necessary adjustments without special help. This cannot be assumed to be the case for a hearing-impaired child unless otherwise demonstrated. Support services to the school child must be provided on the basis of a careful assessment of the child's capabilities and the demands of the learning environment. We must always strive to modify both child and environment to effect maximal compatibility and to minimize the handicap.

We will continue to approach this task within a management framework. First we will examine the assessment of needs. We will try to place ourselves in the position of the teachers to determine what they need to know in order to maximize their contributions to the learning needs of the child. We will examine test information from a functional point of view to determine what implications our findings about the child will have for a classroom teacher. We will then consider the child's needs and discuss how these can be assessed.

The assessment process has as its purpose the identification of needs and the evaluation of resources. The management process involves utilizing those resources according to a well-designed plan of intervention that takes into account the special circumstances of each child, teacher, and learning environment. We will consider how we can use the assessment data to help the teacher help the child, to determine what the parents' role will be in the management process, and to evaluate what the child's specific needs are. Once we understand the needs, we will discuss intervention strategies that may be effective in meeting them. Three major need categories will be considered: receptive communication, expressive communication, and counseling.

The Postprimary School Child

The hearing-impaired child who adjusts well to primary-school education by learning to accommodate the various demands made upon him or her will have made a good start in the educational process. This is true regardless of the type of placement. However, we must not be lulled into complacency by success. Progression through the primary grades involves changing demands and changing expectations for all children; the learning process becomes more complex, the academic content more difficult. At any time, the organization of resources for a given child may become inadequate. This is especially likely to occur when the young person moves from primary grades to junior high, and then to high school. We will consider some of the need changes that occur as a result of different teaching techniques as well as from the student's maturation.

The Hearing-Impaired Adult

Our approach to the problems of the hearing-impaired adult involves the same management philosophy that governed our discussion of the needs of the hearing-impaired child. Although helping a hearing-impaired adult is usually far less complex, the need for a comprehensive approach to problem solving is just as great. To date, adult rehabilitation has not proved to be notably successful. To a considerable extent, this results from a hearing therapists' failure to realize the broad impact of hearing impairment upon the life of an adult. By confining rehabilitation efforts to auditory and visual training, we have failed to address the specific communication problems that arise in work, home, and social environments. We have tried a narrow approach to a problem that requires a very comprehensive one. In explaining how management techniques apply to adult clients, we will cite examples of specific clients who illustrate very differing needs and then explain how such needs can be accommodated.

When you have reached this level of understanding of the problem, and of problem reduction, we will introduce the tool of auditory and visual communication training. The use of this tool is an integral component of communication training for hearing-impaired children; we refer to it as Look-Listen-and-Decide.

My aim with children is to ensure that auditory and visual training blend so completely into the stimulation of cognitive and linguistic development that you perceive it as an important but inseparable part of the overall enrichment process. I have separated auditory and visual communication training from the chapter on management of the adult hearing-impaired person because it remains such a dominant component in present rehabilitation programs. I want to place this valuable tool within the larger perspective of management. To do this it will be necessary to develop a philosophy about auditory and visual training that can be encompassed by the communication and perceptual models presented in the first part of the book. We will identify certain important precepts that must be carefully considered before providing auditory-visual training. Although we will examine the auditory and visual components of communication training separately, this dichotomy is for convenience of discussion only and does not reflect an acceptance of the separation of audition and vision for training, except for such specific purposes as will be described. Finally we will discuss how to plan auditory and visual training as part of the whole task of increasing communication effectiveness.

As you can see, the challenge of providing for the needs of children and adults is a large one. To meet it you need a great deal of information. You need an understanding of normal communication processes and also insight into how these processes are impeded by an impairment of hearing. You must then draw upon your knowledge to develop a systematic program of problem solving. From this point on, we will review the information essential to determining a way in which you can minimize the impact of hearing impairment on the individuals you will have an opportunity to help.

The Human Communication System

2

A Communication Model

The problems of the person with impaired hearing arise from difficulty in understanding what others are saying about an unlimited number of possible topics in a wide variety of situations. When the impairment is congenital or occurs early in life, the child's ability to learn optimally through audition, the manner by which so much of our knowledge is normally acquired, will be affected. The acquisition of verbal language skills particularly will be involved. For a person with a hearing problem, therefore, the overriding difficulty is to define and share experience.

Satisfactory communication is dependent upon two or more people's sharing a common means of interaction. This necessitates the development of a communication system in which the participants have compatibility. The person with impaired hearing will experience a communication handicap in proportion to the degree to which his or her handicap reduces this compatibility. It is the aim of habilitation/rehabilitation procedures to develop compensatory strategies to reduce the impedance between the individual and the larger communication matrix into which that person must fit. In this and the next five chapters, we consider the nature of normal communication in order to better understand how it is affected by impaired hearing.

We remain far from a comprehensive knowledge of the intricate processes of human communication; indeed, we may never fully comprehend them. However, we know enough to be able to construct theoretical models based upon research, empirical data, and reasoning. The purpose of such models, of which there are many types, is not to explain communication. A model serves, rather, to integrate what we know from a variety of fields of study into a holistic picture. We can then use a given model to examine the component units to see how they relate, and to test the model's integrity and usefulness in understanding the communication process.

A model is, therefore, simply a way of examining a process by attempting to incorporate all available information about it. It has the advantage of providing a structure within which to observe and contemplate. Yet the very structure that facilitates perception of the process being considered also serves to inhibit our awareness of other perspectives. Even when it is possible to physically examine each component of a network, a particular orientation or approach is necessary. The particular orientation of an investigator must be founded upon a carefully constructed hypothesis and must be arrived at after systematic evaluation of the factors known to be involved. Ideally it should then be possible to prove or disprove the hypothesis by experimental studies. However, many problems prove to be so complex that they defy experimental study within the limits of current knowledge and equipment.

Certain aspects of the communication process present this problem. Parts of the process are easily observable. We can study the mechanics of respiration, the nature of the laryngeal mechanism, the operation of the middle ear. This still leaves inaccessible to us most of the complex processes concerned with the exchange of information. We are not able to examine the exact nature of the process of formulating ideas, of coding them into language, of analyzing the acoustic signal in the auditory pathway, or of the final perception of the intended message by the listener. For these reasons you must recognize that most of what is presented in this chapter is theoretical. Other models reflect other theories derived from the same information. Nevertheless, the advantage to a model is that it provides the teacher or rehabilitation specialist with the basis for understanding the communication problems associated with impaired hearing and it affords a rationale for the intervention procedures we develop.

With these cautions in mind, we now consider *a* model of the communication process.

THE STORE OF EQUIVALENT EXPERIENCES

When communication occurs successfully between two people, it means that Subject A has managed to cause Subject B to experience thoughts that represent the ideas Subject A wished to communicate. The important point is that the thoughts the listener experiences are his own. They are *equivalent to* those of Subject A and are *evoked by* Subject A, but they were neither sent nor received.

The first requirement for successful communication is, therefore, that each participant possess a store of experiences to which others may relate. Similarity of stored experience is a prerequisite. When experiences between people are noticeably different—as occurs, for example, between racial or cultural groups—communication becomes difficult even when the parties are unable to use a common language code. This is relevant to our understanding of the problems arising from hearing impairment.

When we encounter a young, congenitally severely hearing-impaired child, we are acutely aware of that child's difficulties in using language to express ideas. It is easy for the problems of lingustic proficiency to conceal the fact that the child's communication handicap goes much deeper than the use of structural language. So much of what we know is acquired through use of verbal language. Even our perceptions of direct experience are modified by the manner in which we linguistically encode them. Because of language deficiency, the young hearing-impaired child's experience of his or her world will be less sophisticated than that of his or her hearing peers. Unless special help is provided the child will not be able to participate equally in shared experiences as his or her peers do through their use of language. Thus we must not overlook the fact that although difficulty in the use of the language code appears to be the problem, the situation is even further complicated by the limits placed upon the acquisition and storage of experience. The reduced compatibility between the store of experiences of the hearing-handicapped child and hearing peers places the roots of the problem even deeper than the coding and transmission processes.

This becomes an increasingly influential factor as the growing child with normal hearing adds more and more abstract experiences to knowledge of the concrete relationships of the physical world of people and things. In order to perceive, store, and communicate at an abstract level, use of an increasingly sophisticated language code is essential. The child with a congenital or early-acquired hearing deficit will almost certainly be unable to add to his or her store of experience at the same rate as hearing peers. This is not to say that the hearing-impaired child is less intelligent or less capable than his or her hearing counterparts. The problem lies in the impairment of auditory processing of information resulting from the hearing deficit. The ultimate impact of the impairment on the child's learning rate will depend on many factors. The child's innate intellectual potential, personality, parental and environmental influences, and the age at which intervention is begun are among the most important. However, the amount of useable residual hearing, together with the age at which amplification is provided and the success with which it is used, will exert a highly significant influence on the successful acquisition of knowledge.

Most of what a child comes to know about the world is self-deduced through exposure to events in context. We learn mostly by a process of absorption, similar to osmosis, rather than by direct instruction. Yet for experience itself to influence behavior requires refinement, clarification, correlation, and storage. This is particularly true if experience is to serve to permit a person to predict ahead. We use linguistically stored information about past experience to define what appear initially to be novel situations or problems. The processes necessitate the development of some form of symbolic language, though it need not be spoken language. Without the language tool, the experiences of the child with impaired hearing will be different from those of hearing peers. These experiences will also be impoverished, compared to those hearing peers, and their rate of acquisition reduced. This is so because poor language-coding abilities limit the manner in which the hearing-impaired child can deal with direct experience. The hearing-impaired child will have difficulty in defining an event, in storing information about the event, and in correlating the event with memories of past experiences. The discrepancy will rapidly accelerate as children with normal hearing move from the period of concrete thinking to more sophisticated processes of abstraction. Abstraction involves the ability to deal with things, people, events, and feelings that are not currently occurring. Abstraction allows us to deal instead with the symbolic referents into which those experiences have been encoded. We can thus overcome the limitations imposed by time and space, to deal with what one student aptly referred to as the "not here–not now."

The problems arising from congenital or early acquired hearing impairment thus affect the store of experiences that dominate the compatibility between the hearing-impaired child and those with whom that child must communicate. The degree of impedance, at this most basic level, will depend on the compatibility between the experiences of the communicators. This is why hearing impairment occurring very early in life exerts such a profound influence on normal cognitive and linguistic development. It explains why children who have had hearing for only one or two years, or even for no more than a few months before it is lost, evidence so much more natural auditory responsiveness when amplification is provided than a child with a true congenital hearing deficit. It also explains the concern of audiologists, teachers, and hearing therapists for early diagnosis and intervention.

The effect of hearing impairment on the development of a store of common experiences decreases as the age at which the hearing impairment occurs increases. The effect is closely related to the language level at the age of onset, but its influence is felt even in the older school-age years. At that time, the filtering out of auditory information affects the acquisition and understanding of the more sophisticated forms of language play, such as humor, sarcasm, double-entendre or punning. These more subtle limitations may not be evident in standard test results, but they often show up in anecdotal accounts of difficulties experienced.

The separation of experience and language is thus an artificial dichotomy; they can only really be considered separate in the early years when experience precedes language. As language develops, exposure to new verbal expressions or new vocabulary often initiates a search for an experience or meaning to relate to the language.

Hearing impairment must also be understood in terms of its impact on the learning process. Test results that indicate that a child has adequate language skills do not reflect the difficulty the child is almost certain to have in using those skills under adverse listening conditions. To be able to use linguistic skills successfully, the child must receive the spoken message with a clarity adequate to permit language decoding. The test environment usually provides optimum listening conditions. School classrooms, as we will discuss in Chapter 10, constitute notoriously poor listening environments. Under the conditions of noise and reverberation that the student is likely to encounter in school, even a mild hearing impairment can impair speech comprehension. Difficulty is frequently experienced in following directions and in feeling confident to act even upon what has been heard. The effect of such reduction in the clarity of the speech signal has a still greater impact on the student's ability to learn from orally presented information, which may be difficult to understand even when heard clearly.

A COMMON LINGUISTIC CODE

In discussing the importance of a common store of equivalent experience, some consideration of the influence of language is unavoidable. It is apparent that language and experience are intimately related. Language not only molds experience, it also serves as a valuable tool that facilitates the acquisition of new experience. We use our language system to code experience for storage and easy retrieval. In this way we are able to deal with the world abstractly, which infinitely affects the manner in which we can interact with others. Instead of confining our discussions to things present or to events as they occur, we are able to override the constraints of time and space by tapping into the abstractions of those occurrences now stored in the referential language system. Symbolic coding permits us to transform concrete experiences into abstract ones. When we function linguistically, we do so by manipulating the code to formulate the referential patterns equivalent to the experiences we wish to consider. Communication occurs when two or more people use a language code to cause each other to formulate equivalent coexperiential abstracts. The ability to do this successfully necessitates not only that participants each have a store of equivalent experiences, but also that they share a common language code.

When we think of a language code we automatically think of spoken language because in all cultures, in all societies, spoken language is the common basis for communication. Languages differ in the actual symbols that have evolved, and this presents a communication barrier between people from different language cultures. In addition, different languages result in individuals experiencing the world differently from one another. Nevertheless, all languages are based upon the ability of human beings to restructure experience into a symbolic code.

The potential to do this is almost certainly part of our genetic endowment. The newborn child with normal sensory-motor capacities, capable of learning *a* language, is, therefore, capable of learning *all* languages equally well. As the child begins to develop a particular language, the ability to acquire fluency in others decreases as the years pass. Even so, a child who has a need to learn several languages, will retain far more of the facility that permitted the first language to be learned than will the monolingual person. This decreasing capacity to learn other languages as we grow older does not represent a particular handicap to most of us. Recognition of this phenomenon should, however, have great impact upon our appreciation of the problems of the prelinguistically deaf child. For such a child, the task is not second-language learning, but the acquisition of a native tongue. The longer we wait to take intervention steps to stimulate language learning, the harder this task will be and the more limited the child's potential for optimal achievement.

LINGUISTIC CODING

The language-coding process entails:

1. A set of referents, or values
2. A set of tokens, or symbols, with which to identify those values
3. A set of rules that governs the manner in which the tokens may be combined to form complex patterns to facilitate rapid communication about an unlimited number of values or experiences

Referents

These refer to the semantic level of language, which we have already discussed to some extent. At this level of processing we stand at the boundary, or *interface,* between raw experience and the details of experience encoded into linguistic structures or patterns. Communication begins and ends at this interface, where language evokes perception of experience, or, in expressive communication, where the experience is encoded into the language form. In a way, the concept of a true boundary is misleading, for there is, as we have discussed, a considerable overlap between language and experience. The meaning of experience must mesh with the symbolic level of processing if communication is to occur. Semantic perception involves the evoking of units of speech as large as a phrase or several phrases. At this level the patterns are treated holistically with little or no awareness of the individual components. This is the level of identification of *meaning,* the level of *understanding.* However, holistic pattern processing first requires that a sufficient number of individual components at lower linguistic levels—that is, phonemes, words—be identified in order to predict without ambiguity the future pattern development and to identify the associated meaning. These tokens exist in a layered or *hierarchical structure* and may be identified from the information generated by the speaker and broadcast into several media.

Tokens

Tokens are elements of the language structure that may be identified and reconstructed by the "listener" from the pattern of information received by his or her sensory system. It is again necessary to stress that tokens are learned, that they *exist within the speaker and receiver,* but not in the physical stimulus. The pattern contains only the information necessary to identify the token. This requires that the receiver be sensitive to enough of the physical stimulus to identify the pattern unambiguously. The receiver must also be experienced in transforming the physical pattern of information to the abstract linguistic token. The child with a congenital hearing impairment experiences difficulties with both of these stages, whereas a person with a postlinguistically acquired hearing deficit has trouble with pattern reception only.

Linguistic tokens are the building blocks of linguistic communication. They may be encoded by articulation (speech), broadcast acoustically (sound waves), and received auditorily (hearing and auditory perception). Similarly they may be encoded physically by the hands (signing, fingerspelling), broadcast visually (light waves), and received visually (seeing and visual perception). Visual encoding of token information has also been successful using colored plastic chips to represent different linguistic values (Carrier, 1976; Premack & Premack, 1974). The vibrotactile channel, another avenue for the encoding of linguistic patterns, has relevance in teaching children with minimal residual hearing (Englemann & Rosov, 1975; Erber & Cramer, 1974).

Rules

We mentioned earlier that tokens exist in a hierarchical structure. At each level, a set of rules peculiar to a particular language culture governs the ways in which tokens may be combined. In effective communication both the speaker and listener are familiar with these linguistic rules, which exist at each level of processing of the verbal message and are used both in encoding and decoding. The shared knowledge of these rules permits the tokens to be restructured into patterns of increasing complexity. Thus, the pattern at each level derives from the application of a rule to the tokens at a lower or *deeper* level, changing the form but not the value of the message. The human mind learns to recognize rapidly the implied value of a pattern at a given level. It is not necessary to decode a particular pattern to its essential ingredients because its meaning can be predicted from a knowledge of the rules governing restructuring of tokens.

The size of the tokens vary from phonemes to sentences. There has been much debate over the question of the size of the perceptual unit used in speech perception. It is assumed that the *minimal* elements of speech perception are located below the level of the phoneme (Lehiste, 1972). It is likely, however, that in normal communication we process a chunk of the signal no smaller than is necessary to identify a token at the highest level. Only in phonetic transcription or in spelling are we interested in processing individual sounds. Usually, we do not even have to pay attention to individual words, but listen instead for the meaning.

We will discuss this further when we consider speech perception. It helps to remember, however, that the child with impaired hearing has reduced familiarity with the rules for identifying or generating syntactic patterns. Thus, the ability to process the surface level of the larger pattern is reduced, forcing the child to depend more heavily on the processing of smaller units. A hearing-impaired child, therefore, has much greater need of the extrinsic information contained in the acoustic signal of which, paradoxically, such a child receives less than a person with normal hearing.

INFORMATION PROCESSING

Before we leave our discussion of the role the cognitive-linguistic system plays in communication, it is necessary to examine how the constraints of language structure operate. We need to understand how abstract language patterns in one person's mind can effect the construction of equivalent patterns in the mind of another. This is achieved by the transmission and processing of *information.* Note that the meaning of the term information here derives from statistical theory having to do with probability. Its use, however, is highly appropriate in the context of our discussion because our model of communication is built upon predictions made by the listener on the basis of his or her ability to compute probabilities.

Information was described by Shannon and Weaver (1967), who evolved a mathematical model of information transmission, as "the informativeness of the symbols in a message relative to one's expectation of those symbols." In other words, the components of the pattern at all levels of processing are informative to the extent that they are needed and used to constrain choice.

Phonemic Constraints

That which we expect, whether it be individual speech sounds, a sentence, or a whole phrase, does not convey very much constraint value—that is, information. The unexpected is, by contrast, highly informative. Thus, the role of information is to limit choice on the basis of expectancies computed from a knowledge of probabilities. Carroll (1964, p. 55) illustrates this with three strings of ten-letter messages with the tenth letter missing:

P	R	R	N	W	B	I	T	K	_
A	A	A	A	A	A	A	A	A	_
G	E	N	E	R	A	T	I	O	_

Carroll points out that the informativeness of the missing symbol is great in the first example because the symbols are in random sequence. The probability of a given letter occurring in the tenth position is uninfluenced by those preceding it, and is, therefore, low. In the second example, if the selection of the letter A for the missing symbol proves correct, it will convey little information because one would have had little difficulty predicting it. If, on the other hand, it proves not to be A, the missing letter would be highly informative. The missing N in the third string of letters may be predicted with a high degree of success because the choice of the letters is severely restricted by all of the preceding letters and is further constrained by the imposition of morphological constraints and the semantic criterion—that is, for the result to be a meaningful English word, an N is required for completion.

Structural Constraints

At each level of linguistic processing, a different set of probabilities operates. For a person familiar with the linguistic rules the speaker is using, the linguistic constraints operating at the phonemic level begin to generate probabilities as soon as the first phoneme is identified. This is so because the listener's mind has subconsciously learned the rules that determine the relative statistical probability of occurrence of a given phoneme immediately following or preceding any other given phoneme. As the number of phonemes decoded increases, the probabilities for succeeding phonemes continue to narrow with each additional phoneme until only one is possible. To understand how we narrow the choices to one phoneme, it is necessary to recognize that as phonemic pattern builds, we begin to derive enough information at that level to allow us to shift gears and to begin to process according to the higher constraints of the morphological level. At this level we are concerned with the requirement that phonemes be grouped into meaningful forms such as *ing, ly, ness,* or into whole words. These forms comprise the basic elements of grammatical structure and are slotted into the syntactical constraint patterns until syntactic predictions begin to be possible. As soon as this occurs, perceptual processing begins to operate on probabilities computed at the syntactic level of pattern reconstruction. This obviates the need for time-consuming processing of individual units, shifting the reconstruction process to the generating of much larger patterns on the basis of syntactic constraints.

The role of the structural constraints of language was demonstrated by the author in an experiment using thirty college students divided into three groups of ten (Table 2.1). Each subject was presented a series of dashes which, he or she was told, represented groups of letters. The students were further advised that the letters might or might not constitute meaningful words, and that the units might or might not be related to each other. All of the letters were drawn from the sentence, "The cat sat on the mat."

In the first test item (A), administered to Group I, the letters were arranged at random—that is, they were not subject to any structural constraint. In the second test item (B), administered to Group II, the letter order constituted words, but the word order was randomized; the subjects were therefore subject to phonemic constraint but not to constructional rules. The test item (C), group III, constituted the complete sentence, which obeyed the rules of formal English construction.

Test item A: OTT / TAS / CHA / NE / MTT / EHA.

Test item B: MAT / THE / THE / ON / SAT / CAT.

Test item C: THE / CAT / SAT / ON / THE / MAT.

Each subject was given the following instructions:

The dashes on the sheet represent letters of the alphabet. With one exception these are grouped in threes. You are asked to guess the letters in each group, letter by letter. The letters

TABLE 2.1 Score Sheet for Linguistic Probability Experiment

	Alphabet Lists																									
1.	A	B	C	D	E	F	G	H	I	J	K	L	M	N	O	P	Q	R	S	T	U	V	W	X	Y	Z
2.	A	B	C	D	E	F	G	H	I	J	K	L	M	N	O	P	Q	R	S	T	U	V	W	X	Y	Z
3.	A	B	C	D	E	F	G	H	I	J	K	L	M	N	O	P	Q	R	S	T	U	V	W	X	Y	Z
4.	A	B	C	D	E	F	G	H	I	J	K	L	M	N	O	P	Q	R	S	T	U	V	W	X	Y	Z
5.	A	B	C	D	E	F	G	H	I	J	K	L	M	N	O	P	Q	R	S	T	U	V	W	X	Y	Z
6.	A	B	C	D	E	F	G	H	I	J	K	L	M	N	O	P	Q	R	S	T	U	V	W	X	Y	Z
7.	A	B	C	D	E	F	G	H	I	J	K	L	M	N	O	P	Q	R	S	T	U	V	W	X	Y	Z
8.	A	B	C	D	E	F	G	H	I	J	K	L	M	N	O	P	Q	R	S	T	U	V	W	X	Y	Z
9.	A	B	C	D	E	F	G	H	I	J	K	L	M	N	O	P	Q	R	S	T	U	V	W	X	Y	Z
10.	A	B	C	D	E	F	G	H	I	J	K	L	M	N	O	P	Q	R	S	T	U	V	W	X	Y	Z
11.	A	B	C	D	E	F	G	H	I	J	K	L	M	N	O	P	Q	R	S	T	U	V	W	X	Y	Z
12.	A	B	C	D	E	F	G	H	I	J	K	L	M	N	O	P	Q	R	S	T	U	V	W	X	Y	Z
13.	A	B	C	D	E	F	G	H	I	J	K	L	M	N	O	P	Q	R	S	T	U	V	W	X	Y	Z
14.	A	B	C	D	E	F	G	H	I	J	K	L	M	N	O	P	Q	R	S	T	U	V	W	X	Y	Z
15.	A	B	C	D	E	F	G	H	I	J	K	L	M	N	O	P	Q	R	S	T	U	V	W	X	Y	Z
16.	A	B	C	D	E	F	G	H	I	J	K	L	M	N	O	P	Q	R	S	T	U	V	W	X	Y	Z
17.	A	B	C	D	E	F	G	H	I	J	K	L	M	N	O	P	Q	R	S	T	U	V	W	X	Y	Z

may or may not constitute meaningful words or sentences. The alphabet lists below permit you to record each letter you use for each blank. Beginning with the first dash (examiner indicates this on subject's sheet), which corresponds to Alphabet List No. 1 below, try to guess the missing letter. I will tell you if your guess is right or wrong. If you name the correct letter, fill in the dash. If your answer is incorrect, cross that letter off in Alphabet List No. 1 and try again. Continue guessing until you choose the correct letter. We shall repeat this for each dash.

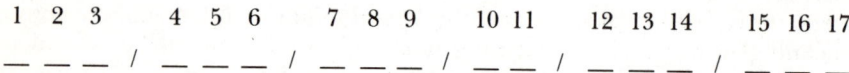

1 2 3   4 5 6   7 8 9   10 11   12 13 14   15 16 17

— — — / — — — / — — — / — — / — — — / — — —

The examiner also checked, on a duplicate sheet, the letters the subject chose. The mean number of guesses required to correctly identify each letter was calculated for each student group. Also computed were the mean number of guesses made by each group per unit and for the complete test item.

The results (shown in Table 2.2) indicate that as the number of structural constraints increases, the ability of a subject to predict missing symbols also increases.

Group I subjects were constrained only by the 26 letters of the alphabet. They tended at first to guess according to the rules of English; for example, most subjects first guessed the initial letter to be *t*, predicting that the word was *the*. Once they realized that the letters did not constitute meaningful words, they resorted to random guessing. In each instance, with the exception of the first letters, the vowels required fewer guesses in this item than any of the consonants. This is because a large number of subjects, when guessing, first ran through the vowels. Therefore, when the missing letter was a vowel, it was quickly guessed. The

TABLE 2.2 The Effect of Different Degrees of Structural Constraint

Student Group	*Mean Number of Guesses Corrected to Nearest Whole Number*	*Test Item*																
										A								
I		O	T	T	T	A	S	C	H	A	N	E	M	T	T	E	H	A
	Letter mean	13	14	13	9	5	12	10	13	3	12	7	10	16	14	8	12	5
	Unit mean		13			9	8		9			9		13			14	
										A								
II		M	A	T	T	H	E	T	H	E	O	N	S	A	T	C	A	T
	Letter mean	8	3	7	12	9	1	11	5	2	7	4	10	3	2	11	3	4
	Unit mean		6			7			6		6			5			6	
										C								
III		T	H	E	C	A	T	S	A	T	O	N	T	H	E	M	A	T
	Letter mean	11	4	1	4	1	1	4	1	1	1	1	2	3	1	4	1	1
	Unit mean		6			2			2		1			2			2	

	Group	Item	
Mean number of guesses per item	I	A	10
	I	B	6
	III	C	2

number of guesses per letter does not improve as the number of known letters increases, because each letter is independent of the preceding or succeeding letter.

The results for Group II indicate that the effect of phonemic constraint is progressively to reduce the number of alternative letters from which the subject may choose. Within each unit (word), knowing the first letter obviously reduces the number of guesses needed to identify the second. Note, however, that correct identification of the first unit does not reduce the number of guesses necessary to identify the succeeding units, because each unit is independent of adjacent units.

In Group III, the effect of phonemic and constructional constraints is clearly seen to reduce the mean number of guesses per letter and per unit.

Contextual Constraints

Even familiarity with the structural rules of a language frequently proves insufficient to permit a message to be understood under conditions of distortion. If, however, the topic of conversation is made known, the distorted signal may be interpreted because it is in context. The effect of contextual and/or semantic constraints is to limit the choice of words and phrases that may be used to convey a particular meaning. A conversation on the topic of baseball eliminates the use of most vocabulary that might be appropriate to a discussion of, for example, music. It is in this way that we often reject a particular interpretation of a distorted message because it appears to be unrelated to its context. Certainly a relationship exists between the semantic and syntactical constraints. We are aided in our interpretation of the signal by the knowledge that nouns are naming words, that verbs designate activities, and adjectives, properties or characteristics. Yet, as Cherry (1957, p. 119) points out, meaning may be conveyed by a chain of nouns—for example, woman, street, crowd, traffic, noise, haste, thief, bag, lost, scream, police.

The reader, by virtue of a knowledge of syntax, can predict the missing elements; but it is also likely that the reader has experience with the types of contexts in which these words may occur, particularly when they occur in this order.

Situational Constraints

In addition to the effect that context has on the choice of vocabulary, the speaker is further limited in the choice of mode of expression by the actual situation in which he or she is to communicate a message. The same message may be expressed in a variety of different ways, and different words and phrases can be used according to the speaker's evaluation of the nature of the audience. A message may be communicated to a roommate in a form that may be totally inappropriate to convey the same information to one's parents. Situational constraints may be considered to be a function of the people present, the relationship of the speaker to these people, and the social structure of the particular environment. The form of expression of a message that passes between a professor and a student may reasonably be predicted as being different from the same message passing from the student to the professor. This will be influenced by the relationship that exists between these two people. Between individuals who have had little or no previous contact, the message will be influenced primarily by the speaker's evaluation of the role and social standing of the listeners.

The influence of environmental factors upon a topic of discussion and upon the manner in which the information is conveyed will be appreciated by the listener if that person imagines him- or herself in each of the following situations: in the main aisle of a large cathedral just before morning service, at an informal student party, in a seminar group, at the question period in a large lecture meeting, or on a first date in a small cocktail bar.

Redundancy

The result of these various constraints is to produce what is known as *redundancy*. This may be defined as that part of a message that can be eliminated without a significant loss of information. Carroll (1964, p. 56) explains it as "the property of texts (language contexts) that allows us to predict missing symbols from the context." It must not be confused with simple repetition of all or part of the message signal, though repetition may affect redundancy. The idea of redundancy is perhaps more easily understood if it is considered as the result of the interaction of certain factors within the speaker (and therefore the message signal), the environment, and the listener. It is not possible to state a redundancy figure for a given message signal without considering these three variables. What may prove to be redundant for one listener may not be so for another. A message signal in one set of environmental conditions may have high redundancy, whereas in a different environment the redundancy of the same message signal may be severely reduced. Similarly, a message spoken by a person whose native tongue is English may become extremely difficult to understand when spoken by a foreigner whose English is characterized by a heavy dialect. The most important factors influencing redundancy are shown in Table 2.3.

Shannon has shown that for the average adult reader, the redundancy of written English over any series of not greater than eight letters is approximately 50 percent. Thus, when we are operating under the constraints of written English, half of what we write is freely chosen, whereas the other half is determined by the structure of the language. In normal conversational speech, under favorable conditions, the level of redundancy is higher. Most of us can recall instances in which we have been able to maintain a conversation with one person while listening to the conversation of two people standing close to us.

Noise and Redundancy

Closely related to the concept of information is the concept of noise. In communication terminology this term is far more inclusive than the concept of audible noise. Noise may be considered the effect of any factor

TABLE 2.3 Factors Influencing Redundancy

Factors within the Speaker
- Compliance of the speaker to the rules of the language
- Compliance to the patterns of articulation, stress, intonation
- Size of vocabulary from which the message is composed
- Appropriate choice of words to convey the message

Factors within the Message Signal
- Number of syllables within the word
- Number of words within a sentence
- Number of different words (type-token ratio†)
- Amount of context
- Amount of repetition
- Frequency bandwidth of acoustic signal
- Intensity of acoustic signal

Factors within the Environment
- Amount of acoustic noise
- Amount of reverberation
- Amount and intensity of other environmental stimuli
- Number of potential clues related to the message

Factors within the Listener
- Familiarity with the language rules
- Familiarity with the speech patterns of the speaker
- Familiarity with the vocabulary used by the speaker
- Familiarity with the topic of conversation
- Fidelity of reception of the acoustic message signal
- Awareness of and ability to interpret related stimuli

†Type-token ratio: $\frac{\text{number of different words}}{\text{(total number of words)}}$

that adds confusion and so reduces the amount of information conveyed. In any communication situation, the listener is faced with varying amounts of noise in the system. This may be inherent within the message signal itself, it may be a function of limitations in the listener's ability to receive and decode the message signal accurately, or it may exist in the channel through which the message signal travels.* Table 2.4 indicates the major sources of noise in oral communication.

The importance of redundancy lies in the role it plays in helping to combat these noise factors. If the redundancy of a particular message is relatively high, then its resistance to noise or distortion is also great, permitting the receiver to obtain enough information to enable him or her to predict the missing elements of the message. The amount of redundancy in any given speech sample is, therefore, a function of the interaction between the speaker, the listener, and the message signal. It must

*The term *channel* refers to the pathway through which the message signal travels. This includes both the neurological and the environmental pathways; for example, auditory channel: hearing and sound waves; visual channel: vision and light waves; tactile channel: touch and low-frequency vibrations.

TABLE 2.4 Sources of Noise

Within the Speaker
- Inadequate vocabulary
- Poor syntax
- Semantic ambiguity
- Imprecise or deviant articulation of speech
- Poor vocal production
- Improper stress and inflection

Within the Environment
- Acoustic signal
  - Acoustic noise resulting in masking of the message signal
  - Distortion of the frequency pattern of the message signal
  - Reverberation
- Visual signal
  - Poor lighting
  - Visual field limited
  - Competing visual stimuli

Within the Listener
- Unfamiliarity with the vocabulary of rules of the language
- Failure to identify correctly the topic of the message
- Incorrect recognition of auditory and/or visual signals because of similarity between sounds or between the visible characteristics of some articulation patterns
- Distracting stimuli
- Psychological factors, such as poor intellectual ability, poor motivation, poor attention span, high distractibility, preoccupation with something else, prejudice against the speaker or topic of conversation, and so on.

be stressed that the value of redundancy is limited by the extent to which the receiver is able to utilize it. Unfamiliarity with the linguistic structure or ignorance concerning the context of the message will seriously affect the benefit that the listener can derive from redundancy of speech material.

An understanding of the role of noise and redundancy in communication helps us to appreciate how it is that a person with what appears to be quite a severe auditory handicap can often function adequately in a communication situation. At the same time, it emphasizes the need for developing in the individual an awareness of an ability to capitalize on other factors that contribute to redundancy.

The concept that human communication is a process based upon the ability to predict the next "bit" of information has been succinctly summarized by Peter Laurie in an article entitled "The Explorers" in the British *Sunday Times Supplement.* Laurie writes:

The idea of the mind computing the probabilities of what's coming next has proved an essential key in the fast-growing new branch of psycholinguistics. One of the problems here is to elucidate the processes of hearing speech and decoding it into ideas. A good deal of experimenting has been done on this now, starting with the work of Professor Colin Cherry at Imperial College, London, at the beginning of the 1950s. It appears that hearing and understanding a spoken message involves several layers of computation. At the first level we can pick out from the noise around us—a cocktail party, say—one voice. We can tell the rate it's speaking and the direction it's coming from. Even something as apparently simple as this is in fact very sophisticated. It involves, to keep track of the tone of voice, making a statistical analysis of the characteristic sounds of that voice, storing this and comparing all the incoming sounds with this to pick out the ones we want. Then to find its direction we have to store the last second or so of this voice's input into each ear and shuffle the two records until they match to find the time delay between the two ears.

The sounds from the selected voice are stored for less than a second and passed on to the next level where they are translated into the equivalent sounds one could make oneself, and stored again—this is how one can make a stab at the last few syllables of something in a foreign language. This transfers again into a store where the sounds are identified with meaningful words—the short term memory we use to hold a telephone number between directory and dial. Unless the number is consciously repeated and reinserted, it fades after six seconds or so. Then the words are recorded again as ideas and transferred into long term memory. Interest focuses at the moment on this transfer from short term into long term store and back again. It is suggested that as one listens to a speaker, one runs ahead, using the statistical structure of the language to throw up the probable next words out of the long term store and matching them in one's head against those in the short term store. What we remember, or understand, is not the sound *of the word we hear, but the* idea *stored in our heads that would generate the sound nearest to it. It's as if we were using a dictionary, flipping through it until we find a word that seems to match the word we hear and reading off the meaning. The fact that there's only one central dictionary is shown by the impossibility of speaking effectively while reading, writing, or listening.*

This dictionary is not, however, arranged alphabetically, but by a continously shifting scale of probabilities, and these are influenced by who is speaking, the situation we are both in, and particularly by what has just been said. So when one goes to answer the phone, one's dictionary already has some likely phrases ready to hear, like "Hold on, I have a call," and when you've got that far you hear "for you" automatically. But if the operator said, "Hold on, I have a call for umbilical hippopotamus," the last two words—having a low assigned probability—would not be found until it was too late, and so wouldn't be heard. That the brain works somehow like this was shown by an English psychologist, David Bruce, who made a record of a voice speaking against a background so noisy that nothing could be understood. He played this to a group of listeners who were told it was a talk about football. Then he played them one about hire purchase, and another about politics. Each time, given a cue, they could follow the sense; they were astonished to be told afterwards he'd played the same record each time (March 19, 1967).

Summary of Information Processing

To summarize information processing, we can say that information refers to the contribution any element of a pattern makes to the identification of the speaker's intent. A message component is said to be highly informative when it is not predictable. Each bit of information contributes to the identification of a meaningful unit of the language. The rules of a language operate at the level of phonemes, morphemes, syntax, and semantics. We process the incoming bits of information at each level only until we identify enough constraints to permit us to move up to the larger, more meaningful units at the next level. The more of the pattern that is apparent, the easier prediction of meaning becomes. The prediction of meaning from phonemic and structural constraints is enhanced by the effect of context, which relates to the rules of semantics. Finally, the constraints generated by the situation in which the communication arises further contribute to the probability of what is said. A given number of constraints is necessary to permit comprehension of a particular message by a particular person in a given place and time.

Constraints in excess of the required minimum constitute redundancy. They reduce the pressure on the listener, who does not have to pay attention to each bit of information. Factors within the speaker, listener, or environment that hinder the encoding, transmission, reception, or decoding of the message are known as *noise.* When noise occurs, the task of comprehending becomes more difficult. The listener is forced to draw upon redundant information to compensate for the increased difficulty. If insufficient redundancy exists to compensate for the effects of noise, the message will be distorted and misunderstood.

ENCODING MESSAGE EQUIVALENTS

We have seen how a thought or idea is encoded into, and to a considerable degree formulated by, the language code. We also saw that language is an abstraction, that phonemes, words, and grammar have no concrete form. Yet their influence can be transmitted to others. It is obvious, therefore, that at every point in the communication process, linguistic patterns must have concrete equivalents.

At the cortical level—the terminal from which outgoing message signals originate and incoming ones terminate—the patterns must be neurally represented. It is inappropriate for us to discuss the nature of neurolinguistics. We will simply assume that this representation consists of patterns of nerve-cell connections that come into being when certain ideas are linguistically coded. The importance of the concept to our discussion is that what begins now is a series of transformations of the linguistic information into different forms of physical representation.

At the level of the cortex, the linguistic pattern, which results from the use of a set of rules appropriate to the idea we wish to communicate, must be recorded. It must be put into a form which will result in the transmitting of encoded information into the environmental media shared by the person(s) with whom we seek to communicate. This information will then flow to the sensory receptors of our audience, where the process of decoding begins.

The essential components of a communication system are shown in Figure 2.1. They are:

1. *Source:* The source or the originator of the information or message that is to be fed into the system. In speech this is the cortex.
2. *Message.* The message constitutes any form of information that may be conveyed by meaningful behavior. Passage through the system is made possible by encoding the message into some form of conventional symbols, at which point we may consider the message to exist in the form of a message signal.
3. *Message signal:* The message signal constitutes the encoded message put into a form appropriate to the particular channel through which it is to travel. In speech communication the message signal travels from the source (cortex) to the transmitter (speech organs) in the form of electrical nerve im-

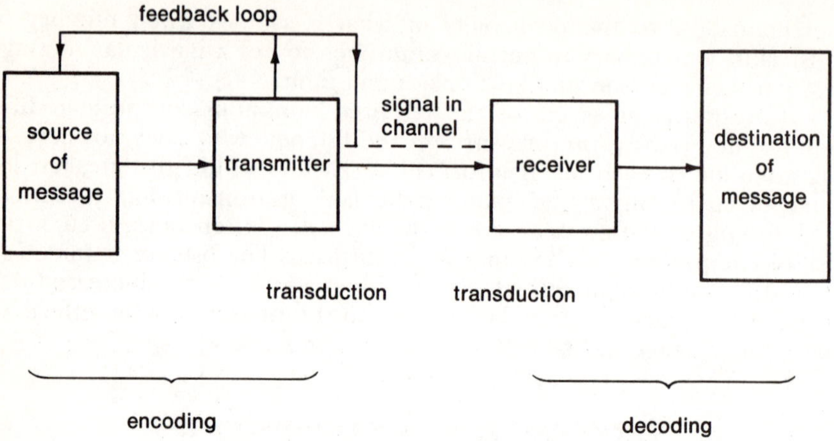

FIGURE 2.1 Simplified version of the basic components of communication through speech.

pulses; the energy is then converted into sound waves. On reaching the ear of the listener, the energy is converted into mechanical movement of the middle ear and finally back into nerve impulses by the inner-ear mechanism.

4. *Transmitter:* A transmitter is a device that projects the message signal from its source into another medium. In speech, the vocal folds serve to change the message signal existing as nerve impulses into the molecular movement of air particles that constitutes sound waves.
5. *Channel:* The channel is the pathway or medium through which the message signal travels, both within the individual (neurological) and in the external environment (physical). In human communication, the auditory, visual, and tactile channels are most frequently used.
6. *Receiver:* A receiver is a device capable of picking up the message signal. In humans the sensory end organs serve as receivers.
7. *Destination:* The destination is the message signal terminal. In humans this is the appropriate area of the cortex where the message signal, which has been partially analyzed at various subcortical nerve centers, is finally interpreted.
8. *Feedback loop:* A feedback loop is a monitoring system that permits the maintenance of a desired quality of production by making possible the constant comparison of the output with a predetermined internal standard.

Figure 2.2 illustrates the application of the communication model to the essential components of a human communication system, utilizing only the spoken word as a means of conveying information. Subject A has a thought or idea to communicate to a friend, Subject B. This thought, which constitutes the message, must be encoded into some symbolic form before it can be communicated. In fact, for most of us it is probably only when we put the idea into words, either aloud or in silent thinking, that we are able to formulate the thought clearly. This process takes place in the brain, where the message is converted into a message signal in the form of language symbols represented by nerve impulses. These impulses activate the vocal mechanism and the articulators of speech, which change the neural message signal into complex sound waves.

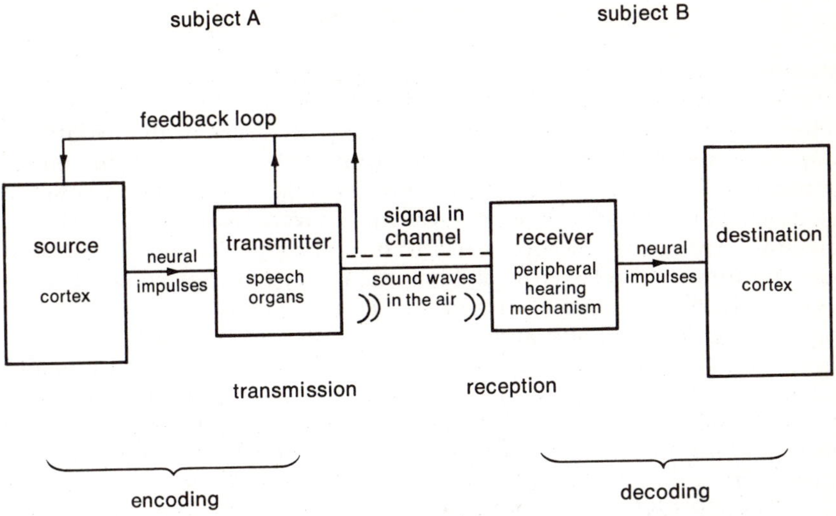

FIGURE 2.2 Identification of the components of the speech communication model.

Subject B, who at this stage in the conversation is playing the role of the listener, receives the message signal through his or her hearing mechanism, which converts the sound waves back into nerve impulses. These travel by way of a series of subcortical nerve centers to the auditory cortex, where they are analyzed and interpreted, providing Subject B with the meaning content.

STRUCTURING THE MESSAGE SIGNAL

The thought, linguistically encoded by the speaker as patterns of neurone activity, must be restructured into a message signal for transmission within the nervous system. We know that when we communicate, the changes we make upon the surrounding media are effected physically; therefore, the information flowing from the cortex must be patterned in terms of neuromoter commands to the effectors—that is, to the speech organs or, in the case of manual communication, to the hands. In Figure 2.2 the basic components of a communication system have been labeled to accommodate speech processing. The last stage of restructuring occurs when the linguistic information for reconstituting the message, now in the form of equivalent neuromoter patterns, is converted into movement of the vocal folds and of the articulators of speech. The articulatory patterning of the visual sound results in the recoding of the original linguistic pattern into sound waves for transmission to the listener.

It is to be expected that a process that involves so many transformations will require careful monitoring and a system of self-adjustment in order to maintain the desired accuracy of output. This quality control is achieved through a feedback system.

QUALITY CONTROL

If we wish to be certain that a production unit maintains a particular standard of operation, then we must devise a means of assessing and controlling the quality of the product. This is as necessary in the production of speech as it is in the production of automobiles. To make this quality control possible, we must feed back into the system information concerning its output. The system must have incorporated within it a means of detecting any errors that occur in the message signal that it is transmitting, and it must also have the ability to make the appropriate corrections. An error is said to occur whenever a discrepancy exists between the generated message signal and an internal standard against which the output signal may be compared. This comparison will reveal any discrepancy that may exist between the intended and actual message signal, permitting immediate corrective action to be taken to eliminate the error. Such self-regulating mechanisms are commonly referred to as *servomechanisms* or *servosystems*.

A much used, but simple illustration of such a system is that which automatically regulates the heat in a house (Figure 2.3). The "message signal" being conveyed is heat, generated by the boiler (source), transmitted into the air by a radiator or warm-air ducts. Feedback of information concerning the air temperature in the room is made possible by a ther-

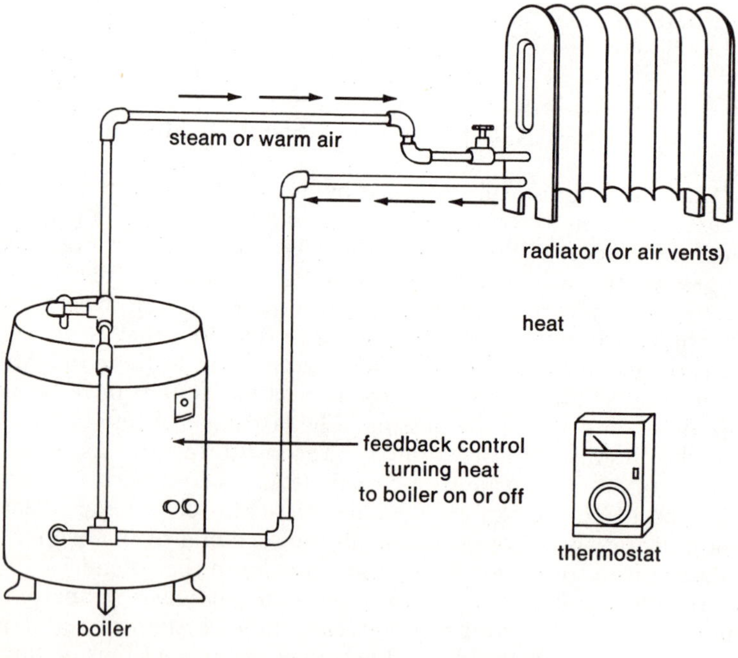

FIGURE 2.3 A common servo-mechanism (boiler and radiator).

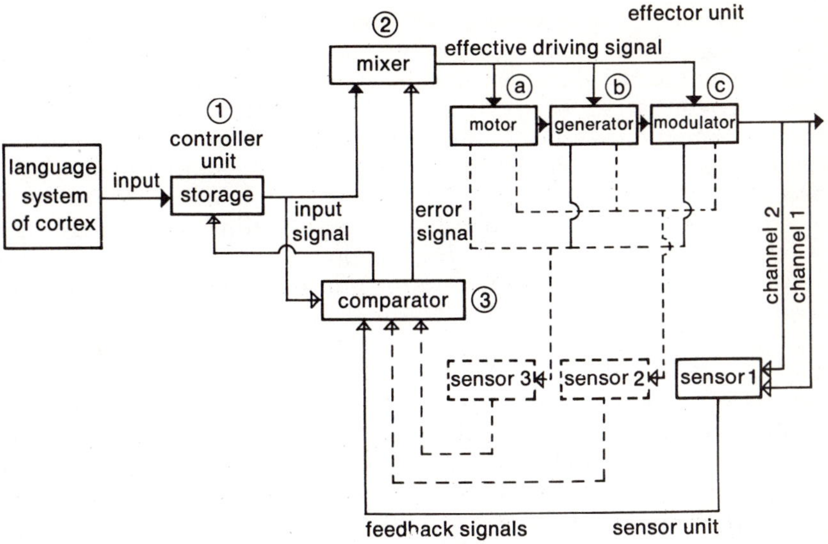

FIGURE 2.4 Model of a closed cycle control system for speaking (proposed by Fairbanks, 1954).

mostat, which we set at a desired temperature. This temperature represents the internal standard of the system. Whenever the output of heat from the boiler causes the heat in the room to rise above the prescribed temperature, the sensing mechanism of the thermostat, detecting the discrepancy (error) between the actual and the desired temperature, operates to turn down the boiler. When the temperature falls below the required level, the thermostat will cause the heat to be turned on again.

Feedback must be considered an integral part of the communication system itself; without it, effective communication is impossible. It is of particular importance to an understanding of the communication problems resulting from impairment of hearing, because these problems result primarily from an impairment of the feedback process. We shall, for this reason, consider it in somewhat more detail than is usual in an introductory chapter on communication.

The continual monitoring of the message signal (speech sound, written symbols, gestures) is necessary to ensure the greatest possible accuracy of the message. Fairbanks (1954) has proposed a model (Figure 2.4) that is helpful in understanding the internal feedback mechanism by which we control the quality of our speech production. The system is divided into two linked units, one concerned with converting the neural message signal into speech sounds (effector unit), the other (sensor unit) concerned with feeding a copy of the output back to a control unit that modifies future signals.

A message signal originates within the language system in the cortex. It first passes through a storage component (1)* that is capable of

*Numbers and letters refer to Figure 2.4.

storing a copy of a few units of the message† for a short period of time. The message-signal then passes through a mixer (2) that provides the impulse needed to drive the effector unit (effective driving signal). The effector unit consists of three divisions: (a) the motor, which corresponds to the breathing mechanism; (b) the generator, representing the vocal folds; (c) the modulator, which represents the articulators and resonators of the speech system.

The effector unit is responsible for transmitting the message signal into the external environment. Information concerning the behavior of the various components of the effector unit is carried by feedback pathways to associated sensor units. The first unit (sensor 1) represents the ear. Information concerning the output reaches it by way of two channels: channel 1 is the airborne route through the middle-ear structures, whereas channel 2 is the tissue and bone conduction route resulting from vibration of the skull and its tissues. The message signal received by sensor 1 travels directly to the comparator (3).

Information concerning the tactile and proprioceptive aspects of the message signal reaches the comparator by individual channels from sensors 2 and 3. Thus, the information arriving at the comparator consists of the total of all the available sensory data concerning the message signal being transmitted. A copy of the original message signal that was fed into the mixer unit also reaches the comparator from storage. In this way, the intended message signal and that which is actually being transmitted are brought together for comparison. Any difference between the two constitutes an error. An error-correction signal is immediately fed into the mixer, where it is combined with the driving signal in such a way as to modify the future impulses to the effector unit. This is done so that future output more closely approximates the input signal. Note that in the diagram the error signal travels from the comparator to the storage unit, where a modified input is established before the previous unit has been utilized by the effector unit. This is necessary, because the storage unit provides the input signals to both the mixer and the comparator.

Fairbanks stresses the importance of this final aspect of the system as a means of providing for the role of prediction of the system's output. He states: "The essence of a speaking system, however, is control of the output, or prediction of the output's future. In this kind of system the significance of the data about the past is that they are used for prediction of the future" (1954, p. 134). This process of prediction of future output has been appropriately referred to as *feed forward.*

Fairbanks' model is only concerned with an explanation of the manner in which the output of the spoken word is monitored by the speaker. This internal monitoring is referred to by Van Riper and Irwin (1958, p. 113) as an intrapersonal communicative circuit. An understanding of the total communicative process necessitates that we expand this model to include the monitoring of other forms of symbolic output, such as those transmitted by the hands, face, and other body parts.

†Message units are the individual components from which the message is constructed. The smallest unit in speech is the phoneme; the largest unit, for the purpose of this discussion, will be considered to be the sentence.

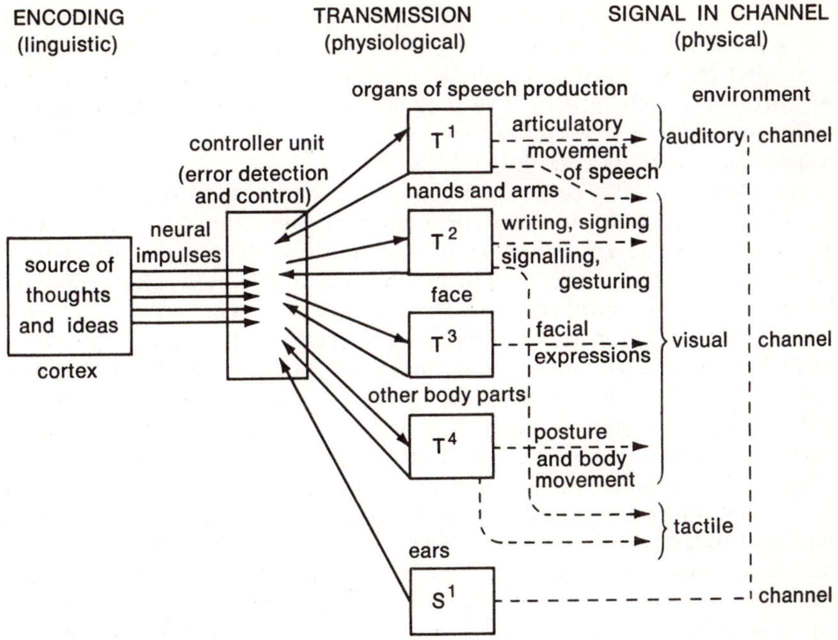

FIGURE 2.5 Model of the transmission processes involved in human communication.

Figure 2.5 illustrates a model that includes the monitoring of communication through such means as writing, gesturing, facial expressions, and bodily movement. The message is encoded into a particular symbolic form and travels as neural impulses to an error-detection and control unit. At this point, a copy of the encoded message is stored while impulses travel to one or more of four transmitters. These transmitters represent the organs of speech production (T1), the hands and arms (T2), the face (T3), and other body parts (T4). At the transmitter, the encoded message is transduced into a signal. The nature of the signal will differ depending upon which transmitter is being used. Speech production involves the movement of the organs of speech, the laryngeal mechanism, and the articulators. The hands and arms are used for such forms of communication as writing, signaling, or gesturing, and the facial muscles transmit the message through facial expressions and grimaces. Impulses to other body parts will be transmitted in a variety of body movements and postures, as is seen in the communication that takes place through the medium of dance or pantomime. Internal sensory feedback of tactile and proprioceptive information travels from each of the transmitters to the error-detection and control unit for comparison with the stored copy of the intended signal. External feedback of the acoustic signal travels by way of the hearing mechanism.

The signal leaving each of the transmitters will travel in one or more of three major channels. The speech signal travels as complex sound waves through an acoustic channel. Simultaneously, the visible aspects of the articulatory movements involved in speech production travel through a visual channel in the form of light energy. Signals transmitted by hands and arms, face, and other body parts also travel in the visual channel. The third channel utilized in human communication is the tactile channel, through which information may be transmitted as in a handshake or embrace, aggressive pounding on a rostrum, or by the tap of a foot on another foot beneath a table.

So far, we have concerned ourselves only with intrapersonal feedback. We must also take into consideration the influence exerted upon the speaker by the reception of information concerning the effect of his or her message upon the person to whom it is directed. This constitutes the interpersonal communicative circuit.

The information transmitted by Subject A in the form of a message signal has passed through the appropriate channels and has been received and analyzed by Subject B, for whom the message was intended. If the message is satisfactorily decoded, Subject B will give evidence of having received the message by some form of change in behavior. The nature of this change will, in itself, be informative to Subject A. Cues to the success with which the message is being received and decoded are, in fact, transmitted by the receiver even as the message is being received. The dichotomy of the communication situation into speaker and receiver is an artificial one. We really assume both roles simultaneously, though one may dominate at a given time. As I am speaking to a person I am also receiving information from that person about his or her response to my message. This necessarily means that in the role of listener or receiver the other person is also sending information. Oral communication involves the constant and simultaneous interaction of people. The behavior elicited by the message may involve the use of a verbal reply, spoken or written, or it may take the form of a nonverbal vocalization, such as a gasp, sigh, or laugh. It may evoke a gesture, a facial grimace, or the adoption of a particular posture, or it may cause the subject to perform a particular task. The effectiveness of the signal carrying the encoded message is therefore evaluated on the basis of how well it brings about a desired response. The response made by Subject B may reach Subject A through sensory end organs of hearing, vision, touch, and pressure. From the peripheral sensory receptors, the encoded message travels to the brain by way of a number of nerve centers situated enroute to the cortex. Thus, a variety of stimuli are reaching Subject A concerning his or her own speech production and its effect upon the listener, Subject B. In addition, Subject A will receive other stimuli from the environment; these may be both related and unrelated to the message. All of these data must be sorted and those which are relevant must be integrated into a meaningful whole, a function that also involves the incorporation of information based on associations drawn from a memory of relevant past experiences. The final result of this process is total perception.

It has been generally held that the process of synthesizing sensory data in order to provide a total perception of a situation takes place only at the association level of the cortex. Research evidence is available, however, that suggests that the specialized sensory pathways are, in fact, neurologically related at levels below the cortex. The concept of the nervous system as comprised of a number of separate circuits, each responsible for a particular function, has been increasingly challenged by research evidence (Pangborn, 1960). It may, however, reasonably be presumed that there exists a complex system involving reception, integration, analysis, association, and interpretation of data from all sensory end organs. Figure 2.6 indicates by dotted lines the existence of interconnecting fibers traveling between the various subcortical nerve centers.

The information that is derived from this process of total perception of the effect upon B of the signal that was originally transmitted by A is then utilized by Subject A to modify future output. The model suggested in Figure 2.7 depicts the total process involved in the act of communication between two individuals. Although at first glance this diagram may appear overwhelming, closer examination will reveal that, in fact, it contains nothing that has not been previously discussed. The diagram simply puts together the information contained in Figures 2.5 and 2.6. It represents two people in a communication situation, each with a transmitting and a receiving system serving the language system.

We have seen how the communication system serves to link the linguistic and cognitive systems of speaker and listener. The shared knowledge of linguistic rules permits internal values, related to experience of the external world, to be encoded into language patterns. These patterns must be familiar to speaker and listener if effective communication is to occur, because they serve to identify equivalent internal values. Our examination of the means by which the linguistically encoded information can be externalized revealed that the patterns pass through several transformations. Represented first as cortical neural organizations, they are recoded as neuromotor commands to body articulators. These articulators

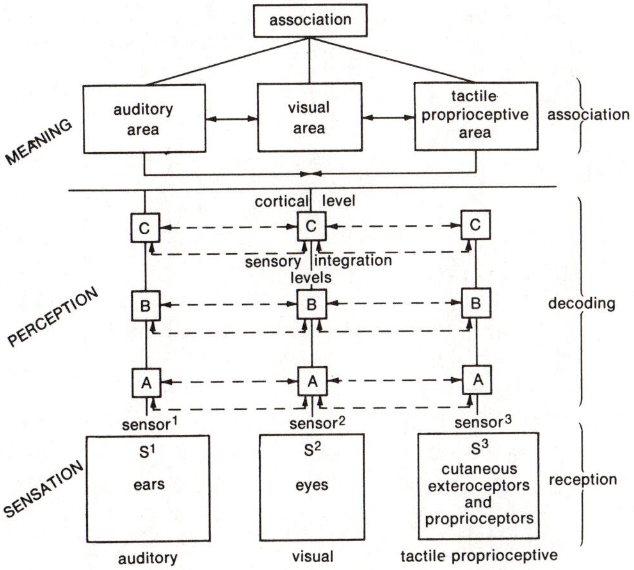

FIGURE 2.6 Schematic diagram of synesthetic perception.

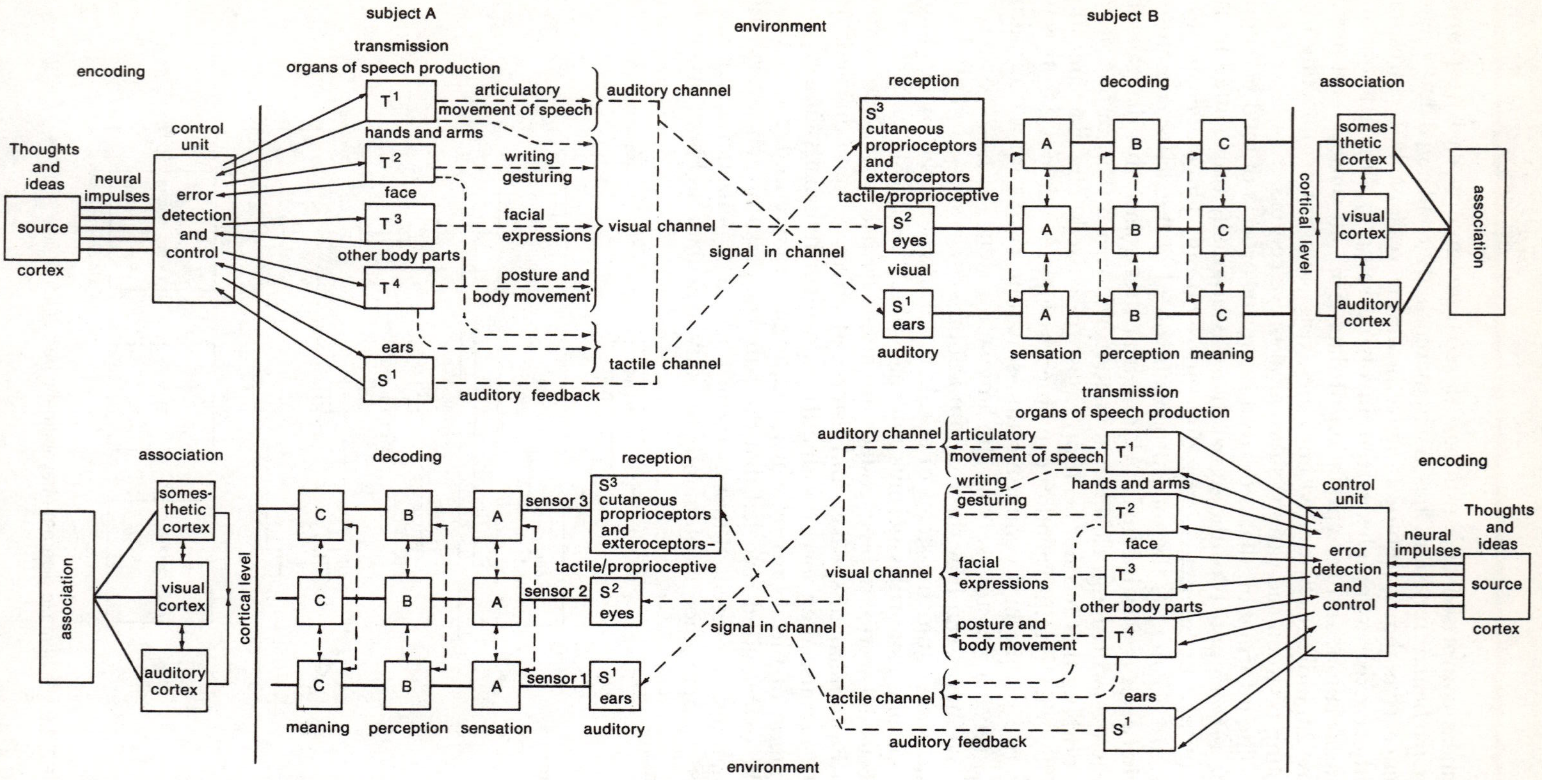

FIGURE 2.7 The communication cycle.

may be those of speech, writing, signing or gesture, or other body movements. It is the constraint on the behavior of these articulators that transforms neuromotor commands into communicative behavior. Behavior modifies the environment of the communicators, an occurrence essential to the flow of information between them. It is the nature of the modification of the auditory and visual environment to which we must now turn our attention.

REFERENCES

Carrier, J. K., "Application of a Non-Speech Language System with the Severely Languaged Handicapped," in *Communication Assessment and Intervention Strategies,* ed. L. Lloyd, pp. 523–547. Baltimore: University Park Press, 1976.

Carroll, J. B., *Language and Thought.* Englewood Cliffs, N.J.: Prentice-Hall, Inc., 1964.

Cherry, C., *On Human Communication.* New York: John Wiley & Sons, Inc., 1957.

Englemann, S., and R. Rosov, "Tactual Hearing Experiment with Deaf and Hearing Impaired Subjects," *Journal of Except. Child., 41,* 1975, 243–253.

Erber, N. P., and K. D. Cramer, "Vibrotactile Recognition of Sentences," *American Annals of the Deaf, 119,* 1974, 716–720.

Fairbanks, G. "Systematic Research in Experimental Phonetics: Speech as a Servo-Mechanism," *Journal of Speech and Hearing Disorders, 19,* 1954, 133–139.

Laurie, Peter, "Your Health: The Mind, the Explorers," *London Sunday Times Magazine,* March 19, 1967.

Lehiste, I., "The Units of Speech Perception," in *Speech and Cortical Function,* ed. J. H. Gilbert, p. 197. New York: Academic Press, Inc., 1972.

Pangborn, R. M., "Influence of Color on the Discrimination of Sweetness," *American Journal of Psychology, 73,* 1960, 229–238.

Premack, D., and A. J. Premack, "Teaching Visual Language to Apes and Language Deficient Persons," in *Language Perspectives—Acquisition, Retardation, and Intervention,* eds. R. L. Schiefelbusch and L. L. Lloyd, pp. 347–376. Baltimore: University Park Press, 1974.

Shannon, C. E. and W. Weaver, *The Mathematical Theory of Communication.* Urbana: University of Illinois Press, 1967.

Van Riper, C., and J. V. Irwin, *Voice and Articulation,* p. 113. Englewood Cliffs, N.J.: Prentice-Hall, Inc., 1958.

Physical Aspects of the Speech Signal

3

Acoustic Aspects of Speech

In the previous chapter we discussed the nature of the human communication system. Although it was explained that in speaking with each other we transmit and receive information in more than one channel, the role of the acoustic signal in speech communication is obviously paramount. In this chapter we will consider the acoustic structure of speech and we will examine the nature of the constraining information it carries.

The extent to which a hearing deficiency impairs the perception of speech will depend on how many of the constraining acoustic cues are eliminated or distorted. Familiarity with the pattern of constraints associated with individual sounds or sound groups will greatly facilitate your understanding of the problems that hearing-impaired individuals encounter in perceiving speech. Furthermore, auditory self-monitoring is very important to the production of intelligible speech, so that a close relationship exists between what we hear and how we speak. Thus, if you are aware of the distorting effects that a hearing impairment may have on the accuracy of the internalized acoustic patterns of speech, you will improve your understanding of the speech production problems experienced both by children with congenital hearing impairment, and by people who suffer a partial or complete loss of hearing later in life. Finally, some knowledge of acoustics is necessary to comprehend the nature of amplification. You must consider the benefits of amplification, as well as the limitations imposed upon it by current technology and the characteristics of various patterns of hearing impairment in terms of what we seek to do to the speech signal.

In testing hearing we use discreet frequency tones to assess the status of the cochlea. The results permit us to chart the sensitivity of the ear at specific points across its frequency range. Even for the purpose of diagnosis, this information is not sufficient. We must examine both the effects of the pattern of reduction of hearing sensitivity upon speech reception, and the ability of the auditory system to analyze and integrate complex speech sounds. It is this latter function, the processing of the complex speech signal, with which we are concerned. We shall follow the changes occurring in the speech signal from its source at the vocal folds through the articulatory resonant system into the air medium that conveys the patterned information to the listener. We will study only as much acoustics as is essential to our task. Readers who wish to obtain a more detailed knowledge are referred to other texts (Minifie, Hixon, & Williams, 1973; Sanders, 1977; Wakita, 1974).

PRODUCTION OF THE VOCAL TONE

Vocal sound arises from neuromotor commands to the breathing mechanism and to the vocal folds. These comprise the generator and motor components of the Fairbanks model (see Figure 2.4). The action of the lungs forces controlled air flow past the vocal folds of the glottis, where a combination of muscular action and aerodynamics produces a pattern of vibratory movement. This movement disturbs the air within the larynx, producing the *glottal tone,* whose lowest frequency is known as the *fundamental frequency.* The glottal tone constitutes the carrier wave upon which the acoustic pattern, representative of coded linguistic information, is impressed.

During speech, the vibrations of the vocal folds vary in rate or *frequency.* The term frequency refers to the number of complete vibrations that occur in one second. The vibrations are usually designated in units called *Hertz* (Hz) after Heinrich Hertz, who confirmed the existence of electromagnetic waves. Each complete vibratory event constitutes a cycle. Therefore, frequency may also be expressed in cycles per second (cps). The rate of vibration of the vocal folds determines the frequency of the glottal tone. The pitch of the voice is perceived to rise as the fundamental frequency increases.

As a person grows from infancy to adulthood, the mean level of the fundamental frequency changes. Both the cries of newborn infants and the speech of children are of a higher pitch level than is the speech of adults. The mean vocal pitch levels of persons of different ages have been studied by many investigators. A composite of the results of these studies is shown in Table 3.1. You can see from this table that the fundamental frequency of newborn babies and of children within the first two years of life is high (McGlone, 1966; Ringel & Kluppel, 1964). As the child grows older, the pitch of the voice decreases, with a marked drop occurring for both boys and girls during adolescence (Fairbanks, Herbert, & Hammond, 1949; Fairbanks, Wiley, & Lassman, 1949; and Hollien, Malcik, & Hollien, 1965). The speaking fundamental frequency continues to lower from age 20 to 40 years, but thereafter, in males between the ages of 60 to 90 years, it rises (Figure 3.1) (Hollien & Shipp, 1972).

TABLE 3.1 Mean Speaking Fundamental Frequency Level and Speaking Frequency Range of Males, Females, and Children

Speakers	*Age*	*Mean Frequency (Hz)*	*Range (S.D. in Tones)*
Children (9)	16.5 mos.	443.3	1.70
Preadolescent girls (1)	8 yrs.	288.0	1.40
Preadolescent boys (2)	8 yrs.	297.0	1.00
Postadolescent girls (6)	17.5 yrs.	211.5	1.67
Postadolescent boys (5)	18 yrs.	115.9	2.21
Females (8)	adult	199.8	1.52
Males (11)	adult	113.2	1.45

For the purpose of our discussion, the significance of the different mean vocal pitch levels in men, women, and children lies in the effect of these differences on the speech discrimination of hearing-impaired persons. It is not uncommon for hearing-impaired people to complain that they seem to have more difficulty in understanding the speech of women than that of men, and that children are particularly difficult to follow. This is understandable because the complete acoustic pattern is impressed upon the glottal tone. Thus, when the mean pitch of the speaker's voice is high, the important identifying speech cues will be even higher. For some hearing-impaired persons, this will mean that the criti-

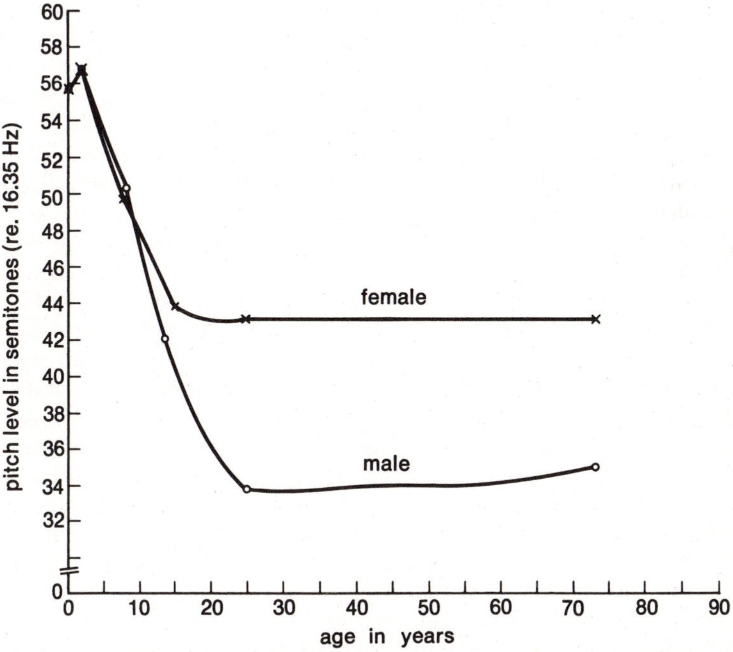

FIGURE 3.1 Pitch-level trend for males and females, from data collected at various ages (after Ringel et al., McGlone, Fairbanks et al., Linke, Hollien et al., Mysak).

cal perceptual information carried by these cues is out of their range of residual hearing, which in most cases tends to be poorer in the mid- and high-frequency ranges than in the low range. However, when the speaker's voice has a low mean pitch, sufficient components of the acoustic pattern may fall within the range of residual hearing to permit improved understanding, because not only the fundamental frequency but all frequencies in the acoustic pattern are shifted downward. A further implication is that children with very severe hearing impairments frequently have residual hearing only in the low frequencies. These children will have particular difficulty in monitoring the quality of their voices. With a mean fundamental frequency of 443 Hz (Table 3.1), even vocal pitch may be barely audible to some. Furthermore, the monitoring of articulation will also be impaired because most of the distinguishing characteristics of speech sounds will lie in the higher frequency ranges, beyond the limits of their residual hearing.

Molding the Glottal Tone

One of the basic characteristics of the glottal tone is that it is not pure. Unlike the sound produced by a tuning fork or by an audiometer, which generate a single-frequency pure tone, the glottal tone is complex. A complex tone results from the sound generator vibrating in parts rather than as a whole, generating component vibrations that interact to produce a complex wave. Figure 3.2 compares a single-frequency pure tone and a complex tone resulting from the interaction of several frequencies.

The complex sound wave generated by the larynx passes into the cavities of the pharynx, nose, and mouth, where it excites the air contained within them. This capacity of air within a cavity to be set in vibration is known as *resonance.* The cavities themselves are called *resonators.* Each resonator has a resonant sensitivity, which differs for cavities of different volume and shape. The energy present within a complex tone is molded by the resonator to accord with its own resonant characteristics, rearranging the distribution of energy across the frequency range. When the energy at a particular frequency in the vibrating sound wave coincides with the sensitivity of the resonator, it will be augmented. However, when there is little or no coincidence between a particular band of energy in the complex tone and the sensitivity of the resonator to that frequency band, the energy at those frequencies will be reduced, or *damped* (Figure 3.3). Even the fundamental frequency is not immune to this effect. There appears to be no resonant chamber in the speech mechanism that is tuned to a frequency low enough to match the voice fundamental. When we compare the spectrum of a sound recorded just above the larynx with a spectrum of the same sound after it has passed through the speech resonance system, we find that the fundamental has always been attenuated, whereas the higher-frequency components have been amplified (Figure 3.4). This occurs even when all, or nearly all, of the energy at the fundamental has been damped. The explanation may be that the hearing mechanism responds to the differences between the higher tonal components and predicts from them the fundamental frequency.

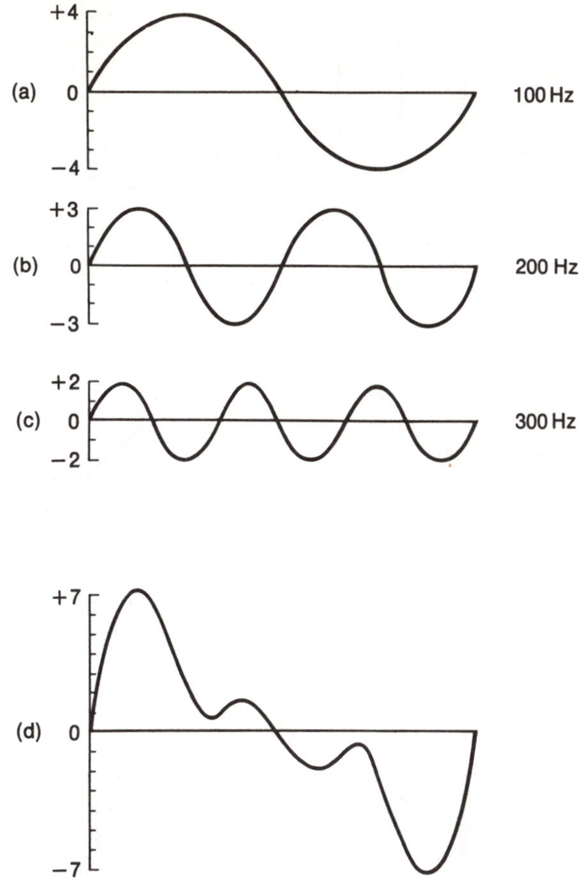

FIGURE 3.2 A harmonic complex wave and its sinusoidal components.

A complex sound produced at various pitches will differ in structure because the fundamental frequencies are not the same. When these sounds pass through the same resonance chamber, they do not produce the same frequency distribution (spectrum) and, therefore, will differ in their perceived quality. The vibration of any segment of a resonance system is dependent on the presence of energy in the vibrating tone at or near the natural resonant frequency. A sound with a fundamental frequency of 400 Hz, and higher components (harmonics) at multiples of this frequency, may not have energy components to activate certain resonant sensitivities that would be activated by the same sound with a fundamental of 100 Hz and a difference of 100 Hz between the harmonics. The resulting spectrum of sounds is shown in Figure 3.5. The wave composition of these sounds is different because the overall spectrum of sounds, including speech phonemes, results from an interaction of the fundamental frequency and the shape and size of the speech resonators.

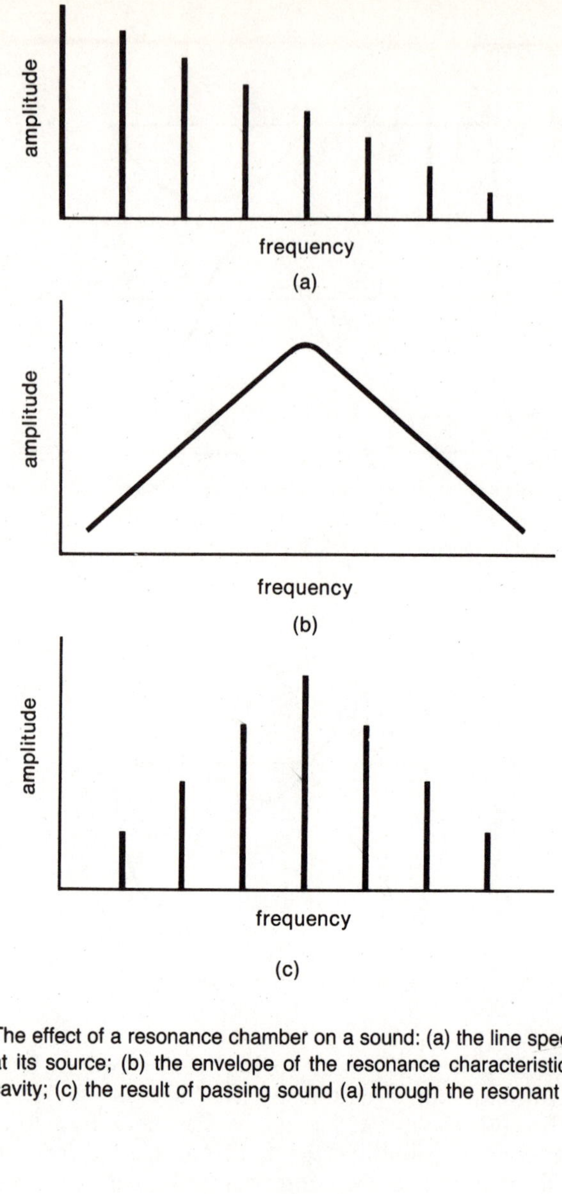

FIGURE 3.3 The effect of a resonance chamber on a sound: (a) the line spectrum of a sound at its source; (b) the envelope of the resonance characteristics of a resonant cavity; (c) the result of passing sound (a) through the resonant chamber (b).

SPEECH MODULATION

Speech is a melodic phenomenon; it varies in frequency, intensity, and rate. We perceive these melodic attributes as continuous changes in pitch, loudness, rate, and stress. These *prosodic* characteristics are known as *suprasegmental components;* vowel and consonant units, by contrast, are identified as *segmental.* It is only recently that the full significance of suprasegmental information has begun to be realized. It was originally believed that the role of suprasegmentals was confined to the conveyance of emo-

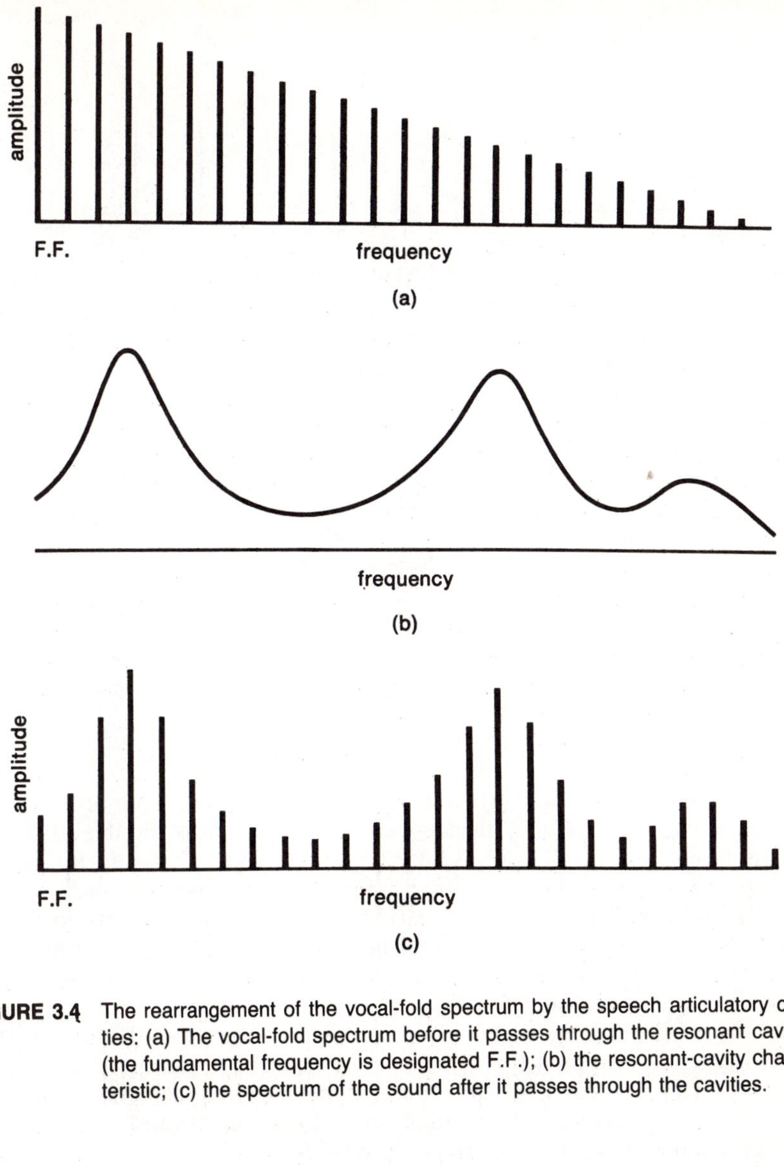

FIGURE 3.4 The rearrangement of the vocal-fold spectrum by the speech articulatory cavities: (a) The vocal-fold spectrum before it passes through the resonant cavities (the fundamental frequency is designated F.F.); (b) the resonant-cavity characteristic; (c) the spectrum of the sound after it passes through the cavities.

tive information or to the resolution of ambiguity that might otherwise exist at the segmental level. Current theory, however, recognizes a close relationship between suprasegmental processing and segmental information (Liberman, 1967; Martin, 1972). It has been suggested that the basic function of the suprasegmental patterns is to establish constraints that facilitate the identification of segmental cues. The rhythm pattern of speech serves to identify the highly encoded and, therefore, highly informative stressed syllables for early decoding.*

*For a discussion of this topic, see Sanders, 1977, pp. 37–38 and pp. 136–139.

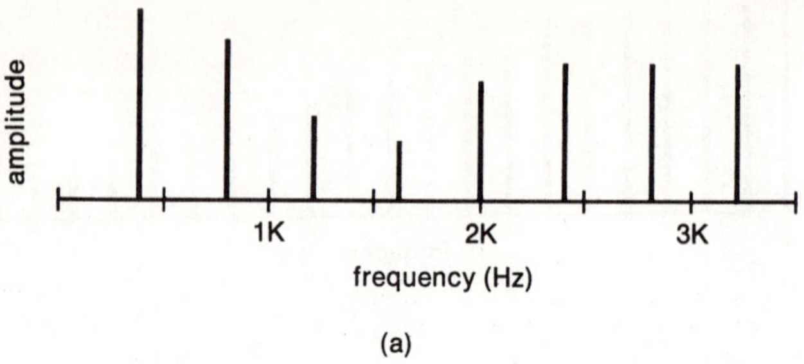

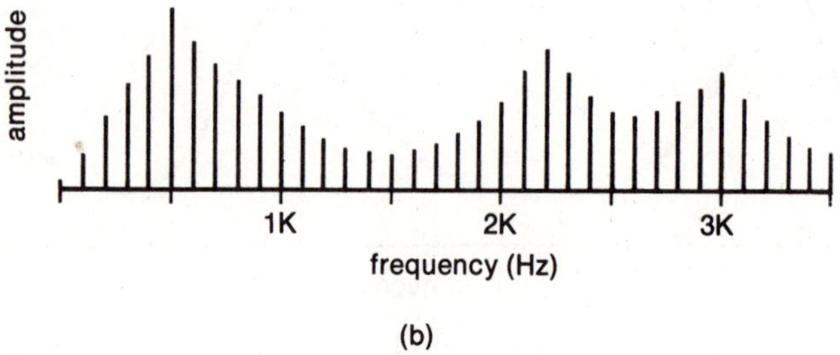

FIGURE 3.5 Spectra of harmonic complex tones with different fundamental frequencies passed through the same oral cavity: (a) a tone with a fundamental frequency of 400 Hz; (b) a tone of 100 Hz.

The suprasegmental information is heavily dependent on the patterning of the vocal tone. This suggests that an infant is capable of learning the basic rhythms of speech long before he or she has the capacity to process its segmental components. Evidence to this effect has in fact been provided by Condon and Sander (1973). These researchers demonstrated that even newborn (one-day-old) babies exhibit patterns of precise and sustained movements that are synchronized with the articulated structure of adult speech. The authors suggest that: ". . . 'infant motor organization' entrained by these organized patterns for many months after birth, may prepare operational formats for later speech" (1973, p. 101). If this assumption proves correct, the effects of hearing impairment on speech acquisition may indeed be maximal from birth. It certainly emphasizes the importance of suprasegmental components, both on the development of speech perception and on the ability to communicate within the normal melodic patterns of the language culture.

The role of early amplification in facilitating perception and production of normal suprasegmental patterning is obviously crucial. Our awareness of the probable importance of the lower frequencies of speech in the acquisition of spoken language is increased by such information. It may lead us, for example, to decide to emphasize frequencies below 1000 Hz for severely hearing-impaired children to provide listening and learning in favorable acoustic conditions.

Early babbling patterns and the subsequent development of jargon depend heavily on control of the vocal tone. Deliberate inflectional use of the voice precedes the ability to produce the specific sounds of speech (Kaplan & Kaplan, 1971), the process we refer to as speech articulation.

SPEECH ARTICULATION

Speech articulation involves molding the vocal tone into distinct acoustic patterns. These patterns are directly related to the linguistic structure into which a thought has been encoded. It is made possible by use of the articulatory resonant system of speech.

The resonators of speech are coupled together in such a way that they constitute a single, tunable resonance system. Unlike rigid cavities, the speech resonance system is capable of a considerable range of changes in shape and volume. This is achieved by the speech articulators. A change in the angle of the lower jaw can enlarge the oral cavity from the "at-rest" position. The movement of the lips and cheeks, the shutting off of the nasal cavity by the elevation of the soft palate, and the shaping and positioning of the tongue all serve to change the resonant sensitivity of the coupled speech resonance system. In this manner, we are able to mold the glottal sound wave into a variety of distinctive patterns, each characteristic of a particular articulatory resonant posture. The pattern of a given speech sound is greatly influenced by the sounds adjacent to it and changes as they change. However, within a given phonetic context, that is between any two particular sounds, the pattern remains constant and is characteristic of that phoneme in that position. We divide the speech sounds into the two major categories of vowels and consonants.

Vowels

When we define vowel-sound production, it is necessary to designate both the amount of jaw opening and the tongue position. The vowel /i/ and the vowel /u/ are considered closed vowels with the maxilla and the mandible in close approximation, whereas the vowel /ɑ/ is essentially an open vowel. As a speaker assumes a particular cavity posture for each of the vowels progressing from /i/ and /u/ toward /ɑ/, the mandible becomes progressively more separated from the maxillary arch. Still another articulator that can affect the shape of the resonance tube is the lips. The most common position used for the production of the /i/ sound is the retraction or spread of the lips; the production of the /u/ sound generally involves lip rounding, whereas for the /ɑ/ sound the lips are unrounded.

In normal speech vowels are produced with vocalization. The complex harmonic sound produced by the larynx is rearranged depending upon the shape of the cavities above the larynx. Figure 3.6 shows the rearrangement of the total energy that occurs when the cavities are in the general shape that they assume for the vowel /i/. When the cavity shape is changed to the configuration for the vowel /ɑ/ and the pitch level is held constant, the spectrum of the sound changes (Figure 3.6).

Actual line spectra of eight different vowels are shown in Figure 3.7. Note that the amplitude of the various frequency components is different

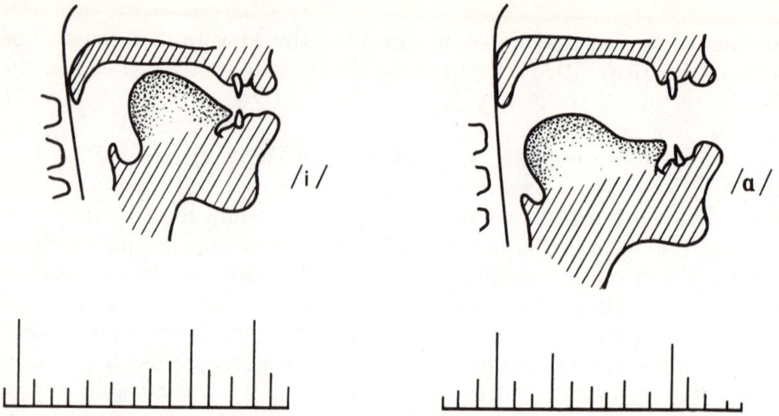

FIGURE 3.6 A diagrammatic representation of the position of the speech articulators of a person producing /i/ and /a/ and the resulting spectra of these vowels.

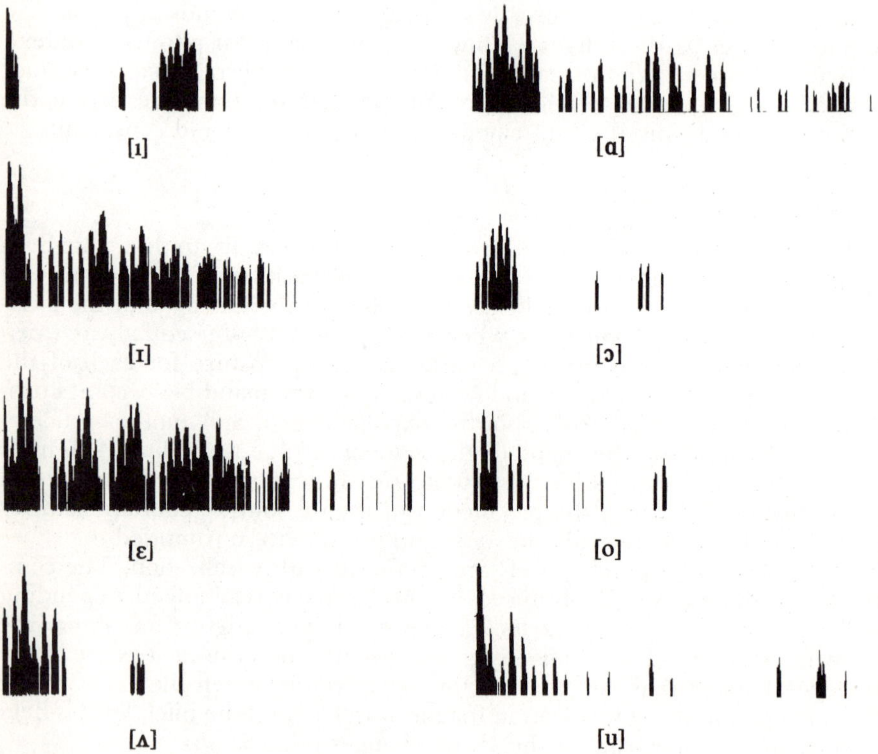

FIGURE 3.7 Actual spectra of eight vowels.

for each vowel sound. Two or three major amplitude peaks occur for each vowel and reflect the natural resonant frequencies of the cavities when articulating these vowels. This concentration of energy around each peak is called a *formant.*

The reception of the first and second formants is essential for vowel identification. Figure 3.8 presents the first and second formant values for each of the vowels shown in Figure 3.7. For example, the vowel /ɑ/ has an F1 value of 680 Hz (ordinate), and a value of 1300 Hz for F2 (abscissa). Seldom, if ever, does an individual or a group of individuals produce the same vowel in the same way. Since vowel-sound production varies, the formants' structure also varies; therefore, a precise statement of the formant frequencies associated with vowel production is not possible. However, formants do tend to fall within a range that can be specified. Cavity configurations that produce this range of acoustic-signal modifications result in phonemes that have been assigned a specific identification value and, within a language, are invariant. That is, if the oral-cavity shape is changed to a configuration outside this range, the resulting acoustic signal is no longer identified as the original vowel. When this occurs, the sound may be confused with another vowel, or it may be considered only as a sound without linguistic value.

Of the two vowel formants, a wider span of frequencies is found for the second formant. Although changes in formant frequency occur from vowel to vowel for F1, these are relatively slight when compared to the variations that occur for the frequency range of F2. The second formant of vowels coincides with the most sensitive frequency range of the ear.

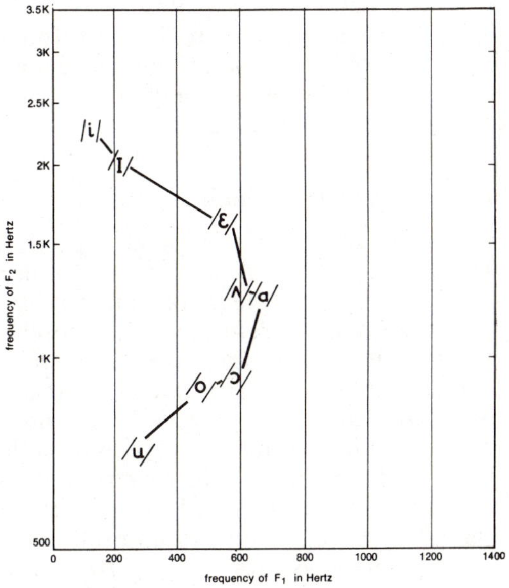

FIGURE 3.8 A plot of the frequencies of Formants 1 and 2.

Consonants

Vowels alone comprise just a small part of the sounds used in speech; in fact, few words consist only of vowel sounds. As previously mentioned, vowel sounds do apparently carry most of the energy of speech. However, consonants contribute the most to the identification of words and phrases. Consonants may, or may not, contain vocalization and therefore may, or may not, have wave forms that have a harmonic complex structure. A few consonants, notably /m/, /n/, /1/, and /r/, present harmonic complex wave forms very much like a vowel. Some of these sounds, depending upon their use in a syllable combination, have a semivowel characteristic. Generally, what discriminates a vowel from a consonant is that a consonant, unlike a vowel, contains an articulatory movement that obstructs or greatly restricts a flow of air from the laryngeal mechanism through the articulatory mechanism. The most common method of describing consonants is by specifying the place and manner of articulation. The place of articulation refers to the major anatomical-structure position for the production of each consonant, whereas the manner of articulation is based upon a subjective description of the acoustic nature of the sound. For example, the consonants /p/, /b/, and /m/ are called *bilabials* because both lips must come together for adequate production of the sounds. The /t/, /d/, and /n/ sounds are made by the contact of the tongue to the alveolar maxillary ridge and hence are called *lingual alveolar* sounds. Definition by acoustic nature describes the phonemes /p/, /b/, /t/, /d/, /k/, and /g/ as *stops* because the air stream associated with their production is completely blocked. Similarly, *fricatives* are made by constricting the air flow, somewhere in the mouth, enough to make the air turbulent, resulting in a sound that has a characteristic hissing quality as /s/. The consonants /m/, /n/, and /ŋ/ are made by directing the air stream through the nasal passages, hence adding the effect of nasal resonance to the production. Many articulatory positions may be used either with or without voicing, thus further delineating phonemic categories.

Transitional Characteristics of Speech

The rapidity of speech precludes the precise production of speech sounds. The ability of our system of speech communication to tolerate slight changes in articulatory placement for both vowels and consonants without affecting their value is, therefore, vital to speech comprehension. Because speech is not made up of sounds used individually, but of sounds put together in a series, this tolerance permits us to maintain values at high rates of transmission. In connected speech, the movement from one articulatory position to another is often as important as the position itself. This movement is called the *transition*. The spectrum of connected speech shows that much of speech is transitional. Figure 3.9 shows a spectrum of a word. The ordinate represents frequency and the abscissa depicts time. The amplitude of the formants is shown by the frequency bars.

The transitions arise from the movement of the articulators, primarily the tongue, between the ideal target positions for the two adjacent speech sounds. As a result, the transitions vary as the phonetic context

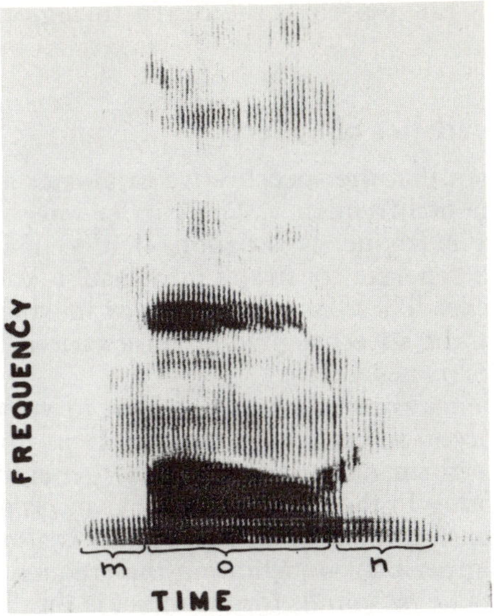

FIGURE 3.9 An actual bar spectrum illustrating transition.

varies. The transition arising from the movement of the articulators from /k/ to /a/ will be different from that generated by the movement from /k/ to /i/. Each transitional movement is, therefore, characteristic of the adjacency of particular sounds. The transition is shared by those sounds and each affects the acoustic pattern of the other in a manner peculiar to that relationship. Thus each speech sound in context not only has its own acoustic structure resulting from the place and manner of its production, but it also embodies information about its neighbors. The speech organs, in preparation for the production of sounds to come, often begin to pattern articulatory movements far ahead of the sound for which those movements are essential. This anticipatory positioning is termed *coarticulation* (Daniloff, 1973). Later in the text, when we discuss speech perception, we will see that coarticulation makes a major contribution to the redundancy present in the speech signal. The effects of coarticulation are of considerable importance to our understanding of the role and nature of auditory training. Coarticulation produces transitional information, which means that it is not essential to perceive a particular sound in order to be able to predict it, providing the listener can perceive the information about its presence that is embodied in the acoustic pattern of its neighbors. This provides the rationale for intensive training aimed at increasing speech perception through improved use of redundant information.

The pattern of energy distribution determined by the articulatory movements is defined by three parameters: frequency, intensity, and duration. These three aspects of the acoustic signal combine to create distinctive sound patterns that are keyed to the phonemic system of the language. Thus analysis of the changing pattern of energy distribution across the frequency range permits the restructuring of the intended linguistic values.

Frequency Characteristics of Speech

We have already seen that the speech wave originates as the glottal tone, which has a fundamental frequency. This carrier wave is perceived as the pitch of the voice. The frequency variations that occur in the pitch of the voice during speech generate constraint information known as the suprasegmental components. These constrain the way in which the listener will linguistically analyze the speech signal, because various linguistic patterns have intonational correlates.

Further frequency constraints are present in voiced sounds in the form of energy concentrations, which we identify as formants. The relationship among the formant frequency bands generates the frequency constraints contributing to the identification of vowels and voiced consonants. The constraint information for consonants is also found in part in the effect of the manner of production on the frequency composition of the sound emitted. The /s/ sound, for example, is produced in a manner which concentrates the energy released into the frequencies above 3500 Hz. Finally, frequency information critical to perception of the acoustic cues to speech is found in the transition patterns arising from coarticulation. The frequency cues in the transitions are important because they provide information about the relationships among sounds in a group—in other words, a linguistic pattern. Because the transition occurs over time, it is a rich source of information about changing relationships, and much data can be computed from the acoustic pattern.

Any reduction in the frequency components will result in distortion of the pattern, increasing a listener's difficulty in recovering the linguistic values from the acoustic signal. A hearing deficit will, therefore, distort speech and make comprehension difficult.

Intensity Characteristics of Speech

The constraints imposed upon the listener's decoding of the acoustic signal by the intensity characteristics of speech are less well defined than those of frequency. Nevertheless, the ability to detect the differential pressure levels of speech contributes to the perception of suprasegmental cues and, to a lesser extent, to the perception of the speech sounds.

The intensity of speech is determined by the amount of energy provided by the lungs and the extent of the movement of the vocal folds. It is perceived as the loudness of the stimulus. The intensity of speech ranges from soft speech, at an approximate intensity of 50 dB sound pressure, to 80 dB for loud conversation at one yard distance. Average conversational speech is approximately 65 dB SPL. Most of this intensity is present in the vowel sounds and is therefore distributed in the mid- and low-frequency ranges. The individual speech sounds vary greatly in intensity, as is shown in Table 3.2. The vowel values were obtained when each vowel was surrounded by the same consonants; however, when the

TABLE 3.2 Relative Phonetic Powers of Speech Sounds as Produced by an Average Speaker

ɔ	680	l	100	t	15
ɑ	600	ʃ	80	g	15
ʌ	510	ŋ	73	k	13
æ	490	m	52	v	12
ʊ	460	tʃ	42	ð	11
ɛ	350	n	36	b	7
u	310	ʤ	23	d	7
ɪ	260	ʒ	20	p	6
i	220	z	16	f	5
r	210	s	16	θ	1

consonants surrounding a particular vowel are changed, the loudness or energy present in the vowel also changes. It is apparent, therefore, that the phonetic environment of a vowel sound significantly affects its perceived loudness. For this reason, specific statements about one vowel's being louder than another cannot be made unless the environment of the sounds is held constant. In speech, the phonetic environment must change in order to communicate; therefore, the intensity or loudness of vowels usually differs within sentences and even within words. Note that the intensity of consonant sounds is considerably less than the intensity of vowels (Gerber 1974b).

Because many of the sounds of speech are vocalized, the intensity of these sounds may be varied by the manner of vocal-fold vibration. Figure 3.10 illustrates the spectrum of a sound recorded just above the larynx and produced at a soft level, compared to the spectrum of a sound produced more loudly, with the pitch of both held at essentially the same level. The difference between these two spectra is seen in the higher har-

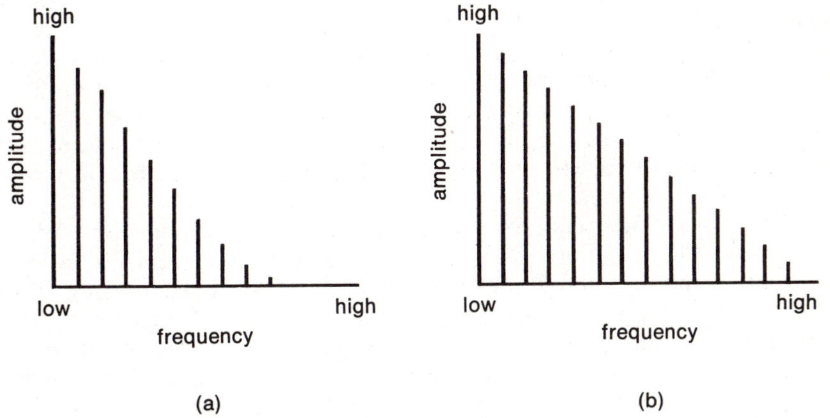

FIGURE 3.10 A line spectrum of the sounds produced by the vocal folds recorded just above the larynx: (a) a soft tone; (b) a loud tone.

monics. More energy is present at higher frequencies and the number of higher harmonics also increases. Therefore, one manner of making sounds louder is to add energy in higher frequencies, where no energy is present for softer sounds.

The contribution that intensity makes to the perception of speech decreases with the pattern and severity of the hearing impairment. Because intensity and frequency are two parameters of the same acoustic event, considering the effects of a reduction in the contraints generated by intensity differences from the interwoven effect upon frequency perception is difficult. It is clear from the information in Table 3.2 that a reduction in the intensity of speech, even when it is equal across frequency, will affect the perception of some sounds more rapidly than others. Because the consonant sounds are the weakest, they are the most severely affected by reduced intensity. The addition of higher-frequency energy—increasing intensity while holding pitch constant—results in a perception of increased loudness for a person with normal hearing. It must be remembered, however, that for persons with sensorineural hearing impairment, sensitivity in the higher-frequency range is commonly reduced.

Durational Characteristics of Speech

Speech is an event that occurs over time. Each component of speech, whether it be a single sound, a syllable, or a phrase, takes a certain amount of time to articulate. The duration of various speech sounds in normal conversational speech varies considerably, thus providing an additional source of constraints. The sounds that have the longest duration are the vowels, which range from 100 to 200 milliseconds in duration (Bode, 1975). Consonants for the most part are of as little duration as 40 milliseconds. The average durations of vowels and consonants are shown in Table 3.3. The amount of time during which a signal is available to a listener—that is, its duration—has been shown to affect its detection level (Gerber, 1974a). Duration is also a measure of pause, the time during which speech energy is absent. The pause serves as a constraint in the identification of plosive consonants in which the energy is stopped prior to the utterance of the plosive sound. The pause, measured by its duration, is also used as one means of marking syntactic units in the otherwise continuous acoustic stream. It serves as a punctuation marker in the spoken message.

The durational characteristics of speech have implications for amplification. The capability of hearing aids to respond faithfully to short-duration sounds is sometimes limited at high levels of output (Bode, 1975). When this is the case, the aid adds additional frequencies, which continue after the short-duration sound has passed. This resonant echo effect consists of transient distortion. It is called *ringing* and may overlap the next speech sound, making it more difficult to hear the critical transients of speech (Pollack, 1975). Short speech-sound duration is therefore a factor that may reduce the intelligibility of amplified sounds, particularly for persons with severe hearing deficits. It is reasonable to conclude that the durational characteristics of speech probably contribute some

TABLE 3.3 The Average Duration Times for Twelve Vowels and Diphthongs and Fifteen Consonants (after Crandall, 1925)

	Phoneme	*Duration*	*Phoneme*	*Duration*
VOWELS AND DIPHTHONGS	u	0.351	æ	0.294
	i	0.341	ɔ	0.290
	ɝ	0.331	ʌ	0.280
	ou	0.325	ʊ	0.249
	ɑ	0.306	ɛ	0.219
	ei	0.305	ɪ	0.211
CONSONANT VALUES FOR TWO SPEAKERS	ʒ	0.28	ʃ	0.18
		0.13		0.17
	s	0.27	f	0.15
		0.19		0.30
	z	0.24	g	0.12
		0.22		0.10
	j	0.22	b	0.12
		0.14		0.19
	v	0.20	tʃ	0.07
		0.25		0.08
	ð	0.20	k	0.07
		0.18		0.08
	d	0.13	θ	0.02
		0.10		0.02
			p	0.02
				0.04

constraint information that adds to the definition of the total pattern. As is the case with frequency and intensity, a group of adjacent speech sounds is characterized by an acoustic pattern peculiar to that combination. The uniqueness of the pattern results from the particular combination of the constraints defined by the parameters of frequency, intensity, and duration. Certain minimal acoustic requirements can be identified for any speech pattern; each helps the listener to differentiate the sound pattern received from all other patterns.

RECEPTION OF SPEECH

Hearing impairment, whether due to a deficiency in the conduction of sound from the eardrum to the organ of hearing or to damage to that organ, results in a reduction in the amount of information available for the process of perceiving. We have seen that the information in the acoustic signal comes from the patterning of the glottal tone by the speech resonators. The resultant complex wave originates from the interaction of a number of simple components. Therefore, over time, the acoustic signal is the direct equivalent of the changing articulatory resonant patterns. To receive this information, the ear must be sensitive across the range of frequencies within which speech sounds fall. Although the normal ear of a young person has a frequency sensitivity range of approximately 20 to 20,000 Hz, the frequency range of speech does not exceed 250 to 3000 Hz, though high frequencies above this may contribute to the learning of speech. The 250 to 3000 Hz range encompasses the first and second formants of vowels and voiced consonants and the major energy concentrations of voiceless consonants.

Figure 3.11 indicates that for any voiced sound, identifying formant information occurs at two or more points along the frequency scale. For example, the phonetic symbol /d/ occurs at approximately 300 and 2800 Hz, whereas the vowel /i/ occurs at approximately 300, 2300, 3300 Hz. The perception of a vowel speech sound as it is transmitted depends on the ability of the peripheral hearing mechanism to be stimulated by the sound wave at each of these frequencies. If, due to hearing impairment, the full frequency information is not recorded by the auditory system, the speech-sound pattern will be distorted. Most hearing impairments do not affect all frequencies equally. The loss of sensitivity characteristic of sensorineural hearing problems usually affects the high and middle range of frequencies more severely than the low frequencies.

We explained previously that the first two formants are essential for the discrimination of vowel sounds; however, consonant-sound identification is more dependent on the ability to receive the higher-frequency components. If these are inaudible, the place of consonant articulation cannot be determined, thus precluding identification. Such a situation can occur when a listener suffers from high-frequency deafness and may be aggravated by the presence of environmental acoustic noise. Under

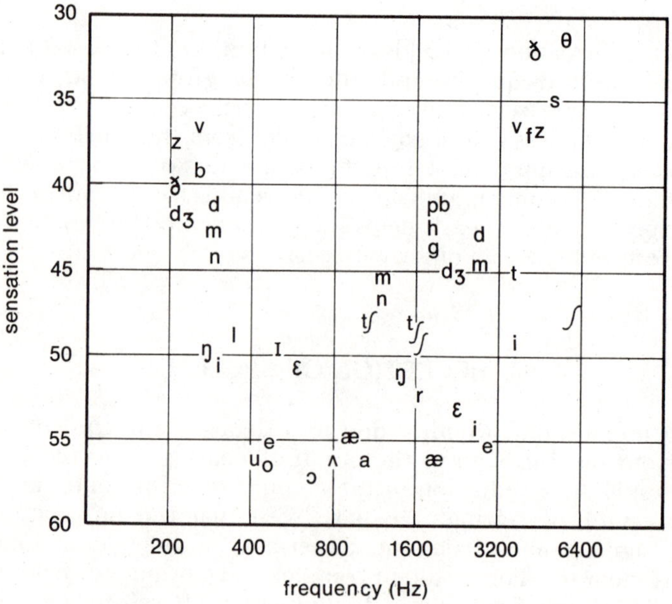

FIGURE 3.11 Sensation level and frequency characteristics of speech and sounds (after Fletcher, 1953).

such circumstances, the listener will become dependent upon other sources of information, both in terms of the linguistic structure and the supplementary use of the visual channel, as a means of obtaining the necessary cues to identify the consonants.

Consonant discrimination may also be significantly affected by a decrease in signal intensity. As Table 3.2 shows, consonant components contain less energy than vowel sounds; thus, they are affected by loss of intensity far more rapidly than are vowels. If a speech signal is made softer, it is often difficult to distinguish the consonant sounds. However, in syllables and words, vowels provide many cues to the recognition of consonants. Actually, it is probably the transitional part of the syllable rather than the vowel itself that assists in this identification. Because vowels contain the greatest energy of all speech sounds, and transitions are similar to vowels, the information transmitted in these sounds requires considerable attenuation before it is lost.

If the reception of speech sounds is in any way interfered with, the intensity of the sound will be diminished, and it will sound softer. For the sound to have full intensity, all of the harmonics must be received. The removal of any harmonic by filtering or by attenuation, including that imposed by an impairment of auditory sensitivity, will reduce the overall intensity or loudness, even though intelligibility may not be affected. The effect that this will have upon the identification of the pitch characteristics of the voice will be minimal, providing the listener possesses enough hearing to permit the reception of several harmonics. Failure to receive either high or low frequencies will not destroy pitch identification. Pitch perception is possible even without understanding what is said.

This chapter has dealt with the production and reception of sounds used in speech. It is these sounds that constitute the basic units of a spoken language. When the sounds are "woven together" in a predescribed manner, communication through speech may occur. Perception of the message communicated requires a more complex process than the simple reception of sounds. However, if the basic units cannot be accurately produced or received, this language cannot be used. Whenever a reduction of information in the auditory channel occurs to a degree that interferes with speech comprehension, it is necessary for the listener to seek supplementary cues. Because speech occurs within an environmental context, and more important, because much of the articulation of speech is observable, the visual channel constitutes a valuable alternate source of information. Next, we consider the nature of those visual-constraint cues.

REFERENCES

Bode, D. L., "Speech Signals and Hearing Aids," in *Amplification for the Hearing Impaired,* ed. M. Pollack, pp. 287–304. New York: Grune & Stratton, Inc. 1975.

Condon, W. S., and L. W. Sander, "Neonate Movement is Synchronized with Adult Speech," *Science, 183,* 1973, 99–101.

Crandall, I., "The Sounds of Speech," *Bell System Technical Journal,* 4, October 1925, 586–626.

Daniloff, R. G., "Normal Articulation Process," in *Normal Aspects of Speech, Hearing and Language,* eds. F. Minifie, and T. J. Hixon, pp. 169–209. Englewood Cliffs, N.J.: Prentice-Hall, Inc., 1973.

Fairbanks, G., E. Herbert, and J. Hammond, "An Acoustical Study of the Vocal Pitch of Seven- and Eight-Year-Old Girls," *Child Development, 20,* 1949, 71–78.

Fairbanks, G., J. Wiley, and F. Lassman, "An Acoustical Study of the Vocal Pitch of Seven- and Eight-Year-Old Boys, *Child Development, 20,* 1949, 63–69.

Fletcher, H., *Speech and Hearing in Communication.* Princeton: D. Van Nostrand Co., Inc., 1953.

Gerber, S. E., "Auditory Temporality," in *Introductory Hearing Science,* ed. S. E. Gerber, pp. 172–186. Philadelphia: W. B. Sanders Company, 1974. (a)

Gerber, S. E., "Intelligibility of Speech," in *Introductory Hearing Science,* ed. S. E. Gerber, pp. 238–260. Philadelphia: W. B. Saunders Company, 1974. (b)

Hollien, H., E. Malcik, and B. Hollien, "Adolescent Voice Change in Southern White Males," *Speech Monographs, 32,* 1965, 87–90.

Hollien, H., and T. Shipp, "Speaking Fundamental Frequency and Chronological Age in Males," *Journal of Speech and Hearing Research, 15,* 1972, 155–159.

Kaplan, E., and G. Kaplan, "The Prelinguistic Child," in *Human Development and Cognitive Processes,* ed. J. Eliot. New York: Holt, Rinehart & Winston, 1971.

Liberman, P., "Intonation and Syntactic Processing of Speech," in *Models for the Perception of Speech and Visual Form,* ed. W. Wathen-Dunn, pp. 314–319. Cambridge, Mass.: M.I.T. Press, 1967.

Linke, E., "A Study of Pitch Characteristics of Female Voices and Their Relationship to Vocal Effectiveness." Ph.D. dissertation, University of Iowa, 1953.

Martin, J. G., "Rhythmic Hierarchical Versus Serial Structure in Speech and Other Behavior," *Psychology Review, 73,* 1972, 487–509.

McGlone, R., "Vocal Pitch Characteristics of Children Aged One and Two Years," *Speech Monographs, 33,* 1966, 178–181.

Minifie, F. D., T. J. Hixon, and F. Williams, eds., *Normal Aspects of Speech Hearing and Language.* Englewood Cliffs, N.J.: Prentice-Hall, Inc., 1973.

Mysak, E., "Pitch and Duration Characteristics of Older Males," *Journal of Speech and Hearing Research, 2,* 1959, 46–54.

Pollack, M. C., "Electroacoustic Characteristics," in *Amplification for the Hearing Impaired,* ed. M. C. Pollack, pp. 21–80. New York: Grune & Stratton, Inc., 1975.

Pollard, G., and R. Neumaier, "Vision Characteristics of Deaf Children," *American Annals of the Deaf,* 119, 1974, 740–745.

Ringel, R., and D. Kluppel, "Neonatal Crying: A Normative Study," *Folia Phoniatrica, 16,* 1964, 1–9.

Sanders, D. A., *Auditory Perception of Speech—An Introduction to Principles and Problems.* Englewood Cliffs, N.J.: Prentice-Hall, Inc., 1977.

Wakita, H., "The Acoustics of Speech," in *Introductory Hearing Science,* ed. S. E. Gerber, pp. 209–237. Philadelphia: W. B. Saunders Company, 1974.

4

Visual Aspects of Speech

We have already discussed the primacy of the acoustic signal in the process of speech perception by normal-hearing persons. Such primacy, however, is predicated upon the ability of the listener to receive more auditory information than is necessary for the reconstruction of the intended linguistic and cognitive values. That is, the system must contain a high level of redundancy. Furthermore, auditory perception is greatly influenced by a person's ability to generate internal probabilities that further reduce dependency upon acoustic cues.

A hearing impairment will most certainly reduce the amount of the acoustic pattern received. When such an impairment is present before the acquisition of language, it will also limit a person's capacity to compensate for acoustic distortion by drawing upon internal linguistic redundancy. Both congenital and acquired (adventitious) hearing impairment necessitate increased dependency on other sensory modalities. This is the only way in which the total amount of information may be raised above the minimal requirements for comprehension.

Any sensory modality can be used to convey information. The extent to which this can be achieved depends upon the compatibility between the nature of the stimulus code and the receiving capabilities of that system (Sanders, 1976). However, the visual system is adapted to the reception of both verbal and nonverbal aspects of communication. For this reason, it assumes a major role as a supplementary source for information processing. Our concern in this chapter is with the nature of the visual constraints operating during speech communication and some of the factors affecting them. Heightening awareness of these constraints is an important aspect of the visual-communication training component of rehabilitation.

The visual system constitutes a major supportive component in the processing of information relevant to the act of communication. The demands placed upon vision by a person who has a hearing impairment are considerable. It is, therefore, of primary importance to ensure that the visual system is functioning optimally. If a person who has difficulty in hearing also has impaired vision, the task of compensatory adaptation is even more difficult.

It is important to note that the two periods in life when visual problems are most likely to appear first are during the early school years and during middle age. These are the same periods when impairment of hearing is also most frequently detected. Some of the conditions that cause deafness are also likely to result in vision defects. Greene's (1978) in-depth screening of the vision of 156 deaf school-age children demonstrated a significantly higher incidence of visual anomalies than is present among hearing children of the same age. The increased incidence was shown for hyperopia (4 times greater), strabismus (2.5 times greater), amblyopia (8.5 times greater), and other binocularity disorders (3 times greater). Pathology among the deaf children was shown to have an incidence 12 times greater than among normal-hearing children. In an earlier study Pollard and Neumaier (1974) reported the incidence of ocular defects among deaf children to be between 20 percent and 60 percent. These findings emphasize the paramount importance of thorough in-depth visual testing of hearing-impaired children.

A notable cause of congenital auditory and visual problems is maternal rubella, which affects the infant, particularly if the mother contracted the disease during the first three months of pregnancy. Increasing age, which produces a deterioration of both visual function (presbyosis) and auditory function (presbycusis), is a condition we can all expect to face. Although many adults become aware that they are experiencing difficulty with visual acuity, the amount of deterioration is often fairly marked before it draws attention to itself. Up to that point, many people unconsciously compensate for the problems they are experiencing. It is possible that some people may, to a certain extent, psychologically reject the idea that they might need glasses. People who already wear glasses might not want to go to the expense of reexamination and possible replacement of their current pair. The visual difficulty may, therefore, only evidence itself in the hard-of-hearing adults as part of the total deterioration in their ability to communicate as a result of the less-than-normal visual acuity. Such people are unable to compensate to any marked degree for the loss of hearing by greater dependence upon visible cues to speech. In a visual-communication training class, they may suggest many different reasons why they have been unable to develop this skill. It may not occur to them that they may be calling upon their eyes to perform a task that is too fine for their visual acuity to handle. Because vision constitutes such an important component in the total information-processing system that we utilize in training or retraining people with impaired hearing, we now consider some of the factors that influence the effectiveness of visual processing of information.

FACTORS INFLUENCING VISIBILITY

Lighting Conditions

The efficiency of the human eye is markedly reduced when the light intensity is strongly increased or reduced suddenly. Consider, for example, the effect of extinguishing the lights in a bright room. The initial reaction is that you are in total darkness. However, you gradually become able to distinguish the shapes of objects that were previously not visible. This phenomenon is known as *dark adaptation.* Similarly, sudden exposure to bright light after a period in a relatively darkened room results in a sensation of glare until your eyes adapt to the new light conditions. Light adaptation is very important to hard-of-hearing subjects in communication, because they are dependent upon the visible aspects of speech as an aid to comprehension. If they move from brightness to a dimly lighted environment, they experience a temporary decrease in visual sensitivity because of the low level of illumination. They experience similar difficulty in bright light.

Visual acuity can be defined as the ability of the eye to distinguish fine details. Perhaps the most important factor affecting visual acuity is the light intensity. The amount of light that needs to be present in the environment to permit the clearest vision varies depending upon the nature of the visual task. Generally speaking, the finer the nature of the work the eyes are required to do, the more illumination is required. For example, you may be able to peel an apple, count coins, or arrange flowers in a relatively poor light. However, threading a needle, removing a splinter from a finger, or reading small print on a label all necessitate a much greater amount of illumination. Up to a point, performance on even larger tasks may be improved by the provision of extra light; however, too much intensity will produce glare, which reduces acuity. The light must be directed on the activity or object being observed; if the light is directed toward the viewer, it will tend to decrease that person's ability to perform the task accurately.

The visual task confronting the listener in a communication situation is to see and utilize the constraint cues arising from facial expressions and, more specifically, from the visible characteristics of speech articulation. The influence that various levels of constant illumination have upon the ability of hearing-impaired persons to speech-read has not been subject to extensive study. Thomas (1962) appears to have been the first to investigate the effect of several constant light levels on the visual recognition of messages with highly familiar content. Thomas found that speech-reading performance of trained subjects was not significantly different under excellent or adverse conditions. At a distance of ten feet from a speaker, Thomas' subjects showed no deterioration in their ability to correctly identify test items until the level of lighting was reduced to approximately one-half foot candle power, which is the minimal amount of light necessary to be able to just see the speaker's face.

Erber (1974) studied the effects of facial and background illumination on the ability of profoundly deaf children to recognize words by visual cues alone. He compared the mean word-recognition scores obtained when the speaker was seated in front of a highly reflective surface with those obtained when a low, reflective, black background was used. Erber's results revealed little difference in the scores obtained by the deaf children when lip-reading under these two conditions of reflected light. He concluded that the intensity of light source at the level of the mouth, which illuminates both mouth and face, only minimally affects visual recognition of the spoken word. Thus, background reflection of light does not appear to be a significant factor in visual-communication performance. Further study by Erber concerned the influence of a highly illuminated background (300 footlamberts) on the ability of the children to visually recognize words presented under varying levels of illumination of the speaker's face. This part of the investigation demonstrated a highly statistically significant effect. The mean difference between the word-recognition scores for low (3 footlamberts) and high (30 footlamberts) facial illumination against the background glare (300 footlamberts) was 49 percent.

The conclusion drawn from these studies is that contrary to conventional wisdom, once appropriate light adaptation has occurred, speech-reading can be performed equally well in high- or low-intensity light levels. However, contrast between the level of illumination of the speaker's face and the background exerts a highly significant effect on speech-reading performance, at least among the deaf children studied by Erber. Erber concluded from this research that the level of contrast between facial and background illumination is the critical factor. Thus, when facial illumination is high, the effect of a bright background on a listener's ability to use visible speech cues will be negligible. However, the reverse is true when, for example, the listener stands with his or her back to a sunlit window with no other light source to equally illuminate the face. Erber makes the important point that persons with normal language abilities do not depend upon the perception of every speech element for speech recognition, even under adverse listening conditions. Young children with impaired hearing, on the other hand, require every available external cue to compensate for their low linguistic redundancy. Thus, concern for adequate contrastive lighting conditions in educational settings is justified.

Another important factor in determining the fineness of details observed by the eye concerns the angle at which the light strikes the retina. When a person focuses on an object, the light reflected from that object is directed on the fovea of the retina. The ability to see an object 20 degrees to one side of the center of focus is reduced to a visual-acuity level approximately one-tenth of the foveal vision, because the light rays at this position will not be as sharply focused (Kendler, 1963). Thus, to teach deaf children the names of objects or to point out a particular picture, try to bring the object close to your face so that it is in clear focus.

Viewing Distance and Angle

Visual acuity is also affected by the angle and distance between the eye and the object observed. The greater the separation, the poorer visual acuity becomes. Keith K. Neely (1956) attempted to quantify the effects of distance and the angle from which the listener observes the speaker. Using a trained speaker and thirty-five male listeners with normal hearing and vision, Neely compared the scores obtained by the subjects on a multiple-choice intelligibility test at nine different seating positions. These positions were 3, 6, and 9 feet and 0, 45, and 90 degrees from the speaker. Distance, within the limits tested, did not affect intelligibility, though the scores obtained by subjects directly facing the speaker were higher than those obtained for subjects at 45- and 90-degree angles. Berger, DePompei, and Droder (1970) extended the viewing-distance factor. These researchers assessed the effect of distance upon the ability of normal-hearing adults to distinguish between vowels in monosyllabic words using only visual speech cues. Their results confirmed those obtained by Neely (1956), but extended to 24 feet the range within which visual speech discrimination is not affected by distance. Using two speakers, Erber (1971) also examined the effect of distance on the lip-reading performance of profoundly deaf children. The speakers' faces were lit directly at mouth level. The test items were monosyllabic words, two-syllable words with the stress on the first syllable (trochaic), and two-syllable words with equal stress on each syllable (spondaic). The study revealed that word-recognition scores for the subjects increased as the distance decreased from approximately 11 percent at 100 feet to approximately 75 percent at 5 feet (Figure 4.1). In a later study, Erber (1974) reported that the scores obtained by his subjects, viewing from angles of 0 degrees and 45 degrees, decreased in a linear manner as a function of increasing distance. However, when the speaker was viewed from the side (90-degree angle), the mean scores were not further enhanced by decreasing the speaker-child distance below 12 feet.

Erber also investigated the effect of the angle of viewing on visual reception scores obtained by the profoundly deaf children tested. He found the best visual reception of speech to occur for either the 0- or 45-degree viewing angle. Erber notes that these findings do not exactly concur with those obtained by other researchers. Neely (1956), for example, found that the 0-degree horizontal viewing angle produced slightly higher scores than the 45-degree angle, whereas Larr (1959) and Nakano (1966) both reported that the 45-degree angle was superior to the 0-degree viewing angle.

In a different approach, Berger, Garner, and Sudman (1971) compared the effect on visual speech discrimination of viewing the subject from below the level of the face (−35-degree angle), which is equivalent to how a child sees an adult, with face-level viewing (0-degree angle). The adult subjects had normal hearing. No significant difference was found in the scores obtained for the two viewing angles.

Thus, for children and adults, the optimal viewing position for visual perception of speech appears to be a horizontal angle of 0 to 45 de-

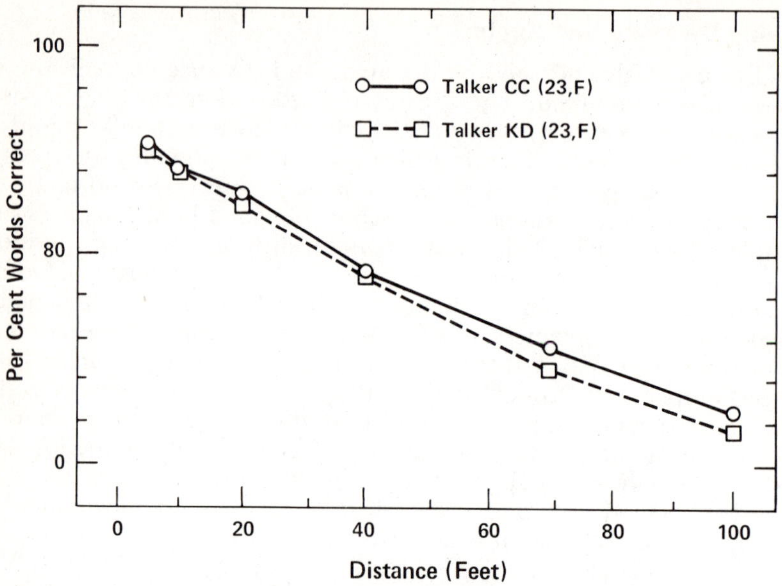

FIGURE 4.1 Mean word-recognition scores of six profoundly deaf children as a function of distance. Intense, shadow-free illumination was provided at mouth level for the speakers. Total vocabulary equals 240 words (after Erber, 1971).

grees at a distance of no greater than 6 feet. A 90-degree viewing angle appears to be disadvantageous to optimal visual recognition of speech, reducing performance by 11 to 22 percent.

Visual Acuity

Despite the obvious importance of vision in the processing of visual speech information, not until 1970 was the report of a systematic investigation that related the performance of the peripheral visual mechanism to lip-reading performance published. Sixteen college students with normal hearing participated in the study by Hardick, Oyer, and Irion (1970). The subjects were drawn from a pool of fifty-two students who had taken a filmed lip-reading test (Utley, 1946). The two equal groups of subjects chosen had obtained the eight highest and eight lowest scores on the test. The original pool of students represented a random sample with respect to skills in visual speech processing. The main purpose of the investigation was to determine whether, on the basis of optometric findings, normal-hearing subjects who demonstrated an ability to process a relatively large amount of visible speech information could be discriminated from those who performed poorly. The measures of visual function included visual acuity, refraction, astigmatism, and ability of the eye to discern form movement and color. Accommodation, peripheral vision, eye-blink rate, stereopsis, and phoria—that is, the tendency of the visual axis of one eye to deviate when the other eye is covered and fusion is prevented—were also assessed. The result of this examination revealed that visual performance varied along only two of the parameters tested, visual acuity and eye-blink rate. Subjects were thus given an optometric rating mainly on the basis of binocular acuity.

The lip-reading scores obtained by subjects with high visual acuity rating and the scores of subjects with visual deficiencies were compared. The results indicated that the subjects in the normal group obtained significantly higher lip-reading scores on the sentence subtest and on the overall test score, but not on single-word identification or the story comprehension.

The authors of the study concluded that their results indicated that even a relatively minor deficiency of acuity will significantly lower scores on a lip-reading test. They question the validity of previous research into visual communication skills because rarely, if ever, were the test subjects controlled for visual acuity.

Visual Defects

The process of focusing light energy upon the retina is achieved through bending or refracting the light waves. When the light is reflected from objects close to the individual, it tends to spread outward. This requires a much greater amount of refraction to obtain the necessary focus than is essential for distance vision.

The relatively few people who possess perfect vision do so because the eyeball is so shaped that it provides focus for distance vision without adjustments to the shape of the lenses. The amount of adjustment necessary for close vision is very small; neither near nor far vision places the eyes under strain. An abnormality in shape or size of the eyeball is liable to result in a distortion of the normal refractive process, and it may cause a decrease in visual acuity, discomfort, or interference with the coordinated action of the two eyes. These defects in vision are known as refractive errors, and they fall under three headings: *myopia* (nearsightedness), *hyperopia* (farsightedness), and *astigmatism.*

Myopia. Myopia results from an abnormal elongation of the shape of the eyeball. As a result, the light rays emanating from distant objects come into focus at a point before they reach the retina. Thus, the image of distant objects is blurred. Near vision remains unimpaired, since the light rays from near objects come into focus farther back and fall on the retina. A child with such a defect would not have difficulty in observing facial expressions and lip movements of a speaker close by, but the child would be unable to make use of these visual clues to speech on a person at 20 feet away. Indeed, faces might be unrecognizable at this distance (Figure 4.2).

In the classroom or therapy session, children with hearing impairments depend heavily on visual aids and information presented on the blackboard. They derive great help from seeing new or difficult vocabu-

FIGURE 4.2 Myopic vision blurs objects at a distance, while near vision remains unimpaired (courtesy of St. Mary's School for the Deaf, Buffalo, New York)

lary written, from seeing the written outline of subject material and key words associated with it, and from written instructions or assignments. Myopic children without glasses will encounter difficulty in seeing the blackboard. They may be unable to read or they may misinterpret what has been written. More serious is the general overall reduction in the amount of information that they receive. A hard-of-hearing person with normal vision may be able to manage adequately in communication situations when supported by a program of aural rehabilitation. The same person deprived of adequate visual information to augment the auditory signal may find it quite impossible to function in the same situations. This is particularly true for children in school.

Hyperopia. Hyperopia results from a shorter-than-normal distance between the cornea and the retina (Figure 4.3). As a result, the visual image is still not in focus by the time the light waves reach the retina. In an attempt to compensate for this loss of focus, the ciliary muscles, which control the shape and thickness of the lens, must contract strongly. This process, called *accommodation,* is necessary even for distance vision, while a much greater amount of contraction is involved in producing a clear image of objects close to the viewer. If the ciliary muscles are strong, as is common in children, a person may be able to make the necessary adjustment to be able to carry out close work without difficulty. This, however, involves placing a strain upon the optic muscles, and it may give rise to such symptoms as periodic blurring of the visual image, a short visual-attention span, or headaches. These symptoms are most likely to occur in

FIGURE 4.3 **Hyperopia results in the blurring of objects close to the viewer, while those at a distance remain clear** (courtesy of St. Mary's School for the Deaf, Buffalo, New York).

connection with tasks requiring fine visual acuity, one of which is the interpretation of the visual articulatory movements of speech. Hyperopia may therefore seriously impair a hard-of-hearing person's ability to capitalize on the visual cues of speech. A speaker may appear quite clear when seen at a distance, as will any visual aids that are used. In a more personal communication situation, however, in which the speaker is much closer, as in a tutoring relationship or in a small group, the face and lip movements will appear blurred, depriving the listener of the cues embodied in the visible articulatory movements of speech.

Astigmatism. An astigmatism arises from an irregularity in the curve of the cornea. This results in the uneven focusing of light rays originating from the same source. The fact that some of the rays are focused farther back than others produces a blurred distortion of the image on the retina. Objects may appear fuzzy, or they may be elongated or flattened. Astigmatism is a condition that may be found both in isolation and also associated with either hyperopia or myopia. With this type of visual problem, the observer may find part of the object viewed to be in focus while other parts are out of focus. This can be particularly disturbing to a person who is attempting to focus vision upon a speaker. As the speaker moves, different parts of that person's image will be in focus.

In addition, problems may arise that affect the fusion of the image from both eyes. These conditions are *impairment of binocular vision.*

Since the human being has two eyes placed in a single plane in the front of the head, the visual images of the same object are focused simultaneously on the retina of each eye. A brain mechanism, unique to humans, fuses these images so that the observer perceives only a single object. An even subtler feature of binocular vision is made possible by the separation of the two eyes by an average of sixty-five millimeters in the adult. Due to this separation, a slight disparity exists in the positions of the two corresponding images on the two retinae. This disparity is responsible for depth perception, known professionally as *steropsis.* There are several visual clues available for the judgment of distance, such as parallax and differences in size and brightness, but true depth perception is possible only as a result of this image disparity associated with binocularity. Any disfunction in this fusional ability and stereopsis, especially in children, will interfere with the spatial orientation of the individual. In severe cases this may result in double vision *(diplopia).*

A loss of binocular vision may also occur if the eyes are crossed, or if a single eye turns outward or inward. This condition may result from a severe refractive error in one eye. If the amount of accommodation necessary to correct this refractive error is too great for the ciliary muscles to achieve, the poor eye will cease the attempt, leaving the task of maintaining visual acuity to the better eye. Since the distorted vision of the poor eye will no longer be of use, that eye will tend to converge. In time, this inactivity leads to a complete suppression of the visual image received from the poor eye, resulting in what may prove to be permanent changes in the function of the ciliary muscles. For all practical purposes, the eye becomes blind. To a hearing-impaired person, either of these conditions would constitute an added handicap, since there would be serious impairment of the sense of distance as well as direction, both of which already may be affected by the hearing impairment.

The problem of poor visual acuity in young children is likely to remain undetected unless the eyes are tested. Children with visual defects may be quite unaware that the world should appear any differently from the way they see it. Furthermore, in the early years most children tend to be farsighted. Thus, the gradual onset of myopia, most commonly occurring during the first years of school, may escape detection. It is not until the visual deterioration evidences itself in the child's failure to make progress in school that visual acuity is questioned. The hard-of-hearing child stands in double jeopardy in this respect. We are only too likely to attribute educational retardation entirely to the hearing impairment and thus completely overlook the role of vision.

The five types of visual problems we have discussed are common to both children and adults. Two additional visual hazards encountered by adults may both result in a serious deterioration of vision. These are *glaucoma* and *cataract.*

Glaucoma. Glaucoma, which affects 2 percent of people over 40, is usually an ailment found in adults, though occasionally it may be present in children and young adults. An increase in the pressure of the fluid in the eye jeopardizes both the optic nerve and its blood supply. Glaucoma may develop so slowly that the subject is unaware of the gradual loss of vision until the condition is fairly advanced. Some early symptoms may be: mild headaches or aching eyes, both of which may occur after viewing television or movies; transitory blurring of vision; poor vision in dim light; halos around lights; or partial loss of side vision.

Cataract. Cataract involves "a cloudiness of the lens of the eye which blocks the normal passage of light rays through the pupil to the retina" (U.S. DHEW, 1963). This may produce blurring of near and distance vision, black spots in the visual field, or the illusion that parts of objects are missing. The symptoms vary according to the part of the lens that is affected. Any of the symptoms listed for either of these conditions necessitates prompt consultation with a medically qualified eye specialist (ophthalmologist).

For the reasons previously stated, the importance of evaluation of peripheral visual function in any child or adult with a hearing impairment cannot be too strongly emphasized. Optimally, corrected vision should be a prerequisite to the enrollment of a person into a rehabilitation management program. This is important because such intervention procedures almost of necessity will include training designed to develop supplemental skills in the visual processing of speech to compensate for information lost as a result of impaired hearing. Thus, in keeping with our concern for the total process of communication, it is essential that we make particularly certain that, in addition to providing the hard-of-hearing subject with all possible help in receiving and interpreting the auditory signal, we also ensure that the visual pathway is operating at its optimum level. This requires that each subject with a hearing impairment receive a thorough examination of visual function by an ophthalmologist or optometrist,* and that reexamination of vision is made every 2 years.

VISIBILITY OF THE MESSAGE SIGNAL

Up to this point we have been concerned with those factors that directly affect the ability of the eye to detect visible cues related to the message signal. We must now consider the nature of the visible stimuli in human communication. Our discussion concentrates upon the properties of visible cues that determine the degree to which they will be visible to the observer. The factors that affect the manner in which this information is actually perceived—that is, the way in which meaning is ascribed to what is seen—is discussed in Chapter 6.

In a communication situation a person is able to encompass a large number of objects and people at a single glance. What a person actually notices, as opposed to what the person sees, will be determined primarily by the expectancies the person has for certain information deemed relevant to the understanding of the situation, and by what is likely to be

**Ophthalmologist:* A medical doctor who specializes in the medical diagnosis and treatment of defects of the eye. This includes the use of surgery and the prescription of glasses.
Optometrist: A nonmedical specialist qualified to test vision, provide glasses, and conduct visual training. An optometrist is not qualified to treat diseases of the eye or to recommend medical or surgical treatment.
Optician: A person trained to grind lenses and fit glasses according to the prescription provided by the ophthalmologist or optometrist.

communicated. When we considered the model of communication in Chapter 2 it was emphasized that the whole process involved the use of information patterns to generate and verify expectations. Listening and looking, unlike hearing and seeing, are active processes guided by our anticipations. This visual-communication training aims to increase the use the hearing-impaired person is able to make of potentially informative visual cues. This requires increasing the efficiency with which visual information is processed. When biology students first look through their microscopes at slides of a cross-section of a plant stem, or at a unicellular organism, they are lucky if they can observe more than a few of its characteristic features. However, with training and experience they begin to learn how to look, they learn to recognize highly informative landmark characteristics, and they start to see things not as an unrelated series of features but as a pattern or gestalt arising from the interrelationship of individual components. Once students are familiar with patterns, they can recognize very rapidly what they see. Even more important, they know what to look for, they know the salient features of a particular slide. This ability to establish an anticipatory set greatly increases the rate of information processing with no decrease in accuracy.

Thus in a communication situation we select from the massive array of stimuli those we consider to have a probable relationship to the content of the message being received. We impose a weighting on the available stimuli which accords with our expectancies. This process is applied in very broad terms to the manner in which we observe the general environment in which the communication event is occurring. It is refined in a very controlled manner when we process the speech stimulus itself.

The visible stimuli with which we are concerned may be divided into three categories:

1. Stimuli arising from the environment in which the communication occurs
2. Stimuli associated directly with the message, but not part of speech production
3. Stimuli directly associated with the production of speech sounds

Environmental Stimuli

Communication between individuals necessarily takes place in a physical environment. It is against this background that the message signal, received by the listener, will be interpreted. Nonspeech stimuli arising from people or objects may, therefore, prove useful in the interpretation of the message signal if they are received by the eye. For the most part, environmental cues suffer least from poor viewing conditions. It is, nevertheless, important to recognize that such factors as low light intensity, dark adaptation, and position of the stimulus object within the viewer's visual field will all influence to some extent the ability of the observer to make use of this background information. In a communication situation, a person is able to encompass a large number of objects and people at a single glance. It is from this massive amount of stimuli that the person will select those that he or she considers to have a probable relationship to the content of the message signal being received.

The role of environment is easily understood if we consider the effect that theatrical scenery and costumes have on the interpretation of the actual words of a play. We interpret what is said in the light of the scene in which it is said. We must therefore be able to see the scenery clearly. The lighting director often makes use of this by opening the scene in darkness and then gradually raising the light intensity level until a background is provided against which the dialogue may be interpreted. Similarly, the director may focus the lighting on one particular section of the stage, thus eliminating the remainder of the scenery from the context, changing the relative emphasis on various actors and items of scenery. In this way, variations of period, time, and place may be conveyed within a stage set.

In a more everyday setting, imagine yourself joining a group of people at a table in a dimly lit restaurant. The phenomenon of dark adaptation, together with the low intensity, may deny you the benefit of interpreting a spoken message about someone or something in the environment against the background of visual clues. Again, the limitations that this places on the already handicapped communication system of the hard-of-hearing person may sufficiently reduce the total amount of information to a level that denies comprehension.

Nonspeech Stimuli Directly Related to the Speaker

Under this category we include body posture; body movement, including gesture; and facial expressions. Each of these aspects of communication behavior is capable of conveying information concerning events that have preceded the sending of a message, and concerning factors that lie behind the message at the time it is being transmitted (Hall, 1959). The actual way in which these may be interpreted will be considered in more detail in the next chapter. At this point it will suffice to say that when a person is denied the benefit of seeing these cues clearly, he or she is denied an additional source of information. We recognize this when, at a lecture or a discussion, we attempt to seat ourselves in a position that permits us to see the speaker clearly. We do this even when we know we will have no difficulty in hearing what is said. When the acoustic conditions are poor, as is frequently true in churches and in some meeting halls, we are particularly anxious to ensure that we are not denied the additional help that we, as normal-hearing subjects, derive from watching the visible aspects of the speaker's delivery.

Poor visual acuity, resulting from defective vision or environmental conditions, is likely to have a marked effect upon the ability of a person to see the speaker's face clearly. If you wear glasses you know how troublesome it is to attend a lecture without them, and as a result to have to listen to a speaker whose face appears blurred. The same annoyance is experienced when a theater stage is poorly lit or a movie is slightly out of focus. In choosing a seat at a play or lecture, we like to sit near the front, since being seated at a distance deprives us of a clear view of facial expressions. This indicates that even persons with normal hearing utilize to some extent the additional information conveyed by the visual channel.

We may therefore conclude that the ability to receive both environmental stimuli and nonspeech stimuli originating from the speaker is important in determining whether we will be able to understand a spoken message, particularly when the acoustic signal is distorted.

Visible Aspects of Speech Production

The production of various speech sounds is made possible by the modification of air flow from the lungs brought about by the changes in the shape and size of the supralaryngeal resonators. These changes involve the movement and positioning of the jaw, lips, tongue, and soft palate. Each speech sound involves a distinctive articulatory movement. Under favorable viewing conditions, part, but seldom all, of this movement will be visible to an observer. A movement may be considered as having a *formative aspect* and a *revealing aspect.* The formative aspect includes the movement of all articulators essential to the production of a particular sound; the revealing aspect involves only those articulators that may be involved in or associated with its production. For example, the formative aspect of the speech sound *sh* /ʃ/ involves elevation of the soft palate, the grooving of the tongue, and the elevation of the sides of the tongue to make contact with the upper teeth. None of these movements are easily visible. The revealing movement associated with /ʃ/ is the puckering and protrusion of the lips, a movement associated with, but not essential to, the acoustic production of the sound.

In a number of phonemes some of the formative movements may also be revealing, as are the lip movements in the production of the bilabial plosives /p/ and /b/, or as is the tongue movement in the production of the voiced and unvoiced lingual dental fricatives /θ/ and /ð/.

Since these visible stimuli arise directly from the production of a specific phoneme, they provide a valuable source of additional information concerning the spoken word. If it were possible for the eyes to receive and identify each phoneme or word spoken purely on the basis of its visible characteristics, and if the conditions for viewing the speaker were always optimal, then the hard-of-hearing subject would not be handicapped by the inability to receive the auditory signal correctly. Rehabilitation of the hearing-impaired person would simply involve training the person to replace the use of ears by eyes in the reception of the message signal. Unfortunately this is not the case. The visible aspects of speech are subject to a number of important limitations that exist within the visual message signal itself, within the environment through which it travels, and within the person who is acting as the receiver. At this time, we are concerned only with the factors that pertain to the message signal and the environment. Factors within the receiver will be discussed later as an aspect of visual perception.

Four major factors influence the usefulness of the visual signal as a conveyor of information:

1. The degree of visibility of the movement
2. The rapidity of articulatory movements

3. The similarity of the visual characteristics of the articulatory movements involved in the production of different speech sounds
4. Intersubject variations in the visible aspects of articulatory movements involved in the production of any given sound

Degree of Visibility. The visual recognition of the speech sound is dependent upon the revealing aspects involved in its production. These vary considerably for each phoneme. The only phoneme that can truly be said to possess no revealing visible characteristic in its production is the aspirate /h/; however, for a considerable number of phonemes, the revealing characteristics are relatively obscure, and accuracy of recognition cannot be absolutely guaranteed even for a trained observer.

A study undertaken by the American Society for the Hard of Hearing (U.S.W.P.A., 1939) investigated the relative visibility of different phonemes. Using a value system that classified sounds into four categories ranging from complete visibility to zero visibility, they devised a system for calculating the measure of visibility for any speech sample. A modified table of the relative visibility of speech sounds, using this scale, is presented in Table 4.1. The percentage visibility of a word or sentence can

TABLE 4.1 Degree of Visibility of Speech Sounds

IV *0–0.25*	*III* *0.26–0.50*	*II* *0.51–0.75*	*I* *0.76–1.00*
CONSONANTS			
[k] as in *k*ite	[s] as in sit	[l] as in let	[p] as in pay
[g] good	[z] zebra		[b] boy
[ŋ] sing	[t] toy		[ʃ] ship
[h] hat	[d] dog		[ʒ] pleasure
	[n] no		[tʃ] church
	[r] red		[dʒ] jump
			[f] fish
			[v] very
			[θ] think
			[ð] the
			[m] mouse
			[j] yacht
			[w] weep
VOWELS AND DIPHTHONGS*			
	[ɛ] as in pen	[er] as in make	[a] as in father
	[ɪ] bid	[i] he	[ɔ] fall
	[ɝ] bird	[ɛɝ] fair	[æ] cat
	[u] put	[ɑɪ] my	[ou] no
	[ʌ] hut	[ɪə] here	[u] move
	[ə] about		[ɔi] boy
			[ɑu] house

*Double consonants, such as [bl], [fr], involve one movement.

be calculated by assigning each phoneme the maximum visibility value for its category; that is,

Category	*Value*
I	1.00
II	0.75
III	0.50
IV	0.25

The individual values are then added and divided by the total number of phonemes. Multiplication of the quotient by 100 provides a percentage-visibility figure. The formula for calculating percentage visibility is, therefore:

$$\text{Percentage visibility} = \frac{\Sigma \text{ individual phoneme values}}{\text{the total number of phonemes}} \times \frac{100}{1}$$

For example: Most speech sounds are fairly visible.
mou s p i tʃ sɑunz ə fɛəlɪ vɪzɪbl

Value: 1 + 1 + .5 + 1 + .75 + 1 .5 + 1 + .5 + .5 + .5 1 + .75 + .75 + .5
1 + .5 + .5 + .5 + 1 + .75

Total phoneme value = 15.5
Total number of phonemes = 21
Percentage visibility = 73.8 percent

$$\frac{15.5}{21} \times \frac{100}{1} = 73.8 \text{ percent}$$

or: Her hat isn't in here Katy.
hə hæt ɪznt ɪn hɪə keɪtɪ

Value: .25 + .5 + .25 + .25 + .5 + .5 + .5 + .5 + .5 .5 + .5
.25 + .75 + .5 + .5

Total phoneme value = 7.75
Total number of phonemes = 17
Percentage visibility = 45.6 percent

From these two examples you can see that the visibility of sentences can vary quite considerably. The range of visibility of normal conversational sentences was found to vary from a minimum of 47 percent to a maximum of 83 percent, with the average falling between 65 and 70 percent.

Rapidity of Articulatory Movements. Edward B. Nitchie (undated) has pointed out that in ordinary conversational speech a speaker averages approximately thirteen articulatory movements per second. The eye, on the other hand, is capable of consciously recording eight or nine movements per second. According to these figures, the eye therefore misses approximately a quarter of all sounds produced, though it must be remembered that not all the sounds are clearly visible to the observer in the first place. Nitchie draws attention to the fact that although the average duration of the articulatory movement is one-thirteenth of a second, speech sounds are produced that are both shorter and longer in duration. Using a motion-picture camera, filming at sixteen frames per second, Nitchie found that many of the speech sounds were too rapid to be recorded by the camera, indicating a duration of less than one-sixteenth of a second. The consonants were found to be of shorter duration than the long vowels, which had a duration of two-sixteenths to three-sixteenths per second, although some short vowels were articulated as quickly as many of the consonants (see Table 3.3).

The importance of the rate of articulation is supported by the findings of Mulligan (1954), who investigated the effect that speed of projection of a movie film had on the viewer's scores on a test of lip-reading. Mulligan showed the film at two speeds—slow (sixteen frames per second) and normal (twenty-four frames per second)—and found that the slower speed resulted in higher scores on the test.

On the other hand, a later study conducted by Byers and Lieberman (1959) produced contrary evidence. These researchers subjected four groups of experienced lip-readers from a school for the deaf to a sentence lip-reading test adapted from the Utley test (1946). By modifying the speed in filming and the speed of projection, they were able to produce controlled variations in the speaker's rate of utterance. Using four rates, normal (120 words per minute), and two-thirds, one-half, and one-third slower than normal rate, they studied the subjects' performance on the test under each condition. The results indicated no significant differences between the four rates of presentation The authors concluded that, within the range studied, variation in rate did not affect the degree of correct recognition of the visible aspects of the spoken word. This was found even though one of the rates was one-third of normal, and despite complaints from the viewers that the films were being shown at too slow a speed. They were of the impression that lip-reading skill is adaptable to quite an extensive range of articulatory rates.

The reason for the discrepancy between the results in these two studies may rest within the subjects used. Mulligan's findings are based on the performance of college students with normal hearing, while those of Byers and Lieberman were obtained from a group of deaf subjects, all of whom had had at least two years of formal lip-reading training. It may well be that we are not justified in generalizing data collected on subjects with normal hearing to the performance of subjects with hearing impairment. It has been demonstrated by Sumby and Pollack (1956), Neely (1956), and Sanders and Goodrich (1971) that for subjects with normal hearing, increased distortion of the auditory aspects of speech results in an increased dependence upon the use of visual cues. It may reasonably be presumed that a subject with a marked congenital auditory impairment will have come to depend heavily upon the contribution that vision is capable of making to speech intelligibility. This dependence will undoubtedly have resulted in a degree of skill—which the subject with normal hearing has not been called upon to develop—in making use of this information. When each of these two groups, the normal and the hard-of-hearing, are presented with a task involving the ability to obtain information through the recognition of visible speech characteristics, the hard-of-hearing subject is at an advantage. As a sophisticated user of information, a hearing-impaired person's tolerance for changes in speech rate is much greater than that of the person with normal hearing, who finds that he or she performs best when the material is presented at a slower speed.

If this is in fact so, then it has important implications for the training of beginning lip-readers. Factors that may not be important for the sophisticated lip-reader may well be crucial in the early learning stages. The role of rapidity of articulatory movements in the learning and maintenance of visual communication requires more investigation before we can confidently say that rate is not important.

Similarity of Visible Articulatory Movements. As was explained in our discussion of the acoustics of speech, each phoneme in the English language has a unique acoustic structure. The phonetic alphabet recognizes this in that, unlike the alphabet of written English, there exists a discrete symbol for each sound. The uniqueness in acoustic structure is that no two sounds are articulated in exactly the same way. In other words, for a given sound the formative movements that constitute the total articulatory movements are different from the formative movements of all other sounds. This is not, however, true for the revealing movements, which are confined only to the articulatory movements that are visible. Many speech sounds are revealed by identical visible movements. Such sounds are known as homophenes.* The adjective *homophenous* may be applied both to individual phonemes such as /p/, /b/, /m/, which are identical in revealing movements; to groups of phonemes such as /nt/ and /nd/; or to words, such as *bad, mat, pan.* In normal conversational speech it is quite impossible to distinguish between homophenous items. A study of the vowels and consonants of English indicates that the vowels do not exhibit any strictly homophenous formation, though some of the vowel sounds do present difficulty and only appear different to a trained observer. A list of homophenous groupings of consonants is given in Table 4.2. The homophenous groupings of consonants indicated in this table were established by Woodward (1957). Woodward made a linguistic analysis of the phonological, grammatical, and lexical aspects of lip-reading stimulus materials and hypothesized that the absolute visibility of a given speech item was dependent upon the area of articulatory placement involved. She presented a filmed series of paired syllables to a group of subjects with normal hearing and asked them to judge the two items as same or different. From an analysis of the results, Woodward established the consonant classifications already indicated. She concluded that, although in context it is possible to distinguish between many of the phonemes within a set, differentiation cannot be based upon visual compari-

*The term *homophenes,* which refers to phonemes that are identical in the visible aspects of their articulation, should not be confused with the similar term *homophones,* which refers to letters or symbols that have the same sound as others.

TABLE 4.2 Homophenous Clusters of Initial English Consonants (after Woodward, 1957)

(a)	p	b	m					
		f	v					
	m	w	r					
(b)	ch	ʤ	ʃ	ʒ	j			
	t	d	n	l	s	z	θ	ð
	k	g	h					

son alone. It must be concluded, therefore, that the visual similarity of homophenes compels the observer to rely on the linguistic redundancy of the material to provide the information necessary to differentiate between them.

On the basis of tests conducted with different passages representing colloquial English, Nitchie (undated) estimated that almost every word contains one or more homophenous sounds, that more than 40 percent of the total number of sounds in the test sample have one or more sounds homophenous to them, and furthermore, that approximately 50 percent of the words in the sample constitute homophenes of one or more other words.

Intra- and Intersubject Variation of Articulatory Movements. Careful analysis of the speech of a given individual reveals that the manner of articulation of a given speech sound varies at each production. It has been demonstrated experimentally that exact duplication of the manner of production is not possible, even when a subject makes a special effort to achieve this. The variation, which always exists to some degree, is frequently found to be quite considerable. Although these deviations are observed in the production of all speech sounds, they are especially noticeable in the production of vowels. In spite of these variations, there exists for each phoneme a fundamental movement pattern, which remains essentially the same. Kantner and West (1941, p. 29) use the analogy of movements involved in writing to illustrate this point. They explain that even though letters of the alphabet may be produced in a variety of different ways, the movements tend to become stereotyped within an individual, making it possible to identify a person by his or her handwriting. An expert is able to recognize these stereotypes even when an attempt has been made to disguise them.

In the production of speech sounds within the individual, this stereotyping occurs as a result of the necessity to ensure that the acoustic characteristics remain within the limits of a phoneme so that the meaning of a group of phonemes (word) is not interfered with. A second factor is the influence of a physiological tendency to stereotype movements.

When we extend our interest in the variability in speech-sound production to the changes occurring in a way in which different people produce a given speech sound, we find that the differences are frequently quite marked. It has been suggested that these interpersonal variations can be attributed to three causes: (1) variations in anatomical structure of the speech mechanism; (2) interpersonal differences in auditory perception of speech sounds; (3) regional or social variations occurring where speech sounds have developed in a different manner from those of people in other areas or social milieux.

Obviously, the stereotyping of sound production between individuals is dependent upon the acoustic factor. Auditory feedback ensures that the output—that is, the acoustic pattern of the speech sound—stays within the person's perceptual limits for that particular phoneme. It is these limits, rather than the specific articulatory movements, that different speakers have in common. Because it is possible to produce a sound in a variety of ways within the phonemic limits, it is understandable that the visible, or revealing, characteristics may vary somewhat from person to person.

As we have already noted, a careful comparison of the visible characteristics of English phonemes indicates that for some, the movements essential to the normal production of the sound—that is, those upon which the phonemic value of the sound is dependent—are quite visible to an observer. In these instances, the sound may be considered to be formed and revealed by the same movement. For other sounds, the formative movement is concealed from the observer. However, it has been demonstrated that the articulation of certain phonemes commonly involves movements of groups of facial muscles that are quite unnecessary for the normal production of the acoustic properties of the sound Light oller (1925). These movements constitute associated, but under normal conditions of oral communication, unessential, accompaniments to the formative movements.

It would seem rather odd that an organism should preserve such apparently useless movements. The answer rests, perhaps, in the underlying philosophy of this text—namely, the totality of the act of communication. We may thus presume that these seemingly unimportant movements do, in fact, have a role to play. Although they do not contribute to the recognition of the acoustic aspects of the sound, they are directly associated with it. They constitute, therefore, part of the total identity of the sound. Under normal listening conditions, we do not need to make use of these visible characteristics; however, under conditions of auditory distortion, recognition of the sound may be dependent upon the ability of the listener to utilize this built-in visual redundancy. For example, for many hearing-impaired subjects, the recognition of such sounds as /sh/ and /s/ is dependent upon the associated secondary lip-rounding and lip-spreading, since the formative movement, which is lingual alveolar, is practically invisible.

It is the secondary movements that are most subject to variation. The visible aspects of a sound that is revealed by its associated rather than by its formative movements may vary sufficiently from one speaker to another to present a problem of identification. As will be explained in the following chapter, the recognition of vowel phonemes is a function of auditory judgment rather than the exact nature or the extent of the movement. The pitch, resonant qualities, and duration are all important contributing factors. The actual articulatory movements of vowel production vary considerably, making it difficult to differentiate between them on the basis of their visible appearance. Consonants, on the other hand, require more exact positioning of the articulators and tend, therefore, to exhibit somewhat less variability of revealing characteristics. When we examine the visual nature of the articulatory movements in consonant production, we find that a number are revealed by their secondary characteristics alone. Those that are considered visible are /r/, /s/, /z/, /t/, /ʃ/, /ʒ/, /j/. It is these consonants which are particularly subject to interspeaker variability.

We have discussed the four major factors that influence the usefulness of speech as a form of visual communication. We have also considered the effect on speech-reading of some of the conditions that are known to affect the efficiency of the human eye. These included the phenomenon of dark adaptation, variations in light intensity, the position of the object in the visual field of the observer, and the distance between the eye and the object viewed. In addition to these, we also discussed the affect of certain defects of vision. Unfortunately, when we look to the literature to provide us with data concerning the interrelationship between these various conditions and the communicative value of the visible aspects of speech, we find little available. This remains an area that requires further systematic investigation.

We may conclude that the value of the visual message signal in communication will be influenced by environmental conditions. Until we have definite evidence to indicate the contrary, we must take these factors into consideration when planning rehabilitational training in the area of visual communication.

REFERENCES

Berger, K. W., R. A. DePompei, and J. L. Droder, "The Effect of Distance on Speech Reading Performance," *Ohio Journal of Speech and Hearing, 5,* 1970, 115–122.

Berger, K. W., M. Garner, and J. Sudman, "The Effect of Degree of Facial Exposure and the Vertical Angle on Speech-Reading Performance," *Teacher of the Deaf, 69,* 1971, 322–326.

Byers, V. W., and L. Lieberman, "Lipreading Performance and the Rate of the Speaker," *Journal of Speech and Hearing, 2,* 1959, 271–276.

Erber, N. P., "Effects of Distance on the Visual Reception of Speech," *Journal of Speech and Hearing Research, 14,* 1971, 848–857.

Erber, N. P., "Effects of Angle, Distance, and Illumination on Visual Reception of Speech by Profoundly Deaf Children," *Journal of Speech and Hearing Research, 17,* 1974, 1, 99–112.

Greene, H., "Implications of a Comprehensive Vision Screening Program for Hearing Impaired Children," *Volta Review, 80,* 1978, 467–475.

Hall, E. T., *The Silent Language.* New York: Doubleday & Co., Inc., 1959.

Hardick, E. J., H. J. Oyer, and P. E. Irion, "Lipreading Performance as Related to Measurements of Vision," *Journal of Speech and Hearing Research, 13,* 1970, 1, 92–100.

Kantner, C. E., and R. West, *Phonetics.* New York: Harper & Row Publishers, Inc. 1941.

Kendler, H. H., *Basic Psychology.* Englewood Cliffs, N.J.: Prentice-Hall, Inc., 1963.

Larr, A. L., "Speechreading through Closed Circuit Television," *Volta Review, 61,* 1959, 19–21.

Lightoller, C. H., "Facial Muscles: The Modiolus and Muscles Surrounding the Rima Oris with Some Remarks about the Panniculus Adiposus," *Journal of Anatomy, 60,* 1925, 2–45.

Mulligan, M., *Variables in the Reception of Visual Speech from Motion Pictures.* Unpublished master's thesis, Ohio State University, 1954.

Nakano, Y. A., "A Study on the Factors Which Influence Lipreading of Deaf Children," cited by S. P. Quigley, "Language Research in Countries Other Than the United States," *Volta Review, 68,* 1966, 68–83.

Neely, K. K., "Effects of Visual Factors on the Intelligibility of Speech," *Journal Acoustical Society of America, 28,* 1956, 1275–1277.

Nitchie, E. B., *Principles and Methods of Lipreading,* mimeographed pamphlet, n.d.

Pollard, G., and R. Neumaier, "Vision Characteristics of Deaf Children, *American Annals of the Deaf, 119,* 1974, 740–745.

Sanders, D. A., "A Model for Communication," In *Communication Assessment and Intervention Strategies,* ed. L. Lloyd, pp. 1–32. Baltimore: University Park Press, 1976.

Sanders, D. A., and S. J. Goodrich, "The Relative Contribution of Visual and Auditory Components of Speech to Intelligibility as a Function of Three Conditions of Frequency Distortion," *Journal of Speech and Hearing Research, 14,* 1971, 154–159.

Sumby, W. H., and I. Pollack, "Visual Contribution to Speech Intelligibility in Noise," *Journal of the Acoustical Society of America, 26,* 1956, 1275–1277.

Thomas, S. L., *Lipreading as a Function of Light Levels.* Unpublished master's thesis, Michigan State University, 1962.

U.S. Department of Health, Education, and Welfare, *Cataract and Glaucoma,* Public Health Service Publication, No. 793, Health Information Series No. 99. Washington, D.C.: Government Printing Office, 1963.

U.S.W.P.A. "Lipreading Project of the Board of Education," *New Aids and Materials for Teaching Lipreading.* New York: U.S.W.P.A. for the City of New York, 1939.

Utley, J. "A Test of Lipreading Ability," *Journal of Speech and Hearing Disorders, 11,* 1946, 109–116.

Woodward, M. F., "Linguistic Methodology in Lipreading Research," *John Tracy Clinic Research Papers, 4,* December 1957.

Perception of Spoken Language

5

Relevant Principles of Perception

We have discussed the physical aspects of the visual and auditory stimuli that are considered relevant to an understanding of the communicative processes. We have also considered the sensitivity of the peripheral receptors of vision and audition and the factors that may affect this sensitivity. It was suggested that this initial receptive level is concerned only with sensations, which arise as a direct result of the stimulation of the peripheral receptor by environmental stimuli. In theory this is a relatively passive procedure. The receptor is acted upon; no part of this organism contributes anything to the sensory experience, which is entirely dominated by the stimulus. In practice, however, the human organism is incapable of remaining passive in the presence of a complex stimulus. Active involvement is invariably evidenced in the form of discrimination, differentiation, and interpretation of the stimulus. The resultant awareness of ourselves and the world around us is known as perception. When you pick up the phone in response to its ringing, turn down the flame when the milk begins to boil, or develop an appetite when you smell and hear bacon sizzling in the pan, you have done more than receive a stimulus; you have responded in a discriminative manner. You have perceived a difference between a particular pattern of stimuli reaching you and all other stimuli present. This initial stimulus identification makes it possible for meanings to be attributed to what would otherwise remain raw sensations. However, if part of the stimulus pattern fails to be discernible, as may occur when a hearing impairment is present, differentiation among speech-sound patterns, and in more severe cases among environmental sounds, will be difficult or even impossible. As a result of the hearing deficiency the peripheral processing of the stimulus pattern will be impaired. It is customary to consider the negative effects of sensorineural hearing impairment as confined to this peripheral stage of stimulus-pattern replication. Yet from the previous discussion of information processing, we know that the manner in which we treat the available sensory data is determined to a considerable extent by our expectancies. The system is set up to process the information in accordance with those expectancies. We shall see that perception is an active process that imposes an organizational structure on the sensory systems; its effects reach all the way to the peripheral mechanisms exerting a selective effect upon which stimulus is processed for perception.

Perception of speech is governed by the expectancies derived from linguistic rules. A child who has not adequately learned those rules will find the task of speech perception a difficult one. Since we learn spoken language through use of the auditory system, hearing impairment inevitably affects language development. Language in turn molds cognitive development. Thus it is reasonable to assume that the perceptual world of the child with congenital or early-acquired hearing impairment will differ from that of hearing peers. The problems experienced by the child with impaired hearing are for those reasons complex. They impinge upon the child's ability to experience, to define experience, and to communicate with others about it.

Each child is called upon to adjust to a society which is heavily dependent upon the ability to learn and communicate in the auditory mode. To develop effective intervention procedures designed to facilitate this adjustment, we need insight into normal perceptual processes. We also need to understand how the hearing deficit changes the experience upon which the child must model a perception of the world. It is important to remember that all aspects of behavior—for example, thinking, learning, communicating, feeling—are likely to be influenced by perceptions. Only a comprehensive approach to management is likely to be effective. It is quite clear that sensory perception constitutes the basis of all forms of adaptive behavior. The adjustment that a person with a hearing impairment has to make to the environment is an instance of this behavior. Ideally, we would like to raise the level of the handicapped person's perception of the environment to the point where it differs from ours, not in its accuracy, but only in the nature of the information upon which the total perception is based. Solley and Murphy point out that "There is a redundancy of environmental information that an individual utilizes in anticipating environmental events" (1960, p. 154). We aim to train the hearing-impaired person to compensate for an auditory communication deficit by the maximum use of this redundant perceptual information.

THE ROLE OF THE SENSES

Though we are particularly concerned with the role of hearing in speech, we must not forget that hearing, together with the other senses, has a more fundamental purpose. The major function of sensory processing is to provide information. This reaches us through our internal and peripheral sense organs, which provide a continual flow of data concerning changes occurring in our bodies and in the environment. We are able to initiate appropriate behavioral responses based upon the analysis of information received.

Awareness

At its most primitive level, perception constitutes a preconscious awareness of our relationship with the environment. An ongoing monitoring of this relationship, together with the resultant adaptive behavior, accounts for the comfortable feeling of being a participant in the world around us. If this coupling is disrupted—for example, if we are suddenly plunged into darkness, or if we enter a sound-isolated chamber—a feeling of anxiety, sometimes acute, is almost certain to occur. The auditory system is particularly important to this background monitoring because the information it receives arrives from all around us. Sound is not easily blocked out by physical objects, as visual information is, nor does the monitoring cease when we sleep.

The child in whom this preconscious auditory monitoring capability is either congenitally absent or deficient as a result of impaired hearing may be expected to feel less confident in dealing with the environment than do his hearing peers. It is essential that we remember this aspect of the role of hearing when we consider providing early amplification for hearing-impaired children. With young children our first concern must be to establish this auditory coupling with the environment at as early an age as possible to ensure increased stability in the child's perceptions of his or her relationship to the physical world of people, things, and events. Thus the fitting of a hearing aid may be justified even when the only benefit it provides is to facilitate environmental awareness. This is so because the way in which the perceptual system and thus adaptive behavior will evolve depends upon the sensory experiences to which the child is exposed during the early formative years.

Deterioration of hearing in children and adults who have had normal hearing reduces the efficiency of the monitoring process. The effects will be most dramatic in cases of rapid loss of hearing, which sometimes produces a state of depression necessitating psychological guidance. In the more common event of a gradual reduction in hearing, the effect tends to be insidious. Unfortunately, feelings of progressive detachment and isolation, which lead to loneliness and insecurity, are frequently misinterpreted both by the person with this problem and by those around him or her (Ramsdell, 1970; Sanders, 1980a and 1980b).

In addition to general awareness of the world, our sensory systems provide us with information about specific changes. Any one of these may constitute a potential threat necessitating immediate action, or it may require less dramatic behavioral adjustment. In either case, awareness leads to attention and a suitable level of information processing. Without awareness neither attention nor appropriate adaptation would be possible. Awareness, therefore, serves as the basis for protection, orientation, and communication.

Protection

The most important information we receive is that which provides warning of a threat to our safety. The ability to perceive and react appropriately is essential to the preservation of the individual. Warnings from our internal sense organs alert us to possible sickness or disease, while those received through our peripheral sensory receptors indicate potential external danger. The startle (moro reflex) and eye-blink (auropalpebral reflex), which occur as reactions to a loud sound, are examples of the most primitive of the auditory defense processes. Children with severe congenital hearing deficits will be unaware of the significance of intense or unusual sounds, since they are inaudible to them and play no part in their perception of the environment. If by use of amplification we are able to bring these sounds within their hearing sensitivity, it will be necessary to train them to recognize and adapt appropriately. Thus gross sound-discrimination training must be an important component of the auditory training of young children. It creates environmental awareness and teaches children to make use of sound to predict what is happening around them. A hearing-impaired child who has received amplification and training in environmental sound awareness and recognition will be safer than a child for whom this aspect of training has been neglected.

Orientation

In addition to awareness and protection, sensory information contributes to spatial orientation, which is dependent upon the integration of data received from internal and external sensory mechanisms. From these sources we obtain not only information relevant to posture and balance, but also information concerning the position of our body relative to objects around us. The role of hearing in spatial orientation is, perhaps, underestimated. You are probably unaware of the number of times you safely cross a road without looking, depending on your ears to tell you that no cars are coming. Your ability to walk confidently down a familiar staircase in the dark without falling is partly due to the auditory feedback you receive from your footsteps, which tell where you are in relation to the bottom. In a strange house, you may literally need to feel your way down the stairs. This use of the auditory aspects of spatial perception is most clearly illustrated in the blind subject. Several experimenters (Cotzin & Dallenbach, 1944; Dolanski, 1930; Kohler, 1944; von Senden, 1960; Supa, Cotzin & Dallenbach, 1944), working under controlled laboratory conditions, have demonstrated that both blind subjects and sighted subjects temporarily deprived of vision are able to detect the presence or absence of target objects placed before them, purely on the basis of echo reflection from the objects. The sound made by a person's body movements and footsteps as he or she approaches an object is sufficient for detection and avoidance (Cotzin & Dallenbach, 1944; Dohler, 1944). There is even evidence that it is possible to discriminate with a high degree of accuracy between various-shaped objects and to a lesser extent between materials of different qualities (Rice, 1967).

Orientation of our systems to sound sources also enables us to adjust rapidly to demands expected from relevant stimuli. In speech communication, awareness that someone has spoken, which can be determined merely by identification of the vocal tone, is followed by orientation to the speaker. We look up when spoken to, we turn toward the speaker. We expect this same behavior when we address someone. Absence of this response, which is often evident in the communication behavior of a blind person or of someone who deliberately ignores us, is disconcerting. As listeners we usually feel more comfortable when we watch a speaker. For a person with reduced hearing sensitivity, rapid visual orientation is even more important, because visual cues may greatly facilitate comprehension of a remark that might not be understood by hearing alone.

Preconscious monitoring, which contributes to basic awareness and orientation, is thus important to the overall level of adjustment. If an ability can be shown to contribute in some way to normal adaptive behavior, impairment of that ability will modify certain aspects of the person's perceptual function. Awareness of these subtle changes may help us to better understand the problems we seek to solve. Certainly the studies referred to previously emphasize the importance of recognizing that sense modalities do not function as independent mechanisms. To consider hearing only in relation to its role in speech perception is to fail to understand the complexity of the problem of hearing impairment.

THE PERCEPTUAL PROCESS

Earlier in our discussion it was pointed out that, in responding to stimuli in a discriminative manner, we show that we have perceived a particular group of stimuli, a "stimulus complex," as different from all other stimulus complexes. This permits us to attribute a particular meaning to it. It may help you to understand this process of perception if you look up from this text for a moment and glance around you. Now ask yourself what you see and hear. Your answer will almost certainly include a list of people, things, and activities that you have observed, together with the sounds associated with them. Depending upon where you are, you may perceive your roommate sitting in a chair studying, a clock ticking on a bed table, a news program on television, or the siren of a fire engine or ambulance in the distance. The first thing to note is that the stimuli reaching you are all complex in nature and that you are aware not of the individual stimuli, but of the objects and activities that give rise to them. You see people, not rays of light, hear voices, not component sound vibrations. Your reaction is to *patterns* of stimuli; you are not usually aware of the component parts. You may look at each of the pieces of this perceptual jigsaw in isolation, but when you put them together they constitute a picture that you are only then able to recognize. As Hilgard says, "The total impression from organized stimuli has properties not predictable from the parts in isolation" (1957, p. 363). We should bear this in mind when we discuss the analytic and synthetic approaches to the teaching of visual communication skills.

The second thing that you may note about your observation of your environment is that you are familiar with almost all of the things you see and hear in it. You have encountered them on previous occasions and in other settings. Nevertheless, your orientation toward them on this occasion may be somewhat different from what it was before. This is because your perception of the object or activity is determined not only by its immediate setting but also by your past experience of the same or similar object, event, or idea. Note how, on separate occasions, you often respond differently to the same stimulus complex, and how different reports of the same event may be received from a number of observers.

We note, then, that we react to groups of stimuli that are seen as an integrated whole, a *gestalt.* This gestalt is the result of the interaction of all the component stimuli; the identity of the individual components may not be consciously perceived. Indeed, in the early stages of learning it may not be possible to consciously isolate and identify them. We respond to the "catness" of a cat, rather than to the individual attributes of a cat, a phenomenon referred to as physiognomic perception (Coleman, 1949). We also notice that we are influenced in what we perceive by our previous experiences. How do we organize these multitudinous stimuli in order to make possible the designation of meaning? In communication two phenomena are particularly important in this process: figure-ground perception and closure.

Figure-Ground Perception

The general constancy of most of our perceptions implies the existence of an underlying organizational pattern. The first of these is the phenomenon of *figure-ground.* This may be defined as the perceptual process by which a particular object or object quality is seen to stand out against a background constituted by the remaining objects or object qualities.

The world of the newborn child consists essentially of a jumble of meaningless stimuli. However, few of these stimuli are processed beyond the peripheral stages. The child's lack of experience of patterns of stimuli, along with an as yet rather unsophisticated neural integration, provide what Broadbent (1958) and Spitz (1965) have referred to as a "sensory barrier," which prevents the child from being overwhelmed by the quantity of peripheral information.To make a start toward perceiving the objects that give rise to this multitude of sensations, it is necessary to learn to organize the stimuli into complexes, to pattern them, to bring order and, therefore, predictability. This is only possible if some of them can be made to stand out more distinctly than the rest. A number of factors within the child and within the stimuli will determine which are most attention getting. The group of stimuli that at a given instance in time command the child's attention become the figure; the remainder constitute the (back)ground. This phenomenon of figure-ground perception appears to occur even when practice has been denied. The research findings of von Senden (1960) on the experience of congenitally blind adults following surgical removal of cataracts showed that after an initial period of recovery, patients evidenced figure-ground perception ability. Without previous visual-perceptual experience, they were able to organize the stimuli into a figure-ground relationship. Lawson has explained this function.

The code interpretation of how an infant learns to differentiate a primitive figure-ground unity to perceive an object as a whole is based on five related assumptions. The first of these is that every perception involves an etiology and a prognosis, i.e., any perception is based on past experience and contains a predictive element. In the code hypothesis both S and T elements are the results of past experience, while the operation of the T element produces the prediction. The initial code of the human infant is presumed to be the result of ancestral experience, i.e., heredity, rather than the infant's own perceptual experience. However, changes in this code that produce new S and T code elements are presumed to result from the infant's own experience.*

The second assumption is that every visual perception includes a figure-ground unity. The third assumption is that every perception results in some behavior. The fourth assumption is that following perception of a unity there results an automatic shift of focus to some part or subfigure within the whole. The fifth assumption is that through eye movement (behavior) other parts or subfigures of the whole are sought and the perceived parts are then related and recorded in the memory code.

If we accept all these assumptions, we may say a human infant begins by perceiving a figure-ground unity. He then changes his focus from the figure as a whole to some part of the whole. If he can differentiate lines and angles and can follow the contours of the figure by eye movement, he can differentiate parts of the whole and relate them. If we assume that each movement of the eye is recorded and that the parts of the figure also are recorded, then after the record is complete, perception of any part of a figure would activate the record, firing the entire sequence and producing perception of the whole (1967, p. 17).

Figure-ground perception is not confined to vision; it also occurs in hearing. It makes it possible for you to attend to a particular sound source against a background of other environmental noises and to shift your attention from one sound source to another. It accounts for the fact that you are able to listen to what one person is saying at a cocktail party, even though everyone is talking, and that you can recognize the melody of a piece of music against the background of accompaniment. It is important to recognize that perception of figure-ground does not constitute the ability to attribute meaning to a stimulus. A person exposed to sound for the first time is able to hear something against a background but will not at first have any knowledge concerning what this something may be. Subjects studied by von Senden were unable to make even the simplest visual discrimination between shapes until they had been given extensive training.

We can find equivalents to the visual code interpretation, described

*S equals elements of the sensory code. T equals a connected code element.

by Lawson, in theories of auditory code interpretation of speech. The infant begins by perceiving figure-ground unity, identifying human speech as an entity. The child responds initially to the emotive content of what Mother says rather than to the language structure itself. The child learns to interpret Mother's mood from the intonation patterns of her speech. Freelander (1970), for example, demonstrated that infants aged 9 to 18 months clearly prefer certain types of speech stimuli. They prefer melodic to monotonic speech, they are more responsive to familiar voices than to unfamiliar ones, and they prefer varied content to repeated content. As children's exposure to speech increases they begin to associate word patterns to intonational patterns. They change their focus to include the key elements of the segmental structure. We saw that the differentiation of the parts of visual patterns is enhanced by the development of the ability to distinguish component lines and angles. Similarly, in auditory perception, the recognition of the underlying phrase markers, cued by intonational patterning, enhances the recognition of syntactic structures.

Cognizant of the role that figure-ground plays in auditory pattern interpretation we recognize the need for such basic perceptual training in auditory discrimination as part of our program of aural rehabilitation for those with impairments of hearing sensitivity. A distinct difference exists in the manner of processing speech and nonspeech. The author concurs with Ling (1976) that the auditory discrimination of nonverbal sounds and speech sounds is not, therefore, part of the same developmental process. However, commitment to a program of intervention directed at facilitating maximum adaptation to the environment, rather than concentrating exclusively on speech discrimination, means that we should provide training in environmental sound discrimination as well as in the recognition of meaning in the speech signal. We may also train the child to make speech and nonspeech discrimination decisions. Rhythm training of nonspeech and speech patterns appears justified because rhythm, both of speech and nonspeech, is perceived in the nondominant hemisphere of the brain, while speech is perceived in the dominant hemisphere. The relationship between speech and nonspeech perception is not, therefore, quite as exclusive as Ling has suggested.

Closure

The second important factor to consider in perceptual organization is *closure.* This term refers to the tendency we have to perceive an incomplete figure as being complete. It accounts, in part, for the ability of a person to recognize a spoken word or a sentence on the basis of limited visual cues, or for a person with a marked hearing loss to correctly perceive certain sounds that are inaudible to him or her. Closure is obviously dependent upon prior experience with the whole figure. It is impossible to correctly complete a figure with which one is unfamiliar. Given parts of a relatively unfamiliar sentence, you may be unable to complete closure:

_____has a_____suffered_____ _____tragedy.*

However, the task is relatively easy if you are familiar with the whole:

Don't_____all_____eggs_____ _____basket.†

When you encounter an unfamiliar situation, you attempt to understand it by analyzing its components. In so doing, you are able to establish the relationship that exists between the whole and its parts. On future occasions it may not be necessary to actually receive the total stimulus complex in order to recognize it. As has already been discussed, perception of part of the stimulus will frequently be sufficient to call forth a memory of previous perceptions of the same or related experiences. Every stimulus complex has, for each of us, a minimal number of component stimuli necessary for its accurate perception (recognition). This minimum constitutes the *minimal perceptual invariant.* The minimal perceptual invariant need not be a consistent pattern of stimuli. It may be different on different occasions, but whichever combination of stimuli is utilized, it provides the essential elements for recognition.

In aural rehabilitation, we utilize this knowledge when we separate the visual and auditory aspects of the message signal. We break each of these down further into their individual parts (analytical approach) so that the person may become familiar with the characteristics of individual speech sounds or groups of sounds. We then present the whole visual complex and the whole auditory complex. Finally, the integrated auditory-visual stimulus is presented (multisensory approach). If we can train the person to obtain through vision, audition, and the phenomenon of closure the minimal component stimuli necessary for recognition, it will be possible for a speech sound, word, sentence, or idea to be perceived, even when only part of the stimulus has actually been received.

A PERCEPTUAL MODEL

Solley and Murphy have proposed a model to help clarify the perceptual process (Figure 5.1). They state that perception is a process that "is extended in time, and which consists of a series of interdependent subprocesses, or stages, which can be partially ordered in their succession" (1960, p. 18). Their schematic model involves five stages: (1) perceptual expectancy; (2) attending; (3) reception; (4) trial and check; and (5) final perceptual organization.

The box on the extreme right in Figure 5.1 constitutes the covert or overt behavior changes occurring as a result of the perception. Also in-

*Never has a man suffered such great tragedy.
†Don't put all your eggs in one basket.

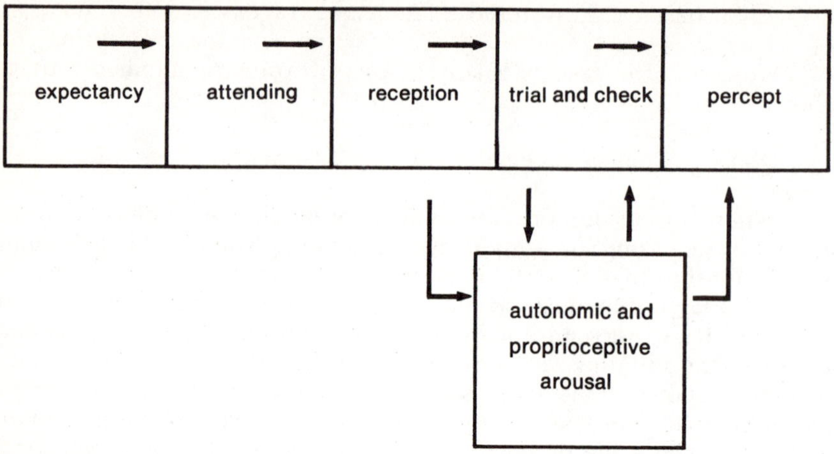

FIGURE 5.1 A model of the perceptual process (after Solley and Murphy, 1960).

corporated in the model is the autonomic and proprioceptive arousal system that, it is suggested, may exert control over some forms of perceptual behavior.

The external factors contained in the box on the extreme left represent those forms of readiness that give rise to "expectancy." Solley and Murphy point out that a perceptual act originates because an individual has certain needs and desires for which fulfillment is sought. This factor serves as the primary motivation for communication between individuals. The perception of language stimuli serves to mediate between our personal needs and our environment. Motivation is, therefore, an important factor in communication since it serves to direct our attention toward the appropriate stimuli and heightens our awareness of them.

The first component of the perceptual model, *expectancy,* involves our ability to predict, with some measure of reliability, the probability of a given stimulus complex occurring in a given situation. According to Solley and Murphy (1960):

> *We know from countless acts of commerce with our environment that we can expect such and such a stimulus to follow or occur with another set of stimuli. Often, before a given source can act as an input to our receptors, we are expecting it. The ebb and flow of experience is such that we are constantly being bombarded by stimuli, and it is only by developing expectancies and schemata that we are able to deal with this array of stimulation* (p. 156).

In human communication the effect of the situational and contextual constraints placed upon a speaker permit the listener to develop expectancy.

In Chapter 2 we discussed how linguistic expectancies, derived from a knowledge of language rules, reduce dependency on the acoustic signal,* thus allowing high rates of information flow while combatting noise

*See Sanders, 1977, Chapter 6, for a discussion of linguistic influences on auditory perception.

in the system. Expectancy of both nonverbal and verbal speech cues is, therefore, particularly important to a person with impaired hearing. The value of expectancy increases considerably when message signals are received under adverse acoustic conditions, such as those imposed by hearing deficiency.

Expectancy directs us to search for a given stimulus or patterns of stimuli and so increases the probability of our becoming aware of them. An examination of the auditory system as a pattern processor (Sanders, 1977) reveals considerable evidence to support the theory that expectancies result in the tuning or "gating" of the neural pathways. This may occur in a manner that raises the threshold of those neuron groups that are not expected to be relevant to the processing of the next segment(s) of the message. As a result, the threshold of expected relevant groups is lowered to facilitate the processing of the anticipated message units. The auditory system may thus be set up as a flow chart appropriate to the expectancies, providing preferential treatment of relevant components of the message signal.

Attention

Attention serves, therefore, to increase our chances of perceiving specific stimulus complexes. It determines the figure-ground relationship by increasing the degree to which we are conscious of certain stimuli. It is important to our consideration of communication to realize that this process of bringing a particular stimulus complex into focus does not exclude all other stimuli from consciousness; it serves, rather, to determine the relative importance of various stimulus groups. Elements of the background do not cease to contribute information, but they do contribute less than the figure. "Successive acts of attending bring stimulations into close contiguity with one another, an important requirement for sensory integration. . . . The perceived environment becomes integrated into a meaningful whole" (Solley & Murphy, 1960).

We should also recognize the possibility of the existence of two types of attention. As Lawson points out:

> *First, there is the awareness essential for carrying out a learned behavior pattern. A person who has driven an automobile for years performs the manipulations of driving automatically, without paying attention to the details of steering, accelerating, shifting, or braking, as long as the pattern unfolds as expected. However, should the accelerator get stuck, or brakes fail, or any other event occur that is contrary to the normal behavior pattern, then the second kind of awareness or attention would go into operation. Specific attention is now directed to the cause of the disruption and the person is alert to new sensory input, unexpected in terms of normal driving behavior, but expected in view of the disturbance* (1967, p. 98).

These quotes from Solley and Murphy and from Lawson relate to the processing of language patterns and have implications for auditory training procedures. We need to constantly remember that the successive acts of attending, in close contiguity with one another, are a prerequisite to the integration of the separate bits of sensory information into a meaningful pattern. Children with impaired hearing must be taught listening habits. The fact that amplification brings acoustic information within their reach does not ensure that they will naturally acquire optimal use of it. It is our role to motivate the children to pay attention while we ensure the repeated sound-pattern presentations they need to fuse the parts into a meaningful whole.

Lawson's reference to two types of attention should remind us that the patterns we present can be processed sequentially or in parallel. It has been suggested by Neisser (1963) that in responding to new patterns of stimulation we use a step-by-step serial procedure to examine the individual features in order. This is a rather slow process, prone to compounding of any error occurring in the early stages of processing. Furthermore, if there are a large number of components, heavy demands are made on short-term memory—something we will discuss later. Nevertheless, it seems we pay attention to detail until we are familiar with the landmark cues and able to see the overall pattern emerging. Once this occurs we shift to the parallel processing of information, possible even when paying scant attention to a familiar pattern. In parallel processing we examine the components by the feature analyzers simultaneously so that the pattern emerges immediately with little need for storage. Familiarity with the pattern means that we can predict it on the basis of little information; thus, tolerance for distortion arises from the inherent redundancy.

Much work with children who are hearing handicapped involves teaching them to become familiar with new auditory-visual speech patterns, and with new linguistic patterns. We need to be aware of the shift in the type of processing that occurs when sensory perceptions become integrated into a meaningful whole and the change in the type of attention that results. Although we must ensure the availability of the complete pattern of information, we also need to have insight into the possibility that the child is processing the pattern serially while we are dealing with the whole in parallel.

Reception

Reception, the third state of the perceptual model, has been discussed in some detail in the two previous chapters. The nature of the stimulus itself is obviously of critical importance. The way in which we perceive stimuli depends on our previous experience in structuring them into complexes. If the receptive process is impaired, or if we lack previous experience, then we may be forced to develop our perceptions on the basis of inadequate information. We may fail to recognize the stimulus complex, or we may develop a misperception, resulting in an incorrect meaning being attributed to the stimulus. Thus, impairment of hearing, which eliminates some components of the pattern and reduces the intensity of others, will result in distortion. The acoustic patterns of speech sounds or groups of sounds that are dependent upon discrimination of certain distinctive features may be so modified as to be unidentifiable. Furthermore, children whose linguistic development is incomplete and whose ability to use linguistic rules to generate the missing or distorted components is thus reduced either may fail to attribute meaning or may designate an inappropriate value. This has definite significance in terms of the next unit of the model, which is concerned with hypothesis testing, a trial-and-check process.

Trial and Check

Before the stimulus is finally structured as a percept, the model depicts a stage in which a hypothesis is made about what the signal pattern will be. An internal model of an expected pattern is synthesized from knowledge of prior components of the stimulus and from more general situational and contextual constraint factors. This ongoing pattern prediction, created from information fed forward from earlier segments, is then compared to the actual signal received. This is the same process that we discussed when we considered the role of the comparator in Fairbanks's model of a closed-cycle control system for speech. Here, however, the comparison is not between desired and actual output, but between expected and actual input. Solley and Murphy have borrowed the term *trial and check* from Woodworth (1947), who states:

> *When a new percept is in the making—when an obscure stimulus-complex is being deciphered, or when the meaning of a cue or sign is being discovered—an elementary two-phase process is observable. It is a trial-and-check, trial-and-check process. The trial phase is a tentative reading of the sign, a tentative decipherment of the puzzle, a tentative characterization of the object; and the check phase is an acceptance or rejection, a positive or negative reinforcement of the tentative perception* (Woodworth, pp. 123–124).

The purpose of this stage, then, is to compare the expected perceptual pattern with what has actually been received. If the predicted event concurs with the perceived event, it is possible to attribute meaning to it. If a discrepancy is revealed, then the organism is directed both to obtain more information through reobservation and to recheck the files of associated memories in an attempt to identify the incoming stimulus complex. Within-channel trial and check might occur, for example, when a friend introduces you to her financé. From your friend's previous description of her fiancé you will have built up an expected perceptual pattern. When you meet him, you may find that he is quite different from what you had envisaged; your predicted image does not concur with what you now perceive: "He's not a bit like I had imagined him." You then seek to eliminate the discrepancy between what you had previously anticipated and what you now observe in order to ensure future recognition. Future recognition thus necessitates your restructuring your image.

The same trial-and-check process has been offered in several mediated theories of speech perception. Each theory postulates that the perception of spoken language involves the active generation by the perceptual system of an internal model against which the incoming speech-pattern information can be compared for verification. The internal model can be synthesized at any level from articulatory to syntactic. The actual level at which we conduct this "analysis by synthesis" depends upon the ease with which we are able to develop accurate predictions at any moment in the process. The poorer our internal prediction function, the more dependent we are on information derived from the acoustic signal. Moving to more detailed analysis slows down and generally impedes communication interaction. Thus the person with impaired hearing is forced to ask for clarification or repetition of what has been said. As a result, communication may be reduced to an unsatisfying level of interaction.

In attempting to understand the trial-and-check (or analysis-by-synthesis) component, remember that it is not confined to any one sensory channel. We recognize that a given object or event simultaneously emits stimuli of various types. We may see, hear, and touch a particular object. In doing so, we initiate a trial-and-check procedure for each channel. If you refer back to Figure 2.6, you will see that it shows interconnecting fibers traveling between various subcortical nerve centers. These interconnecting fibers are indicated because we presumed the existence of a complex system involving reception, integration, analysis, association, and interpretation of data from all sensory end organs. The trial-and-check process occurs, therefore, not simply *within* a sensory channel, but also *between* sensory channels. When we perceive and attribute meaning to something, we do so because there is harmony between the perceptual structures in each channel. If, for example, you were to see what you thought to be a vase of freshly cut roses, but on touching them felt the texture of plastic and noted the absence of any scent, you would reject the visual percept that had already satisfied the trial-and-check process for that sensory channel.

An example of the effect of between-channel trial and check created considerable humor in one of the Candid Camera television programs. In this situation, a young and unwitting participant was sent to a bakery to purchase a custard cream pie. The salesgirl was herself enjoying a slice of pie and offered a piece to the customer. His within-visual channel trial and check was acceptable. He observed a custard filling with a thick cream topping; he also observed the girl obviously enjoying her portion. Not until between-channel trial and check had been carried out, when he bit heartily into his piece, did he reject his perception upon realization that his piece had, in fact, a thick layer of shaving cream for a topping.

Between-channel trial and check would be important in a communication situation in which a speaker might perceive a person to say, "Did you hear that John Smith lost his life in a car accident?" This sentence would make sense in context and would pass an auditory trial-and-check stage. If, however, the observer noted that the word heard as "life" showed lip rounding of the initial sound, he or she would not achieve auditory-visual, interchannel trial-and-check agreement. If the word has lip rounding for the initial sound, it cannot be "life"—it must be "wife." The observer will therefore reject the initial perception and replace it by, "Did you hear that John Smith lost his wife in a car accident?"

The amount of trial and check necessary is a function of the predictability of the event. When redundancy is high, as in favorable listening or viewing conditions, it is not necessary to carry out extensive trial and check. However, when high noise levels in one sensory channel reduce redundancy, then trial and check both within and between sensory channels becomes vital to comprehension. Our justification for training the hard-of-hearing person in visual communication skills is based upon this awareness of the part that intersensory-channel trial and check contributes to the correct decoding of the message signal.

The correct decoding of both incoming auditory and visual information requires that the listener have previous experience with the pattern and that knowledge of the pattern be available in a memory system. The availability of such knowledge is equally essential to the process of generating expectancies based upon the use of linguistic rules. Memory processing is, therefore, a critical factor in auditory perception.

Memory Processing

Because the acoustic speech stimulus is continuous and unsegmented, at no time does the listener have available more than the minutest part of a meaningful segment. Therefore, it is necessary for the brain to record the acoustic information. It must be allowed to accumulate until enough of the pattern emerges for probabilities to be computed and predictions generated. Storage is believed to occur in three stages. The first involves the recording of an image of the acoustic pattern. This is usually referred to as *echoic memory*. The echo of the acoustic pattern is retained for only 2 to 3 seconds (Bjork & Healy, 1970; Crowder & Morton, 1969; Estes, 1970), long enough for the extraction of linguistic features and essential suprasegmental information. The data derived from this information are restructured continuously into *short-term memory*.

Short-term memory differs from echoic memory because the information has been changed from raw data into segmented linguistic form organized according to the rules of the language. It is at this level of processing that we are first able to exert conscious control over memory content. For example, we are able to renew the linguistic pattern by rehearsing what we heard, either overtly or covertly, or we may recode it into a mnemonic key to aid future recall. Short-term memory is, however, also limited in capacity. Miller (1956) has explained that the number of stimulus units which we can hold in conscious memory is limited to between five and nine. This holds true whether we are trying to remember numbers, words, or any other kind of unit. To surmount this limitation we must combine smaller units into larger chunks. Although these are also subject to what Miller refers to as the limitation of the "magical number seven plus or minus two," each unit represents a considerably larger amount of information. In processing of spoken language, chunking into more and more complex units results from progressively restructuring the information up through the linguistic hierarchy from phoneme through morpheme to syntax. In this way we can remember several sentences just as they were spoken, but we cannot retain an equally long string of unrelated words.

Information required for long-term storage is restructured into semantic values and placed in *long-term memory*. Long-term memory records, therefore, the meaning or content, not the structure of a message. The original language pattern fades while the semantic value is retained. Access to that information necessitates that it be restructured back into *an equivalent linguistic pattern.* It is important to recognize that because the original structure was not stored, the accuracy of recall of a topic will depend upon the ability of the person to use knowledge of language rules to restructure an equivalent message. Memory for spoken language content, therefore, is influenced by the ability to construct a linguistic message from an acoustic pattern, and later by the ability to reconstruct an equivalent language pattern when the information needs to be retrieved.

Each of the stages in perceptual processing requires very complex activities. It is not surprising, therefore, to find evidence which suggests that through learning, a part of the process becomes relegated to an internal monitoring system. This system exerts an active influence not only on how stimuli are processed, but also on the sensitivity of the system to different stimulus patterns. This role has been attributed to the autonomic and proprioceptive arousal system.

Autonomic and Proprioceptive Arousal System

The evidence pertaining to the relationship that may exist between stimuli arising from the autonomic and proprioceptive arousal system and our total perception of the external world is at best tenuous. In reviewing the existing literature, Solley and Murphy conclude that the research indicates that specific and diffuse feedback systems exist within the individual. Through the process of conditioning, it becomes possible for these feedback systems to be aroused by specific external stimuli. They explain that "in addition the occurrence of such feedback will also strengthen the perception (cortical integration) of that stimulus" (Solley & Murphy, 1960, p. 242). Referring to the works by Solomon (Solomon, Kamin & Wynne, 1953; Solomon & Wynne, 1950, 1954), the authors suggest the perception may then become "linked or 'locked' to certain specific and general autonomic and proprioceptive feedback mechanisms so that perception and feedback mechanism are mutually excited" (p. 243).

In recent years there has been considerable growth of interest in the role of the feedback mechanism by which the sensory perceptual system monitors its own behavior. Research has demonstrated the existence in the auditory system of nerve fibers that run from cortex to cochlea—that is, in the opposite direction to the afferent sensory fibers. The actual function of this outward flowing *efferent* system is only vaguely understood. It is known, however, that efferent fibers exert a controlling influence over the afferent system. Clear evidence is available, therefore, of the existence of a servomechanism within the auditory perceptual system. This afferent-efferent loop changes a passive sensory system into a dynamic tunable one under the control of higher processing levels. The capability exists for the processing of the input signal, indeed for its very reception, to be preset by higher-order neurons on the basis of computed expectancies. Rather than "feedback" we would envisage a "feedback-feedforward" process preparing the system to respond in a weighted manner to any components of the total stimulus array that are predicted as relevant, while rejecting the upward flow of other stimuli. Thus stimuli are either processed upward to conscious levels of awareness or processed no further than a preattentive level.

According to Solley and Murphy, the organisms' constant sensory scanning activities constitute the heart of perception. These result from homeostatic factors, from specific needs or sets. Initially random in character, this scanning for exteroceptor cues becomes more patterned. It is not unreasonable to assume that scanning becomes more selective, more appropriate, as the neural system becomes tuned in accord with expectancies. As early parts of the incoming signal confirm crude expectancies, more accurate tuning of the perceptual system is possible, resulting in more effective scanning procedures. French (1957) is of the opinion that the internal scanning process probably constitutes part of the function of the reticular formation, which, he suggests, develops differential sensitivity to stimuli. This view is certainly in accord with neurological theories of speech perception (Abbs & Sussman, 1971; Uttley, 1954, 1959, 1966) and with what is known about the efferent system. French proposes that the attention pattern results from the action of both the arousal system and a cortical probability calculation. Solley and Murphy also suggest that we scan for internal memory cues to identify a match between the incoming stimuli and memory traces left from previous stimuli. Active mediative theories of speech perception view the process as more generative (Liberman, Cooper, Shankweiler, & Studdert-Kennedy, 1967; Stevens & Halle, 1967). According to these theorists the system actually generates a pattern based upon probability computations. It is against this pattern that the incoming signal is compared for verification of predictions. Neisser (1967) proposes that "this constructive process is itself the mechanism of auditory perception." Thus those components that do not match constitute the ground, as discussed earlier. "Scanning moves to that which is congruent with established set and excludes that which is noncongruent" (Solley & Murphy, 1960, p. 253). It seems justified, therefore, to modify the model in Figure 5.1 to show the arrows running in both directions between each stage to represent the tuning in the system we have discussed.

We have talked repeatedly about the need to enrich total perception for the hearing-impaired person in all available ways. The question arises whether it is feasible to sensitize the student to such internal cues. If this is possible, we may be able to evoke what Solley and Murphy refer to as a new "search set." The authors are reassuring; they refer to an experiment by Seward (1931) in which it was shown that on a repeated visual-perceptual task in which no results were given to the subject between trials, the number of correct responses increased progressively. This indicates that repeated exposure to the sensory data arising from a perceptual act, even in the absence of external feedback, may lead to the modification of the response to more closely approximate reality. Evidence that this may be true for the perceptual act of interpreting visual speech cues can be derived from the present author's work with Goodrich (Sanders & Goodrich, 1971). Examination of the mean scores obtained by normal-hearing subjects on four successive visual-discrimination tests of monosyllabic words with no feedback given revealed that the mean items correctly identified rose from 6.60 on the first presentation to 8.00 on the fourth. This tendency encourages us to persevere with many aspects of auditory and visual communication training even though to date we lack experimental proof of value. In the words of Solley and Murphy (1960): "To the extent an individual can learn to discriminate and recognize these cues he can gain greater control over his perceptual system and, hence, become more viridical in his perceptions" (p. 260).

The Percept

The ultimate result of these progressive stages is the *percept.* This final structuring of the perception permits meaning to be attributed to the stimulus complex. The stimulus is interpreted in a particular way on the basis of previous experience. The phenomenon of figure-ground and closure play an important role in determining the final percept. We have seen that the determinants of the figure-ground relationship lie both within the stimulus and within the individual. It is a dangerous oversimplification to consider the environment and the individual as independent entities. They are, in fact, so interrelated as to constitute one system. It is rather like stiring chocolate cake batter into a white cake mixture to make a marble cake. In places, the cake is clearly all white or all brown, yet in general, the colors run together so as to be inseparable.

The process by which we finally attribute meaning is highly complex but clearly involves the fusion of selected external stimuli with the memory of past experiences. This brings about an interpretation that most reasonably fits in with the information that has satisfactorily passed the within-channel and between-channel trial-and-check stage. This process is never completed; our perceptions can never be reality, because absolute reality is really nonexistent. We are not attempting to specify a "something" out there, but rather to specify the significance of the result of our interaction with that "something." That is, we perceive in terms of how we process stimuli. So the trial-and-check process constitutes a continuous servomechanism, causing us to constantly reevaluate our perceptions in light of the never-ceasing intake of additional sensory data. The amount of perceptual change must be a function of the ability of the individual to use the additional stimulus input; such ability is determined by motivation, awareness, and a library of perceptual experiences. Through a systematic program of aural rehabilitation, we aim to provide the hard-of-hearing person with an enhanced ability to do this.

We have now set the stage for a consideration of the perception of the auditory and visual speech signal.

REFERENCES

Abbs, J. H., and H. M. Sussman, "Neurophysiological Feature Detectors and Speech Perception. A Discussion of Theoretical Implications," *Journal of Speech and Hearing Research, 14,* 1971, 23–26.

Bjork, E. L., and A. F. Healy, "Intra-Item and Extra-Item Sources of Acoustic

Confusion in Short-Term Memory," in *Communications in Mathematical Psychology*. Rockefeller University Technical Reports, April 1970.

Broadbent, D. E., *Perception and Communication.* New York: Pergamon Press, 1958.

Coleman, J. C., "Facial Expressions of Emotion," *Psychological Monographs, 63,* 1949, 1–36.

Cotzin, M., and M. Dallenbach, "Facial Vision: The Role of Pitch and Loudness in the Perception of Obstacles by the Blind," *American Journal of Psychology, 63,* 1944, 485–515.

Crowder, R. J., and J. Morton, "Precategorical Acoustic Storage (P.A.S.)," *Perception and Psychophysics, 5,* 1969, 356–373.

Dolanski, V., "Les Aveugles Possidentile les Sens d'Obstacles," *Année Psychologique, 31,* 1930, 1–51.

Estes, W. K., "On the Source of Acoustic Confusions in Short-term Memory for Letter Strings," in *Communications in Mathematical Psychology.* Rockefeller University Technical Reports, April 1970.

French, J. D., "The Reticular Formation," *Scientific American, 196,* 1957, 54–60.

Freelander, B., "Receptive Language Development in Infancy," *Merrill-Palmer Quarterly of Behavior and Development, 16,* 1970, 7–51.

Hilgard, E. R., *Introduction to Psychology* (2nd ed.). New York: Harcourt Brace Jovanovich, 1957.

Kohler, I., *American Foundation for the Blind Research Bulletin, 4,* no. 14, 1944.

Lawson, Chester A., *Brain Mechanisms and Human Learning,* The International Series in the Behavioral Sciences. Boston: Houghton Mifflin Company, 1967.

Liberman, A. M., F. S. Cooper, D. P. Shankweiler, and M. F. Studdert-Kennedy, "Perception of the Speech Code," *Psychology Review, 74,* 1967, 431–461.

Ling, D., *Speech and the Hearing Impaired Child: Theory and Practice.* Washington, D.C.: Alexander Graham Bell Association for the Deaf, 1976.

Miller, G. A., "The Magical Number 7 ± 2: Some Limits on our Capacity for Processing Information," *Psychology Review, 63,* 1956, 81–97.

Neisser, U., "Decision Time without Reaction Time: Experiments in Visual Scanning," *American Journal of Psychology, 76,* 1963, 376–385.

Neisser, U., *Cognitive Psychology,* Century Psychology Series. Englewood Cliffs, N.J.: Prentice-Hall, Inc., 1967.

Ramsdell, D. A., "The Psychology of the Hard of Hearing and Deafened Adult," in *Hearing and Deafness* (3rd ed.), eds. H. Davis and S. R. Silverman, pp. 435–446. New York: Holt, Rinehart & Winston, 1970.

Rice, C., "Human Echo Perception," *Science, 155,* February 1967, 656–664.

Sanders, D. A., *Auditory Perception of Speech: An Introduction to Principles and Problems.* Englewood Cliffs, N.J.: Prentice-Hall, Inc., 1977.

Sanders, D. A., "Hearing Aid Orientation and Counselling," in *Amplification for the Hearing Impaired,* ed. M. C. Pollack, pp. 343–391. New York: Grune & Stratton, Inc. 1980(a).

Sanders, D. A., "Psychological Implications of Hearing Impairment," in *Psychology of Exceptional Children and Youth* (4th ed.), ed. W. M. Cruickshank, pp. 218–254. Englewood Cliffs, N.J.: Prentice-Hall, Inc. 1980(b).

Sanders, D. A., and S. J. Goodrich, "The Relative Contribution of Visual and Auditory Components of Speech to Intelligibility as a Function of Three Conditions of Frequency Distortion,"*Journal of Speech and Hearing Research, 14,* 1971, 154–159.

Seward, J. P., "The Effect of Practice on the Visual Perception of Form," *Archives of Psychology, 20,* 1931, 72, 130.

Solley, C. M., and P. Murphy, *Development of the Perceptual World.* New York: Basic Books, Inc., Publishers, 1960.

Solomon, R. L., L. J. Kamin, and L. C. Wynne, "Traumatic Avoidance Learning: The Outcomes of Several Extinction Procedures with Dogs," *Journal of Abnormal and Social Psych., 48,* 1953, 291–302.

Solomon, R. L., and L. C. Wynne, "Avoidance Conditioning in Normal Dogs and in Dogs Deprived of Normal Autonomic Functioning," *American Psychologist, 5,* 1950, 264.

Solomon, R. L., and L. C. Wynne, "Traumatic Avoidance Learning: The Principles of Anxiety Conservation and Partial Irreversibility," *Psychology Review, 61,* 1954, 353–385.

Spitz, R., *The First Year of Life.* New York: International Universities Press, Inc., 1965.

Stevens, K. N. and M. Halle, "Remarks on Analysis-by-Synthesis and Distinctive Features," in *Models for the Perception of Speech and Visual Form,* ed. W. Wather-Dunn, pp. 88–102. Cambridge, Mass.: M.I.T. Press, 1967.

Supa, M., M. Cotzin, and M. Dallenbach, "Facial Vision: The Perception of Obstacles by the Blind," *American Journal of Psychology, 57,* 1944, 142–152.

Uttley, A. M., "The Classification of Signals in the Nervous System," *E.E.G. Clin. Neurophysiol., 6,* 1954, 479.

Uttley, A. M., "Conditional Probability Computing in a Nervous System," in *Mechanisation of Thought Processes,* pp. 121–147. London: Her Majesty's Stationery Office, 1959.

Uttley, A. M., "The Transmission of Information and the Effect of Local Feedback in Theoretical and Neural Networks," *Brain Res., 2,* 1966, 21–30.

von Senden, M., *Space and Sight. The Perception of Space and Shape in the Congenitally Blind Before and After Operation.* London: Methuen and Co., Ltd., 1960.

Woodworth, R. S., "Reinforcement of Perception." *American Journal of Psychology, 60,* 1947, 119–124.

6

Perception of the Spoken Message

We now examine the perception of the auditory stimulus in terms of the perceptual model just discussed. We can divide the components of the model into two stages: (1) reception and identification; (2) perception and recognition. In this section we consider the reception and identification step only. The process of perception involves the integration of multisensory cues; this will be discussed in the next chapter.

RECEPTION

To be ready to receive a speech signal in a communication situation a person must be motivated to do so. You are no doubt familiar with the experience of someone's trying to communicate a message to you when you are simply not interested in listening—the sort of situation that occurs when you are engrossed in an exciting detective story and someone calls you to dinner or, worse, suggests that you set the table. You are simply not prepared to receive the spoken message and will frequently protest that you did not hear the request. The motivation to listen is important, because it gives rise to auditory-perceptual expectancy. This constitutes the adoption of an appropriate auditory set of predictions, based upon an evaluation of the total communication situation. As a result, we direct our attention to the speech stimulus, which then becomes the figure. We have prepared ourselves to receive the acoustic aspects of the spoken message. The factors that affect this receptive process are particularly important to us, since the person with sensory or conductive deafness experiences a breakdown at this first stage of our communication model.

If the speech stimulus is to be received, *the acoustic power must fall within the limits of audibility.* Figure 6.1 shows the range of frequencies and intensities audible to a person with normal hearing. The lower limits of this auditory area are set by the threshold of audibility, while the upper limits are a function of the tolerance of the ear for discomfort caused by high sound-pressure levels. The distance between the threshold of audibility and the threshold of discomfort constitutes the intensity range within which speech sounds must fall to be of use. The effect of a hearing impairment is to reduce this area by raising the threshold of audibility. The problem is further aggravated in some types of sensorineural deafness by the lowering of the threshold of discomfort. The implications this has for aural rehabilitation become clear when we talk about the use of amplification.

In Chapter 3, when we discussed the energy of speech, it was shown that the overall sound-pressure level of conversation averages about 65 dB (Fletcher, 1953). This means that, for the most part, if you have normal hearing, you listen to speech at a level 65 dB above your threshold. You know from experience that you are quite capable of understanding speech at much lower intensity levels than this. It has, in fact, been demonstrated that if you listen carefully to simple, familiar, connected speech, you will be able to understand correctly at only 24 dB above your threshold (Hawkins and Stevens, 1950). It is not, therefore, essential to amplify speech to a full 65 dB above threshold to make the acoustic signal useful to a person with a hearing loss. In fact, quite frequently the loss is so severe that there may not be a range as great as 65 dB between the thresholds of reception and discomfort. The 40-dB range between the level at

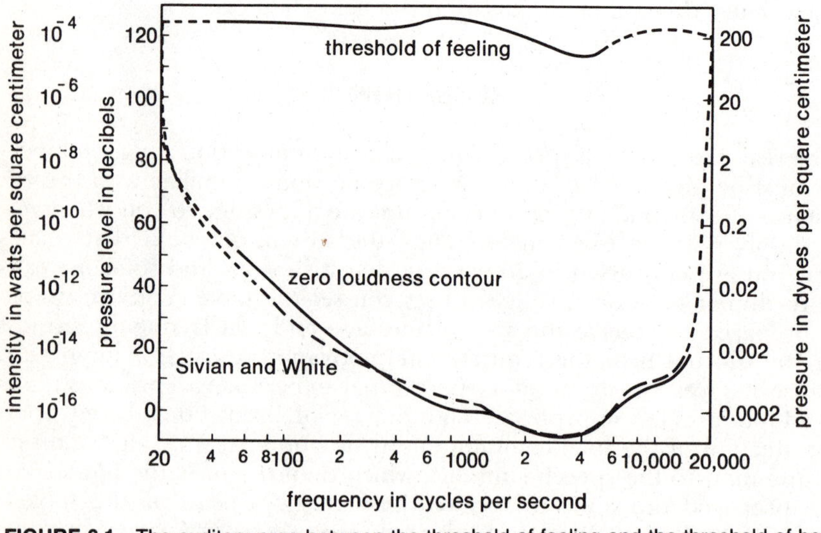

FIGURE 6.1 The auditory area between the threshold of feeling and the threshold of hearing (after Fletcher, 1953).

which speech becomes intelligible and the level at which we normally hear speech constitutes a part of acoustic redundancy without which aural rehabilitation would be considerably more difficult.

In addition to the necessity for the speech stimulus to fall within the auditory area, it must also be of an intensity greater than the acoustic noise in the environment. The figures we have mentioned regarding the audibility of speech were obtained for subjects with normal hearing under conditions of quiet—that is, room noise is less than 20-dB SPL (30-dB sensation level). For levels of environmental noise up to 20-dB SPL, the speech reception threshold of subjects with normal hearing is not affected (Hirsh, 1952). If noise levels exceed this, then the threshold of reception will be raised progressively as the noise levels increase.

PHYSICAL CUES TO IDENTIFICATION

To understand the auditory perception of speech we must first consider the physical properties of speech sounds that serve as cues to identification.

If you refer back to Table 3.2, which displays the relative intensity levels of English phonemes, you will see that a measure of the loudness of a speech sound relative to all other speech sounds makes possible the limitation of the phonemic units into which this speech sound might be placed. For example, there is evidence to show that /s/ and /ʃ/ can be distinguished as a class from /f/ and /θ/ on the basis of intensity alone (Lawson, 1967). Remember that the comparison of loudness between sounds is relative, not absolute. Your auditory mechanism is placing a given sound somewhere on a scale between the weakest phoneme, /θ/, and the strongest. /ɔ/. The raising or lowering of the overall intensity of speech does not normally affect the intensity relationship of the speech sounds to each other. A person with a long-standing hearing loss may have a different pattern of intensity relationships because the auditory impairment weakens some sounds more than others. If, however, the hearing loss is static, then the person's internal perceptual scale is also stable and will permit that person to make judgments, even though their value may be reduced.

The relative duration of speech sounds varies considerably. Table 6.1 (shown previously in Chapter 3) indicates the average duration times for twelve vowels and diphthongs and fifteen consonants obtained from a controlled speech sample (Crandall, 1925). It is clear from these figures that the duration of vowel sounds is significantly longer than the duration of consonants, which permits an initial differentiation between these two categories. Furthermore, sufficient differences exist within each category to be able to further subdivide into groups of vowels and groups of consonants. However, you will observe that not every phoneme is noticeably different in duration from all others. We also know that the absolute duration of a particular phoneme for a given speaker varies with phonetic and semantic context. Stressed syllables, for example, are of longer duration than unstressed syllables. Such variations are not accidental; they occur because a speaker causes them to occur; the encoding processes are

TABLE 6.1 The Average Duration Times for Twelve Vowels and Diphthongs and Fifteen Consonants (after Crandall, (1925)

	Phoneme	*Duration*	*Phoneme*	*Duration*
VOWELS AND DIPHTHONGS	u	0.351	æ	0.294
	i	0.341	ɔ	0.290
	ɝ	0.331	ʌ	0.280
	ou	0.325	ʊ	0.249
	ɑ	0.306	ɛ	0.219
	ei	0.305	ɪ	0.211
CONSONANT VALUES FOR TWO SPEAKERS	ʒ	0.28	ʒ	0.18
		0.13		0.17
	s	0.27	f	0.15
		0.19		0.30
	z	0.24	g	0.12
		0.22		0.10
	j	0.22	b	0.12
		0.14		0.19
	v	0.20	tʃ	0.07
		0.25		0.08
	ð	0.20	k	0.07
		0.18		0.08
	d	0.13	θ	0.02
		0.10		0.02
			p	0.02
				0.04

perceptually known to the speaker and to varying degrees are predictable by the listener. Although we have not been able to understand the exact nature of the duration code that we use so expertly, we are aware that it is an important contributor to speech discrimination, even though speech-sound identification cannot be made on the basis of duration alone.

The third major clue to speech-sound discrimination rests within the frequency spectrum. You are familiar with the form and structure of vowels and know that each may be characterized by the nature of its formants. It is generally recognized that F1 and F2 are of greatest importance in the perception of the quality of a vowel sound. It is these two formants that contribute the information we need to make a phonemic classification. Fischer-Jorgensen (1961, p. 123) explains that for a single speaker, and to a lesser extent for a group of male or female speakers, the decisive element in phoneme recognition from formant structure seems to be the actual frequencies at which the energy concentrations occur. However, a comparison of the vowel sounds produced by adult males and females and by children indicates that the formant pattern for women is 17 percent higher in frequency than that for men, and that for children is even higher. Thus the perception of the position of the formants relative to each other is an important factor in our ability to understand the speech of different people.

Consonants are recognized partly by the frequency distribution of their energy and partly from the effect that they have on the spectrum of adjacent vowels. Fischer-Jorgensen has explained:

The spectra of the consonants proper contain the cues for the distinction between various categories of consonants according to manner of production (e.g., stops, fricatives, nasals), and these differences are sufficiently clearly perceived when consonants are heard in isolation. On the other hand the differences between consonants according to place of articulation are to a great extent perceived by means of the influence exercised on the second (and partly third) formant of the adjoining vowel. There are also differences in the spectra of the consonants according to place of articulation, but except for voiceless fricatives these differences are not always sufficient for recognition. It is difficult to distinguish isolated stop explosions but the vowel "transitions" will often be sufficient for the auditory differentiation between b, d, and g, even if there is no explosion at all (1961, p. 126).

We have seen that speech consists of a continuous wave form. In order to make evaluations of phoneme intensity, duration, and frequency spectrum, it is obviously necessary, at the initial stage of the analysis of the auditory message signal, to break down this wave form into a series of discrete phonemic units. We have just seen that the actual spectrum of a sound may be noticeably influenced by the sound generated by the movements of the speech articulators from the position of the previous sound and toward the subsequent sound. We also know that these transitions are important contributors to the recognition of consonants. The process of breaking down the sound wave into phonemic units cannot therefore be considered as analogous to a phonetic transcription, which provides us with a series of related but unconnected symbols. Each speech sound is intimately related to adjacent sounds by the transitions it shares. The transition belongs equally to the two sounds it links. Recognition of this fact is important, since it means that the transitional characteristics of a sound may be sufficient to enable the listener to identify the sound itself, even when it is distorted. Figure 6.2 (shown previously in Chapter 3) illustrates the principal frequencies present in English sounds. Notice that /d/ and /b/ both contain the same amounts of energy at around 350 Hz, and a second band at about 2800 Hz. Because of the similarity in the intensity and frequency of the lowest component of these two sounds, one might anticipate that it would be impossible to discriminate between them without being able to hear the differentiating second component. However, experiments have shown that one can differentiate between these two consonants on the basis of the transitional changes that they induce in the formant structure of the adjoining vowel (Fry and Whetnall, 1962). Additional transitional cues have been shown to rest in the duration of the transition and in the presence or absence of a silent interval between the steady-state stage and the transition. The contribution of the transitions to intelligibility of other phonemes has been similarly demonstrated. There is, then, sufficient evidence for us to assume that we do not have to hear all of the frequency components of a sound in order to recognize it. It is important that you understand this concept, since it constitutes the basis of the approach to auditory training that we shall develop.

Our discussion of the factors involved in the recognition of speech

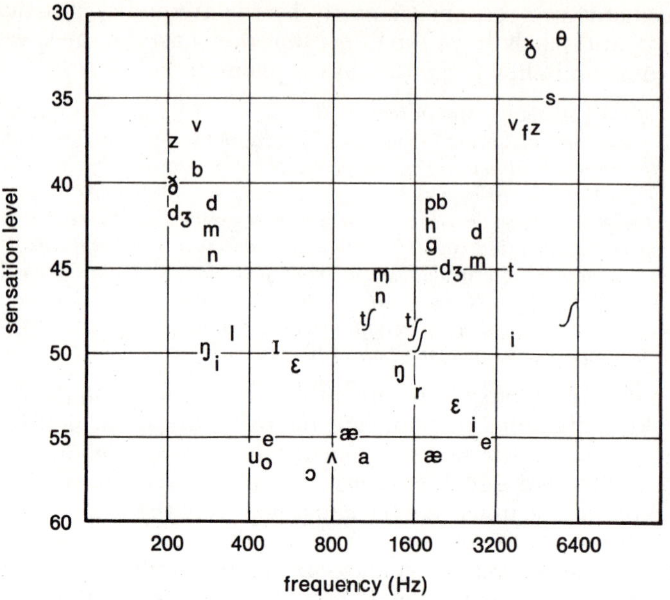

FIGURE 6.2 Sensation level and frequency characteristics of speech sounds (after H. Fletcher, 1953).

sounds cannot be concluded without at least a brief reference to the controversial issue of whether or not motor-kinesthetic feedback plays a role in speech perception. This question involves the relationship that may exist between the articulatory, acoustic, and auditory stages of speech communication.

Research in experimental phonetics has shown that many of the distinctive characteristics that one hears in a speech sample become considerably less identifiable when heard in isolation or in a synthetic speech pattern that closely approximates the sound spectra of human speech. Studies have also shown that even a skilled listener may fail to recognize distinctive characteristics of phonemes if that person is unaware that he or she is listening to a speech sound. On the basis of these findings, Liberman, Cooper, Shankweiler, and Studdert-Kennedy (1967) have suggested that the distinctiveness of a speech sound "is not inherent in the acoustic signal, but is rather added as a consequence of linguistic experience." These findings have led several authors to suggest that speech may be perceived by reference to articulation (Liberman, 1961; Liberman et al., 1967). They maintain that it appears likely that listeners interpret the acoustic signal only after they have mimicked the articulatory pattern that they predict gave rise to the acoustic signal they received. This articulatory mimicry is often observed in an overt form in children, who may appear to be mumbling when being spoken to. In adults, however, Liberman suggests that the process is in some way short-circuited. The sensations of the articulatory movements of speech production may in some way be represented by the corresponding neurological patterns in the brain. These serve to mediate between the acoustic stimulus and the final perception of speech.

It is important for us to reflect upon the implications that these suggestions may have upon our understanding of the speech and hearing abilities of people with hearing losses. It strongly suggests another instance in which we are unjustified in separating out any one particular process involved in the chain of events that constitute human communication. We have argued that vision and audition interact in a manner that produces an end result that cannot be predicted on the basis of data obtained from the two processes functioning in isolation. In light of the theory of motor-kinesthetic speech perception, we also need to consider the relationship between speech therapy for the hard of hearing and auditory-visual training.

In addition to these cues to phonemic identification, information important to meaning is also conveyed by the stress patterns and rhythm of speech. Specific rhythmic patterns of speech are peculiar to particular languages; we learn them when we learn the languages. When we listen to a person from another country who has recently begun to learn English, we often have difficulty in comprehending some of the things that person says because he or she uses unusual stress patterns, both within words and within sentences. As a native of England, I observed, for example, that my American students looked surprised and sometimes puzzled when I used the word "controversy," since I stress the second syllable, con-*trov*-ersy, rather than the first. Given the following three words, you are able to distinguish between them purely on the basis of the stress pattern.

argue   farmer   intent

In fact, the meaning of an isolated word or words often rests ultimately in the ability to identify the stress patterns.

con-tent   con-*tent*
in-*sight*   *in*-sight

Changing the stress patterns of the sentence can also change the meaning:

Where do you think you are going?
Where *do* you think you are going?
Where do *you* think you are going?
Where do you *think* you are going?
Where do you think *you* are going?
Where do you think you *are* going?
Where do you think you are *going*?

DEVELOPMENT OF AUDITORY PERCEPTION

How and why does the child with normal hearing learn to recognize sounds? At birth the hearing mechanism is fully developed. The infant responds to auditory stimulation soon after birth. Within the first few weeks of life the baby is able to respond selectively to sound with a surprising degree of sophistication (Eimas, 1975; Morse, 1977). Eisenberg (1976) showed that infants gave different emotional responses to sounds of different frequencies. High-pitched sounds tended to be distressing, whereas low-pitched sounds were soothing. It has also been demonstrated that babies can discriminate between paired cognate speech sounds such as /p–b/ or /t–d/ (Eilers & Minifie, 1975; Eimas, 1975). Even more important are the findings which show that the infant can use hearing actively in an effort to control auditory events. Butterfield (1968) showed that day-old infants quickly learned to increase their sucking of a pacifier when it was wired to activate a tape recorder which played music. Freelander (1970) also showed that 9- to 18-month-old infants are discriminating in what sounds they listen to, sometimes even selecting taped samples that varied in language content over others that consisted of repetitions of a brief language sample.

It appears, therefore, that at birth the child's mind is not quite that blank slate it was at one time thought to be. The neonate seems to have the ability to discriminate auditorily, and even to have certain innate preferences for sound qualities. Moreover, the ability to discriminate segmental and suprasegmental cues in the acoustic stream grows very rapidly (Freelander, 1970; Spring & Dale, 1977), undoubtedly laying the foundations for both later comprehension of spoken language and the development of speech communication (Condon & Sander, 1974). The child hears; but, as with von Senden's patients after cataract removal, the incoming stimuli, in this case auditory, are devoid of meaning. They are cues to nothing, because the child has no internal schema into which they can be fit, even if he or she were intellectually capable of the task. As the child develops neurophysiologically, the sophistication of the central nervous system increases, permitting the child to process an ever-increasing complexity of stimulus configurations. The developing brain makes it possible for the child to keep a very simple record of experiences—simple because the manner in which the child is able to apprehend things is, in itself, simple. Early experiences are little more than physiological in nature, with no cognitive associations, occurring in an all-or-nothing form. The child is hungry or satiated, warm or cold, threatened by a loud sound or unaware of it.

The increasing sophistication of the mechanism for processing sensory input and the associated increase in awareness of complexity of stimulus patterns impinging upon the organism gives rise to the need for, and stimulates, a rapid growth in the ability to discriminate. As soon as an organism becomes aware that an incoming stimulus complex differs significantly from those that have already been experienced and internalized, the restructuring of internal representations is necessary if the new stimulus complex is to be incorporated into the individual's experience and given meaning. This process may occur by the modification of the existing schemata or by the addition of a new one, associated with existing internal representations of experience, but sufficiently different to exist in its own right.

We can say, then, that the growth in discrimination ability in all sensory channels arises as a combination of a growth in neurophysiological development and the pressures of a complex environment that places ever-increasing demands upon the individual. Joseph Church refers to these two factors as biological and experiential (1961, p. 78). He suggests that "theories which assume that ontogenetic changes in behavior are produced by maturational changes must take account of the possibility that many maturational changes are in turn induced by perceptual stimulation" (p. 30). He goes on to say that "while some part of the change that occurs in infancy can be accounted for in terms of physical maturation, we know that maturation stands in a circular feedback relationship to experience—the things the organism does, feels, and has done to it" (p. 36).

Initially, the infant recognizes the stimulus complex by its gestalt, without awareness of its components. The child is aware of new stimulus complexes by what they are not rather than by what they are, and then later by their overall pattern rather than by their specific components. This is an important concept, and we need to discuss it further in relation to its implications for various approaches to training visual and auditory perception.

The beginnings of auditory-perceptual development, therefore, involve, first, *an awareness of sound,* which results from an ability to internalize auditory stimuli and to integrate them with other sensory stimuli in order for a relationship between the child and the sound source to be established within a context. Mother's voice is recognized first in the context of her visual image, the warmth of her body, and the feel of her arms. Later, the auditory cue alone will provide sufficient information for recognition of Mother. Second, auditory-perceptual development involves *an ability to discriminate between sounds* and, therefore, between sound sources. The initial discrimination is elementary. It involves a decision between "it is" or "it is not" Mother. As the child's repeated contact with other sound-generating people or objects in the environment increases, he or she has reason to differentiate between them in order to control his or her world. This requires internal representation of all sensory cues to the new experience. The child's auditory world consists of, for example, Mother, Father, bottle, squeaky toy, and several sounds in the "not-one-of-these" category. The child is aware of these latter sounds, but is not yet sufficiently familiar with them to have completely internalized them together with their concomitant stimuli and associations. The library of internalized sound patterns and associations grows rapidly in the first year of life as the child becomes increasingly auditorily oriented. It has already been pointed out that sound cues play an important role in orientating the child in space, in providing the child with information about the ever more complex world, and in protecting the child from impending dangers or reassuring the child that all is well.

This is the pattern of the early stages of auditory development in young children with normal hearing. The initially painstaking task of discrimination begins to grow easier as the child's brain learns to process the incoming information with greater and greater sophistication and ease. Meaningful auditory discrimination, which was first only possible between a few of the most dissimilar sounds, begins to be possible between an increasing variety of sounds and between those that differ less and less in acoustic structure. This occurs because of the auditory training that the environment continually provides the child with normal hearing—auditory training of which the hearing-impaired child is deprived.

The factors involved in learning to discriminate between gross sounds may be summarized as follows:

1. Awareness
2. Repeated exposure to the sound within a context
3. Predictable association of the acoustic stimuli with other sensory stimuli arising from the same sound source
4. Internal representation of auditory and other sensory impressions
5. Multisensory or gestalt recognition of sound-generating objects
6. Identification (prediction) of a sound source on the basis of its acoustic characteristics alone

DEVELOPMENT OF SPEECH-SOUND DISCRIMINATION

With a few exceptions, the normal child is born into a family in which speech constitutes the major form of communication. The child's parents presume that the child, too, will develop the ability to utilize this form of communication. Since the infant's parents are themselves very dependent upon the verbalization of ideas and, therefore, feelings, it is natural for them to talk both to themselves and to the child when they are attending to the child's needs and when they relaxed with the child. In addition, the child will be exposed to varying amounts of verbal communication between parents and other siblings. The child exists in a speech environment.

We have already concurred with Church's statement that maturation stands in a feedback relationship to experience. We may postulate, therefore, that the development of auditory-perceptual ability is heavily dependent upon the exposure to environmental sounds and speech sounds, which takes place from birth. We must not neglect the importance of the role of this preverbal auditory experience. It is fascinating to note, for example, that even in some species of birds, exposure to the singing pattern of the parent bird is necessary for the young bird to learn the song of the species, even when the exposure occurs before the young bird is itself physiologically ready to sing (Beach, 1960; Thorpe, 1956).

The same factors that are involved in the learning of gross-sound discrimination are valid in the learning of speech perception. The child must first become aware of speech. This awareness is closely related to the figure-ground phenomenon, which is in itself determined, to a large extent, by the ability of the individual to attribute meaning to certain stimulus complexes.

But figure-ground organization is dictated neither by stimulus intensities (except at disruptively high levels of contrast) nor by the formal organizational laws of Gestalt theory. Those objects, and those properties of objects, stand out which offer some relevance to the child himself, in terms of promise or threat or concrete action. Those things which are meaningless seem also to be beyond perception. The young infant is oblivious to the screaming sirens of the fire trucks that go racketing past, to the hubbub of the thunderstorm, to the clamor of the telephone or doorbell; but he may wail in distress when his mother sneezes in the next room.

Here we are saying two things: that the child perceives only personally meaningful objects, and that what he perceives is not so much the objects as their meanings (Church, 1961, p. 4).

Meaning grows out of association, which results from repeated exposure to particular sensory stimuli in concurrence with other sensory stimuli.

The most meaningful person in a child's early life is its mother, one of whose characteristics is that she speaks. Since, as we have said, the child's early perceptions are in the form of a gestalt or holistic impression, for a child with normal hearing, vocalizations of the mother, both her singing and the words she speaks, will become as integral a part of the child's perception of her as will the visual image, the physical contact, and the way in which she handles him or her. The child is not initially capable of isolating, out of this gestalt, the individual components; this is a much later developmental behavior pattern. The reason the child pays attention to, and becomes aware of, speech is because it is an intimate part of the perception of Mother. Mowrer (1950) has suggested that is is this identification of speech patterns with Mother, combined with a normal autistic need in the child to recreate Mother's image in her absence, that gives rise to early babbling and its modification to an increasingly exact replica of Mother's vocalizations.

Mother's contact with her infant is limited to the child's waking periods and the nature of her relationship limited by the needs of the child. One talks to a baby in a particular way and about particular things, especially in activities that involve the child and the adult. The vocabulary used by the mother is, therefore, fairly restricted by situational constraints that provide the necessary repeated contextual exposure to the sound patterns of certain words. For the most part, when the mother talks to the child, she is with the child, so that the child receives the auditory stimulus together with the associated visual and tactile impression. These permit the child to develop internal representations of the auditory and other impressions. When these have been developed, the child seems able to predict the meaning of certain spoken words on the bases of his or her total perception.

The spoken names of things are first given to the child in the presence of the object. While handling a ball, the child is told, "That's a ball. Isn't it a pretty ball? Throw Mommy the ball"; or, "Where are your shoes? Let's put your shoes on. Here are your shoes. Let's put them on your feet. One shoe, two shoes." Out of these sentences the child focuses attention upon salient words. Certain words in a given situation become salient words because of the natural tendency that we have to stress them, because they are repeated more frequently than other words, and because they refer to objects and events within the perceptual experience of the child. Early speech perception therefore begins to occur in a situation in which redundancy is very high. The child's predictions are greatly aided by information that he or she has received through other senses and by the very limited alternative choices with which he or she is presented. As a result, the child is likely to experience success, and the parents are likely to reinforce attempts to identify things by their names. We say a child knows the name of something when he or she is consistently able to identify it on the basis of the spoken word alone.

This basic process continues to develop and to become increasingly sophisticated. It does so because the ability to make accurate predictions about one's environment and the people within it is greatly enhanced by the comprehension of speech. Even before the child can use expressive speech as a means of directly manipulating the environment, he or she finds that ability to discriminate between the words "cookie" and "milk," contained in a question asked by Mother, considerably speeds up the process of getting whichever he or she wants on a particular occasion. Accurate speech perception is, therefore, a rewarding process and encourages the child to refine and develop skills in this behavior. The increasing ability to differentiate between more and more words and, therefore, between the objects and ideas to which they refer, causes the child to become increasingly dependent upon speech as a source of information. The greater the skill, the better able the child is to function under conditions of reduced redundancy. The child who is initially able to only discriminate a few words under conditions highly favorable to accurate prediction is ultimately able to identify complex ideas by spoken words received under markedly adverse listening conditions.

VISUAL PERCEPTION AND THE SPOKEN MESSAGE

The role of vision in helping the receiver to reconstruct and interpret the message has, to some extent, been covered in Chapter 4. We now consider in more detail the visual cues the listener may make use of and the nature of their contribution to communication.

General Background Cues

Many of you have seen at least a televised performance of a ballet, in which a story is told completely through body movements. Such experiences leave little doubt that information can be and is transmitted in the visible nonverbal form. We may be less convinced that this takes place in a more everyday communication situation. One of the easiest ways to decide whether you utilize visual cues in a communication situation is to sit before a television set with the sound turned off. If, under these conditions, you are unable to obtain any information that you might use in an evaluation of what the speaker might be saying, then you could conclude that vision is unimportant to communication. However, you will probably not find this to be the case. Among the things you might find that you had noted might be whether the speaker was a man, woman, or child; the speaker's approximate age, general appearance, and manner of dress. You may be able to reach a conclusion concerning the type of person you are watching. Further information concerning the speaker's role in the situation will be obtained from the relationship the speaker evidences with other people in the environment and from the speaker's general manner or conduct. We make all of these observations about a person who is engaged in a particular activity in a particular situation. The conclusions we reach may not hold true for another person in the same situation or for the same person in a different situation.

On the basis of our observations, we assign a role to the speaker. We are able to do this most easily when the person wears an easily recognizable uniform, a particular mode of dress, or if the person is engaged in a particular activity, such as conducting an orchestra. "The interpretation of mutual roles serves the purpose of clarifying the verbal, gestural and action messages that people consciously convey to each other. . . . Those who are quick to recognize roles and are aware of the shifting nature of roles are at an advantage in dealing with social situations" (Ruesch & Kees, 1956, p. 72).

This is the type of awareness that Nitchie (1912) advocates we should attempt to develop in the hearing-impaired person. Nitchie refers to it as "intuitiveness"; you will recognize it as the ability of the person to make accurate predictions on the basis of a minimal pattern of verbal and nonverbal cues. Ruesch and Kees emphasize this process when they state:

"I'm trying to remember—did you major in geology or drama?"

FIGURE 6.3 "Those who are quick to recognize roles and are aware of the shifting nature of such roles are at an advantage in dealing with social situations." (Cartoon courtesy of General Features Corporation)

In the practice of communication we are continually assessing our material surroundings, making attempts at identifying others and their roles, their status, and their group membership, in order to arrive at a kind of diagnosis that will combine all these features into an integral pattern: the social situation. *In the truest sense it is the social situation that determines the context and nature of any communicative exchange* (p. 37).

Or, to quote Peters:

We know what the person will do when he begins to walk toward the pulpit in the middle of the penultimate hymn or what the traveller will do when he enters the doors of the hotel because we know the conventions regulating church services and staying at hotels, (1958, p. 7).

These same conventions also regulate the conversation of people and, therefore, considerably increase our ability to predict what may be said.

In summary, we can say that the contextual cues originate from:

1. The physical environment in which the message is communicated
2. The people in the environment
3. The relationship of the speaker to the people in the environment
4. The general appearance of the speaker, including build, age, and type of dress

Cues Directly Related to the Message

Try now to recall what you noticed about the speaker while watching the television without sound. You will almost certainly agree that you observed visual cues that arose from the speaker's physical actions. If you consider these more carefully, you will recognize that they consisted of two types of cues:

1. Those that arise from an activity in which the speaker was engaged, or that are expressive of an emotion
2. Those that were clearly intentional gestures

Cues from Implemental Activities

Implemental activities, such as a person taking out his or her wallet, opening it, and removing three dollars, provide information against which we interpret the spoken message. Of more particular interest to us, however, are expressive movements that connote a particular emotion. These are primarily of an involuntary nature and may be scarcely noticeable as separate entities. We may, for example, find it quite difficult to say exactly which muscular actions are involved in conveying a look of puzzlement. Yet it has been demonstrated by several investigators that we are able to recognize such emotional expressions from photographs either of actors posing (Coleman, 1949) (Fry & Whetnall, 1962), or of emotions elicited by authentic situations (Dolanski, 1930). There is little doubt that we expect certain facial expressions to be associated with the emotion evoked by certain situations (Figure 6.4). Therefore, when seen in context the visual cues help us to predict the verbal message and may considerably increase our accuracy in doing so. They increase the number

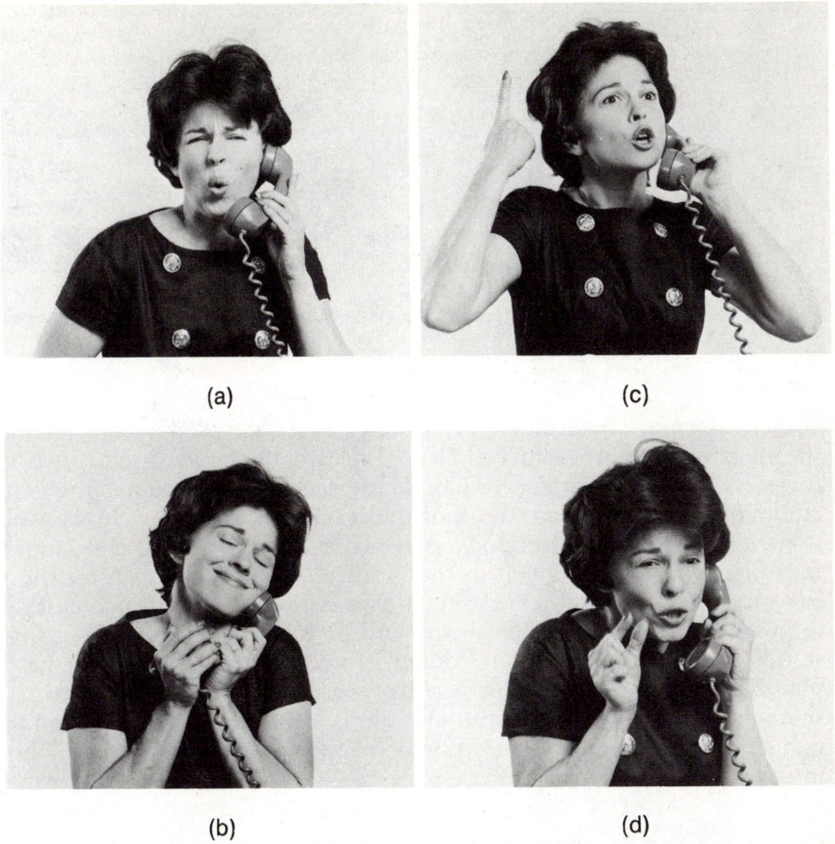

FIGURE 6.4 Information is conveyed in facial expressions and gestures; (a) learn estimate for fixing the fender; (b) learn husband still loves you in spite of fender; (c) get out the vote; (d) tell the store to send those *teeny-weeny* tomatoes for the party (photographs courtesy of Ormond Gigli, Inc.).

of constraints and serve as a source of information upon which intersensory trial-and-check procedures can be carried out.

Gestural Cues

Gestures, unlike expressive movements, are made consciously and are used in a communication situation. They may be made with almost any body part, though we are most aware of those involving the head, face, shoulders, and hands and arms (Figure 6.5). We recognize the significance of the nod of approval or disapproval, the protruded tongue, the shrug of the shoulders, the extended hand, or a raised hand in a classroom. Such gestures may serve as substitutes for the spoken word, though for the most part they accompany speech. "Gestures are used to illustrate, to emphasize, to point, to explain, or to interrupt; therefore they cannot be isolated from the verbal components of speech" (Ruesch & Kees, 1956, p. 37).

FIGURE 6.5 Gestures can often prove very meaningful (cartoon courtesy of King Features Syndicate, Inc.)

In normal conversational speech, gestures are used as signs. That is, the meaning of the gesture is closely related to the act itself. Such gestures are illustrated in Figure 6.6. These serve the secondary function of augmenting or modifying the spoken message in some way. It is possible, however, for gestures to be given symbolic value. When this occurs, the meaning is arbitrarily given to the gesture, which now *stands for* the object, event, or idea, rather than being *an extension of it.* In such cases it is impossible to interpret the gesture unless you are familiar with what it stands for. The gesture is no longer a modifier of the word—it has replaced the word. This is how gesture is used by the deaf in a system of symbolic gestural communication that is misleadingly called sign language. Similar systems are used by bookies at a race track and by jobbers in the stock exchange.

Cues Arising Directly from the Spoken Message

Finally, we must consider the contribution made to speech intelligibility by the visible characteristics of the spoken message itself.

The organs of articulation that contribute most to the visible aspects of speech are:

1. *The lips.* Cues to recognition may be derived from various degrees of lip rounding or spreading, ranging from the marked rounding that characterizes the production of the vowel /u/ as in *boot* and the /w/ in *wind,* to the spread lips for the vowel /i/ in *meek* (Figure 6.7). Protrusion and lip rounding together help in recognition of the /tʃ/ in *church* and /ʃ/ in *ship* (Figure 6.8).
   Cues to the bilabial plosives /p/ and /b/ and the bilabial nasal /m/ are obtained from observing the lips being brought together (Figure 6.9). The contact of the lower lip and the upper teeth facilitates the recognition of the labial dental fricatives /f/ and /v/ (Figure 6.10).

2. *The tongue.* Observation of the tongue position contributes valuable information to the recognition of such sounds as the lingual dental /θ/ and /ð/ in think and these, the /l/ in letter, the lingual alveolar plosives /t/ and /d/, and the lingual nasal /n/ (Figure 6.11).

FIGURE 6.6 In conversation, gestures are closely related to the act itself.

3. *The jaw.* From observation of the degree of opening of the jaw, together with information about other articulators, we obtain cues important in the differentiation between vowels—for example, between /a/ as in *a*rm and /i/ as in h*i*m (Figure 6.12).

To the information obtained from these articulators we must add that contributed by the secondary movements of facial muscles associated with the articulation of certain phonemes discussed earlier.

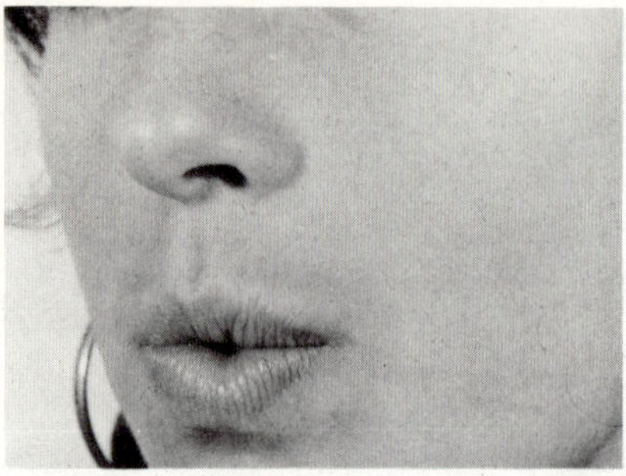

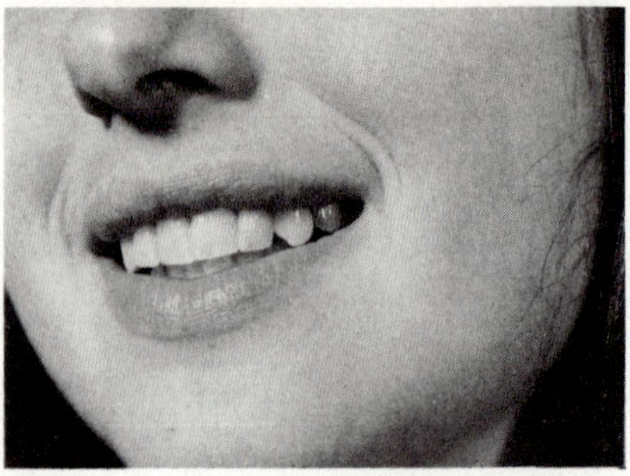

FIGURE 6.7 The posture of the lips helps in the discrimination between /u/ or /w/ and /i/.

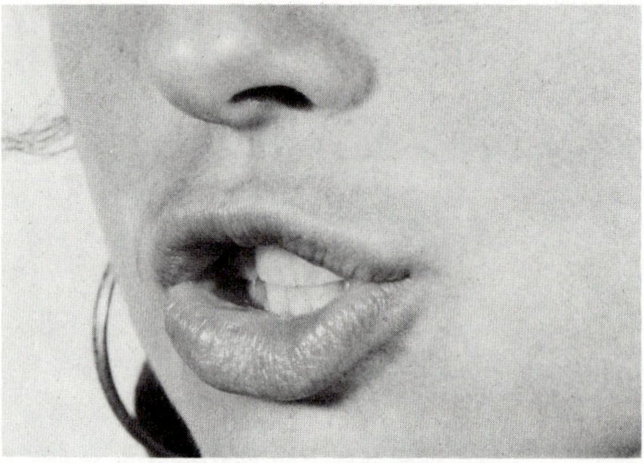

FIGURE 6.8 Protrusion and rounding of the lips assist in the identification of /ʃ/ and /tʃ/.

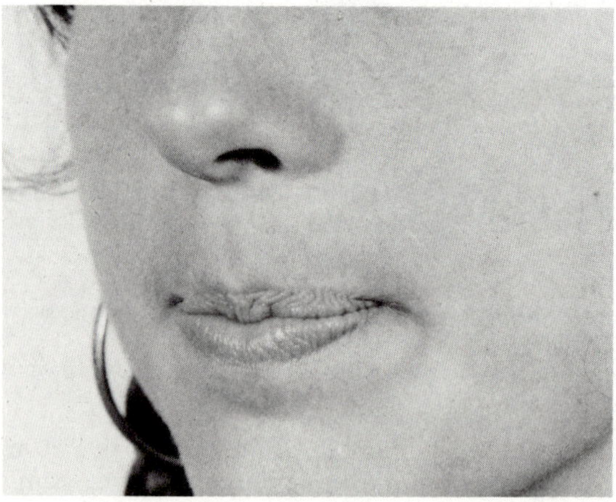

FIGURE 6.9 The phonemes /p/, /b/, and /m/ are characterized by lip closure.

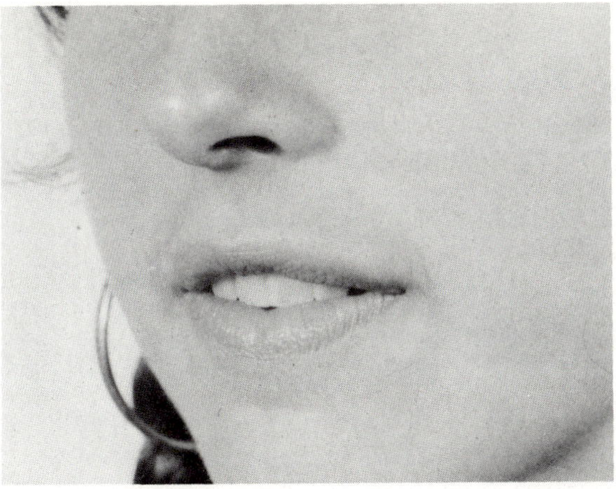

FIGURE 6.10 The contact of the lower lips and upper teeth facilitates the recognition of /f/ and /v/.

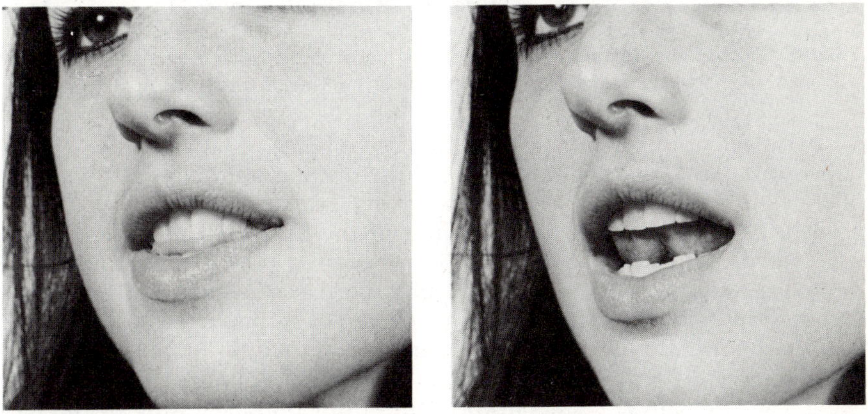

FIGURE 6.11 Observation of tongue movement helps in the identification of (a) /θ/, /ð/ and /l/; and (b) the sound groups /t/, /d/ and /n/.

At this time we are only concerned with the amount of information conveyed by the visible aspects of speech when the auditory components are absent. In an attempt to obtain a little more information about this, we conducted a small project involving twenty college students with normal hearing. We found that when we asked them to recognize phonetically balanced monosyllabic words from visual cues alone, the mean score based upon 100 words was 7.0 words correctly identified. In other words, when visual perception of the spoken word provided the only source of information about the message, only 7 percent of the material was correctly identified.

Utley administered her film test, "How Well Can You Read Lips?"

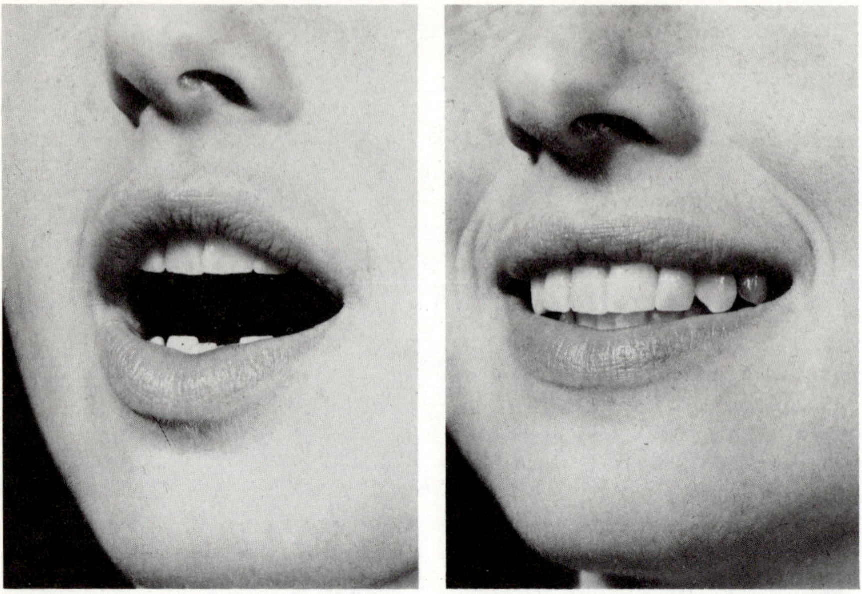

FIGURE 6.12 Differentiation between vowels is made on the basis of jaw opening and lip shaping. The contrast between /a/ and /i/ is shown here.

to 761 deaf and hard-of-hearing subjects (1946). The mean score obtained on the word-recognition part of the test was 6.9 words (19 percent) of a possible total of 36. The words in this test were, however, not monosyllabic, but were selected from a test of the first 1000 most frequently used words. They included a number of bi- and trisyllabic words, which increased redundancy, and a score of correct was given on the basis of recognition either of the test word or of any of its homophenes. Even so, less than one-fifth of the words were recognized by experienced lipreaders.

If we view these results in the light of our understanding of the factors that limit the visual reception of speech, the low scores obtained through vision alone will not be surprising. The little information one is able to obtain from the visible aspects of the spoken message signal itself is derived from the revealing movements of the articulators. Woodward, whose findings we discussed earlier, demonstrated that when we receive only the visible cues to speech, the most we can achieve, as far as consonant recognition is concerned, is to classify them into one of six groups of homophenous clusters. Further classification proved impossible on the basis of visual observation alone.

Another observation made by Woodward (1957) and supported by Brannon and Kodman, Jr. (1959) was that the visibility of movements was related to their place of articulation. Mirror observation of your own speech will illustrate this relationship. You will notice, for example, that the bilabial clusters /p/, /b/, and /m/ and the lingual dental clusters /f/ and /v/ are far easier to recognize than the lingual alveolar clusters /t/, /d/, /n/, and /l/ or the lingual velar sounds /k/, /g/, and /ŋ/. It is, however, not true that the relationship between visibility and place of articulation is on a one-to-one basis. Because the formative movements of the lingual alveolar fricative sounds /s/ and /z/ and the alveolar fricatives /θ/ and /ð/ occur at the same place of articulation as the /t/, /d/, /n/, and /l/ cluster, they should be equally hard to recognize. In fact they possess a high coefficient of visibility (1.0) bestowed upon them by the secondary revealing movements of the lips (see Table 4.2).

TOTAL PERCEPTION

So far in this chapter we have looked at the aspects of the auditory and visual stimuli that contribute to the ability of the receiver to reconstruct the message-signal codes reaching him or her through various sensory channels. To facilitate our study of speech perception, we examined the auditory and visual components independently. You will recognize the artificiality of such a dichotomy. The integral relationship of sensory pathways in the process of perception has already been stressed. We review the research findings concerning the integration of visual and auditory information more fully in the next chapter.

The process of total perception may, therefore, be seen as involving an internal restructuring of the symbolic representation of the situation, event, thought, or idea that occurs in one's external environment. We do this by the use of data reaching us through our various sensory channels. Human communication concerns the process of transmission and reception of a series of instructions. These carry information designed to permit the receiver to predict, with varying degrees of accuracy, the idea that the sender wished to communicate. This stage is concerned with comprehension, with information processing. It requires the ability to sustain recognition over a period of time. In this stage, words and nonverbal cues are stored in order to establish context to permit the occurrence of the probability analysis, which we discussed earlier.

As the data comes in through the sensory pathways and travels up to the central processing area, different parts of it are analyzed at the various substations along the route (Bocca & Calearo, 1963, p. 338). The information from all sensory modalities is then put into a common pool. The important question now is whether, as a listener, using your knowledge of structural, contextual, and situational probabilities, you have enough information within the pool to reconstruct the message.

For communication between individuals with normal hearing under favorable listening conditions, the amount of information in the pool is usually far greater than the minimum required to predict the message. The auditory pathway alone contributes more than enough for this purpose. The data contributed by the other sensory pathways constitute the redundancy factor to which the receiver turns for additional information when the noise level in the system makes accurate reception difficult.

To reconstruct any particular message the person needs a certain minimum amount of instructional information. We have seen in our discussion of communication that it is possible to predict accurately a significant percentage of those instructions on the basis of limited information. We learned earlier that the amount of data we need in order to predict the missing components varies with a variety of factors (see Tables 2.3 and 2.4). If you obtain a minimum amount of information, it is immaterial through which channels it came.

The situation may be considered analogous to that which might occur if a group of three students wished to purchase a second-hand car. The reason they agree to pool their financial resources is that no one person has sufficient funds to purchase the car alone. The actual price of the car may be $600; the minimum needed to obtain the car is a down payment of $150. It is most convenient to assume that each student contributed an equal sum toward the down payment, though it would be perfectly possible for the sum to be obtained by each student's contributing different proportions. No matter how the contributions vary in proportion, providing a minimum of $150 is raised, the car will be obtained. If each of the students contributes $100 to the fund, then the additional $150 is in excess of what they actually require in order to take possession of the car. They may, however, need the additional money if they discover that the price has subsequently been raised or if they failed to allow for the sales tax. In this analogy, the salesperson represents the receiver, the total cost of the car ($600) represents the total message, and the down payment ($150) represents the minimum information necessary to understand the essential aspects of the message. The three students, each contributing a sum of money to the pool, stand for the channels through which the receiver obtains information. The difference between the amount of money the students absolutely have to contribute and the amount they actually have may be considered the redundancy factor that will be reduced if the noise in the system (unexpected sales tax) goes up. The important point to remember is that, just as in the analogy, it is perfectly possible in communication that the information arriving through a single channel is not sufficient for perception to take place. This does not, however, mean that this channel is not important. It may be that no one channel is contributing enough information to permit perception, yet when the various amounts of data from different channels are pooled, the total may be more than adequate to permit the reconstruction of the original message. It must again be stressed that the pooling of data is not a simple additive function, as would have been the case in our analogy of each student's financial contributions to the group fund. The process is one of integration or blending. Each unit of information assumes a different value when combined with the other units. A single piece of a jigsaw puzzle may be meaningless alone, yet when fitted together with several other pieces, it not only adds information, it also modifies perception of the other pieces and may suddenly acquire a meaning of its own, permitting perception to take place. If you now remove the piece and view it alone, you see it quite differently because of what you know about its interaction with the other pieces.

This philosophy underlies the approach to rehabilitation that characterizes this text. We recognize that the hard-of-hearing person in many communication situations receives inadequate information through the auditory channel to permit accurate reconstruction of the idea the speaker wishes to convey. Unfortunately the visual channel alone does not convey enough information for it to serve as an alternative source from which that information may be derived. Our aim must therefore be to establish a program of rehabilitation that integrates all sources of information. Miller, in his chapter "The Perception of Speech," concludes:

Perceiving speech is not a passive, automatic procedure. The perceiver contributes a selective function by responding to some aspects of the total situation and not to others. He responds to the stimuli according to some organization that he imposes upon them. And he supplements the inconsistent or absent stimulation in a manner that is consistent with his needs and his past experience (1963, p. 79).

We aim to provide the hearing-impaired person with a perceptual approach to communication that is more productive. Although during training we function to a great extent on a conscious level of behavior, ultimately the hearing-impaired person must incorporate these patterns into an unconsciously assumed communication behavioral set—what Church refers to a an "organismic mobilization." In subsequent chapters we consider how this may be achieved.

REFERENCES

Beach, F. A., "Experimental Investigation of Species-Specific Behavior," *American Psychologist, 15,* 1960, 1–18.

Bocca, E., and C. Calearo, "Central Hearing Processes," In *Modern Developments in Audiology,* ed. J. Jerger, pp. 337–370. New York: Academic Press, Inc., 1963.

Brannon, J. B., and F. Kodman, Jr., "The Perceptual Process in Speech Reading," *Archives of Otolaryngology, 70,* 1959, 111–119.

Butterfield, E., "An Extended Version of Modification of Sucking with Auditory Feedback," Working paper No. 43, Bureau of Child Research, University of Kansas Medical Center, 1968.

Church, J., *Language and the Discovery of Reality.* New York: Random House, Inc., 1961.

Coleman, J. C., "Facial Expression of Emotion," *Psychological Monographs, 63,* 1949, 1–36.

Condon, W., and L. Sander, "Neonate Movement is Synchronized with Adult Speech. Interactional Participation in Language Structure," *Science, 183,* 1974, 99–101.

Crandall, I. B., "The Sounds of Speech," *Bell System Technical Journal, 4,* 1925, 586–626.

Dolanski, V., "Les aveugles possidentile les sens d'obstacles, Année Psychologique, 31, 1930, 1–51.

Eilers, R., and F. Minifie, "Fricative Discrimination in Early Infancy," *Journal of Speech and Hearing Research, 18,* 1975, 158–67.

Eimas, P., "Developmental Studies of Speech Perception," In *Infant Perception, Volume II,* eds. L. Cohen, and P. Salapatek, pp. 193–231. New York: Academic Press, Inc., 1975.

Eisenberg, R., *Auditory Competence in Early Life.* Baltimore: University Park Press, 1976.

Fischer-Jorgensen, E., "New Techniques in Acoustic Phonetics," in *Psycholinguistics,* ed. S. Saporta, pp. 112–142. New York: Holt, Rinehart & Winston, 1961.

Fletcher, H., *Speech and Hearing in Communication.* New York: D. Van Nostrand Company, 1953.

Fletcher, H., and W. A. Mundson, "Loudness: Its Definition, Measurement and Calculation, *Journal of the Acoustical Society of America, 5,* 1933, 82–108.

Freelander, B., "Receptive Language Development in Infancy," *Merrill-Palmer Quarterly of Behavior and Development, 16,* 1970, 7–51.

Fry, D. E., and E. Whetnall, *The Deaf Child.* London: William Heinemann, Ltd., 1962.

Hawkins, J. E., and S. Stevens, "The Masking of Pure Tones by White Noise," *Journal of the Acoustical Society of America, 22,* 1950, 6–13.

Hirsh, I. J., *The Measurement of Hearing.* New York: McGraw-Hill Book Company, 1952.

Lawson, C. A., *Brain Mechanisms and Human Learning,* The International Series in the Behavioral Sciences. Boston: Houghton Mifflin Company, 1967.

Liberman, A. M., "Some Results of Research on Speech Perception," in *Psycholinguistics,* ed. S. Saporta, pp. 142–153. New York: Holt, Rinehart & Winston, 1961.

Liberman, A. M., F. S. Cooper, D. P. Shankweiler, and M. Studdert-Kennedy, "Perception of the Speech Code," *Psychological Review, 74,* 1967, 431–461.

Miller, G. A., *Language and Communication.* New York: McGraw-Hill Book Company, 1963.

Morse, P., "Infant Speech Perception," in *Auditory Perception of Speech: An Introduction to Principles and Problems.* D. A. Sanders, pp. 161–176. Englewood Cliffs, N.J.: Prentice-Hall, Inc., 1977.

Mowrer, H. O., "On the Psychology of Talking Birds," in *Learning Theory and Personality Dynamics,* ed. H. O. Mowrer, pp. 688–726. New York: Ronald Press Company, 1950.

Nitchie, E. B., *Lip Reading: Principles and Practice.* New York: Frederick A. Stokes Company, 1912.

Peters, R. S., *The Concept of Motivation.* London: Routledge & Kegan Paul, Ltd., 1958.

Ruesch, J., and W. Kees, *Nonverbal Communication.* Berkeley and Los Angeles: University of California Press, 1956.

Spring, D., and P. Dale, "Discrimination of Linguistic Stress in Early Infancy," *Journal of Speech and Hearing Research, 20,* 1977, 224–232.

Thorpe, W. H., *Learning and Instinct in Animals.* London: Methuen & Company, Ltd., 1956.

Utley, J., "A Test of Lipreading Ability," *Journal of Speech and Hearing Disorders, 11,* 1946, 109–116.

Woodward, M., "Linguistic Methodology in Lip Reading Research," *John Tracy Clinic Research Papers, 6,* 1957, 1–32.

7

The Interaction of Vision and Audition in Speech Perception

In the previous chapters we studied some of the general principles involved in the process of perception. Then we looked closely at those aspects of the auditory and visual stimuli that contribute to the listeners' ability to reconstruct the message-signal codes reaching them through various sensory channels. To facilitate our study of speech perception we examined the auditory and visual components independently. You should recognize the artificiality of this dichotomy, for the integral relationship of sensory pathways in the process of perception has already been stressed. We have seen that what we perceive is not the sensations themselves but the values and concepts that those sensations evoke. Once the necessary cues have been received, we perceive the whole regardless of whether the information that elicited the perception reached us through a single sensory channel or through several.

Hearing impairment reduces the sensitivity of the listener to the full range of information in the acoustic signal. Therefore, when communication difficulties arise, they do so because the information that the listener is able to extract from the acoustic signal is insufficient to evoke the appropriate percept. Thus, our interest in the role of intersensory interaction in speech perception is to help the individual compensate for this reduction or distortion of acoustic information.

INTEGRATION OF VISION AND AUDITION

It is generally accepted that information received through one sensory modality can affect the way in which we perceive that received through another. This was illustrated in experiments conducted by Shipley (1954) and by Gebhardt and Mowbray (1959). These researchers studied the effect that the rate of flutter of a clicking sound would have upon a subject's perception of the rate of flicker of a flashing light. They established both the critical flicker and the critical flutter rate. Critical flicker is the frequency at which a flashing light first appears steady, and critical flutter is the frequency at which a clicking sound appears to be uninterrupted. Intersensory interaction was then demonstrated by presenting a light at a specific rate of perceived flicker. Simultaneously the subject heard a complex sound set to flutter at the same frequency as the visual stimulus. The frequency of the auditory stimulus was then gradually increased and decreased. As would be expected, the rate of auditory flutter was perceived to increase or decrease accordingly. However, the surprising observation was that the perceived visual flicker rate also increased and decreased in the same manner, even though the physical stimulus was held constant. It is interesting that it was not possible to reverse the procedure—that is, to modify the auditory perception by varying the visual stimulus. In a later study Brown and Hopkins (1968) used information-theory techniques in an attempt to achieve a precise measurement of the interaction occurring between the auditory and visual sensory modalities. They determined the optimal probability of detection of a 1000-Hz tone presented against a background of white noise as a function of the signal-to-noise ratio. The corresponding visual task required the subject to detect a 1000-Hz signal presented on an oscilloscope trace against a predetermined level of visible noise. Thresholds were first established for the visual and auditory system independently. The signal was then presented to both sensory systems simultaneously and a bimodal threshold was obtained. The two unimodal thresholds and the bimodal threshold were compared. Results indicated that the redundancy of information resulting from combining two sensory channels in a bimodal presentation significantly improves signal-detection performance. In a related study, Karlovitch (1968) showed that the perception of loudness can similarly be enhanced by the introduction of a correlated visual stimulus. These studies indicate that the brain processes the products of sensory integration of information rather than the raw sensory data itself. When information in two different channels is complementary, the integration of sensory data makes possible a reduction in the dependency upon either single channel.

Intersensory interaction does seem to occur in the processing of data obtained through different modalities. Harris (1950) says that this makes sense, at least in terms of visual and auditory processing, because the two systems are directly interconnected along the neural tract to the cortex. It has even been demonstrated that in cats some cells in the auditory cortex require a combined auditory-visual stimulus to activate them, whereas a few auditory cortex cells respond only to visual stimulation (Evans & Whitfield, 1964). Harris (1950) concludes that "The evidence is in favor of one organ enhancing the sensation from another organ, though there are negative findings" (p. 47).

Current discussion of intersensory interaction centers on the level at which this takes place, and whether or not it is an association process dependent upon language. Much of the work on cross-modal interaction has been contributed by Ettlinger (1967). Ettlinger's experiments have been directed toward ascertaining whether the discrimination and perception of an object or event involves a neural system common to all modalities (supramodal), or whether recognition occurs independently in each modality (unimodal). Ettlinger reviews experimental findings pertaining to the following:

1. The transfer of specific discrimination habits from one sense modality to another
2. The transfer of learned principles
3. The ability to match equivalent stimuli in different modalities

A study conducted by Cole, Chorover, and Ettlinger (1961) assessed whether cross-modal transfer of discrimination habits can occur. Cole et al. attempted to determine whether adults' learning of an auditory rhythm-discrimination task facilitated performance of the same task by vision. No evidence of cross-modal transfer was found in this particular experiment. In a similar study by Blank and Bridger (1964), children were taught to discriminate between a single and double flash of light and were then asked to make the same discrimination between a single and double sound. Significant transfer of the learned discrimination habit occurred in only those children whose learning procedure involved verbalization.

The second type of transfer, that of derived principles or hypotheses, involves the subject's developing certain response techniques in one sensory channel and then utilizing those techniques in another sensory channel. For example, a visual-motor task may be based upon the principle that the relationship between stimuli consists of each subsequent stimulus being a multiple of the previous one. When this principle has been learned, the subject can then make correct predictions about others. Thus, if the subject is presented with a task equivalent to the original one, but in a different sensory modality, the time taken to learn the second task can be compared to the time needed to learn the first. A shortened learning time indicates that the principle has been transferred.

The third type of behavior with which Ettlinger has been concerned involves the matching of equivalent stimuli between sensory modalities. In experiments investigating this ability, the subject experiences an object through one sense alone and is then asked to identify the object when it is presented for inspection through a second single channel. The subject may, for example, first taste the object and then be required to select the substance from a group solely on the basis of its visual appearance.

In summarizing the experimental findings, Ettlinger (1967) concludes that "cross-modal transfer of a specific discrimination habit only occurs when language can be utilized" (p. 59). On the other hand, the research suggests that the cross-modal transfer of behavioral tendencies, or the ability to match across sensory modalities, may occur with or without verbalization.

Ettlinger suggests that the processing of sensory information may occur at two levels, and he proposes two mechanisms. The first, a unimodal system, involves a separate neural system for each sensory modality. Each modal system is responsible for the recognition of those sensory attributes relative to its particular function. All systems are related through a higher center, which receives the identifications (specific sensory perceptions) from each subsystem and uses them to evoke the total perception and its associated name or symbol value.

The second mechanism involves a cross-modal process that utilizes a single neural system concerned with those forms of behavior involving a general principle that holds true regardless of the particular type of sensory input.

What relevance do these suggestions have to our understanding of visual and auditory communication? If we follow Ettlinger's proposed model, we would envisage auditory and visual information being analyzed by the neural centers of each appropriate channel. The process of checking information received against the predictions made takes place first within each sensory channel. The individual auditory, visual, or tactile perceptions are then conveyed to a higher neural system, where each is evaluated in the light of the others. This concept is supported by the findings of Miller and Nicely (1955) who, in an analysis of perceptual confusions among some English consonants, found that "the place of articulation, which was hardest to hear correctly in our tests, is the easiest to see on the talkers' lips. The other features are hard to see but easy to hear" (p. 352). This is another instance of the redundancy of intersensory information that the system of human communication has evolved. It is on the basis of these integrated data constituting total perception that the meaning, concept, or word value is assigned.

To incorporate the fact that interconnecting neural fibers exist between the auditory and visual systems at several levels below the cortex, we might suggest that the intersensory comparisons are made at several stages below the level of perception. This would involve the cross-modal matching of equivalent stimuli, which is essential to the interchannel trial-and-check stage that we discussed in Chapter 5. This would be equivalent to a situation in which two students are attempting to solve a common problem. Although the students are using different approaches and the numerical results they obtain are different, they are able to compare their equivalent findings at several stages of the analysis in order to reassure themselves that they are on the right track.

We know that the early stages of learning to communicate involve the acquisition of certain fundamental principles by which sensory data are processed. We might interpret the cross-modal principle as suggesting that a basic processing rule learned with reference to a particular type of sensory information, whether it is visual or auditory, may be generalized to the processing of equivalent data in another channel. It has been shown that this type of behavior is not necessarily dependent upon verbalization and may, therefore, constitute the subconscious learning of communication principles that occurs in the early developmental stages of language learning. Nitchie (undated), in his discussion of visual-communication training, devotes a considerable amount of attention to what he refers to as the "mental factor." Among the labels Nitchie uses for the behavioral characteristics that he includes in this category are such terms as synthetic power, intuitive power, and quickness and alertness of mind. Perhaps the possession of these attributes by an individual is a manifestation of a highly developed system of evaluating sensory information at preperceptual levels. It is known that human subjects are capable of improving their performance on repeated problems without being able to transfer anything specific about the stimuli involved in one problem to subsequent problems. We can attribute this to the establishment of a perceptual set. The improvement in the ability to learn a discrimination task may then be transferred across sensory modalities to a second channel. For this reason, we may be justified in suggesting that analyzing visual and auditory information represents dealing with two aspects of the same behavior. Two levels of information processing appear to be involved: (1) the conscious or perceptual level (cognitive awareness), in which the student and the instructor are dealing with verbalized principles; and (2) a preperceptual level (subconscious), where certain aspects of information processing are carried out automatically without reference to consciousness (Bocca & Calearo, 1963). At present we know very little of the mechanisms involved at this level of analysis, though there is an increasing amount of evidence available to indicate that it takes place. It is this level that is involved in the implementation of discrimination habits. Some discrimination habits may have been consciously learned and then delegated to the habitual level; others are still beyond the awareness of the most distinguished psychologist or linguist. We cannot help being impressed by the realization of how highly skilled in utilizing psycholinguistic principles the human brain is—most of which we are unaware of or consciously know little about.

Auditory-Visual Integration for Speech Perception by Normal-Hearing Subjects

No doubt, future research will eventually clarify our understanding of the processes involved in intersensory interaction during communication and learning. Meanwhile we do have at our disposal a significant amount of current theory and research findings. It appears from the studies of the performance of normal and hearing-impaired individuals that when acoustic information is distorted, considerable improvement in comprehension usually occurs when visual-speech cues are available to supplement the auditory information. It is important that this statement be recognized as a generalization, for there are exceptions that merit serious consideration. Let us first examine the general findings.

One of the earliest investigations of the contribution made by vision to the recognition of speech by normal-hearing subjects was conducted by O'Neill (1954). O'Neill studied thirty-two undergraduate students with normal hearing and no special experience in visual-communication skills. The students were grouped into four listening panels, each of which observed the test items spoken by three speakers from a distance of 8 feet. The materials used consisted of seven vowels, each combined with the initial consonant "p," seven consonants, each preceding the vowel "i," and twenty-four word lists of twenty-one items each. The total test items were presented at four signal-to-noise ratios. This served to progressively reduce the amount of information available in the auditory channel. The test items were presented through the visual channel alone, through the auditory channel alone, and through both channels simultaneously. The results indicated that speech-reading facilitated communication under all conditions. However, the contribution of speech-reading progressively increased as the signal-to-noise ratio decreased—that is, deteriorated. As might be expected, no relationship was found between the visibility of the various phonemes and the intensity at which they were produced. O'Neill provides a detailed breakdown of comparative recognition scores for each of the vowels and phonemes when visual and auditory stimuli were simultaneously presented and when auditory results were superior to the unimodal.

In his conclusions, O'Neill states, "If the auditory channel of communication is employed alone, a high level of noise tends to make communication more difficult. When the visual channel supplements the auditory channel, there is an increase in the understandability of the vowels, consonants, words, and phrases that are transmitted" (p. 439).

Sumby and Pollack (1954) utilized the information found by O'Neill to examine the contribution that the visual aspects of speech make to intelligibility. The speech sample consisted of bisyllabic spondees, monosyllabic words, and trisyllabic phrases, which were presented to 129 subjects with normal hearing and no formal training in visual-communication skills. The materials were also presented through the two unimodal channels of vision and hearing, and then through the bimodal channel of vision and hearing combined. The amount of information available in the auditory channel was varied by the manipulation of a speech-signal intensity against a constant noise level. The results of this experiment confirmed O'Neill's findings, which indicated that as the signal-to-noise ratio is decreased, the visual contribution to intelligibility increases.

Erber (1969) also demonstrated increasing utilization of visual cues by subjects as speech-to-noise ratio deteriorates. Using five normal-hearing adults, Erber compared the auditory and auditory-visual scores obtained for 250 two-syllable (spondaic, equal-stress) words. The evidence is clearly presented in Figure 7.1. Erber observed that as the listening conditions deteriorated, his subjects showed increasing between-subject variability in scores obtained. He attributes this to variable lip-reading skill, a factor that becomes more and more evident as emphasis is shifted to the visual channel as a source of information.

Binnie, Montgomery, and Jackson (1974) used normal-hearing subjects in their study of the role of vision in speech perception. Using broad-band masking, Binnie et al. progressively reduced the signal-to-noise ratio until the noise was 12 dB greater than the speech. At this level the only acoustic features discernible in the speech signal were voicing and nasality. Yet, despite the severe acoustic distortion, with a combined auditory-visual presentation, the subjects were able to correctly identify 83 percent of the consonants presented, compared to only 34 percent by hearing alone.

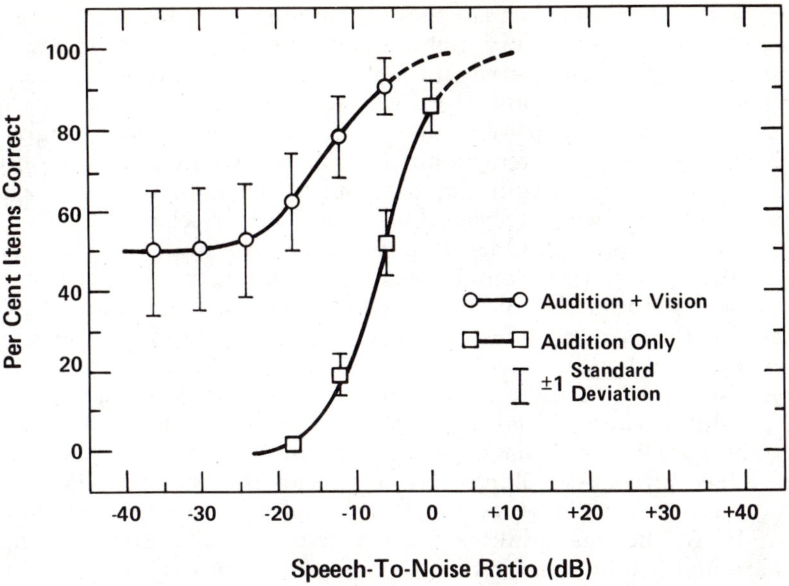

FIGURE 7.1 Auditory and auditory-visual recognition of 250 spondaic words in broad-band noise by five adults with normal hearing (Erber, 1969).

In 1977 two British psychologists reported on a research project that clearly demonstrated the interactive nature of the auditory and visual cues to speech articulation (McGurk & MacDonald, 1977). The results strongly suggest that in normal-hearing subjects, the integration of the two sets of data is achieved through the mediation of linguistic rules. These researchers used a series of videotape recordings on which the auditory speech-sound characteristics of a given consonant in a consonant-vowel syllable were dubbed onto the revealing visual characteristics of a different consonant. For example, the subject would observe a speaker saying the double syllable ba-ba but would be presented with the auditory stimulus ga-ga, and vice versa. A total of 103 subjects were asked to view four such presentations. Each utterance was repeated once per second with a half-second interval between presentations. The following consonant-vowel combinations were used:

ba-ba/ga-ga
ga-ga/ba-ba
pa-pa/ka-ka
ka-ka/pa-pa

The subjects consisted of twenty-one children aged 3 to 4 years, twenty-eight children aged 7 to 8 years, and fifty-four adults aged 18 to 40 years. Each subject was tested individually under two conditions: (1) auditory-visual, in which the subject watched the film and repeated what he or she heard the speaker say; and (2) auditory only, in which the subject only listed to the auditory stimulus and repeated what was heard. Responses were scored correct when the subject accurately repeated the *auditory* component of the audio-visual recording.

The results obtained were unexpected, intriguing, and strongly indicative of intersensory interaction. In the auditory-only presentation utterances were identified with almost complete accuracy. However, when the visual stimulus, which consisted of the articulatory characteristics of a different consonant, was added to the auditory stimulus, a dramatic decline occurred in correct identification. The stimulus that the subjects reported *hearing* under the auditory condition was changed simply by the addition of the incompatible visual cues. Note that although this effect was experienced both by children and adults, the influence of the incompatible visual cues on auditory perception was markedly less in children than in adults. The children in the study appear, therefore, to be processing the auditory information of speech with relatively little reference to its visible aspects. As children grow it appears that they give increasing weight to the visible components of speech under the conditions tested in this study. By the time adulthood is reached, the visible speech components are highly influential in constraining perceptions. The effect of the incompatible visual cues, which varied according to the consonant-vowel syllables used, was most noticeable in the ba-ba (auditory)/ga-ga (visual) and pa-pa (auditory)/ka-ka (visual) combinations. When the auditory-visual conflict resulted in an incorrect identification of the auditory stimulus, the subject seldom simply perceived the syllable revealed by the visual component. The incidence of subjects resolving the problem in this manner was very low for all sound combinations, and nonexistent in half. Instead, when forced to resolve the auditory-visual incongruity, the subjects restructured the information, either by fusing the stimuli to produce the perception of an element present in neither, or by combining elements from each of the two stimuli to result in a compromise. Fusion is evident in the perception that occurred when visual cues for /ga/ were synchronized with the acoustic stimulus /ba/, producing the auditory perception of /da/. Similarly, acoustic /pa-pa/ fused with visual /ka-ka/ to produce the auditory perception /ta/. Fusion responses were almost exclusively confined to the just-described two syllable combinations. Among adults they occurred 98 percent of the time for ba/ga and 81 percent for pa/ka. These perceptual illusions were also experienced by a large proportion of the children tested. The combination of auditory and visual speech cues to resolve incongruity occurred only in the stimulus combinations ga (auditory)/ba (visual) and ka (auditory)/pa (visual). The resultant auditory perceptions were most commonly reported as /gabga/ and /bagba/ to the ga/pa combination, and /kapka/ and /pakpa/ to the ka/pa combination. Once again adults manifest a high incidence of such perceptual illusions whereas children exhibit a much lower incidence. Fusion and combination accounted for almost all the adult response patterns. Among the 3- to 5-year-old children most responses were either explained by a combination process or fell into a category the authors identified as *other*—that is, resolutions that could not be explained by fusion or combination strategies. In discussing the data, McGurk and MacDonald (1977) state:

The burden of our observations, then, is that when conflicting speech inputs are simultaneously presented to auditory and visual modalities, the subjective experience is not of auditory-visual conflict, nor is the outcome the domination of one modality by the other; at all ages tested, but increasingly so with increasing age, the frequent and significant outcome is an interaction at some level of processing, between auditory and visually perceived information resulting in the experience of an auditory illusion.

It would appear, therefore, that the influence of observed visible characteristics of speech on auditory perception increases as a child grows older. In the preschool years this influence, as shown in the test results, is almost nonexistent. By 7 to 8 years of age, it has begun to be evident and continues to increase. McGurk and MacDonald did not investigate the age at which the maximum effect evidenced by the adult group is reached.

The most obvious possible explanation of the process underlying this intersensory interaction in speech-sound perception is that it is related to linguistic sophistication. It seems plausible that the conflicting sensory information from the two sensory modalities is achieved by combining and synthesizing the data to produce a best-fit solution. This, the authors hypothesize, may be achieved by a place-manner analysis. The manner of articulation (voicing, nasality, plosion, and so on) is derived from acoustic information, while place information (bilabial, labiodental, lingual-alveolar, and so on) is derived from the visual constraints. The authors report that these findings lend considerable support to the validity of the place-manner hypothesis, as an explanation of the illusion effects previously described.

In each of the studies already mentioned, the variation in the amount of information available in the auditory channel was achieved through manipulation of the signal-to-noise ratio. By contrast, Sanders and Goodrich (1971) manipulated the amount of information in the auditory channel by subjecting the speech material to four conditions of frequency distortion. Using phonetically balanced word lists drawn from the CID Auditory Test W-22, these authors used three different modes to present normal-hearing students with the test items—vision, audition, and vision and audition together. Comparisons were made of the scores obtained under these three modes for four conditions of frequency filtering. The filtered conditions were:

1. A wide bandwidth passing frequencies from 100 to 3000 Hz
2. A low-pass filter passing only frequencies below 500 Hz
3. A high-pass filter passing only frequencies above 200 Hz
4. A 15,000-cycle bandwidth passing frequencies between 500 and 2000 Hz

The results indicated that the mode of presentation (audition, vision, audition and vision combined), the filter frequency bandwidth, and the interaction of the mode of presentation and the frequency filter bandwidth all affected the subject's discrimination of the speech sample. It was found that, by audition only, the low-pass filter most seriously affected speech discrimination. Both the 1500-Hz band pass and the high-pass filter reduced auditory discrimination performance, but not to any serious extent. The effect of the bimodal presentation was to increase the discrimination performance for all frequency conditions. The increase was greatest for the low-pass condition, which produced the greatest reduction of information in the auditory channel. This is clearly illustrated by the mean and median percentage values for each of the three conditions. By vision alone, the mean percentage of words correctly identified by the twenty subjects was 12.6 percent, the median 11.8 percent; by hearing alone, the mean and median values were each 24 percent; and for the bimodal presentation of vision and hearing, the mean value was 78 percent with a median of 79 percent.

All of the studies reviewed so far used subjects with normal hearing. For this population it is apparent that varying degrees of familiarity with the visual aspects of speech are acquired without training. It is also evident, from the study by Erber (1969) and from the work by Sanders and Goodrich (1971), that the degree of proficiency in visible speech recognition varies considerably among normals. It should be noted, however, that in auditory-visual tasks, this only becomes apparent when the normal-hearing subjects experience high levels of degradation of the acoustic stimulus.

Auditory-Visual Integration for Speech Perception by Hearing-Impaired Subjects

The studies we have examined indicate that among subjects with normal hearing, under unfavorable signal-to-noise ratios, and for several conditions of frequency distortion, the addition of vision to hearing results in better speech recognition than is possible by hearing alone. Furthermore, under the conditions of dual sensory presentation, the tolerance for deterioration of the signal-to-noise ratio is some 5 to 10 dB better than by audition alone (Erber, 1975).

The questions that now arise are: What effect does impairment of hearing have on the ability to synthesize auditory and visual speech cues? Is the process enhanced as a result of the hearing deficit? Does the performance on visual tasks increase with increased hearing impairment in a natural compensatory manner?

A number of studies have sought to investigate the performance of persons with hearing impairment on auditory-visual speech perception tasks. Hudgins (1951) reported on the discrimination performance of a group of children, aged from 10 years, 8 months to 16 years, 2 months, with average hearing losses in speech frequencies ranging from 82 to 108 decibels. The speech sample was presented visually, auditorily, and visually and auditorily combined. The results for each modality are shown in Table 7.1. Note that only four of the fourteen subjects obtained any score at all through the auditory channel alone, and that only one of these received any significant degree of information. Yet a comparison of the visual and the combined visual-auditory presentation clearly indicates that the bimodal condition provides considerably more information than the unimodal channel of vision, even though the scores obtained for hearing alone suggest that the auditory pathway contributes no information. Furthermore, a comparison of the additive scores for lip-reading and audition indicates that for all but three subjects the integrated score is greater than can be accounted for by a simple additive function.

TABLE 7.1 The Average Score of a Group of Profoundly Deaf Pupils Obtained from Tests of Lip-reading, Hearing, and Lip-reading and Hearing (after Hudgins, 1951)

	Average Hearing Loss in Decibels					
Pupils	*Left Ear*	*Right Ear*	*Age*	*Lip-reading*	*Hearing*	*Both*
1	98	95	13–8	58	7	70
2	78	92	14–0	42	0	53
3	87	88	12–7	52	41	72
4	77	78	14–0	40	0	40
5	82	83	11–9	30	0	44
6	108	105	14–8	44	7	74
7	97	97	15–0	40	0	42
8	103	105	14–10	30	0	45
9	78	100	16–2	40	0	66
10	75	78	15–7	36	10	76
11	88	92	11–4	30	0	42
12	93	95	12–3	32	0	76
13	83	87	11–7	37	0	50
14	98	95	10–8	40	0	40

Kelly (1967) reported the scores obtained by six hearing-impaired children required to discriminate and identify spoken words and spoken names of letters of the alphabet. The test items were presented through vision, audition, and vision and audition combined. A comparison of the results is presented in Table 7.2. Note first of all that the scores obtained for the recognition of the names of letters of the alphabet are considerably higher than those for word recognition. This is understandable in light of our discussion of redundancy. The choices available to the subject are limited by the letters of the alphabet. Note also that under both conditions, vision contributed less information than audition. This we would expect, since the visible aspects of speech contain less information than the auditory. Once again, bimodal presentation of speech material conveys more information than either the visual or auditory channel alone. This finding is further supported by Prall (1957), who tested hearing-impaired children in a school for the deaf (Table 7.3). The results indicate that a subject's speech-discrimination performance is substantially enhanced when visual cues are presented together with the acoustic signal.

As part of a larger investigation, the speech-discrimination performance of fifty primary-school-aged children with hearing losses ranging from 55 to 110 dBs was studied by Sanders (1961). The subjects were grouped into four hearing-loss categories: (A) 55 to 64 dB; (B) 65 to 74 dB; (C) 75 to 94 dB; and (D) 95 to 119 dB. Test materials consisted of a muliple-choice picture identification task. Four conditions of presentation were used: (1) aided hearing without visual cues; (2) unaided hearing with visual cues; (3) aided hearing (personal hearing aid) without visual cues; and (4) aided hearing with visual cues. A comparison was made of the group mean scores for each category under each condition. The re-

TABLE 7.2 Visual, Auditory, and Audiovisual Communication of Hard-of-Hearing Subjects (after Kelly, 1967)

	Subject	*Words*	*Letters*
VISUAL ONLY	A	30	65
	B	21	63
	C	33	60
	D	52	75
	E	10	45
	F	50	78
MEAN PERCENT		32.67%	64.33%
AUDITORY ONLY	A	88	98
	B	81	86
	C	56	73
	D	38	77
	E	25	30
	F	19	57
MEAN PERCENT		51.17%	70.17%
AUDIOVISUAL	A	93	100
	B	93	96
	C	82	100
	D	75	96
	E	69	63
	F	88	94
MEAN PERCENT		83.33%	91.50%

sults are shown in Table 7.4. These indicate that the amount of information that the children were able to obtain from the auditory channel without amplification decreased as the hearing loss increased. For hearing losses in excess of 75 dBs, the auditory channel alone was insufficient to permit the recognition of the names of familiar objects on the basis of the auditory cues alone, even when the choice of alternatives was limited to six items. The benefit derived from amplification was also shown to be in an inverse relationship to the severity of the hearing impairment. In other words, even with amplification, the amount of information that the auditory channel is capable of contributing to speech discrimination becomes progressively less as the amount of residual hearing decreases.

In all categories of hearing loss the number of items correctly discriminated without amplification increased when visual cues were made available. The least increase occurred in children with the greatest amount of residual hearing. The possible explanation for this may be that the children in this group had sufficient residual hearing to obviate the need for heavy dependence upon the visual cues of speech and were, therefore, less skilled in speech-reading. This assumption is supported by the score of 79 percent that the children in this category obtained for amplified speech without visual cues.

TABLE 7.3 Average Scores for PBK Lists: Lip-Reading Alone, Hearing Aid Alone, and Lip-Reading and Hearing with Hearing Aid Combined (after Prall, 1957)

Pupils	*Better Ear Average in dB*	*Grade*	*Lip-reading Alone*	*Hearing and Alone*	*Lip-reading and Hearing Aid Combined*
P.A.	70	5	28	0	33
M.B.	63	6	27	10	41
L.C.	57	5	30	27	47
J.C.	68	8	24	3	44
C.H.	52*	2	30	26	43
J.H.	45	5	29	22	47
C.L.	63	7	27	16	45
M.T.	57	8	27	27	45

*Better ear average here represents loss in left ear only. Average loss in right ear for the three frequencies is 70 dB. Pupil uses aid in right ear.

TABLE 7.4 Mean Percentage Discrimination Scores for Hearing Loss against Conditions of Presentation for Fifty Primary School Children (after Sanders, 1961)

Hearing Loss in Decibels	*Unaided with No Speech-reading (Percent)*	*Unaided with Speech-reading (Percent)*	*Aided, but with No Speech-reading (Percent)*	*Aided with Speech-reading (Percent)*
A 55–64	41	60	79	93
B 65–74	21	74	55	90
C 75–94	0	74	36	88
D 96–110	0	78	6	79

Under the most favorable communication condition (amplified speech with visual cues), the children in hearing-loss categories A, B, and C obtained significantly better discrimination scores than under any other condition. The children in category D, however, were clearly so dependent upon the visual channel as the major source of information and derived so much from visual cues (78 percent by vision alone) that the amplified speech signal contributed no significant additional information.

Feature Identification in Visual/Audiovisual Perception

Since the beginning of the 1970s increasing interest has been directed toward experimental research designed to identify which features of speech sounds are enhanced by the addition of visual to auditory information. In 1972 Erber studied the ability of children with normal hearing and children with severe (70 to 95 dB, ANSI) and profound (greater than 95 dB,

ANSI) hearing deficits to discriminate between eight common consonants (/p, b, m, t, d, n, k, g/) when presented between /a/ vowels (for example, /apa/). When presented with only visual cues, all groups of children readily discriminated *between* place of articulation (for example, bilabial, alveolar, velar), but they were unable to discriminate between sounds *within* a place category (for example, /t, d, n/). When only auditory cues were presented, normal-hearing subjects had almost perfect consonant recognition. The severely hearing-impaired children accurately distinguished between voiced and voiceless stops and nasal consonants. The profoundly hearing-impaired group, by contrast, performed extremely poorly, even evidencing difficulty in identifying voicing and nasality cues. When visual cues were added, the severely hearing-impaired groups approximated the nearly perfect scores of the normal-hearing group. Bimodal presentation of vision and audition to the profoundly impaired group, however, failed to significantly improve the scores obtained by vision.

Binnie, Montgomery, and Bodle (1974) also investigated feature recognition in terms of perceptual confusions by studying the performance of ten normal-hearing adults. The speech recognition task involved 320 syllable productions obtained by combining sixteen English consonants with the vowel /a/. Three signal-to-noise ratios (−18 dB, −12 dB, and −6 dB) were used for auditory and auditory-visual presentations. Presentations were also made under auditory-in-quiet and visual-only conditions. Results of the feature analysis of perceptual confusions led the authors to conclude the features most resistant to masking by the side-band noise used were voicing and nasality. Place-of-articulation cues were the most severely affected features. Normal-hearing subjects consistently classified consonants into discrete homophenous (look-alike) groups on the basis of where they were articulated (for example, bilabials, alveolars, and so on). The study clearly demonstrated that vision contributed most to reducing perceptual confusions under the condition of audiovisual presentation at poor S/N ratios. The resolution of the discrimination error was most apparent when the auditory confusion was between phonemes that differed by place of articulation.

Walden, Prosek, and Worthington (1975) followed up on the work of Binnie et al. (1974). They also sought to describe the contribution of visual cues to audiovisual recognition of distinctive features. Their study, however, was conducted with hearing-impaired adults. Their subjects were classified into five groups according to their auditory-discrimination scores on a 400-item auditory-only test. The subjects were asked to identify the consonant in a consonant-vowel syllable (for example, /pa/) when presented in an auditory-only and then in an auditory-visual mode. The results revealed that visual cues enhanced recognition of place of articulation, frication, and duration features of auditorily presented consonant-vowel syllables. However, vision did little to help these hearing-impaired adults identify intervowel glide and voicing features. Most of the help afforded by vision was attributed to additional information that it provides by supplying contrasting cues to resolve auditory confusion. That is, sounds that are auditorily difficult to distinguish by a hard-of-hearing person are more easily identified if characteristic visible articulatory differences are observable.

AUDITORY-VISUAL INTEGRATION AS A FUNCTION OF SEVERITY OF HEARING IMPAIRMENT

It is understandable that the major factor influencing the role of audition in auditory-visual perception of speech is the degree of hearing impairment. Erber has illustrated well the difference that the severity of hearing impairment exerts on the usefulness of bisensory integration. His comparison of the results of a number of researchers (Erber, 1975), reproduced in Figures 7.2 and 7.3, demonstrates that even though simultaneous reception of auditory and visual cues is significantly beneficial to severely hearing-impaired children, it provides little improvement over the performance of profoundly deaf children using visual (lip-reading) cues alone. For children with moderate to severe hearing deficiencies, the auditory channel apparently conveys valuable constraining cues in speech perception. This is evidenced by the improvement (19 to 28 percent) that occurs when hearing is added to vision. By contrast, observation of the performance of children who are profoundly hearing impaired reveals that they derive far fewer additional constraint cues from the auditory signal. When audition is added to vision, these children's recognition of the test words is not markedly improved (1 to 15 percent). Similarly, if a

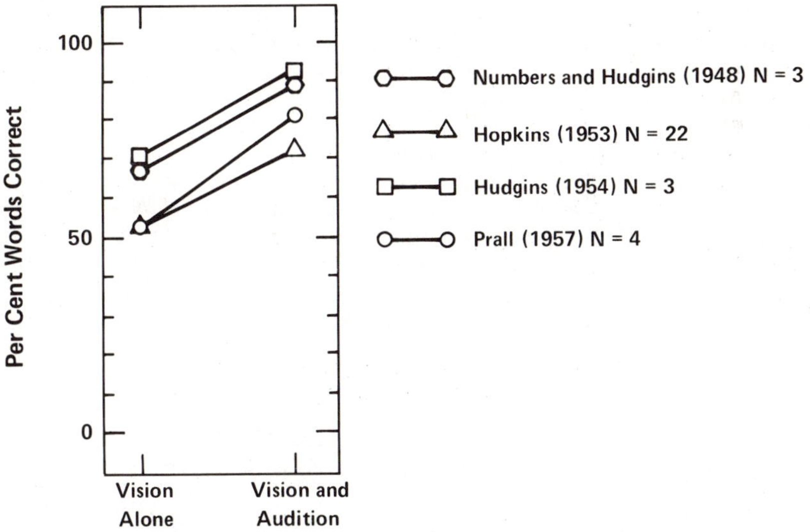

FIGURE 7.2 Mean recognition of spoken words by severely hearing-impaired children through vision (lipreading) and through vision plus audition (Erber, 1975).

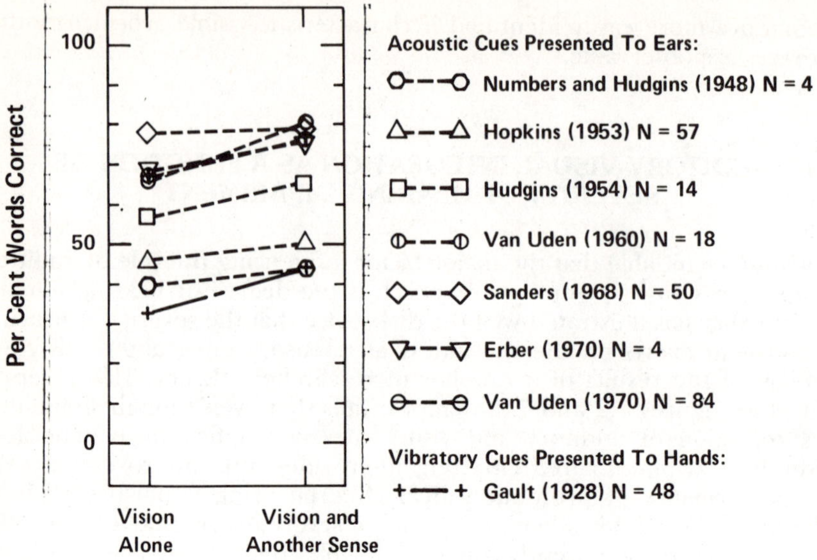

FIGURE 7.3 Mean recognition of spoken words by profoundly deaf children through vision alone and through vision plus another sensory system (Erber, 1975).

hearing-impaired subject scores very high on the auditory-alone presentation, little improvement can be expected when vision is added because the subject is already functioning near maximal level. In Erber's (1974) words, "The important distinction is whether the child receives acoustic information through a hearing aid that complements or only supplements the cues that are available to him through lipreading" (p. 179). Sherrick (1974) reaches the same conclusion:

> *. . . when both residual hearing and lipreading are available to the severely impaired child, he may do reasonably well on a communication task. In fact this group of children could carry on a conversation without too much difficulty. This is not true of the profoundly deaf group. When provided with acoustic information alone, they do not have the ability to classify on the basis of low-frequency voicing and nasality cues, and their errors appear to be quite random.*
>
> *Also when visual and acoustic cues are combined, these children do no better than under the visual-only condition: that is, they are able to make little use of the acoustic cues* (p. 59).

AUDITORY-VISUAL INTEGRATION AS A FUNCTION OF LINGUISTIC CONTEXT

Almost all the work in the assessment of auditory-visual perception has involved the use of syllable or word recognition. We know from our discussion of linguistic constraints that perception of spoken language by normal-hearing persons is heavily dependent on the ability of the listener to capitalize on these rules in order to make predictions. This phenomenon was demonstrated by Miller, Heise, and Lichten (1951), who showed that normal-hearing subjects recognized key words presented against a noise background far more easily when the word was in a sentence than when it was presented in isolation. We also saw evidence of the effect of contextual cues on lip-reading. Unfortunately most studies of auditory-visual perception by hearing-impaired persons have used word recognition as the test measure. This is not surprising. It is difficult to construct sentence tests that provide valid diagnostic information because so many variables are involved and scoring procedures are difficult. However, a few studies in which sentence discrimination was used have been reported. Craig (1964) studied the ability of severely and profoundly deaf children to recognize a single set of sentences presented visually and audiovisually. The results showed that a bimodal (hearing and vision) presentation was, on the average, 5.0 to 8.5 percent superior to presentation by vision alone. Dodds and Harford (1968) used the Utley Lip Reading Sentence Test to provide supplementary information about the benefit derived by a client from a hearing aid. They compared scores with and without visual cues to determine how much lip-reading was improved by amplification. They found that, in general, bimodal was superior to unimodal presentation for subjects with usable residual hearing. Similar findings were obtained in a later study by Ewertson, Neilsen, and Neilsen (1970). In an unpublished study reported by Erber (1975), Gammel (1974) assessed the comprehension of a group of profoundly deaf children who viewed a videotaped reading of a paragraph with and without the audio signal. Gammel found the bimodal presentation to be only 3 percent better than the vision-only presentation.

The factors involved in auditory-visual perception of speech are far more complex than those involved in either auditory or visual speech perception alone. Yet this information is of particular importance to the audiologist and teacher-clinician, for it affects both hearing-aid assessment practices and rehabilitation-teaching procedures. In considering the studies previously reviewed, it appears that although the overwhelming body of evidence supports the claim that audition and vision combined result in speech identification superior to that obtained by vision alone, the amount of improvement varied considerably among subjects and among study reports. Also of note is the significant difference in the auditory-visual speech discrimination of severely and profoundly hearing-impaired children; the latter group derived very limited improvement from the addition of audition to vision. Noticeably absent from the studies reviewed is information pertaining to the effect on a learning task of combining auditory and visual information.

AUDITORY-VISUAL INTEGRATION IN LEARNING

All of the studies reviewed so far in this section have been concerned with the role of bimodal reception of speech on recognition or discrimination. A few researchers, stimulated by the work of John Gaeth (1960, 1963,

1966) at Wayne State University, Detroit, have conducted studies of verbal and nonverbal learning in hearing-impaired children. Gaeth attempted to produce evidence concerning the relative effectiveness of unimodal and bimodal presentation of communication and material to be learned. In a paper presented to the National Symposium on Deafness in Childhood held at Vanderbilt University in 1966, Gaeth reviewed a series of experiments that he conducted between 1957 and 1966. He defined the aim of these experiments: "to investigate bimodal versus unimodal methods of presentation of material to be learned." The results seemed to provide evidence contrary to our basic assumption that bimodal presentation provides a greater degree of information than unimodal.

In his studies, Gaeth used the method of paired-associate models, requiring the individual to respond with the second of a pair of stimuli when presented with the first. He used six to ten paired items, which consisted of simple words, nonsense trigrams, nonsense drawings, and novel noises. The presentation was made auditorily, visually, or audiovisually, with the criterion for learning being either the number of trials taken to reach a certain level of performance, or the number of correct responses obtained for a specified number of trials. In addition to controlling the method of presentation, Gaeth also controlled the method of learning and practicing, providing a total of nine different conditions represented by nine groups of children.

Gaeth provides the learning curves for ninety fourth-grade children divided into three equal groups. The three groups learned by the three methods of presentation. The results showed no difference in the learning curves, regardless of the methods of presentation; that is, the combined auditory-visual presentation was not superior to that achieved by either of the unimodal methods.

When the material was presented to a group of hard-of-hearing children with losses of between 16 and 30 dbs ASA, no significant difference was found between the rate of learning attained through the audiovisual and that attained through the visual presentation. However, a significant deficiency in learning was demonstrated when the material was presented through the auditory channel alone. (These same findings were obtained for two other groups of children with hearing losses ranging from 31 to 45 decibels and from 45 to 60 decibels in the better ear.)

The resultant learning curves for a group of children whose hearing losses fell within the range of 61 to 75 decibels indicated that the combined presentation actually produced a poorer learning rate than the visual presentation alone. In reacting to these findings, Gaeth (1967) comments:

A reasonable inference seems to be that for the groups with the milder hearing loss the auditory material was meaningful or at least intelligible to the children and thus did not interfere with the performance, though it did not help it either. In the case of the children with the hearing losses between 61–75 dB, the material was not intelligible and either confused the tasks somewhat or distracted the children from functioning as efficiently as they did visually (p. 284).

Gaeth goes on to state:

The first major experiment showed repeatedly that the combined method of presentation was not superior to the visual method with hard-of-hearing children, nor superior to either the visual or the auditory with children with normal hearing. Secondarily, it highlighted the fact that hard-of-hearing children, in regular schools, were not performing auditorily as well as might have been expected from their audiograms or from their speech discrimination scores (p. 285).

Using large numbers of children with normal hearing, Gaeth also conducted experiments of a similar nature with the same basic results, using as the items to be learned three-syllable nouns, nonsense syllables, and a set of nonverbal, nonmeaningful visual symbols. Gaeth concluded:

1. The combined auditory-visual presentation of simple words, pronounceable nonsense syllables, or nonmeaningful symbols and noises does not result in improvement of performance over single modality presentations.

2. When there is a difference in performance between the auditory and visual method of presentation, the combined presentation is never better than the better of the two unimodal presentations, although it may occasionally be slightly poorer but usually not significantly so.

3. When different materials are presented via the auditory and visual channels (e.g., the visual symbols with the pronounced syllables), the performance with the combined presentation tends to be between the two individual performances when they are significantly different, or to approximate the better condition when the two unimodal conditions do not deviate markedly (p. 289).

Gaeth's findings cannot be treated lightly for they raise serious questions concerning the effects of different approaches to teaching speech and language to hearing-impaired children. Gaeth suggests that when faced with a new learning situation, the child initially uses only one modality—the one with the highest degree of redundancy—and that a multisensory presentation constitutes two learning tasks that must be separated in order for unisensory learning to occur. Certain factors, however, must be considered when examining Gaeth's results.

1. The bulk of the data presented were obtained from children with normal hearing, although a small sample testing of hearing-impaired children did produce the same results.

2. The visual stimuli presented were printed words. They were not visual correlates of the articulatory production of the acoustic signal of speech. Reading and speech-reading are not similar tasks. The difference is an important one for it means that in the Gaeth study the child was required to process two sets of equivalent information by two different types of skill (Conrad, 1972; Sanders, 1977). Active theories of speech perception have suggested that we perceive speech by reference to an internally generated model, frequently that of neuromotor articulatory commands. If this is true, the visual image first would have to be translated into spoken language by the child before it could be integrated with the speech stimulus. It would be reasonable, under such circumstances, that a combined presentation would not prove superior to the best unimodal performance and would, in fact, prove inferior since it represents a more difficult task.

3. As Berg (1976) points out, Gaeth's experiments limited the amount of learning tasks. Berg hypothesizes that the hearing-impaired subjects in the

Gaeth study might have improved their auditory-learning performance significantly with increased experience. This hypothesis is lent support by Prescott's work (1971, 1972, 1974; Prescott & Turtz, 1975), which Berg discusses at some length (Berg, 1976). Prescott found that children's auditory-learning rates were inversely related to the severity of the hearing impairment, and that some with profound losses showed a long period of no progress before making a dramatic improvement.

Pollack (1970) has been a strong advocate of a unisensory (auditory) approach to the training of hearing-impaired infants. She reviews a number of research studies that support the view that simultaneous presentation of auditory and visual cues to speech may impede the learning of spoken language by the child in two ways. Pollack reasons that by being provided with visual and auditory cues to speech, the child develops an overdependency upon the unimpaired visual pathway at the expense of the impaired auditory system. Thus auditory processing is not developed to optimal capacity. Pollack also maintains that simultaneous processing of auditory and visual speech information is a learning task that places too-heavy demands upon the young child's perceptual capabilities. This concurs with Gaeth's belief that the child blocks out the least useful modality in initial learning tasks.

Ling (1976) has also questioned the extent to which optimal development of unisensory perception can occur when training emphasizes a bi- or multisensory approach. Ling points out that children taught exclusively by a multisensory method generally fail to make optimal use of residual hearing (Babbidge, 1965). Moreover, when given intensive auditory-only training, these same children often make significant, even dramatic improvement in auditory reception of speech. To support this observation, Ling quotes his own experimental work, which demonstrated gains in reception of words (D. Ling, 1968), and the work of Agnes Ling in digit and word sequences (A.H. Ling, 1975, 1976). D. Ling refers to others who demonstrated similar results: Doehring and Ling (1971) found improved vowel recognition; Aston (1972) demonstrated improved discrimination of production and voicing of consonants; and Bennett (1973) showed improvement in recognition of voice-onset time consonants. D. Ling (1976) concludes:

> *These studies suggest that in order to develop ability to perceive many of the acoustic cues that are required for adequate auditory-visual speech reception, prior and parallel training in speech reception through audition alone should be provided* (p. 51).

BIMODAL PERCEPTION OF SPEECH THROUGH VISION AND TOUCH

Bimodal presentation of information to deaf subjects has not been confined to a combination of the visual and auditory channels. Pickett (1963) has reported on experiments involving the encoding of speech into vibrotactile information to provide a source complemental to the visual and the auditory channels. Pickett designed an instrument known as a *vocoder* to transpose the frequency vibrations of the spoken message signal into an equivalent vibratory signal, which is received by the student through the fingertips. Using the vocoder with deaf children, Pickett compared the discrimination of speech sounds through the tactile sense with discrimination of the same sounds through vision. He then compared scores obtained under the bimodal condition of touch and vision with those obtained through vision alone. He demonstrated that sufficient information can be presented by vibrotactile means to permit speech-sound discrimination. Furthermore, he showed that better discrimination can be obtained for some speech sounds using vibrotactile information than can be obtained through visual information. For example, using vibratory information one can distinguish between /m/ and /b/, which is not possible on the basis of differential visual cues. A comparison of the bimodal performance, using vision and touch, and the unimodal scores, obtained through vision alone, indicated that a greater amount of information was received through the bimodal presentation.

Suzuki, Kagami, and Takahashi (1968) also used a ten-channel filter to analyze the acoustic energy into bandwidths for transposition into vibratory energy fed to the fingertips. Children trained to use the vibrator were asked to discriminate among vowel sounds in isolation and in words. No improvement was shown in discrimination obtained through vision when tactile cues were added. Tactile cues were, however, successful in increasing the children's ability to discriminate among some homophenous (look-alike) words.

In an excellent review of multisensory speech perception D. Ling (1976) concludes that:

Although certain advantages appear to accrue from the use of tactile aids which employ several vibratory outputs, it is clear that the devices so far developed have not helped speech readers to learn to differentiate optimally between consonants (p. 53).

SIMULTANEOUS RECEPTION OF SIGNS AND SPEECH

It is not possible to conclude this chapter without briefly discussing the possible effects on speech perception of educating severely hearing-impaired children using a "total-communication" method. Total communication involves the simultaneous presentation of information through speech, lip-reading, finger-spelling, signing, and other manual forms of communication. It is not our concern to study this method or to contrast its effectiveness with the auditory-oral method. A review and critique of studies supporting total communication has been provided by Nix (1975). Our interest here lies only in the compatibility or incompatibility of spoken and manually encoded language.

There exist a considerable number of sign-language systems, each having different rules for forming signs and sentences (Wilbur, 1976). In addition, each system has its own dialect within a community of individuals using it. Thus the purity of any system of sign to which a child is exposed is contaminated by contact with the local dialect. Even systems that have been designed to parallel English sufficiently well to be used in conjunction with normal speech—for example, Manual English—do not exactly replicate the morphological structure of the language (Wilbur, 1976). This makes it difficult to accept the claim that the total-communication method of simultaneous presentation of oral and manual speech provides the child with two mutually supportive forms of information. Total communication necessitates that the child process a common concept encoded into two different linguistic systems and transmitted through two different channels (auditory and visual). This requires, at all levels up to and including the syntactic, that the information that is received be simultaneously processed according to two quite different sets of language rules. Concern has been expressed over the ability of a child to simultaneously process the visual and auditory correlates of articulated speech, in which the two stimuli derive from a single linguistic system and are common at the level of articulatory encoding. Gaeth's findings have proven that difficulty in bimodal processing exists when a child is asked to simultaneously process an auditory stimulus and a paired visual associate, even when the stimuli are spoken and written words. Total communication makes even more demands on the system because, as it is commonly used, the structural linguistic compatibility of what is being said and what is being signed is low.

It seems unlikely in view of all we have learned about speech perception that a child can simultaneously process oral and manual language. This, of course, is not to say that some children may not learn better by total communication than by a purely oral-auditory method. In such cases the child may well be processing the manual component only. If this contains more information than the child could derive from a limited auditory input then the child is likely to make more rapid progress through the processing of visual rather than auditory information.

REFERENCES

Aston, C. H., "Hearing Impaired Children's Discrimination of Filtered Speech," *Journal of Auditory Research, 12,* 1972, 162–167.

Babbidge, H., *Education of the Deaf. A Report to the Secretary of Health, Education and Welfare by His Advisory Committee on the Education of the Deaf.* Washington, D.C.: U.S. Government Printing Office, 1965.

Bennett, C. W., *Discrimination of Stop Consonants by Severely Hearing Impaired Children.* Unpublished doctoral dissertation, McGill University, 1973.

Berg, F., *Educational Audiology: Hearing and Speech Management.* New York: Grune & Stratton, Inc., 1976.

Binnie, C. A., A. A. Montgomery, and P. L. Jackson, "Auditory and Visual Contributions to the Perception of Consonants," *Journal of Speech and Hearing Research, 17,* 1974, 619–630.

Blank, M., and W. H. Bridger, "Cross-Modal Transfer in Nursery-School Children," *Journal of Comparative Physiological Psychology, 58,* 1964, 277–282.

Bocca, E., and C. Calearo, "Central Hearing Processes," in *Modern Developments in Audiology,* ed. J. Jerger. New York: Academic Press, Inc., 1963.

Brown, A. E., and H. K. Hopkins, "Interaction of the Auditory and Visual Sensory Modalities," *Journal of the Acoustical Society of America, 41,* 1968, 1–6.

Cole, M., S. L. Chorover, and G. M. Ettlinger, "Cross-Modal Transfer in Man," *Nature, 191,* 1961, 1225–1226.

Conrad, R., "Speech and Reading," in *Language by Eye and by Ear,* eds. J. F. Kavanagh and I. G. Mattingly, pp. 205–240. Cambridge, Mass.: M.I.T. Press, 1972.

Craig, W. H., "Effects of Preschool Training on the Development of Reading and Lipreading Skills of Deaf Children," *American Annals of the Deaf, 109,* 1964, 280–296.

Dodds, E., and E. Harford, "Application of a Lipreading Test in a Hearing Aid Evaluation," *Journal of Speech and Hearing Disorders, 33,* 1968, 167–173.

Doehring, D. G., and D. Ling, Programmed Instruction of Hearing Impaired Children in the Auditory Discrimination of Vowels," *Journal of Speech and Hearing Research, 14,* 1971, 746–754.

Erber, N. P., "Interaction of Audition and Vision in the Recognition of Oral Speech Stimuli," *Journal of Speech and Hearing Research, 12,* 1969, 423–425.

Erber, N. P., "Effects of Amplification and Illumination on the Reception of Speech by Profoundly Deaf Children." St. Louis, Missouri: Central Institute for the Deaf, 1970 (Unpublished report).

Erber, N. P., "Auditory, Visual, and Auditory-Visual Recognition of Consonants by Children with Normal and Impaired hearing," *Journal of Speech and Hearing Research, 15,* 1972, 413–422.

Erber, N. P., "Visual Perception of Speech by Deaf Children: Recent Developments and Continuing Needs," *Journal of Speech and Hearing Disorders, 39,* 1974, 178–185.

Erber, N. P., "Auditory-Visual Perception of Speech," *Journal of Speech and Hearing Disorders, 40,* 1975, 481–492.

Ettlinger, G., "Analysis of Cross-Modal Effects and Their Relationship to Language," in *Brain Mechanism Underlying Speech and Language,* ed. F. L. Darley, pp. 53–60. New York: Grune & Stratton, Inc., 1967.

Evans, E. R., and I. C. Whitfield, Classification of Unit Responses of the Auditory Cortex of the Unanesthetised and Unrestrained Cat," *Journal of Physiology, 171,* 1964, 476–493.

Ewertson, H. W., H. B. Neilsen, and S. Neilsen, "Audiovisual Speech Perception," *Acta Otolaryngol. Suppl., 263,* 1970, 229–230.

Gaeth, J., "Verbal Learning among Children with Reduced Auditory Acuity." *Office of Education Cooperative Research Project 289. Final Report.* Detroit: Wayne State University, 1960.

Gaeth, J., "Verbal and Non-Verbal Learning in Children Including Those with Hearing Loss," *Office of Education Cooperative Research Project 1001.* Detroit: Wayne State University, 1963.

Gaeth, J., "Verbal and Non-verbal Learning in Children Including Those with Hearing Loss. Part II," *Office of Education Cooperative Research Project 2007.* Detroit: Wayne State University, 1966.

Gaeth, J., "Learning with Visual and Audiovisual Presentations," in *National Symposium on Deafness in Childhood,* eds. M. Freeman and P. H. Ward, pp. 279–292. Nashville: Vanderbilt University Press, 1967.

Gammel, C., *Preliminary Development of a Connected Discourse Speech Reading Test.* Unpublished study, Central Institute for the Deaf, St. Louis, 1974.

Gebhardt, J. W., and G. H. Mowbray, "On Discriminating the Rate of Visual Flicker and Auditory Flutter," *American Journal of Psychology, 72,* 1959, 521–529.

Harris, J. D., *Some Relations Between Vision and Audition.* Springfield, Ill.: Charles C Thomas, Publisher, 1950.

Hopkins, L. A., "The Relationship between Degree of Deafness and Response to Acoustic Training", *Volta Review, 55,* 1953, 32–35.

Hudgins, C. V., "Problems of Speech Comprehension in Deaf Children," *The Nervous Child, 9,* 1951, 57–63.

Hudgins, C. V., "Auditory training: Its Possibilities and Limitations," *Volta Review, 56,* 1954, 339–349.

Karlovitch, R., "Sensory Interaction: Perception of Loudness during Visual Stimulation," *Journal of the Acoustical Society of America, 44,* 1968, 570–575.

Kelly, J. C., *Audio-Visual Reading: A Manual for Training the Hard of Hearing in Voice Communication.* Urbana: University of Illinois Speech and Hearing Clinic, 1967.

Ling, A. H., "Memory for Verbal and Nonverbal Auditory Sequences in Hearing Impaired and Normal Children," *Journal of the American Audiology. Society, 1,* 1975, 37–45.

Ling, A. H., "The Training of Auditory Memory in Hearing Impaired Children: Some Problems of Generalization," *Journal of the American Audiolog. Society, 1,* 1976, 150–157.

Ling, D., "Three Experiments on Frequency Transmission," *American Annals of the Deaf, 113,* 1968, 283–294.

Ling, D., *Speech and the Hearing Impaired Child: Theory and Practice.* Washington, D.C.: The Alexander Graham Bell Assoc. for the Deaf, 1976.

McGurk, H., and J. MacDonald, *Hearing Lips and Seeing Voices: A New Illusion.* Paper presented at the annual conference of the British Psychological Society, University of Exeter, April 1977.

Miller, G. A., G. A. Heise, and W. Lichten, "The Intelligibility of Speech as a Function of the Context and of Test Materials," *Journal of Exper. Psychology, 41,* 1951, 329–335.

Miller, G. A., and P. E. Nicely, "An Analysis of Perceptual Confusions among some English Consonants," *Journal of the Acoustical Society of America, 27,* 1955, 338–352.

Nitchie, E. B. *Principles and Methods of Lipreading.* New York: The Nitchie School of Lipreading, n.d.

Nix, G. W., "Total Communication: A Review of the Studies Offered in its Support," *Volta Review, 77,* no. 8, November 1975, 470–494.

Numbers, M. E., and C. V. Hudgins, "Speech perception in Present Day Education for Deaf Children, *Volta Review, 50,* 1948, 449–456.

O'Neill, J. J., "Contributions of the Visual Components of Oral Symbols to Speech Comprehension," *Journal of Speech and Hearing Disorders, 19,* 1954, 429–439.

Pickett, J. M., "Tactile Communication of Speech Sounds to the Deaf, *Journal of Speech and Hearing Disorders, 28,* 1963, 315–330.

Pollack, D., *Educational Audiology for the Limited Hearing Infant.* Springfield, Ill.: Charles C Thomas, Publishers, 1970.

Prall, J., "Lipreading and Hearing Aids Combine for Better Comprehension," *Volta Review, 66,* 1957, 400–409.

Prescott, R., "Acoustic Puzzles: Auditory Training Games," *Volta Review, 73,* 1971, 51–53.

Prescott, R., *Auditory Patterning Abilities of Young Hearing Impaired Children.* Paper presented at the Alexander Graham Bell Assoc. Convention, 1972.

Prescott, R., *Acoustic Puzzles: Listening at Home.* Washington, D.C.: Federal City College, 1974.

Prescott, R., and M. Turtz, *Auditory Pattern Recognition by Young Hearing Impaired Children.* Washington, D.C.: Federal City College, 1975.

Sanders, D. A., *A Follow-Up Study of Fifty Deaf Children Who Received Pre-School Training.* Unpublished doctoral thesis, Royal Victoria University of Manchester, England, 1961.

Sanders, D. A., "Auditory Training within a Communication Framework," *Proceedings of the 43rd Meeting of American Instructors of the Deaf.* Washington, D.C.: U.S. Gov't. Printing Office, 1968, pp. 254–258.

Sanders, D. A., "Speech Perception and Reading," in *Auditory Perception of Speech: An Introduction to Principles and Problems,* pp. 219–229. Englewood Cliffs, N.J.: Prentice-Hall, Inc., 1977.

Sanders, D. A., and S. J. Goodrich, "The Relative Contribution of Visual and Auditory Components of Speech to Speech Intelligibility as a Function of Three Conditions of Frequency Distortion," *Journal of Speech and Hearing Research, 14,* 1971, 154–159.

Sherrick, C. E., "Discussion: Relation of Speech Perception and Production to Assessments of Auditory Function," in *Sensory Capabilities of Hearing Impaired Children,* ed. R. Stark, pp. 41–89. Baltimore: University Park Press, 1974.

Shipley, T., "Auditory Flutter: Driving of Visual Flicker," *Science, 145,* 1954, 1328–1330.

Sumby, W. H., and I. Pollack, "Visual Contributions to Speech Intelligibility in Noise," *Journal of the Acoustical Society of America, 26,* 1954, 212–215.

Suzuki, H., R. Kagami, and T. Takahashi, *Tactphone as an Aid for the Deaf.* Proceedings of the 6th International Congress of Acoustics, Tokyo, 1968.

Van Uden, A., "A Sound-Perceptive Method," in *The Modern Educational Treatment Of Deafness,* ed. A. G. W. Ewing, Washington, D.C., *Volta Review,* 1960.

Van Uden, A., "New Realizations in the Light of the Pure Oral Method," *Volta Review, 72,* 1970, 524–537.

Walden, B. E., R. A. Prosek, and D. W. Worthington, "Auditory and Auditory Visual Feature Transmission in Hearing Impaired Adults," *Journal of Speech and Hearing Research, 18,* 1975, 272–280.

Wilbur, R., "The Linguistics of Manual Language and Manual Systems," in *Communication Assessment and Intervention Strategies,* ed. L. Lloyd, pp. 423–500. Baltimore: University Park Press, 1976.

8

Some Important Effects of Hearing Impairment on Speech Perception and Language Processing

HEARING IMPAIRMENT AND AWARENESS

The primary effect of an impairment of hearing is to reduce the amount of auditory information available to the individual. This results in a reduction of the person's awareness of the world around him or her. Few, if any, environmental sounds are audible to a child with a congenital profound impairment until amplification if provided. Thus, speech is inaudible, too. Therefore, as the child's perceptual system matures, it becomes organized without incorporating auditory information, and the child develops an appropriate relationship with a soundless world. The longer this situation exists the more stabilized this nonauditory perceptual organization becomes. The child experiences increasing difficulty in readjusting his or her system to make use of amplified sound when it is made available. It is rather like trying to remold clay that has already begun to harden. Lenneberg (1967) has, in fact, referred to this decreasing flexibility as a loss of "plasticity."

The degree to which the child is aware of the environment is determined by the pattern and severity of the hearing impairment. Children with considerable hearing in the low frequencies may respond to many or most environmental sounds, because it is not necessary to hear something clearly to be aware of it. These children, and those who have even more extensive residual hearing, often escape early detection because their awareness of sound approximates that of a normal-hearing infant. In an extensive survey conducted at Northwestern University Matkin (1977) found that an inverse relationship exists between the degree of hearing deficit and the age at which identification of the problem occurs.

Even when a hearing impairment is acquired later in the child's life or in adult years, the general level of environmental awareness is likely to be reduced. Too frequently the resultant behavior is misinterpreted, and is attributed to inattentiveness, daydreaming, laziness, or even senility. Such misinterpretation of behavior results in a pernicious erosion of the individual's self-confidence and, indeed, of the confidence of others in that person. Both the young and the old suffer from our quickness to label such behavior perjoratively. Unfortunately people who gradually acquire hearing deficiencies are frequently not cognizant of the nature of the changes that are occurring, or if they are, they may attribute them to causes other than hearing problems. Reduced auditory awareness frequently places individuals under greater-than-normal stress. Their ability to cope deteriorates and they become increasingly concerned with their decreasing competence, often as though it were the problem rather than the symptom of a problem. Realizing the effect of hearing impairment upon auditory awareness is important both for counseling and for intervention procedures.

HEARING IMPAIRMENT AND LANGUAGE DEVELOPMENT

The most serious effect of a congenital or early-acquired hearing deficiency is on the development of the comprehension and use of verbal language. When a hearing impairment is sufficiently severe as to prevent an infant's awareness of sound, that infant will not learn the concept of sound as a referential agent. Thus, not only will particular sounds be meaningless when first heard through amplification, but sound itself will not initially be useful as a referent to its sound source. It is safe to say that the most important of all sounds in our daily life is that of the human voice because we use it as the major conveyer of information about our thoughts. With it we express emotions, seek to satisfy our physical and emotional needs nonaggressively, and endeavor to define the reality of ourselves and our universe. In other words, we use voice communicatively to convey language. In Chapters 2 and 3 we discussed how language is encoded into speech patterns. The natural acquisition of the ability to use this system of communication is dependent on adequate hearing. Any impairment of hearing during the first few years of life will affect the development of normal communication skills in proportion to the severity of the deficiency. Only through early detection and intervention can we hope to ameliorate the negative effects of hearing impairment on language and speech development.

Current theories of language development propose that children learn by induction. They infer the rules of language by repeated exposure to samples spoken by those around them. They learn how language works. "The induction model of language acquisition emphasizes concept formation or the internalization of those principles that are the rules of one's language" (Hirsh, 1974, p. 3). Deprived of the ability to hear spoken language, or able to hear it only in a very distorted manner, the child with a profound or severe hearing impairment will experience serious difficulty in acquiring linguistic skills. Furth (1974) asks why a deaf child who enters school at four years of age has difficulty in learning spoken language. Furth answers the question by saying:

The deaf child has quite happily advanced in the development of his intellect and of his personality without the acoustic input which the hearing child has had. Language has no place in his development and biologically the deaf child has no need for it (1974, p. 175).

Deprivation of exposure to spoken language results, therefore, not simply in a delay in language development, but, far more seriously, in the establishment of a biological perceptual posture in which verbal language has no relevance. More subtle difficulties in language processing will be experienced by children with mild and moderate degrees of hearing impairment.

It is important to realize that this difficulty with language acquisition lies not in the children themselves, but in the impedance between the medium of transmission of information (acoustics) and the children's ability to receive it. Fry (1977) stresses that for the deaf child, the sequence of reception, abstraction, and organization proceeds just as in a normal-hearing child. Fry emphasizes that:

Although deafness imposes a great obstacle in the path of language acquisition, it is possible to overcome this obstacle to a considerable degree. A majority of children born with a hearing loss are capable of acquiring their mother tongue through the acoustic medium of speech provided they hear enough speech and hear it loudly enough. *Language acquisition is an affair of the brain, and such children have a normal brain even if they have subnormal hearing* (1977, p. 301).

The development by severely and profoundly hearing-impaired children of near-normal linguistic competencies depends, therefore, on early and appropriate amplification coupled with intensive language stimulation. Comprehension and use of speech at a level of competence that makes communication with hearing persons possible is equally dependent on these two major factors. Despite poor performance in the past (Klopping, 1972), there is a resurgence of faith that: ". . . speech communication is a worthwhile goal and that high standards of speech production can be achieved through informed, systematic, and sustained effort" (Ling, 1966, p. 9).

We know that the age at which training begins exerts a considerable influence on the ultimate effect of hearing impairment on language acquisition. The maximum potential for linguistic competence decreases the longer intervention is delayed. McNeill (1966) and Lenneberg (1967) have both argued that there are optimal periods in the child's early life when language can most easily be learned. After these periods pass the task grows increasingly difficult. Lenneberg maintains that these periods are bound at the lower limit by maturation and at the upper limit by the loss of adaptability and the inability to reorganize the brain. Fry (1966), Elliot and Ambruster (1967), Horton (1974), Scheiflebusch and Lloyd (1974), Northern and Downs (1974), and Lloyd (1976) all stress the critical role of the first two years in determining the hearing-impaired child's ultimate potential in developing language and speech skills.

Language competency is a critical factor in all aspects of intervention, for it affects cognitive development, speech perception, and learning abilities within an auditory environment. At no time can we afford to ignore the child's cognitive linguistic competence. We must consider it in our testing procedures and it must underlie our intervention strategies.

HEARING IMPAIRMENT AND AUDITORY DISCRIMINATION

An impairment of hearing that is present in a child at birth immediately results in a distortion of incoming auditory signals. The peripheral hearing mechanism is, in many ways, similar to a microphone of an amplifier. It serves as a sensing device capable of responding to changes in the pressure of the air around it. It is capable of transducing the energy in sound waves into an electrical wave form that embodies coded information directly correlated to the sound wave. We are able to describe the sensitivity of the human ear in the same way as we described the sensitivity of the microphone. Equal loudness curves derived by Fletcher and Mundson (1938) (Figure 8.1) are statements of the sensitivity of the ear at different sound-pressure levels. From these curves we learn that, for input sounds of a sound-pressure level of 50 dBs and above, the sensitivity of the ear is essentially flat across the frequency range of 300 to 4000 Hz. At normal conversational loudness, the normal ear does not favor some frequencies in the speech range more than others. Neither the differences in sound-

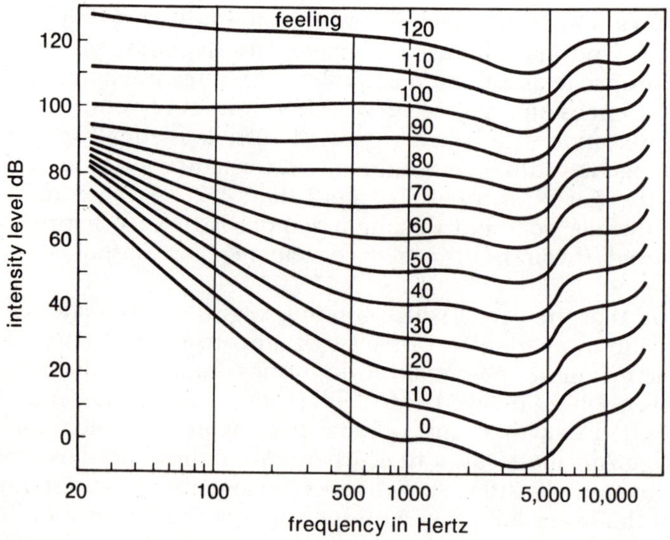

FIGURE 8.1 Loudness-level contours. These lines link points that may differ in intensity but are equal in perceived loudness (after Fletcher and Mundson, 1938, p. 124).

pressure level nor the relative strengths of the formants in the various phonemes is affected by the normal ear. This no longer holds true once the sensitivity curve of the ear is changed by a hearing impairment. A hearing loss always affects the overall loudness of the input signal; frequently, it also affects the perceived frequency spectrum.

Consider first a typical conductive hearing impairment (Figure 8.2), which reduces the hearing sensitivity relatively evenly across the speech frequency range. Even though the sensitivity curve is evenly depressed, a reduction in the loudness of speech affects the perception of some phonemes more rapidly than others. This has been documented by Fletcher (1953), who conducted a series of tests of speech perception for individual speech sounds. Using the average intensity level of normal conversational speech as a reference level, Fletcher derived articulation-gain curves for each phoneme as a function of intensity. In other words, the graphs he derived showed the effect of progressively reducing the speech intensity on the accuracy of speech-sound recognition (measured as a percentage). The results of these studies show that vowels are more easily recognized than consonants, with the exception of the vowel /ɛ/ as in "ten," which is exceptionally difficult, and for consonants, /l/, /r/, /ŋ/, which are easily recognized. The sounds /s/, /θ/, /f/, and /v/ were the most difficult to recognize. The voiced sound /z/, which is easily identified at normal conversational level, rapidly becomes extremely difficult to recognize when the intensity level is reduced. The vowels and diphthongs /i/,

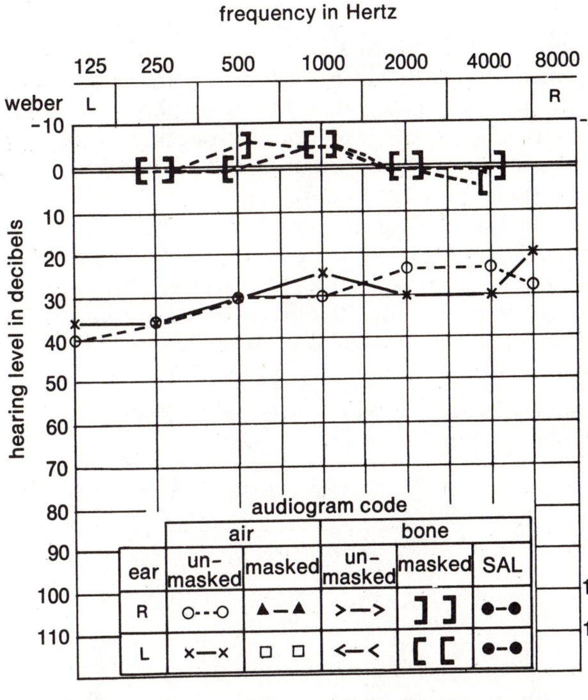

FIGURE 8.2 Audiogram of a person with a typical conductive-type hearing impairment.

/ou/, /ɛ/, and /o/ are extremely resistant to loss of identifying qualities as a result of reduction in intensity. Finally, Fletcher points out that at normal conversational level the sounds /v/, /f/, and /θ/ together represent more than half of the mistakes in recognizing fundamental speech sounds.

These findings indicate that, although a person with a relatively flat conductive hearing loss may not begin to notice difficulty until the impairment reaches a level of 35 to 40 dB ISO (International Standards Organization), there will, in fact, be a loss of information conveyed by the acoustic signal. This results in a reduction of the overall redundancy of the message. We see this in people with a progressive-conductive–type loss, who usually first notice difficulty in situations in which the redundancy of the message itself has already been reduced by adverse listening conditions. Such people have difficulty, for example, in understanding lectures and sermons or conversation in a group. They may hear better when they have glasses on or when they are able to watch the speaker's face. La Benz (1956) has indicated the extent to which the loss of speech discrimination increases as a result of progressive reduction of intensity. LaBenz's findings are shown in Table 8.1. These assume that the loss is fairly flat in configuration. Note how the increased redundancy from visual cues accounts for much better discrimination scores.

Although some sensorineural losses may be as flat in configuration as the characteristic conductive loss, for the most part they tend to result in an uneven threshold pattern. Some frequencies, generally the higher ones, are more seriously affected than others. The sensorineural hearing loss, therefore, results in a loss of sensitivity, coupled with an uneven distortion of the sensitivity of the ear to different frequencies. In attempting to understand the result that this may have on speech discrimination, remember that, with one or two exceptions, speech sounds possess three formants. The first and second formants are essential to recognition of the phoneme, whereas the third is not.

The sensorineural hearing loss will reduce the sensitivity of the ear to certain frequencies. The resultant effect upon discrimination will depend on the frequencies involved and the strength and frequency characteristics of the various formants of a given speech sound. The distortion of a phoneme may make its recognition impossible, or it may be sufficient

TABLE 8.1 Predicted Discrimination Scores for Subjects with Flat Conductive Audiograms (after LaBenz, 1956)

Average Loss 500–2000 Hz (ASA)*	*Discrimination Score for Phonetically Balanced Words*	
	Hearing Alone	*Hearing and Vision*
20–30	75%	88%
40	40%	70%
50	10%	50%
60	less than 10%	20–30%

*American Standards Association

to make the sound inaudible. Numerous research studies on the effect of frequency distortion on speech perception indicate that auditory discrimination for speech sounds is increasingly impaired as more and more of the frequency spectrum is eliminated. The degree of resistance to frequency distortion shown by phonemes varies quite noticeably. This is primarily a characteristic of the pattern of distribution of their sound energy. Fletcher points out, for example, that the sound /i/ as in "team" was correctly identified 98 percent of the time when either the frequencies above or below 1700 Hz were eliminated (1953). By contrast, however, the elimination of frequencies below 1500 Hz only slightly affected a listener's ability to recognize the phoneme. The exclusion of frequencies above 400 Hz made recognition practically impossible. Fletcher showed that, although the frequencies below 1000 Hz appeared to be important to the recognition of short vowels, those above 2000 Hz do not contribute very much to discrimination. Long vowels and the diphthongs appear to possess enough distinguishing characteristics in either half of their frequency range to make recognition possible when there is marked distortion.

The high frequencies were shown to contribute a very high percentage of the recognizable characteristics of fricatives. When frequencies above 3000 Hz were eliminated, the percentage discrimination for the sound /s/ was reduced to 40 percent, for /θ/ to 66 percent, for /z/ to 80 percent, for /t/ to 81 percent, and for /f/ to 85 percent. Other speech sounds experienced less than a 10 percent reduction in discrimination when frequencies above 3000 Hz were eliminated. A further incursion into the frequency spectrum, eliminating frequencies above 1000 Hz, again reduced the discrimination scores for consonants without, in general, seriously affecting vowel-sound discrimination. However, once the cutoff excluded frequencies above 500 Hz, the second formant in most vowels was seriously encroached upon and vowel discrimination dropped dramatically. Under this condition, vowel discrimination was sometimes poorer than the discrimination of some of the consonant sounds that were recognized by transition clues.

The data concerning the effect of frequency and amplitude distortion upon speech-sound discrimination have essentially been obtained by using subjects with normal hearing. It is clear from these findings that the result of such distortion is to reduce the amount of information carried by the acoustic signal as the number of speech frequencies eliminated and the degree of intensity loss increases. Not all speech sounds are equally affected by this; in general, vowels are more resistant to distortion than consonants, and the fricative sounds are the most seriously impaired. However, we already know that speech discrimination is not dependent upon the auditory signal alone. The extent to which a person will be able to compensate for acoustic distortion of connected speech will be influenced by how well that person can predict the missing components. Unlike the adult, or the child who acquires deafness after learning to speak, the child with a congenital deafness will be hampered not only by the limited ability to make use of the acoustic signal, but also because of the resulting impairment in the acquisition of language skills, which further reduces the redundancy of a message signal. In spite of the tremendous strides that have been made toward the provision of enriched experiences for the hearing-impaired child, a congenital hearing loss is still likely to result in an impairment of language, even though, in the case of moderate or mild hearing losses, this may only affect the understanding of the subtler aspects of communication.

HEARING IMPAIRMENT AND AUDITORY PERCEPTION

It is not possible to make a general statement concerning the effect that hearing impairment has upon the individual's perceptual function, because numerous variables are involved. The severity and pattern of the hearing impairments is obviously of paramount importance. If the hearing loss is profound, the child will be deprived of all auditory input without amplification; thus, experience of the world will not include awareness of sounds. The child will be deprived of the information that he or she would normally be able to obtain from environmental sounds; people or objects that do not fall within his or her visual field will be literally outside the immediate environment. When a deaf child's mother leaves the room, all contact with her is lost; the child is unable to derive reassurance from hearing her voice and the sound she makes from performing her various household activities when in another room. Unlike those of us who have normal hearing, the person with a profound hearing loss is unable to predict what is occurring in the environment on the basis of the information carried by the auditory cues. For example, as I sit in my office writing this chapter, I predict that a secretary is in the front office, since I can hear the sound of typing originating from that direction. I am also aware that someone is using a tape recorder in an adjacent therapy room and that the blackboard, which I requested to be mounted in one of the rooms, is being put up.

Experience with very young deaf children who have profound congenital sensorineural hearing losses indicates that in many cases the children have utterly no concept of sound. They develop no awareness of it, and so when they are first introduced to it through a high-powered amplifying unit, they tend to reject it as something that confuses them and, therefore, impairs their ability to function. It serves as no more than an unpleasant distraction. It is imperative that teachers or therapists be clearly aware of the impact that amplification of environmental sounds, including speech, will have upon such children. They must be prepared for this rejection and they must be capable of patiently developing awareness of sound and an understanding of its referential value at the introductory stages of auditory training.

The auditory-perceptual development of children who have a severe hearing loss, but for whom amplification is not provided during the early years of life, may be similar in many ways to that of children with profound deafness. They may also fail to hear most of the environmental sounds at an intensity level at which sufficient information can be derived to make it meaningful. If they are able to hear some sounds they may demonstrate better awareness of acoustic stimuli. They may show pleasure in listening to sound-making toys that may be partially audible when held very close to the ear. They may also have learned to derive some value from loud environmental sounds that they are able to associate with visual or tactile knowledge of a sound-making object. We can expect severely hard-of-hearing children, therefore, to have had a modicum of experience in gross-sound discrimination. The extent to which they will have incorporated this into their system of adjustment will depend upon the degree to which their residual hearing has made it possible for them to use the sounds they hear to identify things in the environment. Speech, on the other hand, may not have been heard as anything more than a faint mumbling. Their inability to derive any meaning from speech suggests that it exists for them only as a noise factor. When such children are fitted with amplification, making them aware of environmental sounds and speech may be somewhat easier than it is when working with profoundly deaf children. In addition, since there is probably considerably more usable residual hearing, the amount of information that amplification will make available is much greater. Increased meaning may, after a while, serve to establish a self-rewarding feedback situation.

For children with mild to moderate loss, the problem is not normally a lack of awareness, since a great number of sounds in the environment have been audible to them. They may be expected to have developed a system of communication with the environment that incorporates the auditory signal whenever it is loud enough to be utilized. Speech, however, by virtue of the fine discriminations that are involved, has probably never been clear enough or loud enough to be of real value. Mildly to moderately hearing-impaired children have probably learned to derive cues from the stress and intonation patterns, and they may listen to the voice even though they are not able to understand the speech. Such children may or may not be using the speech signal to increase the amount of information they are able to obtain about a situation. Careful evaluation of each child's communication system will need to be made in order to know at what level he or she is functioning and the nature of the training that he or she will need.

In all instances, we have presumed that these children have been deaf from birth and have not previously been provided with amplification. For the child who acquires deafness after speech inception, and for the adult, the problem is very different. In this case, the person is well aware of environmental sounds and has developed a communication system that depends heavily upon the use of audition for information. However, the hearing loss considerably decreases the redundancy of the auditory signal to the point at which the child or adult may no longer be able to comprehend speech in all communication situations. Amplification may compensate for this loss of redundancy by raising the signal intensity to an adequate loudness level. However, amplification does not provide a high-quality reproduction and compensates little for the frequency distortion imposed by the hearing loss. The hearing-aid user will, therefore, need training in associating the new sound patterns with previous internal representations.

HEARING IMPAIRMENT AND SPEECH PERCEPTION

The relationship between language and speech is so close that they are difficult to separate into two discrete entities (Kavanagh & Cutting, 1975). One of the major problems in discussing the effects of hearing impairment upon the perception of spoken language is that in normal communication we perceive linguistic values, not a series of discrete sounds. The more we are forced to discriminate the details of the speech signal, the harder the task becomes. As Fry (1977) states: "Intelligibility is to be found, not in the signals themselves, but in the brain's organization of the information that the signals supply" (p. 300). For this reason, the auditory-processing difficulties that arise from congenital hearing impairment occur as much from the resultant linguistic retardation as from peripheral distortion of the acoustic signal. Communication involves the perception of spoken language. As we have seen, there is strong support for the claim that the process depends heavily on the accuracy with which the individual is able to predict the development of the pattern of any event. When the event is a speech event the listener must be familiar with the rules being used by the speaker to generate the speech patterns. It is by reference to a common set of rules that the listener is able to use the acoustic information to identify which particular encoding routines are being used by the speaker. Once the listener has identified these routines, he or she can use them to reconstruct the message.

In normal conversation the rate of information flow is high, 165 words or 440 syllables per minute (Gerber, 1974). This is possible only because so much linguistic redundancy is encoded into the speech signal and because the listener with normal language is able to rapidly generate linguistic and contextual probabilities. Under normal conditions of communication, then, dependency upon the details of the signal is minimal. Children with reduced language abilities are, therefore, in a position of double jeopardy. By virtue of their reduced linguistic knowledge, they are not able to make adequate predictions about the probable message. Thus, they are forced to depend heavily on the acoustic signal. This, however, is inadequate because of distortion arising from the hearing impairment.

This is the problem confronting us as we attempt to train severely and profoundly hearing-impaired children. The amount of difficulty experienced, both in speech perception and speech production, can reasonably be expected to increase with the severity of the hearing impairment. Ahlstrom (1970) reported a high correlation between hearing impairment and speech-recognition and speech-intelligibility scores obtained by deaf school children. Boothroyd (1974) and Levitt (1974) found that speech perception and production skills correlate highly with the average pure-tone thresholds in the speech range, particularly with those at 1000 and 2000 Hz. This correlation also holds true for phoneme and word-recognition tests. Smith (1973) demonstrated that a close relationship also exists between speech perception and production skills.

It is hardly surprising that a correlation exists between the severity of the hearing impairment and speech-recognition performance. Because the initial cues to the message content can seldom be predicted, they must be derived from an analysis of the acoustic signal. Any reduction in the intensity of the signal received will result in a reduction of potential information. A hearing deficit always reduces the overall loudness of the speech signal; frequently, as we have seen, it also distorts the frequency spectrum by removing more energy at some frequencies than at others.

The data available on the effect of frequency and amplitude distortion on speech-sound discrimination have mainly been derived from normal-hearing adult subjects. Clinical experience with adults who have peripheral (cochlear) sensory hearing impairment reveals that the correlation between the degree of impairment and discrimination ability is not absolute. In many instances the discrimination performance of an individual with less residual hearing may be better than that of another person who has 10 to 20 dB more hearing. With increasing age, speech discrimination decreases disproportionately with reference to pure-tone thresholds; this phenomenon is known as presbycusis or phoneme regression (Goetzinger, Proud, Dirks, & Embrey, 1961). Hetherington (1970) showed that this increasing discrepancy between pure-tone thresholds and speech discrimination occurring as a function of age is also found in adults whose hearing remains within normal limits. In most studies, the age of 40 years is taken as the dividing point at which deterioration begins to appear. Normal discrimination ability can legitimately be said to be lost in adults as a result of the loss of hearing sensitivity. Knowledge of language-processing rules, however, remains unimpaired. The problem lies in receiving a sufficiently undistorted acoustic signal to make recognition possible.

In children whose hearing is prelinguistically deficient the effect is far greater. Erber (1974) and Cramer and Erber (1974) have reported upon the relationship of pure-tone thresholds to discrimination performance by these children. Erber (1974) studied seventy-two children and obtained 144 monaural speech-recognition scores. He correlated these with the average pure-tone thresholds for frequencies 500, 1000, and 2000 Hz. The hearing thresholds ranged from 65 to 128 dB. Spondee words were used for test items, because Van Uden (1970) reported that these are easier for severely hearing-impaired children to discriminate than the traditional monosyllabic words. The results of Erber's study indicate that the auditory-discrimination performance produced a bimodal distribution of high (70 to 100 percent) and low (0 to 30 percent) scores. The 90 to 95 dB level of average hearing clearly represents a dividing line between children with good and poor discrimination abilities. However, an overlap of about 5 percent of the ears tested was evident. This suggests that pure-tone averages are not perfect predictors of whether a child has good or poor auditory-discrimination potential. Erber's opinion is that the children in the high-scoring group may be classified as severely hearing impaired. These children, he believes, have true residual hearing. Erber identifies the children in the low-scoring group as profoundly deaf. They lack true hearing but perceive acoustic information by vibrotactile transmission. Although they are able to recognize time and intensity cues, they are not able to perceive the spectral characteristics arising from frequency patterns.

Cramer and Erber (1974), acknowledging that pure-tone averages are not perfect indicators of discrimination ability, sought to develop a recorded test that would employ spondee words in the assessment of discrimination. They tested fifty-eight hearing-impaired children ages 5 to 9 years who had average impairments (500 to 2000 Hz) ranging from 52 to 123 dB (ANSI, 1969). Repeating testing until each child's scores stabilized, Cramer and Erber then plotted the average recognition score for the last four tests. The study confirmed the bimodal distribution found in the Erber (1974) study previously discussed. The clusters were 66 to 100 percent for pure-tone averages up to 93 dB HTL, and 0 to 66 percent for averages of 103 dB HTL and greater. Between 93 and 103 dB, no close correspondence between pure-tone average and discrimination scores was found. For this group the spondee-recognition test provides important information not predictable from pure-tone results. Of particular interest and importance was the finding that recognition scores for some children improved on repeated testing, moving their classification to a higher group. This emphasizes the importance of not making hearing-aid selection or educational-placement decisions on the basis of only one or two speech-recognition tests.

HEARING IMPAIRMENT AND MEMORY PROCESSING

We have seen that the understanding of spoken language depends on several critical requirements. The first is that the perceptual system be sensitive to the physical cues that comprise the acoustic signal and the visible speech articulation patterns. Any reduction in auditory or visual acuity results in the elimination of information from which the message and its meaning must be reconstructed. It is reasonable to assume that the reduction of such information will impair an individual's ability to learn and remember auditory information. Evidence supporting this assumption may be found in the retarded vocabulary development evidenced by hearing-impaired children (Wrightstone, Aranow, & Maskowitz, 1965), and in the reduced short-term memory performance they exhibit (Myklebust, 1960). In an attempt to better understand the effects of reduced auditory information on learning and recall, Novak and Davis (1974) conducted an experiment that measured the rate at which normal-hearing young adults learned to pair visual nonsense syllables with a set of monosyllabic words recorded and played backwards. The auditory stimuli were presented to the experimental group through a system that filtered out frequencies above 960 Hz at the rate of a 25 dB intensity drop per octave. The control group heard an unfiltered recording. Memory for the learned pairs was assessed by asking the subjects to listen to strings of words two, five, seven, and nine items long, and then to identify the equivalent visual string. The findings were that the reduction in the high-frequency information resulting from the filter condition significantly decreased the rate of learning of the unfamiliar auditory items. The study also showed that filtering resulted in greater variability in the number of trials required by different subjects to learn the item pairs than was apparent in the control group.

On the memory task, the experimenters found that the group receiving the filtered stimulus performed significantly more poorly in remembering the five-item string than the control group, who heard the unfiltered stimulus. Even though the performance of both groups in recalling the seven- and nine-item strings was reduced when compared to the recall of five-item strings, no significant difference was evidenced between the filtered and unfiltered conditions.

This study demonstrates that for normal-hearing subjects, acoustic filtering of high-frequency information in speech-like stimuli significantly reduces the rate of paired associate learning. The authors hypothesize that this results from reduced redundancy and increased ambiguity arising from the loss of frequency information important to pattern identification. The absence of these important cues makes the learning task more difficult and more time consuming. Furthermore, it was shown that deprivation of high-frequency information also affects short-term recall of learned items. It is logical to expect that distortion of the acoustic signal by hearing impairment, with a resultant loss of information, will have a similar adverse affect on learning and recall.

The ability to learn and remember, as we have seen, is dependent on restructuring information out of echoic memory, where it exists as an image of the physical stimulus, into short-term memory. For this to be possible it is necessary to translate acoustic data into linguistic data. We can learn and remember only what we can restructure. We have already seen that reducing the information in the external stimulus distorts the pattern, slows down the process, and increases errors in memory among persons with normal linguistic capabilities. Depressed language skills further handicap hearing-impaired children. Not only do they receive less acoustic information than their hearing counterparts, they also have inferior knowledge of the rules by which the acoustic pattern can be restructured into the language code essential to memory storage. An impoverished vocabulary means that even words that are sufficiently well received to be discriminable cannot be restructured into the abstract linguistic tokens, which in turn evoke appropriate referents or meanings (see Chapter 2). Thus, even much of the speech that is heard remains an unsegmented jumble, just as a foreign language sounds to a normal-hearing person.

Segmenting the acoustic stream into meaningful units is an essential prerequisite to the restructuring of information from echoic to short-term memory. To store information it is necessary to restructure it into larger chunks. This necessitates the ability to generate internal language patterns that can accommodate the acoustic information. Whenever a child is unable to reconstruct a linguistic pattern equivalent to the acoustic pattern meaning can neither be assigned nor remembered.

The impact of a hearing impairment on a young child's learning and remembering is twofold. First, the amount of information entering echoic memory is reduced, making pattern differentiation and identification difficult. Second, the resultant deprivation of clear acoustic models of spoken language prevents the child from rapidly learning the rules for processing language. Without well-developed language rules for segmenting, chunking, and restructuring the information, understanding is difficult, and remembering even more so.

THE EFFECT OF NOISE ON LEARNING AND MEMORY

The reduction in speech discrimination caused by impaired hearing and the resultant deficit in linguistic skills are primary factors affecting learning and remembering by hearing-impaired children. Another important contributing factor—the effect of environmental acoustic noise—must not be underestimated. The relative loudness of the speech signal and competing noise, especially speech noise, are of critical importance to amplification. The effect of noise on auditory learning by hearing-impaired children is becoming increasingly relevant as more and more of these children are educationally placed not in the quiet listening environments of special classrooms, but in the noisy conditions of the normal class.

It has been shown that equivalent speech-intelligibility scores can be achieved for different conditions of speech distortion (Broadbent, 1958). However, such similar achievement involves a great deal more effort under some conditions than under others. Rabbitt (1966) has suggested that the increased effort necessary for discrimination under poor listening conditions reduces the amount of attention that is available for processing the cognitive content of the spoken message. Rabbitt demonstrated that when noise was introduced into the acoustic environment, poorer memory recognition of words occurred even when those words could be correctly discriminated in the noise. Downs and Crum (1978) conducted an experiment to assess the effect of degraded listening conditions on learning accuracy and ease of learning. These investigators studied normal-hearing adults who were asked to learn pairs of two-syllable (spondee) words under different signal-to-noise ratios and signal-intensity levels. Their results indicated that the intensity of the signal in quiet (20, 35, and 50 dB SL) had no effect on either accuracy or effort of learning. The introduction of competing speech noise at 6 dB greater than the test words also did not effect the accuracy of learning; however, it did significantly increase the effort exerted in learning the words. Downs and Crum (1978) conclude:

> *This result is an indication that noise present in home or educational environments may produce deleterious effects on learning performance of children. Increased effort would be required to attend selectively to an auditory signal. If this effort is not expended, there will be a concomitant decrease in learning performance. Stated differently, a child can sacrifice optimal learning if the processing demands of a task are increased. This tradeoff relationship could be summed up with the statement "Learning is just not worth the effort." Similarly, if effort is allocated but is not adequate to fulfill attentional demands of a learning task, performance also will falter* (p. 711).

When a child is already handicapped by reduced auditory information and depressed language-processing competency, the effect of noise on learning and memory merits serious concern. The impact of such handicapping conditions frequently is evidenced as inattention, depressed learning ability, increasing developmental language lag, inability to remember the content of auditorily presented information. The child naturally becomes frustrated, loses interest, becomes bored, and either withdraws from the situation or exhibits behaviors that prove distracting to peers and the teacher. Thus, while hearing impairment exerts a direct negative effect upon speech comprehension and auditory-learning skills, frequently secondary effects also rapidly ensue. Solving the problem of hearing impairment necessitates, therefore, an approach broad enough to extend beyond the immediate communication problem.

REFERENCES

Ahlstrom, K. G., "On Evaluating the Effects of Schooling," in *Proceedings of the International Congress on Deaf,* Volume I. Stockholm, Sweden, 1970.

Boothroyd, A., "Sensory Capabilities in Normal and Hearing Impaired Children. Discussion: Relation of Speech Perception and Production to Assessments of Auditory Function," in *Sensory Capabilities of Hearing Impaired Children,* ed. R. E. Stark, pp. 41–89. Baltimore: University Park Press, 1974.

Broadbent, D., *Perception and Communication.* London: Pergamon Press, 1958.

Cramer, K. D., and N. P. Erber, "A Spondee Recognition Test for Young Hearing Impaired Children," *Journal of Speech and Hearing Disorders, 39,* 1974, 304–311.

Downs, M., and D. Crum, "Processing Demands during Auditory Learning under Degraded Listening Conditions," *Journal of Speech and Hearing Research, 21,* 1978, 702–714.

Elliot, L. L., and V. B. Ambruster, "Some Possible Effects of the Delay of Early Treatment of Deafness," *Journal of Speech and Hearing Research, 10,* 1967, 209–224.

Erber, N. P., "Pure Tone Thresholds and Word Recognition Abilities of Hearing Impaired Children," *Journal of Speech and Hearing Research, 17,* 1974, 194–202.

Fletcher, H., *Speech and Hearing in Communication.* New York: D. Van Nostrand Company, 1953.

Fletcher, H., and W. Mundson, "Loudness: Its Definition, Measurement, and Calculation, *Journal of the Acoustical Society of America, 5,* no. 19, 82–108.

Fry, D. B., "The Development of the Phonological System in the Normal and Deaf Child," in *The Genesis of Language: A Psycholinguistic Approach,* eds. F. Smith and G. A. Miller, pp. 187–206. Cambridge, Mass.: M.I.T. Press, 1966.

Fry, D. B., "Language Development in the Deaf Child," in *Childhood Deafness: Causation, Assessment and Management,* ed. F. Bess, pp. 295–304. New York: Grune & Stratton, Inc., 1977.

Furth, H., "Discussion: Language Processing and the Hearing Impaired Child," in *Sensory Capabilities of Hearing Impaired Children,* ed. R. Stark, pp. 173–196. Baltimore: University Park Press, 1974.

Gerber, S., *Introductory Hearing Science.* Philadelphia: W. B. Saunders Company, 1974.

Goetzinger, C. P., G. O. Proud, D. D. Dirks, and J. Embrey, "A Study of Hearing in Advanced Age," *Archives of Otolaryngology, 73,* 1961, 662–674.

Hetherington, J., *The Use of Interrupted Sentences in the Discrimination of Hearing Aid Characteristics.* Unpublished doctoral dissertation, University of Kansas, 1970. (Referred to in Goetzinger, C. P., "Word Discrimination Testing," in *Handbook of Clinical Audiology,* ed. J. Katz, p. 175. Baltimore: The Williams and Wilkins Company, 1972.)

Hirsh, I. J., "Information Processing and the Deaf Child—Keynote Address," in *Sensory Capabilities of Hearing Impaired Children,* ed. R. Stark, pp. 1–7. Baltimore: University Park Press, 1974.

Horton, K. B., "Infant Intervention and Language Learning," in *Language Perspectives Acquisition Retardation and Intervention,* eds. R. L. Schiefelbusch and L. L. Lloyd, pp. 469–491. Baltimore: University Park Press, 1974.

Kavanagh, J. F., and J. E. Cutting, eds., *The Role of Speech in Language.* Cambridge, Mass.: M.I.T. Press, 1975.

Klopping, H. W. E., "Language Understanding of Deaf Students under Three Auditory-visual Stimulus Conditions," *American Annals of the Deaf, 117,* 1972, 389–396.

La Benz, P., "Potential of Auditory Perception for Various Levels of Hearing Loss," *Volta Review, 58,* 1956, 387–402.

Lenneberg, E. H., *Biological Foundations of Language.* New York: John Wiley & Sons, Inc., 1967.

Levitt, H., "Discussion: Relation of Speech Perception and Production to Assessments of Auditory Function," in *Sensory Capabilities in Hearing Impaired Children,* ed. R. Stark, pp. 41–89. Baltimore: University Park Press, 1974.

Ling, D., *Speech and the Hearing Impaired Child: Theory and Practice.* Washington, D.C.: The Alexander Graham Bell Assoc. for the Deaf, 1976.

Lloyd, L. L., *Discussant's Comment: Language and Communication for High Risk Infants and Young Children.* Baltimore: University Park Press, 1976.

Matkin, N. D., "Assessment of Hearing Sensitivity During Preschool Years," in *Childhood Deafness: Causation, Assessment and Management,* ed. F. H. Bess, p. 127. New York: Grune & Stratton, Inc., 1977.

McNeill, D., "The Capacity for Language Acquisition," *Volta Review, 68,* 1966, 17–33.

Myklebust, H. R., *The Psychology of Deafness.* New York: Grune & Stratton, Inc., 1960.

Northern, J. L., and M. Downs, *Hearing in Children.* Baltimore: The Williams and Wilkins Company, 1974.

Novak, R., and J. Davis, "Effects of Low-Pass Filtering on the Rate of Learning and Retrieval from Memory of Speech-Like Stimuli," *Journal of Speech and Hearing Research, 17,* 1974, 270–278.

Rabbitt, P., "Recognition: Memory for Words Correctly Heard in Noise," *Psychnomic Sci., 6,* 1966, 383–384.

Schiefelbusch, R. L., and L. L. Lloyd, *Language Perspectives Acquisition Retardation and Intervention.* Baltimore: University Park Press, 1974.

Smith, C., "Residual Hearing and Speech Production in Deaf Children," *Communicative Sciences Laboratory Report #4.* New York: C.U.N.Y. Graduate Center, 1973.

Van Uden, A., "New Realisations in the Light of the Pure Oral Method," *Volta Review, 72,* 1970, 524–537.

Wrightstone, J. W., M. S. Aranow, and J. Maskowitz, "Developing Reading Test Norms for Deaf Children," *American Annals of the Deaf, 108,* 1965, 311–316.

Amplification for the Hearing-Impaired Person

9

Fundamentals of Amplification

We have stressed repeatedly that amplification is the first and most important consideration in any intervention program designed to minimize the effects of a medically untreatable hearing impairment. The maximal use of an appropriate hearing aid is of primary concern in helping both children and adults with hearing deficiencies. The impact of optimal amplification will naturally be greater on hearing-impaired children than on adults because of its potential in facilitating the acquisition of speech, language, and communication skills. Ross and Tomassetti (1980) have said: ". . . for most hearing impaired children the early and appropriate selection and use of amplification is the single most effective tool available to us" (p. 214). Thus, every teacher, audiologist, and hearing therapist working with a hearing-impaired individual must be knowledgeable about the nature, potential, and limitations of amplification. We must know how to capitalize on the assets of amplification in our determination to improve the client's ability to learn, understand, and use spoken language and to make use of environmental sound cues.

Audiologists must be thoroughly familiar with all facets of amplification; they must be able to identify a particular aid as most appropriate for a given individual and they must be able to select and modify the amplification characteristics as needed. In recent years several texts have been published that provide extensive coverage of this topic (Berger, 1974; Pollack, 1980a, 1980b; Rubin, 1976a). These texts are particularly relevant for students of audiology. They cover the technical aspects of hearing aids and include discussions of assessment and selection procedures and of special applications of amplification. However, only tangentially do they deal with methods of capitalizing on the rehabilitative use of amplification. The text *Hearing Aid Assessment and Use in Audiologic Habilitation* by Hodgson and Skinner (1977) was the first to diverge from tradition by making audiologic habilitation/rehabilitation the perspective from which amplification is viewed. It is hoped that this text will orient audiologists to assess the use of hearing aids rather than to simply select and fit them.

Remember, however, that the audiologist is seldom in a position to monitor daily a child's performance with an aid. Despite the growth of educational audiology it is still the speech pathologist and special teacher who see the child in the day-to-day conditions in which that child must function. It is also mainly the speech pathologist who provides auditory and visual training to hearing-impaired adults. Yet curricula in speech pathology and deaf education seldom include an intensive course on amplification. As a result hearing-impaired children and adults are receiving help from professionals who, despite their dedication to the provision of competent service, have only a rudimentary knowledge of hearing aids and auditory training equipment. It is difficult for these professionals to use the available texts to increase their competency on this subject, because these texts tend to be technically and prescriptively oriented and, for the most part, do not address the principles of using the aid in rehabilitation management. It may be that knowledge of and confidence in using amplification would effect a great change in its successful adoption, at least by children. Even though the optimal use of residual hearing is our primary goal, the evidence clearly indicates that we have not been successful. Studies from 1966 to 1973 have repeatedly shown that less than 50 percent of children who wear aids are receiving adequate amplification. Limited data are available concerning what the figures would be for adults who purchased aids, but clinical experience leads one to conclude that they, too, would reveal an unacceptably high incidence of inadequate or unworn hearing aids (McCandless, 1976).

In referring to the situation as it applies to children, Ross and Tomassetti (1980) poignantly state: "The inescapable conclusion of this sad litany is that for most hearing impaired children, the effective use of residual hearing is a myth shrouded with good intentions" (p. 247). Obviously each of us needs to be well prepared to capitalize fully on the potential benefits of amplification. As a teacher/therapist, it is unnecessary for you to understand the technology of hearing aids, or to devote time to studying the various research findings concerning hearing-aid selection. That is the audiologist's responsibility. Audiologists work with hearing-aid manufacturers to learn how to achieve various acoustic effects through modification of the hearing aid or ear mold. If you are a teacher/therapist, on the other hand, you must be thoroughly knowledgeable about the use of amplification in the educational and rehabilitation process. For this you need to know what can and cannot reasonably be expected from a hearing aid and you must know how to train the hearing-impaired individual to make maximum use of amplification. Most important, you must be sophisticated enough to work closely with the audiologist while he or she seeks first to identify the child's specific amplification needs and then to select the best aid. This is particularly important when you are working with children. An audiologist should not be expected to assume complete responsibility for the hearing-aid selection process when children are involved. The younger the child, the more this is true. The purpose of amplification is to facilitate environmental awareness, speech awareness, linguistic and cognitive growth, and academic learning. The audiologist in a sound booth simply cannot assess the child's performance with the aid in these areas. It is essential, therefore, that you, the teacher or therapist, work with the audiologist and the parents as a team capable of monitoring all aspects of the child's reactions to amplification in both learning and social situations.

THE NATURE OF AMPLIFICATION

Amplification is the process of enlarging the acoustic signal. Its purpose is to raise the signal intensity in order to bring as much of the sound pattern as possible above a person's hearing threshold. This is achieved by changing the acoustic signal to an equivalent electrical signal, amplifying it, and then changing the magnified electrical pattern back into an acoustic pattern for delivery to the ear. To achieve this, any amplification system must consist of three basic units: (1) a microphone; (2) an amplifier; and (3) an output transducer. Figure 9.1 schematically illustrates these components.

The Microphone

In all conventional wearable hearing aids, the microphone is housed within the case of the aid itself. In larger amplification units referred to as *auditory training units* the microphone is often a separate external unit

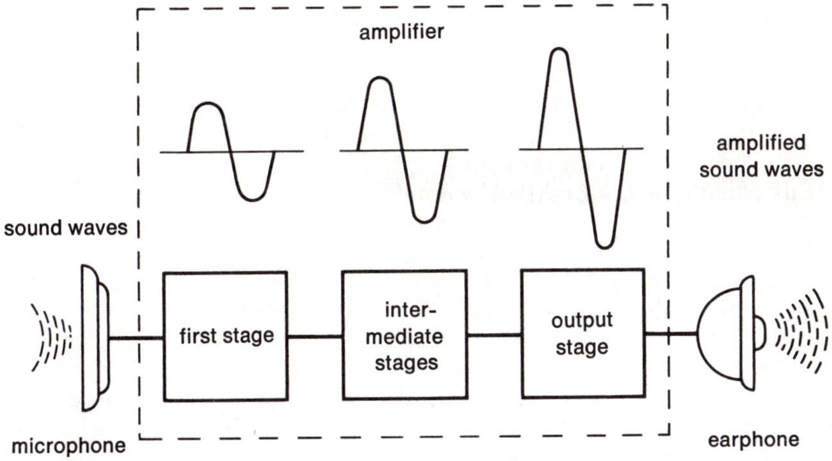

FIGURE 9.1 Schematic diagram of a hearing aid (courtesy of Zenith Hearing Aid Sales Corporation).

connected directly or indirectly to the amplifier. The microphone's purpose is to change or *transduce* the acoustic energy pattern into an electrical replica. Until recently this was achieved by tiny ceramic microphones in which the mechanical movement of a diaphragm that vibrated by acoustic energy was conveyed to a crystal. The resultant distortion of the crystal caused it to generate an electrical current, which was a fairly faithful facsimile of the acoustic wave. Now, more and more hearing aids are fitted with *electret microphones,* which substitute a permanently electrically polarized fluorocarbon plastic film for the crystal. These microphones are sensitive to vibration across a wide range of frequencies, which increases the fidelity of reproduction of the acoustic pattern because it minimizes distortion. Two major advantages of the electret microphone are that: (1) it reduces to a minimum annoyance caused by noise resulting from clothing rubbing against the aid; and (2) it is all but free of *mechanical feedback.* Mechanical feedback occurs when poor shock absorption in the mounting of the microphone in the hearing-aid case results in low-frequency (400 to 500 Hz) mechanical vibrations of the receiver that are transmitted back to the microphone where they are amplified, producing an audible low-pitch squeal. Mechanical feedback should be distinguished from the more commonly occurring higher-pitched squeal or whistle of *acoustic feedback,* which we discuss later.

One further relevant design characteristic is that of directional microphones. Standard microphones are nondirectional—that is, they are equally sensitive to sounds arriving from all directions. The directional microphone, by contrast, is designed to provide greater amplification for sounds originating from the front of the aid than for those arriving from the rear. This is achieved by the use of front and rear sound openings. A resistance device slows down the speed of the sound waves entering from the rear, thus suppressing these sound waves and reducing their level of amplification. Figure 9.2 shows relative amplification as a function of direction. Note that a directional microphone produces a pear-shaped area of sensitivity decreasing from front to rear. The advantage of this pattern of sensitivity is the user's improved ability to discriminate speech against noise background when the noise originates from behind. Under this condition Frank and Gooden (1973) demonstrated a 15 percent improvement in speech discrimination when subjects used a directional microphone compared to when they used a nondirectional one. This superiority of directional over nondirectional microphones was also demonstrated by Lentz (1972) and Sung, Sung, and Angeletti (1975). If, as a teacher therapist, you encounter hearing-aid users who complain that although their hearing aids are helpful under quiet listening conditions, they are not as useful in noisy environments, you should discuss this with an audiologist to investigate whether a directional microphone may be of further help.

To summarize, using microphones is the first stage in the process of replicating the acoustic wave pattern. Any distortion—that is, components added, reduced, or subtracted from the input acoustic signal—will be amplified by subsequent stages. Two sources of distortion that are not uncommon with ceramic microphones—namely, mechanical feedback and noise from clothing rub—are virtually eliminated when an electret micro-

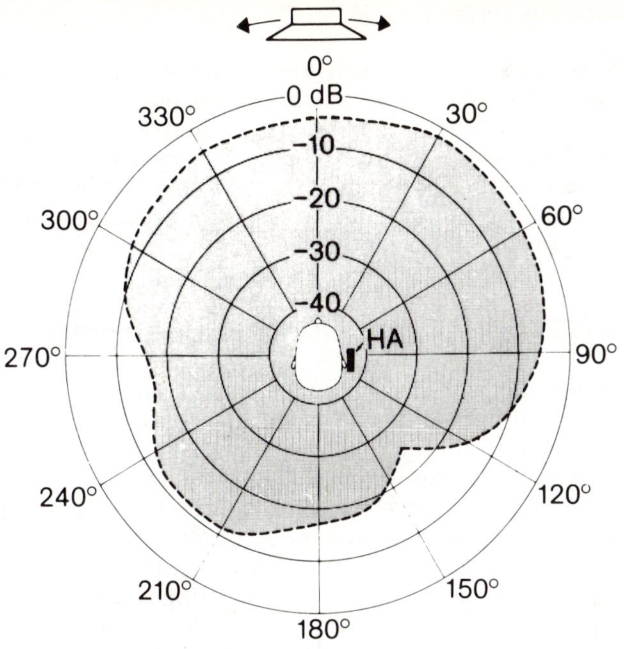

FIGURE 9.2 The characteristics of sensitivity of a directional hearing aid (courtesy of Oticon Hearing Aid Company).

phone is used. Another characteristic of microphones that we considered was directional versus nondirectional sensitivity. For persons who experience particular difficulty with speech discrimination in noise, a directional microphone may result in improved speech comprehension under certain circumstances.

The Amplifier

The amplifier constitutes the most complex part of a hearing aid. Fortunately we do not need to be familiar with the circuitry; if you have an interest in this, you should consult Olsen (1977).

Two stages of amplification occur—the preamp and the power amp. At the preamplifier the weak electrical signal generated by the input microphone is amplified to the level necessary for it to be received by the amplifier. Thus the preamp serves as a means of matching the microphone to the amplifier. In the amplifier the signal is greatly magnified before transmission to the output transducer—that is, the receiver headphones or loudspeaker.

The Output Transducer

The role of the output transducer—that is, the hearing-aid receiver or headphones—is the opposite of that of the microphone. The output transducer receives the electrical signal, magnified many times by the amplifier, and converts it back into an acoustic wave form. The resultant output wave pattern should be an extremely enlarged replica of the input wave transduced by the microphone. The quality of the output signal will depend upon the fidelity of reproduction at each stage of the process. Any components of the input signal that are changed in relative intensity or any components in the output that were not present in the input signal will constitute unwanted distortion.

INTENTIONAL MODIFICATION OF THE SIGNAL

Other than the intensity of the overall pattern, anything added or subtracted from the input signal constitutes distortion. This is true when a change occurs as an unwanted characteristic of the system. However, in order to meet the different needs of persons with various degrees and configurations (patterns) of hearing impairment, hearing aids are built with different amplification characteristics. Most individual aids can be modified further by the audiologist or hearing-aid dealer. Modifications are made by using external controls, by adjusting small screws or switches somewhere in the case, or by changing the selective characteristics of the ear mold. More sophisticated modifications can be made on auditory-training unit amplifiers than on wearable aids. First, let us examine the changes that can be made; then we can consider their significance.

Acoustic Gain

High-Frequency Average Full-On Gain. The term *gain* means exactly what it says: It refers to the increase (gain) in intensity of the input signal to the microphone as a result of amplification. Every wearable hearing aid amplifies an input signal by a certain amount. This amount varies intentionally in the different models of hearing aids manufactured by any given company. The hearing-aid division of a company designs a range of hearing aids to meet the needs of people with mild, moderate, and severe or profound hearing defects. The acoustic gain for an aid is specified by the manufacturer as maximum gain, which is a measure of the amount the aid adds to a 60 dB sound-pressure level (pure-tone) input signal when it is set to the full-on position. An average of the amount of sound-pressure increase in the input signal is taken at 1000, 1600, and 2500 Hz.* The figure obtained is referred to as the *High-Frequency (HF) Average Gain.* The value of this figure is that it provides some idea of the amount of amplification the wearer will derive from the aid in the higher range of speech frequencies, where the need for amplification tends to be greatest.

Saturation Sound-Pressure Level (SSPL 90). The SSPL represents the maximum sound level the aid can generate, regardless of the strength

*Current standards for reporting these measurements are defined by the USA *Standard Methods of Expressing Hearing Aid Performance* (1971) and the Hearing Aid Industry Conference (HAIC) *Standard Method of Expressing Hearing Aid Performance* (1974).

of the input signal or the gain of the aid. This measure has also been referred to as the *maximum power output* (MPO). Above this level the hearing aid cannot increase the input signal.

Peak Gain. This refers to the maximum gain at any frequency—that is, the highest peak of amplification.

Reference-Test Gain. This is a recent specification. It represents the gain added to a 50 dB SPL or 60 dB SPL input signal when the peaks that occur in long-term speech are included in the computation. The 50 dB input is used for aids that limit output by clipping the peaks off the signal; the 60 dB input is used for aids with automatic volume control. These two methods of protecting the listener from amplification to discomfort levels are discussed on pp. 187–189. The practical use of reference-test gain lies in its approximation of the gain that would be added to the intensity of a speaker's conversation at about three feet from the aid. An example of a hearing aid's Full-On Gain Curve is provided in Figure 9.3.

Significance of Gain Specification

The two most important criteria governing the effective use of a hearing aid are that: (1) the instrument delivers enough amplification; and (2) the output does not exceed the person's threshold of discomfort (loudness discomfort level or LDL). We call this range between minimal useful loudness and the LDL the *dynamic range of hearing,* which represents an individual's usable residual hearing. Compare, for example, the dynamic range of two persons, shown in Figure 9.4. Subject A has an average threshold of 35 dB for frequencies 500 to 2000 Hz. If we assume normal LDL of 130 dB, the dynamic range will be 95 dB. If, on the other hand, a person has a far more severe hearing defect, as does Subject B, the range will be much smaller. When we subtract the average deficit of 80

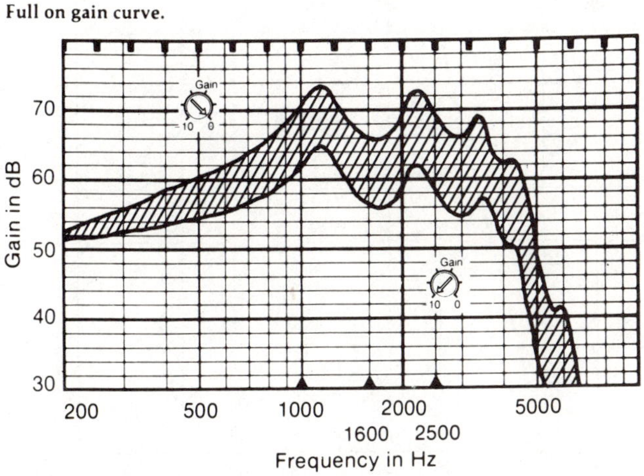

FIGURE 9.3 Gain specifications for Telex Model 33 DA.

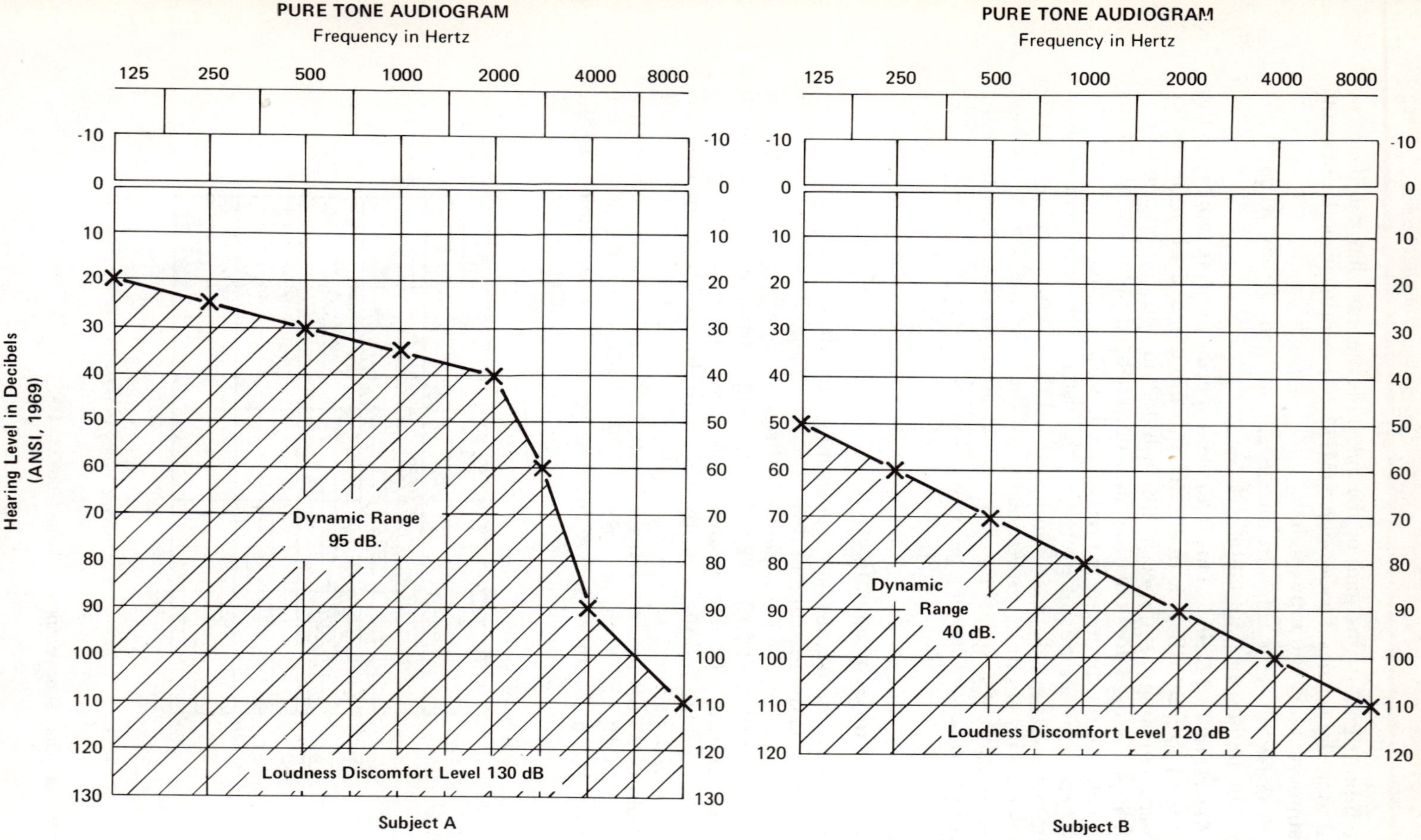

FIGURE 9.4 The comparative dynamic ranges of hearing of two subjects with different hearing deficits and loudness discomfort levels.

dB (500 to 2000 Hz) from a reduced LDL of 120 dB, which is common with severe hearing deficits (Hood and Poole, 1966), the result indicates a dynamic range limited to 40 dB.

If the hearing aid permits sound to be delivered to the ear of an adult at levels that exceed the LDL the person will turn down the volume until a tolerable level of maximum output is achieved. Unfortunately in doing so the person also turns down the intensity of the softer speech signal so that its value is severely reduced. For a young child who wears an aid turned down to a level at which speech is insufficiently amplified, language learning and speech communication will necessarily be jeopardized. If the child is too young to turn down the volume, prolonged overamplification may cause further deterioration of hearing sensitivity (Jerger & Lewis, 1975; Rintelmann & Bess, 1977; Ross & Lerman, 1967).

As previously mentioned, it is essential that sufficient acoustic gain can be provided to amplify speech to usable levels of intensity. The HF average gain of the aid must be adequate for the client's needs. Up to this maximum level, the actual amount of gain may be varied by the volume control on the aid. Thus, for a given input intensity, output may be adjusted by changing the volume control (input + gain = output).

The task of selecting an aid that has appropriate gain for an adult falls to the audiologist. In the rehabilitation process, however, the teacher/therapist must confirm that the aid is living up to the audiologist's expectancies, and must be particularly concerned that the appropriate volume setting is being used. In a study of 200 adult hearing-aid users McCandless (1976) demonstrated that the volume (gain) setting selected for average use proved to be half the intensity of the subjects' average thresholds at 500, 1000, and 2000 Hz. For example, in a group of fifty subjects, the average use-gain for persons with a 30-dB hearing deficit was shown to be approximately 18 dB whereas those with a 60-dB hearing deficit had a use-gain of approximately 28 dB. The hearing-aid users showed a linear increase in gain equivalent to approximately 5 dB for each 10 dB increase in hearing deficit from 10 dB to 95 dB.

It has also been shown that for adults, maximum speech discrimination is achieved when the aid is set to the most comfortable loudness level (MCL) (Markle & Zaner, 1966; Yantis, Millin, & Shapiro, 1966), which is almost identical for pure tone and for speech stimuli (Berger & Lowry, 1971; Ventry, Woods, Rubin, & Hill, 1971). MCL has been described by Skinner (1977) in this way:

> *The comfort level in a hypothetical sense is assumed to be a loudness level at which the input is amplified to a level approximating the center of the subject's dynamic range; that is a signal level that is "not too soft and not too loud,"* (p. 108).

The reliability of MCL as a loudness criterion in hearing-aid gain selection has been confirmed by Hochberg (1975). It should be noted at what point on the volume control MCL is reached. Preferably, this should be somewhere around half to two-thirds of full rotation. If you find that a subject is wearing the aid with the volume barely turned up, then you need to determine why. Either turning it higher would result in unacceptable acoustic feedback, or the aid is overpowered for the client's needs. If, on the other hand, the user wears the aid near to maximum volume, one must suspect that it is providing insufficient gain.

Gengel (1974) has reported that for a group of hearing-impaired adults studied at Gallaudet College in Washington, D.C., maximum vowel discrimination for most subjects occurred 22 dB above the speech detection threshold, whereas the maximum consonant discrimination level was 11 dB higher (that is, 33 dB). Gengel (1974) noted:

> *Typically, however, subjects such as these set their hearing aids to receive speech at 20–25 dB or at most 30 dB above their detection thresholds. They probably set these levels with reference to the loudness of F1. It was possible for them to become accustomed to a higher gain setting; for good speech perception they should be doing just that, but for the most part they did not* (p. 130).

Studies of volume settings used by children with severe and profound hearing deficits reveal the same tendency to set the volume control lower than a position optimal for speech perception (Bess, 1976; Byrne & Fitfield, 1974).

A problem arises when it is difficult to determine the MCL of a child. This occurs with infants, or with children who have very limited language abilities. The method of selecting a gain that represents half the average hearing deficit is helpful if electroacoustic determination of gain at a particular point on the volume control can be measured. Recently the use of aided acoustical stapedial reflex thresholds (ASRT) has been advocated as a means of objectively determining appropriate use-gain for children (Rappaport & Tait, 1976; Snow & McCandless, 1976). Rappaport and Tait demonstrated that when use-gain was determined by the acoustic-reflex method in adults, their aided discrimination scores were equal to those obtained using the subjective MCL method.

Maximum Power Output (Saturation Sound-Pressure Level)

We defined MPO, or SSPL, as the maximum level of output of the aid regardless of the intensity of the input sound. Limitations of the output of the aid are essential to ensure that sounds do not exceed the thresholds of discomfort and do not approach the pain level. It is physical sound pressure rather than psychological loudness that determines discomfort. The tolerance levels of hearing-impaired persons with sensorineural deficits are therefore normal or reduced. Schwartz and Larson (1977) have pointed out that most powerful body and ear-level hearing aids generate SPL's of 130+ dB. Some even reach 149 dB, which exceeds the normal pain threshold of approximately 140 dB SPL. Schwartz and Larson contend, therefore, that MPO is critical to the selection of an appropriate aid, particularly for preverbal children. McCandless (1976) has drawn attention to the fact that 50 percent of hearing-aid users experience some discomfort as a result of too great an output from their aid, whereas 20 to 35 percent use their aids only part-time, or do not use them at all for the same reason. Limitation of MPO is, therefore, most necessary to protect the ear from further damage due to overexposure to intense sound, and to ensure that the output of the aid stays within an individual's tolerance levels for loudness at all times.

Methods of Limiting Output

There are two methods by which the maximum acoustic output of the amplifier can be limited. The first is by a process of *peak clipping*. This involves cutting off peak intensities whenever they exceed the maximum output limit (Figure 9.5). It has been conclusively demonstrated that the peak intensities of speech can be quite severely clipped without producing any significant loss of intelligibility (Davis, Hudgins, Marquis, Nichols, and Peterson, 1946; Licklider, 1946). This is because the vowel sounds, which are more intense than consonant sounds and which contribute less to intelligibility, reach maximum output levels first. Clipping the vowel peaks permits the overall gain to be turned up. Amplification of the relatively weaker consonants can therefore occur without impairment of vowel intelligibility. The spectra of speech sounds subjected to peak clippings have been shown to be only slightly modified by the process (Licklider, 1948). However, although intelligibility remains unaffected by moderate peak clipping the quality of the sound is generally adversely affected. This can be compensated for by providing relatively greater amplification of the high-frequency components of speech sound than of the low-frequency sounds.

The second method of limiting output is by *compression amplification*. This is achieved by an automatic electrical-circuit servosystem, generally referred to as the *automatic volume control* (AVC) or automatic gain control (AGC). When the intensity of the electrical signal at the final stage of amplification (output stage) exceeds a predetermined level, sufficient current flows through a feedback circuit to the first stage or first and second stages of amplification to influence its function in a manner that decreases the gain it provides. The intensity level of the electrical signal at the output stage that will induce this decrease in gain may be modified on a variable resistor similar to the volume control. In some aids this involves the choice of one of several control settings, each of which repre-

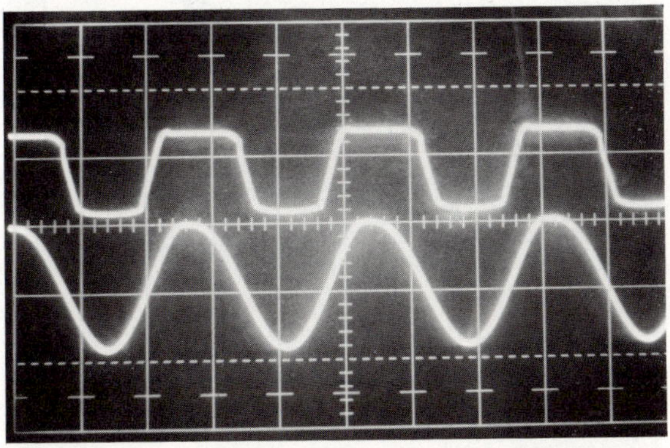

FIGURE 9.5 The effect of peak clipping on the wave form of an acoustic signal.

sents a feedback circuit offering a particular resistance to the feedback current. The current intensity must be sufficient to overcome the resistance before compression of the sound wave will occur. The control that determines this level is sometimes referred to as the *comfort control.* The chart shown in Figure 9.6 illustrates the compression provided by AVC at various levels of gain. For the full-gain curve, changes of 50 to 100 dBs of input intensity at the microphone (a 50-dB increase) result in output changes of less than 10 dBs. This provides protection to the hearing-aid wearer. The compression action for stated gain levels below maximum is also shown. The effect of AVC is to permit restriction of the range of output levels, generated by a wide range of input sound intensities, within one-thirtieth of a second of the arrival of a sound-pressure level that exceeds the selected sensitivity of the AVC. The gain of the instrument has been reduced to prevent the signal from crossing the tolerance level. It takes one-tenth second for the gain to return to normal level when the input sound-pressure-level peak drops.

Skinner (1977) has concluded that:

All forms of compression amplification offer advantages over peak clipping: 1) compression reduces the amount of distortion of the signal; 2) output is limited at a level below the amplifier saturation through gain reduction over the entire signal. In addition, compression amplification permits an expanded dynamic range for the hearing aid user since it provides a wider range of input level to the ear, yet still maintains maximum output levels which can be adjusted to the tolerance levels of the hearing impaired (p. 111).

An important advantage of compression amplification is that the signal-to-noise ratio of the input signal is preserved because both signal and noise are equally reduced. This is a significant benefit in speech discrimination tasks (Pollack, 1980a).

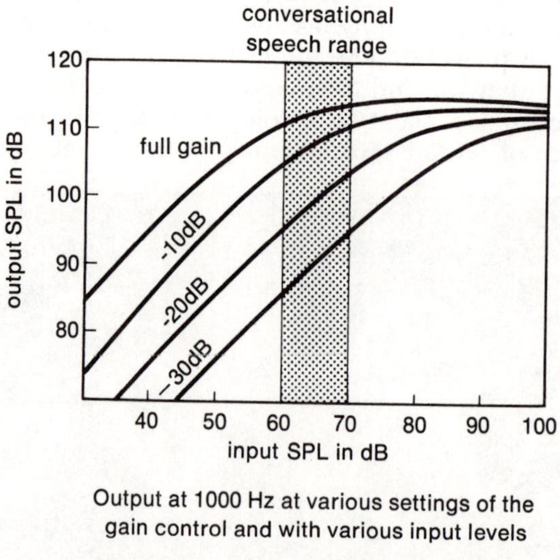

FIGURE 9.6 Signal compression of various degrees resulting from compression amplification at various levels of gain (courtesy of Zenith Hearing Aid Sales Corporation).

You should bear in mind the potential benefits of compression amplification when one of your clients seems to experience difficulty in tolerating his or her aid when it is set to produce sound at a level of loudness necessary for speech comprehension. Hearing-aid users who complain that their aid works well in quiet environments but becomes intolerable where loud noises occur may be candidates for compression amplification. Children who instinctively cover their ears when a loud noise occurs as though this protects them from the amplified sound, or who pull out the ear mold, cry, or wince at loud sounds, or who consistently wear the hearing aid at an unexpectedly low setting should be referred to an audiologist. In the case of both adults and children, your insight into loudness tolerance and your careful justification of audiological referral may result in successful use of amplification by someone who might otherwise not have used the hearing aid optimally.

Frequency Response

Just as hearing aids are manufactured with a variety of gain and output capabilities, so are they available with a range of preset or adjustable frequency sensitivities. A frequency response curve of an instrument depicts for each frequency the amount by which the incoming signal is amplified (that is, gain at each frequency). These frequency-sensitivity curves show how the pattern of amplification provided by a hearing aid may be varied by its component units. In a wearable hearing aid we cannot modify the frequency response by changing the microphone because it is inaccessible. The microphone will, therefore, contribute a constant response to the system. However, remember that if we connect a microphone other than the one designed for a particular auditory training unit to the system, we can no longer expect the amplifying system to function in accordance with the specifications provided by the manufacturer. We may also find that in addition to having changed the frequency-response characteristics, we have changed the overall gain of the system because of an impedance mismatch between the microphone and the amplifier.

The receiver of the type of hearing aid worn in glasses or in a single behind-the-ear unit is, like the microphone, a built-in component not accessible to the user. The receiver of the body-type hearing aid, however, is quite accessible and can be easily detached and replaced with a different one. Because the receiver of the hearing aid also has frequency-response characteristics, it is possible to change the response characteristics of the total system by changing the receiver. This method of altering overall response characteristics is used with some types of body aid. It must also be recognized that the response curve will be affected by the coupling device used to feed the output signal into the ear canal. This includes any plastic tubing connecting the aid to an ear mold, and to the mold itself.

The overall frequency-response characteristics of the aid represent the interaction of the response characteristics of its individual components. Figure 9.7 shows the overall specifications typical of a wearable hearing aid.

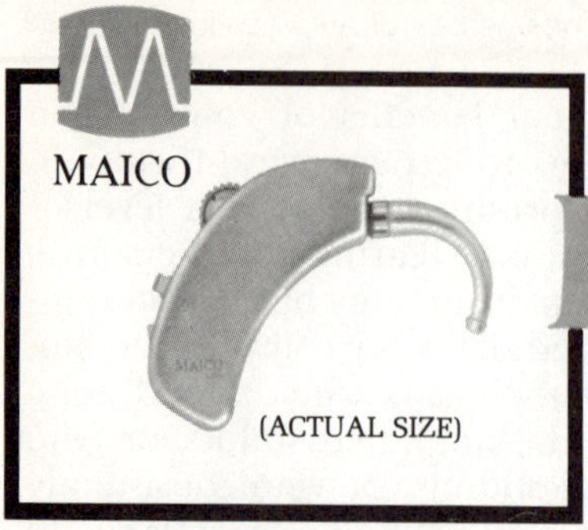

TECHNICAL SPECIFICATIONS

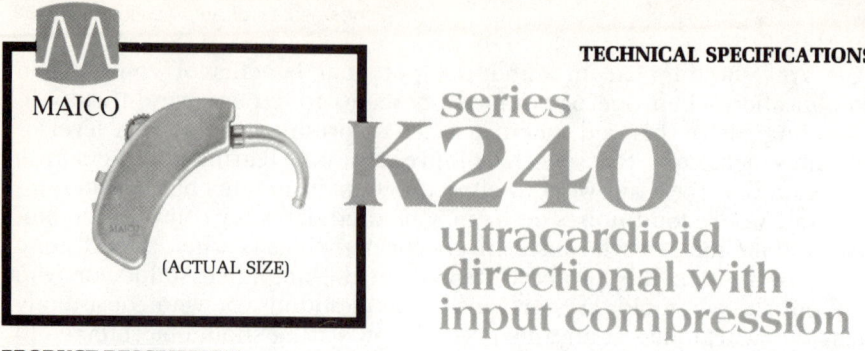

series K240 ultracardioid directional with input compression

PRODUCT DESCRIPTION

The Series K240 is a medium gain, medium output, ultracardioid directional behind-the-ear instrument, with an input compression circuit, having an extended high frequency response and continuously adjustable controls for establishing power output level (SSPL 90) and for reducing the low frequency response. Available with an optional telephone switch, user operated Response Selector Switch or without any external switches, as needed, the Series K240 can be recommended for use in a wide range of applications, especially when non-distorting signals at controlled output levels are required.

SSPL 90 curve

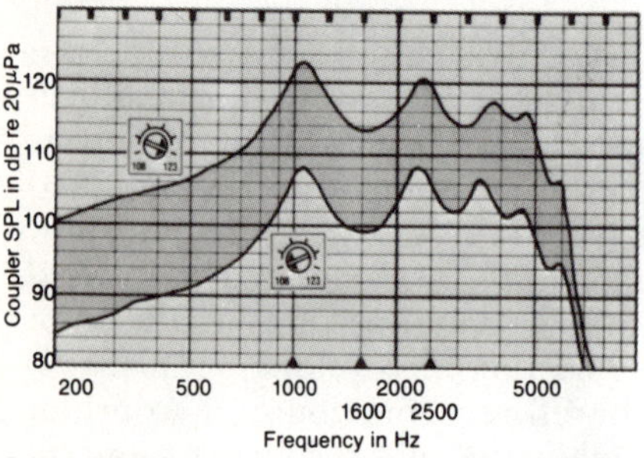

Figure 1 — Shaded area shows range of the Power Level Limiting control. Adjustment of this control reduces HF-Average SSPL 90 approximately 15 dB, from 118 to 103 dB SPL.

Full on gain curve.

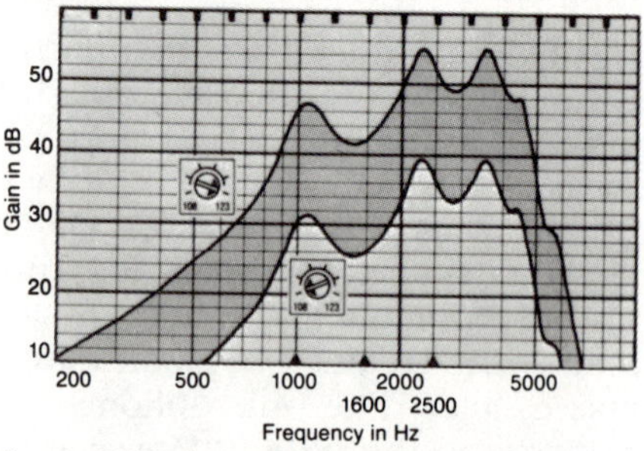

Figure 2 — Wide band receiver provides significant gain at high frequencies (approximately 37 dB at 5000 Hz). Shaded area shows typical effect on gain when Power Level Limiting is reduced.

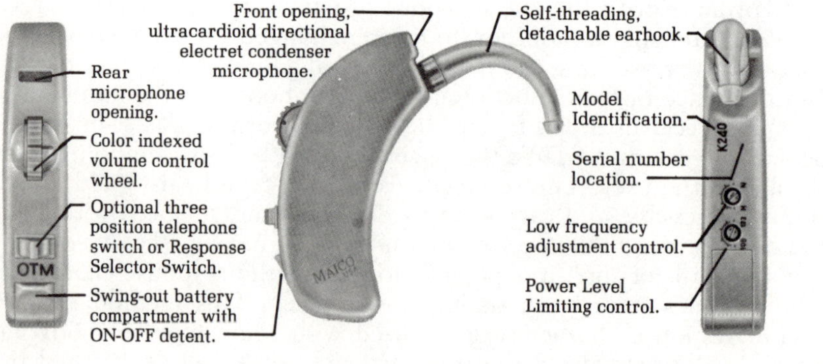

FIGURE 9.7 Overall specifications for a wearable hearing aid (courtesy of MAICO Instrument Corporation).

MAICO

series K240

ultracardioid directional with input compression

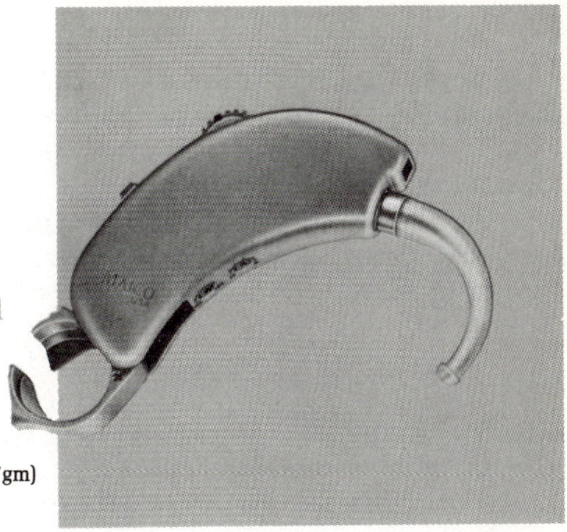

PHYSICAL SPECIFICATIONS

Length: 1.66" (42.2mm)
Width: .590" (15.0mm)
Thickness: .375" (9.5mm)
Weight without battery: .20 oz. (5.7gm)

PERFORMANCE SUMMARY

ASA Standard 7-1976 (ANSI S3.22-1976) Method[1]

MEASUREMENTS	VALUES	TOLERANCES	TEST CONDITIONS
Maximum SSPL 90	127 dB SPL[2] (123 dB SPL typical)	Maximum	A
HF-Average SSPL 90	118 dB SPL	± 4 dB	A
HF-Average full-on gain	46 dB	± 5 dB	B
Reference test gain	NA[3]		
Frequency range	560 to 6000 Hz		B
Total harmonic distortion[4]			
500 Hz	Not Measured[5]		
800 Hz	5% (1.4% typical)	Maximum	D
1600 Hz	9% (4.5% typical)	Maximum	D
Battery current drain	1.6mA (1.4 mA typical)	Maximum	C
Coupler SPL with induction coil	104 dB SPL	± 6 dB	E
Attack time	2 ms	± 5 ms	F
Release time	45 ms	± 22.5 ms	G

HAIC Method (for purposes of comparison)

MEASUREMENTS	VALUES	TEST CONDITIONS
Average output	115 dB SPL	A
Peak output	123 dB SPL	A
Average gain	40 dB	B
Peak gain	55 dB	B

FOOTNOTES:

(1) Test Conditions.

Temperature:	23 ± 5°C (73 ± 9°F).
Relative humidity:	0% to 80%
Atmospheric pressure:	760 (+35, −150) mm of Hg.
Earphone coupler:	HA-2, employing a rigid tube 25mm (.984") long and 1.93mm (.076") diameter with earhook 1005-392 (Kit No. 6466).
Supply voltage:	Mercury 675 battery, 1.30 volts partially discharged to avoid typical high initial voltage.
Control setting:	Power Level Limiting control at maximum (123). (AGC mode is present at all settings of the Power Level Limiting control.) Low frequency adjustment control at normal response (N). Response Selector Switch set at (N).

A. Full-on gain setting, 90 dB input, 0° sound incidence.
B. Full-on gain setting, 50 dB input, 0° sound incidence.
C. Full-on gain setting, 65 dB input, 0° sound incidence. 1000 Hz.
D. Full-on gain setting, 70 dB input, 0° sound incidence.
E. Full-on gain setting, 10 milliamp per meter magnetic field, 1000 Hz.
F. Abrupt increase from 55 to 80 dB at 2000 Hz, 0° incidence.
G. Abrupt drop from 80 to 55 dB at 2000 Hz, 0° incidence.

(2) The maximum SSPL 90 value, i.e., the highest point on the SSPL 90 curve, will always be less than 127 dB SPL as listed above. The typical maximum SSPL 90 value, as shown on the SSPL 90 curve (Fig. 1) is 123 dB SPL.

(3) For AGC instruments, reference test gain is defined as the full-on volume control position, per ASA Std. 7-1976, Section 6.6.

(4) Values shown indicate maximum allowable (upper limit) total harmonic distortion, for any given instrument, lower typical values are shown in parentheses.

(5) The distortion data at 500 Hz is omitted because the response curve rises more than 12 dB between fundamental (500 Hz) and second harmonic (1000 Hz), per ASA Std. 7-1976, Section 6.10.

The aim of the manufacturer is to provide a pattern of amplification that does not distort the input signal. However, although speech contains frequencies across a range from approximately 100 to 8000 Hz, good comprehension of conversational speech can be achieved by a person with normal language, providing he or she receives frequencies in the range of 300 to 3000 Hz. Because of instrument size, the frequency-response characteristics of many wearable hearing aids (standard-response aids) have not generally extended much beyond this range. The fidelity with which the input signal will be amplified may be assessed by the flatness of the response curve. If the aid unintentionally favors some frequencies while suppressing others, then frequency distortion will be present. Remember, however, that frequency distortion is assessed relative to normal hearing. In designing amplification systems to meet the needs of hearing-impaired persons, it is recognized that in most instances the hearing-aid user will already be experiencing frequency distortion due to the greater loss of sensitivity to some frequencies than to others. The auditory-response curve is not flat to begin with. This may present a problem. If a flat pattern of amplification is used, frequencies that may be relatively unimpaired by the hearing problem will be amplified equally with those that are more severely affected. Thus, sounds that are heard at comfortable loudness without amplification become abnormally or uncomfortably loud, while the less audible sounds may still fail to be amplified sufficiently. It seems reasonable, therefore, to ask whether the selective amplification of sound energy in the frequencies where the hearing loss is greatest will improve the value of amplification in oral communication.

In 1947, Davis reported the findings of a study designed to provide information relative to this question. The report, commonly referred to as the Harvard Report, indicated that the most effective amplification was provided by an instrument that possessed a flat response or provided moderate high-tone emphasis across a wide frequency range and that also incorporated true square-top peak clipping (Davis, Stevens, Nichols, Hudgins, Marquis, Peterson, & Ross, 1947).

Similar findings were obtained in a parallel study by the British Medical Research Council (1947). However, these findings did not resolve the controversy concerning the value of varying degrees of frequency response in accommodating the needs of persons with different patterns of hearing deficiency. Thus, both wearable hearing aids and auditory training units available today make provision for the modification of the overall frequency-response pattern. This may be achieved by choosing among aids that have different frequency responses, by changing the receiver on body-type aids, or by using small plastic inserts, which fit into the nozzle of the earphone. The ear mold or tubing that couples the aid to the ear can also be modified. The tone control found on many aids or small accessible switches or screws may also be adjusted to modify the frequency response.

We are obviously not convinced that a flat response is adequate for all patterns of hearing impairment. Carhart (1980) stated:

To generalize, we have moved from an era where selective amplification was unpopular to a philosophy where many audiologists remain alert to the patterns of hearing loss exhibited by their patients and keep in mind a variety of ways for modifying the frequency pattern of the amplification the patient is receiving (p. xxiii).

As Carhart points out, we still lack firm scientific evidence concerning which modifications in frequency response of aids help particular types and patterns of hearing deficiencies. A number of studies directed at this problem have appeared in the literature. Reddell and Calvert (1966) reported on the interpretation of audiometric data as a guide for hearing-aid selection. They found that high-frequency emphasis resulted in improved speech discrimination by subjects with steeply sloping high-frequency hearing patterns. Similar findings were reported by Pasco, Niemoeller, and Miller (1973), who showed that the extension of the upper frequency range of amplification from 3150 to 6300 Hz resulted in an increase in discrimination. For one subject this averaged 12 percent. Triantos and McCandless (1974) also investigated the importance of the higher frequencies for speech discrimination by both normal and hearing-impaired subjects tested in quiet and in noise. A comparison was made between scores obtained when frequencies were cut off at 3800 Hz and those obtained when the range extended to 5200 Hz. Both normal and hearing-impaired subjects obtained approximately 15 percent better scores with the extended range of frequencies when tested in noise. However, this improvement did not occur under quiet conditions. Thomas and Pfannebecker (1974) found that in quiet conditions a significant reduction in low-frequency amplification was effective in producing a marked improvement in the discrimination test scores of persons with sensorineural hearing impairment. However, much intersubject variation was found and the results did not relate clearly to the pattern and degree of the pure-tone thresholds. Pasco et al. (1973) had demonstrated similar improvement from low-frequency suppression in children with a broad band of residual hearing. On the basis of their results these authors concluded that the frequency response of the aid should allow an increase of gain of 7 dB for each octave.

From these studies it appears that noise in the low frequencies, or even amplification of the low-frequency components of vowels, mask out the weaker high-frequency patterns that characterize many of the consonants (Danaher & Pickett, 1975). The significance of this is obvious when you realize that these consonants provide as much as 60 percent of the cues to speech intelligibility (Gerber, 1974). Thus, emphasizing high-frequency components by selective amplification often affords significant help to persons with sensorineural hearing problems.

By contrast Ling (1964) studied the effects of extending the frequency range of the hearing aid downward to 100 Hz where the suprasegmental cues to speech are found. Ling demonstrated that children with bilateral fragmentary hearing were better able to discriminate stress, pitch, vowels, and syllabic structure when extended low-frequency amplification was provided. No improvement in consonant discrimination was demonstrated. Ling's concern was to provide amplification for children with residual hearing only in the low frequencies (below 1000 Hz). For these children it appears that such amplification may be of value in speech perception. Low-frequency amplification is counterindicated in all other circumstances (Danaher & Pickett, 1975). In fact, as we have seen, for adults and children with hearing above 500 Hz some suppression of low-frequency amplification may prove necessary. Furthermore, when residual hearing extends out beyond the 4000-Hz limit of the conventional hearing-aid response, extension of high-frequency amplification should be considered, particularly for children. We know that valuable cues to unvoiced consonants are present above 4000 Hz. It is, as Ross and Tomassetti (1980) point out, ludicrous to adopt an amplification system that filters out potentially valuable acoustic information, particularly because it is technically possible to extend the range of a wearable aid to 6000 Hz or even 9000 Hz (Lybarger, 1977).

Ear-Mold and Tube-Response Characteristics

The final factor that can modify the response characteristics of the hearing aid is the mechanical device used for coupling the aid to the ear—the mold and the tubing. At this point we only need to consider briefly the acoustic influence of the mold. Later, we will examine the types you may encounter.

The purpose of the ear mold is to connect the hearing-aid receiver to the ear. The receiver of the body aid is an external unit; therefore, the mold clips directly onto it. In the ear-level or glasses-type aid, the receiver is internally housed in the aid case, and it must be connected to the mold by a length of plastic tube. In all aids, the ear mold and tubing constitute integral component parts of the amplification system, and they are not merely a channel for sound. The coupling system will either preserve the quality of the amplified signal or distort it. Appropriate modifications can even enhance the signal in terms of a client's special needs. This may be achieved by: (1) varying the size of the channel through which the acoustic energy flows from the receiver to the ear (that is, the bore of the mold and the connecting tubing); (2) varying the depth of projection into the ear canal; (3) inserting filters; or (4) drilling channels (venting) that extend between the cavity adjacent to the eardrum and the atmosphere outside. The research suggests that appropriate modification of the characteristics of the coupling system can favorably influence speech discrimination by as much as 16 percent (Davis & Green, 1974; Jetty & Rintlemann, 1970; McClellen, 1967).

DISTORTION

Faithfulness of replication of the input signal by the amplification system is critical to optimal speech perception. Exact reproduction is not possible because no system is perfect, but distortion in the form of (1) nonlinear frequency or amplitude replication; (2) reduction in the width of the band of frequencies present in the input signal; or (3) addition of harmonic vibrations not present in the original signal must stay within predetermined limits. Significant distortion is present when the output signal differs in wave form from the input signal by more than the specifications of the manufacturer.

Four major forms of distortion exist. The first, *harmonic distortion,* results from the addition of harmonic vibrations not present in the input wave.

The second type, *linear distortion,* occurs as a result of unequal amplification at different frequencies. This is apparent in a sensitivity curve that is not flat across the band of frequencies being amplified.

Intermodulation distortion results when two pure tones occurring simultaneously produce an effect perceived as a warble or beat phenommenon. If an amplification system is subject to the presence of harmonic distortion, the interaction of the input signal with the harmonic distortion may result in the perception of a beating tone known as intermodulation distortion.

Another form of distortion results from the resonant characteristics of the electrical and mechanical components of the amplifier. If these components are not adequately damped, they may give off sympathetic vibrations known as transients, thus creating *transient distortion.*

The electroacoustic performance of an aid should be assessed by an audiologist. Among the measures should be the percentage of harmonic distortion. The audiologist should be able to advise whether the distortion conforms to the manufacturer's specifications for the aid. The total amount of distortion should certainly not exceed 10 percent in any aid (Bode & Kasten, 1971; Jeffers, Behrens, & Rubin, 1973).

Summary

What we have seen is that present hearing aids place a wide variety of gain output and frequency-response characteristics at the audiologist's disposal. To take advantage of these, the client's hearing and amplification needs must be carefully assessed. The assessment must be aimed at obtaining measures of the subject's *functional* use of hearing, because only tentative predictions can be made on the basis of audiometric data alone. We also considered evidence that indicates that for some persons the need for, and advantages of, selective amplification, or use of directional microphones, only becomes apparent when the person must function in noise. The need for functional assessment of the effectiveness of amplification on young children, particularly prelingual children, is clearly critical to the selection of appropriate hearing-aid characteristics. It is important to recognize that an initial fitting of a hearing aid to an infant or even a young child is necessarily exploratory and therefore temporary. Determination of the specific amplification needs must depend on the coordinated efforts of the audiologist, parents, teacher, and therapist to assess the effect of various aid specifications on the child's communicative, learning, and social behavior. Furthermore, the child's needs may well change with age. To participate fully with the audiologist, the teacher/therapist must have sufficient understanding of amplification and hearing aids. This is necessary to permit intelligent, knowledgeable discussion, to raise pertinent questions, and to realize how much, in fact, can be done to overcome a child's or adult's difficulty. It is frequently acknowledged (Carhart, 1975; Matkin, 1977; Ross & Tomassetti, 1980; Swartz & Larson, 1977) that current hearing-aid selection for adults and children alike lacks a systematic general theory as to the specific requirements for optimal amplification. Nor is there a single well-documented method for selecting an aid (Ross & Tomassetti, 1980; Swartz & Larson, 1977). Despite the critical importance of understanding the interaction of the physical characteristics of the hearing aid and the perception of speech, even what we do know does not always influence our selection of appropriate amplification characteristics: "Unfortunately, many audiologists show little concern for parameters such as MPO, frequency range, and distortion relative to the provision of maximum speech information" (Swartz & Larson, 1977, p. 221). Therefore, in some instances you may find it necessary to be very persistent in your relationship with an audiologist or hearing-aid dealer if you are to ensure that your client's difficulties with a given aid are to be remedied.

Your input concerning the child's or adult's functional use of the aid is essential to the determination of optimal electroacoustic characteristics for a given person. As Harris (1976) states: "Even if one has a good candidate and the theoretically ideal prosthesis for him, there is no validated way to measure, much less to predict, what that aid does in the wearer's daily life" (p. 5). You should need no further persuasion to accept the importance of your being familiar with the matters we have discussed so far.

TYPES OF HEARING AID

Having considered the essentials of amplification, let us now examine the types of hearing aids you may expect your clients to be wearing and the controls on these aids.

There are four types of wearable hearing aids available (Figure 9.8). These are (1) the *body* aid, which is worn on a person's clothing or, by young children, in a harness; (2) the *behind-the-ear* hearing aid; (3) the *glasses* hearing aid; and (4) the *in-the-ear* hearing aid.

According to information from the Hearing Aid Industry Conference, New York (1976), the number of hearing aids estimated to be sold annually in the United States almost doubled from 350,000 in 1965 to 600,000 in 1975. The figure for sales for July, 1979 to July, 1980 was 661,359 for the United States and Canada combined, an increase of 8.3 percent over the previous year. Tables 9.1 and 9.2 show how these sales were distributed among the various types of aids.

The data clearly indicate a dramatic decrease in the number of body-type instruments sold. Among the ear-level hearing aids, fewer people are wearing glasses-mounted units, while more are wearing behind-the-ear models. It is of particular note that the percentage of in-the-ear aids purchased has increased fivefold since 1965. The use of the electret

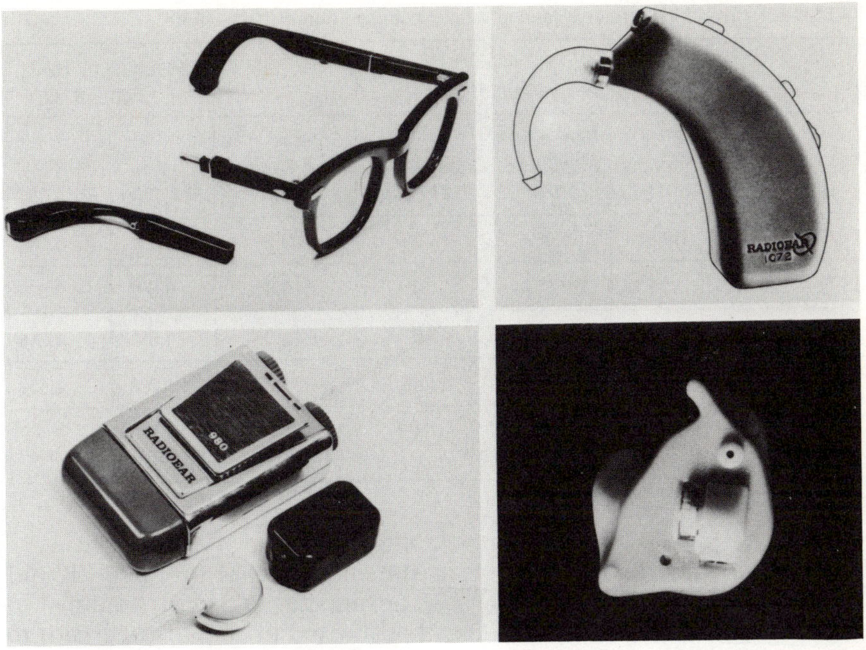

FIGURE 9.8 Four types of personal hearing aids (courtesy of Radio Ear Corporation).

microphone, and improved mounting design, have significantly reduced vibration in this type of instrument and have permitted average gains of up to 40 dB without mechanical feedback. The frequency characteristic usually is a rising one. One would hope that these technological improvements explain the increased sales. However, it may well be that the much advertised cosmetic attraction of this type of aid means that more persons with mild hearing impairment are purchasing it because amplification can be delivered so inconspicuously. Unfortunately, sales figures reveal neither the suitability of the fitting nor its successful use.

The situation concerning behind-the-ear aids, which are also being purchased in increasing numbers, is different. It is now widely recognized that all but the most severe or profound hearing impairments can

TABLE 9.1 Trend in Types of Hearing Aids Purchased during 1965–1976*

	1965	*1976 (January–June)*
Estimated total number of aids sold	352,000	600,000
Percentage of total aids		
Body aids	17.3	4.8
Glasses aids	29.5	16.3
Behind-the-ear aids	46.9	60.9
In-the-ear aids	6.3	18.0

*Source: Hearing Aid Industry Conference, New York, 1976.

TABLE 9.2 Trend in Types of Hearing Aids Purchased during 1979–1980†

Unit Sales by Type of Model					Forecast by HAJ Surveys	
Model Type	*First 6 Months of 1980*	*Second 6 Months of 1979*	*Change in % Total Sales*	*Change in % in Each Class*	*For 1980*	*For 1981*
Behind-The-Ear	59.3%	59.9%	− .6%	+ 3.5%	+4.1%	+ 6.7%
In-The-Ear	31.6%	29.8%	+1.8%	+10.8%	+8.5%	+10.0%
Eyeglass Aids	5.8%	7.0%	−1.2%	−13.9%	−4.5%	− 4.7%
Body Aids	3.3%	3.3%	Same	+ 7.2%	−1.8%	− 4.6%
TOTAL SALES Actual Increase 1979 over 1978 +8.3%					+7.8%	+11.7%

†Source: *Hearing Aid Journal*, 1980.

be accommodated by this type of instrument. Gains of up to 70 dB and outputs of up to 130 dB are available, advantages previously confined to the body aid. In some cases it is even possible to fit behind-the-ear aids to infants, providing special procedures are followed (Rubin, 1976b). Ear-level aids are always preferable for children old enough to eliminate physical fitting difficulties (Madell, 1976).

Body-type aids are usually reserved for very young infants who cannot be satisfactorily physically fit with an ear-level unit, and for those physically handicapped or elderly people who cannot reach or manipulate the small controls on an ear-level instrument.

Binaural Hearing Aids

A growing number of hearing-aid users are choosing to wear two aids, ear level or body type, rather than one. Although it is not possible to determine without careful testing who should wear two aids, the evidence clearly indicates that in general two aids are better than one. The demonstrated advantages of binaural amplification include improved speech discrimination in noise (Dirks & Wilson, 1969; Gelfand & Hochberg, 1976; Nabelek & Pickett, 1974a, 1974b), improved sound localization (Byrne & Dermody, 1975, Dermody & Byrne, 1975a; Heyes & Ferris, 1975), and loudness summation (Dermody & Byrne, 1975b). Ross (1977) suggests that subjective benefits probably also accrue from binaural amplification:

The subjective appreciation of auditory space, the reduction in communication effort, the confidence in one's responses, the speed by which verbal communication may be processed, all of which have been noted by binaural hearing aid users, add dimensions to auditory experience that the clinician should ponder when the question of monaural versus binaural hearing aids arises. Audition is our most important sense, and we should not treat it lightly (p. 246).

The studies already mentioned, among others, all used adult subjects. Research on the effectiveness of binaural aids for children is very limited. Ross and Tomassetti (1980) refer to an unpublished study by Yonovitz (1974), which clearly demonstrated superiority of binaural aids for hearing-impaired children listening at five signal-to-noise ratios. Two earlier studies (Fisher, 1964; Lankford & Faires, 1973) also demonstrated the advantages of binaural aids. Despite the paucity of research relating to children's use of two hearing aids, many audiologists express a preference for binaural amplification. Some centers or schools (Lexington Hearing Center of the Lexington School for the Deaf, New York, and the Peninsular Oral School, Redwood City, California) fit most of their children with binaural aids (Rubin, 1976b). However, each decision must be based on careful assessment of the needs of each child and the benefits derived from the additional instrument.

As a teacher or therapist you should always raise the question of the potential improvement in communication and learning under environmental conditions that may result from binaural amplification. Ross, Hunt, Kessler, and Henniges (1974) have published a rating scale designed to facilitate systematic observation of a child's behavior over time after being fitted with binaural amplification. You may be of considerable assistance to the audiologist by generating such a profile.

Some audiologists continue to be reluctant to fit two hearing aids, fearing that prolonged exposure to high levels of amplification may result in further deterioration due to induced trauma (Jerger & Lewis, 1975). Evidence that this occurs in selected cases has appeared in the literature (Ross & Lerman, 1967). Indeed, careful monitoring of thresholds is necessary when any high-powered aid is fitted to a child, but careful use of output-limiting devices should safeguard most ears. Certainly binaural amplification is not for every child, but neither is it for no child. A comprehensive review of the potential of high-level amplification's inducing further deterioration has been provided by Rintlemann and Bess (1977). Though recognizing that such a hazard does exist for some children, these authors conclude that maximum use must be made of residual hearing in all hearing-impaired children. They state, however: "While the use of amplification is indispensible in the aural habilitative process, it must be employed in a cautious and controlled manner" (p. 292).

Ross (1977) also systematically develops the rationale behind the concern about potential hazard from induced acoustic trauma. He then presents a well-reasoned response in favor of binaural aids providing their use is very carefully monitored. Ross stresses the need for frequent and ongoing evaluation of the audiological status of *all* children wearing hearing aids.

As a clinician or teacher you should be familiar with the potential information about the significant benefits to be derived from effective use of binaural aids appropriately fitted. If the need and benefit can be demonstrated, binaural aids should be fitted. You are justified by the literature in discussing the matter thoroughly with the audiologist responsible for the audiologic management of the child. Your responsibility is to ensure that the child's functional needs in the home and school environment be given heavy weighting among factors that determine the ultimate decision. Too frequently these are not considered by the audiologist. For a comprehensive discussion of the factors to be considered in fitting two hearing aids, see Pollack (1980b), Ross (1977), and Lankford (1970).

CROS Aids

The final type of aid that you will undoubtedly encounter is that in which signals, picked up at one ear, are routed to the opposite (contralateral) ear, where they are amplified and fed to a receiver. These aids are usually identified by the acronym CROS (Contralateral Routing of Signals). This system of amplification, together with its modifications, is used (1) to aid individuals who have monaural hearing impairment in which the poor ear cannot be successfully fitted with amplification and (2) to increase the probability of being able to successfully provide amplification to individuals with steep high-frequency hearing impairment.

A client with a classic CROS fitting wears a microphone on the unusable ear. The microphone is housed either in a case behind the ear, or in the bow of a glasses frame. It is connected by an electrical wire to an amplifier and receiver unit behind the other ear, and looks like a regular behind-the-ear or glasses aid (Figure 9.9). Occasionally you may see the

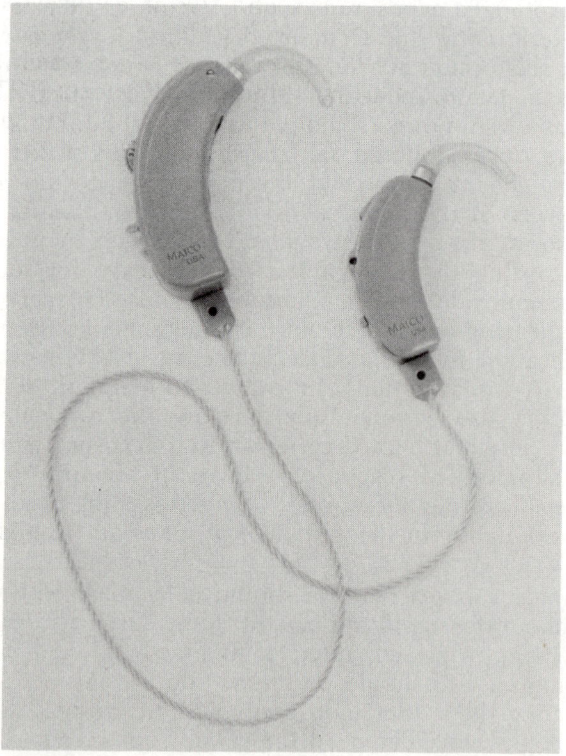

FIGURE 9.9 A typical ear-level CROS hearing aid (courtesy of MAICO Instrument Corporation).

acoustically less satisfactory and cosmetically less attractive plastic tube connection between a regular behind-the-ear aid on the poor ear, and a mold in the good ear. The benefits of a successfully fitted CROS aid are that persons with a hearing deficiency in one ear, and normal or near-normal hearing in the opposite ear, often can benefit from amplification. Even though in the past clients have frequently been assured by audiologists and hearing-aid dealers that they need only one ear to function normally, persons with monaural hearing impairment continued to express feelings of being handicapped in certain situations. Such persons have difficulty in hearing confidently when spoken to by someone on the side of their poor ear, and difficulty with sound localization. The research indicates that CROS fitting does provide significant help to selected clients. It can be quite effective in quiet conditions but appears to be of little or nor help in noisy environments unless noise is located on the side of the good ear while the speaker is located on the side of the poor ear. However, when noise level exceeds the speech signal intensity, CROS generally affords no benefits. In terms of rehabilitation counseling note that the follow-up studies on the successful use of CROS aids are equivocal. In an early follow-up of CROS aid users Harford and Dodds (1966) reported a high level of satisfaction. Aufricht (1972) reached a similar conclusion from the results of a study in which 54 war veterans responded to a questionnaire about their CROS aids. Eighty-five percent of those questioned expressed satisfaction. However, Pollack has (1980b) questioned these results. His personal experience indicates that despite extensive counseling many CROS users cease to wear their aids. He cites the findings of Smedley, von Khaelssberg, and Clement (1974) to support his impression. These researchers reported that approximately 80 percent of the CROS owners studied were not deriving sufficient benefit to justify use of the aid.

The importance of your close cooperation with the audiologist during a trial or postfitting period is emphasized by Harford and Barry (1965) and by Harford and Dodds (1966). These authors concluded that client motivation, careful profiling of the demands on hearing, and the types of environments in which these must be met are highly influential in determining appropriate candidates for this type of amplification and also in determining subsequent successful use. CROS aids are not considered effective for use with most children (Matkin & Thomas, 1971). However, with careful management some may be fitted successfully.

Bilateral Contralateral Routing of Signals (BICROS). This type of fitting is commonly used when a client has a hearing impairment in both ears, but has only one ear suitable for amplification. A complete aid is fitted to the usable ear. A second microphone, located at the unusable ear, picks up sounds for contralateral routing to the usable ear, where the sounds are fed to a single amplifier, which accepts signals from both microphones. These amplified signals are then fed to a single receiver in the usable ear.

There are many subtle variations of the basic CROS system; these have been explained in detail by Pollack (1980).

THE EAR MOLD

The ear mold is as much an integral part of the amplification system as the microphone, amplifier, and receiver. It is far more than a physical device to connect the hearing aid to the ear because it affects the acoustic characteristics of the signal, which must pass through it to the ear canal. Several ear-mold styles are available (Figure 9.10); some of these are intended to effect certain acoustic results, whereas others are designed for cosmetic purposes only. Each ear mold is made from an impression of the ear in which the aid is to be worn. The use of an appropriate fitting mold from a general stock is not an acceptable substitute except in an emergency, such as when a mold is lost or when awaiting delivery of a new one. The decision concerning the type of mold, and the acoustic characteristics to be achieved, rest with the audiologist and hearing-aid dealer. However, you may once again play an important part in drawing attention to problems that may arise as a result of an inappropriate or poor fitting. You may need to urge a hearing-aid user to consult an audiologist about such problems or to persist in attempts to obtain satisfaction rather than accepting that a person simply cannot get used to an aid.

Identifying the most suitable hearing aid and amplification characteristics depends upon expertise, experimentation, observation, and counsel, often over a period of time. Only when the audiologist, teacher/therapist, hearing-aid dealer, client, or child's parents work as a cooper-

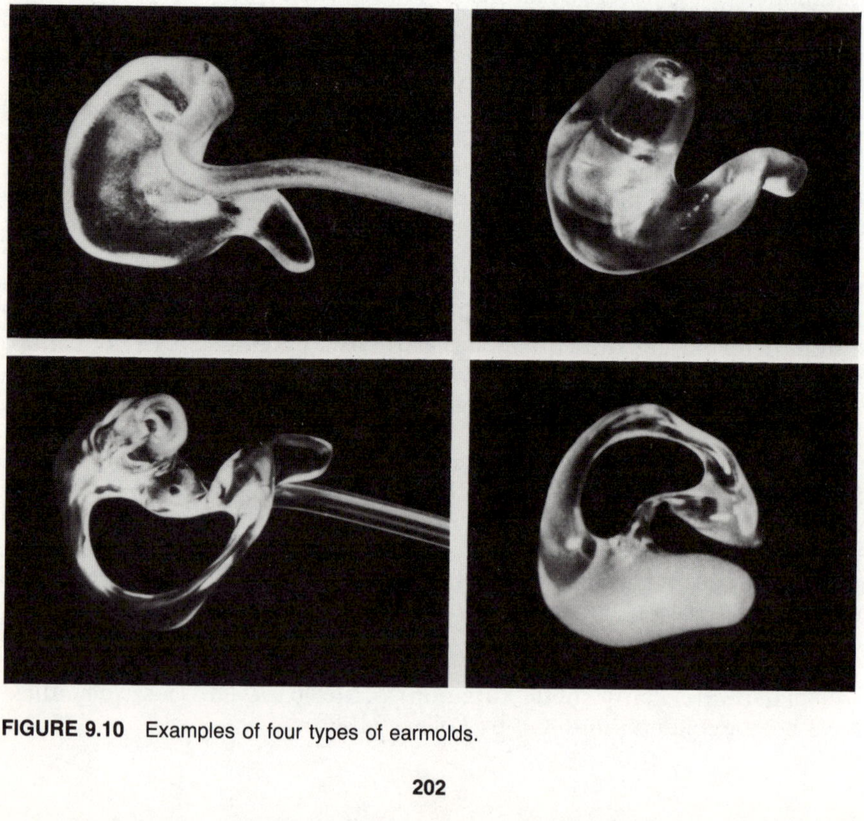

FIGURE 9.10 Examples of four types of earmolds.

ative team can optimal amplification needs be identified and provided for maximal effect. Such cooperation necessitates that all involved in the team be familiar with the practical implications of the theoretical concepts we have examined. These are discussed in the next chapter.

REFERENCES

Aufricht, H., "A Followup Study of the CROS Hearing Aid," *Journal of Speech and Hearing Disorders, 37,* 1972, 113–117.

Berger, J. W. and J. F. Lowry, "Relationships Between Various Stimuli for MCL," *Sounds, 5,* 1971, 11–14.

Berger, K., *The Hearing Aid: Its Operation and Development* (2nd ed.). Livonia, Mich.: The National Hearing Aid Society, 1974.

Bess, F. H., *Characteristics of Children's Hearing Aids in the Public School. Final Report, Dept. H.E.W.* U.S. Office of Education Grant Procurement and Management Division, *41,* 1976, 252 (c), (d).

Bode, D. L., and R. N. Kasten, "Hearing Aid Distortion and Consonant Identification," *Journal of Speech and Hearing Research, 14,* 1971, 323–331.

British Medical Research Council 1947 Committee on Electro-Acoustics, *Hearing Aids and Audiometers MRC Special Report Series No. 261.* H. M. Stationery Office: London, England.

Byrne, D., and P. Dermody "Localization of Sound with Binaural Body-worn Hearing Aids," *British Journal of Audiology, 9,* 1975, 107–115.

Byrne, D., and D. Fitfield, "Evaluation of Hearing Aid Fittings for Infants," *British Journal of Audiology, 8,* 1974, 47–54.

Carhart, R., "Introduction," in *Amplification for the Hearing Impaired,* ed. M. Pollack, pp. VII–XV. New York: Grune & Stratton, Inc., 1975.

Danaher, E. M., and J. M. Pickett, "Some Masking Effects Produced by Low Frequency Vowel Formants in Persons with Sensorineural Hearing Loss," *Journal of Speech and Hearing Disorders, 18,* 1975, 261–271.

Davis, H., C. Hudgins, D. Marquis, R. Nichols, and G. Peterson, "The selection of hearing aids," *Laryngoscope, 56,* 1946, 135–163.

Davis, H., S. S. Stevens, R. H. Nichols, Jr., C. V. Hudgins, R. J. Marquis, G. E. Peterson, and D. A. Ross, *Hearing Aids: An Experimental Study of Design Objectives.* Cambridge: Harvard University Press, 1947.

Davis, R., and S. Green, "The Influence of Controlled Venting on Discrimination Ability," *Hearing Aid Journal, 6,* 1974, 27.

Dermody, P., and D. Byrne, "Auditory Localization by Hearing Impaired Persons Using Binaural in-the-Ear Hearing Aids," *British Journal of Audiology, 9,* 1975(a), 93–101.

Dermody, P., and D. Byrne, "Loudness Summation with Binaural Hearing Aids," *Scandinavian Audiology, 4,* 1975(b), 23–28.

Dirks, D., and R. Wilson, "Binaural Hearing of Speech for Aided and Unaided Conditions," *Journal of Speech and Hearing Disorders, 12,* 1969, 650–664.

Fisher, B., "An Investigation of Binaural Hearing Aids," *Journal of Laryngol. Otol., 78,* 1964, 658–668.

Frank, T., and R. Gooden, "The Effect of Hearing Aid Microphone Types on Speech Discrimination Scores in a Background of Multitalker Noise," *Maico Audiological Library Series, 2,* 1973, 5.

Gelfand, S. A., and I. Hochberg, "Binaural and Monaural Speech Discrimination under Reverberation," *Audiology, 15,* 1976, 72–84.

Gengel, R., "Perceptual and Cognitive Strategies. Discussion: Aiding Speech Reception of Hearing Impaired Listeners," in *Sensory Capabilities of Hearing Impaired Children,* ed. R. E. Stark, p. 30. Baltimore: University Park Press, 1974.

Gerber, S. E., "The Intelligibility of Speech," in *Introductory Hearing Science Physical and Psychological Concepts,* ed. S. E. Gerber, pp. 238–260. Philadelphia: W. B. Saunders Company, 1974.

Harford, E., and J. Barry, "A Rehabilitative Approach to the Problem of Unilateral Hearing Impairment: The Contralateral Routing of Signals (CROS)," *Journal of Speech and Hearing Disorders, 30,* 1965, 121–138.

Harford, E., and E. Dodds, "The Clinical Application of CROS. A Hearing Aid for Unilateral Deafness," *Archives of Otolaryngology, 83,* 1966, 455–464.

Harris, J., "Introduction," in *Hearing Aids Current Developments and Concepts,* ed. E. Rubin, pp. 95–101. Baltimore: University Park Press, 1976.

Hearing Aid Industry Conference. *Hearing Aid Industry Conference Report.* New York, 1976.

Hearing Aid Journal, 26th Annual Facts and Figures, 34, November 1980, p. 3.

Heyes, A. D., and A. J. Ferris, "Auditory Localization Using Hearing Aids," *British Journal of Audiology, 9,* 1975, 102–106.

Hochberg, I., "Most Comfortable Listening for the Loudness and Intelligibility of speech," *Audiology, 14,* 1975, 27–33.

Hodgson, W. R., and P. H. Skinner, eds., *Hearing Aid Assessment and Use in Audiologic Habilitation.* Baltimore: The Williams & Wilkins Company, 1977.

Hood, J. P., J. P. Poole, "Tolerable Limit of Loudness: Its Clinical and Physiological Significance," *Journal of the Acoustical Society of America, 40,* 1966, 47–53.

Jeffers, J., T. Behrens, and M. Rubin, "Task Force 1. Standards for Hearing Aids," *Journal of the Academy of Rehabilitative Audiology, 6,* 1973, 13–19.

Jerger, J., and N. Lewis, "Binaural Hearing Aids: Are They Dangerous for Children," *Archives of Otolaryngology, 101,* 1975, 480–483.

Jetty, A., and W. Rintlemann, "Acoustic Coupler Effects on Speech Audiometric Scores using a CROS Hearing Aid," *Journal of Speech and Hearing Research, 13,* 1970, 101–114.

Lankford, B. G., "Why binaural?" *Audecibel, 19,* 1970, 151–158.

Lankford, S. E., and W. L. Faires, "Objective Evaluation of Monaural vs. Binaural Amplification for Congenitally Hard-of-Hearing Children," *Journal of Auditory Research, 13,* 1973, 263–267.

Lentz, W., "Speech Discrimination in the Presence of Background Noise Using a Hearing Aid with a Directionally Sensitive Microphone," *Maico Audiological Library Series, 10,* 1972, 9.

Licklider, J. C. R., "Effects of Amplitude Distortion on the Intelligibility of Speech," *Journal of the Acoustical Society of America, 13,* 1946, 429–434.

Licklider, J., "The Intelligibility of Rectangular Speech Waves," *American Journal of Psychology, 61,* 1948, 1–20.

Ling, D., "Implications of Hearing Aid Amplification below 300cps," *Volta Review, 66,* 1964, 723–729.

Lybarger, S. F., "Hearing aids—1977," *Audecibel, 26,* 1977, 108–114.

Madell, J. R., "Hearing Aid Evaluation Procedures with Children," in *Hearing Aids Current Developments and Concepts,* ed. M. Rubin, pp. 103–108. Baltimore: University Park Press, 1976.

Markle, D. M., and A. Zaner, "The Determination of Gain Requirements of Hearing Aids: A New Method," *Journal of Audiological Research, 6,* 1966, 371–378.

Matkin, N., "Hearing Aids for Children," in *Hearing Aid Assessment and Use in Audiologic Habilitation,* ed. W. Hodgson, and P. Skinner, pp. 145–169. Baltimore: The Williams & Wilkins Company, 1977.

Matkin, N., and J. Thomas, "Cross Hearing Aids for Children," *Maico Audiological Series, 10,* 1971, Report 8.

McCandless, G. A., "Special Consideration in Evaluating Children and the Aging for Hearing Aids," in *Hearing Aids Current Developments and Concepts,* ed. M. Rubin, pp. 171–202. Baltimore: University Park Press, 1976.

McClellen, M., "Aided Speech Discrimination in Noise with Vented and Unvented Earmolds," *Journal of Auditory Research, 7,* 1967, 93–99.

Nabelek, A. K., and J. Pickett, "Monaural and Binaural Speech Perception through Hearing Aids under Noise and Reverberation with Normal and Hearing Impaired Listeners," *Journal of Speech and Hearing Research, 17,* 1974(a), 724–729.

Nabelek, A. K., and J. Pickett, "Reception of Consonants in a Classroom as Affected by Monaural and Binaural Listening, Noise, Reverberation, and Hearing Aids," *Journal of the Acoustical Society of America, 56,* 1974(b), 628–639.

Olsen, W. O. "Physical Characteristics of Hearing Aids," in *Hearing Aid Assessment and Use in Audiologic Habilitation,* eds. P. Skinner, and W. Hodgson, pp. 17–41. Baltimore: Williams & Wilkins Company, 1977.

Pasco, D. P., A. F. Niemoeller, and J. F. Miller, *Hearing Aid Design and Evaluation of a Presbycusic Patient.* Paper presented at the 86th meeting of the Acoustical Society of America, 1973.

Pollack, M. C., "Electroacoustic Characteristics," in *Amplification for the Hearing Impaired,* (2nd ed.), ed. M. C. Pollack, pp. 21–90. New York: Grune & Stratton, Inc., 1980(a).

Pollack, M. C., "Special Applications of Amplification," in *Amplification for the Hearing Impaired* (2nd ed.), ed. M. C. Pollack, pp. 255–307. New York: Grune & Stratton, Inc., 1980(b).

Rappaport, B. Z., and G. A. Tait, "Acoustic Reflex Threshold Measurement in Hearing Aid Selection," *Archives of Otolaryngology, 102,* 1976, 129–132.

Reddel, R., and D. Calvert, "Selecting a Hearing Aid by Interpreting Audiologic Data," *Journal of Auditory Research, 6,* 1966, 445–452.

Rintelmann, W., and F. Bess, "High Level Amplification and Potential Hearing Loss in Children," in *Childhood Deafness Causation Assessment and Management,* ed. F. Bess, pp. 267–293. New York: Grune & Stratton, Inc., 1977.

Ross, M., "Binaural Versus Monaural Hearing Aid Amplification for Hearing Impaired Individuals," in *Childhood Deafness Causation Assessment and Management,* ed. F. Bess, pp. 235–249. New York: Grune & Stratton, Inc., 1977.

Ross, M., M. Hunt, M. Kessler, and M. Henniges, "The Use of a Rating Scale to Compare Binaural and Monaural Amplification with Hearing Impaired Children," *Volta Review, 76,* 1974, 93–99.

Ross, M., and J. Lerman, "Hearing Aid Usage and Its Effects upon Residual Hearing" *Archives of Otolaryngology, 86,* 1967, 639–644.

Ross, M., and C. Tomassetti, "Hearing Aid Selection for Preverbal Hearing Impaired Children," in *Amplification for the Hearing Impaired,* ed. M. C. Pollack, pp. 213–253. New York: Grune & Stratton, Inc., 1980.

Rubin, M., ed., *Hearing Aids Current Developments and Concepts.* Baltimore: University Park Press, 1976(a).

Rubin, M., "Hearing Aids for Infants and Toddlers," in *Hearing Aids Current Developments and Concepts,* ed. M. Rubin, pp. 95–101. Baltimore: University Park Press, 1976(b).

Schwartz, D. M., and V. D. Larson, "Hearing Aid Selection and Evaluation Procedures in Children," in *Childhood Deafness Causation Assessment and Management,* ed. F. Bess, pp. 217–233. New York: Grune & Stratton, Inc., 1977.

Skinner, P. H., "Relationship of Electro and Psychoacoustic Measures," in *Hearing*

Aid Assessment and Use in Audiologic Habilitation, ed. W. R. Hodgson and P. H. Skinner, pp. 106–126. Baltimore: The Williams & Wilkins Company, 1977.

Smedley, T. C., J. von Khaelssberg, and J. R. Clement, *Success and Failure Patterns among CROS and BICROS Users.* Paper presented at American Speech and Hearing Association, Annual Convention, Las Vegas, 1974.

Snow, T., and G. A. McCandless, "The Use of Impedance Measures," *Hearing Aid Journal* 7, 1976, 32–33.

Standard for Hearing Aids, FDA–MDS–071–0002. Washington, D.C.: Food and Drug Administration, 1974, 1975.

Sung, G., R. Sung, and R. Angeletti, "Directional Microphone Hearing Aids," *Archives of Otolaryngology, 101,* 1975, 316–319.

Thomas, I. B., and G. B. Pfannebecker, "Effects of Spectral Weighting of Speech in Hearing Impaired Subjects," *Journal of Audiological Engineering Society, 22,* 1974, 690–693.

Triantos, T. J., and G. A. McCandless, "High Frequency Distortion," *Hearing Aid Journal, 27,* 1974, p. 38.

Ventry, I. M., R. W. Woods, M. Rubin, and W. Hill, "Most Comfortable Loudness for Pure Tones, Noise and Speech," *Journal of the Acoustical Society of America, 49,* 1971, 1805–1813.

Yantis, P. A., J. P. Millin, and I. Shapiro, "Speech Discrimination in Sensorineural Hearing Loss. Two Experiments in the Role of Intensity," *Journal of Speech and Hearing Research, 9,* 1966, 178–193.

Yonovitz, A., *Binaural Intelligibility: Pilot Study Progress.* Speech and Hearing Institute, Texas Medical Center, Houston, 1974.

10

Practical Aspects of Hearing-Aid Information

Our aim in the previous chapter was to understand the fundamentals of amplification. In this chapter our concern is more practical; we discuss how to make use of the understanding we have achieved.

Let us assume that you have the management responsibility for a new client, child or adult. Your first task is to obtain complete information about the hearing impairment, and about the type of amplification your client is wearing. If the client does not have a hearing aid you need to investigate the reasons why. It is not uncommon for a person to be advised by a physician that an aid will not help, or that the impairment is not severe enough to warrant the use of an aid. Persons with monaural impairment are often told an aid is unnecessary, and parents may be told that they should not consider an aid for a child until the child is older, or until the impairment is more severe. Even when a hearing aid is recommended some people simply cannot face the reality that they are sufficiently handicapped to need one. They claim to get along well enough without one—"I just need a little lip-reading practice." Parents of hearing-impaired children also sometimes reject the idea of their child's wearing an aid in an attempt to avoid acknowledging and broadcasting the fact that their child is "not normal."

In some cases a person may have purchased a hearing aid with or without audiological or medical consultation, a possibility that exists despite new laws governing hearing-aid dispensing. Dissatisfaction with the aid may have resulted not only in its complete rejection, but also in the rejection of the idea that amplification may help. Even individuals who have had appropriate hearing-aid evaluation and fitting may be dissatisfied. Many fail to complete recommended follow-up visits specifically designed to make necessary adjustments to the aid, and to discuss problems and clarify misunderstandings. We cannot even rule out the possibility that the audiologist or dealer who recommended the aid simply may not have provided adequate hearing-aid orientation services.

Children may also express dissatisfaction with an aid. It is not unusual for a child to pass through a stage when, for reasons related to personal or social identity, the use of the aid is rejected. This may occur even when its benefit is indisputable. Acceptance of the aid by a child, as indicated by its daily use, is not conclusive evidence that the child derives maximal benefit from it. The previous chapter discussed the dismal reports which testify that in excess of 50 percent of aids worn by school children are not operating adequately. Perhaps most important to our discussion is a report by Porter (1973) that 77 percent of the malfunctions found in eighty-two aids worn by children in a school for the deaf *could have been detected by simple checks conducted by the teacher or parent.*

BECOMING FAMILIAR WITH THE CLIENT'S AID

If you have ever purchased a household appliance, you know that explanations by the salesperson in the store, intended to demonstrate simplicity of operation, seem to fade before you even get the item home. You turn for help to the operating manual provided by the manufacturer. Unfortunately in most cases this only heightens your sense of incompetence. Similarly, consider the experiences of the parents of a young child recently fitted with a hearing aid, or an elderly person who may have had difficulty hearing the instructions in the first place, or of someone just like yourself. To accommodate the needs of these persons you should be able to assure them of assistance, be able to explain, demonstrate, and teach them the basic things they need to know about and to do with their aid. You should be able to help them be confident, successful hearing-aid users. To achieve this requires that you have confidence in your own knowledge of hearing aids in general.

The sources of information available to you are:

1. *The audiologist who made the hearing-aid evaluation.* Remember, however, that many clients may have purchased an aid without such an evaluation. In these cases you should seriously consider suggesting that a complete assessment be sought. You should be particularly cautious not to accept into a rehabilitation program any person who has purchased an aid after having waived the right to medical examination. We must insist upon medical clearance as an absolute prerequisite to rehabilitation. This situation may arise only infrequently, but professionally it is a very important one.
2. *The dealer who sold the aid.* Hearing-aid dealers vary considerably in qualification and experience. A few provide sophisticated services, some even have their own laboratories. It is unfair to make sweeping generalizations about hearing-aid dealers. That they are businesspeople should not prevent them from having sincere concern for their hearing-impaired clients. Pride in the business is often the motivation for quality service. You should approach the

dealers who service your clients to find out how they believe they can cooperate in your rehabilitation programs. Let the dealers describe the services they offer. Their expertise is in their understanding of what modifications can be made to reduce or eliminate problems experienced with the aid. Only through working with the dealers will you learn the extent of experience they can place at your disposal and the cooperation they will give. A respectful approach to hearing-aid dealers usually results in surprisingly satisfactory working relationships.

3. *The informational booklet that must accompany every aid.* This contains the manufacturer's specifications for the model. Federal law now governs the specifications that the manufacturer must meet. However, it cannot be assumed that the characteristics of the aid being worn by your client are accurately defined by the specification data, even though they may have been when the aid left the factory. The specifications will tell you what you have a right to expect from the aid. It will be necessary for you to ask the audiologist for an electroacoustic analysis of a hearing aid. At the present, few hearing-aid dealers have the equipment to provide this type of assessment of the performance of each aid. Remember that a hearing aid should be monitored periodically for performance. This is particularly true for aids worn by children. Any trauma to the aid is immediate cause for reassessment. It even appears that an electroacoustic analysis is necessary on an aid that has just returned from repair by a dealer or manufacturer. Warren and Kasten (1976) checked forty-one such aids for gain, saturation, sound-pressure level, and frequency response by comparison to the specifications of the aids. Sixty-three percent of the aids repaired failed to meet manufacturer specifications.
   General wear on an aid together with new technical benefits make any aid five years old a candidate for replacement. Ideally, hearing-aid reevaluation should occur every two or three years. Statistics pertaining to the average life of a hearing aid show it to be 3.3 years (Sinclair, 1976).
4. *The manufacturer of the aid.* Feel free to contact the manufacturer of the client's hearing aid. Hearing-aid companies will readily supply you with information about a specific model of hearing aid and they usually have considerable literature directed to hearing-aid users and professionals who work with hearing-impaired persons.

From the sources listed above, you should obtain the following information about the aid:

1. Make and model
2. High-frequency average gain (gain in speech-frequency range)
3. Reference-test gain (gain added to speech at one meter distance)
4. Saturation sound-pressure level (SSPL 90) or maximum power output (MPO) (highest intensity the output can reach)
5. Output limiting, particularly important to know whether automatic gain control is a feature of the aid
6. Frequency-response characteristics for each tone control or internal-adjustment control setting
7. Recommendations concerning the ear in which the aid should be worn. Children particularly are often provided with a mold for each ear together with instructions to alternate the aid between ears for a certain percentage of the time. If this is so, you should discuss the rationale with the audiologist. If you have any difficulty in understanding why the aid has been fitted

to a particular ear, do not hesitate to seek an explanation. Ask if any special modifications have been made to the mold for acoustic reasons.

8. Find out from the audiologist or hearing-aid dealer on which tone-control setting the client should use the aid.
9. Find out which volume-control setting should be used for average noise conditions. What recommendations have been made concerning when and by how much the volume setting should be increased/decreased? Can the recommended setting of the control be visibly marked so a parent or adult has a position to turn it to?

It may seem a rather ambitious project to obtain all this information on each child or adult with whom you are to work. It will certainly take more time than we are used to devoting to this aspect of rehabilitation. However, ethically we are not justified in agreeing to teach or provide special-communication training without having such basic knowledge. It is like driving a car without finding out whether it has power brakes, or even functioning brakes, without knowing where the light switch and dimmer is, or if they are working. What is the point of providing amplification to hearing-impaired persons if we are not diligent in ensuring its optimal use? You cannot slough off this responsibility by assigning it to the audiologist or to the hearing-aid dealer. You have to get involved. You must operate as part of a team, you must monitor all aspects of rehabilitation, and you must have continual feedback among team members. Audiologists probably feel they cannot spend enough time providing adequate counseling to the client about hearing-aid use. Your new client is probably not very familiar with the aid he or she has purchased. This becomes, in part, your responsibility too.

INSPECTING THE AID

Consider now the actual aid itself. Take it in your hand and familiarize yourself with the location of the controls. The following guidelines may be helpful:

1. *On-off switch.* This may either be a separate switch, or it may be incorporated into the volume control. Batteries should be removed whenever the aid is not in use.
2. *Volume control.* Note whether the volume control is numbered or notched. In some way the client, or a young child's parents, should be able to easily determine to what position the control should be rotated for normal use.
3. *Tone control.* It may not be possible for the user to change the frequency emphasis of the hearing aid. However, if variable settings are provided, be sure you have ascertained which setting was recommended for your client.
4. *Input-selection switch.* Many aids are equipped with a special circuit for use when listening on a telephone. This is marked *T*. When the output is switched to *T*, the external microphone circuit is disconnected and the aid is set to respond to the electromagnetic changes occurring in the telephone receiver, which must be placed against the aid. Some aids also have an *M-T* output. This position allows the external microphone to continue to pick up environmental airborne sound while also responding to electromagnetic changes in the telephone receiver.

5. *Battery compartment.* Note where the battery is inserted and the location of the + and − signs to indicate which way the battery should face. In a body-type aid, you should ensure that the terminals are clean and that there is no sign of corrosion either on the terminals, in the compartment itself, or on the battery. Terminals and battery contacts may be brightened by softly rubbing with a fine emery board.
6. *Tubing or cord.* Ear-level aids use plastic connecting tubing to convey the amplified sound from the internal receiver to the ear mold. This tubing should be soft, pliable, and unkinked. Hard, dry tubing is likely to split, and should be replaced by the hearing-aid dealer before this happens. There should be no condensation of moisture in the tube. With body-worn aids you should ensure that the connecting cord is not frayed, that the points show no signs of corrosion, and that they insert tightly into the aid and the receiver.
7. *Receiver.* In body-worn aids, the external receiver should be inspected. It is most important to check that the plastic housing is neither chipped nor cracked. Either of these two conditions indicate that the receiver has been subject to trauma and may be defective. This warrants immediate referral to the hearing-aid dealer.
8. *Ear mold.* This should be inspected to ensure that it is neither chipped nor cracked, and that it is free of earwax. Pay particular attention to the channel through which the sound waves must pass. A blocked ear-mold channel gives the wearer an immediate conductive hearing deficit in addition to his or her own impairment.

CHECKING THE AID

To assist you in performing a listening check on an aid you should have a standard ear mold to listen to body aids and a mold usable with aids that have internal receivers (shell, skeleton, or canal molds). A hearing-aid dealer can make these (this should be considered a professional expense covered by your agency). By fitting the mold in your ear you will become familiar with how it inserts and will be able to help clients who report difficulty in putting the mold in easily (Figure 10.1). First learn to fit your mold while looking in a mirror. Gently lift the pinna of the ear forward and outward. Then insert the canal of the mold into the ear canal with the long projection (helix) facing slightly backwards. Placing gentle pressure on the mold, screw it forward and then back until the helix hooks into the uppermost fold of the ear. The fit should be tight but comfortable. Before fitting a mold to a client be careful to check that the ear shows no sign of soreness caused by abrasion of a chipped or poorly fitting mold.

With the aid connected to your ear, turn it on and gradually increase the volume. The growth in loudness should be smooth without sudden jumps. There should not be scratchy sounds, nor should there be more than a soft internal background noise. Voices—of others and your own—should be clear. However, because of frequency modification the quality may lack richness. If the aid has a cord, check that cutout of sound does not occur when the connection to the hearing aid and receiver are touched. Now remove the mold and check for acoustic feedback.

FIGURE 10.1 The therapist should be familiar with how to insert a mold into the ear (State University of New York at Buffalo).

Feedback

Acoustic feedback is a problem frequently encountered among children wearing hearing aids. It occurs most often in young children, particularly those who have severe hearing impairment. Acoustic feedback results from the leakage of amplified sound, which is picked up by the microphone and reamplified in a reverberating whistle or squeal. The problem arises because of the resonant peaks that occur in any sensitivity curve. When gain must be high these intense peaks often result in sound leakage with resultant acoustic feedback. The closer the microphone is to the output components, the greater is the likelihood of feedback occurring. *The most common source of leakage is a poorly fitting ear mold.* You should, therefore, check to see that there is a tight seal between the mold and the ear canal. The mold should need gentle persuasion to insert and remove. If feedback occurs (the aid whistles) before or at the desired volume setting, gentle pressure from a finger on the receiver or mold will generally indicate whether a loose seal is the problem. You should also remove the mold and place your fingertip over the opening in the tube blocking the escape of amplified sound. Then turn the volume to maximum. If under this condition feedback does not occur, you have reason to recommend that a new mold be made to provide a tight seal.

In a body-type aid, if feedback occurs even when you block the mold opening as just described, then you should check:

1. *The connection between the receiver and ear mold.* This is where the protruding metal nubbin on the receiver button snaps into the metal ring on the plastic

mold. A plastic ring washer will sometimes tighten this connection enough to eliminate the problem.

2. *The connection between the cord and the receiver button and the aid itself.* This may be loose. Plastic washers may also solve this problem, though a new cord or new connecting receptacle may be necessary.

If the aid is a behind-the-ear or glasses type, leakage may occur as a result of cracked tubing. Tubing should be soft, flexible, and unkinked because this will generally prevent cracking. Feedback may also arise from a loose fit of the tubing to the plastic elbow of the aid (or metal nozzle on a glasses aid) or between the elbow and the aid case.

ASSESSING THE EFFECTS OF AMPLIFICATION

Once it has been ascertained that the client has an aid that is both appropriate and is functioning well, you will wish to know what effect amplification has upon communicative function. The purpose of the rehabilitative evaluation, therefore, is to generate information that will suggest how much help we can expect the listener to derive from aided hearing when confronted with the task of daily living. This is important to ensure that the hearing-impaired child or adult, and those that are in close contact with him or her, have realistic expectancies. Test results will permit the formulation of a working hypothesis, the validity of which must be assessed through monitoring subsequent performance. The sources of information will be: (1) the audiologist; (2) the hearing therapist; (3) the classroom teacher; (4) the specialist or the resource teacher; and (5) the parents. In this chapter we consider the types of information that the audiologist can provide. When we examine the management of the hearing-impaired child, we will discuss the contribution of the hearing therapist and classroom teacher to the development for each child of an overall communication/learning profile.

THE AUDIOLOGIST'S CONTRIBUTION

The amount of time an audiologist can devote to the testing of a hearing-impaired child or adult is determined by the expense of the service, and the audiologist's concept of his or her role. The cost of evaluation should not prevent the generation of significant practical information that will contribute to providing effective service to the hearing-impaired individual, particularly to the education of children. The need for careful diagnostic evaluation is seldom challenged, yet there is resistance to the idea that an audiologist must spend time evaluating the child's capacity for auditory-communication processing and particularly for auditory learning. Assessment services that can be shown to be directly relevant to the child's communicative and learning needs will be purchased by parents and paid for by third-party funding sources. The growing field of educational audiology bears witness to this.

The audiologist's perceived role is most often the reason that habilitative/rehabilitative evaluation is not made. Audiologists must reassess the contribution they can make to the intervention process, while teachers and therapists must turn to audiologists for educationally oriented assessment procedures. Together with the parents, we professionals must cooperate in the assessment and definition of the child's auditory capabilities for communication and learning. We must identify and describe areas of difficulty, and must together develop a plan for total management. We should ask the audiologist to provide comparative data indicating the child's unaided and aided performance on a number of tests. The information sought includes:

1. Thresholds for pure tones or narrow-band noise
2. Thresholds of speech awareness
3. Thresholds of speech reception
4. Speech discrimination

Comparing Unaided and Aided Free-Field Response to Pure Tones

To make comparison, adjust the aid to the recommended volume and tone settings. The information you obtain is very helpful when a child has limited language capability. The unaided free-field audiogram should be procured in a sound room using warbled tones or narrow-band noise. This minimizes the effects of distortion that may arise from reflective sound effects (standing waves). It is helpful to record thresholds for the intermediate half octave frequencies (750, 1500, 3000, 6000 Hz) as well as the octave frequencies (250, 500, 1000, 2000, 4000 Hz). The procedure is then repeated with the child wearing the aid(s). The threshold improvement afforded by the hearing aid may be seen by plotting the unaided and aided responses on the same audiogram.

In Figure 10.2 you can observe the "use" gain obtained by a child wearing a single ear-level aid. From this comparative audiogram, some cautious assumptions about the child's receptive ability for sounds can be made. We can observe that without the aid the child may be expected to hear an adult speaker's voice without too much difficulty because the hearing for the low-pitched vocal tone (below 200 Hz) falls close to normal limits. However, thresholds for the speech components in the important 500 to 2000 Hz range average only 60 dB, while those for the higher frequencies of speech (3000 to 6000 Hz) average only 78 dB. This means that even for a person with normal language competencies, speech, though softly audible, will be very distorted and extremely difficult to follow, even under good listening conditions. At a distance of greater than approximately 4 feet, in poor acoustic conditions, or in a group, this person would most probably be unable to follow conversation without a hearing aid unless he or she had excellent visual communication skills.

Now consider the aided audiogram. The shaded area indicates the use gain the aid provides. Average speech-range thresholds are raised by the aid to 22 dB in the 500- to 2000-Hz range. This brings them within the range of comfortable loudness for speech listening. The weaker,

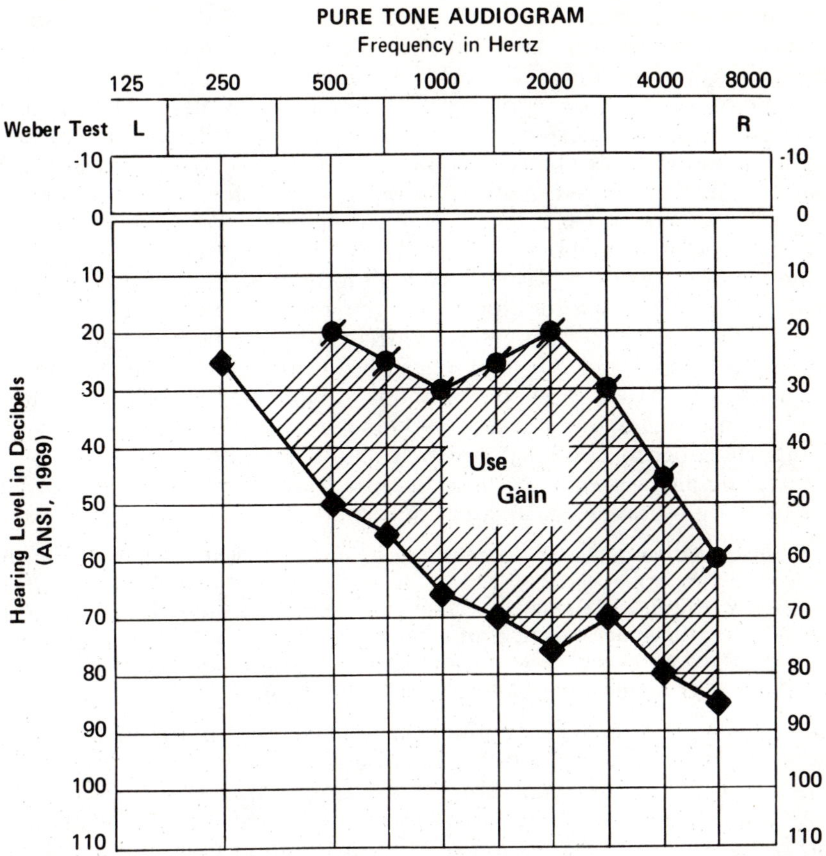

FIGURE 10.2 Gain provided by a hearing aid.

higher-frequency components of speech are raised to 34 dB, which also brings them into audible range. It is reasonable to expect that under favorable listening conditions, the aid would permit the child to follow speech comfortably, providing his or her speech discrimination ability is not seriously impaired.

Comparing Unaided and Aided Speech Processing

The influence of language constraints on perception operates whenever speech is used as a stimulus for testing. Even at the level of awareness the decision is made that someone is speaking. The theoretical division of linguistic processing into discrete functions is fraught with problems, because the act of speech perception is complex, with analysis occurring simultaneously at various levels. Therefore the divisions into which tests have been divided (speech awareness, reception, and discrimination) must be recognized as being defined by the nature of the type of response required rather than by knowledge of the specific internal processes operating. Overlap between categories inevitably occurs. This makes the determination of the most appropriate type of speech materials to be used a difficult task. It is necessary first to decide what it is you wish to know about an individual's ability to process speech, and then to select a response task that most effectively provides the information. Remember that we are not at present concerned with a detailed analysis of the individual's processing abilities at each level. Our aim is to obtain basic information about the effect of amplification on the individual's receptive communication. We want to know how the individual's potential for the receptive use of spoken language is affected by the fact that he or she is wearing a hearing aid. Most significantly we must have information that will help us form some reliable opinions of what we can expect of the individual in terms of communication behavior when wearing the aid. This is important because it will significantly influence the counsel we give to the hearing-aid wearer and those in close contact with that person. The questions we must seek to answer concern:

1. *Speech awareness.* At what intensity level does the hearing-aid user first become aware of speech?
2. *Speech reception.* At what speech-intensity level can the individual begin to identify the general content of a message?
3. *Speech discrimination.* How much of speech can be discriminated and at what level of decision making can discriminations be made?

The three categories just identified have been used traditionally for the diagnostic assessment of hearing disorders. They represent useful divisions of auditory processing. In the diagnostic process, the emphasis is upon the function of the auditory system itself, which in test administration has led to the suppression of the contribution that contextual cues make to speech perception. In rehabilitative assessment our interest is in the interaction of auditory information with the linguistic and cognitive systems of the hearing-impaired person. We want to know how well the person can use aided hearing for language comprehension under normally encountered circumstances. This means that when we test children we must ensure that the test items are within the child's language competence so that auditory linguistic interaction can occur. In testing adults, we can generally assume familiarity with the test items. However, certain vocabulary or concepts may be affected by educational or cultural backgrounds, particularly when English is not the subject's native tongue. A further difference between diagnostic and rehabilitative tests of speech processing is that for diagnosis, speech-discrimination tests are routinely given 40 dB above the speech-reception threshold. However, our interest is in the person's ability to discriminate and comprehend speech within the range of speech intensities he or she will normally encounter (approximately 50 to 70 dB). We will also seek information about the effects of factors within the speaker, the situation, the message, and in the acoustic environment. What we are seeking is a profile of the child's or adult's use of aided hearing.

Let us now consider the test information our audiologist can generate for us.

Testing Speech Awareness

Speech awareness tells us at what intensity the person wearing an aid will first become alerted that a person is speaking. A comparison of aided and unaided speech-awareness thresholds may provide the first indication that amplification contributes to an infant's perception of the auditory world. We discussed the role and importance of awareness earlier (Chapter 5). Even in cases of severe hearing impairment, simply knowing that someone is speaking serves to activate the visual search that is a prerequisite to the use of speech-reading skills.

In testing awareness we ask the child or adult to indicate over several trials when he or she first begins to be aware of the sound of a person talking. Understanding what is said is not important, only the knowledge that someone is speaking. Conversational speech is used as the test sample. Because of the higher fundamental frequency of the female voice, it is helpful to obtain thresholds for male and female speakers. When a child is too young or lacks the language to follow verbal directions, a distraction response is sought. Cessation of activity or searching behavior on the part of the child when the sound is alternated between speakers is convincing evidence of awareness. This behavior may be stimulated by visual reinforcement when correct localization occurs.

Testing Speech Reception

Once it is known at what level of intensity speech evokes attention, we attempt to gain information about the level at which the auditory information, unsupported by visual cues, begins to be useful in understanding speech—that is the level at which speech begins to interact in a significant manner with the cognitive linguistic system to permit understanding. We wish to know how much this level deviates from that required by normal-hearing subjects. We compare the unaided and aided thresholds to see how much amplification raises speech-reception sensitivity. Research has shown that sound alone becomes useful when approximately 50 percent of the auditory speech cues are perceived. To assess the SRT we traditionally use two-syllable words with equal stress on each syllable (spondees). When testing children you must be sure to use familiar words. This requires going over the test words or pictures to eliminate any with which the child is unfamiliar. When language competence is low, you may have to limit the number of test items. A few familiar objects may be used or the list may be comprised of the days of the week or even number pairs (for example, five-two, seven-three). Children with little residual hearing may receive insufficient auditory information to repeat or identify even familiar items. The task obviously requires a minimal capacity for auditory discrimination. When such capacity is present we will wish to obtain an indication of its extent.

Testing Speech Discrimination

Discrimination involves the perception of differences between and among the acoustic patterns of speech units. At its simplest it requires awareness that two units (sounds, words, phrases) sound different even when they are not sufficiently clear to permit recognition—that is, to be repeated or understood. For severely hearing-impaired persons it will be necessary to test this basal level using a same-different choice paradigm. We will consider this more detailed testing later. For the majority of children and adults, we can assess the contribution of the hearing aid to the recognition level of discrimination.

Recognition of speech units permits the identification of objects or ideas on the basis of their acoustic correlates. Remember, however, that the ability to repeat a spoken word does not alone signify recognition. The child must be able to use what he or she hears to identify something within his or her cognitive linguistic experience. We want to know how well the child can discriminate speech at conversational loudness (60 to 65 dB SPL), which is the level at which the test items should be delivered. It is helpful if the audiologist also administers the test at 50 to 55 dB SPL to indicate how well the subject will be able to discriminate quiet speech.

The test may consist of standard monosyllabic words (phonetically balanced lists such as the Central Institute for the Deaf W22 lists for adults or the Kindergarten word list PBK's for children). Often it is necessary to modify a list to accommodate the child's vocabulary, or to use an independent list developed by a teacher as representative of the vocabulary with which hearing-impaired children in that class will be familiar. For younger children or for those with more severe hearing impairment, a picture-identification test such as the Word Intelligibility by Picture Identification (WIPI) test may prove to be most effective. Regardless of the test materials used, it is strongly recommended that test items be presented in language context. Single-word identification by auditory cues alone gives unnatural weight to the acoustic stimulus. Our interest is not in what the child hears, but in what the child is capable of perceiving when given contextual cues. The method of presentation should be:

milk—"We have milk with our cookies"—*milk*

The child is then asked to say *milk,* or to identify the appropriate picture (see Figure 10.3).

The importance of this method of assessing speech discrimination has been emphasized by a pilot study conducted by Weber and Reddell (1976), who modified the WIPI test to incorporate test words into sentences. They then compared the scores obtained on the two forms of the test by seventy-five hearing-impaired children. Their results indicated that for children with either very good or very poor discrimination capacity for speech discrimination, the linguistic context did not significantly improve performance. However, for one-third of the children tested—namely, those with midrange speech-discrimination ability—the sentence form of the test produced significantly better discrimination of the test words than did the isolated word presentation. For this group of children, the scores obtained using sentence items correlated more closely

FIGURE 10.3 The Word Intelligibility by Picture Identification Test is helpful in assessing word discrimination (State University of New York at Buffalo).

with the classroom teacher's estimate of the child's speech-discrimination capability than did the single-word test scores. This resolved many of the discrepancies previously experienced between the audiologist's test findings and the classroom teacher's observation of the child's discrimination performance.

Assessing Ability to Follow Directions

Next the audiologist can assess the effect of amplification on the child's ability to follow simple directions adapted to his or her age and language ability. A young child may be asked to manipulate objects or play people, whereas an older child may be asked to follow directions of the type encountered in class—for example, finding a page or figure in a text, understanding certain items in a list, or indicating certain activities in an action picture (Figure 10.4). The instructions should all be given without visual cues at normal conversational loudness of 60 to 65 dB SPL, free field.

Assessing Ability to Answer Simple Questions about Familiar Material

Greater demands are made upon auditory discrimination when content processing involves decision making. When we ask a child to answer questions about familiar material, we are examining the role amplified hear-

FIGURE 10.4 The child's ability to follow age-related directions should be assessed (State University of New York at Buffalo).

ing plays in the recognition of learned materials. Some information concerning the child's potential to do this through hearing alone will be most helpful to a teacher trying to accommodate the child's needs. First review a familiar story drawn from a nursery rhyme or an abbreviated version of a familiar fairytale with the child. Then ask questions about the story using the free-field speaker as the acoustic input. Older children may answer orally or in a multiple-choice form. Young children may select pictures or items that indicate that they have correctly heard what was asked.

Assessing Ability to Learn Simple Material by Hearing Alone

The final assessment provides the most important information of all. How much does amplified hearing alone contribute to the child's ability to learn by auditory input? To assess this, present a very simple anecdotal account to the child by auditory input alone. The story should include two or three characters involved in events that occur in a sequential manner effecting certain consequences. Read the story several times at conversational level. Then ask simple questions to see how easily the child is able to acquire information auditorily.

Speech in Noise

The most valid criticism that can be leveled at audiological assessment of speech processing is that testing is conducted in a sound-isolated environment. This is totally unrepresentative of any situation that the hearing-aid user will ever encounter in the real world. We know that noise and reverberation both seriously reduce the speech discrimination performance of normal-hearing persons when certain limits are reached. The adverse effects of these two acoustic phenomena are greatly magnified when a person suffers from a hearing impairment. Despite this knowledge, we still lack standardized tests or test data that can be used in assessing a subject's tolerance for the interference that noise causes when listening for speech comprehension. Consequently seldom does an audiologist's report convey information about the possible negative effects of classroom acoustics on the ability of the child to understand and learn through speech. Nevertheless there is reason to ask audiologists to make some assessments of the effect of noise on the child's performance. Bode (1980) has concluded that the confusion that exists concerning the type, level, and signal-to-noise ratios that should be used in clinical assessment requires that each audiologist "make arbitrary but tentative decisions" (p. 293) concerning the choice of noise and the manner in which it is used during testing. Bode urges us to select noises for specific purposes, to obtain normative data for comparison, and to frequently reassess the procedures we use. What we are asking the audiologist to provide is general information that suggests how seriously noise conditions may influence the individual's ability to understand speech. Because we are interested in predicting the child's or adult's probable performance in a particular environment, it is logical to follow Bode's advice and use noise samples representative of that specific environment. Two types of noise are recommended—competing speech and nonspeech. The interference from a competing speech signal is known to exert a significantly more negative effect upon discrimination of speech than does general environmental noise. This is undoubtedly due to the different modes by which we process speech and nonspeech. Speech discrimination, therefore, should be assessed with the child using the hearing aid in the presence of a second speech stimulus. We must select the competing speech signal cautiously. We want to avoid creating a test that mainly emphasizes competing content. It is recommended, therefore, that either speech noise be used (this has equal intensity at frequencies up to 1000 Hz with a 6- to 12-dB decrease in intensity at frequencies above 1000 Hz) or that multiple talkers be recorded (cocktail-party noise). A single talker speaking an unfamiliar language would also be acceptable. The competing speech stimulus is usually presented at S/N ratios of + 10 dB, +6 dB, and 0 dB (Berger & Millin, 1971), to establish whether deterioration in discrimination occurs as the ratio is reduced.

Environmental sound should ideally represent the kind of noise in which the hearing-aid user must function. For the school child, it is desirable to use a sample recording of schoolroom noise selected to represent what a teacher identifies as representative of the background against which the child would usually listen. Experience with measured noise levels in classrooms indicates average levels to approximate 69 dB in kindergarten (Sanders, 1965), 59 to 63 dB in elementary (Paul, 1967; Sanders, 1965), and 62 dB in high school (Sanders, 1965). My study showed S/N ratio to range from +1 dB in kindergarten to +5 dB in elementary and high school. Paul found an average S/N ratio of +3 dB. These figures support the use of the three S/N ratios that it is customary to select in testing. The results of speech-discrimination and speech-comprehension measures obtained against a noise background should suggest the effect that such interference is likely to have on the child's communicative behavior in class.

The information obtained from all tests administered should be interpreted for the hearing therapist, teacher, and parents in a summary

Sample Report Synopsis

Mary was seen for assessment of the benefit she currently derives from hearing alone when wearing her hearing aid. The comparison of her unaided and aided pure-tone thresholds indicates that amplification increases her response to sound to a degree that would justify behavior compatible with a mild to moderate impairment compared to her actual unaided moderate to severe impairment. Specifically, without an aid Mary is able to hear only the voicing component of speech in the low frequencies (125 and 250 Hz). Speech-sound components above this level will for the most part be inaudible, precluding comprehension by hearing alone. Speech is first detected unaided at 50 dB. Without the aid speech does not reach a level of loudness to permit even the gist of the message to be followed. Neither speech reception nor discrimination for simple word items could be tested unaided. When wearing the aid, Mary's detection of speech improves to a level that permits her to be aware of someone's speaking in a soft voice. The greatest improvement, however, is observed by the measurable speech-reception threshold, which indicates the levels at which Mary's hearing begins to be useful for speech comprehension even without visual cues. With the aid she should be able to follow the gist of conversation (using familiar vocabulary) at an intensity level of only 35 dB, which is at minimal voice intensity. Speech intelligibility using familiar single-syllable test words in sentences revealed a percentage score of 84 percent at conversational intensity (60 to 65 dB). This indicates very effective use of residual hearing when using an aid. This observation is supported by test results indicating that Mary can follow simple directions given by hearing alone and can also converse about familiar-content material. When presented with new-content material at her language level, she experienced noticeable difficulty in learning the information involved by hearing alone. This latter observation suggests that care should be taken to avoid underestimating the effects of the hearing impairment in situations involving new learning. When competing speech noise was introduced into the test environment, Mary experienced considerable difficulty discriminating words in sentences, 66 percent (a decrease of 18 percent), and showed difficulty in following directions. For this reason we will investigate possible changes in the aid she uses to attempt to combat this problem.

In summary we would expect that under favorable listening conditions with her aid functioning optimally, Mary will understand most of what is said to her in a 1:1 relationship. She will experience some difficulty in learning new-content matter when dependent upon her aided hearing alone. Unfamiliar vocabulary, group situations, and particularly less-than-good listening conditions may be expected to reduce her performance. Her ability to discriminate speech by hearing alone may reasonably be expected to decrease as distance from the speaker increases. I recommend assessment of her language and speech skills and of her ability to benefit from visible speech cues (lip-reading) by the speech and hearing therapist. The information obtained can then be correlated with audiological findings and checked against the classroom teacher's observations of Mary's performance in the learning situation.

report, which should serve as a prediction of reasonable expectancies for the child. The accuracy of these predictions will be determined by the observations and experiences of teachers, therapists, and parents, and in follow-up assessment by the audiologist working in concert with them.

This type of testing and report writing may appear to require more of an audiologist's time than can be expected. Such concern, however, is not justified. It arises from a clinical view of what an audiologist can and should contribute to the management of the needs of hearing-impaired persons and in particular to the educational management of hearing-impaired children. The audiologist must become part of the team of specialists who evaluate and monitor the child's communication and learning progress throughout the school years. This necessitates new concepts concerning the role of the audiologist, a readiness to accept the need for more frequent and more applied evaluative procedures closely correlated with educational demands, and above all team management.

REFERENCES

Berger, K., and J. Millin, "Hearing Aids," in *Audiological Assessment,* ed. D. E. Rose, pp. 471–517. Englewood Cliffs, N.J.: Prentice-Hall, Inc., 1971.

Bode, D., "Speech Signals and Hearing Aids," in *Amplification for the Hearing Impaired,* ed. M. Pollack, pp. 309–324. New York: Grune & Stratton, Inc., 1980.

Paul, R. L., *An Investigation of the Effectiveness of Hearing Aid Amplification in Regular and Special Classrooms under Instructional Conditions.* Unpublished doctoral dissertation, Wayne State University, 1976.

Porter, T., "Hearing Aids in a Residential School," *American Annals of the Deaf, 118,* 1973, 31–33.

Sanders, D. A., "Noise Conditions in Normal School Classrooms," *Exceptional Child, 31,* 1965, 344–353.

Sinclair, J. C., discussion in *Hearing Aids: Current Developments and Concepts,* ed. M. Rubin, pp. 207–220. Baltimore: University Park Press, 1976.

Warren, M., and R. Kasten, "Efficiency of Hearing Aid Repairs by Manufacturers and by Alternative Repair Facilities," *Journal of the Academy of Rehab. Audiology, 9,* 1976, 38–47.

Weber, S., and R. Reddell, "A Sentence Test for Measuring Discrimination Ability in Children," *Audiology and Hearing Education, 2,* 1976, 5, 25–27, 30, 49.

11

Amplification for Education

Since the publication of the first edition of this text such dramatic changes have occurred, both in the philosophy of educating hearing-impaired children and in the technology of amplification systems, that much of what was discussed at that time has become outdated. It is not unreasonable to assume that within the next decade, as the sophistication of the personal hearing aid increases, the whole concept of special amplification for education may become redundant. It has been most encouraging to observe the success that the hearing-aid industry has had in developing systems of amplification that possess increasing flexibility and are thus effective both in and out of the classroom.

This progress toward the development of a multipurpose hearing aid is rapidly making obsolete the concept of special classroom amplification systems. In view of the increasing philosophical and political pressures to educate more and more hearing-impaired children in regular public schools (mainstreaming), these developments are most timely. In fact it is currently unwise to consider classroom amplification out of the context of the philosophy of mainstreaming. It is acknowledged that for the foreseeable future severely hearing-impaired children will be educated in separate special classes or schools. Yet we must recognize the great shift away from special-education placements. We must consider the implications that mainstream education has upon a hearing-impaired child's need for amplification in school.

A useful way of examining the topic of amplification for education is by raising a series of questions whose answers should provide you with an understanding of the main issues involved.

In what way does amplification for education use differ from normal hearing-aid use?

Ideally there should be no difference between the two. The conditions of amplification that we seek to provide should be optimal at all times. In the past, limitations in the acoustic characteristics of wearable hearing aids necessitated the development of special amplification systems for classroom use. The units that were developed were not confined by the limitations of size and cosmetic appearance that affect the fidelity of sound reproduction by a wearable aid. Classroom units therefore provided considerably better sound amplification. This remains true of most of today's units despite the dramatic advances in hearing-aid technology. Unfortunately, this real difference between the wearable aid and the classroom system obscured the fundamental principle that both are designed to serve a single purpose—namely, to increase the child's ability to use and to learn by his or her auditory system. The very term "auditory trainer," by which classroom units are commonly identified, evidences the fact that they have been accepted not as substitutes for the lower-fidelity wearable hearing aid, but as special units for a specific purpose. They have come to be identified with special periods in which auditory-discrimination training is coupled with speech training. As Ross (1977) points out, auditory training in special schools and classes became "a regularly scheduled classroom activity which presumably took care of the child's auditory needs" (p. 223). "Because of the emphasis on 'classroom' amplification, the exploitation of residual hearing in many special programs evolved into an academic topic with formally structured sequential lessons . . . " (p. 222). This negates the whole purpose of amplification, which is to make possible the optimal use of residual hearing *at all times.* Amplification must serve an ongoing functional purpose. It cannot be divorced from the learning process to be associated only with special lessons in auditory training and speech production. Focusing attention upon the acoustic signal and speech articulation or voice production is justified only as part of the overall management plan.

Amplification for education, then, differs from amplification for daily use only in the capabilities of the instrumentation. It differs not at all in its purpose.

Why then do we need special amplification for educational purposes?

In part, we have already answered this question. The reason that educational amplification systems were developed is because the quality of sound necessary to permit the auditory learning of language and academic content far exceeded the specifications of wearable hearing aids. Wearable hearing aids were designed primarily to meet the needs of the very large adult population with acquired hearing impairment. They were not designed specifically to enable young, severely hearing-impaired children to develop spoken language nor to meet the needs of a child attempting to compete with hearing peers in a learning environment. For this reason classroom amplification systems were developed to meet the particular needs of children in learning environments.

Ideally, what characteristics should amplification for the learning environment possess?

1. Such systems must be able to accommodate the amplification needs of groups of children with hearing impairments differing in severity and frequency configuration. This necessitates the electroacoustic flexibility necessary to vary the gain, frequency response, and output at the receiver units of individual children.
2. The unit must provide high-fidelity sound reproduction ideally with true binaural amplification. Individual controls should be provided for each ear.
3. A classroom system must have a high internal signal-to-noise ratio.
4. It should be designed so that a child can receive the voices of classmates with the same degree of fidelity as he or she receives the teacher's voice.
5. The instrument must permit the child to monitor his or her own speech production, which must be faithfully reproduced.
6. It should ensure that the negative effects of room reverberation and room noise are combatted. The distance between the input microphone and the person speaking, particularly the teacher, should therefore be kept to a constant distance of no greater than 6 inches. This produces an approximate S/N ratio of +24 dB when noise is at 60 dB (Ross, 1977). As Ross reminds us, such a high S/N ratio has been shown by Gengel (1971) and by Gengel and Faust (1975) to be essential for optimal auditory reception by hearing-impaired students. Hearing students, by comparison, can achieve the same level of performance with S/N values as low as +6 to +12 dB. For self-monitoring, the child's microphone should be no further than 6 inches from the mouth.
7. The unit must be easy to operate and maintain. An instrument that meets all of the preceding requirements may fail to be used by the teacher because he or she perceives it as technically too complicated. Thus the requirement that the unit be simple to use is certainly as important as all other requirements because if it is not met, the system's other assets are never operative. With few exceptions, teachers and speech and hearing therapists feel threatened by instrumentation. Moreover, it is unreasonable that an aid to teaching, because of the complexity of its operation, should impede the very process it is intended to facilitate. Classroom amplification units must, therefore, be designed so that simple demonstration by a sales representative or an audiologist, augmented by a clearly written manual, will permit even the newest teacher to quickly grasp how to operate the unit effectively and with confidence. The design of the unit should, in fact, be simple enough to permit a child in the upper primary grades, a teacher's aide, or a volunteer parent to set the unit appropriately after only a few demonstrations.

What types of classroom amplifying units am I likely to encounter?

For financial reasons, amplification units are not suddenly replaced when a more effective system becomes available. You may encounter types that are still in use despite their recognized limitations and despite the availability of superior equipment. It will be of value, therefore, to outline briefly the full range of classroom amplifiers even though many are rapidly disappearing from use.

TYPES OF EDUCATIONAL AMPLIFICATION SYSTEMS

Hard-Wire Systems

Historically the first system developed used wires to connect the children and the teacher to the amplifier. Such units are referred to as "hard-wire systems." These are still found in many schools for the deaf though fewer and fewer are actually in use. The layout of such a unit is shown in Figure 11.1.

Every system of amplification has both advantages and disadvantages. For the hard-wire group-amplification units, the advantages are:

1. The quality of the signal in a well-maintained hard-wire unit can be excellent, because the size of the unit does not force the manufacturer to exchange high-quality amplification for mobility or cosmetic appearance.
2. The electroacoustic characteristics at each pupil position can be modified for individual needs of gain, maximum output, and, to some extent, frequency emphasis.
3. The reliability of a quality hard-wire unit is good if well serviced.

The disadvantages of hard-wire group-amplification units are:

1. *Microphone placement.* In Figure 11.1, a floor stand or ceiling microphone is depicted. This microphone picks up the voices of the teacher and children but it does so at a distance. The microphone also picks up all other sound in the classroom and is subject to the negative effects of reverberation. The clarity of amplified speech and the signal-to-noise ratio with this type of microphone placement is not favorable. The use of a microphone around the teacher's neck, reducing the distance from the mouth to the microphone, would provide an excellent S/N ratio for the teacher's voice. Unfortunately, by this arrangement children can adequately hear neither themselves nor their classmates. The addition of a group microphone close to the students' desks still does not provide the necessary S/N ratio either for the child's voice or for the voices of his or her classmates. Appropriate microphone placement for such units requires that each child have an individual microphone attached to a headphone unit. This personal microphone permits the child to hear his or her own speech, to receive input from the teacher, and to receive a clear signal of the other children's speech by way of the amplifier. Only a few manufacturers provide this facility.
2. *Teacher/child immobility.* Hard-wire units allow little or no mobility of the students or the teacher, who are attached to the unit by headphone or microphone wires.
3. *Lack of portability.* Because of the size of the units, and the practice of incorporating output jacks into desks, the system cannot easily be moved from room to room.

As a result of its limitations the hard-wire system tends to be useful only in formally structured, small-group teaching situations. This all but

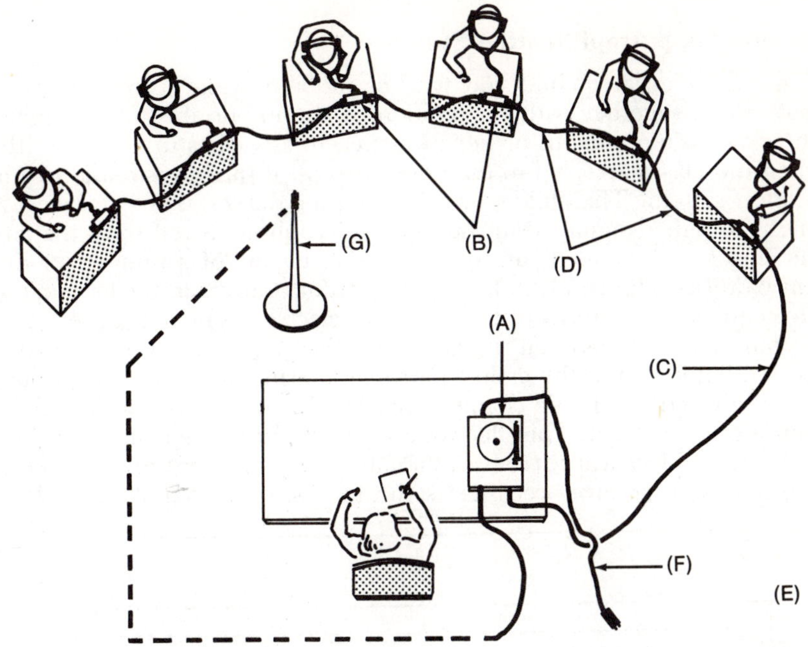

(A) Binaural amplifier or control unit (1450), located at teachers desk. May be installed in any other convenient place.

(B) Student control boxes (1451), each equipped with dual volume controls for individual student sound level adjustment.

(C) 12-foot-long interconnecting cable (1457), connects control unit (1450) to first student control box (1451).

(D) 4-foot-long interconnecting cables, connects student control boxes.

(E) 25-foot-long microphone cable, connects control unit to ceiling-mounted microphones.

(F) 8-foot-long AC cord, equipped with adapter where grounded 3-conductor wall socket is not available.

(G) Ceiling-mounted microphones (floorstand is optional). For the ceiling-mounted microphones we recommend a height of approximately 7 feet above floor level.

FIGURE 11.1 Typical classroom layout for use of hard-wire amplification system (courtesy of Ambco Electronics).

precluded their use at the preschool and kindergarten/first-grade level when optimal amplification is so essential for language and speech acquisition. Hard-wire units were compatible with an educational philosophv and methodology that is fast fading. These units may soon be completely surplanted by more flexible alternative systems of classroom amplification.

Induction-Loop Amplification Systems

The need for greater child and teacher mobility while using classroom amplification, together with recognition of the importance of the ability of the child to monitor his or her own speech, as well as to hear both the teacher and classmates, led to the development of the induction-loop amplification system. The child's own hearing aid serves as the receiver. A strongly amplified signal from the input microphone is fed from the amplifier into a coil "looped" around the room in one of a number of different patterns (Figure 11.2). Electrical current changes in the looped coil induce equivalent patterns of change in an electromagnetic field set up in the room. The link between the child and the amplifier is then provided by an induction coil in the child's personal hearing aid. This coil is sensitive to the electromagnetic changes that induce an equivalent pattern of current flow in the aid. This electromagnetic input to the child's aid, converted into an electrical current, is then amplified and sent to the receiver of the aid. The receiver reconverts the magnified electrical signal back

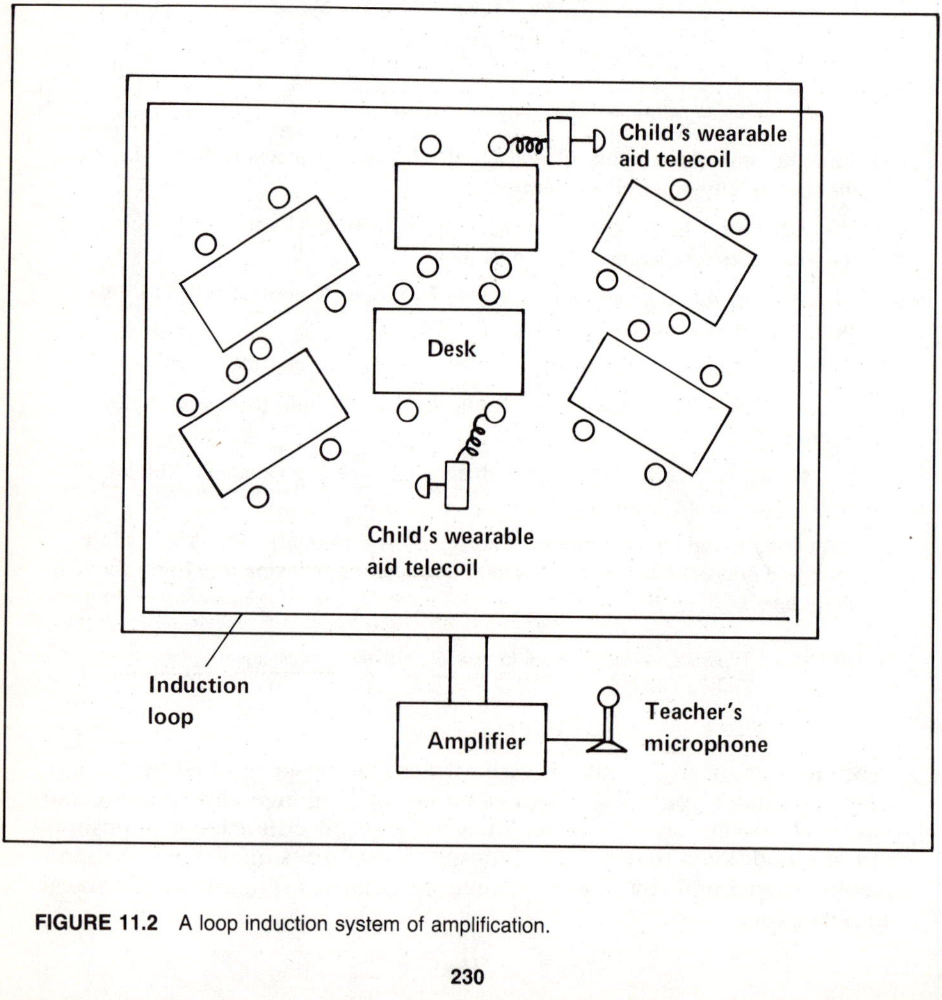

FIGURE 11.2 A loop induction system of amplification.

into sound waves for delivery to the ear. Initially the induction coil used in the hearing aid was the same one used for the telephone pickup. However, by switching the aid to the *T* (telephone) setting, the external microphone circuit is cut out, preventing the child from hearing his or her own voice, or that of others, except as they are picked up by the teacher's microphone. To overcome this limitation, manufacturers produced aids that have an additional microphone-telephone (*M/T*) setting. This allows both the external microphone pickup and the telecoil to be active simultaneously.

The loop-induction system, which uses the child's own hearing aid adapted to receive both acoustic and electromagnetic signals, sought to overcome the limitation of hard-wire systems. However, to date its disadvantages appear to have outweighed its advantages. Its advantages are:

1. *Teacher/child mobility*. The greatest advantage of the induction-loop system is that it permits complete mobility by the child. By using a wireless microphone to beam speech to the amplifier, the teacher can also have complete mobility.
2. *Use of the child's own aid*. By using his or her own personal hearing aid, the child is listening with the amplification specifications selected by the audiologist as best suiting his or her needs. This ensures that the child receives constancy of amplified sound as provided by the personal hearing aid, thus avoiding the variation in characteristics encountered when moving from one amplification system to another.
3. Because the teacher is always speaking directly into the microphone, the S/N ratio and reverberation effects remain highly favorable.

The disadvantages of the loop-induction system are:

1. *Variations in the electroacoustic characteristics of the M, M/T, and T settings*. The first limitation arises from a demonstrated discrepancy between the acoustic characteristics of the hearing aid when using the microphone, microphone-telephone, and telephone settings. Frequently the result is reduced output intensity, undesirable emphasis of low-frequency components, and reduced sensitivity to high frequencies when the telecoil circuit is used for pickup of the teacher's voice (Matkin & Olsen, 1970a, 1970b; Sung & Hodgson, 1971; Sung, Sung, & Hodgson, 1974). Recently manufacturers have been producing hearing aids in which the correlation among the microphone, microphone-telephone, and telephone sensitivity and output curves is much higher and more acceptable.
2. *Inconsistency of signal*. A second disadvantage of the loop-induction system is the variation in the electromagnetic signal in various parts of a looped room. This results in variation of the signal received by the child as the child moves about the room.
3. *Overspill of signal*. A further problem arises from overspill of signals between adjacent classrooms using induction-loop amplification systems. The resulting intermixing of speech signals is highly deleterious to a child's ability to understand the teacher.

The limitations of induction-loop amplification systems probably could and would eventually have been minimized. However, technological advances that have led to the development of radio-frequency amplification systems have shifted the emphasis away from pure induction-loop amplification, though many schools still use this system.

Frequency-Modulated (FM) or Radio-Frequency (RF) Systems

It is difficult to think ahead 10 or 15 years to imagine what amplification systems will be like. It would have been equally difficult 15 years ago to have envisaged the possibility of children's receiving their teacher's voice, broadcast to them on a radio frequency, picked up and amplified to a desired output level by each child's receiver unit. Yet this is what frequency-modulated classroom-amplification systems do. They represent miniature FM radio stations or Radio Frequency units, broadcasting to a classroom audience who listen to the teacher's "station" on their private wearable FM hearing aid. This may be fitted to one ear or both. The teacher wears the transmitter microphone around his or her neck (Figure 11.3). At this

FIGURE 11.3 An FM System of amplification constitutes a miniature radio station on which the teacher's voice is broadcast to the children's radio receivers (courtesy of Phonic Ear Inc.).

time the FM system of amplification appears to have sufficient advantages to compensate for its limitations. The system is gaining widespread acceptance by educators, particularly for the child in a mainstream placement.

The advantages of a frequency-modulated system are:

1. *Teacher/child mobility.* The signal is broadcast by a radio beam from an antenna that is part of the teacher's neck microphone. The teacher, therefore, has complete mobility. The children also receive the signal by radio input so they have equal freedom.
2. *Constant favorable signal level.* The constancy of the distance of the teacher's microphone to his or her mouth ensures that the S/N ratio is always optimal. Furthermore because signal strength varies little in the room the signal received by the child does not change as he or she moves from place to place in the room. This, you recall, was frequently not true with the loop-induction system.
3. *Compatibility for use with personal hearing aid.* It is possible to feed the amplified electrical signal from the child's FM receiver into an induction coil worn around the neck. In this manner the child can listen to the signal through his or her own personal hearing aid set on *T* or *M-T*. Because the field of the loop moves with the child, variations in signal intensity are not a problem.
4. *Self-monitoring.* Most FM units incorporate into the child's receiver pack either a single microphone or two microphones. This permits the child to receive the FM signal while listening to monophonic or stereophonic amplification of airborne sound. Thus the child may monitor his or her own speech and that of others around him or her while receiving the teacher's voice at a highly favorable S/N ratio.
   The receiver can be switched to FM only, to external microphone only, or to a combination of both. This gives the teacher flexibility in conducting the class. For example, if the teacher desires to have only some of the children listen to FM transmission, he or she instructs the remainder of the class to switch to the environmental microphone. If children are reading out loud, or participating in discussion, they can monitor their speech and listen to others nearby yet still receive the teacher's comments or requests clearly by FM reception.
5. *Multiple channels in a single classroom.* The receiver units may be tuned to different stations by a frequency selector switch or by color-coded modules that plug into the child's receiver. In this way, using two microphones broadcasting on separate frequencies, a teacher's aide or resource teacher can work independently with a small group of children in the corner of the room. The class teacher may then work with the remainder of the children using a different frequency. Further, as children change classes, they simply unplug the insert-frequency module, turn on their binaural environmental microphones, and listen to environmental sounds as they walk along the corridor. When they get to the next class they plug in the colored module that matches the teacher's microphone.
6. *Portability.* The units are perfectly portable. They may accompany the teacher and class on field trips where communication with a group wearing personal hearing aids is often difficult (Figure 11.4). The signal limits of the FM microphone are determined only by the strength of the microphone transmission. Power for these units is provided by rechargeable batteries. At the end of school each day the units are replaced in a charger, which ensures they are fully powered by morning.

FIGURE 11.4 Portability of FM units permits the system to be used wherever the class goes (courtesy of Phonic Ear Inc.).

The disadvantages are:

1. *Limited choice of response curves.* With the current FM systems, the possibilities are limited for modifying the electroacoustic characteristics of either the FM receiver or the hearing-aid unit to suit the needs of individual children.
2. *Lack of true binaural FM amplification.* Although the FM signal can be fed to both ears, true binaural amplification is not provided because there is only one input signal. The hearing-aid unit of the receiver may be monophonic or truly binaural with two separate microphones and amplifiers.
3. *Cosmetic appearance.* The units are all body type, necessitating that they be worn with a strap, neck cord, harness, or belt clip. Some children, particularly older ones who have become accustomed to ear-level aids, find this cosmetically unacceptable.
4. *Need for checking operational controls.* Problems can arise if the teacher neglects to turn off the microphone when, for example, a parent or another teacher comes into the room to speak privately with him or her. In fact, the same situation can occur if the teacher steps out of the room for a moment to speak confidentially with someone. The result is that the private conversation is broadcast clearly to the whole class. In class the teacher must also become accustomed to controlling which group of children are tuned into

the microphone. These, however, are teaching techniques that most teachers can accommodate without a great deal of difficulty. Similar procedural problems occur when the child is in a normal classroom rather than with other hearing-impaired children in a special class.

The use of an FM unit can make normal classroom placement possible for a hearing-impaired child who, using a personal aid, would not be able to cope with the average classroom acoustics and signal-to-noise ratios. There is no superior system of amplification for use in the normal school classroom, college, or university learning environment. FM units maximize the educational use of residual hearing. Ross (1977) fully concurs with this view, yet as he has bluntly stated, "its correct utilization is often a pain in the neck" (p. 240). For a child too young to assume responsibility for its operational use, this can be true. The teacher in the normal class must constantly monitor use of the microphone and the child's changing needs to adjust the input-selection control. The teacher must also ensure that the unit is recharged each night. Yet, when we place a given hearing-impaired child into the mainstream of normal education, we do so because, for that child, it represents an optimal learning environment. We should not agree to less. If the use of FM makes this placement possible, management procedures must be brought to bear on the situation to convince the teacher of the value of efforts to accommodate the child and the FM unit. We must work with the teacher in a fully supportive manner to resolve the inconveniences and to help the teacher feel comfortable in using the system. The child's educational and social success in a normal school will be enormously influenced by the effective use of residual hearing (Ross, 1976). The research findings of Ross and Giolas (1971) and Ross, Giolas, and Carver (1973) clearly demonstrate the superiority of FM amplification over the hearing-impaired child's hearing aid when used in a normal school classroom. Speech discrimination was significantly better when reception was by FM transmission. We have no choice but to work diligently and patiently in cooperation with classroom and special teachers to ensure the effective use of this system where appropriate.

Where, then, does the personal hearing aid fit into the plan for use of amplification in school?

We have examined classroom amplification systems, stressing that they have been designed to combat the unfavorable listening conditions encountered in school. To varying degrees all classroom amplification systems are superior to the personal hearing aid in their capability for doing this. It is reasonable, therefore, to ask what role the personal hearing aid should play. Is it realistic to use a high-quality system for training a person to make use of the acoustic aspects of speech, when in normal communication situations that person will have to make predictions on the basis of the reduced information that he or she is able to obtain through the personal hearing aid? Perhaps we should train the individual on the instrument with which he or she will have to function in most communication situations.

We have already recognized that speech perception and speech comprehension are not achieved solely on the basis of the analysis of the acoustic stimulus. This complex process also involves making predictions on the basis of linguistic cues and, possibly, on the association of the incoming auditory pattern with the motor pattern we would use in order to produce such a sound wave. It has also been stressed that communication between individuals involves a great deal of built-in redundancy. It is not necessary to receive the complete message signal in order to perceive what has been said and to be able to attribute meaning. It would seem, however, that when we are attempting to learn a new activity we require a great deal more information in learning to discriminate between sounds and words than we do to perform the same act of discrimination once we have learned these sound patterns. This is not difficult to understand when we remember that speech discrimination is dependent upon our ability to make predictions and that, in order to be able to do this effectively, we must be familiar with the rules that make these predictions possible. The amount of information necessary to verify a reasonable prediction is considerably less than that needed to learn to make such a prediction. We are justified in using a high-quality unit for teaching purposes because our aim is to provide the hard-of-hearing person with an acoustic signal that contains the greatest amount of information. During the process of learning to discriminate between acoustic signals that may be completely or relatively unfamiliar, hearing-impaired persons will need as much information as possible to guide them in their predictions. Increasing familiarity with the acoustic patterns will be augmented by an unconscious, but nevertheless important, awareness of the linguistic rules that determine the ways in which we may sequence these patterns. In a good program students will also be encouraged to reproduce what they hear in spoken and, when possible, in written form. In this way the acoustic signal will be associated with its tactile-kinesthetic and visual-motor aspects. An efficient aural rehabilitation program that integrates sensory information through several channels through a program of listening, watching, saying, and writing will build up sufficient message-signal redundancy to permit individuals to tolerate the reduction in the information available through the auditory channel that may be expected when the performance of the high-fidelity unit is replaced by that of the wearable hearing aid.

This rationalization of the use of high-fidelity amplification in training situations can only be supported if we accept the concept of the information pool and the associated threshold of comprehension. Some writers have cautioned therapists about the apparent waste of money represented by using wide-frequency, high-fidelity amplification with subjects for whom no thresholds have been determinable at frequencies about 1000 Hz. This is an acceptable criticism providing we recognize that, unless modifications of an individual audiometer have been made, the pure-tone audiogram seldom represents the maximum limits of hearing, since it is not usually possible to test at sensation levels of greater than 100 dB re: audiometric zero. Thus, before we rule out the value of high-intensity amplification of high frequencies, we must be quite sure that we have demonstrated, beyond reasonable doubt, that the hearing-impaired person is incapable of detecting sound at these frequencies.

We are, however, justified in showing concern if our training program is carried out exclusively with a classroom amplification unit without any comparative training in the use of the personal hearing aid. In addition to aiming to provide the subject with the best possible acoustic conditions for learning, we must teach the person the relationship between the acoustic patterns received through the classroom system and those received through a personal hearing aid. Thus, part of our training program will involve using speech materials with which the subject is familiar through training on the classroom unit to train that person to perform the same task of discrimination using his or her personal hearing aid. Similarly early lessons conducted under good listening conditions will be modified to provide experience in auditory discrimination under listening conditions of increased difficulty.

In summary, we may say that whenever possible we should provide our subject with the experience of listening to amplified speech through the best available system. We should design our management program to permit the subject to use residual hearing to the maximum possible extent in the process of learning to represent internally the acoustic patterns of speech. Once this has been achieved, we must then teach the subject to associate a signal containing less information with the internal speech patterns learned. In order to do this we must also conduct listening training with the personal hearing aid. Once again, the concept of a pool of information is strongly stressed. Learning auditory discrimination using a high-fidelity amplifying system involves learning the linguistic and contextual probabilities that are essential to the process of attributing meaning to speech. Furthermore, because learning the identifiable characteristics of speech sounds normally occurs simultaneously with learning the visual characteristics, teaching the person to correlate the visual and acoustic aspects of speech will enhance the total amount of information available to him or her.

POTENTIAL COMPATIBILITY OF PERSONAL HEARING AIDS AND CLASSROOM AMPLIFICATION SYSTEMS

We may conclude that the demands of learning combined with the effects of classroom acoustics will usually exceed the ability of the personal hearing aid of most children with moderate or severe hearing deficits to provide optimal amplification for learning. Recognizing the gap that exists between classroom amplification systems and personal hearing aids, manufacturers have sought to marry the two. An example of an aid that is compatible with various classroom amplification systems and models is the Maico Instruments Series 325 ear-level power aid.

This series of personal hearing aids has various optional features (Figure 11.5). One version of the S325 provides three input-selection choices identified as *T-M-E*. These letters stand for:

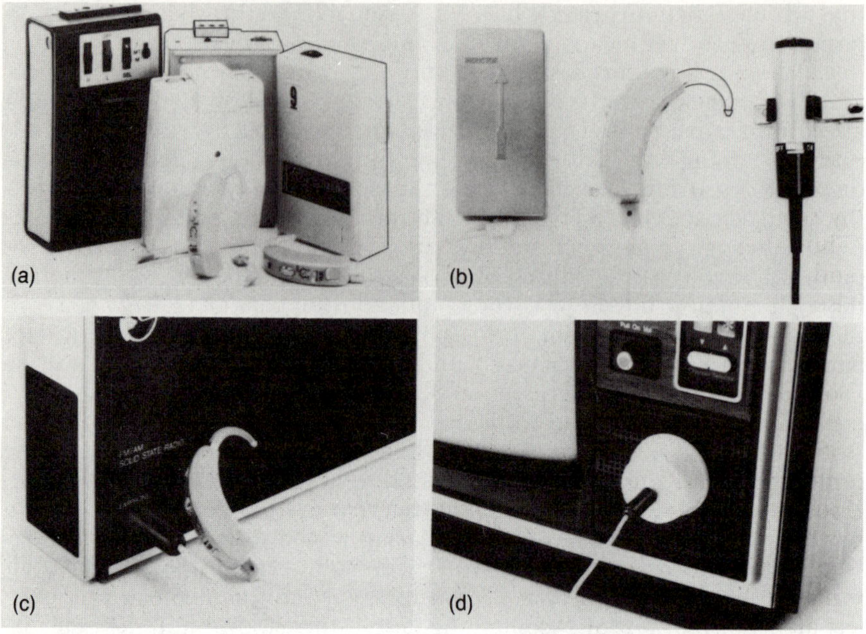

FIGURE 11.5 The personal hearing aid can now provide several options: (a) hearing aids such as the Maico 325 series can be connected by direct audio input to a variety of FM units; (b) an external extra strength telecoil accessory placed under a telephone receiver and an external detachable microphone with On/Off switch can provide improved speech comprehension; (c) direct audio input can link a hearing aid to a radio or cassette tape recorder, improving signal quality; (d) an external adhesive microphone that picks up the signal at the TV speaker can provide direct audio input to the hearing aid. TV volume levels can remain acceptable to other, normal-hearing persons in the same room (courtesy of MAICO Instrument Corporation).

1. *Telephone*. This switch position permits the user to use the telephone induction coil to listen to telephone conversations without picking up airborne environmental noise. The same setting permits the aid to be worn in a classroom that has induction-loop amplification.
2. *Microphone*. This provides for normal hearing-aid use.
3. *External detachable accessories*. The external-accessory position allows for a direct audio input by a wire connection from the output of a tape recorder, movie projector, record player, television, or radio. Using an extremely thin wire cord, an external microphone also can be directly connected to the aid set in the *E* position. With this accessory a teacher or therapist can ensure optimal S/N ratios by speaking 2 to 3 inches from the microphone. This is very important when the child is endeavoring to match speech models, or to monitor his or her own speech in a therapy session. The external microphone also permits the child to listen to a tutor in a noisy environment in which communication might not otherwise be possible. A further accessory is a detachable high-strength telephone neck coil, which, when attached to

an FM receiver, permits a child to join a hearing aid to any make of classroom FM unit.

A second version of the S325 has input selector settings labeled *M-B-E, in which the B* stands for both microphone and external accessory used simultaneously. This version differs from the *T-M- E* version in that it provides for simultaneous listening to environmental sound picked up by the external microphone and whatever accessory input is being used. Thus a child can receive an FM signal yet still hear his or her own voice and that of other children. The child can listen to a TV program while also hearing clarifying comments made by the teacher.

For children in classrooms that use induction-loop amplification or for children who choose to wear an FM neck-induction loop, a third version of the S325 provides a *T-B-M* input combination.

Another company, Phonic Ear, has developed what it calls a Personal FM System, which joins the personal hearing aid to an FM transmitting-receiving system. The Personal FM System is designed to improve speech intelligibility in environments where competing room noise and reverberation are a problem. The system allows maximum utilization of the person's own hearing aid while providing optimal S/N ratios. The unit can be used in school, home, and social environments. When used by an adult it can be worn at work where appropriate. The system consists of three component parts—two different FM receivers and a microphone/transmitter. These components can be combined with a personal audio input hearing aid or with a telecoil loop and a personal hearing aid with telecoil induction capability (Figure 11.6). The microphone-transmitter consists of a miniature lapel microphone connected to a small transmitter. It transmits the FM radio signal to one of two types of receivers. In both types the receiver picks up the radio signal from the speaker's unit and feeds it to the wearer's hearing aid(s) where it is amplified according to the personal hearing-aid specifications. The difference between the two receivers is that one is designed for use with aids that permit a direct hard-wire audio input or a microphone/telecoil input through a neck teleloop accessory. The other receiver has an environmental microphone for use with aids that have a telecoil position (*T*) but not a microphone/telecoil *(M/T)* position. The receiver unit, like the transmitter component, can be worn in a pocket or clipped to a belt (Figure 11.7).

These two commercially available systems represent a serious attempt by hearing-aid manufacturers to accommodate the special listening needs created by special environments. The classroom and other school environments generate very special needs. Whether a child is joining a personal hearing aid to an existing educational amplification system using an aid like one of the Maico Instruments 325 series, or whether the child is creating a personal FM system as manufactured by Phonic Ear, he or she is coming closer to always having available a quality signal, consistent in intensity, frequency emphasis, maximum loudness, and signal-to-noise ratios. The effects of such an improved signal on the child's potential for learning in classroom environments can be dramatic.

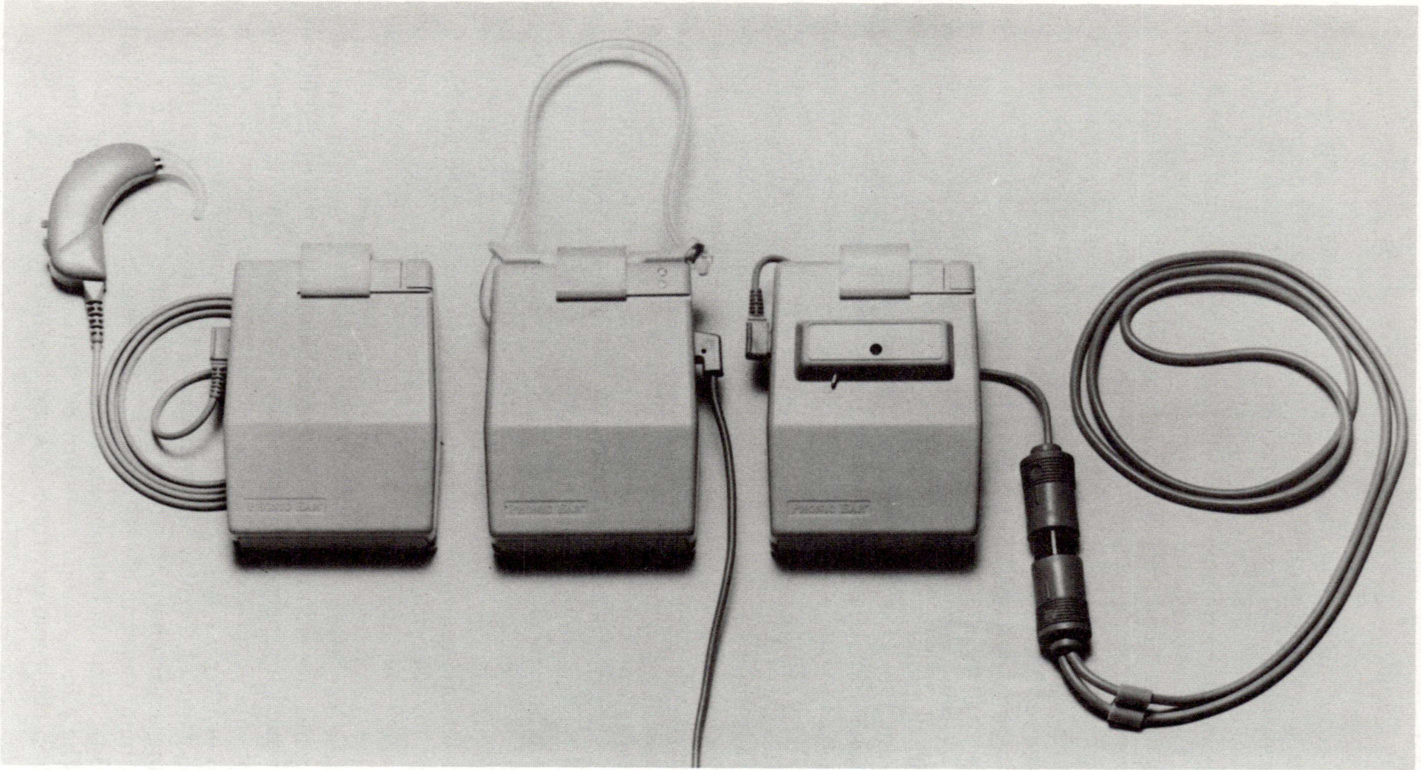

FIGURE 11.6 Personal FM systems permit the wearable hearing aid to be coupled to any FM system by direct audio input or by a telecoil loop (courtesy of Phonic Ear Inc.).

FIGURE 11.7 The receiver unit, like the transmitter shown in this student's hand, may be worn in a pocket or on a belt (courtesy of Phonic Ear Inc.).

REFERENCES

Gengel, R., "Acceptable Speech-to-Noise Ratios for Aided Speech Discrimination by the Hearing Impaired," *Journal of Audiological Research, 11,* 1971, 219–222.

Gengel, R., and K. Faust, "Some Implications of Listening Level for Speech Recognition by Sensori-Neural Hearing Impaired Children," *Language Speech and Hearing Services in Schools, 6,* 1975, 14–20.

Matkin, N., and W. Olsen, "Induction Loop Amplification Systems: Classroom Performance," *ASHA, 12,* 1970(a), 239–244.

Matkin, N., and W. Olsen, "Response of Hearing Aids with Induction Loop Amplification Systems," *American Annals of the Deaf, 115,* 1970(b) 73–78.

Ross, M., "Assessment of the Hearing Impaired Prior to Mainstreaming," in *Mainstream Education for Hearing Impaired Children and Youth,* ed. G. Nix, pp. 101–108. New York: Grune & Stratton, Inc., 1976.

Ross, M., "Classroom Amplification," in *Hearing Aid Assessment and Use in Audiologic Habilitation,* eds. W. Hodgson, and P. Skinner, pp. 221–243. Baltimore: The Williams and Wilkins Company, 1977.

Ross, M., and T. Giolas, "Effect of Three Classroom Listening Conditions on Speech Intelligibility," *American Annals of the Deaf, 116,* 1971, 580–584.

Ross, M., T. Giolas, and P. Carver, "Effect of Three Classroom Listening Conditions on Speech Intelligibility: A Replication in Part," *Speech Hear. Serv. Schools, 4,* 1973, 72–76.

Sung, R., and W. Hodgson, "Performance of Individual Hearing Aids Utilizing Microphone and Induction Coil Input," *Journal of Speech and Hearing Research, 14,* 1971, 365–371.

Sung, R., G. Sung., and W. Hodgson, "A Comparative Study of Physical Characteristics of Hearing Aids on Microphone and Telecoil Inputs," *Audiology, 13,* 1974, 78–89.

A Model for the Management of Problems Resulting from Hearing Impairment

12

A Case Management Model

INTRODUCTION

It is the purpose of this chapter to present a philosophy of habilitation/rehabilitation that greatly expands the usual concept of our role as speech and hearing specialists. It has been customary to view these responsibilities as being confined to training persons with impaired hearing to make effective use of amplification and to improve auditory- and visual-communication skills. It is true that we have taken a somewhat broader view of our role with preschool children, because we have also been concerned with helping the parents to facilitate their child's adjustment and to deal with the many frustrations that result from congenital hearing impairment. Nevertheless, each of us—audiologists, teachers of the deaf, speech and hearing clinicians—has tended to accept rather restricted roles defined by our training. The result has been that the child and adult have received specialized services that have not been well integrated. Furthermore, the service each of us offers has not been tailored to provide for the special needs of our fellow professionals also working with the client in different capacities. This is so both in the evaluative and in the habilitative/rehabilitative stages. Our approach to helping the hearing-impaired person to deal with the broad impact of a disability has been fragmented and, therefore, less than optimally effective. It is on this situation that we focus our attention in this chapter. We will consider a model of assessment and intervention based upon the premise that our charge is to contribute to the improvement of the client's level of function within that person's normal, everyday environment. We must be familiar with the nature of the communication demands the person must meet at home, in school, at work, and in play or social environments, and we must understand the many factors that influence the person's ability to succeed in these settings. Our emphasis is upon actual overall communication function rather than upon performance on such individual communication skills as speech-reading, auditory discrimination, or speech articulation. That is not to say that these more traditional concerns are to be ignored, only that they must assume a place in the larger, holistic concept of meeting total adjustment needs. Regardless of our own particular area of specialization, we cannot meet all the needs of our client, but neither are those needs to be met by several specialists who each confine intervention efforts to his or her own area of expertise. To be optimally effective, services must be interactive. This necessitates an overall management approach to meeting the needs of the child or adult with a hearing handicap. In this chapter we will be concerned with the model and its rationale. The detailing of methods will be found in subsequent chapters. It is necessary here only to illustrate the concepts under discussion.

CASE MANAGEMENT

The purpose of the discussion in previous chapters has been to provide a level of insight and knowledge that will equip you to help a person with an impairment of hearing. For the remainder of the text our concern shifts to the integration and utilization of what you have learned. The task that confronts us is how to effectively modify the relationship between an individual and the environment in a manner that will prevent or reduce the effects of the hearing deficit. We need to consider specific techniques and procedures. Yet these can only be optimally successful when they are part of an integrated plan of intervention directed at all aspects of adjustment. The critical impact of a hearing impairment is on communication, but communication is so interwoven with our transactions with the world that its effects reverberate throughout our daily living. Furthermore, since we come to know and define our personal selves through the reflections we receive from interpersonal contacts, our self-image, our concept of self-worth, will also be affected by a communication problem. Thus, our potential effectiveness as helpers depends heavily on our concept of the scope of our responsibilities. Concern is often expressed by students and professionals over the matter of role definition and territorial rights. It appears that neither our responsibilities nor our role have been clearly defined. As a result many teachers and clinicians are reluctant to approach certain areas of need manifest by the person with hearing impairment. It is feared that professional boundaries, which are so ill-defined, may be overstepped. In general our training programs fail to address this very important issue. Yet it is one that has serious implications both for helping professions as a group, and for individual professionals.

In a presidential address to the American Speech and Hearing Association, Doeffler addressed the issue in terms of the profession of speech pathology and audiology:

> *We must on the one hand not set our boundaries so narrowly that we preclude responsibilities which might fall within our scope in the future, while on the other hand we must not set them so broadly that they extend beyond our present or probable capabilities* (Doeffler, 1968, p. 3).

Ainsworth (1965), considering the role of the professional, and in particular that of the speech clinician in the school, identified two alternatives: The clinician may act either as a *separatist* or as a *participant.* Ainsworth defines the separatist role as:

> *An independent professional who is responsible for diagnosing and treating the speech disorders of children. This point of view assumes that the responsibilities of the specialist are fulfilled when he successfully carries out the clinical activities for which he has been trained* (p. 495).

The participant role, by contrast, is defined by Ainsworth as one which:

> *. . . conceives of additional responsibilities which can be summarized by saying that the speech specialist is obligated to make a direct contribution to, and thus be an integral part of the ongoing educational program* (p. 495).

Referring specifically to audiology, Schultz (1972b) places the blame for the narrowness of role definition on its concentration on a single model, which he identified as an "acute-disease-oriented medical model" (p. 119). This model, he says, operates on the assumption that therapy involves the use of objective but not subjective characteristics of the hearing-impaired person. Intervention procedures have traditionally involved the client only in a passive role. Schultz argues that the implicit use of this medical model in training and service has deterred the development of effective aural rehabilitation because few of the necessary intervention procedures can be accommodated by the prevailing model. The important point to be derived from Schultz's argument is that when we consider alternatives to the medical model of audiology, we are forced to take a dramatically different approach to the task before us, to our role as rehabilitators, and to our relationship with the person with a hearing impairment.

The remarks of Doeffler, Ainsworth, and Schultz focus our attention on our responsibility for viewing both our profession and our helping role as involving us in the larger framework of the family, social, educational, and vocational system within which the individual we seek to help must function. We must conceive of our responsibility as a broad commitment to the overall management of the problems of the person with impaired hearing. This requires that our intervention strategies be relevant to the needs of each individual child or adult. These needs arise as a direct result of the demands made by the people and situations encountered by a person in his or her particular environment. If the environment or part of it changes significantly, there will be a change in the demands and, therefore, the needs. For this reason appropriate intervention strategies can be determined only after the specific nature of the individual needs are known. Furthermore, constant monitoring will be necessary to ensure relevance in the presence of changing demands. Thus it is necessary to consider the individual as a system functioning within a system. As with any ecosystem, the interaction between subcomponents varies, since each makes different demands upon the organism. The subcomponents with which we must be concerned may be identified as communicative, psychosocial, educational, and vocational. We must recognize that although communication impairment rests at the base of the problems confronted by the person with hearing difficulty, other problems also stand on that base. We must direct our attention to those problems if we are to have any impact on the person's ability to function maximally despite the hearing impairment. This places a burden upon us to develop intervention approaches that are:

1. Specifically need fulfilling
2. Broad enough to effect an overall improvement in the individual's adaptation to his or her environment(s)
3. Immediately relevant to the situation
4. Defined in operational terms

ADDRESSING THE PROBLEM

It is assumed that our services to the hearing-impaired child or adult only become necessary when the disability somehow affects the individual's ability to function in one or more of his or her everyday environments. Our responsibility is to use every available means to reduce the problems encountered, since it is the *effect* of the hearing impairment that intervention procedures are intended to mitigate against. Thus the overriding consideration that should govern any intervention procedure is that it should be based upon as thorough an understanding of the problem as possible. This is essential to ensure the relevance of the intervention, both in form and content. Developing a broad concept of the problem of hearing impairment necessitates that audiological data alone will not suffice in the determination of the specific intervention procedures that will be effective. We need, therefore, to survey the interaction between the child or adult and the environment in order to identify those areas in which current function is not adequate. It will be in these areas that environmental and/or behavioral management will be necessary.

At this stage our goals are:

1. To identify those communication demands, made on the individual in normal daily activities, that are not being met adequately
2. To describe the nature of the environment in which the demands arise
3. To assess the manner in which the individual is currently attempting to deal with the difficult situations
4. To identify the impact of failure to adequately meet demands on the person's perception of the situation, of him- or herself, and of significant others

THE PROBLEM HISTORY AND PROFILE

Our most immediate concern is to obtain a general, overall picture of the client's problem. The information we solicit should provide a meaningful profile of the relevant history of the communication problem, rather than of the hearing deficit alone. In determining the history, emphasis must be upon relevance. It is not justifiable to waste a great deal of the client's time and money obtaining a lot of information of doubtful significance merely because certain questions appear on a textbook case-history form. You must focus your interview. Try to avoid asking a series of specific questions, but instead identify the topic areas you wish to cover and then enter into a dialogue in which you guide the discussion. An easy give-and-take exploration of the nature of a client's difficulties as perceived by the client will do much to develop a relationship of trust and confidence. It will also serve as an unidentified counseling session because, as is discussed later, informational counseling does much to reduce anxiety. Case management has problem solving as its goal. Problem solving must be preceded by careful problem identification and definition. In the process of describing a problem to you, the client, often for the first time, is required to put into an organized manner the experiences he or she has had since first realizing he or she was experiencing difficulty. The client is beginning the process of problem definition and in so doing will gain insight into problems that often have been no more than vague apprehensions about what might be wrong. This is particularly true for the parents of a child suspected of being hearing impaired or of one who has recently been diagnosed as such. For this reason, at appropriate points, it is often helpful to inquire about the client's feelings or reactions. This will provide useful information in determining counseling needs. You will communicate to your client your interest in him or her as a person, and will help to establish a practice of discussing situations and events both objectively and subjectively. Later we consider counseling as an ongoing process that, for the most part, is interwoven into the fabric of the helping relationship rather than being separated from it. It is helpful to lay the foundations of this model from the earliest contacts.

Open the interview session by briefly defining your purpose. For example, you might say:

> What I would like to do this afternoon is to get some information from you which will help us both to understand the type of difficulties you (your child) are experiencing. We need to try to describe these as carefully as possible. We need to know what problems the difficulties are creating so we can consider ways of solving them. It will help me also to know how you (in fact, how both parents) feel about the various problems, and how you have been dealing with them. Tell me first, when did this all begin? . . .

As you move through the interview guidelines, make notes for your report. Explain to the client that you will be doing this and that you will share your summary report later. However, it is important not to allow note-taking to interfere with your relationship with the client; thus, you should confine it to essential points.

PROFILING THE CHILD AND THE FAMILY

The relative emphasis you place on different aspects of the history will depend upon circumstances peculiar to each person and family. You must use your judgment to determine whether it is important to spend the limited available time in obtaining medical details of the pre- and postnatal history of a hearing-impaired child, or whether that time might not better be invested in exploring the early developmental communication patterns between the child and the family.

The areas in which, over time, you will wish to develop a profile are:

1. Medical history
2. Developmental behavior
3. Communication abilities
4. Educational communication abilities
5. Personal adjustment
6. Audiological history including use of amplification
7. Environmental factors and resources

Medical History

In terms of management it should not be necessary to conduct an extensive medical-type interview. When possible such information should be sought from the pediatrician or otologist in charge of the medical care of the child. Certain medical evidence is, however, relevant to understanding the possible underlying nature of difficulties manifest by a child. For example, pay specific attention to the age of the subject at the time of the deafness. This is particularly relevant in terms of the child's auditory-perceptual development. A child who was born profoundly deaf may have developed a communication system that ignores auditory phenomena. Such a child may not be capable of utilizing amplified sound until given intense training designed to develop auditory behavior. When the onset of deafness has occurred after birth, the amount of auditory cues that have been unconsciously internalized and structured will depend upon the period of learning before the deafness was acquired. The longer the period of normal hearing, the greater the auditory-perceptual resources we have to tap.

Also note the etiology and type of deafness. In as much as 50 percent of all cases of deafness the causation of the auditory disorder is unknown. Among those for whom there is an established etiology, be particularly alert to children whose problems have been attributed to maternal rubella (German measles during pregnancy), especially when it occurred during the first three months of pregnancy; incompatibility of the maternal and fetal blood groups (Rh factor); prematurity; anoxia; and encephalitis. These etiologies are frequently associated with specific and generalized defects of pre- and postnatal development. With this group of children in particular, you should remember that a clear-cut diagnosis of sensorineural deafness as the single cause of the child's communication problems is often difficult. This is especially true during the early years of the child's life. No otologist would wish a diagnosis of sensorineural deafness to inhibit a teacher or therapist from observation of behavior that tends to suggest that the problem is more complicated than it originally appeared to be. A great deal of information concerning the nature of the child's problem can be learned by attempting to teach the child to overcome it. Every classification of the child's difficulty must be tentative, made within the limits of information available at the time. It should most certainly be open to reappraisal in the light of further information obtained by the teacher or therapist through observation and testing.

You will also need to be aware of active middle-ear pathology under treatment or a history of such conditions. Frequent buildup of ear wax and frequent colds or allergies are important factors, all of which should alert you to fluctuations in hearing that may give rise to marked or subtle changes in communicative, educational, and social behavior. Management requires that some person monitor all aspects of the child's overall adaptation, thus ensuring that medical attention is sought whenever a change in hearing status is suspected from an observed change in adaptive behavior.

Developmental Behavior and Communication

Auditory processing involves both reception and perception, and is, therefore, closely related to cognitive function. As I have emphasized elsewhere (Sanders, 1977), the behavior of children whose problems are exclusively due to peripheral hearing impairment is not always readily distinguishable from those with more central involvements. It is extremely important, therefore, that when working with hearing-impaired children, particularly preschool children, you should always be alert to developmental patterns, particularly speech and language patterns, that are not typical of a child whose problem is confined to peripheral reception. We have already noted that many etiologies responsible for impairment of hearing are also responsible for other sensory and/or motor defects. It is frequently impossible at the time diagnostic audiological testing is conducted to rule out conclusively other difficulties, particularly when the child is quite young. The intervention process constitutes, therefore, a natural extension of the diagnostic stage of management. Indeed, to consider these two stages as separate is to create a dangerous dichotomy. It is extremely important that the audiologist and the educational personnel establish and maintain cooperative monitoring of the child's development. You will expect a child diagnosed as having a peripheral hearing impairment to develop in a manner commensurate with that problem. You will expect the child to respond normally through other sensory channels, to be aware of all but the auditory components of the environment, and to be motorically close to age norms. If your expectancies fail to be met, your reassessment of the situation should question whether other sensorimotor problems in addition to hearing impairment may be present. Occasionally you may even have cause to suspect whether a peripheral hearing deficit exists at all. Therefore, you should include in your profile information about the child's overall development. Your main concern will be with the progress shown in response to sound and the receptive and expressive growth in language. These should evidence definite change as a result of amplification and intervention procedures. To ensure that such change can be noted it is recommendable to collect base-line evidence and to set short-term goals. For this reason the initial profile should contain carefully elicited information concerning:

1. The environmental sounds to which the child consistently shows awareness
2. The child's ability to localize sound sources when attention is attracted
3. The environmental sounds to which the child repeatedly responds in a meaningful manner
4. The child's awareness of people speaking to him or her when visual cues are not provided
5. The child's attentiveness to speaking voice
6. The child's ability to respond when familiar objects are named in situational context
7. The ability to find absent objects when named
8. The ability to follow simple directions
9. The ability to follow complex directions

You will need to obtain specific information about how the parents manage their communication interactions with the child.

Is speech in a situational context sufficient for the child to comprehend instructions?
Is it necessary to make heavy use of natural gestures and pantomime in order to be understood?
Can simple conversations be held about immediate or recent events?
How does the child make basic needs known? Does the child mainly point, gesture, use words, use sentences?
Is the child able to tell about simple experiences?
What happens when communication is difficult? How do the parents handle the situation? What does the child do when he or she experiences such situations?

You should consider the parents' reports in the light of your observations of the child in the activities in which you will involve him or her. Discrepancies between the parents' reports and your observations should not be dismissed cursorily as errors in parental reporting. Parents know their child far better than you will as a helper. Often a child behaves differently when with a nonparent in a different environment. Even if the parents' perceptions are colored by their concerns or hopes, the discrepancy can be helpful in familiarizing you with their counseling needs. Parent and helper should work together to bring their differing perceptions of the child's communicative and social behavior into accord through increased mutual understanding of the total situation.

For the older child the communication profile will need to be specific to the child's age level. The parents will be able to provide information concerning the degree of difficulty they experience in communicating with their child under a variety of situations in the home and outside the home. It is necessary to obtain a picture of how much frustration the child and family are having in communication interaction. You should inquire in what situations, if any, communication between parents and child is easy. Can the child understand when called from another room, or from the bottom of the staircase? Is the child able to participate in dinner-table conversations, to understand remarks made about a program while watching television? Can the child converse in the car and understand when spoken to in a busy department store? How much difficulty does the child have communicating with brothers and sisters and with nonfamily members? Can the child use the telephone satisfactorily, enjoy a movie, communicate with peers?

These are parent observations. When the child is old enough, the parents' views may be compared with the child's own perceptions of communication difficulty. This will provide further insight into the nature of the problems being confronted and the child's ability to meet the communication demands of the environment.

Communication Function of the Adult

An adult's profile will need to be less detailed. The information will be derived primarily from the client, though it is helpful to obtain comparative information from a husband or wife, or an older son or daughter who may perceive the client's communication difficulties differently. Remember, the hearing difficulty that creates communication problems for an individual also creates problems for those with whom that person wishes to communicate or who wish to communicate with that person. What we are seeking is as comprehensive an understanding of the individual's difficulties as is possible.

Essentially the same format can be followed for the development of a communication profile for an adult as has been illustrated for the child; only the questions need be different. The profile should reflect the communication situations that present difficulty at home, at work, and in social activities. You may wish to pursue in some detail the particular nature of the important situations in which difficulty is experienced. It is advisable to obtain impressions of the environment, the acoustics and noise conditions, the number of people usually involved, the distance from the speaker, the difficulty of the topic under discussion, and so on. Such information is particularly helpful in pre- and post-hearing-aid fitting when a client needs to make judgments concerning the benefit provided by amplification (Sanders, 1980). The degree to which being able to see the speaker's face clearly reduces the degree of difficulty in the situations mentioned should be noted. Remember, too, that asking the client to reflect upon the specific conditions in which he or she experiences difficulty in communication will not only provide you with useful information, but it will also help the client to see the problem in more objective terms. Before a plan of intervention can be developed it is necessary for both you and the client to understand the factors that give rise to that person's difficulties.

Educational Communication profile

For school-age children—which for our purpose encompasses those in nursery school through college or vocational training—we are particularly interested in the effect of the hearing impairment upon ability to function in an educational setting. Intervention efforts on behalf of the school child should be directed primarily at improving ability to effectively meet the demands of an educational environment. To achieve this we need a profile of the child in school. We need to become familiar with the learning environment and the competencies the child must have or must develop in order to perform adequately. If you are an itinerant or resource teacher, speech clinician, or educational audiologist working within the school system you can acquire such information by making a classroom visit and discussing a child with the classroom teacher and other teaching faculty. If you are a hearing clinician who sees the child in a speech and hearing center or hospital clinic, however, your task is more difficult. It is no less important, though, for only by ensuring the maximum relevance of your intervention procedures are your efforts likely to have a significant effect. We will discuss methods for achieving this when we consider intervention procedures with school-age children in Chapter 17.

Your inquiries should help you become familiar with:

1. The type of classroom(s) in which the child must function
2. The minimal competencies—"minimal survival skills"—that the child must have in order to be considered appropriately placed
3. The different approaches to learning that the child encounters
4. The child's present level of function
5. Specific difficulties the child experiences in meeting demands arising in class

The details pertaining to each of these categories will be considered later. It is important at this point only that you consider the idea of an overall plan for management so that when we consider intervention specific to the preschool or primary/secondary child, you will be able to evaluate the ideas within this framework. Your role should be defined in terms of the child's needs and your abilities, which may not be synonymous with your qualifications. You must try your best to meet the child's needs. If others are available who are qualified and prepared to assume responsibility for certain aspects of specialized intervention, it is your responsibility to ensure that such services are made available. However, you will often find that you do not have such good fortune. In that case you should try to work under the guidance of a specialist (psychologist, guidance counselor, remedial reading teacher, resource teacher, and so on) providing for the needs of the child. Your prime responsibility is to improve the communication abilities of the individual in the environments in which he or she must function. To fulfill this responsibility you must integrate your services to the child into the total educational process; to do less is to make what you do irrelevant. Your responsibility is to achieve *functional* communication, not to develop skills appropriate only to the artificial environment of the "therapy" room.

Personal Adjustment Profile

One of the reasons people with hearing impairment are reluctant to enter into certain communication situations is because of their feelings about revealing themselves as handicapped. They often experience justifiable apprehensions about the potential embarrassment arising from misunderstanding what is said. Adjustment to the reality of the hearing impairment is thus an important factor in determining how well the child or adult can cope with its effects. Similarly the feelings and attitudes of the parents of a child with impaired hearing, and those of a husband or wife of a person with a hearing deficit, can significantly influence the effectiveness of intervention procedures. You should be prepared, therefore, to accept responsibility for helping the individual to express, examine, and deal with feelings about hearing difficulties, or in the case of parents, feelings about their hearing-impaired child. Problem definition usually proves to be a source of initial counseling. The imparting of information about the significance of test findings and profiles often does much to relieve anxiety. Beyond this, some persons and some families need help in working through their feelings about their hearing impairment and the problems arising from it. Usually the difficulties constitute an integral part of the whole experience of having impaired hearing. The client, or the parents of a child, seldom feel that psychiatric or psychological consultation is what they need; they may even be shocked by such a suggestion. What they want is no more than to be able to talk about situations and feelings related to their experiences. You are the person who is knowledgeable about hearing handicaps; it is natural that your client should look to you for guidance. It is your responsibility to equip yourself to meet this need. A management approach includes meeting these subjective needs as well as more objective ones. In discussing counseling in subsequent chapters, we will examine the type of profile that will help you relate to the client's feelings. Such a profile will be more subjective than objective, but it should include information obtained not only from the client, but also from the family, and for a child, from teachers and guidance counselors.

Audiological Profile

The audiologic information about the client is usually the first topic discussed in compiling a profile. You should read what audiological information is provided and you should form some impression from it. However, note that there are some very definite limitations to the data usually available. First, the audiological evaluation is often not current. It is most unwise to depend upon test results that are not up to date. It is even more significant for you to recognize that the purpose of the traditional audiologic evaluation is the *assessment of the auditory system* to identify the site of an impairment of function. Audiologists performing a diagnostic role strive to obtain as much objectivity, as possible in the testing process. When possible, removing the client from the decision-making process is considered desirable. An example of this is the use of *impedance audiometry,* which assesses middle-ear function by studying the response of the middle-ear mechanism to pressure changes. The results of such testing provide reliable information more easily than bone-conduction audiometry. Schultz (1972a) has emphasized that:

Consciously or unconsciously, the point of view has been nourished in audiology that the less the results of any procedure are influenced by the idiosyncracies of the individual patient, the more scientific would be the discipline and the clinical examination (p. 67).

The type of audiologic information that can significantly contribute to helping an individual adjust to the effects of an impairment of hearing must be very different from that derived from a diagnostic evaluation. Our concern must be with *functional behavior in actual environmental situations* rather than with the integrity of the auditory system alone. It is, in fact, with those very idiosyncracies, which the clinical audiologist seeks to avoid, that we must be concerned. It is true that the client's problems stem from an impaired ability to process auditory information normally, but communication, as we have seen, involves more than auditory processing. The degree of redundancy encoded into the communication act, together with the listener's ability to generate expectancies computed from familiarity with the relevant situational, contextual, and linguistic rules, ensures that to some extent improved communication can result from auditory training alone. However, our attention should not be focused on the training of skills. Important as such training may be, skills remain tools. Our concern centers on the enhancement of overall adjustment. When we are familiar with the needs, we will be in a position to request or provide audiologic evaluation of the client's present ability to use residual hearing to satisfy the demands made upon that person. We will also be able to use the information obtained to make a guarded assessment of the potential contribution that residual hearing may contribute to function.

The point is that once diagnostic assessment of the auditory system has been completed, it is necessary to undertake a very different kind of diagnostic evaluation of the nature of the person's communication difficulties and the situations in which they occur. In this assessment, evaluation is concerned with auditory function and must be made within the larger context of overall communication adaptation. The environmental situations peculiar to a given child or adult must be taken into consideration. Schultz (1972a) makes the same point:

. . . *There is little relationship between formalized audiologic assessment and audiologic therapy, so that the individual clinician is more or less successful depending upon the additional observations he makes and the individual insight with which he interprets his observations. In other words audiologic evaluation is a highly complex process and very little of the observational material necessary to these clinical decisions arises from the formalized results of audiologic assessments* (p. 69).

Environment and Resources Profile

We have thus far concentrated our discussion of management on the need to display a comprehensive view of all aspects of those client needs related to or affected by communication difficulty. However, it has been stressed repeatedly that these are environmentally related needs. In order to develop management strategies you need all the information you can obtain about the environments in which the person must function. You also need to identify all the resources available to you in your attempt to reduce the impedance between the individual and the environment. The profiles you develop for each client provide the bases for determination of present function and do much to help you appraise the client's potential for adaptation. You will be able to determine where the greatest need for intervention lies and to develop strategies that you predict will have the greatest effect in optimizing communication performance.

The resources available to you are not limited to those of the client alone. In addition to your work with the individual, you can, to some extent, modify the client's environment and the nature of the demands arising from it. This presents the major difference between a clinical model, which concentrates on training the individual, and a management model, which involves the manipulation of all resources that may effect communication performance. In our study of intervention strategies and methods we will consider the types of environmental resources that should be investigated and how they may be used. A management model calls for the marshaling of these resources in the most efficient manner in order to clearly define and solve problems.

SUMMARY

This chapter has stressed that while the problems of the hearing-impaired child or adult arise from an impairment of communication, their impact is felt in many aspects of the individual's life. Thus our perception of the problem of hearing impairment cannot be limited to its effects upon speech comprehension. Our responsibility to the person with a hearing deficit must not be confined to attempts to improve the ability to understand speech. We must accept the far more challenging and potentially far more effective and rewarding tasks of intervening in all aspects of adaptation that are affected by the communication difficulty. This includes the audiological, communicative, educational, vocational, social, and emotional aspects of a person's life. The present independence of audiological assessment from rehabilitative intervention, and the separation of procedures from the child's educational communication needs or the adult's social and vocational needs, is inexcusable. To avoid this situation we must move away from a clinical model of habilitation/rehabilitation, which limits our intervention to procedures involving communication training. We should instead broaden our intervention strategies to approximate a more sociologically oriented management model. This necessitates careful profiling of each area of the client's communication function that is affected by the hearing impairment. It requires that the information gathered be relevant to the client's daily communication needs in a variety of settings. In this way intervention procedures can be directed at well-defined functional difficulties in a manner that is most likely to effect a meaningful change in the client's level of adaptation.

REFERENCES

Ainsworth, S., "The Speech Clinician in the Public Schools—Participant or Separatist," *ASHA, 7,* 1965, 495.

Doeffler, L., "The Association and the Profession." Presidential Address, 1967 National Convention, *ASHA, 10,* January 1968, 3–6.

Sanders, D., *Auditory Perception of Speech: An Introduction to Principles and Problems,* pp. 177–190. Englewood Cliffs, N.J.: Prentice-Hall, Inc., 1977.

Sanders, D., "Hearing Aid Orientation and Counseling," in *Amplification for the Hearing Impaired,* ed. M. J. Pollack, pp. 323–372. New York: Grune & Stratton, Inc., 1980.

Schultz, M. C., *An Analysis of Clinical Behavior in Speech and Hearing.* Englewood Cliffs, N.J.: Prentice-Hall, Inc., 1972(a).

Schultz, M. C., "The Bases of Speech Pathology and Audiology: What are Appropriate Models?" *Journal of Speech and Hearing Disorders, 37,* no. 1, 1972(b), 118–122.

13

Management of the Very Young Preschool Child

The needs of the preschool hearing-impaired child can only be considered in terms of the impact that diagnosis of hearing impairment will almost inevitably have upon the child's family. In the preschool years of a child's life the foundations for subsequent learning are laid. This occurs as the result of normal developmental processes occurring within the environment of the home, and, most particularly, as a result of the child's contacts with the immediate family (Cazden, 1972). It is at this time that the interactive effects of nature and nurture are at their strongest. The child grows in certain ways and develops certain abilities, attitudes, and behaviors by virtue of the experiences he or she has, the models to which he or she is exposed, and the feedback he or she receives. For the very young preschool child these are provided predominately by the family. Later, nursery-school experiences may be expected to contribute to developmental behavior. *The first principle of management of the young preschool hearing-impaired child must be, therefore, that it be family centered.*

Your initial concern is to help the family, particularly the parents, achieve an effective pattern of adjustment. This should serve to minimize the negative effects that may arise from the knowledge that their child has a physical disability. It is not possible to achieve this goal optimally unless everyone concerned with the child and the family cooperates in the management program. Our efforts must be coordinated to achieve well-defined objectives. These must be known and understood by the parents, the audiologist, teacher and/or hearing therapist, the hearing-aid dealer, and the family physician or pediatrician. The parents must not be exposed to conflict among the professionals with whom they deal; they must not be used by us to defend our particular opinions against other professionals. If genuine differences of opinion occur, we are obligated morally to present, not prejudiced or righteous dogma, but information and rationales. We must meet together with the parents to discuss alternatives and to help them decide how they wish differences to be resolved. The involvement of the parents in the process of preschool management is crucial to the success of many, if not all, aspects of the intervention program. Bronfenbrenner (1975) reported on an extensive longitudinal study of early-intervention programs. He concluded that active involvement of parents in the preschool management of their children resulted in a level of child function superior to that of children from programs that were mainly child centered. The superior performance of children from family-centered programs was reflected not only during the preschool period, but continued into the early school years. By contrast, children from preschool programs that trained the child but did not emphasize, or in some cases even include, parent involvement, demonstrated that early gains tended to be lost on entry to school. Similar conclusions have been reached by Gordon (1976), Radin (1972), Schaefer (1972), and Gilmer, Miller, and Gray (1970).

When applied to the problem of the young hearing-impaired child these findings indicate that training programs will be most effective when they are designed to develop an understanding of the nature of the child's problem, of the task the child faces, and of possible ways of managing the growth and learning environment. The effectiveness of such programs seems to lie in fostering self-confidence and managerial skills in the parents, who must be the child's leading advocates during the school years. They also suggest that by assuming the major responsibility for the child's early development, the parents regain respect for their role as parents. At the same time they develop the competence and confidence necessary to be successful in that role. By contrast, programs that are child centered usurp the parents' role at a time when the parent-child relationship is most critical. A child-centered program may cause the parents to conclude that they are unfit for that role. This, in turn, engenders feelings of guilt. To avoid such problems early-intervention programs should be parent and family centered, a philosophy supported by other educators of the hearing-impaired child (Horton & Hanners, 1977; Ling & Ling, 1978; Simmons-Martin, 1978). As the child progresses toward kindergarten age the relative emphasis will shift to more structured learning in preparation for school. Direct parent involvement will naturally decrease for hearing-impaired children, as it does for hearing children. The parent role shifts to a supportive one but is in no way less important. The management strategies proposed in this text incorporate this philosophy.

AN INTERVENTION PLAN

Your first responsibility as the teacher/hearing therapist is to develop an intervention plan addressed to the needs of a specific family. These needs may be classified as:

1. Informational
2. Personal adjustment
3. Audiological
4. Communication
5. Behavioral
6. Educational planning

You must consider the needs of each family in a highly individualized manner. This calls for sensitivity on your part. Your early contacts with the family unit should be concerned with both giving and receiving information. Your attitude and approach should make clear that: (1) you and the family constitute a team; (2) you seek to develop a plan of action specifically geared to their family situation; (3) your purpose is to support and guide the family in their role as the major providers of the child's needs.

You must avoid the feeling that it is important to begin immediately to do something, anything, with the child. Although some parents will pressure you to begin immediately to work with the child, you must resist, because precipitous action is seldom effective. Moreover you may soon find yourself trapped into a child-centered model in which all the responsibility has shifted from the parent to you. Initially, a carefully planned approach may be hard for anxious, impatient parents to accept. However, usually they soon recognize its value and appreciate the confidence they gain from it.

Let us now consider the categories of needs we have just identified.

Informational Needs

In most instances by the time you first meet with the parents they have gone through the early stages of shock resulting from the discovery or confirmation that their child is hearing impaired. They have begun to make an initial adjustment to the situation as they perceive it. Occasionally an audiologist makes a referral of a family that has only just learned of the hearing impairment. In this case informational counsel should be delayed until the parents have been given support in coming to terms with their feeling of helplessness. Every physician and audiologist who has responsibility for imparting to parents a diagnosis of hearing impairment should either be available to give initial personal support counseling, or should be able to arrange an emergency referral to someone who can provide it. *Continuity of support from the day of diagnosis is very important to parental adjustment* (Figure 13.1).

Assuming that the initial shock has passed, the primary need is to work to inform the parents of the nature of the impairment and the task before them. It is not possible to completely separate informational from personal counseling because the end goal of both is to facilitate adjustment. Much of the anxiety and apprehension these parents experience arises from confronting what is essentially an unknown situation. They do what we all do under such circumstances: They envisage the worst possible outcome. All the negative images and stereotypes they have had about deaf children and adults come to mind. It is essential that you in-

FIGURE 13.1 Continuity of support is important to parental adjustment. (Courtesy of Language Development Program of Western New York)

tervene in this process by providing the parents with factual information that can serve as the basis for realistic discussion of their hopes and fears. The first stage of positive adjustment is dependent upon understanding the problem. You must ensure, therefore, that you have before you details of the otological and audiological findings and background information concerning events leading up to diagnosis. You will also need a report on the recommendation concerning amplification as well as information about the hearing aid(s) and what effect they have, or are expected to have, on the child's potential for auditory processing. It is helpful in the first interview with the parents of a preschool child to begin by asking them what they have already been told about the nature of their child's problem. This will help you determine the extent of the information you need to provide. The following questions, which are characteristic of those many parents ask, or later say they wish they had asked, may prove of help to you in empathizing with parents. Note that the approach to each answer is always in a positive form. Concentrate on the child's potentials, communicate a sense of hope, even optimism, tempered by honesty, concerning the evidence currently available. You should avoid emphasizing the severity of the problem but should stress instead the predicted potentials of the child. This does not mean that you should adopt an overly positive approach, but neither is there ever cause to condone a despondent or despairing attitude, regardless of the severity of the disability.

Following are some guidelines to follow in dealing with parents' questions:

1. Listen carefully and attentively. Each question will give information about the parents' perceptions, concerns, and level of understanding.
2. Treat each question with respect, however simple it may seem to you. Communicate to the parents that you will treat whatever seems important to them in a like manner.
3. Rephrase questions or seek clarification when the intent of the question is not clear. Parents may need help in formulating their questions to more accurately reflect their anxiety. Be prepared to say, "Let me see if I have understood what you are concerned about (or what you wish to know)."
4. Accept questions whenever the parent wishes to ask them. Your role is to facilitate learning, not to deliver a lecture.
5. If a question suggests a deeper reference than its superficial appearance, rephrase it to allow the parents to acknowledge that what you are asking is what they are trying to get at.
6. If a question appears to have jumped several stages in a process of reasoning, phrase and answer the intermediary steps, then answer the parents' original question.

Parental Questions

Let us now consider the types of questions that may arise. Remember, these are phrased in parent terms:

The audiologist said that Becky is deaf. Does that mean she will never hear anything?

The aim of your answer should be to defuse the negative connotations of the stereotypic label "deaf," to shift the parents' concern away from the hearing that is deficit (or "lost" as people so often say) toward the concept of usable residual hearing. The effectiveness of hearing aids in making sound available to the child should be mentioned.

How much can she hear then?

This is the time to discuss residual hearing more specifically. You first need to explain the difference between hearing sound and attributing meaning to it. Even what we pick up by our ears is affected by our listening behavior. From the audiologic data, which you should have available, you will be able to explain how much is known about the child's hearing capacity. With infants and young children definitive hearing profiles are often not yet obtainable. However, approximate thresholds of response to various sounds are usually known. With an older preschool child you may have fairly reliable pure-tone audiograms and even speech audiometric data. You should talk to the parents about the available data, explaining what it suggests in terms of functional auditory behavior. For example, say whether it appears that the mother's and father's voices are audible without amplification. Consider whether this is true from about 4 feet, 2 feet, or only when speaking directly into the child's ear. Does the child receive enough of the component sounds of speech to make vowel discrimination a possibility? Which sounds of speech are either not heard at all or are likely to be very distorted? This information can be obtained by plotting the pure-tone thresholds onto the chart showing distribution of speech-sound energy across frequency (see Figure 3.11). Make your explanations practical and understandable in terms of the present contribution of residual hearing without amplification. Do not present academic explanations of frequency, intensity, decibels, formants, and transitional characteristics. Explain, rather, that speech sounds are perceived in terms of patterns of sound that occur because many different vibrations occur simultaneously at different strengths. When the ear is sensitive to all these vibrations, the speech sound is heard clearly. When some components are not picked up, the sound becomes blurred and difficult to recognize. In some cases none of the pattern is received; the sound is simply inaudible. You can show the parents how this information is reflected on the audiogram where low- to high-frequency components are shown horizontally and strength of signal is depicted vertically. Explain that the normal range of sensitivity is −5 to +20 units of intensity (measured in decibels—dB—as milk is measured in pints). Point out that comfortable loudness for those with normal hearing is between 50 to 70 units of loudness (dB) above detection, and that conversational speech varies from 55 to 65 dB. Then show how close to this the child's hearing comes. Explain how environmental sounds tend to be fairly loud, contain many low tones, and have energy patterns more easily recognizable than the fine patterns of speech. This will explain why the child may respond well to some loud environmental sounds but appear not to respond to speech.

At this point it is important to seek the parents' observations. Do they corroborate what the audiological data imply? Stress that the parents are now part of a team and that test findings and behavioral observations must concur before maximum confidence in the perception of the child can be achieved. This cooperative monitoring, you should point out, will be an integral part of the ongoing management program.

Will the hearing aid that has been recommended correct the hearing problem?

This question relates very closely to the discussion of residual hearing. It arises from the ever-present hope of parents of young children that the hearing problem is reversible or that the child will ultimately function normally without a hearing aid. The answer to the question should be an unequivocal "NO." The aid will not correct the hearing, though by virtue of what it permits the child to hear it will do much to help in the development of effective auditory behavior. Unlike glasses the aid does not have a corrective or restorative function. It is akin to a magnifying glass, which makes more of the details available to its user. The aid is a device that permits the child to receive and process more of the auditory world than is possible without it. It will facilitate the growth of oral-language comprehension and use, and will greatly enhance learning within the limits of the child's ability to comprehend speech. But it will not permit Becky to hear as though she had no impairment.

Will Becky become dependent upon the aid?

This question, sometimes phrased in terms of how long the aid will have to be worn, again reflects the hope that the child's ability to hear will in some way ultimately be normalized. The answer to give is, "I sincerely hope so." Explain that you hope that with the aid Becky will achieve a level of communicative function and environmental awareness impossible without amplification. It is this level of performance and self-confidence that you hope she will become dependent upon. The fact that the aid makes it all possible makes dependency upon it a very positive factor.

What exactly does the aid do for her?

It is necessary for you to draw a comparison between what you have learned from the parents, from the tests, and from your own observations about Becky's unaided response to sound, and what you predict she will hear with the aid. Stress that this is a prediction, the validity of which you and the parents must check through observation. You can first compare the aided and unaided pure-tone audiograms showing the increased area of audibility under the aided curve. You should draw attention to the aided thresholds in the all-important 500- to 4000-Hz range with particular reference to the extent to which conversation (60 to 65 dB) will be audible. If speech-processing measures are available compare them for unaided and aided scores. You should emphasize that a picture of what the aid is contributing can only really be determined in terms of spoken-language acquisition, comprehension, and use. Parents should be encouraged to carefully monitor the child's response to speech and to environmental sounds when wearing the aid.

Will she learn to speak?

This is one of the most difficult questions to answer, for the specific elements critical to the acquisition of intelligible speech and the development of a rich auditory/oral language become less and less common as the severity of hearing deficit exceeds 95 dB. Yet many children's achievements frequently flaunt the general rule. For this reason always try to present cautious optimism, even when a child has limited residual hearing. When a child has considerable usable residual hearing, you can afford to be less cautious. The question is best answered not in terms of the severity of the hearing impairment, but rather in terms of how much residual hearing is predicted to contribute to speech perception and the degree of effort and training you perceive will be necessary. Differentiate for the parent between language and speech, and between comprehension of spoken language, which, as you are aware, involves more than auditory reception, and the ability to communicate orally. Stress that adequate communication skill is the main goal of your contribution to management. We will examine the implications of this when we consider the topic of communication needs. The answer to the question, "Will she learn to speak?" will vary, therefore, according to the information you have available. Assisting a child to learn to understand and communicate by speech should be the ideal toward which you strive. Thus, you should certainly make every effort to help Becky learn to speak. Also bear in mind her urgent need to communicate, and consider the possible need to introduce a supporting manual system if this appears necessary. Dealing with Becky's problems requires a flexible, pragmatic approach with the major emphasis on auditory-oral communication. At the same time, reccognize that for some children use of manual communication may prove to be advantageous.

Will Becky be able to go to our local grade school?

Although you may think this question to be premature if the child is only an infant, it is understandable that the major concern of the parents is that their child will be normalized. (We will consider the educational aspects in the appropriate section.) At this point emphasize to the parents that your goal for their child is to ensure maximum exploitation of potentials. You will guide the parents in the placement of their child in the educational setting most likely to allow for maximal learning and the best possible personal adjustment. Hopefully the public school will prove appropriate for these requirements, but stress the necessity of keeping an open mind. It is most important to impress on the parents that they will be actively involved in the process of reaching educational-placement decisions. As preschool guidance proceeds, you and they together will conduct an ongoing assessment of the child's abilities and needs. Later you will examine the possible school placements that can provide for these needs.

The parents will have many other questions, some of which we will consider under other subsections of our discussion. Those raised here do, however, identify some of the major concerns. Provision of clear information in a confident manner will help to define the problem in a way that makes it manageable. This will do much to allay many anxieties, some of which may be quite unfounded. The knowledge that you are a well-informed professional, that you are patient and understanding, that you are willing to listen to questions in a manner that evidences your respect for the parents, represents the beginning not only of an ongoing informational component to management, but also of a personal guidance component.

Personal Adjustment Needs

Hearing and speech therapists, audiologists, and teachers of preschool hearing-impaired children have an important role to play in helping parents express and deal with their feelings about having a hearing-handicapped child. Few, if any, of us are trained counselors or psychiatric social workers. We should not ever assume that role. We must recognize, however, that the birth of any child into a family is invariably followed by a period of adjustment for all parents, new or old. If that child is found to be handicapped the adjustment is much greater and somewhat different. In almost every case the reactions of the parents, first to the diagnosis and later to the perceived ramifications of having "a child who is not normal," are justifiable, understandable, and to a great extent predictable. *It is the normality of the reactions that justifies our readiness to listen and to provide support to these parents.* At this time of stress most parents need to be reassured that it is normal, even necessary, to experience the feelings that they are encountering. To refer parents to a clinical psychologist at this point tends to repudiate the normality of their reactions. The feelings most parents experience are directly related to the fact that they have learned that their child is hearing impaired. It is natural, therefore, that they should turn to you for support in coming to terms with this. It is, after all, the child who is different. Only by virtue of their child's problem do the parents feel abnormal. In most cases the parents are as well adjusted as we are, yet, like us, in times of stress they need support.

However, the occasion will arise when you feel unable to cope with the parents' reactions. Referral to a psychiatrist or psychologist will be necessary. Generally, this becomes necessary when the parents:

1. Exhibit reactions that are clearly far more severe than appropriate for the situation
2. Appear not to be responsive to your attempts to help them deal with their feelings
3. Appear to have problems that existed before and are aggravated by the diagnosis of hearing impairment in the child
4. Appear not to be making progress in coming to terms with the reality of the child's disability

You should be frank in explaining that you feel limited in dealing with their needs for parent training by the difficulties you are having in helping them handle the emotional effects of their child's problem. You should tell them that you feel it necessary to refer them to someone who can advise both them and you in how to approach the problem. Such a consultation results either in the parents' receiving professional psychological counseling or in your continuing to work with them under the indirect supervision of a specialist.

Parental Reactions to a Diagnosis of Hearing Impairment. The impact that a less-than-perfect child has on the parents, particularly the mother, is documented in the literature (Gordeuk, 1976; Kvaraceus & Hayes, 1969; Mackeith, 1973; Ross, 1964). The major impact is upon the mother's image of herself and of her child, and on her perception of her ability to be a "good" mother. Negative reactions produce a disruption of the early stages of the development of the parent-child bond. This interferes with the establishment of the mother's normal role. Gasson (1966) considers this to be extremely serious, and he feels that unless adverse family reaction to the child is resolved, it may be potentially more damaging than the disability itself. This is so because the child's self-concept in the preschool years is derived almost entirely from the parents' reactions to him or her (Worby, 1971).

If the parents come to you soon after they have learned that their child is handicapped, it will be reasonable for them to be low in spirits. The trauma and grief they experience has been described as very similar to that experienced by parents when a child dies. This is understandable because, in fact, they no longer have the normal child they had dreamed of, and planned for.

In many cases the diagnosis of deafness is delayed by as much as a year from the time of the parents' first suspicions (Northern & Downs, 1974; Shah, Chandler, & Dale, 1978). Many parents, therefore, learn to relate with confidence and pride to what they believe is a normal child.

Diagnosis of hearing impairment often threatens this established relationship, replacing the child who was known with one who is unknown. The parents find they must face "... the uncertainty of how to relate to one different from the norm ... all without knowing what the difference means for the future" (Altschuler, 1974, p. 369).

The process of parents' cognitive and emotional adjustment after being told that their child is hearing impaired usually follows a common pattern characterized by four stages (Gordeuk, 1976; Simmons-Martin, 1976; Solnit & Stark, 1961).

Shock and Disbelief. To protect themselves from its reality, the parents in this initial stage often deny that the child has a problem. They may be critical of the audiologist, question the validity of results, appear unappreciative of the help you are offering. They wish above all to regain their normal child. This feeling coexists with those of intense disappointment (Kapke, 1970). During this period it is unrealistic to expect the parents to be able to become involved in intervention procedures. Your main role at this time is to encourage the frank expression of feelings and concerns. The parents need the acceptance of their anger, disbelief, and frustration. Do not refute what they say. Do not feel that your integrity or that of your audiologist is threatened. It may help for you to agree that further testing will be necessary, that a definitive statement on the child's hearing will take time to develop. Stress, however, that from this point on you and the parents, together with the audiologist and otologist, will be working as a team to accurately describe the child's abilities and needs. Insist that the parents' best hope lies in working with this team; seeking many different opinions is likely to prove counterproductive and will delay the provision of essential services. Above all acknowledge the reasonableness of the parents' reactions, and express understanding of their feelings. Mostly, try to listen sympathetically.

Awareness of the Reality of the Loss of the Normal Child. The parents now begin to acknowledge the facts with which they have been presented. They are trying to cope both with the reality of their felt loss and with the fact that they have a handicapped child. Although continued supportive acceptance is necessary during this stage, parents have moved to a more active role in problem solving. Instead of simply lashing out in anger, or withdrawing into grief, they begin to talk about their perceptions of the child's handicap in contrast to a normal child. Through guidance you can gently influence those perceptions to bring them into accord with known facts. You can begin slowly to involve yourself in the problem-solving task. Your confidence, realism, and invested authority can be very reassuring to the parents at this time.

Mourning of the Lost Child. This represents a very difficult stage during which the parents suffer grief over the negation of their reasonable hopes and aspirations for their believed normal child. This stage is, therefore, characterized by feelings of despair and emptiness. The parents have accepted the reality of the handicap, but they either have only negative references toward which to orient their ideas of the future, or they face a void. It is in this stage that parents first begin to be able to develop a relationship with their "new" child. Yet they are also aware that doing so may constantly evoke images of how things might have been had their child been normal.

As a support counselor you can do much to help the parents learn to feel comfortable in relating to their child, to accept the child for what he or she is. This means that the parents must know what the child's needs are, and they must be aware of how helpful their behavior to the child can be in the pursuit of self-awareness and self-definition. During this period the parents will be receptive to and appreciative of practical guidance that helps them to develop confidence in knowing that what they are doing is appropriate for the child. You should observe the parents' behavior with the child, watching for aspects of it that you can reinforce to give confidence.

"I notice that you give a lot of physical contact to David; that will be very reassuring to him."

"You are helping him a lot by becoming part of his play. That is building a sound basis for the language communication which we will begin to work on."

"It is extremely important that you continue to talk to David in the way you are doing—that is just what he needs."

In any parent-child relationship, you will observe behaviors that can justifiably serve as the basis for communicating your respect for the parent role. A sound foundation of positive reinforced behavior allows for subsequent suggestions for modifying other behaviors.

Reacceptance of the Parental Role. The fourth stage is one in which the parents have worked through their grief and have reaccepted their role as parents. They usually still have considerable anxiety and doubts concerning their adequacy to meet the challenge, but they have accepted it. It is at this point in the adjustment process that you can begin to work out the plan of intervention with the parents. They are now ready to learn appropriate child-management techniques, and to work with you as part of the team. This stage seldom occurs suddenly nor are all traces of previous stages erased. Each stage generally blurs into the next, and each retains some residuals of the earlier ones. However, there comes a time with all parents when the traumatic experience has been lived through sufficiently to permit them to want to spend more of their energies looking forward than looking back.

Personal adjustment lies at the base of intervention procedures. Until the parents feel secure in their roles, and until they develop confidence in their ability to cope and to be effective parents to their hearing-impaired child, they will be unable to meet the child's needs fully. This growth comes through successful experiences. You cannot endow them with the confidence necessary to begin. You must assume that the parents with whom you work have the necessary capacity to fulfill their roles well. The shock of the diagnosis of hearing impairment will have drained, to various degrees, their self-confidence. Being provided with an opportunity to express, understand, and work through those feelings, coupled with the acquisition of knowledge and guidance in the use of appropriate techniques for helping their hearing-impaired child, will restore the parents' confidence necessary for success. This is an ongoing developmental process that we will continue to refer to in our discussion of other needs. The important point is that your responsibility is to help parents to be effective, not to assume their roles for them.

Audiologic Needs

Although it is possible to obtain some approximate measure of auditory behavior even in newborn babies, the task of defining the audiologic needs of the child is complex. It involves periodic assessments by the audiologist with ongoing monitoring of the child's auditory behavior by the hearing therapist or teacher in cooperation with the parents. A team approach to management is especially important in assessing residual hearing and selecting appropriate amplification. Matkin (1977) has stressed that the reliable assessment of hearing sensitivity is only the first step in comprehensive pediatric audiologic evaluation. He states:

In other words, once the hearing loss has been described in terms of degree, configuration and type, it becomes essential that the focus be shifted from the hearing loss, to the child's usable residual hearing (p. 129).

Your concern is no longer with auditory sensitivity but with auditory behavior. You are interested in documenting the relationship between a particular hearing aid or aids, and the child's use of residual hearing.

The prerequisite to fully meeting the child's audiologic needs is the parents' understanding and acceptance of the hearing aid. If they have not yet reached this stage, then the greatest audiologic need is for informational and personal-adjustment counsel. The task of coming to terms with having a handicapped child places heavy emotional demands upon the parents. It is natural to experience disappointment and a sense of failure. There is a strong desire not to admit to the reality of the hearing impairment. You can understand how hard it is for many parents to broadcast the child's deficiency publicly by having the child wear the stigma symbol of a hearing aid. This is particularly true when a body aid is fitted. An initially negative reaction to the child's wearing a hearing aid should be accepted as normal and reasonable. Even hearing specialists, despite their knowledge, would probably experience the same feelings, though they would either conceal them or seek to work them through. Many parents also conceal such feelings. In some cases the aid may only be put on the child in the privacy of the home, or only when visiting the center for parent guidance. Any number of excuses may be offered to explain the child's nonuse of the aid. These may include: "It does not fit well," "She keeps pulling it off," "It hurts his ear," "It pulls on his clothing," "I am afraid she will lose it." Such objections are most often justified by a valid reason. Therefore you must investigate and attend to each objection. When the complaints appear not to be justified objectively, then you can assume that equally valid subjective reasons lie behind them. You should, therefore, help the parents explore their feelings about the aid and what it signifies. Try to bring underlying attitudes to the surface. Accept the parents' feelings but do everything possible to separate them from the child's critical need for amplification. This is particularly necessary because you have shared responsibility for meeting the child's needs and failure to do so now will result in enormous feelings of guilt later. Make sure that the need for amplification as the keystone in the intervention program is both understood and accepted by the parents.

The second greatest audiologic need after parental acceptance is to ensure that the hearing aid is worn constantly by the child. This necessitates that you check that the parents are competent in fitting the mold into the child's ear, have an appropriate harness for fitting a body aid on the young child, and know how the audiologist wishes the aid to be worn. Parents should understand the philosophy of changing the ear in which the aid is worn, if this has been recommended, and should be aware of how often to do this. They should know the recommended settings for the frequency and volume-control settings and feel confident that they can take care of the aid as explained in Chapter 10 (Figure 3.2). It is the responsibility of the parents to keep the aid functioning, so you must go over with them the checks they should make to ensure that it remains in good condition (Downs, 1971). It is particularly important that the fit of the ear mold be checked regularly. Frequent replacements tend to be necessary in the growing infant if optimal acoustic quality is to be maintained. Unfortunately, the problem of acoustic feedback resulting from a

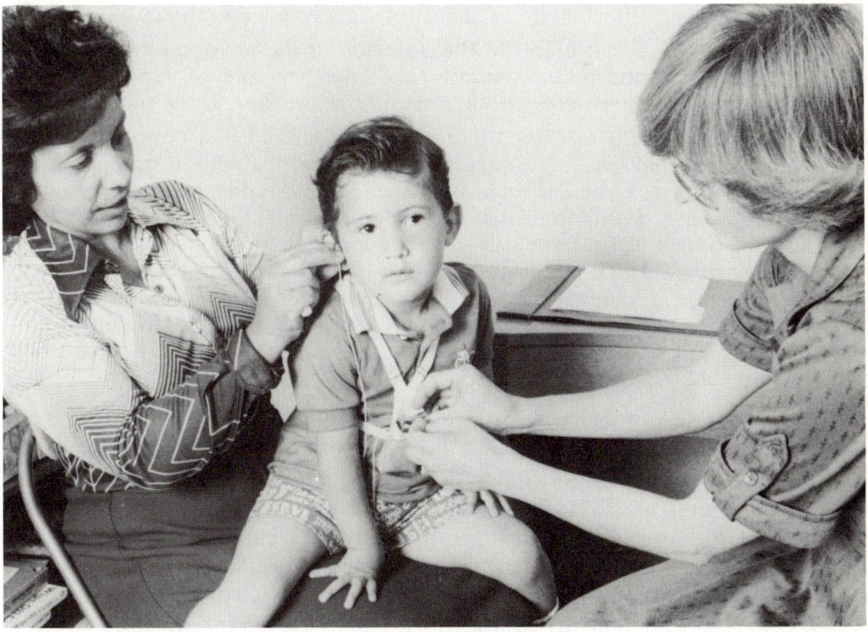

FIGURE 13.2 The parent should be competent in putting the hearing aid on the child. (Courtesy of Language Development Program of Western New York)

poorly fitting mold is often solved by the highly undesirable procedure of turning down the volume control. Parents must be cautioned against this.

Part of your responsibilities will often be to work with the parents in getting the child to wear the aid willingly. The younger the child, the more easy obtaining acceptance is likely to be. In essence, success in persuading the child to wear the aid lies in your own confident handling of the parents and child. Some guidelines to follow have been suggested by Downs (1966):

1. Convey quite clearly to the parents that the child simply must learn to accept the aid. Without it the development of thought, language, and oral-communication skills will be severely limited. There must be no hesitancy or ambivalence on your part concerning the need to get the aid on the child.
2. Handle the child gently but firmly. Do not be deterred by the child's reluctance to have the mold inserted. If you waiver in your firmness you will increase the child's resistance.
3. Do not be afraid to constrain the child in order to insert the mold. Hold the child firmly but kindly. Talk in a relaxed, reassuring manner. Use touch to soothe the child while holding him or her.
4. Demonstrate to the parents how to insert the mold. Then work with them until they are confident in their ability to fit it. If the child objects to the mold, insist that the parents insert it into the ear for 5 minutes four times a day, under physical restraint if necessary. The child must learn not to be bothered by the mold. Avoid fighting the child, accept negative reactions, and do not react negatively to them. Try to occupy the child with some pleasant diversion while he or she is learning to tolerate the mold.
5. If the child does not object to the insertion of the mold, and most do not, the aid may be attached to it and turned on at low volume. A parent should talk soothingly to the child while holding the aid close to the mouth.
6. If the aid is readily accepted by the child, it should first be worn at home during the child's waking hours. However, careful attention should be paid to the comfort of the ear mold. Any evidence of redness of the ear caused by abrasion warrants immediate consultation with the audiologist or hearing-aid dealer. A sore ear will soon cause the child to reject the mold and the hearing aid. The parent should also avoid exposing the child to loud sounds close at hand, such as to a vacuum cleaner. The aim is to make early experiences with amplification pleasant. Once the child seems comfortable with the aid, its use can be extended to visits to friends' houses and to shopping expeditions.

You should consult the audiologist to ascertain how often he or she wishes to reevaluate the child and hearing aid. Dated records should be maintained in a hearing-aid log book, and changes by the audiologist should be clearly marked. In this way there can be no misunderstanding about what the audiologist said. Similarly, before each visit to the audiologist, you should make note in the log of any observations, concerns, or questions you might have about the aid or its use. It is also important to record any significant information the parents have communicated to you.

To summarize, audiologic needs concern:

1. Parental acceptance of the aid
2. Parental understanding of the importance of the aid, how the child should wear it, and how to check and set it for daily use
3. Acceptance and constant use of the aid by the child
4. Monitoring of the aid in terms of its appropriateness and fidelity
5. Assessment of the child's use of amplification

The assessment of the child's use of amplification should occur as an integral component of the program to meet communication needs. For most children, effective use of the hearing aid serves as the basis for the development of oral-language comprehension and use. It is the primary tool in meeting the child's communication needs.

Communication Needs

One of the most serious forms of psychological punishment is isolation from other human contact. Congenital hearing impairment isolates children from auditory contact with our world. It cuts them off from the main channel through which they relate to others and others to them. As social beings we are dependent upon interaction with others. We learn about ourselves, and we learn to understand our feelings and our experiences through communicative interchange. Our knowledge of the world in which we live and of the ways to function in it is heavily dependent on the ability to communicate. Communication depends on the acquisition and use of the tools of language, which, in turn, make possible abstract thought, releasing us from the constraints of time and space. It is the ability to think in abstraction that permits past experience to influence not only our behavior, but also our ability to develop expectancies and thus to plan ahead. The development of language, and the tools of communication that permit the use of language, constitute, therefore, the core of a preschool management program for the hearing-impaired child. Their importance lies in the impact that language and communication have upon cognition, learning, and psychosocial adjustment.

Children learn about their environment through all their senses. You should encourage the parents with whom you work to enrich all aspects of their child's sensory experience since it is on those experiences that the child will build the cognitive concepts and their associated language patterns. The tool of spoken language permits the sensory experiences of the hearing child to be refined, clarified, and coded for storage in memory. For the hearing child, this learning occurs from birth through natural exposure to normal models, and it triggers the innate mechanisms of language learning. For this reason hearing impairment occurring before language skills have developed greatly impedes their acquisition. Part of the difficulty lies in the child's lack of awareness of the power of language as a tool for learning about and negotiating relationships with the environment.

The models that children hear and see during the first few years of life are provided almost exclusively by the immediate family. Preschool management procedures are directed, therefore, at shaping the child's home environment and related experiences to maximize the learning process. You will work to train the parents of the young preschool hearing-impaired child to relate to the child in ways that increase the frequency of the child's exposure to desirable models in natural context.

THE PARENT-TRAINING ENVIRONMENT

To construct a model of parent home training you must deal with actual or surrogate home situations. Ideally you should work with parents in their own homes, operating at least partially as an itinerant home visitor. Utilizing such a model ensures that the training you provide is realistic, and is compatible with the environment in which the parents and child interact. It permits you to demonstrate to the parents that their work with their child is to be an integral part of their natural relationships with the child, not an addition to them. Once you are familiar with the family environment as a home teacher and the parents have experienced the fundamental principles of the role they are being asked to play, many of the demonstration-training sessions may be conducted in a clinic or center. Even in a center it is desirable that the environment represent that of a home. This allows for reenactment of actual home-learning situations. The degree to which this is possible will, of course, vary with your facilities. Some centers, such as the Mamma Lear Demonstration Home at the Bill Wilkerson Hearing and Speech Center, Nashville, Tennessee, and the Home Demonstration Center at Central Institute for the Deaf, St. Louis, Missouri, use actual model homes that encompass all the experiences of daily home living for parent-training activities. Few centers can afford such desirable conditions. However, each agency working with preschool children with delayed language development should seek to set up a room or two with home-like characteristics—for example, limited cooking facilities such as a bench-top stove, a sink, and running water; a table and chairs; cooking and eating utensils; cleaning materials; a small bed for the child, and so on. The aim is to allow you to develop intervention procedures for use by the parents in their home. What occurs must be relevant to the child's actual home experiences and must build on existing parent skills.

Goals of Parent Training

It is most important that the parents fully understand that you do not wish them to become teachers. It is even more important that you avoid working with them in a manner that might imply that this is your goal. The goal of parent training is to modify normal behaviors in everyday activities to optimize opportunities for the growth of thought and language in the child.

Horton (1974, p. 483) defined five general categories of program objectives for early intervention with very young hearing-impaired children as:

1. To teach the parents to optimize the auditory environment for their child
2. To teach the parents how to talk to their child
3. To familiarize parents with the principles, stages, and sequence of normal language development and how to apply this frame of reference in stimulating their child
4. To teach parents strategies of behavior management
5. To supply effective support to aid the family in coping with their feelings about their child and the stresses that a handicapped child places on the integrity of the family

Optimizing the Auditory Environment

This objective is worked toward first by focusing the parents' attention on the sounds that naturally occur in the home environment. Since early-language acquisition arises from events observed, objects that make noise in the home provide a natural basis for the child's early experiences with amplified sound (Figure 13.3). They also give rise to verbal comment:

Listen. Oh, what a lot of noise! It's the blender.

Oh, the telephone is ringing.

That's the doorbell. Someone's at the door.

Look. Mommy's going to turn off the alarm clock.

Daddy's home. Listen, hear the car?

FIGURE 13.3 Naturally occurring sounds around the home provide a basis for early listening.

Parents should be encouraged to take the child with them when responding to environmental sounds. When the phone rings, suggest that they take the infant to the phone, let it ring several times while they point first to it then to an ear indicating that they hear it. Then they should say, "The phone is ringing. Hear the phone?" They should treat the dog barking, the water filling the bathtub, the toilet flushing, and the lawn mower being used in the backyard in the same way. Parents can anticipate or create environmental sounds for the child to listen to in the presence of the sound-generating object or event—they can wait for the clock to chime, make the whistling kettle boil, the alarm clock ring, the paper bag pop, the doorbell ring, the cup and saucer rattle, the spoon bang, the saucepan drop. The child needs to become aware of the world of sound, limited or distorted though it may be. The child needs to learn the referential function of sound. Your role is to convey to the parents that they need to orient their child to sound so that the child learns its value, begins to pay attention to it, and makes use of it in predicting events that he or she cannot see. You must guide the parents specifically in how to choose sounds that are likely to be significant to the child. This is why awareness of the child's daily experiences is so important. The sounds selected for special attention should:

1. Have a pitch and loudness that the child can hear
2. Arise from experiences that have significance to the child
3. Originate from objects with which the child is familiar
4. Occur frequently in or around the house
5. When possible, be capable of being started and stopped by the child

The parents must be shown how to respond to the sounds in a consistent manner that motivates the child to want to participate in the listening, discriminating, learning, doing activity. They can do this by visual and verbal communication. The parent ceases activity when the sound is made, adopts a listening attitude by placing a finger at the ear, pauses, gives a look of puzzlement followed quickly by happy enlightenment, then identifies the sound source. Initially it will be necessary to take the child to the sound source; later the child will begin to respond to the acoustic referent and to adopt recognition behaviors, indicating learning has occurred. Babies should always be taken to the source of the sound and be allowed to observe the parents' response behaviors. Both parents need to be encouraged to become involved in these behaviors. When a working father arrives home, for example, he should blow the car horn when he gets out of the car and the mother should try to anticipate the arrival: "Daddy's coming soon. Where's Daddy? He's coming. There's Daddy. I hear him. Let's go see." He should ring the doorbell, repeating long rings several times in a pattern code that will become identified with him. He should call loudly when he comes in, "Hello, I'm home, where's my Sarah?" Father should familiarize Sarah with the sounds of his activities around the house—for example, using an electric razor. Unfortunately, fathers are too frequently not brought into the parent training, which is assumed to be the mother's responsibility. Because you are aiming to mold the family environment, you must involve the father in a manner compatible with his normal daily contacts with his children and in terms of his normal home activities. Both parents should also be encouraged to involve their other children in these techniques for optimizing the auditory environment.

Talking to the Child

Speech is a part of the auditory environment. It is acoustic and has a referential function despite its greater complexity and capacity for abstract reference. Even when we discussed making the child aware of environmental sounds we stressed that it was necessary to involve the parents in talking about the events. Early-language stimulation must be event related. Speech provides a linguistic commentary that presents the child with examples of the language pattern appropriate to the event. The basis of language acquisition will be the semantic concepts the child learns (Miller & Yoder, 1974). Both cognitive and semantic values are derived directly from the child's nonverbal and verbal experience. First the child perceives objects, object functions, object relationships, and events conceptually—that is, the child attributes meaning to them. At the same time the linguistic commentary provides the appropriate language patterns associated with the object or event. When the concept is correlated to the linguistic pattern, the child has developed a semantic value for the experience. That semantic value, which is an abstract, can then be evoked by the appropriate spoken-language patterns. Later the semantic value can be correlated with its linguistic equivalent, allowing the child to communicate orally. Parents must understand, therefore, the importance of talking about what is happening, about what they are doing, and about what the child is doing or experiencing. This, it should be pointed out, is a natural behavior exhibited by parents (Ling & Ling, 1974). You are only seeking to reinforce what they would normally do. The hearing-impaired child needs this even more than hearing peers. Early-language training, therefore, does not involve lessons, but the provision of appropriate linguistic commentary on events meaningful to the child. Turton (1974) states: "In terms of the hearing impaired child, the parents must be sensitive to his experiential background as it provides stimuli for language acquisition" (p. 497).

The use of spoken language in context greatly enhances the potential situational redundancy. It is necessary to guide the parents in how to talk to their child. This requires that you observe the rate, complexity, grammatical correctness, and articulatory clarity of the parents' speech. Explain to the parents that certain communication behaviors by them are known to be potentially very helpful to their child's development of language skills. These include using speech directly related to what is happening, being physically and actively involved (sharing in) their child's experience, praising their child's vocalizations and verbalizations, verbalizing for their child what has happened and why and how it happened. Research has shown that parents speak differently to young children than they do to older children and adults (Broen, 1972; Frayer & Roberts, 1975; Phillips, 1973; Snow, 1972). When we speak to very young children we do so more slowly than to older children; we use more one-word sentences, more incomplete sentences (for example, "Go bye-bye?", "Come see Daddy"), and shorter sentences in general. The vocabulary and sentence structure of our utterances is simpler, and we often repeat or rephrase what we have said. It may be necessary through demonstration and commentary on parent-child communication for you to attempt to modify the parents' existing behaviors to reflect the natural characteristics just described. This must be done cautiously so as not to imply rejection of the parents' speech. You should stress that speech that is acceptable for young hearing children must often be further modified to meet the special needs of the young child with impaired hearing. You will need to train parents to encode linguistic redundancy into their communication. They should learn to talk about events, not just to label them. For example, in bathing the child the parent might say:

Where's the soap?

Where's the soap gone?

Oh, here's the soap.

I found it. I found the soap.

or in a play situation:

There's the teddy bear. Listen to teddy bear squeak. Squeak, squeak, teddy bear. Here, you hold teddy bear. Squeeze it there. Squeak, squeak, squeak.

Then, hiding the toy behind your back:

Where's teddy bear gone? Where's teddy bear? Squeak, teddy bear.

Then when you squeak the toy:

I hear it, listen. Do you hear teddy bear squeak? There it is. Hi, teddy bear."

Communication with the child should be simply worded but not distorted into baby talk. Statements should be linked together in a constructive supportive manner:

Let's put on your shoes.

Here are your two shoes.

One shoe, two shoes.

Now we'll tie your shoes.

First tie this shoe—now tie this shoe.

There, all done. Your shoes are tied. Down you go.

Guidance should be given to the parents to ensure that they use natural, melodic speech, clearly articulated but not exaggerated, and that they do not speak unnaturally loudly to their child. Before a hearing aid has been fitted the parents should be encouraged to talk and sing to their baby with their mouths within an inch or two of the baby's ear. This raises the intensity level of normal voice to 95 to 100 dB without distortion. It also encourages close physical contact between parents and child. Once the aid has been fitted the infant can be played with as a hearing child—

for example, held on the lap facing the parent. This ensures optimal listening distance and allows the child to enjoy and respond to the visible pleasures of parent-child communication, which are shown by accompanying facial expression. Most important, however, is that the parents should talk to the baby whenever they are with the child during waking hours. The closer the parents are to the child, both physically and psychologically, the better the learning opportunity. The sooner the parents assume the role of natural habitual commentators of events and experience, the sooner the child is likely to become speech oriented. The younger the child is when this pattern of parent communication is established, the greater will be the optimal potential for the learning of auditory/oral communication. It takes time before the effects of talking to the child begin to be rewarded in terms of early attempts at speech. Parents need support and encouragement during this long period of waiting. Counsel them to look for reassurance in the child's nonverbal responses to auditory/visual speech input, in the child's increased attention span, and in the child's signs of pleasure when stimulated. In most cases the child will give observable evidence of processing the auditory/visual input. Eventually the child will give signs of spontaneous vocalization and imitation. This calls for reinforcement behavior by the observer.

Responding to the Child's Communication

Hearing-impaired babies, even those with profound deficits of hearing, do not differ from their hearing peers in their vocalizations in the first five to six months of life (Northern & Downs, 1974). Cooing, gurgling, and even babbling appear to be innately preprogrammed. However, beyond this initial stage, auditory feedback from self and others is critical to the activation and shaping of early-linguistic behavior. The parents should be taught and encouraged to reinforce the child's earliest vocalizations. Both auditory and visual reinforcement should be given. When the infant vocalizes the parents should respond with pleasure that can be seen by the child. The child should be responded to verbally: "Are you talking to Daddy? There's a good girl. Ah ba ba ba ba (repeating the utterance). Come on, tell me some more . . ." Touching, patting, or stroking the baby can help to reinforce such early vocalizations. The parents should also echo the child's babbling patterns, allowing pauses for the child to begin to babble again. The idea is to encourage consciousness of vocalizations, which in the hearing-impaired child tend to die out if not strongly reinforced. As soon as the child begins to attempt linguistic utterances, words, sentences, and meanings likewise should be reinforced by pleasurable responses.

Early stimulation of spoken language as distinct from vocalization is directly related to experience and to thought processes. The child's first use of words can be prompted, reinforced, molded, and expanded. If the parents have been given early training, or if they have perceived the importance of talking to the child about what is happening, the child will have repeatedly heard natural-object and event-related language. As soon as the child attempts to imitate the parents, either by vocalization or by spoken words, the communicative behavior must be reinforced. These early utterances can be molded by the parents, who should provide the child with several repetitions of the correct model (Figure 13.4).

PARENT: *Here's your milk. Don't spill it, don't spill your milk.*

CHILD: *ma ma*

PARENT: *Good,—milk—say milk, milk.*

CHILD : *ma ma*

PARENT: *Good girl, you said milk.*

Next time milk is given to the child, the parent should prompt the child to name it, asking, "What's this? What have I got for you?" If the child does not respond, the parent should name the object: "It's your milk—you say it—milk, milk—come on, tell me, milk."

Always accept the child's attempt to imitate even if it is only an approximation or indeed if it is no more than a vowel sound, but always reinforce by providing several repetitions of the correct model. Encourage, but do not pressure, the child to say the word. Do not overload the child by continuing the interchange at the expense of the child's willing participation in this language game.

Once words or word approximations become consistently associated with appropriate objects, the parents can begin to expand on the child's utterance. According to Schumaker and Sherman (1978), an expansion is "a parent utterance that uses what the child has said to form a more adult-like utterance" (p. 300). For example, when the child volunteers "ma" for milk the parent may expand the one word to include an extended but better-defined experience with the milk—Parent: Yes, that's milk—drink your milk—drink it up. The word drink will be used with other liquids; thus, a concept begins to emerge through association.

Similarly when an infant playing with a doll says "bei-bei" the parent smiles and says:

Yes, that's a baby—baby.

Sarah has a baby—love the baby.

Oh nice baby.

On a subsequent occasion the parent may expand the semantic content:

Look baby's crying—poor baby, she's crying.

Don't cry baby—love her so she doesn't cry.

Look, Mommy's crying (mother pretends to cry).

Don't cry Mommy (Mother smiles again, takes child's hands, puts them to her eyes, and speaks) Poor Sarah, Sarah's crying, don't cry Sarah.

Research by Slobin (1968) and Schumaker (1976) has shown that parents of young hearing children use expansions following 30 percent of their children's utterances. In reviewing this research Schumaker and Sherman (1978) recommended that this form of modeling should be used frequently with children who are potentially linguistically handicapped.

The role of parents in the stimulation and molding of the child's

FIGURE 13.4 The parents should take every opportunity to reinforce and model the child's early utterances.

language development is paramount. Parent guidance in this aspect of management is extremely important. For further information refer to Simmons-Martin (1978), Ling and Ling (1978), Schumaker and Sherman (1978), and Meers (1976). To further improve the effectiveness of parent intervention, it is helpful to familiarize the parents with the general principles and stages of language development in children.

Familiarizing Parents with the Principles and Stages of Language Development

Parent training will be most effective when the language-stimulation activities of the parents are underpinned by an understanding of the principles involved. Parents should be helped to understand why they are learning certain behaviors and how they relate to the child's cognitive and linguistic development at each stage. They must be taught the manner and order in which language forms are acquired and must be shown the direct relationship between what the child is capable of and what they are doing with the child. Later the parent must learn to relate the child's early utterances to what the child is experiencing at the time. Obviously, formal instruction of the parents in developmental linguistics is inadvisable, though small parent-discussion groups are often helpful for explaining the nature of the developmental aspects of language acquisition.

Mostly, however, you will explain principles as you guide the parents in relating to their child. Describe what the child is doing, identify the cognitive-linguistic stage this represents, explain the next stage, give examples of what the child will progress to, and demonstrate the techniques for facilitating the gradual introduction of the more advanced language form. It is important to stress the difference between comprehension and use of language in the presence of the subject or event, and understanding and use of the same language form in the absence of context (Bloom, 1974). The principles that are known to govern language acquisition in the hearing child should govern intervention procedures with the hearing-impaired child. Parents should be helped to learn, understand, and implement these procedures.

BEHAVIORAL MANAGEMENT NEEDS

One of the problems of being a parent is knowing how to mold your child's behavior in ways acceptable to society. The most common form of control is through verbal explanations, warnings, and reprimands. During the period before language comprehension permits verbal control of behavior, some parents use physical control of the child—that is, restraint or removal from the situation. These parents feel that physical punishment used as a conditioning technique is necessary to protect the child. In general, parents do not like to have to smack a child, and may do so only when verbal control is ineffective.

It is easy to appreciate the problem that faces the parents of hearing-impaired children. Because the child's language is delayed, the parents are forced to exert more direct control over their child's behavior than parents of hearing children (Schlesinger & Meadow, 1971). As a result they have been shown to be less flexible in the way they respond to the child's behavior, to allow the child less freedom, and to give less encouragement and reward than parents of hearing children. Difficulty in communicating with the child often results in an autocratic model of behavior control. The parents are unable to explain to the child why he or she must behave in certain ways. They cannot persuade or console the child into the desired behaviors. The child has, therefore, to adopt patterns of behavior simply because the parents demand them. This type of control is usually achieved through punishment. To minimize this, the parents often do for the child things the child should be capable of doing. Such a solution does little to foster self-confidence through self-reliance.

A less frequent reaction to the difficulty of molding the behavior of the nonverbal child is to become overprotective and overly accepting of the child's behavior. The family that adopts this model tries to accept and adjust to a child's increasingly unsocial behaviors at an age when linguistic bargaining should be modifying such behavior. The parents accept the aggression and temper tantrums, yielding to demands and rearranging family priorities in an understandable but misguided attempt to solve the problem. Both models of behavioral management arising from the difficulty in parent-child communication almost always exaggerate the normal development behavioral problems of the preschool years of any child (Vernon, 1969). The child, reacting to the conflict and frustration he or she experiences, often converts the resultant stress into symptoms of irritability, temper, aggression, or eating and sleeping problems. All of these are quite normal reactions to stress.

The effects of behavior-management problems also frequently give rise to secondary problems of interpersonal relationships among family members. Parents often disagree over how the child should be handled. The mother may feel that her husband does not share responsibilities, avoids the problems and blames her for the child's unmanageable behavior. The father may feel that after a day's work he should not be expected to deal with problems his wife should have worked out during the day. Siblings resent the family disruptance caused by their handicapped brother or sister, object to the amount of parental attention the child receives, protest about the way in which meeting the child's needs interferes with what they see as their family rights, and are often embarrassed to bring friends into this atmosphere.

The child's behavior problems cannot, therefore, be viewed in isolation; they are as much problems of the family as they are his or her own (Altschuler, 1974; Northcott, 1975). They can be understood only in terms of an action-reaction model based on family expectations, management strategies, and reactions. Similarly, help can only be provided in these terms. The problems that arise do so because the parents feel they lack the experience necessary to cope with what they believe to be the child's abnormal behavior. You have the information and objectivity necessary to help them to understand what is happening. In almost every case the parents have the capabilities to make the adjustments necessary to reduce the conflicts they are having in dealing with their child.

Your first aim is to communicate the normality of the situation. The child's behavior is understandable in terms of the frustrations he or she experiences. Similarly, it is equally easy to appreciate the parents' reactions to the situation. They have attempted to cope with the situation but the methods they have used have not effected the desired results. The situation has become increasingly more difficult and they now find frustration, even resentment and anger, affecting their behavioral management of their child. They feel badly about this but seem trapped in the situation. You should communicate to them that the difficulty is not in their failure as parents, but in the management strategies they have adopted. The solution lies in techniques that reduce the frequency of stress-creating situations and in identifying alternate ways of reacting in those situations when they occur.

The steps to helping parents evolve more effective behavioral-management strategies are:

1. To encourage the parents to describe in detail the behavioral problems they are having with the child
2. To discuss what the parents expect in terms of the child's behavior
3. To consider the appropriateness of such expectations in terms of the child's age and communication abilities
4. To encourage reassessment of expectancies if this appears appropriate

5. To encourage explanation of the ways in which the parents react to unacceptable behaviors in specific situations
6. To encourage evaluation of their management procedures in terms of their effectiveness
7. To identify particular problems and problem situations and to break them down into components
8. To identify and, when appropriate, to modify the goals of behavior management for a particular problem situation
9. To consider the various management alternatives for the achievement of these goals
10. To use situations that occur in the center, or in the home, or to reconstruct situations that give rise to the problem, and to demonstrate a new technique to evaluate for effectiveness

Parents should clearly understand that their difficulties are not exceptional, that they have reason to feel what they do, and that it is their dissatisfaction with the way things are not working that justifies discussion of the problem. It is most important that both parents agree on what behaviors are unacceptable in the child and that they both subscribe to the ways of dealing with such behavior. It is unwise for you to "show them how they should handle the child." This demeans them as parents and ignores the feelings they have about the situation, feelings you are spared. You should instead encourage them to try new responses to their child's behavior, help them to evaluate the interaction that takes place, and suggest further possible changes in the strategies they use. They should be encouraged to strongly reinforce positive behaviors in their child using verbal praise with associated gestures of affection and pleasure. Specific situations should be selected for the parents to evaluate the effects of modifying their expectancies and of giving the child greater freedom of behavior.

The normal problems of early childhood are frequently exaggerated and prolonged in the hearing-impaired child due to the lack of adequate communication skills. It is to be expected that as methods of communication between the parent and child become more sophisticated, the intensity and frequency of behavioral problems will be reduced. It is necessary, however, to provide support to the parents until the influence of increased language skills is felt. Ongoing discussion of problems as they occur, and the opportunity to verbalize their own frustrations and feelings of resentment and guilt will do much to help the parents see the problems in an objective light. Association with other parents whose children have passed through this very difficult stage frequently provides greater support than you can give because such parents have high credibility. It is advisable, however, that discussion groups meet under your guidance, as not all parents make good counselors. Some structure must be given to discussions and some statements will require clarification.

You will find you have much to offer parents in terms of meeting the child's behavioral needs even if you are not yourself a parent. The key to effectiveness is the same as the key to adjustment counseling: You must serve as a facilitator in a problem-solving situation, not as an expert capable of providing solutions.

REFERENCES

Altschuler, K. Z., "The Social and Psychological Development of the Deaf Child: Problems, Their Treatment and Prevention," *Social and Psych. Development,* August 1974, 365–376.

Bloom, L., "Talking, Understanding and Thinking," in *Language Perspectives—Acquisition, Retardation and Intervention,* eds. R. Schiefelbusch and L. Lloyd, pp. 285–311. Baltimore: University Park Press, 1974.

Broen, P. A., "The Verbal Environment of the Language Learning Child," *ASHA Monograph,* No. 17, 1972.

Bronfenbrenner, V., *Is Early Intervention Effective: Report on Longitudinal Evaluations of Preschool Programs, 2,* Dept. of HEW Pub. No. (OHD), 75–125. Washington, D.C.: U.S. Dept. of Health, Education, and Welfare, Office of Child Development, 1975.

Cazden, C. B., *Child Language and Education.* New York: Holt, Rinehart & Winston, 1972.

Downs, M.P., "The Establishment of Hearing Aid Use—A Program for Parents," *Maico Audiology Library Series, 4,* 1966, 5.

Downs, M.P., "Maintaining Children's Hearing Aids—The Role of the Parents," *Maico Audiology Library Series, 10,* 1971.

Frayer, C., and N. Roberts, "Mothers' Speech to Children of Four Different Ages," *Journal Psycholing. Research, 4,* 1975, 9–16.

Gasson, W., "Psychopathological Environmental Reaction to Congenital Defect," *Journal Mental Nervous Disease, 142,* 1966, 453–459.

Gilmer, R., J. O. Miller, and S. W. Gray, *Intervention with Mothers and Young Children: Study of Intra Family Effects.* Nashville: Darcee, 1970.

Gordeuk, A., "Motherhood and a Less than Perfect Child," *Maternal Child Nursing Journal, 5,* 1976, 57–68.

Gordon, I. J., "Parenting, Teaching, and Child Development," *Young Children, 31,* 1976, 173–184.

Horton, K., "Infant Intervention and Language Learning," in *Language Perspectives—Acquisition, Retardation and Intervention,* eds. R. Schiefelbusch, and L. Lloyd, pp. 469–491. Baltimore: University Park Press, 1974.

Horton, K., and B. Hanners, "Trends in Educational Programming: The Early Years of the Hearing Impaired Child Zero to Three," in *Childhood Deafness Causation Assessment and Management,* ed. F. Bess, pp. 313–319, 483. New York: Grune & Stratton, Inc., 1977.

Kapke, K. A., "Spina Bifida Mother-Child Relationship," *Nursing Forum, 9,* 1970, 310–320.

Kvaraceus, W. C., and N. E. Hayes, *Is Your Child Handicapped?* Boston: Porter Sargent, 1969.

Ling, D., and A. Ling, "Communication Development in the First Three Years of Life," *Journal of Speech and Hearing Research, 17,* 1974, 146–159.

Ling, D., and A. Ling, *Aural Habilitation,* The Foundations of Verbal Learning in Hearing Impaired Children. Washington, D.C.: The Alexander Graham Bell Assoc. for the Deaf, 1978.

Mackeith, R., "Parental Reactions and Responses to a Handicapped Child," in *Brain and Intelligence,* ed. F. Richardson, Hyattsville, Md.: National Educational Consultants, 1973.

Matkin, N., "Assessment of Hearing Sensitivity During the Preschool Years," in *Childhood Deafness Causation Assessment and Measurement,* ed. F. Bess, pp. 127–134. New York: Grune & Stratton, Inc., 1977.

Meers, H., *Helping Our Children Talk.* New York: Longman, Inc., 1976.

Miller, J., and D. Yoder, "An Ontogenetic Language Teaching Strategy for Retarded Children," in *Language Perspectives—Acquisition, Retardation and Intervention,* eds. R. Schiefelbusch and L. Lloyd, pp. 503–528. Baltimore: University Park Press, 1974.

Northcott, W. H., "Normalization of the Preschool Child with Hearing Impairment," *Otolaryngology Clinic of North America, 8,* 1975, 195–196.

Northern, J. L., and M. P. Downs, *Hearing in Children.* Baltimore: The Williams & Wilkins Company, 1974.

Phillips, J. R., "Syntax and Vocabulary of Mothers' Speech to Young Children: Age and Sex Comparisons," *Child Development, 44,* 1973, 182–185.

Radin, N. "Three Degrees of Maternal Involvement in a Preschool Program: Impact on Mother and Children," *Child Development, 43,* 1972, 1355–1364.

Ross, A. O., *The Exceptional Child in the Family.* New York: Grune & Stratton, Inc., 1964.

Schaefer, E. S., "Parents as Educators: Evidence from Cross-Sectional, Longitudinal and Interventional Research," *Young Children, 27,* 1972, 227–239.

Schlesinger, H., and K. Meadow, *Deafness and Mental Health: A Developmental Approach.* San Francisco: Langley Porter Neuropsychiatric Institute, 1971.

Schumaker, J., *Mothers' Expansions: Their Characteristics and Effects on Child Language.* Unpublished doctoral dissertation, University of Lawrence, Kansas, 1976.

Schumaker, J., and J. Sherman, "Parent as Intervention Agent: From Birth Onward," in *Language Intervention Strategies,* ed. R. L. Schiefelbusch, pp. 237–315. Baltimore, University Park Press, 1978.

Shah, C. P., D. Chandler, and R. Dale, "Delay in Referral of Children with Impaired Hearing," *Volta Review, 80,* no. 4, 1978, 106–215.

Simmons-Martin, A., "Demonstration Home Approach with Hearing Impaired Children," in *Professionals Approach Parents of Handicapped Children,* ed. E. Webster, ch. 4. Springfield, Ill.: Charles C Thomas, Publisher, 1976.

Simmons-Martin, A., "Early Management Procedures for the Hearing Impaired Child," in *Pediatric Audiology,* ed. F. Martin, pp. 356–385. Englewood Cliffs, N.J.: Prentice-Hall, Inc., 1978.

Slobin, D., "Imitation and Grammatical Development in Children," in *Contemporary Issues in Developmental Psychology,* eds. N. S. Endler, L. R. Boulter, and H. Osser, pp. 437–443. New York: Holt, Rinehart & Winston, 1968.

Snow, C. E., "Mothers' Speech to Children Learning Language," *Child Development, 43,* 1972, 549–565.

Solnit, A. J., and M. H. Stark, "Mourning and the Birth of a Defective Child," *Psychoanalytic Study of the Child, 16,* 1961, 523–537.

Turton, L., "Discussion Summary—Early Language Intervention," in *Language Perspectives—Acquisition, Retardation and Intervention,* eds. R. Schiefelbusch, and L. Lloyd, pp. 493–501. Baltimore: University Park Press, 1974.

Vernon, M., "Sociological and Psychological Factors Associated with Hearing Loss," *Journal of Speech and Hearing Disorders, 12,* 1969, 541–563.

Worby, C. M., "The Family Life Cycle: An Orienting Concept for the Family Specialist," *Journal Medical Education, 46,* no. 3, 1971, 198–203.

14

Management of the Older Preschool Child

The model of management of the very young hearing-impaired child has been centered on the family unit. The role of the family will continue to be great as the child grows, but other influences also begin to be important. The most significant of these are the child's developing capacity for independence, and the increasing sophistication of the behavioral competencies that society expects of the child as he or she grows. These increasing expectancies during the preschool years culminate in the basic competencies necessary to begin formal education at the first-grade level. Intervention procedures with the older preschool child must reflect recognition of these influences. Thus, from about age three, the focus of your efforts moves progressively from parent to child. This shift is motivated by a need to encourage the child's growing independence by assisting the child's development of the cognitive, linguistic, and social skills necessary for full participation in structured learning situations. The later preschool years prepare the child for school. This is a period during which you must be concerned with "*the implementation today of procedures designed to prepare the child for the demands he will encounter tomorrow*" (Sanders, 1977). You must gradually adjust your intervention model toward that of the kindergarten, which, ideally, is designed to provide the child with the social and learning skills and competencies necessary for the beginning of primary school.

The thrust of your efforts with the older preschool child will be:

1. To provide experiences that stimulate cognitive awareness
2. To provide the vocabulary and language forms by which those experiences can be described and defined

3. To increase the child's comprehension of spoken language
4. To stimulate the child to use spoken language as a means of exploring the world
5. To stimulate, encourage, and refine the child's early communications
6. To stimulate the development of sociolinguistic behaviors appropriate to the child's age
7. To mold the child's social behaviors to expectancies for his or her age

When a hearing impairment is diagnosed in infancy you teach the parents how to turn the home, and excursions outside the home, into language-stimulation experiences. This helps to ensure the child's readiness for more structured learning environments. You can expect the child to be aware of spoken language, to have learned its referential functions, and to absorb spoken language as a part of the total situation in which it occurs. Early parent guidance will have stimulated the child's development of an orientation conducive to the use of spoken language for increasing understanding and, in most cases, for augmenting attempts to communicate to others. Hopefully, the parents will have become so used to providing language models in appropriate forms that this will now be part of their natural behavior with their child. Encourage them to continue these behaviors, stressing the importance of their role in providing the child with the capabilities of dealing with the naturally occurring experiences of real life. A shift of focus from parent to child must in no way diminish the importance of the parents' continued activities. No one expects the orchestra to stop playing when the soloist in a concerto makes an entry. The home continues to be the major source of support for learning.

When the child is identified as having impaired hearing at a later age (2 to 3 years old, for example), the principles discussed in the previous chapter will still operate. Parent influence is always potentially great, so that a home-centered preschool program must be established regardless of the age at which the diagnosis of hearing impairment is made. With the older preschool child, however, you will be under pressure to intensify efforts to develop levels of language competence commensurate with the child's cognitive abilities. Thus, you will introduce the more structured experiences earlier in the intervention program. However, these must be in conjunction with, not in place of, a parent-guidance program. The child's needs remain the same as those of the child diagnosed early, it is just that the needs have been intensified by delayed identification and that you have lost ground to make up.

BEGINNING STRUCTURED COMMUNICATION TRAINING

Providing Experiences and Associated Language

The hearing-impaired child approximately 3 years of age and older needs selected and structured learning experiences. You should choose these experiences to teach the child to deal with the basic concepts of the world in which he or she must function. Be sure that the conceptual and linguistic experiences you select are appropriate for developmental norms. When structuring activities remember that the development of cognition and language are intimately related. Together they follow a progression from concrete to abstract experience. At first the child is aware only of things present, things that can be experienced directly through the senses and through manipulative involvement. First we know, then we know about. Language provides the information that permits us to know about experience. It is first understood and used to describe immediate experience. Later the child learns to relate to toys, pictures, and models that represent the real things in their absence. Language becomes more important in filling out this less-concrete type of experience. Finally verbal language alone permits experience to be restructured in complete abstraction. At this level experiences can be evoked and manipulated purely linguistically. It is this stage that presents the greatest difficulty to the hearing-impaired child. Through structured activities you will control experiences, highlight relationships, and provide appropriate language models for the child. You will create opportunities for the child's mind to test the validity of the hypotheses he or she will begin to make about ways to use language.

The child also needs to be exposed to peer-group situations, which generate communication needs and stimulate the growth of social-interaction skills. These two needs—structured learning and social interaction—are appropriately met by including the child in group activities. Initially these may consist of small groups of preschool hearing-impaired children. As far as possible the children in the group should be compatible for age and communication abilities. Mixing children with widely differing communication skills makes it hard for the teacher to accommodate individual needs. However, if it is not possible to match children fairly closely, a mixed-ability group may derive benefit under the guidance of an experienced teacher. The availability of a trained aide or experienced parent is also essential to permit the teacher the flexibility necessary to individualize influence. Placing a child in an integrated or even a normal nursery school is also a possibility.

In the home, situational language—that is language in natural context—arises from the ongoing activities of the parents and other family members. Language is provided when events occur. In contrast, a structured learning environment controls experience. You choose the cognitive and linguistic experiences you wish the child to have and then you create specific situations to generate the appropriate language needs. In Mecham's (1969) words, you should aim to:

> . . . *create an atmosphere of specific geographic locations or events which would be similar to particular experience units for the child in daily life. Structure experiences which might approximate the normal environment. The advantages of structured experiences in the classroom or therapy is that labels can be supplied at the moment of experience and therefore can more easily become part of the experience concept* (p. 53).

Even though you are structuring experiences they are generally seen by the preschool child as play, which indeed they will be. But play is work when the child learns through doing. Choose activities that foster an awareness of the properties of things—color, size, shape, quantity, texture, and so on. Have the child match and group objects by color and then color pictures of things that are, for example, green (trees, grass, familiar green vegetables) or red (tomatoes, ketchup, fire, fire engines, and perhaps city buses or the child's sweater). Let the child distinguish big and small objects: making oneself big and then small, opening the small box, finding the big apple, filling the big glass, emptying the little one. Then let the child choose, match, and group pictures according to these properties. Expose the child to experiences of quantity by pouring water into big jars and little jars, putting beans or beads into big boxes and little boxes, choosing a large pile of candies instead of a small one. Each experience you provide must be stimulating and meaningful, and it must create appropriate language models. Seek to stimulate the child's awareness and attention to spoken language as it relates to concrete experiences. For example, when you involve the children in activities aimed to teach the concepts of size and quantity, verbalize what is occurring, emphasizing the relevant language vocabulary and forms:

Look the jar is full—it's full of water—you have too much water. Put some in the little jar. Now the big box is full—you have no more beans—the beans are all gone. This little box has no beans, it's empty. The little box is empty. Let's put some beans in the little box. There, now it's not empty. Is it full? No, it's not full, look we can put some more into it. The big box is full, we can't put any more beans in the big box, it's full. Let's make it empty—you

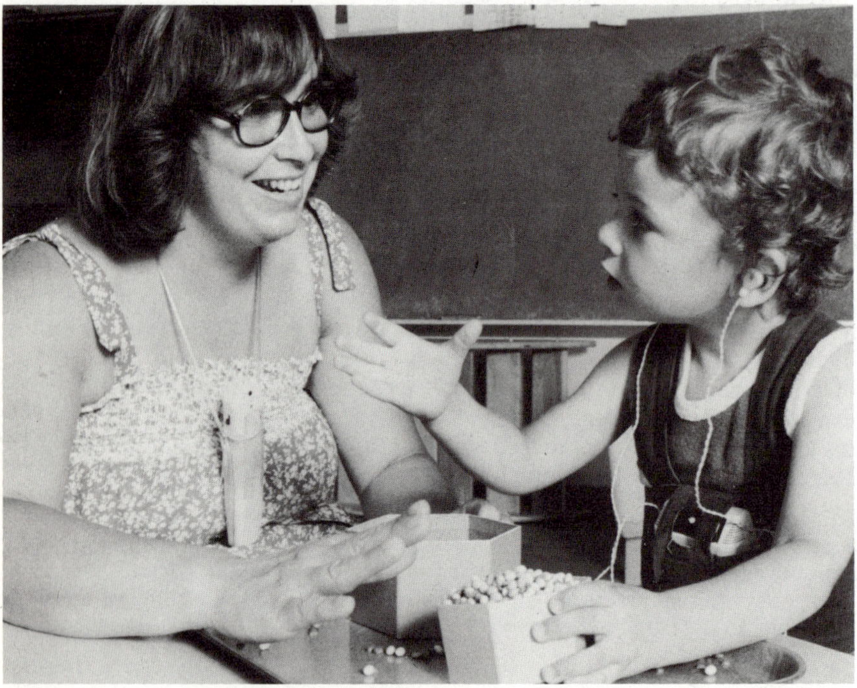

FIGURE 14.1 Language stimulation must be related to cognitive experience. (Courtesy of Language Development Program of Western New York)

empty it. There, now the big box is empty. Let's put all the beans in the little box—now the little box is full—the little box is full, the big box is empty. Give me the empty box (Figure 14.1).

You can also teach categories of objects by grouping them according to *function*. Center play activities on washing and dressing a doll, for example, by letting the child choose what one uses to wash:

Let's find the bath—here it is. Where's the water? We have to get some water to fill the bath. Come, we'll get some water to fill the bath. There, now the bath is almost full. We need some soap. Can you find the soap, Mary? We need the soap to wash the baby. Good, you found the soap. Now we need a cloth and a towel. Where is the towel, John? Can you see it? That's right—that's the towel. Now we can wash the baby with the soap and cloth (Figure 14.2).

Similar categorization along with associated language can be structured around dressing, eating, cooking, and so on—all activities with which the child has become familiar at home. New activities may be centered on such categories as animals and birds, fruit and vegetables, people who help us, things we use when we cook, garden, fix the car, or build a play house, ways we travel, types of buildings (schools, hospitals, libraries, firestations).

Children also need to be aware of the concept of roles in society. Roles and functions are related to categories. Each has associated vocabulary and language expressions. In the family the child learns the names and roles of mother, father, brother, sister, grandma and grandpa, aunt and uncle. Outside the family the children should be taught the language

FIGURE 14.2 Play activities should provide for the functional use of language. (Courtesy of St.Mary's School for the Deaf, Buffalo, New York)

associated with the people they are most likely to encounter: teacher, letter carrier, doctor, nurse, shop assistant. Thus, you should develop activities that deal with "Who does this? What does he or she use?" By coordinating activities with the parents, you can reinforce experiences the child has had outside the class, such as a visit to the doctor or shoestore. Use such visits as the stimulus for teaching the concepts and language appropriate to roles and events. Similarly, planned visits to the zoo, circus, a children's play or parade, or to take someone to the airport can provide further relevant language units. When you plan or recreate these language-stimulation experiences, try to capture not simply the vocabulary but also the event. Imagine yourself in the experience so that you can react as if you were actually there. You need to think in terms of natural language even though you will ensure redundancy through repetition and rephrasing. If you are talking about a visit to the airport, talk about more than the planes. Airports are busy places with parking lots, taxis, buses, luggage, check-in counters, coffee shops, bookstores. Encourage the parents to let the older child experience these broader aspects of a central concept in order to expand cognition and to provide an extended base for language needs.

Planned activities should be deliberately structured to provide such *expansion of concepts* over several sessions. This ensures that vocabulary and language structures can be reinforced and presented naturally in different forms. For example, the topic of food can encompass types of foods, categories of food, meals, what we eat at each meal, which foods we cook, ways of cooking, what we use to cook with, shopping for foods, ways of preparing food, and so on.

Lesson experiences should use real objects, play objects, pictures from commercial kits (for example, the Peabody Language Development Program), cutouts from magazines, and even photographs of the child visiting places being talked about or participating in activities at the center. Whenever possible, illustrate new vocabulary by acting it out or by using pictures. For example, you can demonstrate verbs such as fall, run, laugh, hit; adjectives such as angry, sad, happy, hungry, big, square, hot; adverbs such as quickly, quietly, loudly; prepositions: such as in, under, behind, on top of. Exaggerated demonstrations that are funny and make the child laugh are always well received. Use examples in which the child can participate and can later copy and imitate. The visual images you create are hooks on which to hang concepts to keep them tidily placed with an appropriate experience. These examples provide the keys to generalization and categorization.

Use pictures only when real experiences are not possible, when concepts and vocabulary have been well learned, or as a record to remind the children of what they experienced. Things that can be illustrated should go into a scrapbook (workbook), which the parent(s), who should participate in lesson activities, can use with their child at home. The book should remind the parents of the concepts, vocabulary, and language structures that need to be reinforced and generalized to other similar objects and events at home. The integration of activities in the structural sessions with those of the child's daily experiences is essential to rapid learning. In the structured sessions draw on parental information about what the family has been doing. Likewise, the parents should reinforce what occurs in the preschool program (Figure 14.3).

Stimulating the Child to Use Language

The intensive stimulation you give the child will usually result in attempts by the child to imitate what you say. You must reinforce these attempts in a developmental manner. The following list identifies the progression of your stimulation goals:

1. The child attempts to use voice to communicate.
2. The child tries to mold vocalizations by appropriate inflection.
3. The utterance is related to an object or event (that is, has definite referential function).
4. The utterance is made using articulated speech.
5. The language usage is appropriate.
6. The articulation is appropriate.

Note that how the child phrases communication and how the child articulates it do not become important until communicative behavior is well established. What the child needs during early attempts at communication is acceptance, encouragement, success, and clear examples of appropriate speech and language models. The child does not need inter-

FIGURE 14.3 Children's scrapbooks help to reinforce memories of actual experiences. (Courtesy of Language Development Program of Western New York)

ruptions in the attempt to communicate in order to correct the model. *Communication involves understanding each other.* Modification of form becomes necessary only after basic communication has been established. Formal drilled correction of the child's utterances in the initial stages of oral communication, therefore, is inappropriate. What the child says should be accepted and responded to strongly and positively. Correct models of the child's utterance can be provided along with the gestures of acceptance—for example:

CHILD: *Me down.*

PARENT: *You want to get down.*

CHILD: *Down.*

PARENT: *Get me down, Mommy—get me down. There, Mommy will get you down.*

Early utterances are difficult for the child to formulate and articulate. Thus, after you have accepted and praised the child, it is appropriate to provide the correct model, thus expanding the child's utterances as we discussed in the previous chapter. Repetition of the correct model with correct, clearly articulated speech is essential. At no time should articulation be exaggerated.

Developing Communication Skills

For older children who have acquired some basic verbal communication, it is advisable to begin to provide structured speech discrimination and production training associated with language stimulation. As Ling and Ling (1978) point out, the one-to-one parent-child or teacher-child relationship of the early years of preschool training is no longer a viable method of teaching when a child enters nursery school. At this time the amount of adult-child interaction is drastically reduced in a class of eight to ten children and one special teacher. The teacher/therapist will, therefore, need to plan group learning experiences that emphasize communication skills. These activities can be broken down into the components:

1. Listening, watching, and deciding
2. Molding and correcting

LISTENING, WATCHING, AND DECIDING

This is usually referred to as auditory- and visual-communication training. Visual communication is synonymous with lip-reading or speechreading. We use the terms listening and watching here because they describe perceptual behaviors rather than skills. The ultimate purpose of your efforts is to increase the perceptual behaviors that contribute to the comprehension of spoken language. Speech is the articulatory acoustic correlate of language forms; therefore, the perception of speech involves language processing. Your training must capitalize on the role that situational and linguistic constraints play in speech perception.

Earlier, we discussed whether to train children by a unisensory or multisensory method. In some cases bimodal stimulation might result in an amount of stimulus information that exceeds the child's attentional or processing capacity. Similarly, when the information in a single channel provides relative ease of speech comprehension, the child may elect to ignore or suppress information in the second modality. Thus a teacher may report of a child who "is such a good lip reader that he doesn't use his hearing" or conversely, that "the child hears enough with her aid that it is hard to get her to watch the speaker." The politics of this issue of unisensory versus multisensory processing have been responsible for confusion and for unjustified conclusions. We must remember that physical constraints (auditory and visual) are only used when they have the capacity to reduce choice, to contribute information. This is determined by the need and ability of the individual to fit the bits of information into the perceptual jigsaw, and by that person's familiarity with the total pattern to which they relate. In circumstances in which audition provides all the bits necessary to satisfactorily predict the picture, visual cues will be redundant. Conversely, if the auditory information has not been available, or has long been distorted for the undiagnosed hearing-impaired child, it may be ignored even when made available by amplification. Dependency in this case will be entirely on the visual channel. This will be particularly true for the child whose hearing difficulty fails to be diagnosed until two to three years of age. Your task is to activate the system to process both auditory and visual cues to spoken language.

The aim of training in listening, watching, and deciding should be:

1. To make the children aware of sound made available to them by amplification
2. To establish listening (attention) behavior
3. To make the children aware of the referential function of sound
4. To train the children to discriminate between and among sound patterns
5. To make the children aware of speech as communicative behavior
6. To encourage the children to pay attention to speech
7. To relate speech patterns to conceptual values, thus forming semantic values
8. To increase the children's ability to use auditory patterns to identify semantic values
9. To integrate new auditory perceptual skills into the language-acquisition process by fostering the development of feed-forward competencies (that is, using cognition—linguistics and auditory perception—in an integrative manner to predict meaning)
10. To develop awareness of the visible characteristics of speech behavior
11. To train the children to watch for visible speech cues
12. To train the children to discriminate among the visible patterns of units of speech
13. To facilitate integration of auditory and visual constraint patterns
14. To develop strategies for processing auditory and visual information

You must assess each child's needs carefully to determine at what stage he or she is functioning. The amount of residual hearing and the age at which amplification and intervention begin will greatly influence the child's acquired abilities. However, you do not know what a child needs until you have carefully observed his or her behavior and have assessed the level of function at each stage. You should first emphasize the utilization of residual hearing. However, naturally occurring visual cues to speech should be suppressed only for short periods during an activity; this concentrates listening and highlights the acoustic characteristics of the speech pattern. What you have isolated temporarily should very soon be fitted back into the total integrated conceptual pattern. Even the strongest advocates of a unisensory auditory approach to training do not suggest eliminating visual information. Pollack (1970) writes: "His energy is directed towards listening, and the rewards and reinforcements are for listening. True, he is not blindfolded, and visual perception can take place, but only in the same natural way it occurs during a normal hearing child's activities" (p. 87).

Listening and watching should, therefore, be treated as a single behavior. You should not deny the child the visual cues to speech, but you should focus attention on them only when the child appears to need more information than can be derived from auditory cues.

Listening, Watching, and Deciding (Environmental Sounds)

Motivation is a prime factor in focusing and sustaining attention. The children should enjoy the activities you select. For this reason gross-sound discrimination provides an excellent way of introducing children to listening and watching behaviors. Recorded environmental sounds are most appropriate for this age group. These may be taken from commercially available records, such as the "Sounds Around Us" available from Scott, Foresman & Company, or they may be recordings that you have made yourself. It is important to make recordings on a good quality high-speed tape recorder. Select the sounds on the basis of how commonly they may be expected to be encountered in the children's environment. Your choice will also be influenced by how easily you will be able to find an illustration of the object, person, and/or event that gives rise to each sound or group of sounds.

Your first task is to ensure that the children are aware of the sounds you have recorded and to check that each child is familiar with them. In the first session present each sound three or four times with a short pause between each presentation. For example, the first sound may be a telephone ringing. As you play and repeat the recording, show the children a picture of a telephone. You listen, point to the picture and say, "telephone—the telephone's ringing—telephone." If you have any doubts whether a particular child can hear the sound, play the game with that child alone. "John—listen, point to the telephone when it rings—that's right, it's ringing—listen again—good boy." Repeat the procedure for a small group of different sounds which you should present one by one—for example, telephone ringing, dog barking, fire engine clanging, vacuum cleaner going. These then constitute the sounds for a first lesson in listening and watching. Put all pictures of all four sounds on a stand and play the next part of the tape, on which the sounds are recorded several times in different order. Ask the children to listen, then point to the picture associated with that sound. It is helpful with the older preschool chil-

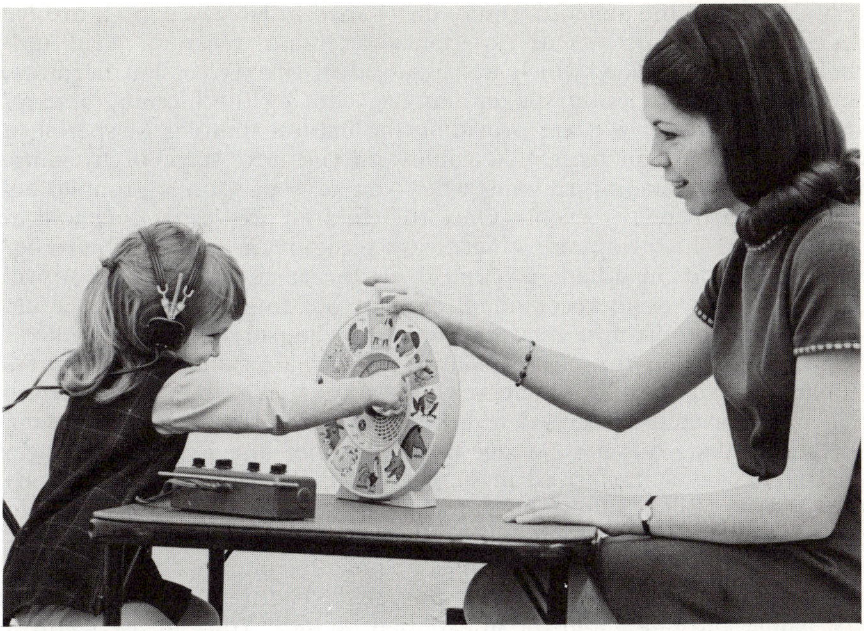

FIGURE 14.4 As the child begins to utilize auditory cues more efficiently, confidence in predictions grows. (Courtesy of The State University of New York at Buffalo)

dren to be able to move from single pictures to clear drawings on ditto sheets, or better still, to individual photocopies of professionally drawn illustrations so that each child can point to the object on his or her own sheet. To increase auditory attention vary the interval between the sounds. Sometimes plan for two presentations to follow each other closely in time, but pause before the next one, encouraging the children to listen carefully:

Wait, listen (pointing to your ear). No (shaking your head and frowning as you listen hard). Ah, there it is (smiling and rewarding the child for a correct identification).

It is important to note if any of the children appear to be having difficulty in paying attention, or in correctly identifying the sounds. Do not let a child become discouraged in the group. It may be necessary to provide individual sessions for such a child to bring that child up to the level of performance of the group. An individual session frequently provides the stimulation and success necessary for the child to gain confidence in the use of residual hearing (Figure 14.4).

Some children entering the preschool program late, particularly those with limited residual hearing, may need to work with actual noisemakers rather than taped sounds. Drums, bells, keys, or rattles may prove more stimulating initially than recorded sounds, because the child experiences the actual noise source, can see and hold it, and can make the sounds himself or herself.

Remember that discrimination of nonspeech sounds does not directly influence the ability to discriminate speech. However, both involve the perceptual processes of expectancy, attention, reception, trial-and-check, and perception, which we discussed in Chapter 5. Furthermore, because you use relevant spoken language during the listening and responding activities, you are providing the natural stimulus of speech in context. You will increase that context in the next stage of listening, watching, and deciding training when you present sounds grouped according to activities or events. Once the children are responding well to short sessions involving individual sound recognition, move to the recognition of sounds in situational context. At this stage of training, you will integrate gross sound recognition, concept building, language training, and speech. To do this, group sounds according to a common context. For example, you may select sounds usually associated with mothers (cooking, cleaning, drying hair, sewing, washing dishes), or you may use the sounds usually associated with fathers (hammering, sawing, mowing the lawn, taking out the garbage cans). It is not intended that mothers and fathers be characterized in stereotyped roles. However, the sounds the young child hears around the house during the day are most likely to be made by the mother or mother substitute. You may select sounds animals make, or sounds that occur in the home (telephone, doorbell, alarm clock, radio or television, clock). Encourage the children to listen to, identify, name, and talk about the appropriate sounds. You can use pictures depicting, for example, mother working in the kitchen, father building something at the workbench, police officers or fire fighters at work, to provide the basis for explaining and talking about the activities to which these sounds relate. As the children learn the names of people and objects that generate the sounds, they listen to those sounds again. You want to develop a level of performance at which the sound cues the appropriate semantic values and evokes the associated linguistic structures.

Listening activities can progress from "Who or what makes this sound?" (mother, father, baby, dog, telephone) to "What is happening?" (mother is sweeping, father is hammering, the telephone is ringing). A child may respond by pointing to the appropriate picture of the sound source (for example, father) and then may choose from among pictures showing that person (father) doing different things that make sounds. Each time a correct response is made, provide the child with a language model appropriate to the event:

That's right, Mother is vacuuming *the carpet.*

Good, baby is crying.

Yes, the dog is barking.

Building a Bridge to Speech Perception

The next step is to have the children learn to listen, watch, and respond to the language structures that identify the sound in its absence. First, train the children to identify the objects and people by name. Select one picture representing each object or person. In the beginning, put only three pictures on the stand. Ask the children to listen and then to point to the appropriate person or object. In order to avoid separating words from spoken-language forms, present the person or object in a sentence as well as alone.

Dog—dog *is barking*—dog. *Mary, show me the* dog. *Where's the* dog?

As the children begin to gain confidence in their responses, increase the number of pictures to which you refer. When a child experiences difficulty, the first thing to do is to draw attention to the visual appearance of the spoken word. Require the child to watch carefully as you name the object or person that is difficult to identify auditorily. Frequently the child has already made use of the additional visual cues. In this case drawing attention to them may not result in correct identification. You need to increase the extrinsic redundancy by providing situational constraints. Say the sentence: "Dog—the dog is barking," play the nonspeech cue of the dog barking, then repeat the sentence. Hopefully, more concentrated auditory-visual processing within tighter constraints will help the child gradually build the level of expectancy, permitting him or her to predict the meaning of the communication from the minimal speech, auditory, and visual cues received. This may take many auditory exposures while listening intently. Do not rush into deciding that the auditory and naturally processed visual cues are insufficient for comprehension to be possible. *Auditory-visual perception of speech is so linguistically and cognitively related that what a child cannot perceive today may be perceived tomorrow if appropriate holistic stimulation fosters growth.*

Always try to provide the children with experience in listening to and identifying the nonverbal auditory and visual situational cues to speech. However, most listening and watching training will involve recognition and interpretation of spoken language. Always keep in mind that the tasks you are asking the children to perform must be useful, relevant to their experiences, correlated to their cognitive and linguistic levels of function, related to their ability to model the sound they hear. Hearing, language, and speech are interdependent processes and should always be treated as such. When you focus on one of these three components, your purpose is to enrich the sophistication of all three. You must avoid training procedures that treat one component independently to ensure that your efforts do not prove disruptive to the integrity of the whole.

Listening, Watching, and Deciding (Spoken Language)

Listening, watching, and deciding is an activity that cannot be separated from cognitive and linguistic growth. We listen to spoken language, which identifies relevant concepts. This activity consists, therefore, of auditory-visual stimulation to reinforce the child's cognitive and linguistic experience. Your aim is to focus on the auditory and visual components of the language related to these experiences. In so doing you will:

1. Provide repeated examples of the relevant spoken language, reinforcing the child's perceptions

2. Provide the necessary structure to refine those perceptions
3. Build the child's confidence in the ability to understand speech

To do this you need to be familiar with the unit that is being worked on in school and, hopefully, is being reinforced at home. The teacher may be concentrating on foods we eat (when we eat them, how we cook them, how things taste), on colors, on action verbs, on prepositions, on people who help us, or on the experience of a class trip. Seasons and season holidays, outdoor activities, and clothes we wear are all frequently occurring topics, too.

The level of language of the children in the group will influence your approach. First you will need to reinforce key words and phrases. When you do this, emphasize listening. Have the children close their eyes as you say the name or phrase appropriate to the picture; then have them open their eyes and watch your face as you repeat it. Now have them close their eyes and listen again very carefully to the same message. The children should be encouraged to listen and attempt to repeat what you say. Link listening to speech production whenever possible because listening and watching aim to develop the most accurate internal image of the spoken message. It is from this internal model that speech will be generated.

Your activities with very young or severely language-delayed children of necessity may be confined to auditory-visual recognition of primary concepts. These may be built around physical activities in which the children participate—for example, walking, jumping, hopping, running. They may involve such basic concepts as up and down, in and out, under and over. The activities may be accompanied by played or recorded music (Whitehurst, 1971). After physical involvement you can present the constraint cues in the form of pictures. Then ask the children to listen, watch and listen, and listen again as you say about the picture:

The little dog is under the table.

The little bird goes hopping, hopping, hopping.

Pussycat's up on the roof.

Then ask the children to choose the relevant pictures, or to make the appropriate cut-out picture animal perform the described activity. Children learn by action (Menyuk, 1976). Whenever possible, use activities in which the child does something in response to speech. For example, first place a box, a hat, a toy bird, a cardboard ladder, a toy dog on a table.

Lisa, come and find the hat—hat—hat—put it on your head—put the hat on your head. Good girl, you put the hat on your head.

David, the bird hopped into the box. Bird—make the bird hop—hop, hop, hop into the box. Make it hop into the box. That's right, into—into the box.

Sarah, the dog goes up the ladder—listen, dog, dog, the dog goes up—up, up—up the ladder—the dog goes up the ladder. Here I'll help you. Here's the dog—dog, dog,—listen and watch—dog. Make the dog go up (pointing up) up, up, up the ladder (guiding Sarah's hand). Good girl, you made the dog go up the ladder—now make the dog come down—down, that's right, down. Up and down (Figure 14.5).

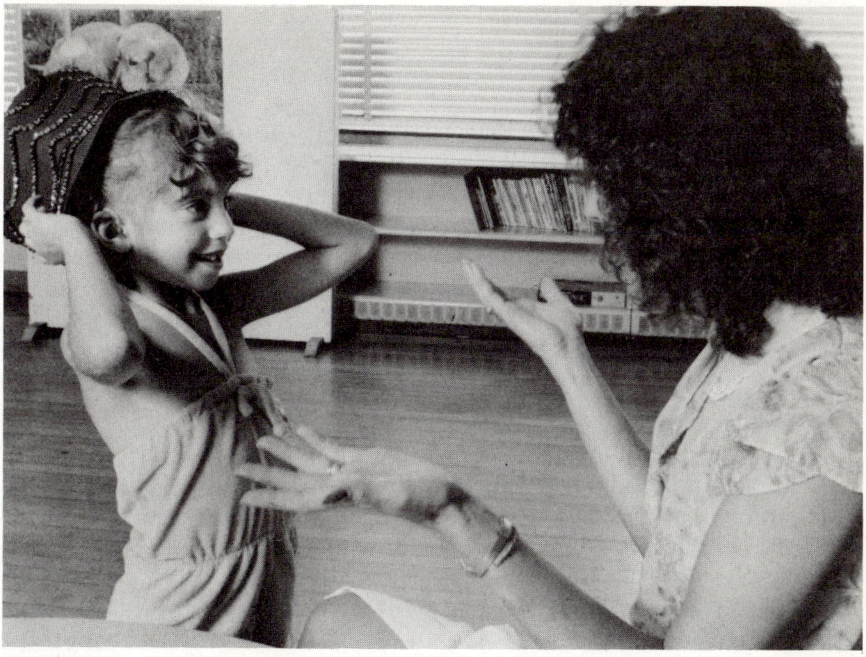

FIGURE 14.5 Whenever possible, have the child do something in response to what you say. (Courtesy of Language Development Program of Western New York)

You will need to modify the cues and support you give depending on the capabilities of individual children in the group. Concentrate on listening and watching behavior. Increase auditory attention by having the children wait in anticipation for a few seconds before you give the message. Tell them:

I'm thinking (adopt an exaggerate thinking pose)—about—the pussycat. Are you ready? Are you listening? Are you listening, Jane?

The pussycat—jumps—into—the box. Pussycat into the box. Make the pussycat jump into the box, David.

Keep sessions short enough to hold the group's attention, ensure success and reward by providing appropriate redundancy and support, and repeat short lessons several times during the school session.

As the children show increasing conceptual and linguistic growth, listening and watching training can become more complex. It will be possible to have the children listen to simple descriptive sentences and then to act out the descriptions.

This morning when I got up I
rubbed my eyes
stretched my arms
brushed my teeth
combed my hair

put on my socks

put on my dress/shirt and trousers

put on my shoes.

The children can listen and participate as a group. Sometimes an individual child can be named to listen, watch, and decide. You can modify the game to ask children to listen for absurdities (Figure 14.6).

I stretched my teeth. No we don't stretch our teeth (shaking your head and laughing). What do we stretch, Mary? That's right, we stretch our arms. Stretch everyone, stretch your arms.

I put on my hair. We don't put on our hair. What do you do to your hair, John? You comb it. Good boy. Comb—let's comb our hair.

I combed my shoes. Do we comb shoes Dena? No. What do we comb? Right, we comb our hair. What do we do with our shoes? We put them on. We put our shoes on our feet.

David, did you put on your dress? Do you wear a dress, David? No. Mary wears a dress. What do you wear David? A shirt—good.

In a unit on Thanksgiving you would first review vocabulary to ensure understanding; then, using pictures identifying key concepts, you can ask the children to identify the picture that is the topic of your message.

The Pilgrims first celebrated Thanksgiving. For Thanksgiving we have a big turkey. We eat cranberries with our turkey. Mother makes pumpkin pie. We sit around a big fire at Thanksgiving.

Other special holidays can also be identified by auditory or auditory-visual recognition of such statements as:

1. I have a big chocolate egg.
2. The presents are under the tree.
3. We get dressed up in funny clothes and we collect candy.
4. We watch the fireworks.

Progressively developing an idea by feeding more information to the children will help hold interest and attention and will thus encourage good listening and watching behavior. For example, you can place an object in a paper bag, and then progressively name its characteristics:

We eat it.

It is oval (show the oval shape with your fingers and repeat—oval, it is oval).

It is sour (pucker your face).

It is a fruit (point to illustration of various kinds of fruit).

It is yellow.

If a child cannot identify the fruit ask:

Is it an orange? No, an orange is not yellow. An orange is orange. An orange is not oval. An orange is round. Is it a banana? (And so on.)

Let the child feel the content of the bag without looking. If the child still does not guess correctly, first show the fruit, then name it. Finally, repeat what you said about it while the child listens, and then listens and watches carefully. You may then show the lemon contrasted with an or-

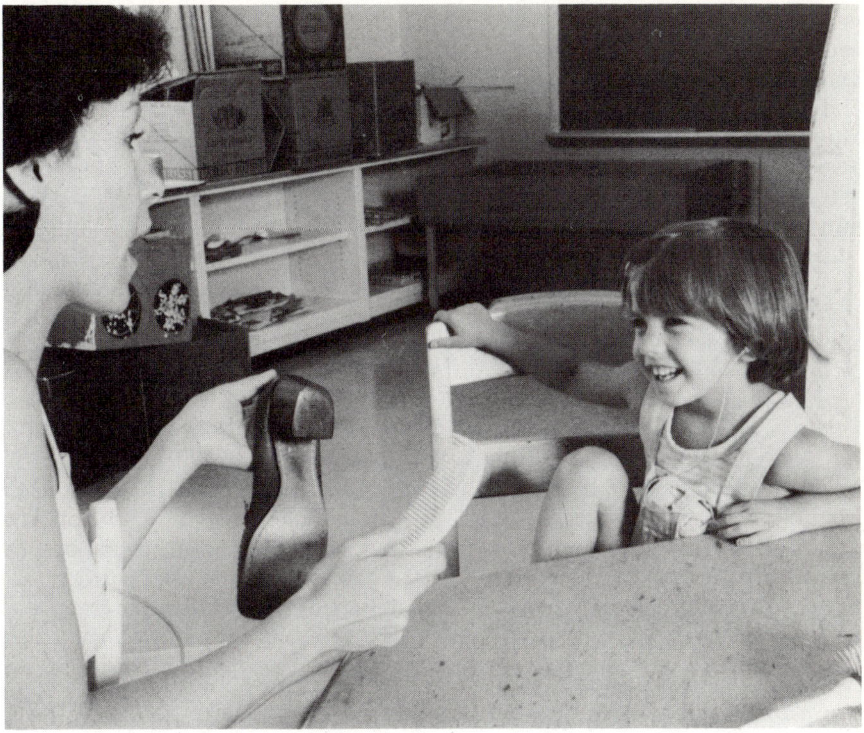

FIGURE 14.6 Absurdities help children to remember correct language models. (Courtesy of Language Development Program of Western New York)

ange. Help the child compare orange to oval, feel the shapes, draw the shapes, discriminate between the shapes, learn the words. Then choose round or oval to describe: like a lemon, like a ball, like an orange, like an egg. Expansion of this lesson could involve auditory-visual discrimination of the names of tastes: sweet, sour, salt, juicy, dry, hot, cold; and of shapes: round, oval, curved, square, all as related to foods and food packages.

In another activity you may encourage the children to listen, watch, and decide by giving each child two objects or pictures. You then tell a simple story involving one of the objects. When you name or tell about the object, the child who has it must give you that object. Receiving the object you say, "Good, Mary, I was talking about the egg. I said, The robin had three eggs in its nest."

As the child begins to acquire the perceptual behaviors that permit correct prediction of meaning from samples of spoken language your concern will be for finer discrimination. You will wish to assess ability to discriminate between similar sounding words and eventually to discriminate between syllabic units. The perception of individual speech sounds is not essential to speech comprehension. In fact, we are seldom aware of the phonological components of speech because we perceive at the level of meaningful units—morphemes, words, or phrases. Sometimes we listen for a sound that has morphological value (for example, lady: lady's, ladies; laugh, laughed), but it is not often that we need to perceive an individual sound to resolve ambiguity. Nevertheless, improved discrimination between sounds similar in acoustic structure will contribute to redundancy. Even more importantly, when successful it greatly facilitates teaching correct speech articulation. We articulate speech in order to enhance the transmission of the message intent. Once again, therefore, we must remain cognizant of the inseparable relationship between language and speech.

We have stressed the importance of structuring listening, watching, and deciding training around school and home experiences and language. A session that concentrates on these receptive skills differs only from a general class activity in the amount of emphasis placed upon them. In the classroom situation, overall communication is the main concern. Concepts and language are presented, experiences are provided and talked about. Total learning is taking place. Although the teacher will encourage watching and listening, it would be disruptive to concentrate on how a word or phrase sounds and looks when spoken. Spoken language must flow with the experience. The listen, look, and decide session allows you to intensify perception of the auditory-visual characteristics of the spoken message. It permits you to build internal perceptual images at a time when a child can pay full attention to watching and listening within the framework of well-structured language and content. Yet listening and watching are part of the larger task of experiencing learning and communicating. It is an ability essential to full classroom participation. You are seeking to improve each child's ability to participate fully so that when the teacher says, "Are you listening David? Watch me." David will have the perceptual organization that permits him to attend closely.

MOLDING AND CORRECTING SPEECH

Ling (1976) has emphasized that in normal speech development children use a comparison of the acoustic effects of their own articulation to the speech of others as a bridge between the phonetic level (speech-sound production) and the phonologic level (the systematic combination of sounds into meaningful patterns). That is, children model their own speech production, at the phonetic level, on the examples of adults. They refine it by comparing their own articulatory efforts with what they hear others say. These adult models are internalized and ultimately serve to permit self-correction. Gradually, with refinement, speech-production patterns become experience linked and acquire linguistic value, first phonologically, then semantically.

You must strive to mold the child's spoken language from your earliest contacts. This molding will occur at two levels:

1. *Phonetic.* At this level you are concerned with the child's ability to correctly and easily produce the sounds of English. To do this the child must first be able to produce the vocal articulatory features of which vowels and consonants are composed—for example, voicing, plosion, friction, nasalization,

and so on. The child must be able to produce these easily and rapidly in the combinations that comprise the articulatory patterns of the sounds of English in the full range of phonetic contexts within which each sound may occur.

2. *Phonologic.* Once the child can produce combinations of sounds easily and acceptably, he or she must learn to apply the skill to the articulation of meaningful words and groups of words.

Your overall goal is to develop the child's ability to comprehend and generate spoken language. However, teaching vocal-articulatory skills is most likely to be successful if the task is not compounded by requiring correct grammatical and syntactic composition. Thus, during the speech lesson, focus on accuracy of vocal-articulatory patterning, not on the correctness of grammatical and syntactic composition. This does not suggest that you divorce speech training from language. On the contrary, you should tie speech training to the linguistic level of development of the child, and you should use materials to stimulate phonologic use of articulatory skills that are contemporary with the child's cognitive linguistic experiences in the classroom.

Phonologic Assessment. Speech should be assessed first at the phonological level, so that you know the current status of the child's speech competency in naturally occurring communication. In this way you obtain a measure of what the child *does* as compared to what the child is capable of doing. You should evaluate the suprasegmental aspects of speech, such as appropriate use of pitch, intensity, intonation, rate, stress, and the quality of production as indicated by breath control and voice quality. Then, you should analyze the sample of natural communication to determine the use and accuracy of consonants and consonant blends. Ling (1976) has provided a detailed record form that facilitates recording the correct articulation, or absence, of each component. Ling and others (Lee, 1974; Tyack & Gottsleben, 1974) advocate the use of a tape-recorded sample of naturally occurring speech for both phonologic and phonetic analysis. These researchers agree that a fifty-word-long sample is adequate for this purpose. The same sample can then be used for phonetic analysis.

Phonetic Assessment. Phonologic assessment is concerned with determining which vocal-articulatory characteristics occur correctly in natural speech. Phonetic assessment aims to provide detailed information about the speech sounds that do not appear to be correctly used. The assessment is concerned with:

1. The child's awareness of each speech sound
2. How closely the sound can be approximated
3. How this approximation is affected by different phonetic contexts (for example, blending and alternating sounds
4. Whether the child can articulate the sound with the rapidity of normal speech

In other words, you seek an assessment of the nature and quality of the child's articulation. You wish to know how closely the child approximates normal vocal-articulatory competence for his or her age level. Beneath the phonetic evaluation lies the level of fundamental speech skills. These fundamental skills are the tools with which speech sounds are constructed. They represent articulatory placements, articulatory movements, articulatory transitions, vocal control, breath control, and so on. To produce any speech sound, or category of speech sounds, several of these tools will have to be combined in a pattern unique to that sound or group of sounds.

Discrimination Assessment

The importance of audition in the development of normal speech articulation has already been emphasized. Its potential as the major avenue of speech learning remains when hearing is deficient except for the child with profound deafness. Assessment of the child's current auditory speech-discrimination ability is, therefore, essential to planning intervention. The evaluation should provide information about:

1. The sounds that, in at least some contexts, are perceived correctly
2. The phonetic contexts in which correct identification occurs
3. The nature of the errors that occur in discrimination, described in terms of articulatory production (for example, fails to voice voiced consonants after weak vowels)
4. The speech sounds that are readily confused and the phonetic contexts in which this occurs

The correct reception of the full-frequency components of speech requires the ability to hear across the frequency scale from 100 to 5000 Hz and perhaps above. Ling (1976, 1978) suggested that sensitivity to speech within this range can be quickly screened by testing the ability of the child to hear the sounds [u, a, i, ʃ, s]. These speech sounds span the acoustic spectrum of speech. The acoustic makeup of all other sounds falls within this range. (Refer back to Table 3.11, which illustrates the component frequencies necessary for the full reception of other sounds.)

A major difficulty in assessing auditory discrimination of speech sounds by young children arises from their limited language development, which makes the use of standard tests impossible. To test discrimination it is necessary to show that a child can decide whether two sounds are the same or different. If the child has sufficient vocabulary to permit this assessment by choosing between pictures, the names of which differ by only one sound, then items may either be drawn from standard tests or compiled from other sources. Usually it is difficult to represent pictorially all the sounds and sound combinations one wishes to test. You may find it easier to develop a listening game that allows you to assess auditory discrimination at the nonsense-syllable level. The concept of same/different is a difficult one for preschool children. It is necessary to train the child to respond to the task by first presenting sounds with associated visual cues. Because the vowels are most likely to be correctly discriminated in an auditory-visual presentation, they make an appropriate entry point for assessment. The response, "same" or "different," can be facilitated by using colored tokens that the child gives to the teacher when he or she makes a decision. Two red tokens mean the two sounds, heard and seen, are the same. A red and a blue token means they are different. So, intially you train the child to make the decision same/different to the auditory-visual stimulus of vowel pairs:

/a/ - /i/
/a/ - /a/
/a/ - /u/
/i/ - /u/
/ε/ - /æ/, and so on.

Once it is clear that the discrimination task can be performed by the child, the stimuli are then presented by hearing alone. When a child fails to make a decision, visual cues are restored to prevent frustration. Incorrect judgments are accepted with a comment such as "Good try, you are listening hard." Testing in short sessions of two or three minutes avoids boredom and fatigue. A total of five presentations for each pair will minimize the effects of guessing. You can record the responses on a chart:

	a	i	I	ε	æ	ʌ	o	ɔ	v	u
a										
i										
I										
ε										
æ										
ʌ										
o										
ɔ										
v										
u										

Such a record will show which vowels a child can discriminate between and which the child confuses.

Consonants can be assessed in the same manner if you pair them with each vowel in initial, medial, and final positions:

ba-da da-da da-ba ba-ba
ad-ab ad-ad ab-ab ab-ad
dad-dab bab-dab bab-bab dab-dab

Conduct the testing using the best possible amplification system to ensure that you have a measure of the potential of the child's residual hearing, which may prove superior to performance with a personal aid. You may check this by comparing discrimination of the consonants with higher-frequency components obtained using the two different systems.

Developing a matrix that shows discrimination of each sound as a function of phonetic context is a large task. Unfortunately this observation often deters a teacher or therapist from undertaking it. Yet the information derived can be of great value for speech training. The data will indicate which sounds can be perceived in which phonetic contexts, it will show which sounds are indiscriminable auditorily despite context, and it will indicate whether visual cues resolve ambiguity when auditory confusions occur. This knowledge helps you to plan speech-teaching strategies. It will help you to analyze confusions and to select strategies of teaching that are in accord with the child's sensory-processing capabilities. The task is not as difficult as it initially seems to be. The key is the systematic use of a series of very short test sessions spread over a number of days.

Speech-Sound Discrimination and Articulation Training

Preschool children in the 3- to 6-year-old age group will invariably show improvement in communication skills if you devote part of each session to specific training in speech-sound production. Teachers and therapists need to be clear about the role of speech training in the preschool program. The following guidelines should be observed:

Speech-production training should not interfere with the child's desire to communicate and experience. It is essential that a teacher not restrict a child's desire to communicate an idea by stopping the child in the middle of a sentence to demand correction of a speech sound. Speech molding in classroom activities designed for language and concept enrichment must be quite unobtrusive.

Classroom and individual speech training should be integrated and mutually supportive. To facilitate the achievement of this goal the class teacher and the teacher/therapist must work together. Speech must not become a special subject. It is an extension of the child's daily communication behavior. The two teachers should discuss the results of the analysis of the child's use of voice (pitch, intensity, modulation, rhythm) and articulation. The classroom teacher should know which sounds the child can hear, which the child can discriminate easily, and which the child perceives only in particular combinations. The teacher should know which sounds the child articulates correctly, which the child can produce in speech if stimulated, and which sounds the child is currently working on. The teacher should be advised what demands can be made on the child for correct speech articulation in class. Techniques of modeling phrases, words, and sounds should be discussed.

The classroom teacher will contribute information about the child's particular communication problems in class activities. The teacher will also identify activities that can serve to integrate individualized speech work into the classroom.

Speech correction in the classroom should be judicious and planned. During class activities the teacher should always provide correct articulation models for words or phrases. When a child has difficulty with correct articulation of a sound or group of sounds in a word the teacher should say the words two or three times with the child watching and listening. This procedure should be incorporated smoothly into the flow of communication between teacher and children. In the early stages of speech training the child should not be required to imitate the correct model, though spontaneous attempts to do so should be praised. As the child's articulation abilities improve, the classroom teacher, guided by information from the teacher responsible for providing individualized speech training, will begin to expect the child to use the speech sounds he or she has learned to articulate in communication. These demands must be made unobtrusively. The teacher must be encouraging rather than critical. The demands made on the child must be monitored judiciously so that they do not overload the child's capacity for correction. They should never interfere with a child's desire to express an idea or ask a question. Correct modeling can always be provided *after* the communication has been accepted and responded to.

In class, group speech activities can serve to support the work of the speech teacher. For example, the children make speech-sound charts. To do this, each child collects and mounts pictures that illustrate words containing the sound(s) he or she is working on. Each child's chart may be used in class and in individual speech-training sessions. In class the children listen as the teacher names one of the objects depicted by using its name in a sentence. A child may then be called upon to identify the appropriate picture on the chart and to articulate the same word and sentence. Help and encouragement can be given. All the children can then join in repeating the word and sentence. Children working on the same sound(s) may have overlapping, interchangeable charts. Children may be asked to find new pictures illustrating their sound(s).

Individual or small group-training sessions should be based upon careful analysis of the child's auditory-visual speech-sound recognition abilities. Speech training aims first to build in the child's mind as clear an auditory image of a speech sound as possible. Careful listening to those sounds that can be heard is an essential prerequisite to teaching or improving articulation of the sound. You should alternate simultaneous listening and watching of the speech-sound production with periods of intense listening to the amplified sound given without visible cues. Simply ask the child to close his or her eyes and "listen hard." You can easily communicate this by closing your eyes, pointing to your ear, and saying the speech sound. Present the sound several times to illustrate both the listening-only condition and the listening-and-watching condition. Allowing the child to feel your vocal vibrations or the fricative flow of air onto the back of his or her hand may sharpen the child's awareness of the role of voicing and friction. You may emphasize plosion by demonstrating the effects of the plosive burst of air on a small piece of tissue on the back of a hand placed near the lips. Nasality may be felt if a child places a finger on the teacher's nose while the teacher produces a strong nasal sound.

Speech sounds should be taught and improved in phonetic context. Recognizing the important role of coarticulation and perception of normal speech demands that you teach and correct consonant production in syllabic units rather than as isolated phonemes. A child may be able to perceive a speech sound better in some consonant-vowel or vowel-consonant combinations than others. You should use the speech-discrimination data to select the combination that provides the best consonant-discrimination condition. Once the child has learned to articulate the sound in that context, you should pair it with each of the vowels in patterned articulation:

ma—mama—ma-ma-ma-ma
mi—mimi—mi-mi-mi-mi
mou—moumou—mou-mou-mou-mou

Repeat this patterning with vowel-consonant (am—am-am-ama) and vowel-consonant-vowel (ama—ama-ama-ama-ama) combinations. Finally, combine the consonant with different vowels:

mami mamou mima mimou
moumi mouma moumu moumi
ami amou ouma oumi
imi aemi eimi oumi

This rhythmical patterning of speech sounds is naturally pleasurable. It can be reinforced by clapping, tapping, or beating out the rhythm. Teaching speech-sound production in this relaxed form, isolated from the need to simultaneously communicate meaning, is likely to effect the most rapid progress in articulation.

When the child has become fluent in the articulation of a sound in a full range of phonetic contexts, success will likely be experienced in transferring the sound into meaningful words. Select the words to represent as many consonant-vowel combinations as possible. It is helpful to select words that can be illustrated:

man mower moon meat
milk mouse men mitten

Once the child can pronounce the words in isolation, they should be introduced into simple descriptive sentences:

The cat drinks the *m*ilk.
The *m*itten is blue.
This is a *m*ouse.

The child can sort pictures to identify those words that begin with the sound being studied; then the list can gradually be expanded. Once the child has established the sound well in the test items, you should plan short periods of careful monitoring of the child's production of the sound. These should fall midway between highly structured speech training and uninterrupted communication. Provide only as much intervention as necessary to cause the child to remember to use the new skills. When obvious difficulty is experienced, isolate the word, model it for the child, then help the child to produce it. If necessary isolate the consonant and vowel and rehearse its articulation as a nonsense syllable:

mitten—mɪmɪmɪmɪ-tən-tən-tən-tən
mɪ-tən mɪ-tən mɪ-tən
mɪtən mɪtən

Selecting Consonants for Teaching

The consonants selected for the earliest intervention should be those that you have demonstrated are audible to the child and, in at least one consonant-vowel combination, can be discriminated with some success. You may have shown that in some phonetic contexts the child articulates the sound acceptably. The concern then is to generalize the use of the consonant to all phonetic contexts, even though it may not be audible in some. Beyond the criterion of audibility, it is helpful to select sounds that can be contrasted in some way. Cognate pairs—for example, /p-b/, /t-d/, /k-g/,/s-z/,/θ-ð/,/f-v/—differ only by the voicing feature. Once one is learned, acquiring its partner should not be difficult because the vocal component will be audible to most children and will clearly identify the voiced member of the pair after the unvoiced plosive or fricative has been learned. The manner of production between, for example, nasal and plosive sounds can also be contrasted. The difference in the manner in which voicing is initiated is a major cue to discrimination between these sounds. Moreover, the difference in manner of production of the plosion and nasality characteristics can be felt if the child places fingers on the nose and before the lips during production. Auditory discrimination among sounds produced in the same manner—for example, plosives, nasals, fricatives—but in different places in the mouth—for example, labial, nasal, velar—will be possible only for children with usable residual hearing for the higher frequencies. Therefore teaching speech-sound articulation requires that you be familiar with all the sensory cues with which the child may be stimulated—that is, auditory, visual, tactile cues. It is necessary for you to know the acoustic cues to each phoneme and to determine whether these fall within the child's auditory range. It is also necessary for you to be aware of how to compensate for inaudible acoustic information by the use of visual and tactile cues. You must individualize the process for each child on the basis of a careful analysis of his or her auditory-discrimination potentials when using optimum amplification.

Almost every child can benefit from speech training, some more noticeably than others. When there is considerable residual hearing, optimal amplification and carefully planned speech training can effect remarkable improvement in a child's communication ability. Tied to training in listening, watching, and deciding and to language stimulation, speech training can result in improved auditory comprehension of speech. However, this requires that a systematic approach be taken. You must assess each child's ability to perceive individual speech sounds across a wide range of phonetic contexts. Then you must assess the child's ability to articulate the full range of speech sounds. Once a profile of speech-sound discrimination and speech-sound production is available, you can systematically plan speech training for each individual child. The speech-teaching methods detailed by Ling (1978), Calvert and Silverman (1975), and Vorce (1974) provide excellent models from which to develop your intervention program.

MOLDING LANGUAGE

Language originates from the exposure to linguistic forms within a meaningful context. The greater part of the child's language acquisition will occur as a result of the influence of language models provided by the class teacher and by the child's family. Because of our commitment to a holistic model of communication, speech comprehension and production cannot be divorced from language. Thus, the teacher of communication skills must be able to contribute to the constant effort to upgrade the child's language abilities.

For each hearing-impaired child, a profile of language capability and performance should be completed by someone experienced in language assessment. The profile should be developed from more than one source, drawing upon standardized tests, developmental scales, and nonstandardized tests supported by behavioral observation (Miller, 1978). For children under three years of age, standardized tests are usually not suitable because appropriate norms are not available. For the older preschool child (3 to 6 years old) who has developed early language skills, the Auditory Test of Language Comprehension (Carrow, 1973) and two tests by Lee—The Northwestern Syntax Screening Test (Lee, 1969) and Developmental Sentence Analysis (Lee, 1974)—provide useful tools for describing young children's nonsentence and sentence constructions.

You must know the types of constructions with which the child is experiencing difficulty. This will permit you to accommodate the child's language needs in your development of new concept categories and new vocabulary and phrases appropriate to those categories, and in the training of auditory and visual recognition and speech articulation of those words and phrases. For example, if a child is still at the stage of using single words, language molding will aim to develop the subject-verb-object structure. It would be inexcusable to concentrate on single-word auditory and visual discrimination of new vocabulary. You should not pursue activities that simply require the child to identify new objects or activities by name, or even to name the objects. You must seek to mold the child's language, first through listening and watching, then through use of the grammatical parts of speech. Thus, listening and watching activities may concentrate on the child's selecting pictures named in a S-V-O construction:

The boy is running.
The bird is flying.
Mother is cooking.
John is swimming.

When an item is correctly identified, or has been identified for the child, you should ask the child to repeat the sentence after you. You can reinforce the model for the child by giving look-listen-and-decide tasks that hold part of the sentence constant while you identify the remainder:

Mother is cooking.
John is cooking.
Father is cooking.
or Mother is cooking
            is reading
            is laughing.

If a child has difficulty formulating questions, you may choose to develop a lesson plan that combines the use of question forms with, for example, listen-look-and-decide training on the topic of *People Who Help Us*.

Does	*Do*	*Can*
Does the letter carrier bring us letters?	Do cats climb trees?	Can an elephant fly?
Does the dog say meow?	Do we eat turkey for breakfast?	Can a fish swim?
Does a ball bounce?	Do we wear a banana?	Can a cat bark?
Does a cup have a handle?	Do mice have tails?	Can children laugh?
Does a bird have four legs?	Do chairs have legs?	Can a dog laugh?
	Do trousers have sleeves?	

You can use photographs to identify the nouns used, or you may draw pictures to illustrate both the truth and the absurdities. Encourage children to ask the question by repeating it with you, then later by asking a question about a picture with minimal prompting by you. Similarly, use *who-what-which*, and *where-when-how* questions to structure a look-listen-and-decide activity. Things and people can first be classified into *who* and *what* categories. The children listen while you name an object or person, and then give a sentence. "Ball—the ball bounces." They then find and place the picture in the "What" category. Later you can expand to Who *does* what and Who *has* what. *Which* can also be introduced to identify the appropriate category. "Which bounces—the ball or the egg?"

"Who brings letters—the doctor or the letter carrier?

Where, when, and *how* can be taught in the same way.

Remember, your role is to reinforce language use. Your primary concern is to increase speech understanding through listening and watching and to improve speech articulation through speech training. However, because both are performance skills based upon the child's language competence, it would be illogical to use materials or activities for speech perception and production training that are not supportive of cognitive and linguistic needs. For the teacher/therapist who must assume responsibility for a much greater role in language development, books by Meers (1976), Wood (1976), and Schiefelbusch (1978, 1979a, 1979b) may prove very helpful. The stimulation and molding of language of the hearing impaired are discussed in texts by Lee, Koenigsknecht, and Mulhern (1975), Blackwell, Engen, Fischgrund, and Zarcadoolas (1978), and Kretchmer and Kretchmer (1978).

MOLDING SOCIOLINGUISTIC BEHAVIORS

The ultimate goal of language and speech-development training is communication. This requires not only that children learn the rules of language, but that they also learn the social rules governing its use. Society has expectations concerning when and how we may communicate in a variety of different situations. We use different communication strategies to achieve different goals. In the early preschool years we are so delighted to find a hearing-impaired child attempting to communicate that we set aside the normal rules. We encourage the child to communicate orally in any form at any time. However, as the child grows older, he or she must learn the social rules for communication—when to speak and when to remain silent, how to ask a question, how to make a request in an acceptable manner, how to use language manipulatively (Wood, 1976).

Acceptance of the hearing-impaired child by normal-hearing peers and adults will be determined not only by the intelligibility of what the child says, but also by how it is said. The pragmatic value of the communication skills acquired by the child becomes increasingly important as the school years approach. This is particularly true for the growing number of children who are being mainstreamed into normal school classes. Thus, during the later preschool years we must begin to help the child gain the experience necessary to cope with a variety of communication situations in ways that will be socially acceptable. As Meers, (1976), puts it: "The fuller the range of language uses and styles available to the speaker, the greater the number of informed choices that are open to him; thus he is able to influence his environment as well as knowing himself to be subject to its laws" (p. 147).

In his book, *The Presentation of Self in Everyday Life*, Goffman (1959) views social behavior in terms of a wide range of roles that we learn in order to cope with others. Knowledge of these roles and the associated sociolinguistic behaviors is learned by hearing children through daily exposure to people in context. The children observe the subtleties of communication and learn from the nature of the verbal interaction. They learn from the different ways in which they are addressed, as well as by the occasions on which they are all but ignored, sometimes even when they are the topic of conversation. They also learn from the control exerted on their verbal and nonverbal behavior by adults who reward and punish such behavior differently in different situations. Hearing-impaired children will need training to develop this sociolinguistic awareness acquired naturally by hearing peers.

Wood (1976) advocates that the social-communication competence of language-delayed children be developed through a situational approach. Attention must be paid to (1) *the goal of the communication*—to effect a course of action (for example, to gain praise, sympathy, understanding, or affection); and (2) the *critical-communication situations* that the child encounters (Wood, 1976). It is necessary to identify these situations for preschool children. Hopefully, as the children grow older, they will begin to assume responsibility for identifying and seeking help in dealing with such critical situations themselves.

Communication is analyzed by Wood in terms of the four categories:

1. *People I talk to*: parents, siblings, playmates, teachers.
2. *Places I talk in*: school (classroom, playground, hall); home (my room, family room, kitchen, garden); public places (church, library, supermarket, children's theater, or movie theater). These two categories are further broken down into the times of the communication—at breakfast/lunch/dinner, when I come home from school, before I go to bed, when Daddy comes home.
3. *What I talk about*: objects, events, people, ideas.
4. *How I talk*: how I use my voice, how I say things, whether I must wait my turn, whether I can call out.

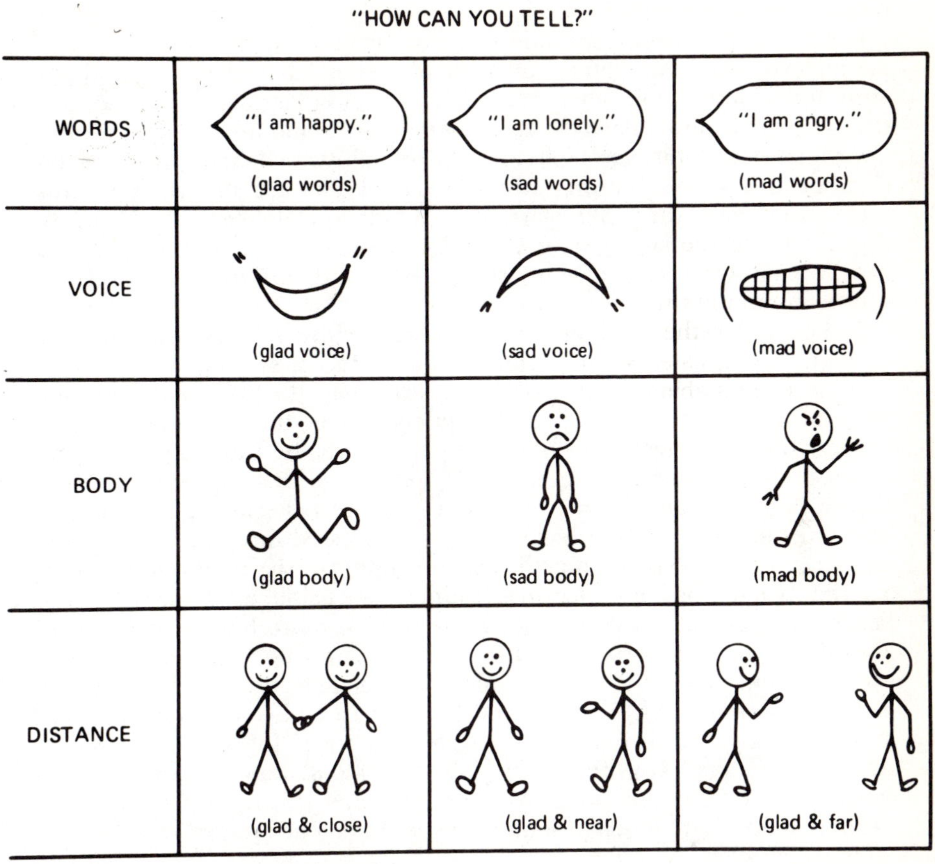
"HOW CAN YOU TELL?"
WORDS
"I am happy."
(glad words)
"I am lonely."
(sad words)
"I am angry."
(mad words)
VOICE
(glad voice)
(sad voice)
(mad voice)
BODY
(glad body)
(sad body)
(mad body)
DISTANCE
(glad & close)
(glad & near)
(glad & far)

FIGURE 14.7 Illustrations can stimulate the child's awareness of options for communicating feelings (Wood, 1976, p. 296).

We learned in Chapter 2 that in communication, we transmit information with our voice, our articulators, and our bodily gestures and postures. Wood (1976) presents the options for communication for young children in illustrated form (Figure 14.7). By using charts such as Wood's, you can stimulate a child's awareness of the behavior of others during communication, thus enhancing understanding of message intent. At the same time, you can begin to foster awareness of the child's own behavior and you can teach the child how to mold it to be appropriate to the demands of various communication situations.

For example, you might have the child consider the times *when* we try to be quiet: for example, when someone is sleeping, when people are already talking, when someone is talking on the telephone, when you have special quiet work to do in school. The child can also learn *where* to be quiet: in a movie theater, in a library, in a doctor's office, at a concert. The child can then learn *what types of voices* are appropriate in different places: quiet voice in a movie, library, and so on; ordinary voice at dinner table, in the classroom, in the hallways; loud voice in the playground, on a busy street, at a fair. Attention can be focused on behaviors, such as taking turns to talk, waiting until someone has finished talking, raising your hand in a group when you wish to answer or ask a question, addressing a teacher by name to attract attention. Communication behaviors appropriate for various situations can be illustrated and practiced by small groups of children preparing for school. Play activities can be introduced that help the child learn how to manipulate people acceptably through spoken language: how to obtain someone's attention politely, how to make a request, how to ask a question in a group, how to refuse, how to communicate displeasure.

Feelings, bodily postures, gestures, and words and phrases can also be identified through pictures illustrating different situations. Recognizing the feelings experienced by others can help the children work out some of their own feelings. Hand puppets may be used to help children express their feelings both nonverbally and verbally. Happy, sad, angry, puzzled, surprised, paper faces can be pinned to the puppets to reflect appropriate feelings. Then, each child can select the faces. You should verbalize for the child the feelings being expressed through the puppet. Similarly, during classroom activities you should verbalize the feelings of a child when possible—pleasure, sadness, surprise, excitement, impatience, puzzlement, as well as anger. It is even more helpful if you can also identify and express the cause of the feelings for the child. Parents should be encouraged to do the same at home. The acceptability of forms of expression of feelings can also be communicated by depicting children in situations to which they react in different ways. In this way, positive strategies for dealing with anger, disappointment, impatience, and fear can be reinforced while inappropriate strategies can be modified. Children with adequate levels of language should be encouraged to verbalize their feelings.

In summary, we can conclude that your concern as a hearing teacher/therapist is for the effectiveness of the child as a communicator of information, ideas, and feelings in a variety of situations. To achieve effective communication behaviors, it is necessary for the child to have adequate receptive language to permit understanding of what is happening in those situations, and to have sufficient language and adequately intelligible speech to be able to meet the demands of the situation. Furthermore the child must have available a range of communication behaviors and the ability to select strategies appropriate to the situation at hand.

The ultimate goal of preschool training is to maximize the development of the child's cognitive, linguistic, and communicative skills. Preschool training has the potential for significantly affecting a child's capacity for learning when that child enters the full-time educational system. Those professionals who have participated in the child's preschool management, therefore, have a major contribution to make to the important task of determining what constitutes the most appropriate educational placement at school-entry age.

REFERENCES

Blackwell, P., E. Engen, J. Fischgrund, and C. Zarcadoolas, *Sentences and Other Systems: A Language Learning Curriculum for Hearing Impaired Children.* Washington, D.C.: Alexander Graham Bell Assoc. for the Deaf, 1978.

Calvert, D., and S. Silverman, *Speech and Deafness.* Washington, D.C.: Alexander Graham Bell Assoc. for the Deaf, 1975.

Carrow, E., *Test of Auditory Comprehension of Language.* Austin, Tex.: Learning Concepts, 1973.

Goffman, E., *The Presentation of Self in Everyday Life.* Garden City, N.Y.: Doubleday, Inc., 1959.

Kretschmer, R., and L. Kretschmer, *Language Development and Intervention with the Hearing Impaired.* Perspectives in Audiology Series. Baltimore: University Park Press, 1978.

Lee, L., *The Northwestern Syntax Screening Test.* Evanston, Ill.: Northwestern University Press, 1969.

Lee, L., *Developmental Sentence Analysis.* Evanston, Ill.: Northwestern Universtiy Press, 1974.

Lee, L., R. Koenigsknecht, and S. Mulhern, *Interactive Language Development Teaching.* Evanston, Ill.: Northwestern University Press, 1975.

Ling, D., *Speech and the Hearing Impaired Child.* Washington, D.C.: Alexander Graham Bell Assoc. for the Deaf, 1976.

Ling, D., and A. Ling, *Aural Habilitation: The Foundations of Verbal Learning in Hearing Impaired Children.* Washington, D.C.: Alexander Graham Bell Assoc. for the Deaf, 1978.

Mecham, M. J., *Development of Audiolinguistic Skills in Children.* St. Louis: Warren H. Green, Inc., 1969.

Meers, H., *Helping Our Children Talk.* London and New York: Longman, 1976.

Menyuk, P., "Cognition and Language," *Volta Review, 78,* 1976, 250–257.

Miller, J. F., "Assessing Children's Language Behavior—A Developmental Process Approach," in *Bases of Language Intervention,* ed. R. L. Schiefelbusch, pp. 269–318. Language Intervention Series. Baltimore: University Park Press, 1978.

Pollack, D., *Educational Audiology for the Limited Hearing Infant.* Springfield, Ill.: Charles C Thomas, Publisher, 1970.

Sanders, D. A., "Educational Programming for the Older Infant," in *Childhood Deafness: Causation, Assessment and Management,* ed. F. Bess, pp. 321–331. New York: Grune & Stratton, Inc., 1977.

Schiefelbusch, R., ed., *Bases of Language Intervention.* Language Intervention Series. Baltimore: University Park Press, 1978.

Schiefelbusch, R., ed., *Developmental Language Intervention: Psycholinguistic Application.* Baltimore: University Park Press, 1979(a).

Schiefelbusch R., ed., *Early Language Intervention.* Language Intervention Series. Baltimore: University Park Press, 1979(b).

Tyack, D., and R. Gottsleben, *Language Sampling and Analysis.* Palo Alto, Calif.: Consultant Psychologists Press, 1974.

Vorce, E., *Teaching Speech to Deaf Children.* Washington, D.C.: Alexander Graham Bell Assoc. for the Deaf, 1974.

Whitehurst, M., *Teaching Communication Skills to the Pre-School Child. A Manual.* Washington, D.C.: Alexander Graham Bell Assoc. for the Deaf, 1971.

Wood, B., *Children and Communication: Verbal and Nonverbal Language Development.* Englewood Cliffs, N.J.: Prentice-Hall, Inc., 1976.

15

Planning for Educational Placement

A number of excellent books are available that deal with the Public Law 94-142 and its impact on the decision-making process in educating hearing-impaired children. These sources also consider the educator's role in the decision-making process. A list of Suggested Readings that you will find helpful in learning more about alternative educational placements, the process of making an appropriate placement decision, and other important aspects of educating hearing-handicapped children appears at the end of this chapter. The purpose of this information is to familiarize you with the process of planning for educational placement and to stimulate you to investigate this aspect of management in greater depth.

The process by which a decision is made about the educational placement of a child is now well defined. The appropriateness of the initial placement will depend upon the amount, relevance, and accuracy of the information used by those who must make the decision. Your input can be extremely valuable. For this reason you should understand what the alternatives for education are, and how the decision process operates. At this point in our discussion we focus attention on the initial educational career. Complete reevaluation of the child and his or her progress must be made every three years. Whenever a change in educational placement is under consideration, the legally defined process must be followed.

TYPES OF PLACEMENT

Basically, we wish to treat the hearing-impaired child as normally as possible. Thus it is desirable to allow the child to be educated with little deviation from normal educational procedures. It is important to realize, however, that no type of educational setting is intrinsically better than another. The criterion by which a placement decision must be judged is the degree to which it achieves compatibility between the child and the learning environment.

It is helpful to view placement alternatives for the hearing-impaired child as lying along a continuum from *no special support services* to *a highly specialized learning environment.* The task then becomes one of matching the child's needs to the alternatives available in a search for an educational placement. The ideal placement will:

1. Provide the specific services needed by the child
2. Exert only minimal limitations on the child's ability to learn and to grow socially
3. Stimulate growth of self-sufficiency
4. Provide for the development of abilities, skills, and behaviors appropriate to functioning in a less-specialized educational setting

The types of educational settings on the continuum are identified in Table 15.1.

Normal School with or without Special Services

Northcott (1973, p. 3) has identified four characteristics that a hearing-impaired child must evidence if he or she is likely to be successful in a normal school setting:

1. Active utilization of residual hearing and full-time hearing-aid usage if prescribed
2. Demonstrated social, academic, cognitive, and communicative (auditory and oral) skills *within the normal range of behaviors* of hearing classmates at a particular grade level
3. Intelligible speech and the ability to comprehend and exchange ideas with others through spoken, written, and read language
4. Increased confidence and independence in giving self-direction to the tasks at hand

In considering a normal school placement for the hearing-impaired child it will be necessary to provide a profile of his or her abilities in each of the aforementioned areas. We will discuss this profile in more detail later in this chapter.

The child with a mild to moderate hearing impairment who has had early successful preschool guidance may be able to manage successfully in the local primary school with support only from the speech, hearing, and language therapist. Some schools also have a general resource teacher and/or a remedial-reading teacher who helps hearing children with learning problems. The services of these teachers will increase the hearing-impaired child's chances of success.

TABLE 15.1 The Continuum of Options and Services

Maximal Support ←		*EDUCATIONAL PLACEMENT OPTIONS*			→ *Minimal Support*
Specialized Residential or Day School	Special Classes Housed Within a Normal School	A Single Special Class at Primary or Secondary Level	Normal School Placement with a Special Resource Room	Normal School Placement with an Itinerant Special Teacher	Normal School Placement with only those Special Services Available to all Children
Increased Services ←		*SERVICES PROVIDED*			→ *Decreased Services*
Full-time special education by specialist teachers. Small classes 8-10 children. Full range of audiology services usually available; hearing-aid monitoring and basic repair. Educational amplification systems. Special curricula. Specialist services in speech and language. Oral or combined oral/manual teaching. Social and activity clubs. Possibility of some mainstream experience for selected children. Career education.	Full-time special education by specialist teachers. Small classes 8-10 children. Education amplification systems. Special curricula. Access to services of speech, hearing, and language therapist. Teaching may be by oral or total-communication method; choice sometimes available. Mainstream experiences where appropriate.	Full-time special education by special teacher. Small class size but usually up to 3-year age spread. Special curricula. Speech, hearing, and language services from regular speech therapist for school. Teaching usually oral. Educational amplification. Mainstreaming as appropriate.	Normal educational program among hearing children. Possible use of FM amplification in selected cases. Daily services of specialist teacher of hearing impaired for at least 1 hour per day individually or in groups no larger than 5 children. Services of school speech, hearing and language therapist.	Specialist resource teacher available at prescribed times. Usually provides individualized support or in groups of 2 or 3 children. Services of school speech, hearing, and language therapist.	Only such services as are available to all hearing children. These include the speech, hearing, and language therapist and in some schools a nonspecialist resource teacher or remedial-reading teacher.

The Resource-Room or Itinerant-Teacher Service

The child who has a more severe handicap, but who has the potential for meeting, or already meets, Northcott's four criteria for mainstreaming will need the additional help of a specialist teacher of the hearing impaired. Help may be provided on an itinerant basis, or the child may be bussed to a school that has a specialist resource room with a teacher of the hearing impaired on the staff. This teacher will not only be able to provide tutorial support and language enrichment, but will also serve as the manager of the child's academic needs. The specialist will be able to aid the classroom teacher, modify the child's curriculum appropriately, and coordinate the child's individual work with that of the classroom teacher. This child may have sufficient problems of understanding speech in the classroom to merit the use of FM amplification.

Separate Classes for the Hearing Impaired

For children who do not yet possess the characteristics important to success in a normal school, such a placement would limit their potential for learning. These children need continuous specialized teaching, intensive language and speech training, the use of educational amplification, and auditory-visual communication training. Such education should be available in special classes for the hearing impaired usually housed in normal schools. It is important to know whether the special classes in a school district use a purely auditory-oral method of teaching or a total-communication approach, which accompanies speech with manual signs. Some urban school districts offer both types of education; other districts offer only one of the two methods. Ideally a child capable of learning by the auditory-oral method should not be placed in a total-communication environment, which is intended for children who need a supplementary or alternative communication system. This ideal may, however, not be achievable in a particular district.

For children with appropriate communication-learning skills, partial mainstreaming into selected subjects in the regular classes is often possible, thus exposing them to the normal educational environment into which some of them may later enter given appropriate resource support.

The advantage of the special class is that the child remains at home, maintains normal social interaction with neighborhood children, and has at least some contact with hearing peers in school. Although the child does not receive the constant spoken-language stimulation of the normal classroom, he or she is exposed to the hearing world for most of the day.

Residential/Day-School Placement

The number of hearing-impaired children attending residential/day school has dropped considerably since school districts have been required to provide increased local services. The population of residential/day schools now consists mainly of children from rural communities, where low-density population makes provision of a full range of special services very difficult, of children who need a total-communication teaching method when one is not locally available, and of children with multiple handicaps of which severe or profound hearing impairment is a major factor. Despite the disadvantage of living away from the family and being separated from the hearing world a residential placement provides many children with an opportunity for an education of which they would otherwise be deprived. For some children it truly represents the least limiting environment for learning. Such a placement may provide the only opportunity for the child to learn and to develop socially to his or her maximum capacity. It also makes available specialized preemployment training from teachers trained to educate young severely or profoundly hearing-impaired persons.

Residential schools may be state operated or state supported, or they may be approved private-school programs. In either case no charge is made to parents for room, board, and tuition.

THE DECISION-MAKING PROCESS

The Committee on the Handicapped

The parent of a preschool child known to be or suspected of being handicapped has as a resource a Committee on the Handicapped. The Committee must include a school psychologist, a teacher or administrator of special education, a physician, and a parent of a handicapped child. They have the responsibility for ensuring that handicapped children in their school district are identified and that their special needs are determined and provided for.

Before the child enters school, the Committee must obtain complete test data about him or her. They must have the parents' written permission to have the child evaluated. The parents must be advised how the child will be evaluated and be informed about the tests to be used. If the parents do not consent to the described evaluation, they have the right to discuss it with the Chief School Officer. If that does not satisfy their objection, they also have the right to an impartial hearing.

The Committee must determine:

1. Whether special services are necessary
2. Which placement would be appropriate
3. Which specific services should be provided
4. The degree of mainstreaming the child should have

Intelligence Testing

One or more intelligence tests is almost always included in the test battery administered to the hearing-impaired child. Intelligence testing often causes the parents greatest concern. This concern is justified because the hearing impairment and its effects on language and communication can often cause a child to function below capacity on standard intelligence tests. Moreover, parents have legitimate reason to wonder whether the psychologist who administers the evaluation has the necessary experience with hearing-impaired children to ensure valid test results.

In 1974, Levine investigated the extent of the special qualifications of 172 psychologists working with children with impaired hearing in 48 states. She found that 83 percent of the psychologists surveyed had no special training to work with the hard-of-hearing or deaf children whom they tested. Sullivan and Vernon (1979), psychologists with extensive testing and research experience with the hearing-impaired population, in discussing Levine's findings state, "The obvious conclusion from Levine's study is that psychologists lack the necessary training, skills, and specialized knowledge to provide adequate psychological services to hearing-impaired children" (p. 272). These authors emphasize that failure to be aware of certain crucial considerations in making psychological assessments of hearing-impaired children ". . . . can result in gross psycho-diagnostic errors of tragic consequences to the child, parents, and educational personnel" (p. 172).

You should be prepared to provide the parents of a hearing-impaired child with the information necessary to determine whether an intelligence evaluation meets the criteria identified as crucial to obtaining valid results. Vernon (1970, 1976) and Vernon and Brown (1964) have carefully described and explained the essential components for valid test administration. They have also identified and evaluated appropriate intelligence tests, achievement tests, and neuropsychological tests for use with hearing-impaired children. Sullivan and Vernon's assessment of intelligence tests appropriate for preschool and school-age populations is reproduced in Tables 15.2 and 15.3 at the end of this chapter.

Make a concerted effort to establish a working relationship with the psychologists who serve the children you work with. Usually you will find that a psychologist will appreciate an offer from you to work with him or her in obtaining an accurate measure of the child's intellectual capacity. Offer your services by informing the psychologist about the child's communication skills. Describe his or her language level, auditory comprehension, auditory-visual comprehension, and ability to follow directions. Discuss the mode of communication by which the child is most likely to comprehend, and how much the hearing aid contributes to the child's communication ability. Offer guidance concerning the conditions and methods that optimize the child's performance in a communication situation. It will be a long time before all psychologists who assess hearing-impaired children have had the training and experience necessary to ensure accurate test results. Until such time, you should make what contribution you can to ensure that the gross psycho-diagnostic errors to which Vernon refers are avoided.

Your Input to the Committee. The parents are invited to meet with the Committee to discuss the child's needs, to present relevant information, and to ask questions. Prior to this you should provide the parents with a carefully written description of the child's performance at the preschool level. All formal test results including audiologic data, measures of aided-hearing function, language level, and speech intelligibility should be given and explained. Pay particular attention to the child's ability to understand spoken language when wearing the aid(s). Comment on the effect of distance from the talker and poor signal-to-noise ratios if possible, as well as the child's dependency on visual cues to speech. Include an overall statement about the child's ability to communicate effectively with others. Discuss the child's speech intelligibility when communicating with adults not familiar with his or her speech patterns and when talking with other children.

Describe the child's social behavior in structured activities and in free-learning/play situations, as well as his or her interaction with other children. Assess general behavior and personality, noting the child's level of curiosity, motivation to understand things, perseverance, friendliness to children and adults, self-sufficiency, and contentedness. Include copies of preschool progress reports in your case summary.

You should also communicate your evaluation of the anticipated support needs. Discuss whether the child will need intensive cognitive and linguistic training, whether special amplification will be necessary for learning, how much supplementary teaching will be needed, whether full-time special education will be necessary. You should relate your assessment of support needs to the description you have given of the child's preschool performance.

It is necessary for you to carefully go over the report with the parents to explain the significance of the information given and the nature of your recommendations. The parents will then have information that they understand to present to the Committee on the Handicapped.

The parents may request that you accompany them to their meeting with the Committee, and that you present their case. You may perform this service as an audiologist, speech and hearing therapist, or teacher. Whatever your profession, if you agree, you should become fully familiar with the federal and state laws governing the educational decision process. Write to your State Education Department's Office for Education of the Handicapped to request all literature pertaining to special-educational placement and particularly to request materials written for parents. It is especially important for the parents to know their rights to an independent evaluation of their child's educational needs, and to know the process by which the Committee's recommendation can be appealed.

Individualized Education Program (IEP)

The IEP is a required written statement of the intended educational program for an individual child. It is required of the school district at the time the child enters special education. Ideally, for a child entering school the IEP should be developed as soon as the placement decision has been finalized. Because the parents have a right to participate in the planning conference, you should discuss with them what you feel would constitute appropriate goals. Justify your opinion by referring to your report.

The IEP should include the following data:

1. *A Statement of the Child's Present Educational Performance Level.* This consists of descriptions of language development, communication skills, motor development, social development, learning behaviors, and information about number skills and prereading skills. The preschool teacher will have this information. Working through the parent, or through direct contact with the

primary school or special-class teacher (with written permission of the parents), the preschool teacher should ensure that what is already known about the child's performance is available at the IEP planning meeting.

2. *The Short- and Long-Term Goals and Objectives for the School Year.* These should be related to the child's identified areas of learning and performance deficits. They should consist of general objectives to be aimed for over the long term and specific objectives whose attainment should lead to the achievement of the long-range goals. These goals should relate to the areas listed in the preceding paragraph. They should also include such specific areas as, for example, increasing the amount of time the hearing aid is worn, increasing the amount of time the child watches the speaker, improving the production of fricative sounds, improving sentence structure in written and spoken communication, increasing the number of communications the child makes in class. Because these goals should be based on needs that will have become apparent during the preschool experience, it is important that the teacher have the information you can provide.
3. *The Specific Support Services and Teaching Materials to Be Provided.* This should include specification of the amount of specialized tutoring the child will receive from the itinerant or resource-room teacher, the amount of speech-improvement training and special remedial-reading instruction that will be provided. Also included should be the recommendation about the child's need for educational amplification. These are clearly specialized aspects of IEP planning about which the audiologist and the preschool staff can offer valuable help to the teacher.
4. *The Amount of Mainstreaming the Child Will Experience.* The IEP must identify whether the child will participate in regular classes with hearing children, for which subjects, and for how many periods. The preschool teacher and hearing therapist will be able to advise the school district about the child's known learning capabilities and the extent to which the child can keep up with normal children. The likelihood of success in a full or part-time mainstream placement can be addressed by the preschool personnel.
5. *The Way in which the Progress Toward Goals Can Be Objectively Determined.* The classroom teacher will have his or her own methods for evaluating the progress of a child. However, he or she is usually very receptive to suggestions as to how to assess the handicapped child in a manner that provides a fair evaluation. Certainly, it would be helpful to suggest guidelines to help to ensure that the method of test administration will be appropriate for the child's communication abilities.

The guide for parents of handicapped children published by The University of the State of New York (1978) suggests that the parents make a list of questions and concerns about the program being proposed. Among the questions parents should ask are:

What do the test results show about my child's abilities?
What academic subjects will my child be studying?
What services will be provided to my child to help him or her reach these goals?
What type of physical education will he or she be offered?
What regular classroom experiences will be available to my child?
What extracurricular activities will my child participate in?
How do other children in the class react to my child?
What behavior problems has my child shown?

How is the teacher handling these problems?
How often will my child's progress be checked?
When will I receive a report on his or her progress?

Finally you may be asked by the parents to aid them in an appeal of the placement recommendation made by the Committee on the Handicapped. If so, you should consider the following points:

1. Did the Committee follow all the requirements of the State Law on due process?
2. Were the parents fully advised in writing and in detail of their rights?
3. Was a detailed description of the recommendation provided?
4. Was a full list of tests and reports used in reaching the placement decision provided?
5. Were all tests administered by appropriately licensed professionals?
6. Were tests and test procedures appropriate for assessment of a hearing-impaired child?
7. Were a full range of tests administered?
8. Were the test data used current?
9. Were the parents informed in writing of their right to an independent evaluation, and advised where to obtain it?
10. Were the conclusions reached by the Committee based on the concrete evidence of the available data?
11. Were any important data lacking?

We have yet to clearly define the optimal role that the audiologist, speech and hearing therapist, and/or specialist teacher can play in the educational process. We do know that the law does not require that they be members of a Committee on the Handicapped even when the child being considered is hearing impaired. However, the parents can request that appropriate specialists be added to the Committee in order to fairly assess their child's needs. The parents may also request that a professional appropriately qualified in hearing impairment accompany them to a meeting with the Committee on the Handicapped or to a subsequent appeal hearing. The parents are essential in ensuring a fair and thorough consideration of their child's educational needs and placement. Unless proven otherwise, the Committee should be considered to be as concerned as the parents about ensuring the best possible placement for the child. You can be very influential in helping the parents relate to Committee and in facilitating the Committee in the achievement of its goals.

Once an educational placement has finally been made and accepted, the task becomes one of managing the child within a structured educational setting. This is the topic to which we will next turn our attention.

REFERENCES

Levine, E., Psychological Tests and Practices with the Deaf: A Survey of the State of the Art. *Volta Review,* 1974, 76, 298–319.

Northcott, W., ed., *The Hearing Impaired Child in a Regular Classroom.* Washington D.C.: The Alexander Graham Bell Assoc. for the Deaf, 1973.

State of New York, *Your Child's Right to an Education: A Guide for Parents of Handicapped Children in New York State.* The State Education Department Office for Education of Children with Handicapping Conditions. New York: The University of the State of New York, 1978.

Sullivan, P., and M. Vernon, "Psychological Assessment of Hearing Impaired Children," *School Psychology Digest, 8,* 1979, 271–290.

Vernon, M. "Psychological Evaluation of Hearing Impaired Children," in *Communication Assessment and Intervention Strategies,* ed. L. Lloyd. Baltimore: University Park Press, 1976, pp. 195–223.

Vernon, M., "The Psychological Examination," in *The Hard of Hearing Child,* eds. F. Berg and S. Fletcher. New York: Grune & Stratton, Inc., 1970, pp. 217–231.

Vernon, M., and D. Brown, "A Guide to Psychological Tests and Testing Procedures in the Evaluation of Deaf and Hard-of-Hearing Children," *Journal of Speech and Hearing Disorders, 29,* 1964, 414–423.

SUGGESTED READING

Abeson, A. N. Bolick, and J. Hass, *A Primer on Due Process: Educational Decisions for Handicapped Children.* Reston, Va.: Council for Exceptional Children, 1975.

Advisory Council for the Deaf, *A Comprehensive Plan for the Education of Hearing Impaired Children and Youth in Massachusetts.* Massachusetts Department of Education, Division of Special Education, 1975.

Bascaglia, L., and E. Williams, eds., *Human Advocacy and PL 94–142. The Educator's Roles.* Thorofare, N.J.: Charles B. Slack, Inc., 1979.

Berry, K. E., *Models for Mainstreaming.* Sioux Falls, S.D.: Adapt Press, 1972.

Bishop, M., ed., *Mainstreaming, Practical Ideas for Educating Hearing-Impaired Students.* Washington, D.C.: Alexander Graham Bell Assoc. for the Deaf, 1979.

Griffing, B. L., "Planning Educational Programs and Services for Hard of Hearing Children," in *The Hard of Hearing Child: Clinical and Educational Management,* eds. F. Berg, and S. Fletcher, pp. 233–244. New York: Grune & Stratton, Inc., 1970.

Healy, W. C., "Integrated Education," in *A Bicentennial Monograph on Hearing Impairment,* ed. R. Frisina, pp. 68–75. Washington, D.C.: Alexander Graham Bell Assoc. for the Deaf, 1976.

Ross, M., "Assessment of the Hearing Impaired Prior to Mainstreaming," in *Mainstream Education for Hearing Impaired Children and Youth,* ed. G. Nix. New York: Grune & Stratton, Inc., 1976.

Torres, S., *A Primer on Individualized Education Programs for Handicapped Children.* Reston, Va.: Council for Exceptional Children, 1977.

Yater, V., *Mainstreaming of Children with Hearing Loss: Practical Guidelines and Implications.* Springfield, Ill.: Charles C Thomas, Publisher, 1977.

TABLE 15.2 Assessment of Intelligence Tests for Infants and Preschoolers (Sullivan and Vernon, 1979)

Test	*Age Range*	*Publisher*
Bayley Scales of Infant Development (Bayley, 1969)	2 mos.–30 mos.	New York: Psychological Corporation
Evaluation The Mental Scale, Motor Scale and Infant Behavior Record are well standardized developmental measures for hearing children and meet satisfactory reliability standards. Although not valid for predicting later functioning or achievement, the three scales provide valuable estimates of *current* developmental status that may be used with hearing-impaired infants. Approximately 36 of the 163 items on the Mental Scale require auditory and/or language skills. These items should be corrected in final scoring according to the procedure employed on the Merrill Palmer Scale of Mental Tests (Stutsman, 1931). The items should be attempted to gain data on language skills using the child's communication mode. However, many hearing-impaired children may be expected to fail most auditory/language related items. All items are arranged developmentally. If the child passes a performance item at a higher level than a language item, the language item(s) should be credited that precede the successfully completed performance item.		
Developmental Activities Screening Inventory (DASI) (Du Bose and Langley, 1977)	6 mos.–5 years	New York: New York Times Teaching Resources Company
Evaluation This is a valuable performance *screening* measure of cognitive development. Test items tap a variety of skills including fine-motor coordination, cause-effect and means-end relationships, number concepts, size discrimination, and association and seriation abilities. Limitations include an inadequate description of normative data and procedures in the manual and the composite developmental quotient in a psychometrically weak quantification of test performance. Concurrent validity appears to be adequate but reliability data are not reported. Items are untimed, easily administered, and do not penalize children with auditory impairments or language disorders. Administration adaptations are also available for visually impaired youngsters. The test appears to be appropriate for use with multiply handicapped hearing-impaired children. Instructional suggestions for the concepts assessed are included.		
Hiskey-Nebraska Test of Learning Aptitude (Hiskey, 1966)	3–17 years	Lincoln, Neb.: Union College Press
Evaluation The Hiskey is one of the best tests available for use with hearing-impaired children. Hearing-impaired and hearing norms are provided and comparisons, when appropriate, can be made of a given child's performance. Deaf norms are to be used, regardless of the child's degree of hearing loss, when pantomime administration directions are employed. Hearing norms should be used when the verbal subtest directions or total communication are employed. The discrepancy between scores using hearing and deaf norms is most probably due to the use of pantomime instructions. Although useful at younger age levels, the Hiskey should be supplemented with another measure on this table at 3 and 4 years of age. Pantomime subtest directions are easy to master. However, the test should be administered by skilled examiners familiar with its administration procedures. Although normative data are inadequately described, reliability and concurrent validity data are adequate.		

Merrill-Palmer Scale of Mental Tests (Stutsman, 1931)	2–5 years	Chicago: Stoelting Company

Evaluation

This test requires a skilled examiner with a thorough knowledge of the psychology of hearing impairment. Although the norms are dated, the variety of items have interest appeal for both language-impaired and hearing-impaired children. Adjustments in scoring can be made for items that are refused, omitted, or failed because of language difficulties. The time factor in scoring some items, however, is a weakness with hearing-impaired children. The Merrill-Palmer is a useful screening test to ascertain developmental functioning and may be used as a supplemental performance measure with another test on this table with young hearing-impaired children. This is one of the few tests with an adequate number of 2- and 3-year-olds in the standardization sample. Subtest instructions may have to be given in pantomime or total communication.

Smith-Johnson Nonverbal Performance Scale (Smith and Johnson, 1977)	2–4 years	Los Angeles: Western Psychological Services

Evaluation

This is an excellent test for use with young hearing-impaired children. Sex, hearing, and hearing-impaired norms are provided. However, the hearing norms are somewhat dated (1960) and the hearing-impaired normative sample included 36% with profound hearing losses and 64% with mild and moderate loss. The majority of hearing-impaired subjects were hard-of-hearing rather than severely and profoundly deafened. The test may be more appropriate for use with the hard-of-hearing. Subtest directions are presented in pantomime and many repetitions may be given. Although not recommended by the authors, total communication is suggested in the administration of this test to children who use this communication mode. Fourteen categories of subtests are presented and the child's performance level is categorized as below average, average, or above average in comparison to peers of the same sex and chronological age. As may be expected in preschool measures, test-retest reliabilities are low. Both reliability and validity data with hearing-impaired children are inadequately described in the manual. This test might also be used with hearing children who exhibit language difficulties.

Wachs Analysis of Cognitive Structures (Wachs and Vaughn, 1978)	3–6 years	Los Angeles: Western Psychological Services

Evaluation

This test is based upon Piagetian theories of cognitive development and is primarily nonverbal in format. It appears to have promise for use with the hearing impaired although they were not included in the normative sample. This test might be used to supplement another measure on this table.

Wechsler Preschool and Primary Scale of Intelligence Performance subtests (Wechsler, 1967)	3 years, 11 mos.– 6 years, 8 mos.	New York: Psychological Corporation

Evaluation

This Scale is not recommended for use with hearing-impaired children. Most subtest directions are difficult to explain either orally, in pantomime, or in total communication.

TABLE 15.3 Assessment of Intelligence Tests for School-Age Children

Test	*Age Range*	*Publisher*
Arthur Adaptation of the Leiter International Performance Scale (Arthur, 1950)	2–18 years	Chicago: Stoelting
	Evaluation	
The Leiter is not appropriate for use with very young and preschool hearing-impaired children because norms for these age ranges are extrapolated from those for older children. In general, the test is psychometrically inadequate, inappropriately standardized, and lacking in reliability and validity for use with all hearing-impaired children. These limitations offset the ease of pantomime administration. See Ratcliffe and Ratcliffe (1979) for a review of these issues.		
Hiskey-Nebraska Test of Learning Aptitude (Hiskey, 1966)	6–17 years	Lincoln, Neb.: Union College Press
	Evaluation	
This test is excellent for use with all school age hearing-impaired children.		
Progressive Matrices (Raven, 1948)	9 years to adulthood	Los Angeles: Western Psychological Services
	Evaluation	
Raven's Progressive Matrices are most appropriate for use as a second test to substantiate another more comprehensive intelligence test. The matrices are easy to administer and score. However, care should be taken to insure that the child is not responding impulsively to subtest items.		
Wechsler Intelligence Scale for Children—Revised Performance Scale (Wechsler, 1974)	6–16 years	New York: Psychological Corporation
	Evaluation	
The WISC-R Performance Scale is an excellent test for use with school-age hearing-impaired children. It is ideally used with the Hiskey-Nebraska Test of Learning Aptitude as a supplementary performance test. The Performance Scale has been standardized with a hearing-impaired sample (Anderson & Sisco, 1977). However, research is needed to demonstrate the efficacy of these norms. A variety of sign systems and administrations were used in the standardization procedure which may account for the population mean IQ of 95 and standard deviation of 18. These parameters must be considered in interpreting scores. Previously recommended administration modifications such as pantomime and visual aids should not be employed if the child is instructed in total communication. All six subtests should be administered. If the child has undue difficulty with Picture Arrangement and Coding only, which is frequently the case with the hearing impaired, the PIQ may be prorated from the other four subtests. If the child has difficulty with Coding only, Mazes may be substituted and the PIQ computed from 5 subtests. However, these procedures affect test reliability and underscore the importance of administering more than one performance intelligence measure.		

16

Assessment of the Primary School Child

The roles of the audiologist, speech and hearing therapist, and teacher of the deaf in the management of the school-age child are changing rapidly. This reflects evolving philosophies and models for the education of hearing-impaired children. The greatest changes originate from the increasing mainstreaming of handicapped children into normal school classrooms. As a result, many teachers of the deaf, who previously would have taught academic content to hearing-impaired children in a separate class, now find themselves called upon to provide, instead, a support service to the normal classroom teacher. Many speech and hearing therapists, who previously saw few hearing-impaired children with more than moderate difficulties, are now expected to assume a major role in providing speech and language services to children with complex communication and learning needs. Even when such children are served by an itinerant or resource teacher of the deaf, they also may be eligible for extra speech and language training. Likewise, the concepts of the responsibilities and capabilities of the audiologist in contributing to the management of school-age children with impaired hearing are undergoing change. Models have been developed and implemented that, in addition to utilizing the audiologists' clinical diagnostic competencies, also seek from them input into the educational planning and monitoring of the children's school experiences. Audiologists are expected to be capable of not only diagnosing a hearing impairment, but also of advising administrators and teachers about its nature and the effects it is likely to exert on a child's ability to learn in an auditory-oral environment. Thus they must be able to anticipate the special learning needs the child will encounter, to explain the contribution that amplification makes to the child's potential performance, and to assist teacher/therapists in maximizing the child's residual hearing.

These changes have made obsolete many of our previous models for providing aural rehabilitation to school-age children. No longer can we confine our intervention to the provision of lip-reading and auditory training. Nor can we continue to work in isolation from the classroom teacher. We will be effective only when our concern is for the improvement of the children's communication skills in the learning environment, and for their attainment of the adjustment necessary for the optimal use of those skills. This is a task that calls for integrating communication training with classroom learning. What we say and do as audiologists and as teacher/therapists must have a direct educational impact. It must facilitate the learning process and increase the child's viability in the classroom. This philosophy necessitates that our intervention program be designed (1) to meet the needs of the teacher in accommodating the child in the regular or special classroom; and (2) to provide the child with the communication skills and strategies needed to succeed in class.

THE NEEDS OF THE TEACHER

The placement of the hearing-impaired child in the classroom necessitates adaptive behavior on the part of the teacher. The teacher's ability to accept and help the child will depend on his or her understanding of how the hearing impairment will handicap the child's ability to learn in the structure of the class. This is as true for the teacher of a separate class for hearing-impaired children as for the teacher in the normal classroom. Without a meaningful profile of the child's communicative-learning abilities, it is extremely difficult for the teacher to accommodate the child's special needs. The placement of a hearing-impaired child in any classroom without providing such information puts the teacher in an untenable position and seriously jeopardizes the child's chances of success.

The information required by the teacher relates to the child's capacity to function in the learning situation. It concerns the child's ability to receive, process, and impart information. The teacher needs to know about the child's

1. Ability to hear the teacher when he or she speaks to the class
2. Ability to hear other children
3. Level of language competency
4. Ability to follow spoken directions
5. Ability to receive, comprehend, and learn from orally presented information
6. Need to use visual speech cues
7. Ability to comprehend in classroom noise, particularly speech noise
8. Ability to understand speech in a group situation

It should be the responsibility of the audiologist to interpret test data and to provide a statement of the child's expected performance in terms of these factors. The teacher should be asked to observe the child over a period of weeks to determine whether the expectations are being fulfilled. If the child fails to perform as expected it will be necessary to consider modifying intervention practices. Integrating the services of the teacher, audiologist, and speech and hearing teacher/therapist can be surprisingly successful. It allows for the pragmatic monitoring of the effectiveness of the various intervention procedures, which become dynamic as the result of constant review.

Audiologic Description and Monitoring of the Child

The audiologist has the key role of ensuring that the child's use of residual hearing is optimal at all times. This necessitates careful assessment of the amount and pattern of residual hearing, and periodic monitoring to detect any changes that may occur. Audiometric and impedance monitoring of the function of the middle ear to detect the occurrence of any conductive overlay is essential to ensure early medical intervention to minimize the period of increased hearing deficit that results. Less frequently, monitoring will detect further sensorineural deterioration, which may necessitate a change in the amplification specification. Teachers, speech and hearing therapists/teachers, parents, and the child must be counseled to be alert to any apparent changes in the child's ability to function auditorily. Although annual or semiannual audiologic reevaluations are recommended, it is often an alert observer who first notices a change in the child's auditory behavior when a problem arises. All of us who serve the child can thus contribute to audiologic monitoring.

As important as monitoring the child's hearing level is checking the hearing aid(s), which constitutes an extension of the child's auditory system. It, too, must be kept functioning at maximum efficiency. Thus, in addition to the daily checks of the hearing aid that parents, teachers' aides, or the older hearing-impaired child should perform, periodic electroacoustic analysis of the hearing aid is important to ensure that it continues to meet specifications. If the aid is subjected to trauma (for example, if it is dropped, left on a hot radiator, allowed to get wet or damaged in any way), it should be reassessed as soon as possible. If a child has an individual FM unit, the audiologist should talk with the teacher in person or by phone to check that he or she feels confident about using the microphone transmitter. If not, the audiologist should arrange for a person familiar with the unit (special teacher or manufacturer's representative) to provide the teacher with the understanding needed. Even trained teachers of the deaf are often unfamiliar with educational-amplification units. Until each school district has its own educational audiologist or consultant, each audiologist must be prepared to offer assistance to the professional staff in schools of the children he or she tests.

In the chapter on the practical applications of amplification we considered the information that the audiologist can generate about the communication abilities of a child. We can now review that information in terms of its usefulness to the teacher and therapist/teacher (Figure 16.1).

The Unaided and Aided Audiogram. This information will help the teacher and therapist/teacher to better appreciate the extent to which the hearing aid brings sound close to normal levels of loudness. The thresh-

Figure 16.1 The audiologist must be prepared to offer assistance to the teacher. (Courtesy of Buffalo City School System)

old curve for aided hearing should be explained in terms of how loud normal conversational speech will sound when the child is wearing the aid. Frequency ranges in which even amplified sound remains inaudible or barely audible should be explained in terms of the resultant distortion of speech sounds and the heavy dependence of the child on other cues to compensate for the missing units. The audiologist should emphasize the improvement obtained with the hearing aid, stressing the importance of its continuous use. Conversely, it should be emphasized that, even with the aid, the child does not hear normally, only better. The teacher should be left with a realistic impression of how much the aid reduces the handicapping effects of the hearing impairment on communication, and how much difficulty the child will continue to have even when wearing the aid.

Speech-Audiometric Results. The audiologist should translate the findings of speech-awareness discrimination and comprehension tests into estimated behavioral capabilities.

Awareness. The audiologist should predict how readily the child in class will be aware that he or she is being spoken to and how easily the child's attention may be gained by calling his or her name. The audiologist should also explain whether awareness will decrease as the speaker-child distance and the signal-to-noise ratio decreases.

Discrimination/Comprehension. The therapist/teacher should be ad-

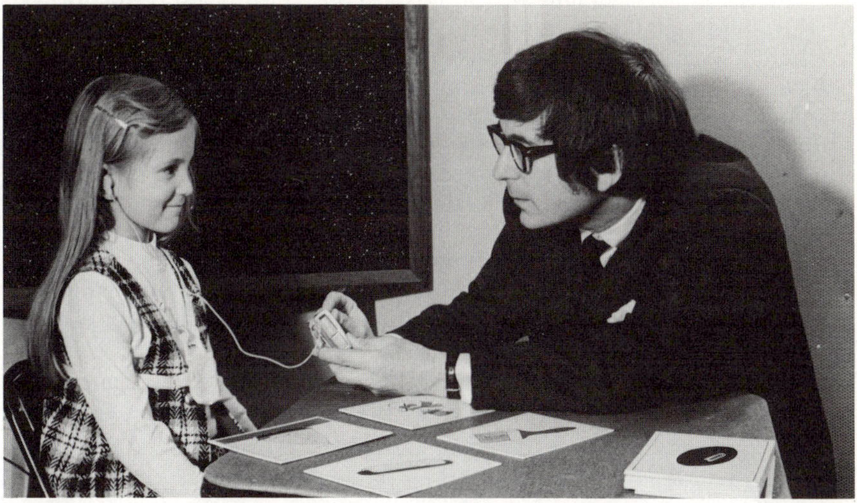

Figure 16.2 The audiologist can assess approximate discrimination percentage using familiar words embedded in sentences. (Courtesy of The State University of New York at Buffalo)

vised how much of what is said directly to the child will be intelligible when the child is wearing the aid(s) and by how much this will be reduced when the child is not familiar with the topic. The approximate percentage discrimination using aided hearing can be derived from the discrimination scores for familiar words in simple sentences (Figure 16.2). The audiologist must stress that discrimination and comprehension are not synonymous. The percentage discrimination represents a measure of auditory function prerequisite to comprehension of words in sentences. Comprehension is a cognitive linguistic ability that makes use of auditory information and cognitive linguistic experience to predict intended meaning. Thus a child may easily comprehend familiar or restricted messages by aided hearing alone, but may have considerable difficulty in comprehending new or unfamiliar content and language. The audiologist should also explain the extent to which the child is dependent upon visual cues to augment comprehension of speech. This information should be used to help the teacher become aware of the extent to which watching the speaker will influence the amount of speech information the child can process successfully. It should be pointed out that such classroom activities as following the text of a book while the teacher explains certain ideas, taking dictation or notes while the teacher is talking, understanding what is said by classmates not within the child's visual field, watching movies or videotapes when the speaker is not on screen, listening to audiotapes, or watching filmstrips when the teacher's face is not visible all limit the child's ability to follow speech to a degree dependent on the child's need for visual speech cues. Monitoring the child's performance in such situations will identify specific problem settings and permit problem-solving strategies to be developed by the management team.

Speech in noise. Finally the audiologist should use the results of tests of the child's ability to understand speech in noise to explain to the teacher how classroom noise levels may affect the child's communication behavior. The comparative quiet/noise condition scores for sentence discrimination, ability to follow topics, to follow instructions, and to answer simple questions should be used to predict how much difficulty the child will encounter under high, average, and low signal-to-noise ratios. Classroom activities likely to result in these different listening conditions (for example, high signal-to-noise ratios during quiet study or when the teacher and child are in one-to-one close contact) should be identified. The increased difficulty the child will encounter in learning from oral presentation of new material, particularly at poor signal-to-noise ratios, should be stressed.

The following report on Elizabeth is an example of how audiologic test findings might be interpreted for a classroom teacher:

Elizabeth

Elizabeth has a moderate, permanent hearing impairment in both ears. She is able to hear the low tones of speech and noise quite well. Thus she is aware of things going on around her, including people speaking. However, her difficulty hearing middle- and high-pitched tones makes it very hard for her to comprehend speech without a hearing aid. Without the aid she hears conversational speech at a just-audible level; a very loud voice would be necessary to make speech comfortably loud.

Elizabeth now has two hearing aids. With these aids she hears speech at a comfortable listening level. She is able to discriminate most of what she hears without needing to watch the speaker. However, you should know that:

1. In a noisy situation when others are talking, Elizabeth's discrimination by hearing alone drops to 65 percent. She misses over a quarter of what is said.
2. When Elizabeth is 15 feet from the speaker she hears clearly only a little over half of what is said. At this distance in noise, she barely understands speech.
3. Even with the aid, Elizabeth has difficulty hearing high-pitched speech sounds such as s, z, f, v, sh, ch, t. The s and sh are noticeably defective in her speech because she does not hear them well.
4. Elizabeth compensates well for her hearing impairment by watching the speaker. When she can clearly see the speaker she scores 100 percent on a word-discrimination task in quiet, 88 percent in noise, and 78 percent in noise at 15 feet percent in noise.
5. Because of her long-standing hearing impairment Elizabeth's language level is 1½ years below her age. This makes understanding what she hears more difficult. Complex sentences, new vocabulary, unfamiliar concepts, even in good listening/watching conditions, cause Elizabeth to appear confused, to be afraid to volunteer a response, or to guess wildly. When she misunderstands you will need to determine whether it is because she has not heard or does not understand what has been asked.

Elizabeth will understand you best when:

1. Within 4 feet of you;
2. Able to see your face clearly;
3. The language and topic are familiar;
4. The noise level is low.

She will have difficulty understanding:

1. Group conversations;
2. Speakers whom she cannot see
3. Tape recordings
4. Television when she cannot see the speaker
5. New material presented orally

In summary, the audiologist's information should provide the therapist and teacher with a forthright and realistic assessment of the child's predicted potential for learning from oral presentation of information. It should identify, as specifically as possible, the types of classroom learning situations in which the child might be expected to manage acceptably well. It should also identify those classroom activities in which the child will probably have difficulty and in which special assistance or allowances will need to be provided.

The audiologist should guide the speech and hearing therapist/teacher in establishing a plan to systematically explore the child's auditory and auditory-visual speech-sound recognition across a full range of phonetic contexts. The therapist will usually appreciate help in determining the relative emphasis to place on auditory and visual speech-recognition training. The therapist will need guidance in the types of auditory-training activities that will be helpful, how to make best use of amplifying units, and when to use the hearing aid rather than an educational amplification unit. The implications of the child's pattern of aided hearing for speech and voice monitoring, along with predictions concerning which sounds may most easily be corrected or learned, should be discussed with the therapist/teacher.

The classroom teacher, as well as the speech and hearing therapist/teacher, should be encouraged to keep in contact with the audiologist and to communicate when any problems or questions arise concerning the child's hearing, the hearing aid, or the child's use of hearing in the classroom. It is also helpful to establish a relationship in which the classroom and special teacher have input into the periodic audiologic reassessment procedures. This can be achieved through feedback to the audiologist of information concerning the child's auditory learning behavior in school.

THE NEEDS OF THE CHILD

The needs of the hearing-impaired primary-school child can be identified as:

1. Audiologic description and monitoring
2. Provision and monitoring of amplification
3. Language and cognitive enrichment
4. Improvement of communication skills
5. Academic support
6. Informational counseling
7. Adjustment counseling

Audiologic Needs

We have already discussed describing and monitoring the child's hearing, together with assessing and checking the use of amplification. The only further comment necessary is to stress the importance of involving the child in this process to the extent of his or her ability to participate. The audiologist or therapist/teacher should train the school-age child to know what his or her capabilities with the hearing aid are. The child should be able to determine when he or she is not hearing or understanding as easily as possible. The child should also learn to assess new situations in terms of the type and extent of difficulty they present for following spoken communication. Educating the child to understand his or her problem will be discussed in the section on counseling later in this chapter.

Linguistic and Cognitive Needs

When a child enters the primary-school grades a dramatic acceleration of the complexity of the demands made upon language use occurs. Moreover language increasingly becomes the primary mode for stimulating conceptual growth. Instead of concrete experience's serving as the basis for increased cognitive awareness, with a complementary growth in language to define new experience, a reversal takes place. Language now progressively becomes the tool with which vicarious experiences are created. Learning increasingly becomes dependent upon a child's knowledge of language and upon the child's ability to acquire new concepts and associated vocabulary rapidly through spoken and printed forms. The language thus acquired is then used by the teacher and by the textbooks to create abstract experience, and to build additional new concepts. This is true both for the child in a special class and for the child mainstreamed into the regular classroom.

Although special classes are small in size (eight to ten students) the children usually vary in age and abilities, often by several years. Children are placed in special classes because the degree of their communication handicap is still too great to make full-time normal-class placement advisable. The rate of acquisition of knowledge, therefore, is slower than in a comparable class of hearing children because much time must be spent teaching concepts and language that are easily acquired by a hearing child.

The situation for the hearing-impaired child mainstreamed into a regular classroom is complicated even more by his or her reduced language abilities. The child will be one of anywhere from twenty-eight to forty children, all of whom usually have normal hearing. The child's ability to learn as a participative member of the class will depend upon his or her cognitive linguistic and communication skills. Unless you can document otherwise, you must assume that the child will experience difficulty in hearing all that is said in class. The child will also have trouble comprehending some of the things he or she does hear. Because the child's language competence is often not up to the level for his or her age, it is likely that he or she will experience reading difficulties due to restricted vocabulary and reduced comprehension of syntactic structures. Reading is often laborious and unrewarding for the young hearing-impaired child. It becomes more of a problem as the ideas expressed and the language in which they are explained become increasingly complex. Poor reading skills will affect performance in all subjects. Texts, which are frequently poorly written, fail to motivate children with normal reading abilities. The hearing-impaired child will simply not learn from them without individual help. With whom does the responsibility for providing that extra support lie?

Only when each professional who works with a child accepts his or her role as a member of a coordinated resource team will the child achieve success. This team should include the parents, the teacher, speech and hearing therapist/teachers, the remedial-reading teacher, and the audiologist. In a special class the teacher of the hearing impaired, together with an aide, will play the major role in teaching new concepts and associated language. They will also teach basic communication skills and reading. The needs of the children in the special classroom are usually too great, however, to permit the teacher to accommodate them all so that support and guidance from the audiologist in the terms we have already considered are always necessary. In addition the special-class teacher will also look to the speech and hearing therapist/teacher to provide extra services to most, if not all, of the children. The needs of each child will have to be defined in order that an integrated support plan can be agreed upon. The therapist/teacher must be prepared to reinforce understanding of concepts taught in class, to review and reinforce the vocabulary and phrases by which those concepts are described and discussed, and to reinforce the grammar and structure of those expressions. In particular the therapist/teacher must be ready to train the child to recognize the spoken forms of those words and phrases through vision and audition, and through audition only. The therapist/teacher must be able to recognize potential perceptual confusions between and among words and phrases, and he or she must train the child to improve the ability to resolve such problems through better use of contextual cues and improved use of auditory and visual-speech cues. Finally the therapist/teacher must help the child to articulate the speech sounds with which he or she has difficulty, and to help the child approximate normal, suprasegmental patterning of well-constructed spoken language. The parents will need to be kept informed of what is being learned in class, of the particular type of extra support being given. They must be advised how they, too, can contribute to the reinforcement of content and skills through home stimulation and support of communicative and learning behavior.

In normal classrooms the teachers cannot be expected to make major changes in their teaching techniques to aid hearing-impaired children. Each teacher's primary responsibility is to the class as a whole. The teacher has only limited time to give to hearing-impaired children, and has not had training in how to deal with their special needs. For most mainstreamed children, success in school is dependent on the effectiveness of the services of the support team. The resource teacher of the hearing impaired and the therapist/teacher must be prepared to coordinate their intervention procedures with classroom academic content. The resource teacher reviews and reinforces what is learned in class by working on the appropriate concepts involved, and is responsible for ensuring that the children have acquired the subject skills necessary to the course.

The therapist/teacher will use the same content and language to train auditory and auditory-visual recognition skills. He or she will work with the child's ability to communicate the ideas acquired. To this end the therapist/teacher will help build language skills to improve the child's ability to articulate clearly and to modulate the voice effectively. The therapist/teacher will also work with the functional uses of language, helping the children to improve interpersonal communication skills in the classroom.

To achieve these goals the teacher and the therapist/teacher will be concerned with the child's ability to comprehend and use spoken and written forms of language. Comprehension involves both the ability to recognize common linguistic principles and the ability to make judgments about the correctness of grammar and structure. As the teacher/therapist, you should aim to assess both components. Production of language requires:

1. An understanding of age-related concepts
2. Vocabulary, grammar, and syntax appropriate to the verbal expression of those concepts
3. Awareness of the pragmatics of language—that is, its use in a variety of communication situations for a variety of purposes

Assessment of the child's language competencies is necessary for two reasons: (1) it permits you and the teacher to better understand the nature of the difficulties the child may be expected to encounter in class; and (2) it permits you to select intervention procedures specific to the child's needs.

Unless you have been well trained in language assessment, your first need will be to overcome the sinking feeling of inadequacy that we all feel when confronted with an essential task for which we know ourselves to be less than well prepared. Such evaluations are often not made at all for hearing-impaired children, and after you have completed the first two or three, you will begin to feel more confident not only in assessment, but also in the validity of your work with the child.

You should begin by referring to several excellent reviews of language-assessment practices. These will familiarize you with the principle of testing and will identify some of the standardized tests and descriptive methods you can use. The recommended readings are: Miller (1978), Kretschmer and Kretschmer (1978), Rees (1978), Rice (1978), Crystal, Fletcher, and Garman (1976), Cicciarelli, Broen, and Siegel (1976), Siegel and Broen (1976), Tyack and Gottsleben (1974).

Your aim in assessing language is to develop a profile that permits you to identify the type of language structures that present difficulty to the child in comprehension and production. The profile should also indicate the extent of the child's knowledge of the concepts and words represented by those structures.

Vocabulary. It is helpful to know the child's level of general vocabulary. For this purpose you can use such standardized tests as the *Peabody Picture Vocabulary Test* (Dunn, 1965). In this test the child is shown four pictures on a page and is asked to identify the picture that illustrates the test word spoken by the examiner. The child's score can then be used to determine vocabulary age. Under no circumstances should this score be used to determine a hearing-impaired child's verbal intelligence quotient.

Another standard vocabulary test is the *Full Range Picture Identification Test,* Forms A and B (Ammons & Ammons, 1948). This test provides a measure of vocabulary comprehension from two years of age to adulthood. Like the Peabody test, it requires the child to identify a picture that correctly illustrates the word named by the tester.

The *Assessment of Children's Language Comprehension Test* (Foster, Giddan, & Stark, 1973) Part A comprises a fifty-item vocabulary test. Parts B, C, and D extend the use of this vocabulary to assess comprehension of sentences containing two, three, and four elements. The norms are provided for each six-month interval for children from 3 years 0 months to 6 years 11 months along with mean scores for educationally handicapped children.

A more complex measure of the child's vocabulary comprehension in relation to the norms is provided by two subtests—Auditory Reception and Auditory Association—of the *Illinois Test of Psycholinguistic Abilities* (Kirk, McCarthy, & Kirk, 1968). To test auditory reception the child is asked to respond to simple sentences such as "Do dogs eat?" "Do children climb?" The auditory association subtest asks the child to complete the second of two analogous sentences.

1. A daddy is big; a baby is ________.
2. Grass is green; sugar is ________.

Note, as Siegel and Broen (1976) point out, that the ITPA test requires the child to demonstrate more than knowledge of pertinent vocabulary. The child must also be able to deal with the syntactic and semantic relationships involved. Thus, failure to correctly complete an item is informative in terms of the norms, but it does not necessarily indicate that the missing word is not known.

More important to your task of selectively upgrading the child's ability to perform school tasks is the assessment of subject-specific concepts and vocabulary. To achieve this you, the student, a parent or older sibling, or an aide must go through a lesson in a text book, an assignment topic, an instruction manual, or other source books to identify in context key vocabulary and phrases essential to a particular task. Over time, you will use these lists to develop a teaching curriculum and accompanying texts, which can be used to identify deficits in the child's conceptual and vocabulary knowledge as they apply to present and projected class needs. Adopting this approach Englemann (1967) developed an inventory, *The Basic Concept Inventory,* to assess a child's knowledge of concepts essential to beginning academic learning. The test, which ranges from preschool to 10 years of age, requires that the child: (1) point to a picture or give a yes-no response; (2) repeat sentences spoken by the tester and answer questions; and (3) be aware of patterns.

Boehm (1971) also developed a nonstandardized test that assesses the child's basic understanding of concepts fundamental to the ability to function in kindergarten and first grade. *The Boehm Test of Basic Concepts* presents words in the context of directions that may be expected to occur in school. The child is instructed to identify meanings of words such as: "more," "below," "at the top," "first" by following spoken directions in which these words are used. You can add to such concepts to assess the abilities of older children by giving directions such as "last but one," "opposite," "above," "odd numbers," "column," "previous," "every other one." The principles of the Boehm and Engelmann tests have been incorporated into a commercially available concept-development program STEP (CC Publications, Inc., 1978), which allows for the assessment of a base-line level for a child beginning the development program.

When a child is old enough to complete written assignments, these can be used to gain further insight into the types of vocabulary deficits and confusions experienced.

By combining standardized and nonstandardized tests with inventory information you can gain insight into the child's concept-word needs. You then can develop a program of specific and general concept and vocabulary enrichment with high relevance to academic demands (Figure 16.3).

Knowledge of Grammar and Syntax. A number of standardized tests exist to permit assessment of the child's understanding of the grammar and syntactic structures of language. *The Northwestern Syntax Screening Test* (Lee, 1969) provides a means of screening a comprehension and expressive use of morphologic and syntactic structures in the age range from three to eight years. The test screens such grammatical components as personal, reflexive, and possessive pronouns, plurality, verb tenses, types of questions, negatives, and so on. Identification of an appropriate picture by pointing in the response mode for the comprehension section; spoken responses are required for the expressive section.

Test for Auditory Comprehension of Language (Carrow, 1973) uses picture identification to test a child's comprehension of vocabulary and a wide range of grammatical structures. Responses are scored correct or incorrect with age norms given for 3 years, 0 months to 6 years, 11 months.

Carrow Elicited Language Inventory (Carrow, 1974) is a test of the child's ability to use grammar in expressive language. Norms are provided for the age range 3 years, 0 months to 7 years, 11 months. The test consists of the child's imitating sentences modeled by the examiner. Responses, recorded on audiotape, are subsequently scored for a wide range of grammatical categories.

Developmental Sentence Analysis (Lee, 1974) uses samples of the child's spontaneous speech to identify the presence of a range of eight syntactic categories comprising parts of speech and types of sentences. The test items are developmentally weighted and scoring allows for comparison of the child's performance to that of the normative sample. The age norms range from 2 years, 0 months to 6 years, 11 months.

Figure 16.3 Formal and informal tests provide a baseline for beginning a developmental language program. (Courtesy of Buffalo City School System)

Illinois Test of Psycholinguistic Abilities (Kirk, McCarthy, & Kirk, 1968), subtest Grammatic Closure, consists of thirty-three incomplete sentences. The child is asked to complete each sentence spoken by the examiner to correspond to a picture shown simultaneously.

Structured Photographic Language Test (Werner & Kresheck, 1978) uses colored photographs to elicit a sample of the language of children in the 4 years, 0 months to 8 years, 11 months age range. A wide variety of syntactic and grammatical structures are assessed and analyzed to provide a developmental age and expressive language profile for the child.

None of the tests currently available provides for a detailed analysis of the child's specific weaknesses in the use of grammar and syntax. Few teachers or therapist/teachers have either the linguistic training or the time to perform such a task. The extent of such an analysis is documented by Kretschmer and Kretschmer (1978). Nevertheless, selective and experimental use of some of the tests identified will provide you with an understanding of the general areas of language processing in which the child needs assistance. Given this information you will be able to develop an intervention program designed to provide the child with the specific cognitive and linguistic knowledge without which academic content cannot be comprehended. You will be able to teach or reinforce subject specific concepts and foster vocabulary acquisition. The results of tests of grammar and syntax will alert you to the types of structural rules with which the child experiences difficulties, thus making it possible for you to teach or review these in terms of the child's school-work topics.

Pragmatics. To be accepted by any group an individual is expected to know and conform to the behavioral expectancies of that group. Just as there is a code for nonverbal behavior, so is there a code for verbal behavior. This code governs how and when we are permitted to communicate in a wide range of social situations. Rees (1978) has provided an excellent introduction to this topic with an explanation of the implications of pragmatics for normal and disordered language development. Rees refers to Hymes's description of the pragmatics of language as pertaining to knowledge of "who can say what, in what way, where and when, by what means and to whom" (Hymes, 1971, p. 15).

The hearing-impaired child who is in a regular school class will benefit greatly from being aware of the different types of communicative behaviors and language use that are expected in different situations. The need for discriminative communicative behavior grows as the child moves through the upper grades into the postprimary years.

As Rees (1978) notes, although pragmatic approaches to the study of language disorders have demonstrated that many hearing-impaired subjects indeed perform more poorly than is normal in the use of the structural language, few specific suggestions have been advanced as to appropriate training methods. It would seem logical, therefore, to consider the specific types of communicative behaviors expected of the hearing-impaired child in the school situation. This is an extension of the principles concerning the molding of sociolinguistic behaviors, which we considered in Chapter 14. It is important to discuss with the teacher and the parent the child's use of the language so far acquired. Find out whether the child is able to use language effectively for the six functions suggested by Halliday (1975). These are:

1. *Instrumental.* the use of language to obtain objects or services.
Does the child know how to ask for information or help? Can the child phrase questions effectively? Can the child identify needs clearly through the use of language?

2. *Regulatory.* the use of language to modify or control the behavior of others.
Does the child know that he or she is expected to wait his or her turn before asking for help, that he or she must look at the listener when making the request? Is the child able to give directions to others clearly and in an acceptable manner? Can the child make requests, tell others not to do certain things, admonish others for unacceptable actions?

3. *Interactional.* the use of language to relate to important others in the environment.
This involves knowing how to address teachers, visitors, and other children. It demands the ability to persuade, to suggest, to thank, to congratulate, to give verbal approval and support.

4. *Personal.* the use of language to admit the speaker into communication situations.
Can the child enter into a conversation acceptably, can the child orient him-

or herself to the topic, offer acceptable comment? Can the child enter a discussion without drawing undue attention or engendering negative reactions? Can the child make appropriate contributions to discussion?

5. *Heuristic.* the use of language to gain information.
   Does the child know how to formulate effective questions, how to elicit information, how to express the nature of difficulty in understanding the meaning of something?
6. *Imaginative.* the use of language creatively, as in role playing, story telling.
   Is the child able to contribute to class activities that demand imagination expressed verbally? Can the child create word pictures, tell about a visually depicted event? Can the child recount an experience?

The amount of attention you will be able to devote to pragmatic use of language will be limited. It is important, however, that you learn from the teacher how effectively the child is able to use verbal language to interact with the teachers and peers in school. Identifying problems in one or more of the categories just listed would justify your devoting some of your efforts to improving the child's function in that behavior.

Communication

Communication involves the receptive and expressive use of the knowledge of the language system. To achieve this, certain skills or abilities are necessary to interpret the incoming auditory and visual components of the speech signal, and to generate a signal through speech articulation. You will have obtained from the audiologist useful information about the child's communication abilities. In the intervention program you may recognize a need to explore these in more detail. Similarly you will wish to assess the child's competence in making use of the visual cues to speech.

The assessment of auditory and visual speech-recognition skills should move from speech comprehension to speech discrimination. You wish to determine:

1. What is the child's present ability to use hearing, and hearing with vision, in a functional sense?
2. What is the nature of the specific speech-sound combinations that the child cannot perceive auditorily?
3. Does the integration of vision and audition permit perception of speech-sound combinations not auditorily discriminable?

Functional Receptive Communication Skills. The communication needs of each child arise directly from the demands placed upon that child in the classroom. It is logical, therefore, that your first concern is to assess the extent to which the child can meet these demands. To do this you need to identify the nature of the demands and to develop test items that provide information about the child's competence in meeting them. Classroom demands in primary grades can be categorized generally as:

1. Responding to name when called
2. Following directions given to the class as a whole
3. Following in a book as the teacher reads

4. Learning new information presented orally
5. Answering questions asked about content that has been presented orally
6. Taking down homework assignments

This general list should be supplemented by demands specific to particular grades. For example, it may be necessary to assess whether a child can be expected to learn information from an audio cassette often used for individualized, programmed learning in the primary grades. You can develop test items to assess each category. Present each task first without the child's being able to see your lips. Hold a sheet of paper in front of your mouth at a distance of about 9 inches (holding the paper close to your lips will distort the acoustic signal). The child's not being able to see you speaking will replicate the most adverse condition in which he or she will have to function.

An example of a test of the category "Following classroom directions" would be: The therapist/teacher stands approximately 10 feet from the child and gives the following directions:

Take out your math book. That's the blue book, Mary.
Turn to page 91, exercise 6.
I want you to do the even numbers in that exercise.

On page 26 of your Word Wealth workbook, you will find an exercise on prepositions. That's exercise 6A near the bottom of the page. I want you to complete numbers 5 to 25.

An example of the category "Answering questions about orally reviewed material" would be: The therapist/teacher first reviews with the child a unit that has been completed in school. Key vocabulary and phrases are reviewed for language comprehension. A number of questions are then asked by the therapist/teacher standing approximately 10 feet from the child. Questions that might be asked about a unit on explorers that deals with the discovery of America by Columbus include:

1. What was the name of the man who discovered America?
2. From where did Columbus sail?
3. Who paid for his trip?
4. How many ships did he have?
5. What were the names of his ships?
6. How many ships reached the continent of North America?
7. Where did Columbus think he was when he first sighted land?
8. In the days of the sailing ships how did the sailors preserve food?
9. What problems did they have from using salt as a preservative?
10. How did they prevent this problem?

From the information obtained from such a test, you should be in a position to predict the ability of the child to meet the receptive communication demands of his or her classroom. You will be able to communicate with the teacher about your expectations for the child and to help the teacher to adjust the management approach accordingly. You should make it clear that your evaluation was made under favorable listening conditions and that you need the teacher to confirm or reject your predictions about the child when he or she has to function in the less-favorable listening conditions of the classroom.

To help the teacher become aware of how the child manages in class, you can use a profile questionnaire of the type illustrated at the end of this chapter. Ask the teacher to rate the ease or amount of difficulty the child experiences in various classroom communication/learning conditions and the frequency of occurrence of those situations. By multiplying the value of an answer to a question—for example, "some difficulty" (+1)—by frequency of occurrence—for example, "often" (+2)—you can determine a value of importance. By adding all response values algebraically (that is, allowing for +'s and −'s) and dividing by the number of questions, you can obtain a mean value. You can then use this as a baseline figure for future comparisons.

Specific Speech-Sound Discrimination. You need this information in order to know

1. Which sounds are not discriminable to the child in certain phonetic contexts
2. In which contexts they are discriminable
3. With which sounds they are confused
4. For which sounds auditory stimulation can be used to reduce perceptual confusions
5. For which sounds recognition of visible articulatory patterns will be necessary for identification
6. For which sounds auditory stimulation can be used for correction of articulation

A number of standard tests are available for testing discrimination ability in children. Lists of monosyllabic words have been developed by Haskins (1949) and Myatt and Landes (1963). Picture identification tests are also available to assess auditory discrimination—for example, Siegenthaler and Haspiel, *Discrimination by Identification of Pictures Tests* (1966); Ross and Lerman, *Word Intelligibility by Picture Identification Tests* (1970); Goldman, Fristoe, and Woodcock, *Test of Auditory Discrimination* (1970). Other tests—Butler, Hedrick, and Manning, *Composite Auditory Perceptual Test* (1973) and Goldman, Fristoe, and Woodcock, *Auditory Skills Test Battery* (1974)—contain subtests of auditory discrimination. The results of such tests are helpful in assessing the amount of discrimination difficulty a child experiences. It is necessary, however, to keep a record of the types of errors the child makes so that you can understand difficulties better. *The Goldman-Fristoe-Woodcock Auditory Skills Test Battery: Diagnostic Auditory Discrimination Test* is helpful in this respect because it provides a scoring method that permits analysis of the errors in terms of distinctive features.

The Larson Recorded Test (Table 16.1) provides for a comparative discrimination between pairs of phonemes that are likely to be confused. Where appropriate, the lists represent an attempt to present the phoneme in the initial, medial, and final positions of a word. In administering the test, one word of each pair within each set is presented to the child, who is asked to identify the spoken word by drawing a line through its printed form.

You can develop similar tests to accommodate the vocabulary limitations of individual children. For example, you can test vowels and diphthongs using multiple-choice lists such as:

TABLE 16.1 Larson Recorded Test (after Larson, 1950)

Name: ____________________ Score: (Errors) __________/__________

Date: ____________________ With Aid __________ (__________)

Without Aid ____________________

Directions to be given the listener: "Draw a line through the words that are pronounced to you from each box."

Box 1	f and ch	*Box 2*	l and z	*Box 3*	l and n	*Box 4*	d and n	*Box 5*	m and l
few	chew	lip	zip	lame	name	dot	not	mine	line
fin	chin	loan	zone	light	night	die	nigh	mast	last
filed	child	dale	daze	loan	known	deed	need	moan	loan
calf	catch	mail	maze	pail	pain	ode	own	name	nail
four	chore	hail	haze	rail	rain	did	din	home	hole
Box 6	b and m	*Box 7*	l and v	*Box 8*	k and g	*Box 9*	p and b	*Box 10*	m and v
bill	mill	lane	vane	coal	goal	pin	bin	mice	vice
boast	most	lie	vie	came	game	pie	by	ham	have
bake	make	lace	vase	coat	goat	pole	bowl	glum	glove
robe	roam	lull	love	luck	lug	cap	cab	mine	vine
tab	tam	rail	rave	rack	rag	rope	robe	mile	vile
Box 11	n and v	*Box 12*	sh and f	*Box 13*	f and k	*Box 14*	f and b	*Box 15*	s and sh
nice	vice	show	foe	fit	kit	fun	bun	lease	leash
nurse	verse	shore	fore	four	core	fig	big	sew	show
nine	vine	shade	fade	find	kind	cuff	cub	sigh	shy
loans	loaves	cash	calf	cliff	click	calf	cab	sip	ship
lean	leave	leash	leaf	laugh	lack	graph	grab	save	shave

Box 16	p and f	*Box 17*	s and z	*Box 18*	v and f	*Box 19*	ch and sh	*Box 20*	b and d
pour	four	ice	eyes	five	fife	chop	shop	bid	did
pile	file	seal	zeal	vase	face	chair	share	big	dig
par	far	bus	buzz	leave	leaf	watch	wash	buy	die
cap	calf	lice	lies	view	few	catch	cash	rob	rod
cup	cuff	juice	Jews	loaves	loafs	cheap	sheep	robe	rode
Box 21	d and g	*Box 22*	t and p	*Box 23*	f and s	*Box 24*	b and v	*Box 25*	v and z
doe	go	tail	pail	fine	sign	bet	vet	live	lies
date	gate	cat	cap	flat	slat	dub	dove	have	has
drove	grove	cut	cup	cuff	cuss	base	vase	rave	raise
bud	bug	tar	par	knife	nice	bigger	vigor	view	zoo
dad	gag	toll	pole	lift	list	robe	rove	wives	wise
Box 26	th and f	*Box 27*	t and th	*Box 28*	k and t	*Box 29*	k and p	*Box 30*	m and n
thin	fin	tie	thigh	kick	tick	pike	pipe	mine	nine
thirst	first	tin	thin	kite	tight	car	par	mew	knew
three	free	trill	thrill	code	toad	crock	crop	time	tine
thought	fought	mitt	myth	shirk	shirt	cry	pry	dime	dine
thrill	frill	pat	path	park	part	coal	pole	dumb	done
Box 31	Word endings			*Box 32*	th and s	*Box 33*	th and v		
store	stores	stored		thumb	sum	than	van		
will	wills	willed		truth	truce	thy	vie		
start	starts	started		path	pass	that	vat		
cough	coughs	coughed		thing	sing	thine	vine		
cap	caps	capped		thank	sank	loathes	loaves		

well	wall	wool
bat	beat	boat
pin	pen	pan
moon	main	man
bud	bead	board
boy	bow	bean
bear	barn	beer
pain	pine	pin
man	mine	mean
been	burn	born
cat	cut	caught
like	look	lick
low	lie	lay
tea	two	tie
rat	rot	rut

Sounds that present discrimination difficulty can be analyzed in detail to determine in which phonetic contexts and combinations they are indiscriminable to the child (the procedure has been described in Chapter 14). Conduct the testing using nonsense syllables, which permit as accurate a measure as possible of the amount of information derived from the acoustic signal at the phonetic level. Consonants are systematically assessed against all vowels and diphthongs in the combinations cv, vc, vcv, cvc. The use of nonsense syllables does present certain difficulties, however, because some combinations are difficult to record in writing. On the other hand, if the responses are given verbally by the student, you are in essence testing not only the ability to recognize, but also the ability to reproduce the nonsense syllable. This also involves the auditory-discrimination ability of the tester who is scoring the responses. Nevertheless, if these limitations are borne in mind and allowed for, valuable information can be obtained from such a detailed analysis. Figure 16.4 shows the results obtained on such a test by a hearing-impaired student. A section of the test was presented at the beginning of each of five sessions. This was considered necessary in order to avoid any learning influence and to counteract the rather rapid boredom that arises from having to repeat a series of nonsense syllables.

Notice that the first test items are comprised of various consonant sounds combined with the vowel /a/. In each instance the consonant sound is placed in the initial position. Three patterns of responses can be observed on the record sheet. The first type of response was correct recognition of the sound on all of the five tests. This suggests that the person had no difficulty in identifying this consonant by its acoustic pattern alone. In the second type of response the sound was not correctly recognized at all, indicating that the acoustic message signal provided insufficient information for the correct recognition of the sound in any of the test items presented. In the third pattern the response was not consistent, as indicated by correct recognition of the sound on some presentations and incorrect identification on others. It is reasonable to expect that a subject with normal hearing might also incorrectly identify a particular sound on one of the five occasions. One false identification was, therefore, not considered to be significant.

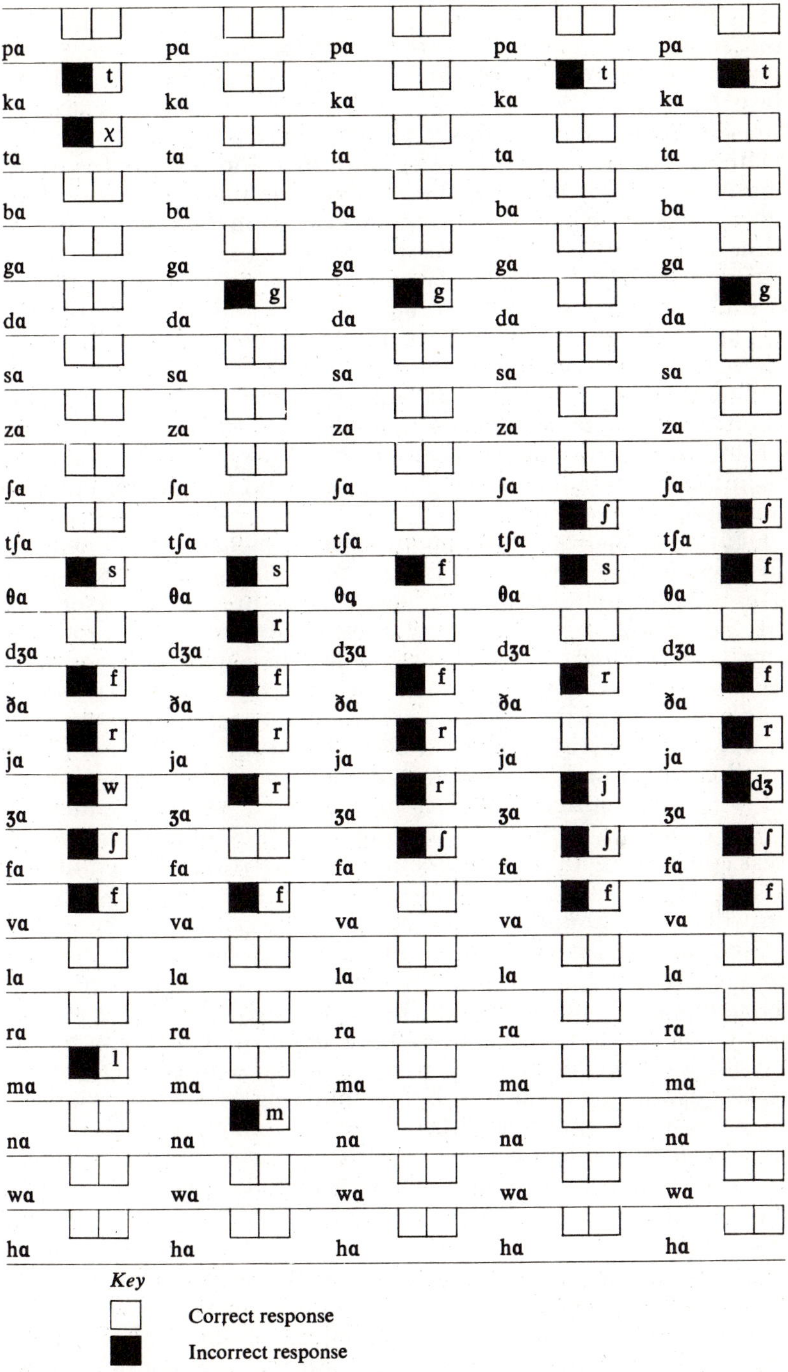

Figure 16.4 Test results for phoneme discrimination test.

Let us examine a little more closely the results that were obtained for this subject. We observe that the phonemes /θ/, /ð/, /j/, /ʒ/, /ʃ/, /v/ all fall under the category of total failure to be recognized. This allows for the fact that two of these sounds were correctly identified on one of the five presentations; however, this might have been a fortuitous recognition rather than a definite discrimination and, therefore, was not considered significant. When we examine the substitutions that were made for the sounds we find a degree of consistency in that on four of the five occasions the voiced "th" sound /ð/ was recognized as an /f/, the /j/ sound was identified as an /r/, and the /v/ was identified as its unvoiced counterpart /f/. Within the other sounds there was not such a high degree of consistency. The unvoiced "th" /θ/, for example, was confused with both /s/ and /f/, whereas the /dʒ/ sound was confused with /w/, /r/, and /j/.

When we turn to the second category, those sounds that are identified part of the time but not consistently, we find that the /k/ and /t/ sounds are confused, though the /k/ appears to be more difficult to identify than the /t/. Note that although the /d/ sound is often mistaken for a /g/ sound the reverse is not true.

Figure 16.5 shows what happens when we isolate the phonemes that the first test indicated was presenting discrimination difficulties and test them in combination with other vowels. The first two phonemes, the voiced and unvoiced "th" sound /ð/ and /θ/ were not made more discriminable by changing the vowel. Essentially, the same confusion pattern existed with /s/, /f/, /v/, and /z/, which constitute the sounds that were predicted on the basis of the distorted acoustic signal received by the subject. Note, however, the difference that occurred in the recognition of the /j/ sound when the vowel was changed. When /j/ was combined with the /a/ sound, it was recognized only once in five trials. When the same consonant was combined with the diphthong /ou/, it was missed only once, whereas combined with the short vowel /ɪ/, it was correctly identified each time. The consonant /f/, which was recognized only once when in combination with the /a/ sound, was not recognized at all in combination with the /i/ sound, when it was consistently confused with the /s/ consonant. Surprisingly, when the /f/ sound was combined with the diphthong /ou/ it was recognized 100 percent of the time. Similarly, the voiced sound /v/, recognized only once in five presentations when combined with the vowel /a/ and only once when combined with /e/, was recognized on three of the five occasions when combined with the diphthong /ou/. The consonant /k/, which presented significant difficulty when combined with the vowel sound /a/, with a resultant confusion between /k/ and /t/, presented no difficulty for discrimination when combined with either the long vowel /i/ or the diphthong /ou/.

The Effectiveness of the Visual Contribution to Discrimination. You should immediately present again each item not correctly perceived in the tests described in the two preceding sections of this chapter, allowing the child to watch your face. This serves two purposes—it minimizes the child's frustration that arises from being shut off from needed visual cues, and it allows you to assess the child's capacity to function on the tasks when watching the speaker.

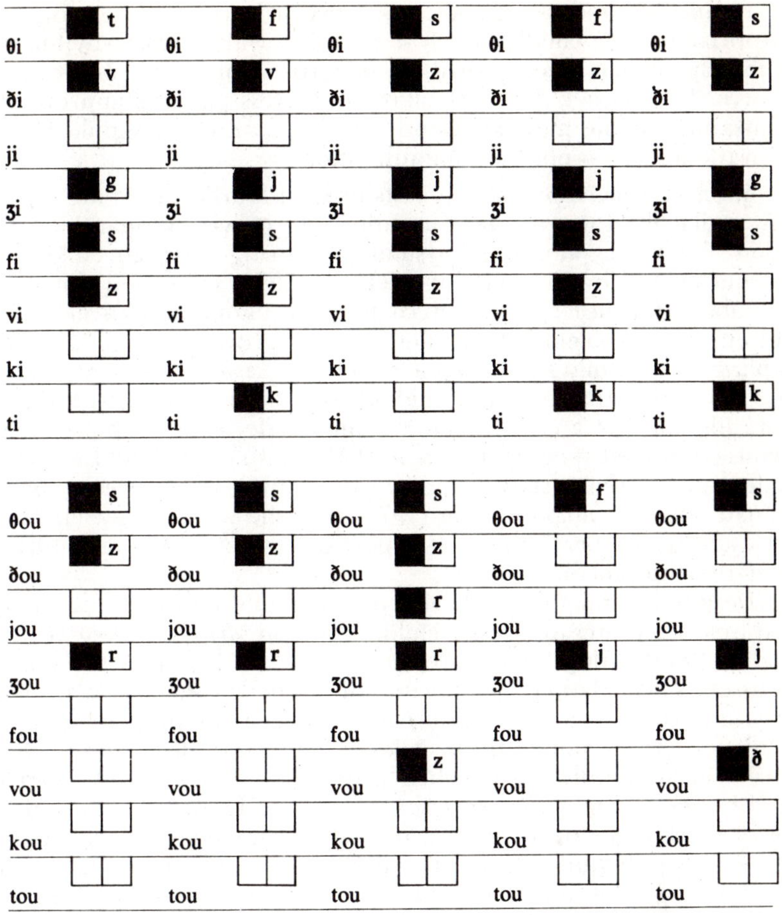

Figure 16.5 Test results illustrating the effect upon consonant discrimination when the vowel is changed.

Voice Production and Control. The expressive use of verbal language through speech requires that the child approximate the normal pitch and intensity patterns that are part of suprasegmental structure. To assess whether the child does this, you can tape a sample of the child's normal conversational speech, which you can elicit by asking the child to tell about the day in school or what he or she likes to do on a weekend, or by prompting the child to tell a story associated with a sequence of pictures. In evaluating the tape you should make a subjective judgment concerning the range, control, and appropriateness of the pitch and intensity modulation. The quality of the voice should also be assessed for such characteristics as too much or too little nasality, breathiness, or harshness.

The control of voice is intimately involved in the suprasegemental patterning of spoken language. It is necessary to note, therefore, whether the child uses correct stress and intonation patterns, whether the child is grouping words and phrases correctly, and whether the child uses pause and disjuncture (indicating contrasts between words, clauses, and so on) appropriately. The child's speech should flow with an easy rhythm made possible by normal speech-breathing patterns. Words and phrases should be correctly grouped, with intonation and stress patterns appropriate to the meaning of the message. Loudness, pitch, and rate should fluctuate within the limits for normal communication.

Speech Articulation. Many tests of speech articulation are commercially available. However, their usefulness in providing quantified information about the phonologic system of hearing-impaired children has been questioned by Ling (1976). McLean (1976) expressed similar concerns about the use of commercial tests with communicatively delayed children. The problem is that standard tests provide only a very limited sampling of the child's phonologic system. McLean (1976) cites Faircloth (1973) as stating that the only valid assessment of all aspects of the phonemic adequacy of a child's speech is one made from a sample of spontaneous connected speech. Dickerson (1971), also cited by McLean (1976), has determined that a sixty- to ninety-word sample of connected speech is adequate for this purpose. Ling (1976) cites the work of Lee (1974) and Tyack and Gottsleben (1974) to support the use of a sample of fifty representative utterances.

Despite its limitations, you will probably find a standard test helpful when first beginning to assess a child. If so, the *McDonald Deep Test of Articulation* (McDonald, 1964) is recommended because it is the only test that assesses articulation as a function of phonetic context. This is particularly important in evaluating hearing-impaired children. In most cases articulation errors among these children arise from distortion of the auditory speech stimulus, both when produced by others and when produced by the children themselves. You need to know, therefore, the degree of consistency of a child's error across phonetic contexts. You can then compare this information to the data you will already have generated about which sounds the child can recognize in which phonetic combinations. Such analysis will undoubtedly influence the method of stimulation and feedback you will use in intervention. It also will affect the context in which you begin to modify a defective speech-articulation pattern. The Goldman, Fristoe, Woodcock *Test of Auditory Discriminations* (1970) will provide you with distinctive feature information about articulation errors, which you can then compare with an analysis of discrimination errors by using the "Auditory Discrimination" subtest of the Goldman, Fristoe, Woodcock *Auditory Skills Test Battery* (1974).

Later, you can obtain and analyze a sample of the child's conversational speech for patterns of errors. Such patterns indicate the nature of the system of speech-sound generation being used by the child. The errors can be identified as omissions, distortions, or substitutions. The substitutions can be examined in the light of the pattern of hearing impairment, the auditory discrimination data, and the distinctive features of place, manner, and voicing.

The generation of a fairly complete profile of the child's receptive expressive language competencies may take time. However, without such specific knowledge of a child's communication difficulties, you will lack the information necessary to plan a maximally effective intervention program for each individual child.

Academic Support

Although many hearing-impaired children need academic support, it is not something for which the therapist/teacher should be directly responsible. Your role is not to serve as a tutor. If a child is experiencing significant academic difficulties, then you should lend full support to efforts to obtain extra help, or to reassess the educational placement. Language and speech cannot legitimately be separated from cognition. It is inevitable, therefore, that you will be involved in helping a child understand content in those subjects that are heavily language based. You will do so because of the nature and structure of your language and communication-skills upgrading program. Academic support will be relevant to you, therefore, to the extent that you wish to select the content materials for your lessons from those school subjects in which reduced competency in language-communication abilities is most seriously handicapping the child.

Counseling

Of all the people who need counseling concerning the nature and effect of hearing impairment, the one who is usually overlooked is the hearing-impaired school child. The goal of habilitative/rehabiliative management is to do everything possible to help the child develop self-sufficiency. You try to train the child to deal with communication, learning, and social situations independently. Despite this goal, educating a child about his or her hearing impairment and the feelings and reactions that he or she and others experience as a result of it are far too often either completely neglected or only given minimal attention. You will need to determine what the child does know about the hearing difficulty and its effects, and what the child knows about his or her hearing aid. We will discuss the nature of counseling in the next chapter; at this point our concern is only with the task of assessing the need for counseling. You have four sources of information from which you will be able to assess how much counseling the child may need: (1) the child; (2) the teacher; (3) the parents; (4) yourself.

The Child. You can ask the child questions about the hearing impairment and the hearing aid to discover if the child knows anything about these aspects of him- or herself. Does the child know

1. The kind of a hearing problem he or she has
2. Whether it is equal in both ears
3. What the hearing difficulty does to speech sound
4. Why he or she wears an aid
5. What kind and make of aid it is
6. How much the aid helps
7. What the aid cannot do
8. How to take care of the aid
9. How much he or she uses the eyes to help the ears

Understanding how and why he or she is different is very important to the process of developing self-respect and, therefore, self-confidence. Explaining and discussing factual information with a child provides a basis for discussing feelings and reactions that would not normally be expressed.

The Teacher. The teacher will usually be able to describe the child's attitude and behavior in class, and should be able to tell you how the child relates both to the teacher and to classmates. You are interested in the amount of self-confidence the child shows, and whether the child is eager or reluctant to participate in class activities individually, and as part of a group. You should try to find out if the child's behavior changes during nonacademic activities such as gym or during lunch period.

The Parents. It is often parents who express greatest concern about their child's general adjustment. At home they observe the effects of stress, anxiety, fatigue, disappointment, and discouragement experienced in school. Similarly they observe positive reactions to increasing academic success, social acceptance, growing self-confidence. They also are usually aware of stress symptoms others may not see, such as fatigue, despondency, sleeplessness, poor appetite, lack of desire to become involved in activities, anger, or crying.

Yourself. As you become sensitive to the problems that hearing-impaired children encounter daily, you will be able to contribute to the pool of information about the child's adjustment. In your meetings you will observe positive and negative attitudes and behaviors that may not occur in the classroom or at home. This comparison of behaviors often proves very helpful in determining how to intervene to facilitate the adjustment of the child in school. Counseling should be part of every intervention program. It will be a natural part of your relationship with the child and should not, therefore, be a demand that you feel incompetent or ineligible to provide for.

In this chapter we have examined what the primary-school classroom teacher needs to know about the hearing-impaired child or children in the class and how that information can be presented effectively. We also considered, in much greater detail, the needs of the hearing-impaired child. We devoted most of our time to a consideration of how these needs can be assessed. Our task now is to correlate and use the information obtained to develop an effective plan of habilitative/rehabilitative intervention.

REFERENCES

Ammons, A., and S. Ammons, *Full Range Picture Vocabulary Test, Forms A and B.* Missoula, Mont.: Psychological Test Specialists, 1948.

Boehm, A., *Boehm Test of Basic Concepts Manual.* New York: The Psychological Corporation, 1971.

Butler, K., D. Hedrick, and C. Manning, *Composite Auditory Perceptual Test.* Hayward, Calif.: Almeda County School Dept., 1973.

Carrow, E., *Test for Auditory Comprehension of Language, English/Spanish Versions.* Austin, Texas: Urban Research Group, 1968, 1973.

Carrow, E., *Carrow Elicited Language Inventory.* Austin, Tex.: Learning Concepts, 1974.

Cicciarelli, A., P. Broen, and G. Siegel, "Language Assessment Procedures Appendix A," in *Communication Assessment and Intervention Strategies,* ed. L. Lloyd, pp. 777–799. Baltimore: University Park Press, 1976.

Crystal, D., P. Fletcher, and M. Garman, *The Grammatical Analysis of Language Disability.* New York: Elsevier North-Holland, Inc., 1976.

Dickerson, M. V., *An Investigation of a Method of Sampling Spontaneous Speech for Evaluation of Articulatory Behavior.* Unpublished doctoral dissertation, Florida State University, Tallahassee, 1971.

Dunn, L., *Expanded Manual for the Peabody Picture Vocabulary Test.* Circle Pines, Minn.: American Guidance Service, 1965.

Englemann, S., *The Basic Concepts Inventory.* Chicago: Follet Educational Corporation, 1967.

Faircloth, M. A., *Articulation for Communication.* Paper presented at the Special Study Institute on Articulation Disorders in School Children Revisited. April–May, San Diego, 1973.

Foster, R., J. Giddan, and J. Stark, *Assessment of Children's Language Comprehension.* Palo Alto, Calif.: Consulting Psychologists Press, Inc., 1973.

Goldman, R., M. Fristoe, and R. Woodcock, *Test of Auditory Discrimination.* Circle Pines, Minn.: American Guidance Service, 1970.

Goldman, R., M. Fristoe, and R. Woodcock, *Auditory Skills Test Battery: Diagnostic Auditory Discrimination Test.* Circle Pines, Minn.: American Guidance Service, 1974.

Halliday, M. A., *Learning How to Mean: Explorations in the Development of Language.* London: Edward Arnold, 1975.

Haskins, H. L., *A Phonetically Balanced Test of Speech Discrimination for Children.* Unpublished masters thesis, Northwestern University, Evanston, Ill., 1949.

Hymes, D., "Competence and Performance in Linguistic Theory," in *Language Acquisition: Models and Methods,* eds. R. Huxley, and E. Ingram, pp. 3–28. New York: Academic Press, Inc., 1971.

Kirk, S., J. McCarthy, and D. Kirk, *Illinois Test of Psycholinguistic Abilities.* Urbana: University of Illinois Press, 1968.

Kretschmer, R., and L. Kretschmer, *Language Development and Intervention with the Hearing Impaired.* Baltimore: University Park Press, 1978.

Larson, L. L., *Consonant Sound Discrimination.* Bloomington, Ind.: Indiana University Press, 1950.

Lee, L., *The Northwestern Syntax Screening Test.* Evanston, Ill.: Northwestern University Press, 1969.

Lee, L., *Developmental Sentence Analysis Test.* Evanston, Ill.: Northwestern University Press, 1974.

Ling, D., *Speech and the Hearing Impaired Child.* Washington, D.C.: Alexander Graham Bell Assoc. for the Deaf, 1976.

McDonald, E. T., *Articulation Testing and Treatment: A Sensory-Motor Approach.* Pittsburgh: Stanwix House, 1964.

McLean, J., "Articulation," in *Communication Assessment and Intervention Strategies,* ed. L. Lloyd, pp. 327–370. Baltimore: University Park Press, 1976.

Miller, J., "Assessing Children's Language Behavior," in *Bases of Language Intervention,* ed. R. L. Schiefelbusch, pp. 269–318. Baltimore: University Park Press, 1978.

Myatt, B., and B. Landes, "Assessing Discrimination Loss in Children," *Archives of Otolaryngology, 77,* 1963, 359–362.

Rees, N., "Pragmatics of Language Applications to Normal and Disordered Development," in *Bases of Language Intervention,* ed. R. L. Schiefelbusch, pp. 191–268. Baltimore: University Park Press, 1978.

Rice, M., "Identification of Children with Language Disorders," in *Language Intervention Strategies,* ed. R. L. Schiefelbusch, pp. 19–55. Baltimore: University Park Press, 1978.

Ross, M., and J. Lerman, "A Picture Identification Test for Hearing-Impaired Children," *Journal of Speech and Hearing Research, 13,* 1970, 44–56. Test available from Stanwix House Inc., 3020 Chartiers Ave., Pittsburgh, Pa., 15204.

Siegel, G., and P. Broen, "Language Assessment," in *Communication Assessment and Intervention Strategies,* ed. L. Lloyd, pp. 73–122. Baltimore: University Park Press, 1976.

Siegenthaler, H., and G. Haspiel, *Development of Two Standardized Measures of Hearing for Speech by Children.* Cooperative Research Program, Project 2372, U.S. Office of Health, Education and Welfare. Houston: University of Houston, 1966.

Tyack, D., and R. Gottsleben, *Language Sampling and Analysis.* Palo Alto, Calif.: Consultant Psychologists Press, 1974.

Werner, E., and J. Kresheck, *Structured Photographic Language Test.* Sandwich, Ill.: Janelle Publications, 1978.

PROFILE QUESTIONNAIRE FOR RATING COMMUNICATIVE PERFORMANCE IN A SCHOOL ENVIRONMENT

1. **a** When I am working with Mary individually at my desk, she is able to understand what I say with:

+2	+1	−1	−2
little or no difficulty	some difficulty (but not a lot)	a fair amount of difficulty (quite a lot)	great difficulty

b) This happens:

1	2	3
seldom	often	very often

2. **a)** When she is one of a small group of children in a learning situation, she understands what I say with:

+2	+1	−1	−2
little or no difficulty	some difficulty (but not a lot)	a fair amount of difficulty (quite a lot)	great difficulty

b) This happens:

1	2	3
seldom	often	very often

3. **a)** In a small group, she understands what the other children say with:

+2	+1	−1	−2
little or no difficulty	some difficulty (but not a lot)	a fair amount of difficulty (quite a lot)	great difficulty

b) This happens:

1	2	3
seldom	often	very often

4. **a)** When I speak to the class as a whole, Mary is able to understand with:

+2	+1	−1	−2
little or no difficulty	some difficulty (but not a lot)	a fair amount of difficulty (quite a lot)	great difficulty

b) This happens:

1	2	3
seldom	often	very often

5. **a)** When we watch a movie film, television program, or filmstrip, she seems to understand with:

+2	+1	−1	−2
little or no difficulty	some difficulty (but not a lot)	a fair amount of difficulty (quite a lot)	great difficulty

b) This happens:

1	2	3
seldom	often	very often

6. **a)** In playground or gymnasium games or in activities, she is able to follow verbal directions with:

+2	+1	−1	−2
little or no difficulty	some difficulty (but not a lot)	a fair amount of difficulty (quite a lot)	great difficulty

b) This happens:

1	2	3
seldom	often	very often

7. **a)** In her contact with the other children in class an in social activities during break periods, she seems to understand with:

+2	+1	−1	−2
little or no difficulty	some difficulty (but not a lot)	a fair amount of difficulty (quite a lot)	great difficulty

b) This happens:

1	2	3
seldom	often	very often

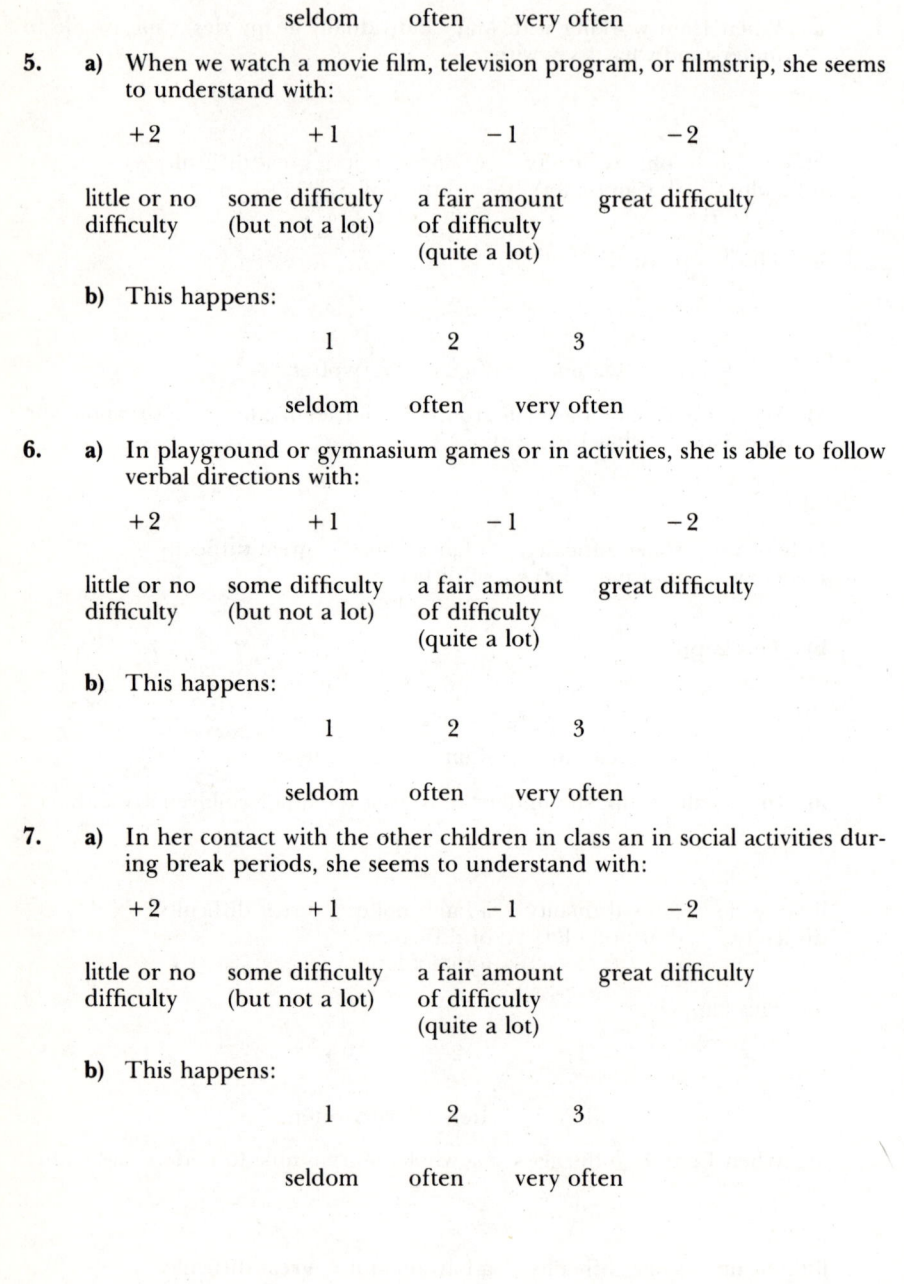

17

Intervention Practices for the Primary School Child

You now have available to you a fairly comprehensive profile of the child. The next step is to determine how to organize the information you have and how to develop an effective plan for intervention. It is helpful to think of your ability to help in terms of

1. Modification of environmental factors, including how others relate to the child
2. Modification of the child's behavior

It is not your responsibility to effect all the desirable changes in the child's environment. It is your responsibility, however, to determine that whatever steps are necessary to optimize environmental influence are taken. Each child must have one person who assumes the role of coordinator of services, who functions as a manager. In far too many instances, each professional assumes that to be the role of another.

DEVELOPING AN EFFECTIVE PLAN FOR INTERVENTION

Summarize and Interpret Test Findings

This information is extremely important in helping the parents and the teacher understand the implications of the test results. Although the audiologist should be responsible for translating audiological test results into behavioral terms, this is often not done, at least not in writing. As a therapist/teacher you will probably have to discuss the results with the audiologist and then write your own profile of the child. Send a copy of your report directly to the teacher. The official copy to a school district is often filed in the child's health file in school or in the County Health Department Office and thus has no educational impact. Your summary report should:

1. Briefly explain the severity of the child's hearing impairment and its influence on the child's ability to understand familiar spoken language by hearing alone.
2. Explain how much improvement occurs when the hearing aid is worn and is functioning well.
3. Give examples of the situations in which the child will probably still have difficulty understanding by hearing alone even with the hearing aid.
4. Explain the extent to which being able to see the speaker makes comprehension easier for the child.
5. Identify the kinds of classroom activities in which you feel the child will manage well or adequately and those in which difficulty can be anticipated; indicate specific learning situations (audio-cassette listening, movies, television presentations, filmstrips or slide projections, auditorium presentations) that will probably present difficulty.
6. Indicate the child's receptive vocabulary age, grammatical competence, and ability to understand syntactic constructions appropriate to his or her chronological age.
7. Indicate expressive language skills, particularly the child's pragmatic use of language.
8. Estimate the extent to which difficulties in comprehension in favorable listening and listening-watching conditions are likely to be due to language deficit.
9. Identify the child's areas of greatest need and explain the goals you will be working to achieve with the child.

Identify Practical Steps the Teacher Can Take to Help

The teacher will appreciate any help you can give if it is presented in a constructive manner. Try to indicate clearly how the teacher can reduce difficulties in dealing with the child. Do not make demands on the teacher; instead try to offer helpful suggestions. Following are some sample suggestions for the teacher:

1. Seat the child in a favorable listening and viewing position within 6 feet of where you will usually be when addressing the child. There is no such thing as a set advantageous seating position. This will depend on the seating plan and where you stand when teaching. In small groups the child needs to be seated diagonally from you. If possible the child should be allowed to move his or her chair to an advantageous position and to turn around to listen to another child speaking. In formal seating arrangements, as in a lecture room or auditorium, reserve a front seat from which the speaker's face can be seen. Avoid facing the child toward the glare from windows.
2. Attract the child's visual and auditory attention before speaking. Arrange for a buddy to alert the child. Help the child locate the speaker in group-discussion situations.
3. Try to position yourself with light on your face when speaking (this provides the favorable contrast conditions discussed in Chapter 4). Try to en-

sure that your face is visible to the child. Remember, the child may not understand at all when you speak while writing on the board or look down at a book on your desk.

4. Speak naturally and clearly. This will help to reduce the rate at which you give information, but you should not speak unusually slowly. Raising your voice or exaggerating lip movements will make understanding more difficult for the child.
5. Be alert to special auditory learning situations or tasks that may make demands on the child that exceed his or her auditory-perceptual capabilities.
6. Rephrase what you said if the child does not understand, use different vocabulary, simplify sentence structure, shorten sentences. When the child understands, repeat what you said the first time. You cannot assume that the child has understood what you have said, particularly when dealing with new or complex information or when listening conditions are poor. Therefore, whenever possible you should ask a question to check the child's ability to use or apply what has been learned. Assignments or activities that require application of knowledge will help you to determine what has been understood. Even the simplest concepts are often not grasped immediately by the child who hears the explanation. The child hears you in a distorted manner, and encounters unfamiliar vocabulary and language structure, as well as new cognitive content. You will find that it will be necessary to go over any verbal instructions or directions given to the child.
7. Appoint a trustworthy pupil to ensure that the hearing-impaired child understands assignments. If possible give homework assignments in writing.
8. Establish a management diary that provides a means of communicating with the parents, daily if necessary. Homework assignments, lesson topics, study-support suggestions, questions or concerns about the hearing aid or other matters all can be dealt with, at least initially, in this way.

Meet with Parents to Determine their Role in Cooperative Planning and Management

The involvement of parents in the planning and implementation of management procedures is a major goal. To achieve this you should meet with the parents to review test findings and discuss with them your plans for supporting and training their child (Figure 17.1). The parents must understand what services their child will receive and by whom these will be coordinated. You should identify what you consider to be the child's most urgent needs and outline the ways in which you plan to meet them or arrange for them to be met. The parents' perception of primary needs should be discussed and you should modify your plans to reflect their constructive suggestions or to accommodate their strong desires when appropriate. You will need to describe and explain how the parents can reinforce the intervention procedures that you and other professionals will initiate. You should outline and discuss how they can reinforce

1. The understanding of new concepts
2. The comprehension and use of new vocabulary, grammatical, and syntactic structures
3. The learning of new patterns of language behavior (pragmatics)
4. The use of oral communication

FIGURE 17.1 Involvement of parents in the planning and implementation of management procedures is a major goal. (Courtesy Buffalo City School System)

5. Speech articulation and voice control
6. Social growth
   a. Developing responsibility
   b. Developing independence
   c. Developing social graces
   d. Participating in extracurricular activities in school and in the community

As a therapist/teacher in the management team you should also contribute to the management diary, dating your entry. This ensures that each member of the team sees a brief summary of what each other member is doing. It provides a means of communication, allowing the parents to know what is being worked on, and to receive guidance in home-reinforcement needs.

Periodically make an appointment with the parents to discuss the child's progress in all aspects of communication as it relates to learning and social interaction. At this time you can give further guidance to help them provide more effective support.

Determine the Most Pressing of the Child's Needs

We have acknowledged that the child's overall level of communication and learning effectiveness result from the interaction of a number of elements we have discussed. However, it often becomes clear that a child is having more difficulty in some areas than others. Intervention procedures will be most effective when addressed to these high-need areas. You should study the assessment findings to determine your priorities. The needs we determined to be characteristic of the hearing-impaired school child were:

Receptive communication. auditory and auditory-visual speech recognition, linguistic and cognitive comprehension
Expressive communication. use of language to express ideas (grammar syntax, pragmatics), speech articulation, and voice production
Counseling. understanding of the nature of the hearing impairment and its effects on communication, understanding one's own feelings and reactions to the handicap, ability to resolve negative feelings, ability to deal with negative reactions by others

The priorities you determine for each school child will be different. An example of identifying need priorities is provided by the management of Jane.

Jane is 5½ years old and has just been mainstreamed into kindergarten from a preschool program. She has a 75 dB hearing impairment. With binaural aids (fitted at age 4 years) she has an aided threshold average of 35 dB and a word-picture discrimination score of 68%. She appears not to use visual speech cues effectively. Her comprehension of spoken language is limited, though she grasps what is expected very quickly. Her measured intelligence on a performance task is 128. Jane is an oral child. She has good control of volume but some difficulty with voice modulation patterns. Her speech can be understood but only with difficulty. She has trouble making herself understood when the teacher does not have situational cues. Jane's language age is 3½ years. Vocabulary, grammar, and syntax are all depressed. She has been mainstreamed experimentally with resource-room support.

Jane will only succeed in her present placement if all available resources are coordinated to support her. Your goals for Jane would be:

1. To involve the parents in a home-support program to reinforce and augment school and training-session activities
2. To increase basic concepts fundamental to kindergarten and first grade
3. To increase vocabulary and language relative to basic concepts
4. To plan and implement a language curriculum to improve comprehension and use of grammatical structures and syntactic forms
5. To coordinate the intervention plan for cognitive-linguistic stimulation with the kindergarten classroom teacher's activities
6. To begin auditory training (a) to increase sentence discrimination of basic concept-vocabulary; (b) to increase speech-sound discrimination in nonsense syllables as a prerequisite to speech-articulation training
7. To increase Jane's ability to make use of visual cues to speech recognition
8. To increase her ability to integrate visual and auditory speech cues
9. To begin speech-articulation training

Melissa, age 8, and Mark, age 12, present different needs.

Melissa has a mild to moderate hearing impairment (average 45 dB) and has recently been fitted with an ear-level hearing aid. Audiologic findings indicate good discrimination for words in sentences (92%) and an aided speech-reception threshold of 15 dB. Language age is twelve months below chronologic age. Vocabulary is below grade level, and her knowledge and use of parts of speech is mildly depressed. Some syntactic forms are incorrectly used. Voice production is normal, articulation errors are confined to /s/, /θ/, /ʃ/. Melissa is described as a shy child who has been a daydreamer in class. She is not cooperating in wearing the aid, often comes to school without it. Her school work, including reading, is a grade below age level.

Your order of priority for dealing with Melissa's needs would be:

1. To counsel the parents and endeavor to persuade them to become part of the management team, to demonstrate to them the importance of the constant use of the aid in learning situations and its selective use outside; to win their support in your attempt to have Melissa accept the aid, and to increase her self-confidence and class participation.
2. To demonstrate to Melissa the benefits the aid can provide, and to ensure she becomes familiar with the operation and care of the aid; to provide pleasurable listening experiences using the aid; to provide auditory training with the aid; to provide successful experiences with the aid.
3. To increase the number of successful experiences Melissa has in communication and learning situations in the training sessions and in the classroom.
4. To provide support to Melissa in a coordinated plan involving the teacher, therapist/teacher, remedial-reading teacher, and parents, to increase cognitive-linguistic competency.
5. To provide academic-content enrichment support through auditory-visual training based on classroom subject content.
6. To increase Melissa's confidence in the use of expressive language in small-group situations.
7. To provide speech training to improve her ability to produce correctly the speech sounds presently misarticulated.

Mark is 12 years old and is in sixth grade. He has a 60 dB hearing impairment and wears binaural aids. His aided SRT is 26 dB, discrimination for words in sentences is 86%. His speech-reading skills are not good. Academically Mark functions at the lower level of his grade expectancy. However, he demonstrates above-average intelligence on a combined verbal-nonverbal test (Wechsler Intelligence Scale for Children). He has a positive attitude to the use of his aids and to school. He works hard. Despite this he is disappointed that he is not achieving better. Mark's language is commensurate with his chronologic age. His use of syntax is good with the exception of a few complex structures. His general vocabulary is slightly depressed but he has difficulty with subject-specific concepts and vocabulary. He reports some difficulty in following everything that is said in class and is shy about taking part in class discussion. Mark experiences difficulty in doing project assignments, in expressing himself easily in small-group situations and in written assignments. His speech shows mild errors in the articulation of predominantly high-frequency consonants. He will move to Junior High School in 10 months' time.

Your goals for Mark would be:

1. To concentrate on improving his understanding and knowledge of subject-specific concepts, vocabulary, and phrases, to provide auditory-visual training on the words and phrases and correct articulation and use of these items in spoken communication.
2. To provide experience in dealing with question-and-answer activities pertaining to newly acquired concepts and language.

3. To provide discussion experience using new concepts and language.
4. To provide small-group discussion experience; to discuss strategies for entering discussions and for keeping up with the topics.
5. To help Mark organize and express ideas in writing.
6. To improve speech articulation.
7. To discuss the new demands he will meet in Junior High School and to provide readiness training to meet these.
8. To begin to establish contact with a Junior High School counselor to plan for transition from sixth grade.

Each of these children requires an individualized program of management to alleviate specific needs. The children described also highlight the fact that if you are to be effective in helping them you will have to be prepared to deal with all aspects of communication from specific to general. You will have to deal with new concepts and associated vocabulary, increase awareness of visual and auditory cues, and improve speech articulation. You will also have to help them adjust to hearing aids, learn to understand why they are not like other children in some ways, and understand and deal with their feelings about themselves, their handicap, and the reactions of others to them. In practice it is neither possible nor advisable to isolate one need from all others. Communication is an integrated function. It is necessary, however, to determine which needs should be focused upon for a given individual. You may decide that a child has very limited conceptual understanding of a subject component and that you need to deal with understanding before dealing with the related language and how it sounds and appears when spoken. For another child, or for the same child at a later date, the knowledge and understanding may have been acquired, but communication about it may be handicapped by lack of appropriate language. Again, the language may be present but the child's articulation and use of voice may make it difficult to communicate intelligibly.

INTERVENTION PROCEDURES

Plan Intervention Strategies and Procedures for the Individual

Now that we have emphasized the integrative nature of communication, we can examine the components independently and discuss intervention practices. The major components are:

1. Language
2. Auditory and visual speech processing
3. Speech articulation and voice
4. Counseling

Language

Language consists of content and skills. At the semantic level, language content is intimately related to cognitive knowledge. Language skills involve the ability to use the formalized system of rules for encoding ideas and experience, for manipulating the environment, and for communicating with others about ideas and experiences. Language and its use pervade all aspects of the child's relationship with the world. It is difficult and unwise, therefore, to assign to any one person the responsibility for upgrading language competency in a hearing-impaired child. You should not ask, "Is language enrichment a part of my responsibility?" but "What is the nature of the contribution I should be making to the growth of language in this child?" This section contains some guidelines to help you answer this question. Consider these ideas critically and modify them to suit your role and the situation in which you work.

We are considering the hearing-impaired primary-school child who may be in a regular classroom with or without the resource of a teacher of the hearing impaired, or the child in a special class for hearing-impaired children. In either case the primary source of language stimulation will be the classroom. Activities will generate the need for communication, which in turn calls for the use of language by the participants. The teacher will present the appropriate vocabulary and expressions and will provide informal models for their use. It is not expected that the teacher of a hearing class will be able to provide individualized instruction in language to the mainstreamed hearing-impaired child. This will be increasingly true as the child moves into the higher grades. If the child receives support from a resource teacher that teacher will almost certainly provide a program for language enrichment. Your contribution as a hearing and speech therapist/teacher will be to augment the resource teachers' efforts by building communication skills, training around the language content currently being worked upon. If a child is receiving no support other than what you are providing, then you must assume primary responsibility for supportive language training correlated with the class subject material.

The child in a special class should be receiving language training as part of every lesson. The teacher will develop concepts and teach vocabulary, phrases, and grammar. She may teach separate language lessons, or she may teach language as part of each subject as the need arises. For children in these classes, your emphasis will be more on the recognition and use of acquired language than on the development of new concepts. However, you must never fail to take advantage of naturally arising opportunities to expand concepts, vocabulary, and language form.

In determining the nature of your contribution, you may be guided by the answers to the following questions:

1. Is the child receiving language instruction specific to his or her needs?
2. Is this instruction a part of daily classroom learning (as in a special class) or is it part of an individualized program provided by a resource or itinerant teacher of hearing-impaired children?
3. Are you the primary support person to a child mainstreamed into a regular class?
4. What is the present status of the child's language competencies in terms of classroom demands?
5. Is deficiency in language content the major handicap?
6. Is deficiency in language skills the major handicap?

The extent to which you must assume responsibility for language training will depend on how much the child is already receiving. You will either assume a primary or a secondary responsibility.

In the majority of instances, children in need of extensive language training will either be in a special class, or will be provided with the services of a resource or itinerant teacher of the hearing impaired. Should you identify a child who is not receiving such service, you must do everything possible to assure it. If, for any reason, you are unsuccessful in obtaining the necessary support for the child, then you must insist on the right to allocate as much of your time to that child as he or she would be entitled to from a resource teacher. The need for you to do this should be increasingly rare. Most of the children for whom a therapist/teacher must assume such primary responsibility for language training will not need extensive language help. You should consider the following steps in developing an intervention program for these children.

Look at the Basic-Concept Test Results. Determine whether the child has the language concepts associated with the demands that will be made in class. If the child does not understand the functional vocabulary essential to teacher-child transactions, he or she will have difficulty in participating in the learning situation. It will be important for you to begin to help the child acquire those essential concepts he or she lacks, to provide the language that identifies all relevant basic concepts, and to train the child to recognize the concepts when spoken about in a natural context.

Examine the Vocabulary Scores. Determine whether the child has a deficit in general vocabulary. Note also the results of subject-vocabulary assessment. You will probably need to develop a vocabulary-enrichment program for both general and specific vocabulary.

Examine the Results of Formal Tests of Language Comprehension. Determine the types of language content the child cannot extract from the structure. For example: Does the child understand subject-object relationships, time relationships (expressed by verb tense, adverbs, and adverbial clauses); location (expressed by prepositions or prepositional clauses); possession (expressed by possessive pronouns); plurality (expressed by verb conjugation and plural nouns)? The formal-test results heavily emphasize difficulty with language form. That is, they deal only with the surface structure. Therefore, in addition you will need to examine the child's errors to determine underlying difficulties with meaning or deep structure.

Examine the Expressive Use of Language. Use both test results and samples of spontaneous speech and written work to identify the types of structural deficiencies that appear. You may observe that the child does not use tense appropriately or that the child may use only the present tense. Verbs may not be conjugated appropriately. The child may omit the infinitive marker "to" in using for example, "He want eat cake." "Mommy like go shop." "She try hit ball." The child may not use the negative form correctly—for example, "He not have a friend." The child may leave out the word "do" or "does" in support of the question form—for example, "Why (do) they laugh?" "How (does) he do it?"

Only by identifying the particular structural errors evident in the child's speech will you be able to write an intervention plan specific to that child's needs.

Intervention Strategies. Your intervention program should follow these stages:

1. *Identify those basic concepts, relative to the child's environment with which he or she is not yet familiar.* Confine your selection to concepts that are functionally important and that occur fairly frequently. First teach these concepts in the situational and linguistic contexts in which they will be encountered most often. *Put away* your books. *Take out* your homework. *Fold* the paper in *two. Do* the *odd-numbered* questions. In the last two sentences you will need to discuss the differences between to, two, too, and should explain how the word "do," when used as a command, replaces the verb—for example, "Do the questions" = Answer. "Do the exercises" = Carry out or complete. Having dealt with the concepts in specific contexts, expand them to cover other situations in which they can occur. "*Put away* your toys, the groceries, your clothes." "*Fold* your arms, hands, the napkins, the newspaper." "*Take out* the garbage, a splinter, a tooth, the dog." Consider concept opposites: open-close; take out-put away, bring in; fold-unfold, undo, unwrap. Consider situations in which these concept words can be used. Whenever possible involve the child physically in the concrete experience in which the word or expression occurs. Among published kits that may prove helpful to you in developing concepts are *Concepts for Communication* (Wright, Norris, & Worsley); *Concept Formation* (Tabaka-Juedes, 1978) *A Basic Concepts Development Program* (Collins & Cunningham, 1978).

2. *Plan to increase general functional vocabulary.* Systematically expose the child to new concepts and words in context. Contrast these words with words of opposite meaning. Compare words of similar meaning. Classify the words into higher-order categories (for example, cat—mammal—animal). Introduce related terms (cat—fur, purr, curl up, hunt, crouch, nine lives). Subdivide and classify words by category (vegetables: cabbage, potatoes, peas, beans; fruit: apples, bananas, oranges). You may find published language-development kits (see Fristoe, 1976, for listing and description) and commercial products such as the *Basic Vocabulary Study Cards* (McCarr) helpful in providing general vocabulary lists. Another source for new vocabulary is age-related children's literature. The school librarian or local public-library staff are invariably most helpful in advising parents on the selection of well-illustrated, interesting books appropriate to a description you can provide of the child's needs. Initiating a daily reading period in which the parents or an older sibling reads to the child will do much to foster general language comprehension. The parents should be guided in how to conduct these listening periods. Stress the need to sit so the child can watch and listen, choose a quiet, relaxed time and environment, combine reading and explaining or discussing what is happening as appropriate to the child's needs, read slowly but naturally, do not let the child become lost or bored, note in writing unfamiliar words for later review. If the child can read sufficiently well to derive pleasure from books, then the guidance of the reading teacher and/or remedial-reading teacher should be involved in developing a progressive reading plan.

3. *Increase subject-specific vocabulary.* Each school subject requires a specific vocabulary. It is necessary to ensure that the hearing-impaired child is familiar with the vocabulary appropriate to each subject and that the child under-

FIGURE 17.2 The librarian can be a helpful resource person in guiding parents in the selection of children's books. (Courtesy of Buffalo City School System)

stands the concepts identified by that vocabulary. This requires that you identify and present relevant terminology. For example, in arithmetic you would check that the child knows and understands such terms as add, addition, subtract, subtraction, multiply, multiplication, multiplier, multiple, divide, divisor, dividend, fraction, numerator, denominator. You should relate these terms to their concepts in the broadest possible way, extending their meanings into general language use. For example: *add* means increase, make larger, but *multiply* also means to increase or make larger. "John added his money to the pile." "Sue added the idea that we should take lunch with us." "The rabbits multiplied rapidly." "The tool had multiple uses." When possible use the word in a colloquialism. "It all added up." "Now I understand how the things I have seen fit together." "*Divide* means to cut up, to section, to share." "I will divide this apple in two." "The children divided the last of the chores among them." "The teachers were divided in their opinion about what to do."

Illustrate the use of each term in general communication, bearing in mind the child's general vocabulary and language level. Then reapply the word to the subject context in which it is used.

In social studies, for example, the following words might be expected to appear: mountains, mountain range, lakes, shoreline, border; or, in a different project, tribes, councils, reservation, chief; or, Pilgrims, traders, explorers, colony, settler. The concepts and vocabulary you select must relate to what the child encounters in the classroom. You should parallel the topics being covered by the teacher. Your role is to ensure that the language concepts and vocabulary essential to subject learning are familiar to the child. You are not expected to teach subject content though you may review the ideas discussed in class. The vocabulary acquired must then be incorporated into language use.

4. *Teacher or correct missing or incorrect grammar and syntactic structures.* Careful analysis of formal test results, as discussed earlier, will reveal the types of omissions and errors made by the child. Samples of the written English of the older primary-school child will also illustrate the types of difficulties encountered in language structure. The teaching and correcting of grammar and syntax necessitates that specific help be given to teach the child to use appropriate rules for expressing the relationship among words. The child does not need to be concerned with the rule itself but must be familiar with its function and must observe the effects of its use. For example, language intervention for the children who have difficulty in understanding complex sentences will probably be most successful if you first approach the individual concepts being conveyed by the surface structure—for example, John was very tired. John overslept. John was late for school. "Because John was very tired he overslept and was late for school." First deal with the underlying concepts of being tired, oversleeping, being late. Then discuss the causal relationship indicated by "because" and by the clause ". . . and was late for school." Examine and generalize sentences that show causal and dependent relationships using various forms: "*Since you are ready* to go I will not wait. "*Now that you have finished your work,* you may play." "This is your reward *for being good.*" "*If you go to the library* don't forget to return these books."

Next work with other simple sentences that can be combined into complex sentences. Have the child combine the simple sentences. Then examine complex sentences to discover the deep structure. Suppose, for example, that a child has difficulty in understanding the difference between the transitive and intransitive forms of the verb: John broke the window. The window was broken. To help the child deduce the functional difference between these forms you may classify a series of pictures into action-transitive:

Mary hit (what?) the boy.
The dog bit (who?) the letter carrier.
Mother cooked (what?) the hamburger.
The teacher praised (who?) the boy.

or action-intransitive:

The window (what happened to it?) broke.
The trick (what happened to it?) failed.
My watch (what happened to it?) stopped.
David (what happened to him?) was hurt.

A number of kits are available to help you improve the child's use of various syntactic constructions. Coughran & Liles; Fokes; Gotkin; Peterson, Brenner, & Williams; Wilson. One kit (Quigley, Steinkamp, Power, & Jones) has standardized norms for prelingually profoundly deaf children 10 to 18 years old. You will need to select from them those items that directly address the problems of an individual child.

To conclude this discussion of language intervention, let us stress again the need for individualized programs to avoid wasted effort. You need to differentiate between errors that the child makes in the use of existing language, and the needs the child has to learn developmentally more complex forms. Kretschmer and Kretschmer (1978) have provided an outline of the sequences for teaching developmental language which serves as a useful guide to the various stages of language growth.

In focusing on language structure it is easy to forget that its purpose is to permit individuals to communicate about their experiences, and to facilitate transactions with their environment. For this to be possible the participants must have adequate communication skills to permit the reception and restructuring of the message, and to encode an appropriate response. Language, therefore, cannot be separated from the decoding and encoding stages of the communication process. We are now ready to consider how to assess and improve the effectiveness of auditory and visual speech processing by the primary school child.

Auditory and Visual Speech Processing

Cognition and language cannot logically be viewed as independent functions. Similarly, speech perception and language processing are intimately related. For this reason it is impossible to think of auditory and visual communication training as representing processing skills that can be worked upon independently of the child's cognitive and linguistic needs. General training programs applied to all children are, therefore, inappropriate.

We saw earlier in the text how the acoustic and visual speech signal constrain or guide the listener in reconstructing the linguistic message. The external signal-constraint cues are rapidly restructured into the language system, allowing the listener to generate linguistic expectancies at increasingly higher levels of language processing. We use the external signal only to the extent that we cannot generate and confirm appropriate expectancies. Ironically, reduced language capabilities in the hearing-impaired child increase dependency upon the details of the very signal that the hearing impairment distorts. Your first goal, therefore, is to do everything possible to optimize the child's use of the auditory information that does get through. Training cannot improve hearing, but it can improve auditory behavior, auditory language processing, and auditory perception.

Both experimental evidence and educational experience strongly support a language-based approach to auditory-visual training. Kretschmer and Kretschmer (1978) have stressed the need for auditory training of young hearing-impaired children to be predominately linguistically based. The extension of this philosophy to the school-age child is supported by Ling (1978), Boothroyd (1978), Levitt (1978), and Villchur (1978), who participated in a discussion of auditory management of hearing-impaired children. Boothroyd, in that discussion, refers to his experience in adopting a global approach to teaching. He states:

Everything had to do with comprehension and communication. We did not use discrimination tasks or multiple choice responses. The children's reactions were interesting. They were all children whom we felt ought to be doing better auditorily than they were. They hated training at first, but later came to enjoy it, and they succeeded. When we tested their per-

formance using both analytic discrimination tests and global comprehension tests we didn't get any improvement in discrimination. The improvement was in the perception of words in sentences and not in isolated words (p. 327).

This, you may recall, is exactly what Blesser (1972) found in his study of the perception of an inverted speech spectrum by persons with normal hearing. It clearly indicates that our concern must be for auditory-visual-contextual perception of meaning rather than for auditory discrimination alone.

The ability of the child to make a prediction about the language content of the signal will depend on the child's having sufficient information to satisfy the minimal criteria for comprehension. This minimal amount of information from all sources will vary as a function of noise and redundancy. We can expect, therefore, that as the factors that determine noise and redundancy change, so will the amount of information the child can derive from residual hearing. There will always be situations in which auditory information alone is insufficient to permit comprehension. In those situations the child must turn for support to the second avenue of information about speech, the visual channel. We seek to train the child to develop the behaviors conducive to the optimal integration of visual cues to speech into the total-information pattern.

Both auditory and visual cues to speech arise from speech articulation; thus they relate to the same code. We aim to train the child to perceive the auditory-visual information as a single pattern, to integrate the information into a single linguistic and semantic value. Thus, *auditory and visual communication can be defined as a systematic procedure for increasing the amount of information that a person is able to extract from the auditory and visual speech signal in reconstructing meaning from the patterns of spoken language.*

In planning to enhance the child's use of auditory and visual cues keep in mind the following considerations:

1. Prerequisite to use of auditory and visual speech cues is familiarity with the concept and language to which the acoustic and visual correlates of articulation refer. Auditory and visual communication training, therefore, must be preceded by cognitive-linguistic teaching of the content and language structure of which the speech pattern is symptomatic. Training must take place within the limits of the child's cognitive-linguistic competency.
2. The prime purpose of auditory and visual training is to facilitate identification of linguistically encoded concepts. For this reason training will be most effective when it concentrates on teaching the child to derive meaning from what he or she hears and sees. Although there is some justification for very short drill activities on the recognition of individual words and speech sounds, most of your efforts should be in training the child to recognize the meaning embedded in patterns of speech.
3. Speech perception requires ability to draw upon internal language redundancy. Lessons should, therefore, use samples large enough for the child to recognize syntactic and semantic constraints.
4. Lessons should work from the general to the specific, from semantic to phonologic discrimination. Aim first for the identification of general meaning, then meaning at the sentence level, then finally the reduction of ambiguities at the word level.

5. Since speech patterns arise from coarticulation, even at the level of phonological discrimination, you must train children on units large enough to permit coarticulatory cues to be capitalized upon.
6. Confusions between sounds may be reduced if the particular sounds are contrasted auditorily and auditory-visually in nonsense syllables. As soon as you have identified contexts in which discrimination between these sounds is possible, shift training to the word-in-sentence level. Consonant-discrimination training as a precursor to speech-articulation training should use a full range of phonetic contexts.
7. Auditory and visual speech recognition must be considered as two complementary aspects of a single message signal. Do not separate the two modalities except briefly. Other than for speech articulation training do not reduce the message signal to a level below which a meaning pattern can be recognized. Reintegrate the auditory-visual information as soon as possible to relate the sensory pattern back to the linguistic and cognitive values.

Integrating Auditory-Visual Training into Language Enrichment. Auditory and visual communication represent a means of processing language. It is in this context that you should plan lessons. Rather than planning separate auditory and visual communication sessions, you should include this aspect of intervention as a significant component of all language-training activities.

From your assessment of the child's receptive communication for familiar language content, you will have an idea of the ease or difficulty with which the child can understand spoken language. You will have an idea of the relative contributions that vision and audition make to speech intelligibility, and you will be aware of the particular speech sounds that present difficulty or are inaudible. With this information you can plan your intervention strategy. You should aim to achieve the following goals:

1. To develop or enhance listening and watching and to increase auditory attention
2. To teach the child to concentrate on deriving meaning from what is said rather than trying to follow word for word
3. To increase awareness of the auditory patterns of meaningful speech units by isolating them from visual cues
4. To increase awareness of visual patterns of the same units by isolating them from auditory cues
5. To integrate auditory and visual cues into meaningful spoken-language units
6. To enhance the child's recognition of familiar words and phrases
7. To ensure that the visual and auditory patterns of all new vocabulary, phrases, and syntactic structures are learned to the child's maximal capacity
8. To develop in the child an attitude toward receptive processing that is as relaxed as possible
9. To increase the child's competence in following instructional and conversational speech under less than optimal conditions

Following are some guidelines for auditory-visual training:

Training should begin under the most favorable conditions.
Use a quality educational amplification system if available. If not, sit close to the child in favorable viewing conditions.

When talking to the child, look up. Try to communicate naturally.
The content of your lesson should be, for the most part, that of your language-enrichment plan. Thus auditory and visual training will include ability to discriminate general and key vocabulary in sentences, subject-related phrases and descriptions, and classroom and textbook instructions.
Write new vocabulary and phrases on the board. Put new words into sentences that clarify their meaning (Figure 17.3).
After you have dealt with the semantic value of key words, phrases, or sentences have the child close his or her eyes and listen.
Repeat the words, phrase, or sentence several times clearly and deliberately. Key words should be spoken first in isolation, then in a clarifying sentence, then in isolation. Have the child open his or her eyes; repeat the item several times. Repeat this procedure with several key items, then pair the items.
Ask the child to select a word in a sentence, a phrase or a sentence when spoken. Provide first two, then three alternatives until he can select one item from among many. Do this first with auditory cues only. Add visual cues if the child cannot discriminate by audition alone.
Select two key words or key phrases and tell the child that you will say something *about* one of them, or that you will paraphrase one of the written statements. The child must identify the word or phrase related to what you say. Present the statement several times allowing the child to listen only. If the child cannot relate the statement to one of the two selected items, repeat your statement while he or she is watching you. Increase the number of items from which the selection must be made.
Ask questions relevant to a particular topic and its key vocabulary, first allowing only listening, then adding visual cues as necessary.
General and subject-specific vocabulary building should include auditory and visual training in the recognition of all words. The words may be presented by auditory and auditory-visual modes, first in isolation, and then in sentences. *Do not ask the child to repeat what you say.* This develops insecurity in predicting. Ask the child either to identify the item or, better still, to respond to questions that require more than a yes/no answer.

Auditory and auditory-visual training should also be conducted using the verbal instructions that the child may encounter in the classroom. First write up the directions on the board, or on individual cards you place before the child. Say each direction several times. The child first listens, then listens and watches. Next have the child identify a direction from among two or three. Increase the sample. Have the child act upon directions given.

Increasing Comprehension under Conditions of Reduced Redundancy. We have not advocated training a child to comprehend speech by visual cues alone because the deprivation of auditory cues puts the hearing-impaired person in an unreal situation. Furthermore, separating audition from vision for training purposes may lead to counterproductive perceptual strategies. There will be situations in which auditory information alone will be insufficient to permit comprehension; thus auditory-visual integration training has been recommended. Dependency upon use of visual cues increases as auditory information decreases. You need to provide training activities that encourage the hearing-impaired child to develop processing strategies appropriate to conditions of reduced redundancy.

FIGURE 17.3 Training in speech comprehension must take place within the child's cognitive and linguistic competencies. (Courtesy of Buffalo City School System)

You can control redundancy by varying: (1) The fidelity and intensity of the acoustic signal; (2) The environmental noise and reverberation; (3) The complexity of the listening task; and (4) The continuity of the listening task.

1. *Signal fidelity and intensity.* Fidelity is affected by the system of amplification used, and is related to the need to train the child first with high-quality amplification and then with the wearable hearing aid. Intensity refers to the range of intensity of normal speech. You need to train the student to follow speech when the intensity is lowered for short periods to a level of confidential speech. It should not be necessary to constantly adjust the volume of the hearing aid. Moving closer to the speaker to receive a confidence and watching more attentively should suffice. Conversely, training should be carried out at different distances from the microphone of the hearing aid. Moving from a distance of 4 inches from the microphone to a distance of 3 feet and then 9 feet will reduce signal fidelity and therefore redundancy. This recognizes that the wearable aid must be used at less than optimal talker-microphone distance (Figure 17.4).
2. *Environmental noise and redundancy.* A child will need to raise speech-perception skills to a level at which he or she can function in normal-listening environments. Many environments have background noise or are rather reverberant. Both factors lower the redundancy of the message. It is important in training sessions to approximate these real-life situations. At the appropriate stage of training you should use one or two tape recorders to provide

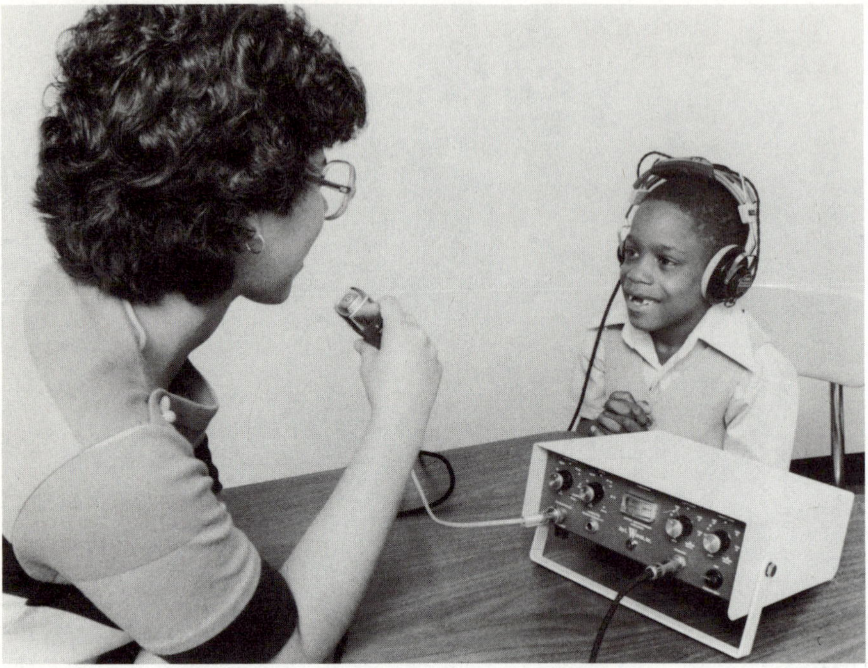

FIGURE 17.4 Use quality amplification and favorable viewing conditions for auditory-visual training. (Courtesy of Buffalo City School System)

background noise. (Refer back to the discussion of the evaluation of speech comprehension in noise in Chapter 10.) If measured S/N ratios can be set you should duplicate those recommended. If not, set the background noise first at what you judge to be quiet, then gradually increase the loudness until you begin to notice it as intrusive to your listening to a speaker conversing at normal loudness. The test results that the audiologist obtained for the child's speech discrimination in noise will help you select levels you should use. Try to obtain records of classroom noise as your background stimulus. You may also wish to use a recording of cocktail-party speech babble because speech is particularly potent as an interference source.

3. *Task complexity.* Pay attention to the complexity of the language and content of the lessons you present. In the early stages you should ensure that material is rephrased to reduce complexity. However, your goal is to help the student handle increasingly complex cognitive-linguistic content up to the level of textbooks and class presentation. Try to increase the amount of information the student can process by auditory-visual reception. Begin by presenting short units of the whole; then gradually increase the length of each unit. Questions and discussion, therefore, should cover larger and larger amounts of information, thus making greater demands upon the student's ability to restructure information into long-term memory.

   You may also increase complexity of the task by raising the demands for decision making. Recognizing content requires less information than processing and responding to directions, answering questions, or making decisions. Work toward increasing the student's willingness to take judicious risks in predicting content. To encourage this you should incorporate the teaching of communication strategies for obtaining further constraints and verifying predictions. For example, encourage the student to ask:

Could you please go over that once more?
How many days did you say the trip took?
Did you say I should do the even-numbered exercises?
or
Let me check that I have understood the homework assignment.

4. *Task continuity.* Hearing-impaired persons often experience difficulty in understanding what is being said when they are unaware of the subject topic. This is particularly noticeable when the topic under discussion changes. Develop training exercises that require the student to identify the general topic without initially worrying about detailed content. For example:
Which topic am I discussing?
   a. The early Pilgrim settlements;
   b. The wars with the Indians;
   c. The trade products of the southern British colonies;
   d. The exploration of the western part of the North American continent.

   The task can be made more difficult by increasing the number of choices to three or four topics.
   You may also identify a topic, and begin to discuss it, asking the student to indicate when the topic changes.

Training in Speech-Sound Recognition. Having stressed so strongly that the perception of spoken language appears to be a holistic, integrated function, it may seem illogical for us to even consider analytical training in speech-sound recognition. Even with a commitment to a language-based intervention model, there is still a place for analytic training. In the discussion in Ross and Giolas' (1978) text, other professionals support this view. The results of analytical assessment of speech-sound discrimination shown in Figures 16.4 and 16.5 testify to the complexity of the process of auditory discrimination. The essential problem that faces you is how to reach some conclusion concerning the relative importance to the child of the information in the acoustic message signal itself for the correct identification of phonemes. It is important that you carefully consider this question, because it is fundamental to the way in which you set up your auditory training program. Should you ignore the fact that a child experiences auditory-discrimination confusions between certain phonemes when they are presented in the form of nonsense syllables? You might justify doing so by saying that speech perception never requires the individual to make discriminations between meaningless sound units. Because the child will always have access to structural and contextual cues, you need not be concerned with the confusions that he or she is likely to make when these are absent. Your lesson plans should concern themselves only with meaningful materials. The drill-type approach, involving the careful comparison of sounds that may be confused, might be considered meaningless to the student and a waste of the student's and the therapist/teacher's time.

On the other hand, verbal communication involves utilizing "bits" of information. We know these are derived from a variety of internal and external sources. The contribution they make must exceed a given amount of information for the threshold of comprehension to be crossed. Therefore, you are not justified in jettisoning even a limited amount of acoustic information that, with training, the subject may be able to use to augment the amount in the pool. It is not true that the listener will never need to utilize the maximum informational context that can be wrung out of the acoustic signal. Since the cushion of redundancy that we have built into our communication system is severely reduced in a person with a significant hearing impairment, the amount of information that can be derived from all available sources becomes critical. This is particularly true for children with reduced linguistic competency. For this reason, you may wish to investigate whether some intensive training in the auditory discrimination of phonemes might not result in an improvement in the phonemic discrimination that would be reflected in an overall increase in the child's communication ability. Follow these guidelines in training to encourage speech-sound discrimination:

1. Train only the discrimination of those sounds the child has been shown to have difficulty discriminating between.
2. Use a high-quality amplifier for training.
3. First identify the sound(s) to be discriminated by presenting words that begin and end with the sound(s) or have the sound(s) in the middle position.
4. Present the sound combination (consonant-vowel, vowel-consonant, or consonant-vowel-consonant) five or six times with a brief interval between presentation; then repeat, adding visual cues.
5. Present the sound combination five or six times, pause, repeat, then ask for identification of the sound pattern. If recognition is not possible, repeat with visual cues.
6. Contrast the sound with other sounds. Begin with dissimilar sounds; then move to the sounds with which the phoneme you are working are confused.
7. Integrate your training with speech-articulation training because sounds not correctly heard are likely to be incorrectly articulated.

Voice and Speech Improvement

The guidelines for speech improvement outlined for the older preschool child (Chapter 14) are equally valid for the primary-school child. The only difference in working with the primary-school child is that you can structure the sessions more and make them a little longer than those for the preschool child.

Correcting speech and voice-production errors should be an integral part of your plan for general improvement of the child's communication skills. Thus, although individual sounds will be isolated and worked on as nonsense syllables in various phonetic combinations, once the child has mastered them they should be worked upon in the general vocabulary and subject-specific vocabulary that constitutes your language-enrichment and support curriculum for the child. The words should then be placed in short informative sentences, relevant to the topic materials. In this way you can monitor production of the sound during sentence production. Finally you can monitor the articulation of the sound for reinforcement during selected periods of conversation during which you w reinforce the correct production of the sound and you will c These periods should be short to avoid frustrating the c something to communicate.

Speech correction and speech-discrimination training must be coordinated. Unless taught differently, we speak as we hear speech. Furthermore we know that production of speech occurs in terms of internal models against which output is compared for acceptance or rejection. We aim to produce speech that matches the model. When hearing distorts speech reception, a deviant model is established. Thus, even though a speech sound is incorrectly articulated, if it matches how the child expects it to sound, it will be accepted. Auditory training, if successful, should result in greater awareness of the acoustic pattern and enhancement of the internal model. Articulation training will bring the production of the sound in closer accord with the correct model. This, in turn, will tend to sharpen the criteria for discrimination.

Training should aim first to maximize the use of auditory information. After concentrating on the auditory information, visual cues may be added to help the child clarify articulation postures. First examine the child's phonetic discrimination test results to identify any contexts in which the sound in question can be discriminated auditorily. If such contexts are found, the consonant and vowel combinations will provide the base for teaching or correcting the child's articulation of that sound. Once the child can produce the sound acceptably in those contexts, he or she can transfer it to other contexts in which it is not discriminable but in which it can be monitored by motor kinesthetic, tactile, and, if necessary, visual feedback.

Voice production of children with severe hearing impairments most likely will need attention. Exercises may be given to help such children improve pitch and intensity control to better approximate normal speech-sound durations and to remediate vocal deviancies such as breathiness, excessive tension, excessive vocal attack, or falsetto vocalization. Suggested approaches to remediation may be found in texts by Ling (1976), Calvert and Silverman (1975), and Wilson (1972). Hearing-impaired children may also need help in using voice and the suprasegmentals of speech to communicate feeling or mood. Exercises may be necessary to help the children learn to put expression into speech—to exhibit surprise, anger, excitement, tiredness. To accomplish this you could extend the types of activities suggested in Chapter 14 to help older preschool children learn to deal with their own and with others' feelings.

Educational Amplifier versus Personal Hearing Aid. Throughout our discussion of intervention practices we have stressed the need to use the highest quality amplification to ensure that the child receive as much of the auditory pattern as possible. Similarly, the acoustic conditions under which training is given should provide optimal signal-to-noise ratios. Ultimately, however, the child must function with the unit that he or she routinely wears. The importance of this must not be overlooked. Some experts (Børrild, 1978) have reservations about training a child on a high-quality amplifier or even simply one with a response characteristic different from the child's own aid; we have already addressed this topic in our discussion of amplification for education (Chapter 11).

Boothroyd's (1978) account of the reaction of severely hearing-impaired children to shifting from group hearing aids during global auditory-discrimination training illustrates how important it is that you understand the relationship between the educational amplification system and the wearable hearing aid:

All this work was done with group hearing aids: ideal signal, ideal signal-to-noise ratio. Halfway through the study we felt guilty. Personal hearing aids were taking a back seat. Once again we were in danger of letting the children believe that hearing aids aren't important. So I asked the teacher to do some of the evaluations with their personal hearing aids and it was a complete disaster. Two of the children were in tears and the rest were angry because they couldn't hear the message (p. 327).

The responses of the children with whom Boothroyd worked indicate several things:

1. The children clearly derived more acoustic information from the group hearing aid than from their personal aids.
2. They came to expect this higher quality of amplification with the resultant increased acoustic information.
3. The better acoustic signal permitted improved speech comprehension.
4. The children were aware of their improved ability to comprehend and were distressed by its reduction when asked to use their own aids again.

You should learn from this experience that the purpose of educational amplification systems is for learning new concepts and language, for acquiring new knowledge, and for improving speech. Until wearable hearing aids afford the same quality of amplified sound as the larger units, you must depend on auditory trainers for teaching purposes. However, the impracticability of their use in everyday situations makes personal hearing aids invaluable despite their acoustic limitations. You must not let the student become so dependent upon high-quality amplification that the effectiveness of the personal aid is reduced. The ultimate goal of your training is to improve comprehension of spoken language in everyday situations. You must incorporate into your training sessions procedures to facilitate transition from comprehension of information learned on a high-quality system to recognition of that content information through the personal hearing aid. The student must know and understand your philosophy regarding amplification. You are partners in this project and the student must fully understand why you do what you do. In this way you will reduce the frustration the child will experience and ensure that you both work cooperatively in pursuit of common goals.

Counseling

During the primary-school years children become increasingly concerned with the need to find out about themselves. Initially self-discovery involves exploring physical characteristics and capabilities. Later they begin to question the kind of people they are. All children are going to learn about their limitations as well as their assets as they gradually find their roles in the social group constituted by classmates and by neighborhood children within a compatible age range (Elkind, 1971). This period of exploration and self-definition will expand self-image when a child experiences success in social acceptance, leadership, academic performance, and athletics. When success is not achieved in one or more of these areas, the natural tendency will be to define the self-image to accord with the reality of the situation, or to rationalize the lack of success. Failure to achieve at least average performance in any area almost always results in a limiting of self-concept. This process continues throughout childhood, adolescence, and young adulthood. Each new opportunity demands that a child or adult assess perceived ability to meet the demand. Success in doing so expands the self-image; failure results in a barrier to self-expansion in that direction. These barriers are sometimes realistic—for example, those imposed by physical limitations. Usually, however, we tend to erect barriers below the level of our optimal performance and fail to extend our growth maximally. The boundaries of self, defined by these barriers, become more and more firmly established as a child becomes an adult. The area represented within these boundaries will serve as the basis for our sense of self-worth. Although few boundaries are rigid, expansion proves increasingly more difficult in every area as the individual matures. Reality forces an increasing degree of acceptance of the image we form of ourselves. Together, the sum total of boundary values in an adult constitute a formidable barrier to self-expansion. Limiting though we may feel our boundaries are, they represent a level of security with which we feel we can live. Expanding personal boundaries involves the individual in a period of insecurity until he or she can reconsolidate those boundaries and redefine his or her self-image to accommodate them. It is awareness of this process that emphasizes the importance of counseling as an integral component of a management program for the hearing-impaired school child. We can do much to affect the factors that influence the developing self-concept of the young child.

The Nature of Counseling. Counseling should be seen as an ongoing personal interaction between you and the child, supported by periodic consultations with the parents and teachers. Your sensitivity to the concerns, apprehensions, and feelings of the child about the handicap, his or her achievement level, and the ways others react to him or her will foster a climate in which things can be talked about when they arise. Effective counseling results from acceptance of the legitimacy of feelings experienced and situations perceived. It requires that you understand how the child feels. To achieve that understanding you must be prepared to listen nonjudgmentally.

The Goals of Counseling. Examine your goals in terms of informational counseling and personal-adjustment counseling. Informational counseling should aim to help the child become thoroughly familiar with the nature of the handicap. Ultimately the child should know all there is to know about the hearing impairment, how it affects the ability to learn, and what actual limitations it imposes upon him or her in school and in the world outside. It is very important that as soon as is practical you begin the process of helping the child to learn what the hearing impairment is. The child needs to know why it cannot be cured, and, if true, that it will probably not grow worse. The child needs to know what the hearing aid does and does not do, how you expect it to affect his or her ability to understand speech in different situations, and why it is so important to make certain that it is working well at all times. The child should be told in which situations he or she should feel free to turn it off or even take it off.

Publications that can help familiarize the child with a hearing aid are: *Hearing Aids and You* (Craig, Sins, Rossi, & Neisworth (1976); *Tim and his Hearing Aid* (Ronnei and Porter, 1951); *Your Child's Hearing Aid* (Craig, Sins, Rossi and Neisworth, 1976); *My Friends Big Talk and Little Talk Hearing Aids* (Costello, 1970); *I Hear the Day* (Johnson, 1977) (Figure 17.5).

A child in the upper grades should be familiar with his or her audiogram and know what it means. The child should also understand the aided/unaided audiograms so he or she is aware how much additional sound the aid makes available. You should explain speech-reception and speech-discrimination test results, showing how much knowing the contexts helps him or her and how much visual cues facilitate speech comprehension. Similarly the child should be well familiar with the aid, the type and model, how to operate it, check it, and take care of it (Figure 17.6).

Obviously the extent to which a child can absorb information of this type will depend upon his or her age, level of language comprehension, and general intellectual ability. It will also depend upon your ability to

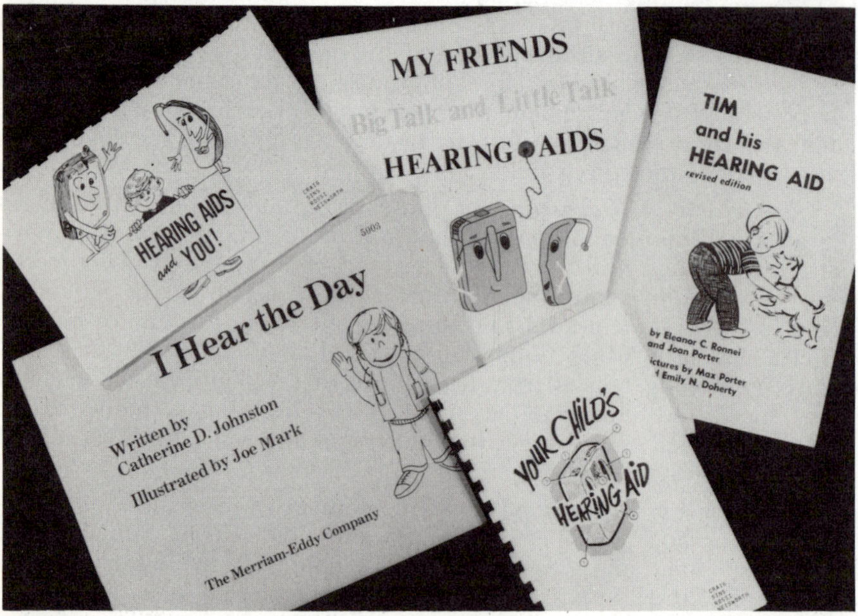

FIGURE 17.5 Children's publications about hearing aids are helpful in familiarizing young children with their hearing aid.

FIGURE 17.6 The older child should be familiar with the nature and extent of his hearing impairment and understand its effects.

simplify information and to make it interesting. Helping a child to understand the disability adds a sense of dignity to it. Too often, we test and work with these children without telling them what we know about their handicap. We counsel teachers and parents about the child, sometimes even in the child's presence, and ignore the child's right to understand. Frequently, hearing-impaired college students have little or no understanding of their hearing impairment. Whenever you test or work with a school-age child you should explain not only what is going to happen in the test, but what you found out. Providing you carefully judge what the child can absorb, and present the information simply in language the child can understand, he or she will gain not only respect for you, but also self-respect. Children respond well to informational counseling judiciously and appropriately given. Such counseling has been integrated into a structured rehabilitation program in at least one school (Poulos, 1960).

Personal-adjustment counseling with primary-school children is usually an unstructured process that you weave throughout the sessions you spend with the child. It is more a relationship with the child, a personal sympathetic interaction, than a formal component of management. The goals of adjustment counseling can be defined as:

1. Providing a comfortable climate in which the child feels free to express both negative and positive feelings without penalty
2. Facilitating the definition of the situation(s) and event(s) that give rise to the feelings
3. Helping the child discuss, analyze, and evaluate those feelings
4. Helping the child explore various ways of dealing with feelings and evaluating the effectiveness of those methods
5. Encouraging the child to express feelings about him- or herself, the handicap, frustrations, and aspirations
6. Encouraging the child to verbalize what he or she feels others think of him or her
7. Exploring the nature of interpersonal relations and how having a hearing handicap affects these

Opportunities will occur naturally for you to enquire how a child is managing in class and with friends. Often the child will express frustration or concern verbally, or may show it through behavior in class or in your sessions together. Usually the most effective method of working with feelings is by your reflecting how you think the child feels, verbalizing what the child may find difficult to express:

You look as though you feel sad, Mary. Have you had a hard time in class today?

You are really angry this morning, John. What happened to make you so mad?

Do you feel that you'll never learn this, Lee? Do you feel you work so hard and it does not make a difference? Does it seem like nobody understands?

This type of counseling is an extension of the intervention techniques we considered when we discussed the molding of sociolinguistic behaviors in the older preschool child (Chapter 14). You may find it helpful to use pictures, illustrated stories, or simple prose passages to provide a basis for discussing how other children feel and react in difficult situations. This permits emotions to be dealt with in a less threatening way. The situation can then often be related directly to the child's experience.

SUMMARY

Intervention practices for the primary-school child derive directly from the analysis and interpretation of the assessment data. The task is best approached within a problem-solving framework. You must carefully consider and weigh each aspect of the child's needs in terms of its present influence on adaptation to school demands. The child must be understood in terms of those demands. You must address problem-solving strategies in terms of the interaction of child and environment. Where possible, environmental modification should be sought in order to reduce the child-environment impedance to learning. Seeking the cooperation of the teacher and parents is the best way of effecting change in the learning and communication environment.

Intervention strategies you direct at the child should be targeted to improve the ability to understand and learn. This necessitates a clear understanding of the task and the situation in which difficulty is experienced. Intervention effectiveness will depend upon the extent to which training can better equip the child to meet the demands of the task.

Language and cognition lie at the base of speech comprehension. Therefore, the approach recommended here depends upon increasing conceptual and language skills. Training in auditory and visual processing is the means to an end rather than an end in itself. Communication training, including speech-articulation training, aims to improve the utility of the available auditory and visual cues to the language structure and content of spoken messages, thus increasing comprehension. Training is primarily integrative in nature because it is believed that speech perception is a holistic process. Counseling is included as a component part of intervention because it seeks to increase understanding of the problem and approaches to its ameliorization, and to reduce anxiety and frustrations that impede relaxed behavior in communication interaction.

REFERENCES

Blesser, B., "Speech Perception under Conditions of Spectral Transformation: I. Phonetic characteristics," *Journal of Speech and Hearing Research 15,* 1972, 5–41. See also discussion of Blesser's work, "Discussion: Perceptual and Cognitive Strategies," in *Sensory Capabilities of Hearing Impaired Children,* ed. R. Stark, pp. 129–153. Baltimore: University Park Press, 1974.

Boothroyd, A., "Speech Perception and Sensorineural Hearing Loss," in *Auditory Management of Hearing Impaired Children: Principles and Prerequisites for Intervention,* ed. M. Ross and T. Giolas, pp. 117–144. Baltimore: University Park Press, 1978.

Børrild, K., "Discussion Summary," in *Auditory Management of Hearing Impaired Children: Principles and Prerequisites for Intervention,* eds. M. Ross and T. Giolas, pp. 145–179. Baltimore: University Park Press, 1978.

Calvert, D., and S. Silverman, *Speech and Deafness.* Washington, D.C.: Alexander Graham Bell Assoc. for the Deaf, 1975.

Collins, P., and G. Cunningham, *A Basic Concepts Development Program.* STEP. Cat. No. 531. CC Publications Inc. (1978), P.O. Box 23699, Tizard, OR.

Costello, M., *My Friends Big Talk and Little Talk Hearing Aids.* Detroit: Henry Ford Hospital, 1970.

Coughran, L., and B. Liles, *Developmental Syntax (Coughran-Liles Syntax Program).* Learning Concepts, 2501 N. Lamar, Austin, Texas 78705.

Craig, H., V. Sins, S. Rossi, and R. Neisworth, *Your Child's Hearing Aid.* Dormac Inc., Box 1622, Lake Oswego, OR. 97034. (1976)

Craig, H., V. Sins, S. Rossi, and R. Neisworth, *Hearing Aids and You.* Dormac Inc., Box 1622, Lake Oswego, OR. 97034. (1976)

Elkind, D., *A Sympathetic Understanding of the Child Six to Sixteen.* Boston: Allyn & Bacon, Inc., 1971.

Fokes, J., *Fokes Sentence Builder Kit.* Teaching Resources, 100 Boylston, Boston, Mass. 02100.

Fristoe, M., "Language Intervention Systems: Programs Published in Kit Form.

Appendix D," in *Communication Assessment and Intervention Strategies,* ed. L. Lloyd. Baltimore: University Park Press, 1976.

Gotkin, L., *Language Lotto.* New Century Ed. Corp., 440 Park Avenue South, New York, New York 10016.

Kretschmer, R., and L. Kretschmer, *Language Development and Intervention with the Hearing Impaired.* Baltimore: University Park Press, 1978.

Levitt, H., "The Acoustics of Speech Production," in *Auditory Management of Hearing Impaired Children: Principles and Prerequisites for Intervention,* eds. M. Ross and T. Giolas, pp. 45–115. Baltimore: University Park Press, 1978.

Ling, D., *Speech and the Hearing-Impaired Child: Theory and Practice.* Washington, D.C.: Alexander Graham Bell Assoc. for the Deaf, 1976.

Ling, D., "Discussion Summary," in *Auditory Management of Hearing Impaired Children: Principles and Prerequisites for Intervention,* eds. M. Ross, and T. Giolas, pp. 295–332. Baltimore: University Park Press, 1978.

McCarr, D., *Basic Vocabulary Study Cards. Units 1 & 2, Nos. 602–603.* Dormac Inc., P.O. Box 752, Beaverton, OR. 97005.

Peterson, H., R. Brener, and L. Williams, *SYNPRO (The Syntax Programmer).* Mercury Co., Division of EMT Labs, 8564 Airport Road, St. Louis, MO. 63100.

Poulos, T., "A Short Term Aural Rehabilitation Program," *Volta Review, 62,* 1960, 345–347.

Quigley, S., M. Steinkamp, D. Power, and B. Jones, *Test of Syntactic Abilities.* Dormac, Inc., P.O. Box 752, Beaverton, OR. 97075.

Ronnei, E., and J. Porter, *Tim and his Hearing Aid.* Alexander Graham Bell Assoc. for the Deaf, The Volta Bureau, Washington, D.C., 20007.

Ross, M., and T. Giolas, eds., *Auditory Management of Hearing Impaired Children: Principles and Prerequisites for Intervention.* Baltimore: University Park Press, 1978.

Tabaka-Juedes, E., *Concept Formation: Steps up to Language for the Learning Impaired.* Communication Skill Builders Inc. (1978), 815 E. Broadway, P.O. Box 42050H, Tucson, AR.

Villchur, E., "Signal Processing," in *Auditory Management of Hearing Impaired Children: Principles and Prerequisites for Intervention,* eds. M. Ross and T. Giolas, pp. 219–237. Baltimore: University Park Press, 1978.

Wilson, D. K., *Voice Problems of Children.* Baltimore: The Williams and Wilkins Company, 1972.

Wilson, M., *Wilson Initial Syntax Program (WISP).* Educators Publishing Service, 74 Moulton St., Cambridge, Mass. 02138.

Wright, J., R. Norris, and F. Worsley, *Concepts for Communication.* Developmental Learning Materials, 7440 Natchez Avenue, Niles, Ill. 60648.

18

Special Considerations for the Postprimary Student

The adolescent years in western society are notable for the adjustment demands they make on the individual. The child must move from the relative stability and protection of childhood through a period of intense biological, psychological, and social change to the independence and responsibility of adulthood. The extent of the upheaval varies from child to child as a result of a complex of interacting factors. These include the child's personality, previous level of academic and social success, the attitudes and support of the family, whether one or both parents are closely involved with the child, the ages of brothers and sisters, and the cultural mores of the peer group. The hearing-impaired child will be subject to these influences as well as to additional factors arising from the hearing impairment. It is important to remember, however, that each child is different, and no general description can be written to accommodate the personal experiences of every child. You will encounter the same range of difficulties and reactions among hearing-impaired students in the postprimary years as are apparent among hearing students.

DEFINING THE PROBLEMS

The special needs that may arise for young hearing-impaired persons in the postprimary-school years occur in several categories. They relate to the need for the students to define themselves and to develop the self-confidence necessary to handle the increasing independence they must assume on the way to adulthood. The maturing students also will need to deal with more sophisticated social relationships with peers. As they move through junior high and senior high school, they will have to accommodate increasing academic demands, and ultimately, they will have to face the question of career choice.

We ended our consideration of the needs of the primary-school child by discussing the need for counseling. This need increases when the child moves into the adolescent years. At this time the child must find an answer to the question "Who am I?" (Cohen, 1978). This answer will be sought in relation to the child's aspirations for the kind of person he or she hopes to be, in the expectations of the parents and peers, in the child's social success, and in his or her academic achievement. At this stage of life the potential for a personal metamorphosis exists, as is evidenced by the unpredictable changes we frequently observe in hearing children. Although adolescence is a period of upheaval, often turbulent, it is also a period of great potential, a period of optimism. As a person whose training and experience makes you sensitive to the special difficulties associated with hearing impairment, you will be viewed by the hearing-impaired student differently from other normal-hearing adults. You know about the handicap, and are sympathetic toward the person who suffers it. When this is recognized, the young handicapped person will usually categorize you among the group of family and close friends to whom Goffman (1963) refers as "the wise." This acceptance of you provides the potential for frank, open discussion of the feelings and anxieties, hopes and despairs that the young adolescent will experience. Your uncritical acceptance of these confidences will create a neutral climate that will encourage the hearing-impaired adolescent to explore his or her feelings. It will encourage the individual to verbalize the fear of not being accepted, to express any doubts about self-worth, to externalize anger about the way others treat him or her. It will permit the student to express aspirations and to explore how realistic they are, to assess assets, and to identify and test what he or she perceives to be personal limitations.

It is important, therefore, that in your early contacts with the postprimary student you define your role in the broadest terms. Explain that you hope to provide support in whatever form it is likely to be effective. Establish a cooperative interaction rather than a teacher-child relationship. Explain that you will adopt a problem-solving approach.

The student, with your encouragement, will attempt to identify and define trouble areas as carefully as possible. Together you will explore and test ways of reducing problems. Make it clear that your goal is to help the student to learn how to define and resolve difficulties, and to assume responsibilities that in the primary school were assumed by others. Depending on the needs of the child much of your time may be spent discussing such expressed opinions as:

> Most of the kids don't have much time for me because I don't hear everything they say.

I'm afraid to tell the other kids that I'm hearing impaired. They don't know I wear an aid.
I'm always afraid to speak up in class in case I didn't understand. I'm afraid I'll make a fool of myself.
There's this cute boy who my friend says likes me, but I'm afraid to talk to him because when he finds out I'm hard of hearing, he won't want anything to do with me.
I've stopped wearing my aid to school because I'm embarrassed by it.
Kids call me deaf. Am I deaf or hard-of-hearing?
I'd like to try out for cheerleading, but I don't think my speech is good enough.
The teachers never call on me to give oral reports because my speech embarrasses everyone.

You cannot, and should not, in any way minimize the significance of the feelings expressed. Your role is to accept what the student says and to help explore the feelings more carefully, to try to describe them more specifically, to consider the situation that gave rise to those feelings or perceptions and to discuss their implications, and to investigate ways of dealing with the difficulties.

You may find it helpful to stimulate self-exploration of feelings and attitudes by using inventories that help to structure the students' thinking about themselves. Libbey (1978) developed an inventory to identify the attitudes of hearing-impaired adolescents in mainstream situations. This inventory contains information about how a student reacts to the types of situations encountered in school and provides a means of comparing the responses of an individual student with those reported by other hearing-impaired students in similar situations. Alpiner (1978) developed a scale of communication function that is heavily weighted in terms of the client's attitudes about the effects of the hearing impairment on his or her own ability to communicate and of the attitudes of others toward him or her. Although the Denver Scale developed by Alpiner was designed for use with adults who have acquired hearing losses, the judicious selection of appropriate items, the modification of others, and the addition of some items specific to the age group we are discussing will provide you with a useful inventory to help the student explore self-perceptions.

An increase in self-confidence can only arise from a better understanding of oneself. The insight gained then permits one to control the degree of risk-taking so that the risk is assumable and the consequences of failure are manageable. Each situation that represents a threat to the student's sense of security must first be examined and understood and then approached with a management strategy with which the student feels comfortable.

The limitations the student perceives will be those that:

1. Jeopardize relationships with peers, including participation in peer-group social activities
2. Limit developing relationships with members of the opposite sex
3. Affect acceptance by teachers
4. Limit academic achievement

Your plan of intervention must grow out of an understanding of the way the student perceives the difficulties encountered in these areas. The student's perceptions are always legitimate in terms of selection and interpretation of the evidence. Your task is to work with the student to determine whether there is evidence that has not been taken into consideration and whether the existing evidence can be interpreted differently. To the extent that the student's perceptions arise from objective evidence, both of you together should attempt to modify either the situation that gives rise to the difficulty, or the strategy the student is using to deal with it. When insufficient concrete evidence is available to justify the student's feelings, then you need to discuss other feelings that are contributing to the perception of the problem, and about other ways of viewing the difficulty. Let us now examine some possible areas of difficulty that may result from any of the categories we have already identified.

PEER RELATIONSHIPS AND SOCIAL EXPERIENCES

In the early adolescent years there is a very strong desire not to deviate in any way from what the group determines is acceptable. This is clearly seen in the vagaries of teenage fashions, which suddenly label a certain type of shoe or brand of jeans as prerequisite to acceptance—the criteria by which crazes are determined. Not only is there a desire on the part of the individual teenager to conform, there also appears to be an almost malevolent determination to root out differences among one's peers. This is behavior to which every teenager is prone. The difference may be as obtrusive as wearing a dress when slacks are identified as the uniform of the event, or as subtle as having eyebrows that meet above the nose. A hearing aid that is visible is obtrusive. Its identification by a peer who comments upon it negatively frequently results in a rejection of the aid that has been worn unprotestingly for years. This rejection must not be met with entreaties to wear it, or threats of the dire consequences if it is not worn. Rather the feelings about it must be accepted and discussed. The normal teasing behavior must be talked about. It can be counteracted by the student's understanding the nature of the hearing impairment and the use of amplification, accepting the need for the aid, and examining the limitations he or she will experience communicating with friends without it. If through informational and adjustment counseling you can restore the student's self-dignity he or she will probably feel able to minimize the significance of the teasing and by so doing may indirectly contribute to its reduction.

A more serious threat to the student's relationship to hearing classmates will arise if he or she experiences difficulty in using the telephone. In Junior High School the telephone begins to be a major means of social contact as well as a way of cooperating on homework assignments. It may be essential to consider whether the hearing-impaired student can benefit from a hearing aid with a telecoil amplification circuit on the aid or, if he or she has one, whether its use is understood. It may be important to explore commercially available modifications, which are designed to improve the ability of a hearing-impaired person to use the telephone.* Parents should encourage a child who simply cannot communicate over the phone to invite a friend to do homework at the house, and to have friends over just to keep up with school gossip.

Participation in extracurricular activities in school and within the community should also be encouraged and facilitated. Talk with the student about the types of activities he or she wishes to pursue. Discuss what such activities demand, whether the student feels the hearing impairment is preventing participation, and, if so, in what ways. Explore ways of overcoming perceived problems. Suggest that you both discuss the situation with a hearing student club or activity member, a club advisor, or activity leader. The hearing-impaired student's reluctance to participate in peer-related activities often lies in a lack of understanding of the demands of the situation. The group leader often has an incorrect perception of what the hearing-impaired student can handle and does not know how to limit difficulties. Both parties need support and help in working together to ensure that the hearing-impaired student has a satisfactory experience. Most handicapped persons are subjected to the limited expectancies non-handicapped persons have encouraged them to accept. Their limited aspirations are often a reflection of others' perceptions of them. It is up to you to help change that situation. It is likely that hearing-impaired girls will experience fewer acceptance difficulties than boys, because boys in general are under heavy social pressure not to manifest weakness. A hearing impairment may be considered as an imperfection resulting in negative feedback from the group.

Acceptance by the peer group will be greatly influenced by the image the young people project of themselves. Hearing-impaired students must be able to counteract the assumption that their handicap generalizes to all areas of competence. They must be encouraged to explore their abilities in as many areas as possible, never assuming limits until they have tested them. You must help them express how they feel about themselves and their abilities and must provide support in their experiments to expand their experiences. You will need to work with their parents, who will be the major source of stability and encouragement even though these are not easy years for them. It is not be easy for parents to avoid being overprotective toward hearing-impaired children out of concern for their physical and emotional well being. It is important to recognize this as a normal reaction, but it can be tempered by the parents' evaluating the assets and competencies of their teenage sons or daughters. They must understand the importance of encouraging peer relationships and of being sympathetic to appeals from their sons or daughters for the material prerequisites to serious participation in group social activities, whether this be shorts and sneakers for the track team, skis to join the ski club, or financial support to permit participation in an overnight school trip.

*An informative booklet entitled *Aids for the Hard of Hearing* is available from the American Telephone and Telegraph Company. For copies, write to AIDS, 195 Broadway, Room 540, New York, N.Y. 10007.

It may not be possible for parents to finance the more expensive activities. It is necessary, however, for the children to realize that the parents would like them to participate but that money rather than lack of confidence is the deciding factor. When support can be given it should be in proportion to the students' commitments. Parents should not feel that they can compensate for their children's handicaps by giving them everything they ask for.

RELATIONSHIPS WITH THE OPPOSITE SEX

These are difficult for most preteen and teenage students. They will be somewhat more difficult for hearing-handicapped students. These students' concepts of self will determine how they think others will receive them. Helping the students to decide what makes a person attractive to others and to identify the characteristics they value most will permit them to better evaluate their own attributes. You can consider the criteria of physical appearance, dress, styles, personal grooming, interests, general behavior, attitudes and behavior to others, choice of friends, willingness to participate in group activities, willingness to reach out to others, ability to handle disappointment. Discuss how they rate themselves in these categories. Consideration of each student as a whole person is important if you are to counteract the tendency to make a self-evaluation exclusively on the basis of the hearing impairment.

Assessing the effectiveness of communication skills and sociolinguistic competencies may motivate greater concern for improvement of auditory and visual speech-recognition abilities, speech articulation, voice quality, and modulation and linguistic competence, particularly in terms of current teenage usage.* The quality of a student's present hearing aid, the possibility of changing the aid, to add a telephone circuit, automatic volume control, or directional microphone may need to be discussed along with the possible advantages and disadvantages of binaural aids.

You should talk about ways of getting to know members of the opposite sex in a social context, of currently acceptable ways of inviting a girl/boy to a school dance, to a party, or to a movie. How and when to raise the issue of the hearing impairment is often a problem faced by a teenager who begins to relate to members of the opposite sex. "If I talk about it, will they be embarrassed?" "Should I tell him/her the first time we go out if he/she does not know? If so, how?"

In a mainstream situation in which several hearing-impaired students attend the same school, a small group discussion of these topics may prove possible and valuable. It may also be helpful to invite hearing friends to one or two sessions.

If you can serve as a resource person with whom a student can raise problem issues and discuss feelings as they occur, you have the potential for contributing to the student's adjustment to the reality of the significance of the hearing impairment rather than to an unacceptable perception of it.

*General vocabulary needs for junior and senior high-school students can be provided for by a commercially available kit by McCarr (1978).

ACCEPTANCE BY TEACHERS

During the primary-school years we tend to show considerable concern for helping the classroom teacher understand the needs of the hearing-impaired child. Unfortunately we do not usually extend such counsel in the postsecondary grades. One of the reasons for this is that instead of a single teacher, the student must relate to several teachers of different subjects. As more students with hearing handicaps are mainstreamed, in-service training becomes increasingly necessary. At least at the beginning of each school year, the staff should consider the special needs of the handicapped students. There should be discussion concerning how these can realistically be provided for. Handicapped students should receive counseling from a person who has an in-depth appreciation of the functional effects of impaired hearing. Such counseling information should be shared with the teachers. Realistically, at present, the most likely route to success is for the itinerant or resource teacher or the therapist/teacher to work closely with a school guidance counselor selected for his or her interest, sensitivity, and willingness to work with the hearing-impaired students. The counselor may then use you as a resource, just as the classroom teacher uses the counselor. It is highly valuable for those who serve the hearing-impaired child to meet at the end of each school semester to assess the student's progress, to identify difficulties experienced by both student and teachers, and to coordinate intervention approaches.

It is equally important that Junior and Senior High Schools encourage the student to participate in planning for his or her own needs. The ultimate goal is the preparation of a student with sufficient knowledge and self-confidence to pursue career training commensurate with abilities and interests. The older the student, the more essential it is that he or she should be involved in a cooperative program of problem identification, definition, and solution. If the student is to gain acceptance by teachers, then those teachers must have an understanding of the impact of the hearing impairment on the student's ability to learn in class, and they must have guidance and support in making reasonable adjustments necessary to accommodate the student. This will mainly involve attempting to accommodate special needs and to minimize those factors that the student perceives as limiting academic performance.

ACADEMIC LIMITATIONS

As for the primary-school child, a comprehensive evaluation should be made of the older student's communicative learning abilities. These should be compared to a profile of the learning demands the student will encounter in each of the classes he or she takes. These demands should be assessed in terms of

1. The subjects involved
2. The course requirements
3. The environment in which the class is taught
4. The method of teaching

Special note should be made of the level of language complexity represented by the textbooks in the various subjects, the nature of the homework assignments, the size of the class, whether the class is taught in a room, laboratory, or auditorium. Note also whether independent or group projects are assigned and what the student is expected to do in order to complete these assignments.

From such an assessment you should be able to identify the student's primary needs for support.

Additional supportive help may include audiologic referrals for improving present amplification and recommendations concerning possible use of an FM system; provision of academic tutoring, either by the regular extra-help sessions given by teacher, itinerant-teacher service, or if appropriate, private arrangement; special note-taking privileges or the substitution of alternate means of fulfilling course requirements.

The need profile also will allow you to determine how you can best serve the student. While one may need intensive help in the expressive use of language, another may primarily need speech and voice improvement, or help in resolving feelings of frustration arising from particular communication situations.

A high-school student finally will need help in career guidance. This should be the role of the guidance counselor. However, since school counselors are not trained to know the effects of hearing impairment on the student's potential for higher education or on the potential for pursuing a particular course of employment training, your input will be very valuable. You will have an understanding of the student's communication and learning abilities, and of the effects of various listening environments and communication situations upon the ability to understand speech. The guidance counselor will be aware of the many career opportunities and what each demands of its applicants. Increasingly the counselor will be familiar with the types of support services available in colleges and of the role of Vocational Rehabilitation Services. Together with the student and parents, you and the guidance counselor should be able to identify realistic opportunities that neither underestimate nor overestimate the student's potentials. The counselor should outline the procedures for pursuing those opportunities.

Adjusting your services to the changing needs of the maturing student through adolescence and young adulthood represents a management approach. This is as challenging and rewarding for you as it is meaningful and effective for the student and the parents.

REFERENCES

Alpiner, J., "Evaluation of Communication Function, Appendix 3D, The Denver Scale of Communication Function," in *Handbook of Adult Rehabilitative Audiology,* ed. J. Alpiner, pp. 53–56. Baltimore: The Williams and Wilkins Company, 1978.

Cohen, O. P., "The Deaf Adolescent: Who Am I?" in "Deafness and Adolescence: A Monograph," eds. A. Nehers and G. Austin, *Volta Review, 80,* 1978, 265–274.

Goffman, E., *Stigma: Notes on the Management of a Spoiled Identity.* Englewood Cliffs, N.J.: Prentice-Hall, Inc., 1963.

Libbey, S., *Attitudes Toward Communication of "Mainstreamed" Hearing-Impaired Adolescents.* Unpublished master's thesis, Boston University, Department of Special Education, Boston: 1978.

McCarr, D., *Vocabulary Building Exercises for the Young Adult.* Dormac Inc. (1978), P. O. Box 752, Beverton, Or. 97005.

Assessment and Management of the Hearing-Impaired Adult

19

Aural Rehabilitation Assessment of the Hearing-Impaired Adult

Working with the hearing-impaired adult lacks the immediate dramatic appeal of working with the young child. Unfortunately it is commonly felt that the adjustment the adult must make is not great. After all, it is reasoned, he or she already has the communication abilities that we often must work so diligently to develop in the child. The needs of the adult tend to be seen as adjusting to the use of amplification, and acquiring some speech-reading skills. This view is supported by the fact that many hearing-impaired persons, once fitted with a hearing aid, are able to compensate for their hearing handicap. They become satisfied hearing-aid users who need no more than periodic attention to their hearing aid by a hearing-aid dealer. Many audiologists even assume that hearing-impaired adults are capable of making this kind of adjustment themselves. Apparently, this is also what hearing-impaired adults expect of themselves. As a result, comprehensive management programs for hearing-impaired adults are not characteristically found in centers that fit clients with hearing aids. Nor does the management of the needs of the adult with acquired hearing impairment figure largely in the training of speech, hearing, and language therapists or audiologists.

Realistically it is probably true that the majority of hearing-impaired adults, when carefully fitted with appropriate amplification, are able to adapt successfully to its use with only minimal guidance. Certainly when approached, few hearing-impaired adults express an interest in a program of aural rehabilitation (Rossi & Harford, 1968).

Why are hearing-impaired adults not motivated to participate in rehabilitation? Is it because:

1. When correctly fitted with a hearing aid they no longer experience significant communication difficulties?
2. They do not wish to emphasize to themselves or others that they are hearing handicapped?
3. We fail to convince them of the nature and benefits of a program of effective management, leaving them with the impression that aural rehabilitation means lip-reading training and is mainly for elderly persons?
4. A lack of understanding of rehabilitation leads hearing-aid users to assume that they are now hearing as well as possible and that the residual difficulties are not sufficient to warrant the time and money involved in going to classes?
5. We fail to clearly define and offer an individualized plan for identifying and addressing the difficulties experienced by each client?

Oyer, Freeman, Hardick, Dixon, Donnelly, Goldstein, Lloyd, and Mussen (1976) sought to identify the reasons underlying clients' failure to follow through on recommendations for aural rehabilitation. Of the forty-five adults interviewed, 66 percent gave lack of motivation as the reason for not entering therapy. The second two most frequently occurring reasons were lack of awareness of the service and its value (approximately 25 percent) and scheduling difficulties (approximately 25 percent). Audiologists apparently are failing to convince clients of the value of effective rehabilitation management. Oyer et al. (1976) interpret their data as suggesting that audiologists themselves may be unconvinced of the value of such programs and thus devote little time to demonstrating their worth. The authors also suggest that programs are not tailored to individual needs and that unnecessary recommendations for aural rehabilitation may be made. The implications of these observations are clear. You must ensure that you do not make blanket recommendations for lip-reading and auditory training for every client you fit with a hearing aid. You must neither incur unnecessary expenditure of time and money for the client who is capable of making a satisfactory adjustment with minimal support, nor must you withhold comprehensive management support to a person who is having considerable difficulty in coping with the effects of the handicap. To motivate a client you must address his or her particular needs with specific suggestions as to how a management program would help to reduce or obviate existing difficulties. This type of approach has been described by Fleming (1972) as a "progressive" approach to therapy.

Determining what should constitute a tailored management program for a hearing-impaired adult is facilitated by viewing the task according to a problem-solving model. This involves the following stages:

Defining the problem
Assessing the needs
Establishing goals
Determining methods of goal achievement
Evaluating effectiveness of intervention strategies

DEFINING THE PROBLEM AND ASSESSING NEEDS

In diagnostic audiology, the goal is to determine the nature of the hearing disability. In rehabilitative management, it is the *effects* of the disability—that is, *the handicap*—upon which you focus your attention. An adult experiences a hearing handicap when: (1) Communication abilities are no longer adequate to permit the client to meet the demands encountered; (2) The psychological cost of meeting daily demands is judged to be too high; (3) The present level of communication abilities, though adequate for current demands, are recognized to limit the adult in the pursuit of advancement. The three areas that encompass most communication situations are:

1. The home environment
2. The work environment
3. The social environment

The relative importance of these three areas differs from each client as a function of his or her life style and as a function of the degree to which the communication demands arising in the situation can be met. It is necessary, therefore, to obtain a profile of the demands of each area and then to evaluate the extent to which those demands fail to be met. In other words, you need to be familiar with:

1. The nature of the physical environment
2. The activities in which the client participates in that environment
3. The nature of the communication situations
4. The nature of the difficulties the client experiences

The aim of the profile is to focus your attention on specific communication problems that the client experiences, and to examine those difficulties within the setting and situation in which they occur. The profile of the communication environment in which the client must function will do much to ensure that you adopt a realistic approach to problem solving and that you identify appropriate rehabilitation strategies. Consider first the nature of the physical environment.

THE HOME ENVIRONMENT

Physical Layout

Assessment would include such information as:

1. The number and layout of the rooms
2. The existence of a family room, workshop, study, sewing room, furnished basement
3. Rooms equipped with television, radio, record player, telephone, telephone extension, or extension bell
4. Size of garden

If the client is an elderly person living in a residential home or nursing home, you will need to gain some insight into the living environment. You should ask:

Does the person have a single or shared room?
Are meals taken in a large dining hall or in smaller dining rooms?
Is there a lounge, recreation room, dayroom, chapel?
How large is each room?
How reverberant do the rooms seem to be?
How noisy does each room tend to be?
What is the furniture arrangement in public rooms?

Answers to these questions are best obtained by visiting the home, but they can be provided by the director, by staff, or by relatives of the client if the client is unable to provide the information.

Family

1. Single, widowed or divorced, living alone
2. Sharing a house or apartment with one, two, or three persons
3. Number of family members at home, including ages of children at home
4. Sharing a room in a residential home

Family Activities and Communication Situations

1. Assisting children with homework
2. Dinner-table discussion
3. Conversation in family or living room
4. Television viewing
5. Conversation in garden
6. Watching slides or movies
7. Entertaining guests, dinner parties, card parties, cocktail parties
8. Telephone conversations
9. Hobbies pursued in workshop or basement, work-related activities pursued in office at home

For the person living in a residential accommodation for senior citizens, you should inquire about activities and communication situations that occur in a typical week. These include the interactions at meals and at organized social situations such as bingo, card games, social entertainment, dances, slide shows, films. You should know about informal social contacts and where they occur (own room, dayroom or lounge, library, garden). Other information would include the person's remedial programs—physiotherapy, occupational therapy, speech and hearing therapy, reality training.

Nature of Communication Difficulties

Following are some of the common communication difficulties that may occur:

1. Difficulty in conversing on the phone, which is located in the kitchen, if any other activity is going on there—for example, cooking, children doing homework or playing, radio playing

2. Difficulty in conversing with husband or wife when he or she is involved in an activity that generates noise, when the radio is playing, when the children are talking
3. Difficulty in participating in dinner-table discussion
4. Difficulty in conversing while watching television, movies, or slides
5. Difficulty in understanding in groups involving more than one other couple
6. Difficulty in hearing bids or remarks at card games
7. Difficulty in hearing when called from another room, particularly when working in the office, sewing room, basement, garden

In a residential home, difficulties might occur:

8. In the dining room; the noise level is too high
9. In bingo; the numbers can be heard but not discriminated
10. In the dayroom; it is so reverberant
11. In the library; the air conditioner makes so much noise
12. In the lounge; the birds in the aviary make it hard to hear speech
13. At film shows; the sound is not clear
14. At religious services; the minister/priest/rabbi cannot be heard

THE OCCUPATIONAL ENVIRONMENT

The difficulties experienced at work can be similarly profiled.

Place of work: office, factory, school, department store, shop, beauty parlor, outdoor location.
Physical environment: large open area, small room, partitioned office, small store, machine area.
Acoustic environment: hard versus carpeted floors, acoustic tiling versus hard ceilings, large window areas draped/undraped, soft-cushioned furnishings versus hard wood or metal.
Noise sources: machinery, loud air conditioning or heating appliances, piped music, loud outside noise sources such as traffic, aircraft, heavy equipment.
People involved: work alone, work in room with small group of people, work among many people, number of people present is highly variable.
Communication activities: work activities involve person-to-person discussion, instructional or consultative communications, interviewing, taking dictation, selling, audiostenography, group discussion, information gathering, telephone conversations, equipment or plant monitoring by audio cues.

Nature of Communication Difficulties

At work, communication difficulties may include:

1. Difficulty in groups of more than three people in quiet office, in larger meeting room
2. Difficulty at committee meetings
3. Difficulty while working around machinery, in sorting office or typing pool, while driving truck or car, in hospital or school corridors
4. Difficulty in using telephone, dictaphone
5. Difficulty in understanding instructions given from a distance
6. Difficulty when speaker is on the side of unaided ear
7. Difficulty in hearing questions from an audience
8. Difficulty in hearing in court, in surgery, in the classroom, in the stockroom

THE SOCIAL ENVIRONMENT

This refers to all social activities outside the home. The activities can be identified by type rather than by place because each occurs in a particular environment. Social activities include:

Social visits to the homes of friends: dinner parties, cocktail parties, coffee hours
Organizational or business functions: dinners, receptions, social hours
Participation: in games, sports, hobby groups
Visits: to movies, theaters, concerts or other entertainment shows
Attendance: at religious services

Nature of Communication Difficulties

These will need to be defined in terms of the particular social activities involved. They may include:

I am unable to catch the funny lines in a movie or play.
I cannot understand what is said to me in a theater unless the person is seated next to me on my aided side.
I find it hard to understand the instructor in my hobby group when slides are being shown.
I have difficulty at coffee hour when several conversations are going on around me.
I cannot follow conversation at a dinner party.
I understand nothing at a cocktail party.

You can collect information of this nature through an informal interview approach or you can obtain it by using a structured questionnaire. The interview format, when sympathetically and efficiently conducted, will represent the beginning of a process of informational and adjustment counseling. The act of describing, in an orderly manner, one's communication effectiveness and one's feeling about communication situations does much to clarify the problem. The informal discussion provides you, the counselor, with an opportunity to develop a trusting relationship with the client. The information obtained can be augmented at future meetings, facilitating the introduction of an informal counseling component into the rehabilitation program. The disadvantage of this informal approach lies in the absence of quantifiable data, which is important for obtaining a base line against which the effectiveness of intervention procedures can be measured later.

A number of attempts have been made to overcome this limitation by using inventories that profile a client's perception of his or her communication abilities and his or her feelings about them. Alpiner, 1978; Ewartsen & Birk-Nielsen, 1973; Giolas, Owens, Lamb, & Schubert, 1979; High, Fairbanks, & Glorig, 1964; Noble & Atherley, 1970; Sanders, 1980; Schein, Gentile, & Hass, 1965. Illustrations of Sanders' 1980 profile method, which we discussed when considering profiling the hearing-impaired child's communication difficulties in the classroom (Chapter 16), appear later in this chapter. There, the procedure is extended to the adult at home, at work, and in social situations. Once again, the severity of the communication difficulty is assessed on a four-point scale ranging from "little or no difficulty" to "great difficulty." This value is then weighted by the frequency with which the situation arises. Multiplication of the two figures provides a positive or negative value. The more negative the value, the greater the significance of the problem. Adding the positive and negative values algebraically and dividing them by the number of questions provides a base line quotient for each environment assessed. The profile can be used to help determine the effectiveness of intervention strategies in reducing communication difficulties. The profile offered here is merely a guide. To obtain an accurate profile of the difficulties encountered by a particular person you will have to add items that describe the specific communication situations with which your client must deal.

Inventories in general have been criticized for a number of limitations: failing to provide accurate, comprehensive assessment of the subject's communication effectiveness in a variety of everyday situations, use of too few questions, and failure of the authors to subject the questions used to item analysis (Giolas, 1970; Giolas, Owens, Lamb, & Schubert, 1979; Oyer & Frankman, 1975).

Giolas, Owens, Lamb, and Schubert (1979) have sought to minimize the deficiencies that they identify in existing communication profile tools. They have developed the *Hearing Performance Inventory*. This inventory contains six sections: (1) Understanding Speech; (2) Intensity; (3) Response to Auditory Failure; (4) Social; (5) Personal; (6) Occupational. The client is asked to respond to a total of 158 questions using a multiple-choice answer sheet. Each response indicates how frequently the problem is encountered. The choices are: Practically always, Frequently, About half the time, Occasionally, Never, or Does not apply. Questions include such items as:

Q11 *You are playing cards, Monopoly, or some similar game with several people and the room is fairly quiet. Can you understand what a friend or family member is saying to you when his/her voice is loud enough for you and you can see his/her face?*

Q14 *You are watching your favorite news program on television. Can you understand the reporter (male) when his voice is loud enough for you?*

Q70 *You are in a quiet place and the person seated on the side of your better ear whispers to you. Can you hear the whisper?*

Q144 *You are at work with five or six co-workers and there is background noise such as music or a crowd of people. One person talks at a time and the subject of conversation changes from time to time. Can you understand what is being said when the speaker's voice is low?*

The ways in which the person attempts to adapt to situations that present difficulty are tapped by such questions as:

Q149 *You are with your employer (foreman, supervisor, etc.) at work. When you miss something important that was said do you pretend you understood?*

Q150 *At the beginning of a conversation do you let your co-workers know that you have a hearing problem?*

Administration of the complete 158 questions covering home, social, and occupational communication situations takes just under an hour. For nonemployed persons, the occupational questions can easily be omitted because they comprise items 132 to 158. Scoring the full range of items also takes an hour.

The authors of the HPI state that the inventory is ready for clinical use, though they plan further work on it when adequate field test data have been generated. Clinically it is presently being used to identify items for opening discussion with clients—that is, as a lead into relevant problem solving. Giolas, Owens, Lamb, and Schubert acknowledge the conclusions of Silverman, Thurlow, Walsh, and Davis (1948) that the responses of clients heavily reflect their feelings about a situation and their difficulty in it and are not, therefore, a direct measure of the actual communication difficulty experienced. It is, of course, desirable to have a measure of actual communication difficulty. It is this measure that most directly relates to the effect of such intervention procedures as modifying the hearing-aid fitting, improving auditory-visual communication training, or teaching new strategies for dealing with difficult situations. However, the experience of the client is defined in terms of his or her perceptions. These, we know, are heavily influenced by feelings.

Helpful information about feelings can be generated by the use of the Denver Scale of Communication Function (Alpiner, 1975, 1978). In the Denver Scale, the client is asked to make a judgment on a seven-point scale indicating how strongly he or she agrees or disagrees with each of twenty-five statements. These include, for example:

Q1 *The members of my family are annoyed with my loss of hearing.*

Q8 *People sometimes avoid me because of my hearing loss.*

Q10 *I tend to be negative about life because of my hearing loss.*

Q15 *Other people do not understand what it is like to have a hearing loss.*

The answers are plotted on a profile chart reflecting judgments under the four categories: Family, Self, Social-Vocational, and Communication.

The development of any profile must be undertaken cautiously. Questionnaires structure the search for information and make it possible for the status of a person to be assessed before and after a management program. However, this method of information gathering easily becomes impersonal and tedious. You cannot afford to subject every client to intensive profiling when the need for rehabilitation may be minimal. Caution should also be shown in requesting the client to spend a lot of time working through a series of questions before he or she knows how the answers will be interpreted and used. Use common sense. The following guidelines may be helpful:

1. Relate to the client in a sympathetic, open, but professional manner that encourages him or her to explain the type of help he or she hopes to receive.
2. Ask for a brief description of the particular situations (home, work, or social life) in which communication difficulties are experienced.
3. Ask the person how serious the difficulties are and what the effects of the difficulties are likely to be.
4. Use your judgment to determine whether the difficulties experienced might reasonably be expected to be overcome with effective use of amplification.

5. Decide whether a program of rehabilitation based upon achieving specific goals will be necessary to reduce the client's difficulties.
6. Explain to the client how you interpret the information you have already obtained.
7. Explain your need for a better understanding of the client's difficulties.
8. Request cooperation in completing the profile questionnaire(s) most likely to be helpful.
9. Aim to spend only as much time developing a profile as you consider to be appropriate for an individual client.

The purpose of rehabilitative assessment is to determine the type and extent of the client's needs. It is on the basis of this information that you will develop a specific rehabilitation plan. To facilitate this process it is helpful to write a synopsis of each client's present status. Chapter 20 provides synopses for three clients which illustrate the planning and implementation of rehabilitative intervention procedures.

REFERENCES

Alpiner, J. G., "Hearing Aid Selection for Adults," in *Amplification for the Hearing Impaired,* ed. M. Pollack, pp. 145–205. New York: Grune & Stratton, Inc., 1975.

Alpiner, J. G., "Evaluation of Communication Function," in *Handbook of Adult Rehabilitative Audiology,* ed. J. G. Alpiner, pp. 30–66. Baltimore: The Williams and Wilkins Company, 1978.

Ewartsen, H. W., and H. Birk-Nielsen, "Social Hearing Handicap Index," *Audiology, 12,* 1973, 180–187.

Fleming, M., "A Total Approach to Communication Therapy," *Journal of the Academy of Rehabilitative Audiology, 5,* 1972, 28–31.

Giolas, T. G., *The Measurement of Hearing Handicap: A Point of View.* Audiological Library Series, 8. Minneapolis Minn.: Maico Hearing Instruments, 1970.

Giolas, T., E. Owens, S. Lamb, and E. Schubert, "Hearing Performance Inventory," *Journal of Speech and Hearing Disorders, 44,* no. 2, 1979, 169–195.

High, W. S., G. Fairbanks, A. Glorig, "A Scale of Self Assessment of Hearing Handicap," *Journal of Speech and Hearing Disorders, 29,* 1964, 215–230.

Noble, W. G., and G. Atherley, "The Hearing Measurement Scale," *Journal of Auditory Research, 10,* 1970, 229–250.

Oyer, H. J., and J. P. Frankman, *The Aural Rehabilitation Process.* New York: Holt, Rinehart & Winston, 1975.

Oyer, H. J., B. Freeman, E. Hardick, J. Dixon, K. Donnelly, D. Goldstein, L. Lloyd, and E. Mussen, "Unheeded Recommendations for Aural Rehabilitation," *Journal of the Academy of Rehabilitative Audiology, 9,* 1976, 20–30.

Rossi, J., and E. Harford, "An Analysis of Patient Attitudes and Reactions to a Clinical Hearing Aid Selection Program," *ASHA, 10,* 1968, 283–290.

Sanders, D. A., "Hearing Aid Orientation and Counseling," in *Amplification for the Hearing Impaired,* ed. M. Pollack, pp. 343–391. New York: Grune & Stratton, Inc., 1980.

Schein, J. D., A. Gentile, K. W. Hass, "Development and Evaluation of an Expanded Hearing Loss Questionnaire," *Vital and Health Statistics* (PHS Pub 1000 Series 12 Public Health Service). Washington, D.C.: U.S. Government Printing Office, 1965.

Silverman, S. R., W. R. Thurlow, T. E. Walsh, and H. Davis, "Improvement in the Social Adequacy of Hearing Following the Fenestration Operation," *Laryngoscope, 58,* 1948, 607–620.

PROFILE QUESTIONNAIRE FOR RATING COMMUNICATIVE PERFORMANCE IN A HOME ENVIRONMENT

1. **a)** In my living room, when I can see the speaker's face, I have:

+2	+1	−1	−2
little or no difficulty in understanding	some difficulty (but not a lot)	a fair amount of difficulty (quite a lot)	great difficulty in understanding

b) This happens:

1	2	3
seldom	often	very often

2. **a)** If I am talking with a person in my living room or family room while the television, radio, or record player is on, I have:

+2	+1	−1	−2
little or no difficulty in understanding	some difficulty (but not a lot)	a fair amount of difficulty (quite a lot)	great difficulty in understanding

b) This happens:

1	2	3
seldom	often	very often

3. **a)** In a quiet room in my house, if I cannot see the speaker's face, I have:

+2	+1	−1	−2
little or no difficulty in understanding	some difficulty (but not a lot)	a fair amount of difficulty (quite a lot)	great difficulty in understanding

b) This happens:

1	2	3
seldom	often	very often

4. **a)** If someone in my house speaks to me from another room on the same floor, I experience:

+2	+1	−1	−2
little or no difficulty in understanding	some difficulty (but not a lot)	a fair amount of difficulty (quite a lot)	great difficulty in understanding

b) This happens:

1	2	3
seldom	often	very often

5. **a)** If someone calls me from upstairs when I am downstairs, or from the window when I am in the garden, I will experience:

+2	+1	−1	−2
little or no difficulty in understanding	some difficulty (but not a lot)	a fair amount of difficulty (quite a lot)	great difficulty in understanding

b) This happens:

1	2	3
seldom	often	very often

6. **a)** Understanding people at the dinner table gives me:

+2	+1	−1	−2
little or no difficulty in understanding	some difficulty (but not a lot)	a fair amount of difficulty (quite a lot)	great difficulty in understanding

b) This happens:

1	2	3
seldom	often	very often

7. **a)** When I sit talking with friends in a quiet room, I have:

+2	+1	−1	−2
little or no difficulty in understanding	some difficulty (but not a lot)	a fair amount of difficulty (quite a lot)	great difficulty in understanding

b) This happens:

1	2	3
seldom	often	very often

8. **a)** Listening to the radio or record player or watching TV gives me:

+2	+1	−1	−2
little or no difficulty in understanding	some difficulty (but not a lot)	a fair amount of difficulty (quite a lot)	great difficulty in understanding

b) This happens:

1	2	3
seldom	often	very often

9. **a)** When I use the phone at home, I have:

+2	+1	−1	−2
little or no difficulty in understanding	some difficulty (but not a lot)	a fair amount of difficulty (quite a lot)	great difficulty in understanding

b) This happens:

1	2	3
seldom	often	very often

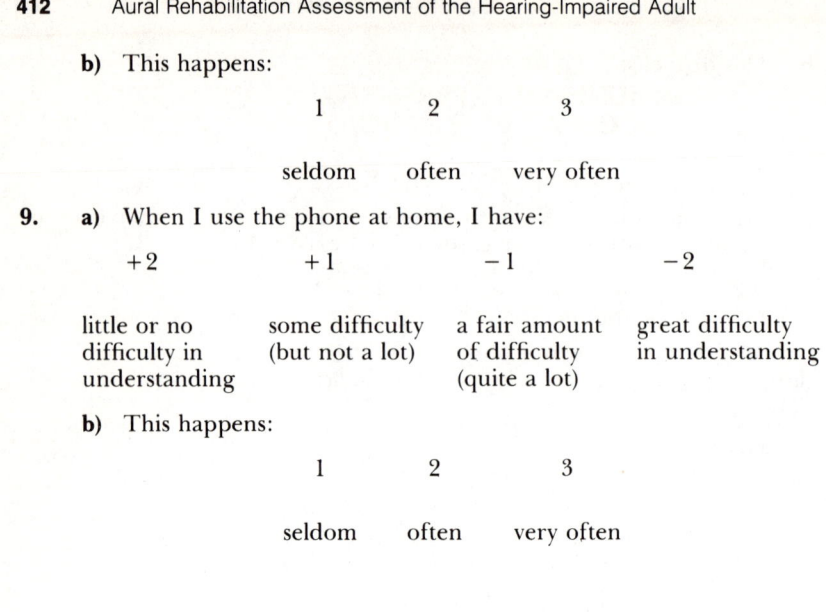

PROFILE QUESTIONNAIRE FOR RATING COMMUNICATIVE PERFORMANCE IN AN OCCUPATIONAL ENVIRONMENT

1. **a)** In talking with someone in the room where I work, I have:

+2	+1	−1	−2
little or no difficulty in understanding	some difficulty (but not a lot)	a fair amount of difficulty (quite a lot)	great difficulty in understanding

b) This happens:

1	2	3
seldom	often	very often

2. **a)** When I am in a room at work where there is noise, I have:

+2	+1	−1	−2
little or no difficulty in understanding	some difficulty (but not a lot)	a fair amount of difficulty (quite a lot)	great difficulty in understanding

b) This happens:

1	2	3
seldom	often	very often

3. **a)** When I am at a meeting with a small group of people, around a table in a fairly quiet room, I have:

+2	+1	−1	−2
little or no difficulty in understanding	some difficulty (but not a lot)	a fair amount of difficulty (quite a lot)	great difficulty in understanding

b) This happens:

1	2	3
seldom	often	very often

4. **a)** If I have to take notes by dictation in a fairly quiet room, I have:

+2	+1	−1	−2
little or no difficulty in understanding	some difficulty (but not a lot)	a fair amount of difficulty (quite a lot)	great difficulty in understanding

b) This happens:

1	2	3
seldom	often	very often

5. **a)** If I have to take notes at a meeting, I have:

+2	+1	−1	−2
little or no difficulty in understanding	some difficulty (but not a lot)	a fair amount of difficulty (quite a lot)	great difficulty in understanding

b) This happens:

1	2	3
seldom	often	very often

6. **a)** If I have to use the phone at work, I have:

+2	+1	−1	−2
little or no difficulty in understanding	some difficulty (but not a lot)	a fair amount of difficulty (quite a lot)	great difficulty in understanding

b) This happens:

1	2	3
seldom	often	very often

PROFILE QUESTIONNAIRE FOR RATING COMMUNICATIVE PERFORMANCE IN A SOCIAL ENVIRONMENT

1. **a)** If I am entertaining a group of friends, understanding someone against the background of others talking gives me:

+2	+1	−1	−2
little or no difficulty	some difficulty (but not a lot)	a fair amount of difficulty (quite a lot)	great difficulty

b) This happens:

1	2	3
seldom	often	very often

2. **a)** If I am playing cards, understanding my partner gives me:

+2	+1	−1	−2
little or no difficulty	some difficulty (but not a lot)	a fair amount of difficulty (quite a lot)	great difficulty

b) This happens:

1	2	3
seldom	often	very often

3. **a)** When I am at the theatre or the movies, I have:

+2	+1	−1	−2
little or no difficulty in understanding	some difficulty (but not a lot)	a fair amount of difficulty (quite a lot)	great difficulty in understanding

b) This happens:

1	2	3
seldom	often	very often

4. **a)** In church, when the minister gives the sermon, I have:

+2	+1	−1	−2
little or no difficulty in understanding	some difficulty (but not a lot)	a fair amount of difficulty (quite a lot)	great difficulty in understanding

b) This happens:

1	2	3
seldom	often	very often

5. a) In following the conversation when I eat out, I have:

+2	+1	−1	−2
little or no difficulty	some difficulty (but not a lot)	a fair amount of difficulty (quite a lot)	great difficulty

b) This happens:

1	2	3
seldom	often	very often

6. a) In the car, I find that understanding what people are saying gives me:

+2	+1	−1	−2
little or no difficulty	some difficulty (but not a lot)	a fair amount of difficulty (quite a lot)	great difficulty

b) This happens:

1	2	3
seldom	often	very often

7. a) When I am outside talking with someone, I have:

+2	+1	−1	−2
little or no difficulty in understanding	some difficulty (but not a lot)	a fair amount of difficulty (quite a lot)	great difficulty in understanding

b) This happens:

1	2	3
seldom	often	very often

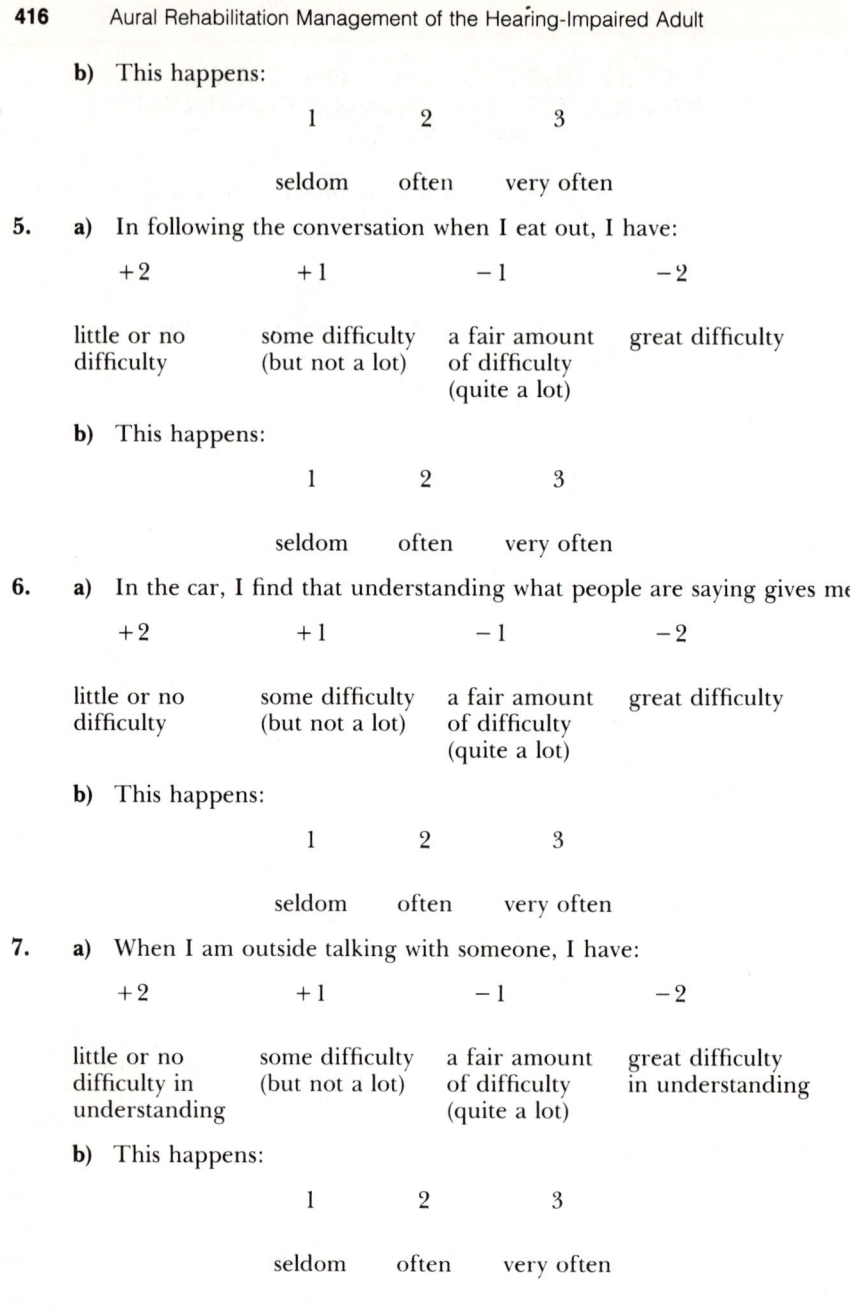

20

Aural Rehabilitation Management of the Hearing-Impaired Adult

This chapter summarizes the management intervention process for three hearing-impaired adults. As you read the synopses of each of these clients, bear in mind that their stories are special. Each person you seek to help will also have special needs arising from individual circumstances. At the rehabilitation-management stage you condense your understanding of the types of problems and needs generally experienced by hard-of-hearing adults into a knowledge of the problems and needs of a particular individual with impaired hearing. Notice, in considering the problems and needs of these three adults that intervention is justified only to address specific needs.

CLIENT ONE

> Mr. David Johnson. Age 52. Postal clerk.
>
> Mr. Johnson has a moderately severe bilateral sensorineural hearing impairment. Progression has been gradual over the past twelve to fifteen years. Communication difficulties have begun to be of significant concern during the past eighteen months.
>
> The average hearing impairment without a hearing aid is 45 dB in the left ear; 55 dB right. Speech discrimination scores for monosyllabic words are 94 percent right ear, 86 percent left ear. Most comfortable loudness level is 75 dB right, 80 dB left.

Mr. Johnson states that until recently he has been able to "get along" in most situations. He admits feeling "drained" at the end of the working day, and that he is experiencing some frustration and anxiety when working with the public. Specifically he notes difficulty in being sure of what customers have requested, increasingly misunderstands, and must cover his mistakes. He also experiences difficulty at work in the letter-sorting area where he misses many of the comments and asides that are part of the joking-around which occurs. He admits to feeling that he may be the butt of some of the humor. He has become less active in union meetings because he does not always follow what is asked or said by a speaker in the audience.

At home his family complains that he always turns the radio and television too loud, does not always catch what is said in conversation, cannot be spoken to from another room.

Mr. Johnson has never been very active socially. However he says he finds the sermon in church hard to follow and feels people mumble at the after-church coffee hour. His most serious concerns are occupational communication.

The difficulties experienced by Mr. Johnson are relatively mild but their impact is serious because they threaten his occupation. He has some hearing problems at home but they are only just beginning to bother family members. Social restrictions arising from his hearing impairment are mild because of his limited interest in outside social activities.

Management Needs

The first step is to explain to Mr. Johnson and his wife that the audiological findings confirm the sensorineural deficiency diagnosed by the physician. The problem, now of moderate severity, appears to have progressed very slowly with the aging process. To this point, extra effort on Mr. Johnson's part has made it possible for him to adjust to the impairment. The price of this adjustment has been Mr. Johnson's having to pay extra attention for increasing periods of time and the tiredness this causes. This is no longer an adequate or desirable solution. Recently irritability and anxiety have resulted at work, along with a certain amount of irritation at home. Test results indicate good potential discrimination when speech is loud enough. This suggests that amplification will probably replace the information being missed and result in a restoration of a normal life style.

The intervention strategies suggested for Mr. Johnson are limited to accord with his limited needs:

1. Informational counseling, including explanation to Mr. Johnson that his feelings and behaviors in communications are fully expectable because his hearing handicap is exhausting his ability to compensate.
2. Trial fitting initially with a monaural hearing aid in the right ear with subsequent opportunity to evaluate binaural amplication. A directional microphone might be considered for the work situation if background noise is a problem at the counter.

3. Instruction in the effective use and care of the hearing aid.
4. Some limited auditory/visual communication training and an opportunity to discuss any feelings he may have that may influence his attitude toward wearing the aid.
5. A follow-up visit three weeks after the purchase of the aid to ensure all is going well. This will allow for consultation prior to the expiration of the 30-day trial of the aid allowed by the dealer.

CLIENT TWO

Margaret Simpson's hearing handicap has an even more significant impact on her life.

Mrs. Margaret Simpson. Age 38. Middle management company executive.

Mrs. Simpson has a congenital, bilateral, sensorineural hearing impairment. Her hearing deficit in the right ear is 52 dB in the speech range, discrimination 82 percent. The left ear average is 72 dB, discrimination 68 percent. Mrs. Simpson has worn a hearing aid in the right ear since childhood. Her aided threshold is 26 dB, discrimination 80 percent.

Until recently she has found that she has been able to adapt to most communication situations at work and at home, where she lives with her husband and two teenage daughters. The communication difficulties she has encountered at home and in her social life have occurred in group situations, at dinner parties, and cocktail parties. Problems arise in the car or at the theater when a speaker is on the side of her unaided ear. These have not presented unmanageable difficulties.

At work problem situations have proved relatively easy to handle until just recently. Mrs. Simpson was an assistant to an advertising executive. She worked in a quiet office where she had control over seating arrangements. She has always been able to use the telephone effectively.

A recent promotion to executive level has threatened Mrs. Simpson's ability to function well in her professional role. She has moved into a larger office with an assistant of her own. The office is not as easy to hear in. Her new responsibilities include participation in frequent meetings involving groups of up to ten persons. She also spends as much as half her time visiting clients outside her office and outside the agency. In these situations she encounters a variety of conditions presenting various degrees of difficulty.

Her employers are aware that she wears a hearing aid but since it did not affect her performance it did not limit their recognition and reward of her abilities.

Mrs. Simpson states that since accepting her promotion she has been experiencing considerable stress. She finds the new responsibilities difficult to cope with. As a result she has begun to question seriously her managerial capability. She has been in two situations in which she felt she jeopardized a contract by less-than-adequate management of the negotiations. She finds herself exhausted upon return home from work, has become irritable with her husband and children, and appears to have increased difficulty in home and social-communication settings. Mrs. Simpson is becoming quite depressed about the whole situation. She wishes she had not accepted the promotion, but does not know whether her previous position would be open to her. Her husband has been sympathetic and supportive. It is at his urging that she has sought guidance.

Management Needs

Mrs. Simpson clearly is in need of immediate help directed at changing her effectiveness in difficult communication situations in her business day. However, it must be noted that this client is not convinced that her present problems are directly attributable to her hearing impairment. This is probably because her previous success obviated the need to consider herself "handicapped." Instead, Mrs. Simpson is doubting her professional capabilities as an executive. Intervention strategies require recognition that this client is in a crisis situation.

The strategies recommended are:

1. *Counseling.* Efforts must first be directed at helping the client understand that all of the difficulties she is experiencing in office and home communication, along with the associated feelings of inadequacy, can reasonably be attributed to the increased demands on her ability to comprehend speech. It needs to be explained that a change in acoustic environment, a significant increase in the sophistication of communication content, and the increased responsibility for decision making have invalidated her existing routine and communication strategies. The resultant anxiety, exhaustion, and depression have aggravated a difficult situation at work and have spilled over to home and social functions, decreasing her effectiveness there. Thus the first aim is to help Mrs. Simpson acknowledge the reasonableness of the difficulties she is having and her feelings about them. She must be asked to reassess her problem in the light of the information you can provide.
2. *Improving amplification.* The possibility of improving her present use of amplification would be a priority. Recommend comparing binaural amplification with a BICROS aid. It is possible that amplification to the poorer ear may decrease performance when wearing a second aid, thus favoring a BICROS fitting. Testing would include speech in noise and speech against a competing speech or speech-noise signal. A very carefully monitored trial of an alternate to the present monaural fitting should be conducted in the troublesome work situations.
3. *Identifying problem situations.* Intervention procedures would be directed at detailing the environments and types of communications she must deal with in her new appointment, including the number of persons present, arrangement of the furniture, type of content of communications, special characteristics—for example, note taking, use of figures, layouts—decision making, question-answer situations, room size and acoustics, room noise.
4. *Implementing environmental modifications.* Follow the analysis of the communication situations causing difficulty by considering how to minimize them. The possibility of modifying the room acoustics of Mrs. Simpson's new office should be considered. Heavy drapes, thick carpeting, an acoustic ceiling, acoustic, absorbent decorative wall patches should not automatically be ruled out, particularly at the executive level. Also explore rearranging the furniture to reduce speaker-listener distance, using natural light optimally, and improving the use of artificial light to facilitate speech-reading.
5. *Making better use of existing resources.* Developing a system for communication management in her new role should be a part of Mrs. Simpson's planning. Determining how to make best use of the assistant, deciding whether the assistant can be present at important discussions, having shorthand notes taken, recording conversations (with permission) when appropriate, ensur-

ing optimal seating position at meetings, using a floor microphone or repeating questions at larger meetings, and choosing favorable acoustic and lighting environments for meeting clients are all potential intervention-management strategies.

6. *Developing new communication strategies*. Personal strategies should also be explored. For example, Mrs. Simpson should consider ways of dealing with situations in which she finds herself unsure of what was said relevant to a particular issue. She may request: "May we go over that point once more?" or "Can you rephrase your suggestion (comment) so I am sure I understand your meaning?" "Could you put that proposal in writing for me?" or "Let me see if I have understood your objection. You disagree that . . . " Mrs. Simpson should try to control the communication situation in a subtle manner that does not disturb her listener(s). She must examine ways of clarifying information without irritating her listeners. She must also consider how to increase her confidence in what she decides has been said. Auditory and visual communication training may help to improve her confidence in comprehension. This should be directly relevant to the content of the situations encountered, as we will discuss later.

CLIENT THREE

The final client presents a very different set of needs.

> Mrs. Amster. Age 80. Retired.
>
> Mrs. Amster is a resident of a nursing home. Her health is not good. Among other problems she suffers from arthritis, which limits her mobility. Mrs. Amster has had a sensorineural hearing impairment for years. Her discrimination is poor in both ears, her tolerance for loudness reduced. Her main interest in life is to visit with one or two friends in the home, to receive visits from some of her family members on the weekends, and occasionally to watch a little television. The staff of the home say it has become increasingly difficult to communicate with Mrs. Amster since she refuses to wear her ear-level aid because it is not working properly and she cannot adjust the controls. Her eyesight is also poor.

Management Needs

Mrs. Amster's communication needs are limited, as is her lifestyle. They are confined mainly to one-to-one relationships in quiet environments, and occasionally to watching television. Intervention strategies should be limited to accommodate these limited needs:

1. *Improving amplification*. The first intervention procedure is to improve the suitability of Mrs. Amster's hearing aid. She needs a model with moderate gain and appropriate maximum output. Changing to a body aid may facilitate manipulation of controls. Once the aid is fitted Mrs. Amster should be shown several times how to operate it. Demonstrations should be sensitively handled and guidance in carrying out the instructions must be given with much patience. Mrs. Amster must be worked with in a manner that prevents

her from feeling overwhelmed. The demonstrations and instructions should be given while a staff member is present. This staff member should be someone willing to assume responsibility for conducting simple checks on the aid and helping Mrs. Amster to replace the battery. Mrs. Amster's difficulties should be explained to this staff member, with whom techniques for enhancing comprehension (speaking slowly and clearly, identifying topic of conversation, standing in good light, speaking close to the hearing aid, paraphrasing statements or questions not understood, and so on) should be identified.

2. *Providing limited communication training.* Visual-communication training for an elderly lady with poor vision can lead only to frustration. However, with a well-fitted hearing aid, some short auditory-training sessions may be helpful.

   Training sessions will need to be short to avoid fatigue. Care should be taken not to overload Mrs. Amster and to realize when the limits of training have been reached. Lessons should include discrimination of the vocabulary, phrases, instructions, and questions that occur in such situations as physiotherapy, occupational therapy, at meals, at a religious service, and so on.

3. *Improving staff-client communication.* It will be helpful to outline in writing or in person ways in which staff members may help reduce their difficulty in communicating with Mrs. Amster. They should be advised to speak into the hearing aid. If the aid is a body aid, it can be held 4 inches from the mouth. If Mrs. Amster agrees to wear an ear-level aid, the staff member should be close to her when speaking. Identifying key words in the question to be asked or the topic to be discussed, as well as providing visual cues, may improve the patient's ability to predict what is said.

THE NATURE OF THE REHABILITATION MANAGEMENT TASK

Now that we have emphasized the importance of addressing the personal needs of each client, we can look at the management task more generally. Rehabilitation management can be subdivided into two categories (but helping the client make the necessary psychological adjustment to a changing situation must be woven throughout all categories):

1. Understanding the problem
2. Developing and implementing the management plan, which includes:
   a. Ensuring optimal use of amplification
   b. Modifying the environment
   c. Modifying communication strategies
   d. Improving information processing

Understanding the Problem

A major concern when discussing the problems clients may encounter as a result of hearing impairment is that you may create anxiety where none exists. It is extremely important that you concentrate on the problems that the client identifies. Do not attribute to your client feelings or attitudes that you have learned from the literature, or even from experience, are "characteristic of persons with impaired hearing." In other words, do not treat an individual as a statistic. The issue of whether to prepare a client for possible negative reactions by others is not one upon which you will find a unanimous opinion. For example, Kasten (1978) refers to a study by Blood, Blood, and Danhaner (1977) that examined college students shown two sets of photographs of normal-hearing teenage children—one in which they were wearing hearing aids and one in which they were not. The college students' judgments of the children's intelligence, achievement, personality, and appearance were significantly more negative when the children were seen wearing the aids than when they were not. This occurred even though simultaneously to viewing both sets of photographs, the students heard the same recording of the speech of these normal hearing-children whether they were wearing the aids or not.

Kasten (1978) suggests that the general population may react in the same way, and he urges the counselor to discuss these matters.

The adult must realize before he encounters unfavorable biases, that some people may react to the acquisition of a hearing aid in this fashion. It is imperative that the perceptive hearing aid user and his family be aware of this possibility before they are confronted with potentially negative reactions. In particular it is imperative that both the hearing aid user and his family realize the hearing aid user will have to prove himself and will have to demonstrate his abilities and strengths to an unsophisticated population in order to maintain his own feelings of self esteem (p. 85).

Kasten's statement presents a contrast to the approach suggested in this text. Kasten's recommendation is not wrong; however, it represents a very different point of view, one that you need to evaluate. You should provide a client and his or her family an opportunity to express their feelings about wearing a hearing aid and about real or expected difficult or embarrassing experiences arising from communication difficulties. However, do not focus attention on *possible* negative reactions by others. These may not occur, they may occur and be treated as not important by the hearing-aid user, or they may occur and be dealt with positively by the user. Likewise, the client should not feel he or she has to prove him- or herself or demonstrate strengths and abilities any more than we each have to do. You should provide a sympathetic climate that encourages your clients to explore their feelings and what they perceive to be those of their families, friends, coworkers, employers, and others. However, you may offer a disservice if you deal with possibilities they may simply not consider relevant to their particular situations.

Your goal for effective management must be to foster independence. Each client must be able to assume responsibility for working out problems that arise from being impaired, just as he or she must resolve difficulties that occur for a variety of other reasons. The hearing impairment is a factor additional to normal attributes and capabilities that does not negate them, but must, in fact, be dealt with by them. For this to be possible the client must have a *practical* understanding of the nature of his or her particular disability and its resultant handicapping effects. The understanding *must* be practical. A client understands little from only being told that he or she has a 50-dB hearing loss, or that he or she has a 60 percent loss in the better ear. Rather, the client must understand how a hearing deficit of the severity and configuration his or her test findings demonstrate is known to affect a person's ability to process spoken information in a variety of communication settings. You must explain the influence that reduced loudness and distortion have on speech comprehension. A hearing-impaired person is often relieved to find that the difficulties he or she has been experiencing arise from the hearing handicap and not, for example, as a result of deteriorating mental abilities. The reduction in the range of usable residual hearing bounded by detection and maximum comfort level should be explained so that the role of amplification can be better understood. It is most important that the client realize that the amount of improvement experienced when using a hearing aid will be determined by this range. It will also teach the client, when appropriate, why speech may suddenly seem too loud and why it may still lack clarity even when amplified. The specific gains and limitations of the amplification provided should be explained and general counseling in the care and maintenance of the aid should be given.

Your main concern is to be sure that the client feels comfortable about wearing, using, and caring for the aid. He or she should know what to expect of the aid; this prevents frustration and disappointment arising from unrealistic hopes.

Make use of the profile to help the client clearly define the types of environments and communication situations that have presented difficulty prior to his or her being fitted with a hearing aid. A person who has been wearing amplification but has just been fitted with a new aid, or has had modifications made to an existing unit, also needs to detail these areas of difficulty. You should determine with the client which are of prime concern and have the client reassess performance in those situations when wearing the aid. If difficulties persist, with or without a reduction in severity, you will need to attempt additional problem reduction.

When you examine the profile with the client, separate out the difficulties experienced in the home, work, and social environments. Encourage the description of specific events that illustrate the problems encountered. Through interested questioning find out as much as you can about these situations. Inquire how the client reacted, and how the reactions were in turn reacted to by others involved. How did the client feel about the situation, his or her management of it, the effect of these reactions, and the way others responded? How does the client think the other persons involved felt about him or her in that situation? Remember that your goal in this first stage is to help the client define difficulties in practical terms. You are attempting to get the client to clarify what initially tend to be gross perceptions and feelings about difficulties encountered. These must be stated as specific problems before they can be approached with particular strategies for reducing them. Once a problem has been understood, the client will wish to know how you can help him or her to reduce its severity.

Understanding the Management Plan

The management plan is a partnership. If it is to work, the client and his or her family must understand the process. The plan must be based upon practical objectives. It must be directed at the ameliorization of problems identified in the assessment stage. Having outlined and discussed the problem with the client, the client's spouse, or other significant relatives, you must now propose a plan of management. You need to describe the steps you recommend be taken. Define these under the categories previously identified—namely, ensuring optimal use of amplification, modifying the environment, modifying communication strategies, improving communication processing. It helps to propose the management program in writing. This ensures that the proposal is well organized, that it is simply and concisely described, and that it provides you and the client with a contract. Rehabilitation management should not be open ended; plan six-week units, which may consist of one or more weekly sessions. After the first unit, you should then reevaluate the plan, modify it, and implement another six-week unit, perhaps with fewer sessions. Finally, reduce your sessions to a single monthly or six-week maintenance visit. At the end of any unit, a mutual agreement may terminate direct management and place the client on an annual recheck list. It is often more satisfactory to taper the sessions to the annual recheck stage. This avoids feelings of severance anxiety, which may occur when therapy is abruptly terminated. Realistically, however, you may find that the client terminates therapy before you feel it to be advisable. This is what a tightly organized, meaningful program well understood by the client is intended to prevent.

INDIVIDUALIZED MANAGEMENT PLANS

Let us reconsider the situations faced by each of the clients we discussed earlier and formulate a management plan for each.

Mr. Johnson

Problems:

1. Reduced speech comprehension of customers at sales counter
2. Difficulty in following group conversation and repartee at work and at church social hour
3. Difficulty in hearing radio and television at normal volume settings
4. Difficulty in hearing sermon in church
5. Apprehension about ability to continue employment
6. Frustration and irritability with his listeners

Proposed management goals (three visits):

1. To fully exploit the benefits that may be derived from amplification, including possible use of (a) monaural ear-level aid; (b) ear-level aid with directional microphone; (c) both an omnidirectional and a directional aid selectively worn according to the communication demands of the situation; (d) binaural aids.
2. To thoroughly discuss the possible benefits to be derived from the various am-

plification alternatives. To work in concert with the audiologist to assess the actual effect of the hearing aid upon increasing speech comprehension and in reducing anxiety in each of the communication situations already identified as presenting difficulty.

3. To encourage the client to talk about the communication difficulties he has been experiencing, and to rank them on a communication profile scale before and after wearing the aid.
4. To discuss feelings of frustration, embarrassment, and anxiety that have been experienced as part of those communication breakdowns, and to rank them on a rating scale.
5. To help the client objectify the reactions he feels others manifest as a result of his difficulties.
6. To provide thorough training in the use and care of whatever aid(s) the audiologist recommends.
7. To provide one or two trial listening sessions involving the use of competing environmental and speech noise. If possible, to conduct a lesson in the agency cafeteria.
8. To provide one intensive session of auditory-visual speech comprehension over the vocabulary and phrases pertinent to his work as a postal clerk. Care should be taken to include some of the less frequent requests, such as "Can I renew my passport here?" "Do I need a customs declaration for this package?" "Have the *T.V. Guides* been delivered this week?"
9. To include in the two sessions just discussed an analysis of present ways of reacting to comprehension difficulty, and to consider alternate ways of handling those situations should difficulties persist.
10. To arrange a follow-up visit 6 to 8 weeks after initial management procedures have been completed, at which time a reassessment of Mr. Johnson's communication function will be made.

Mrs. Simpson

Problems:

Mrs. Simpson's needs are more complex. Her problems have been identified as:

1. Speech comprehension difficulty in a new office
2. Difficulty in understanding speech in group situations at work and in social situations
3. Difficulty in adapting to the changing communication demands in changing environments
4. Decrease in ability to cope with communication demands at home
5. Difficulty when addressed from side of unaided ear
6. Doubts about competence to handle new professional demands
7. Increased tiredness and irritability at end of day

Proposed management goals (initially, two visits in first week, then five further weekly sessions, then a complete status review):

1. To involve Mr. Simpson and, to a lesser extent, the two daughters in the management-support program. Mr. Simpson is sympathetic and supportive; he and the daughters are being affected by Mrs. Simpson's difficulties, and they will benefit from her enhanced professional status when the difficulties are resolved.
2. To help Mrs. Simpson objectify her feelings about the demands and effects of the new position. Particular attention should be paid to the short period she has had to develop new organizational structures. She should evaluate the extent to

which she has been able to systematically examine the specific demands of the position and to work out operational procedures. She should be asked to consider whether the early difficulties in adjusting to new communication demands and environments have prevented her from objective analysis of the professional demands of the position. Part of the counseling goal will be to encourage an evaluation of professional competencies as they apply to the defined demands of the role. Mrs. Simpson must be encouraged to systematically evaluate professionally what her new role is to be, how to make maximum use of her assistant, and how to delegate responsibilities. The hearing demands must be addressed as separate problems. Mrs. Simpson's previous professional success and her selection for this position suggest at least the basic competencies necessary to successful handling of the new appointment.

3. To ensure maximal use of appropriate amplification working in close relationship with the audiologist. To develop a procedure and criteria for systematic evaluation of the comparative benefits to be derived from binaural versus BICROS aids.
4. To ensure a thorough understanding of what to expect from amplification and how to use and take care of the aid(s).
5. To investigate what acoustic changes might be made in Mrs. Simpson's office.
6. To consider the most favorable arrangement of office furniture to facilitate communication. Special attention should be given to where a listener would sit if Mrs. Simpson were seated at her desk. Is an across-the-desk seating plan preferable to having a chair placed at the side of the desk? Is there a favorable small-group seating arrangement? If a table is used for small committee meetings, would a round table provide better speech-reading and listening opportunities than an oblong table?
7. To consider seating arrangements that favor auditory-visual speech processing.
8. To discuss strategies for obtaining favorable seating at interviews or meetings outside the building—for example, requesting ahead of time to reserve a position, arriving early to ensure a satisfactory seat, asking "Do you mind if I move my chair? I have a little trouble hearing you." or "Would you mind if we sit over there? I am a little hard of hearing, which makes seating positions important for me." (Mrs. Simpson's feelings about revealing her hearing impairment in such circumstances should be explored in early counseling sessions.)
9. To review and discuss strategies for increasing Mrs. Simpson's confidence in deciding what has been said (see the earlier discussion of Mrs. Simpson's case). Person-to-person and group situations should both be considered.
10. To consider how to make best use of stenographic and recording services when possible.
11. To work with the family to discuss the situations at home that present communication difficulty. To explore and expand the family's understanding of Mrs. Simpson's problems, and to help them assess their feelings and reactions at times when communication with her is hard. To consider how to facilitate communication with Mrs. Simpson in troublesome listening situations at home—for example, by remembering not to talk from another room, by sitting so each person can see each other person while watching television, by ensuring favorable lighting, by turning the radio or television down or off before beginning a conversation, by being willing to repeat or rephrase when what one said was missed even though it was not terribly important or even worth saying again.
12. To develop a visual- and auditory-communication training program centered upon the vocabulary, phrases, and situations that are likely to occur in business meetings. Mrs. Simpson should generate the training items. At home it may be possible to establish short practice sessions 10 to 15 minutes long in which, in the family group, questions are asked and statements made from the list developed.

This procedure should be demonstrated so that Mrs. Simpson learns to respond to, not to repeat, what is said. Practice sessions can be carried out with the radio or television on low to increase difficulty if necessary.

13. To encourage the keeping of a diary to describe any troublesome situations encountered during the day.

Finally we can consider the help that can be offered to Mrs. Amster. Although her needs are the fewest of these three hearing-impaired persons, they are by no means less important. The challenge is to increase the quality of Mrs. Amster's life in the environment of the nursing home in a manner that does not overload her.

Mrs. Amster

Problems:

1. A hearing aid not acceptable to the client
2. Poor tolerance for loudness
3. Reduced speech discrimination
4. Arthritis, which makes it difficult to handle the hearing aid
5. Poor eyesight, which makes speech-reading difficult

Proposed management goals:

1. To work with an audiologist to demonstrate to Mrs. Amster the extent to which she can benefit from appropriate amplification. This will involve a trial with a body aid selected for simplicity of manipulation of controls. The aid should have automatic volume control (AVC), which the therapist should know how to adjust.
2. To monitor the use of the aid during the trial period to identify the optimal AVC setting. This will allow for maximal desired amplification of speech while reducing loudness of intermittent environmental sound.
3. To help Mrs. Amster learn to insert the ear mold if possible. If this is not possible for her to manage, a permanent staff member should be taught to do it for her, and then to instruct a nurse or aide as necessary.
4. To make sure Mrs. Amster and a staff member know how the aid should be set.
5. To identify environments and situations in the home when Mrs. Amster would be advised to turn off the aid.
6. To obtain a television amplification adapter.
7. To demonstrate the improvement in quality of speech if the aid is spoken into quietly when held 4 inches from the mouth. Mrs. Amster may then decide if there are occasions when this procedure would be helpful.
8. To ensure that the glasses Mrs. Amster wears are a current prescription.
9. To provide two consultations after the aid has been fitted (a) to encourage its selective use; (b) to demonstrate what can be expected of it; (c) to assess whether visual cues improve comprehension and, if so, to orient Mrs. Amster to their use.
10. To discuss with the staff the importance of not increasing the loudness of their voices when communication difficulties with Mrs. Amster arise. To advise speaking closer to the aid, repeating and rephrasing what has been said, identifying the topic in question before repeating what was said.

This chapter has outlined the practical procedural steps to rehabilitative management of adults with impaired hearing. Although this approach is a departure from the traditional model of aural rehabilitation management, which focuses on communication training, it does not suggest that there is no role for auditory and visual training. Rather, such training is a tool to be used selectively and judiciously in a total management plan. Thus before concluding our consideration of management practices with the hearing-impaired adult, we need to discuss auditory and visual communication.

REFERENCES

Blood, G., I. Blood, and J. Danhaner, "The Hearing Aid 'Effect,' " *Hearing Instruments, 28,* 1977, 12.

Kaster, R., "Hearing Aid as Related to Rehabilitation," in *Handbook of Adult Rehabilitative Audiology,* ed. J. Alpiner, pp. 67–87. Baltimore: The Williams and Wilkins Company, 1978.

21

Auditory-Visual Communication Training for the Hearing-Impaired Adult

UNDERSTANDING THE PROBLEM

Unlike congenitally hearing-impaired children, adults who acquire impairment of hearing already have intact language systems. They have well-formed internal representations of the sound patterns of spoken language. They also have developed communication behaviors adequate for personal needs. These abilities will depend primarily on the recognition of the acoustic patterns of speech, which are used by the listener to reconstruct meaningful units of language. Normal listeners process what they hear in context, utilizing available visual cues to augment or clarify the spoken message. The use of visual cues is not essential to speech comprehension under favorable listening conditions. However, when listening conditions deteriorate, the language content is difficult, the language structure is obtuse, vocabulary is unfamiliar, or the articulation is deviant, normal listeners attempt to compensate by listening to the speaker more closely and by processing visual cues related to the spoken message. Hearing impairment reduces the amount of information available in the acoustic signal received. It is thus reasonable to assume that more careful listening, together with processing available visual cues to speech, will compensate to some extent for the lost auditory information. The question one must answer, therefore, is: "Does systematic training in auditory and visual speech processing improve the client's ability to do this?"

For many, this question will be considered heretical because conventional wisdom has bred faith in this approach to aural rehabilitation. For years it has been almost standard practice to recommend "lip-reading and auditory training" for hearing-impaired adults who experience communication difficulties. Even within the limits of this approach to rehabilitation, emphasis has tended to be on lip-reading lessons rather than on auditory training.

Auditory training has been included as part of the process of traditional remediation therapy for the adult with acquired hearing loss. In practice, however, our impression is that its use is not widespread (McCarthy & Alpiner, 1978, p. 103).

This emphasis on speech-reading can be seen by comparing the statements made by the author of a widely used current text in audiology. About auditory training Newby (1979) says:

Whether or not the adult will require any auditory training depends of course on the severity of his loss, the length of time he has been hard of hearing, and also the audiometric configuration of his loss (p. 456).

In discussing the need for speech-reading training, by contrast, the same author states unequivocally:

Regardless of the extent of hearing loss, or whether or not the patient can profit from a hearing aid, instruction in speech-reading will be beneficial (Newby, 1979, p. 452).

Does the research literature justify such strong advocacy of speech-reading? The answer appears to be that it does not. In 1969 Binnie and Alpiner conducted a study to assess whether different approaches to "lip-reading" instruction produced different levels of competence in their subjects. They selected two of the major lip-reading teaching methods. The Jena method, as described by Anna Bunger (1944), was selected to represent the analytic school of lip-reading instruction. This method is based on the assumption that development of the ability to recognize individual speech components rapidly and accurately carries over into the recognition of those same characteristics when encountered in connected speech.

The Nitche (1912) method represented the synthetic approach, which is predicated on the belief that the ability to predict meaning, rather than identifying individual speech components, should be the paramount aim in speech-reading training.

Binnie and Alpiner provided nine 1-hour weekly lessons to ten hearing-impaired adults who had had no previous lip-reading instruction. Half the subjects were trained by the Jena method and half by the Nitche method. A third group of five hearing-impaired adults received no instruction whatsoever. At the end of the experiment a comparison was made of the pre- and postinstruction scores on the Utley silent-film word and sentence test, and on an individual phoneme-recognition test. Statistical analysis showed no significant difference between pre- and post-test conditions for any of the three groups. *The subjects who had received lip-reading training proved no better at recognizing the test items than those who had received no training.*

Alpiner (1978) also examined the pre- and post-therapy speech-reading test scores of one hundred clients who had received eight 1-hour per week therapy sessions that included speech-reading and auditory training, communication training, and counseling. Eighty-nine of the clients reported better communication ability after therapy, yet *there was no significant change in their speech-reading test scores.* O'Neill and Oyer (1973) have pointed out that even though aural rehabilitation centers upon speech-reading and auditory training, we have no body of research findings to provide evidence of its effectiveness or lack of it. Thus in Alpiner's (1978) words: "We find ourselves utilizing techniques which have no supportive documentation for their success" (p. 4). This places the hearing therapist in a dilemma, for it is hard to justify asking a client to pay for a therapy for which we have no demonstrable evidence of success. If anything, the little evidence we do have suggests its ineffectiveness. Why, then, do we persist in providing auditory and visual communication training? Should we continue to include this type of instruction as part of our rehabilitation program for adults? If so, how much time should be spent on such training? These are difficult questions to answer because we lack objective evidence upon which to base decisions. Once again you are forced to use your own judgment in each individual case.

From our discussion we have seen that communication involves the ability to predict the meaning the speaker wishes to convey. We do this by using information inherent within patterns of nonverbal and verbal cues that the speaker transmits. These cues have informational value when correctly decoded. The greatest information is encoded into the acoustic cues of speech. These acoustic patterns are equivalent to linguistic patterns, which, in turn, identify semantic and cognitive values—that is, meanings and concepts. Speech articulation, the means by which we generate the acoustic pattern, is visible to varying degrees. Thus, what we can observe of speech articulation is directly correlated with the acoustic pattern being produced. This makes the visible cues to speech potentially informative. However, at the level of individual phonemes, the visible articulatory information is insufficient to permit identification of each speech sound. Moreover the visual revealing characteristics of speech sounds, like their acoustic correlates, vary with coarticulation. Thus it seems reasonable to assume that visible speech cues, like acoustic cues, are processed in syllable-sized or larger chunks.

We have discussed the fact that we are capable of processing speech at several levels, ranging from listening to the actual sounds (phonetic) to listening only to extract the meaning (semantic). In normal communication we listen for meaning. This is necessitated in part by the rate at which the speech signal is generated. The rate of transmission precludes auditory or visual analysis of individual sound units, so that we must scan for patterns that can be accommodated by syntactic structures. In conversation we listen linguistically rather than acoustically. For this reason our perception of speech is heavily influenced by what we know about the language rules governing the speaker.

Finally, we know that communication does not take place in a vacuum. The study of the pragmatics of language has shown how the choice of topics for communication, the ways in which we introduce and terminate discussion of a topic, as well as the manner in which conversations are developed are all rule bound. Communication takes place in context. Context is determined by content and by the relation of content to previous content. Simultaneous to broadcasting verbal information, the speaker frequently encodes nonverbal cues in the form of gestures. These may be deliberately encoded to clarify the spoken message or they may occur naturally as part of the situation. These visual cues potentially constrain the listener in predicting what is being said.

We know from the study of normal communication that for the reasons just identified, speech involves a high level of redundancy. We know that as the acoustic signal is progressively degradated, the normal listener begins to draw more and more upon that redundancy. This is clear from the studies reviewed in Chapter 7, in which we saw that as the auditory signal deteriorates, normal-hearing subjects increasingly use visual cues to help retain the ability to process the linguistic pattern. Of particular relevance to this discussion is the unequivocal evidence that on tasks involving recognition of spoken language samples, both normal and hearing-impaired adult subjects scored higher when auditory and visual cues to speech were simultaneously available. The bimodal processing of information appears to be integrative rather than additive, resulting in a better definition of the linguistic pattern on the basis of the sensory cues.

PRECEPTS BASIC TO AUDITORY-VISUAL PROCESSING

From this discussion we can identify a number of precepts basic to a rationale for providing auditory and visual communication training.

1. Speech communication involves the identification of cognitive values.
2. These cognitive values are tapped by use of the language code.
3. In normal communication the system attempts to process units in chunks as large as possible.
4. Comprehension occurs as a result of reconstructing language patterns.
5. Providing meaning can be correctly attributed to a pattern. The actual components of the pattern are not relevant and have probably not been paid attention to or processed.
6. In communication, information already understood will facilitate the processing of new, related information. The greatest dependency on the details of the auditory-visual speech pattern occurs, therefore, when the topic has yet to be identified.
7. The acoustic signal is the primary vehicle for speech information. It far exceeds the visual-speech signal as a source of speech information for all but the severely hearing impaired.
8. Speech comprehension through the recognition of individual speech sounds by their visible characteristics is not possible due to factors discussed earlier (Chapter 4).
9. The available visible aspects of articulation can, in many instances, serve to increase the total amount of linguistic constraints upon which prediction of message content is made.
10. Because visible speech articulation is part of spoken language, it is subject to the same factors discussed in items 1 to 5.
11. If the visual intelligibility of speech is low, and visual constraints are inte-

grated with auditory constraints under conditions of acoustic degradation, the overall level of information exceeds that available in either modality alone.

12. Visual and auditory cues are computed by an interactive, not an additive, formula.

These are the precepts pertaining to the perceptual process that we will use to justify auditory and visual communication training. Now let us consider the client's abilities and needs.

THE AUDITORY COMPONENT OF COMMUNICATION TRAINING

Hearing impairment progressively distorts the acoustic signal as the severity of the deficit increases. Hearing-impaired listeners adapt to reduced auditory constraints by increased dependency upon the structural and semantic information. They will probably also pay closer visual attention in an effort to make use of visual cues. By the time they purchase hearing aids, they can no longer sustain the effort necessary to have the confidence in their understanding of speech in essential daily contacts.

Amplification, if effective, will raise the level of auditory information. How much the level is raised will vary from client to client. For some it will surpass the level necessary to restore normal communicative function in all or most situations; for others it will facilitate communication but only under favorable listening conditions. For no client will amplification make speech sound normal. Therefore there will always be a period during which the client will need to become accustomed to the sound of amplified speech. The difference between the sound of amplified speech and the sound of normal speech will vary from client to client as a function of the hearing impairment. For some, amplified speech will be fully intelligible, lacking only the quality of normal speech. For others, not only will quality be different, but clarity will remain less than normal, perhaps even less than necessary for comprehension under all circumstances.

For this reason, the following procedures are recommended:

1. Every hearing-aid candidate should be given a realistic assessment of how much amplification will aid speech comprehension.
2. Every new hearing-aid user can benefit from one or two listening-orientation sessions to help adjustment to the new sound and loudness of environmental noises and most particularly to the new sounds of speech.
3. Many hearing-aid users need no more than this initial single or double listening session.
4. More severely hearing-impaired persons will frequently experience difficulty in adjusting to amplified speech, particularly in less-than-ideal listening conditions.
5. For such clients psychological and motivational support will be essential to the successful use of the aid.
6. These clients can benefit from a structured program of auditory training.

7. Such training should involve listening, deciding, and responding to speech representative of the messages they will encounter in their work, home, and social environments.
8. Priority should be given to the language of problem environments or situations.
9. Auditory training should involve the use of meaningful questions or phrases. These must be responded to in a manner that indicates understanding. Repetition of what has been heard is inadequate and should be discouraged.
10. Auditory training must attempt to approximate the daily situations in which auditory comprehension presents difficulty. Thus if group conversation or speech in noise present the major concern, training should move rapidly from a single speaker talking in quiet conditions to more difficult listening tasks.
11. Single-word discrimination should be used only:
    a. To sharpen the auditory image of key vocabulary before an auditory-comprehension exercise. Each word should first be presented in a sentence, then repeated several times in isolation, then repeated in the sentence.
    b. To help distinguish words auditorily confused by the client. Use the same procedure as in (a).
    c. To stress the topic of a communication—for example, "*Layouts,* I am going to ask you about advertising layouts."
12. Individual speech-sound discrimination is rarely justifiable. It is a boring task that has little to do with comprehension of spoken language.

Auditory training should be presented to the client in terms of clearly defined goals. For example:

I am going

1. to try to help you to become adjusted to the sounds you will hear amplified when you receive your own aid of this type
2. to see if you can learn to accept a little more volume so that speech will be easier to hear
3. to help you to concentrate on what the speaker is saying while you suppress the background noise
4. to teach you to concentrate on identifying the new topic when the speaker changes the subject
5. to train you to listen more effectively when there is more than one speaker

The number of sessions should be limited to six-week blocks. Reappraise the value of continuing upon completion of each block.

THE VISUAL COMPONENT OF COMMUNICATION TRAINING

Some persons with severe hearing impairment or with auditory-discrimination problems that exceed those caused by the hearing-loss configuration alone, as occurs in the aging process (presbycusis), may never derive sufficient auditory information from the amplified signal to make speech adequately intelligible. Others who hear well in quiet may have difficulty understanding speech in group situations, in noise, or in poor acoustic environments. You must investigate the extent to which you can help such persons use visual cues to facilitate the interpretation of what they hear.

As any test of a population of normal-hearing persons will reveal, the ability to capitalize on visual cues to speech varies from almost no ability to a surprisingly high level of competence. The normal-hearing population evidences a distribution of speech-reading ability according to a normal curve. Because the hearing-impaired adult population is a part of the normal-hearing population, it likewise manifests the same range of abilities. We do not know the essential elements for success in speech-reading (O'Neill & Oyer, 1961). We know that there are good speech-readers and poor speech-readers, but we do not know how to make good speech-readers from poor ones. Thus we must base our training procedures upon what seem to us to be logical assumptions.

Except for the person with little or no usable residual hearing, visual communication training is inseparable from auditory training. To consider it as a separate aspect of communication requiring separate training sessions is to ignore the indisputable finding that audiovisual speech processing is superior to auditory or visual processing alone under degraded listening conditions. Under no circumstances are we justified in depriving listeners of the opportunity to make use of residual hearing. They should be encouraged to use their hearing aid(s) during all training sessions. If we can show that with aided hearing a client experiences little or no communication difficulty in any of his or her daily environments, training in visual recognition of speech will be unwarranted.

When the client still experiences difficulty in understanding amplified speech under certain listening conditions, then training to increase the effective use of visual cues is justified. *Training should concentrate on listening more effectively while watching the speaker carefully.* It must aim to increase speech comprehension in those listening situations in which the client reports difficulty. Thus, if you seek to upgrade visual processing of speech in noisy environments, you must introduce noise to the training session. If you wish to enhance speech-reading skills in group situations, you must enroll the client in a group and develop training tasks that involve shifting attention from one speaker to another. If you wish to train a client to use visual cues in a quiet environment, such as at a religious service or in a library, use a very soft voice for training. *You should not turn off the client's hearing aid or simply mouth the training items.*

It is important that you are clear about the goal of visual communication training. Two possible tasks can help the client. The first is to have the client identify quickly and accurately a number of rehearsed items from a closed set. The items in this limited repertoire may be words, statements, requests, questions, or instructions that relate to a given topic or situation of high relevance to the client. The items may, for example, be job related, may pertain to a forthcoming interview, or may consist of the bids made at a bridge game. First familiarize the client with the complete list, which you then divide into smaller units. Ask the client to respond meaningfully (reply to a question, use a word, respond to a request, follow a direction, react to a statement, and so on) to a test item selected from a unit. Increase the number of items in the unit as familiarity with their visual patterns improves. Sims and Jacobs (1976) and Sims (1978) have reported successful use of this approach with severely hearing-impaired young adults at the National Technical Institute for The Deaf, Rochester, New York. After 20 hours of programmed self-instruction on 20-minute videotaped lessons, the students' recognition of job-related practice sentences increased from a pretest range of 0 to 50 percent to a posttest range of 58 to 100 percent. The motivation of the students to learn was considered an important factor.

We have no evidence to show that improved recognition of closed-set, topic-linked items generalizes to improved use of visual speech cues in understanding the infinite range of conversational topics that a client encounters in daily situations. We do not know how to achieve that goal. Such improvement, if it occurs, cannot be demonstrated conclusively on pre- or post-test scores on any existing speech-reading test. If we are able to help the client, our efforts will be reflected in an overall improvement of function in daily communication situations, and in a decrease in the level of anxiety and tension related to communication in general. This conclusion is borne out by the findings of Binnie and Alpiner (1969) that clients who reported improvement in communication performance did not demonstrate improvement on post-test speech-reading scores. Moreover the improvement a client experiences may derive from the complex interactive effect of all of the components of the management support program. It may not be discernible in any one component alone. For this reason you should think not of speech-reading lessons, but of the additional visual cues to a message that, if perceived, may raise the total amount of information above the comprehension threshold. You may decide to isolate vision from hearing in order to sharpen the perception of certain visible characteristics of a phrase or sentence, or to contrast the visual characteristics of speech-sound combinations auditorily indiscriminable to the client. However, to be of maximum value the visual constraints, once identified, must be made part of the auditory-visual pattern. It is necessary, therefore, to present the stimulus again with auditory-visual input in order that the whole may be perceived as greater than the sum of the parts.

Basic Assumptions Underlying Visual Communication Training

Training the client to take advantage of visual cues to speech is predicated on certain assumptions.

1. Visual communication involves sizing up the communication situation by eye.
2. Watching the speaker makes it easier to understand what he or she is saying.
3. Visual cues to communication are an adjunct to the acoustic cues, not a substitute for them except for the person with a profound hearing deficit.
4. There is no justification for completely depriving a listener of auditory cues in an attempt to increase lip-reading skills.
5. The most important goal is to listen and watch for meaning.
6. The reduction of the training materials to word or phoneme identification is only justified for the purpose of:

   a. Identifying new vocabulary or words that will serve to key the context of the message;
   b. Seeing whether ambiguity can be resolved by contrasting words that are confused.
7. Ambiguity is most likely to be resolved by thinking about the context and by obtaining further clarifying information.
8. The ultimate goal of your activities is to improve the manner in which the client integrates visual information into the total pool of available cues to meaning.

PLANNING AUDITORY-VISUAL TRAINING

What separates the auditory from the visual components in a training session cannot be indicated on paper if you agree that both are merely aspects of the larger function of speech communication. As you prepare your outlines for a training session you should try to be aware of how you can highlight the visual and auditory aspects at each step of the lesson. Try to keep in mind the sequence listen, listen and watch, decide. Present key words in a unit in that sequence. Present the word in isolation, then in context:

The word is conference, conference. Listen, conference (without visual cues). Now listen and watch, conference, conference. What is the date of the conference you have to attend?

Determining Goals

Determine your goals for a lesson for an individual or group. Following are some examples.

Encourage Identification of the Topic. To begin it may prove helpful to list two topics and then begin to talk about one. All you ask the client to do is identify to which topic you are referring.

Baseball Game	*Cost of Living*
Did you catch the game on T.V. last night? I missed the beginning. Wow, the Dodgers were really in good form. I couldn't believe those two home runs in a row. And those weren't easy balls.	It seems like every time I go shopping things have gone up again. I can't believe the price of clothes. It's outrageous what they want for a simple cotton dress. I've bought hardly anything this summer.

You can present topics that contrast less sharply, and you can increase the number of topics. If the client lacks confidence, even at this level of decision making, write the script on the board.

The second stage requires topic identification when the topic choice is not made known. Discuss how the client approaches the task. Consider and practice strategies designed to identify the topic by intervening in the conversation in acceptable ways.

Dealing with Changes in the Topic. First ask the client to determine when the topic of your conversation changes. Discuss and practice acceptable ways of verifying that the client has correctly identified a new topic.

Play a taped discussion of a given topic. Then ask the client to shift attention on request from your conversation to identify as quickly as possible the topic being discussed on the tape. The tape should consist of a speaker discussing a series of short topics unrelated to each other. Using two tape recorders you may record a series of questions, each on different topics. Ask the client to reply to the next question on the tape you point to.

Listening and Watching against a Noise Background. Even clients who have little difficulty in comprehending speech in quiet frequently encounter problems in noisy environments. To encourage the client to maintain a figure-ground relationship, repeat lesson units for which topic content, vocabulary, and phrases have been successfully comprehended in quiet. Present these units against a background of noise, preferably of the type the client encounters in difficult listening environments. Introduce the noise at a level that is audible but not disturbing; then raise it until it begins to just bother the client. If you are using a single, taped noise source begin with the noise on the side opposite the amplified ear. Then move the tape recorder in stages around to the front of the listener.

Try communicating with the client against this noise, using what you judge to be an appropriate loudness level. Raise your voice slightly when the client exhibits difficulty in comprehension; then repeat at the lower level. The client should be encouraged to watch you while listening. When hard words or phrases are encountered, isolate them for a concentrated listen, watch, decide presentation. Then go back and repeat those units in their original contexts. Then, use those words or phrases in a different context. Note these items for subsequent review.

Listening and Watching in Poor Acoustics. Whenever possible you should consider giving one or two advanced training sessions in less-than-favorable acoustic environments. Probably the most commonly used environment is the hospital or clinic cafeteria. At this stage of training you need to concentrate on such practical matters as the client's most favorable seating: "Can you see the speakers' faces?" "Are you seated so that you are not visually-distracted by the environment?" "Can you identify a better table or seating position?" "What strategies will you use when a topic changes or you are not certain what has been said or asked?"

If you do not have access to a real-life environment you can increase the difficulty of the listening task by lengthening the distance between the client and yourself. This allows reverberation to exert its full negative effect on the speech signal, thus increasing the client's need to use visual cues.

Listening in Group Situations. Grouping clients for rehabilitation management serves multiple purposes. Among these is the client's opportunity to analyze with you and the other group members the nature of group communication, the difficulties it presents, and the techniques for reducing these difficulties. For the advanced student it can be helpful to observe and critique the communication strategies of others in the group, to hear how others see his or her communication behavior, and to explore the feelings and reactions each experiences while in the group-communication situation. The members of the group should be selected for compatibility of communication-training needs. The group should not exceed seven or eight persons if maximum interaction is to be achieved. In a group situation explore the effects of various seating plans for formal and informal communication. Discuss how seating position fosters or inhibits communication. Identify who can easily be seen for visual cues to speech from the various seating positions.

Have each participant talk to the group for 2 or 3 minutes about an item of topical interest. Then have the group ask questions and discuss the topic. When difficulties occur examine their nature and discuss how they might be managed.

The group situation provides an excellent model for blending communication training with counseling. When problems arise, the feelings associated with the difficult situation can be examined and compared among group members. This provides an excellent opportunity to explore other situations in which negative feelings are experienced if you gradually move the session from discussing management of the situation to management of the feelings it evokes.

This blending of communication training with counseling in which the situation, the communication event, the difficulties experienced, the emotions felt, and the strategies used to handle the situation are all dealt with as a whole is the goal of a management approach to aural rehabilitation.

The separation of the auditory-visual communication training from the total management model is purely artificial and justified only for didactic purposes. Management is concerned with helping people solve problems. People cannot easily be divided into separate components. To attempt to do so, except for the briefest of periods, is to lose sight of the humanistic factors that determine behavior.

CONCLUSION

These twenty-one chapters have been devoted to an examination of the knowledge relevant to understanding hearing impairment, its effects, and the management of the difficulties it creates. The task of integrating all of this information into a practical model of management is a demanding one. It is, however, as rewarding as it is challenging

You should now have a working model with which to approach the task of helping the hearing-impaired person surmount his or her handicap. You should feel comfortable with the knowledge that you will not be responsible for finding solutions to *all* problems. It is a cooperative endeavor you are undertaking, a partnership with your client. Drawing on your understanding of the factors contributing to the degree of hearing handicap, you should now be able to develop an effective management plan. You should be able to marshal existing resources in meeting your clients' everyday communication needs.

The concepts and theories you have learned serve only as the foundation of rehabilitation. It now falls to you to apply and to modify them as needed. Your own insights, coupled with your own creativity, will serve you well in your effort to develop an approach to management with which you feel comfortable, one which will really prove successful.

REFERENCES

Alpiner, J., ed., *Handbook of Adult Rehabilitative Audiology*. Baltimore: The Williams and Wilkins Company, 1978.

Binnie, C., and J. Alpiner, *A Comparative Investigation of Analytic versus Synthetic Methodologies in Lipreading Training*. Paper presented at the annual convention of the American Speech and Hearing Assoc., Chicago, 1969. Cited in Alpiner, J., "Adult Rehabilitative Audiology: An Overview," in *Handbook of Rehabilitative Audiology*, ed. J. Alpiner, pp. 1–16. Baltimore: The Williams and Wilkins Company, 1978.

Bunger, A. M., *Speech Reading: Jena Method*. Danville, Ill.: The Interstate Press, 1944.

McCarthy, P., and J. Alpiner, "The Remediation Process," in *Handbook of Adult Rehabilitative Audiology*, ed. J. Alpiner, pp. 88–120. Baltimore: The Williams and Wilkins Company, 1978.

Newby, H. A., *Audiology*. Englewood Cliffs, N.J.: Prentice-Hall, Inc., 1979.

Nitche, E. B., *Lipreading: Principles and Practice*. New York: Frederick A. Stokes, Co., 1912.

O'Neill, J., and H. Oyer, *Visual Communication for the Hard of Hearing*. Englewood Cliffs, N.J.: Prentice-Hall, Inc., 1961.

O'Neill, J., and H. Oyer, "Aural Rehabilitation," in *Modern Developments in Audiology*, ed. J. Jerger, pp. 211–252. New York: Academic Press, Inc., 1973.

Sims, D., "Visual and Auditory Training for Adults," in *Handbook of Clinical Audiology*, ed. J. Katz, pp. 565–580. Baltimore: The Williams and Wilkins Company, 1978.

Sims, D., and M. Jacobs, *Speechreading Evaluation at the National Technical Institute for the Deaf*. Paper presented at the Annual Convention of the Alexander Graham Bell Assoc. for the Deaf, Boston, 1976.

Index

AUTHOR INDEX

SUBJECT INDEX

Sanders, Derek A.

Aural Rehabilitation $28.95+5.00

RF297
S35
1982